THE TURK IN AMERICA

Utah Series in Turkish and Islamic Studies
M. Hakan Yavuz, Series Editor

A Religion, Not a State:
Ali 'Abd al-Raziq's Islamic Justification of Political Secularism
Souad T. Ali

Armenians and the Allies in Cilicia, 1914–1923
Yücel Güçlü

Debating Moderate Islam: The Geopolitics of Islam and the West
Edited by M. A. Muqtedar Khan

The Armenian Massacres in Ottoman Turkey: A Disputed Genocide
Guenter Lewy

The Turk in America: The Creation of an Enduring Prejudice
Justin McCarthy

The Armenian Rebellion at Van
Justin McCarthy, Esat Arslan,
Cemalettin Taşkiran, and Ömer Turan

Autobiographies of Orhan Pamuk: The Writer in His Novels
Michael McGaha

Sustainability of Microstates: The Case of North Cyprus
Ozay Mehmet

Turkish Foreign Policy, 1919–2006: Facts and Analysis with Documents
Edited by Baskin Oran
Translated by Mustafa Aksin

The Ottoman Army, 1914–1918: Disease and Death on the Battlefield
Hikmet Özdemir
Translated by Saban Kardaş

The Search for God's Law: Islamic Jurisprudence in the
Writings of Sayf al-Dīn al- Āmidī, Revised Edition
Bernard G. Weiss

The Emergence of a New Turkey: Democracy and the AK Parti
Edited by M. Hakan Yavuz

The Turk in America
Creation of an Enduring Prejudice

Justin McCarthy

Utah Series in Turkish and Islamic Studies

THE UNIVERSITY OF UTAH PRESS

Salt Lake City

The Defiance House Man colophon is a registered trademark
of the University of Utah Press. It is based upon a four-foot-tall,
Ancient Puebloan pictograph (late PIII) near Glen Canyon, Utah.

14 13 12 11 10   1 2 3 4 5

LIBRARY OF CONGRESS CATALOGING-IN-PUBLICATION DATA

McCarthy, Justin, 1945-
The Turk in America : creation of an enduring prejudice / Justin McCarthy.
p cm.
Includes bibliographical references and index.
ISBN 978-1-60781-013-1 (pbk. : alk. paper) 1. Turks—Public opinion. 2. Turkey—Foreign
public opinion, American. 3. Armenian massacres, 1915-1923—Foreign public opinion,
American. 4. Public opinion—United States. 5. Prejudices—United States. 6. Stereotypes
(Social psychology)—United States. 7. Missionaries—Turkey—History. 8. Missions to
Muslims—Turkey—History. 9. United States—Relations—Turkey.
10. Turkey—Relations—United States. I. Title.
DS26.M33 2010
305.89'435073—dc22
2010021755

Printed and bound by Sheridan Books, Inc., Ann Arbor, Michigan.

To Don and Ruth

CONTENTS

Maps and Illustrations

All other illustrations follow page 202

Acknowledgments

Initial funding for this project came from the University of Louisville and the Baykan Foundation. A grant from the Istanbul Chamber of Commerce; the Istanbul Chamber of Industry; the Istanbul and Marmara, Aegean, Mediterranean, and Black Sea Chamber of Shipping; and the Istanbul Commodity Exchange provided major funding. The Turkish Coalition of America supported research.

I thank Caitlin McCarthy and John McCarthy for their research assistance; Carolyn Lamka for both research and editing; Melih Berk for his help and friendship; Turhan Baykan for his support; John McLeod, Jon-Paul Moody, and Lee Keeling for every kind of technical assistance; and Kathy Burford Lewis, editor extraordinaire. Librarians and archivists of the University of Louisville Library, the Library of Congress, the U.S. National Archives, the British Library, and the British National Archives gave much-appreciated help and access to the materials that made this study possible.

The Turk in America has taken many years to write. I especially thank my family for their support and their tolerance of research trips and long periods of isolation in my study. As always, everything depends on them.

THE MISSIONARIES DEPART

Pliny Fisk, the first American missionary to the Middle East, gave the following description in his farewell sermon as he left Boston:

> Judea is inhabited by several interesting classes of men. The principal of these are Mahommedans, and Jews; and Roman Catholic, Greek, Armenian and Syrian Christians.
>
> The Mohammedans, who are masters of the country, who possess most of its wealth, and who have the exclusive management of political concerns, are, as you well know, the followers of that artful imposter, who arose in Arabia, about the commencement of the seventh century. Their religion was first propagated, and is still defended, by the sword. Cruelty and blood are among its most prominent characteristics. Mahommedan piety consists very much in fasts, ablutions, pilgrimages to Mecca, and the persecution of infidels and heretics...
>
> [The Jews] still continue a distinct people, and retain their ancient language, customs, and religion:—not their religion as it was exhibited in the piety of David, Daniel, and Nehemiah, but as it appeared in the unbelief and self-righteousness of those Jews who rejected and crucified the Lord Jesus...
>
> The Roman Catholics are scattered in small numbers throughout Judea. At Jerusalem, Bethlehem, and various other places, they have churches, convents, and priests; and enjoy the exercise of their religion. But though they bear the Christian name, and believe the leading facts stated in the Bible; though they hold the doctrine of our Savior's divinity and atonement, and many of the fundamental doctrines of Christianity, yet they are extremely ignorant of the true spirit of the Gospel; are almost entirely destitute of the Scriptures; and to what they retain of real Christianity they add many inventions of their own... Their religious worship consists principally of pompous, insignificant, unscriptural ceremonies.
>
> The Syrian Christians are nominally under the Pope's jurisdiction, though they are said to pay very little deference to his authority, and are much more inclined than the Catholics, to the true doctrines of Christianity, and to the diffusion of them.

The Greeks, in the number and insignificance of their ceremonies, very much resemble the Catholics; but in their doctrines they have not by any means departed so far from the simplicity of Gospel truth. They do not admit the Papal infallibility, indulgences, dispensations, or purgatory.

The Armenians derive their name from the country in which they dwell, and differ very little from the Greeks.

All these sects, though they call themselves Christians, are still destitute almost entirely of the Scriptures, and deplorably ignorant of real Christianity.[1]

The creation of the American image of Turks was primarily the work of Calvinist missionaries sent to the Middle East and the Balkans by the Congregationalist and Presbyterian churches. They drew on a long-standing prejudice against Turks and Muslims, amplified it, and brought it to the American public. What began in Fisk's almost humorous bigotry became more sophisticated but remained an anti-Turkish and anti-Muslim crusade. From start to finish, the American missionaries viewed the Turks as their enemy. They carried their feelings to the American people.

Fisk, one of the first two American missionaries to the Ottoman Empire, delivered his judgments in a sermon in 1819, just before he left to take up his labors as a missionary in Palestine. Obviously, there was much work to be done. But Fisk felt certain that his work would prosper, because Palestine offered comparatively fertile ground: "Every where [*sic*] you see a faint glimmering of light, through the gross and almost impenetrable darkness. Nor are the inhabitants of this region sunk in such stupidity and such brutal ignorance, as are the Hindoos of India, and the Hottentots of Africa."[2]

Fisk's companion on that first American mission to the Middle East, Levi Parsons, was particularly confident about converting the Jews. He saw history as leading all the Jews to become Christians, as exemplified, he believed, by the conversion of Jews in Russia under what he considered to be the benevolent tutelage of the tsar: "While enumerating the blessings, which have descended upon the Jewish nation, we cannot forget the unexampled benevolence of the Emperor of Russia, whom Divine Providence has raised up as a second Cyrus, to gather together the outcasts of Israel. And what is more remarkable, and auspicious, we find among the advocates for the conversion of the Jews, the Allied Sovereigns of Europe!"[3] Parsons felt that all the Jews would soon gather in Palestine and convert to Christianity. Nothing was keeping them from that end but the Turks, who stood in their way: "Destroy, then, the Ottoman Empire, and nothing but a *miracle* would prevent their return from the four winds of heaven."[4]

Bringing about the Millennium

The belief of early American Calvinists that the Ottoman Empire soon would be cast down, the Jews would return to Palestine to become Christians, and the Reign of Christ was at hand was based on faith in their interpretation of the Book of Revelation.[5] Among New England Congregationalists and other Protestants of the time it was commonly felt that the End of Days as foretold in Revelation was working itself out in their time. The rule of the Antichrist was coming to an end, to be followed by the Millennium. At that time the Antichrist would be struck down and the Jews converted. The Protestants were divided as to the identity of the Antichrist. Some felt that he was the pope, others the "sultan of Turkey." Some thought him to be both the pope and the sultan, mystically conjoined into one Antichrist. Many felt that the dates of the reign of the Antichrist were known exactly: 606 to 1866. Both papal authority and the Turkish Empire were believed to have been founded at the earlier date, and the Antichrist's reign was to have been 1,260 years. Although 606 was not an especially significant year either for papal authority or for Islam and the Turks, this does not seem to have been a hindrance to belief.[6] American Protestant authorities generally agreed that both the pope and the sultan would be overthrown when the Millennium approached, believing that "the career of Mohammedanism runs parallel to that of Popery, and that, taking their rise from a common era, they are destined also to synchronize in their fall."[7]

Calvinists always had a problem with what to do in the world. Many Calvinists felt that God's plan was unchangeable and in no need of help from humans. This might make philosophical sense, given the belief in predestination, but it was never palatable to most of the avowedly Calvinist Christians. A doctrine of "universal benevolence" even evolved, saying that Christians should do good works even if they knew they were damned.[8] Of course, few probably were really convinced that they were damned. Human nature was activist. Preachers and congregations believed that they could and should do something to change the world for the better. They felt it was their duty as Christians to contribute to the eschatological process through missions to the heathen and the infidel. To that end, a committee of graduates of Williams College met in 1810 and proposed a mission society, which was officially incorporated in Massachusetts in 1812: the American Board of Commissioners for Foreign Missions (ABCFM). While organizing, the committee addressed the public in 1811 on the need of missions: "Prophecy, history, and the present state of the world seem to unite in declaring that the great pillars of the Papal and Mohametan impostures are now tottering to their fall...Now is the time for the followers of Christ to come forward boldly, and to engage earnestly in the great work of enlightening and reforming mankind."[9]

Parsons and Fisk departed for the Middle East in 1819. Their mission was the first to the Middle East sponsored by the American Board of Commissioners for Foreign Missions, which had previously sent missionaries to India and Hawaii. The mission was financially supported by collections from the public, particularly by New England Congregational churches. Reports sent home by Parsons and Fisk convinced the American Board that there was a great need for missions to the Middle East and a great opportunity to preach the gospel there. In 1823 missionaries Isaac Bird and William Goodell were sent to Beirut. Goodell went on to Istanbul in 1831 to open the mission there. Both the Beirut and the Istanbul missions were soon joined by other missionaries sent from the United States. Although they at first made few converts, the missionaries began to open schools and print the Bible in local languages.

The American Board missionaries were primarily drawn from the Congregational and Presbyterian churches. The two churches shared similar theologies, both based in Calvinism, and cooperated in America as well as in the mission field. When the Presbyterian Church decided in 1870 to oversee its own missionary contributions, the Middle Eastern field was amicably divided. The Presbyterians took over the mission effort in Ottoman Syria (particularly in what is today Syria and Lebanon) and Iran. The American Board Congregationalists took Anatolia (today approximately the area of modern Turkey in Asia) and the Balkans as their field. Cooperation between the two was complete.

Missionary language necessarily became more temperate on the matter of the Second Coming once it was obvious that the end of the world was not imminent.[10] Nevertheless, the commitment of missionaries to the cause of evangelism continued. Some even believed that God had created the United States as part of His plan. The country had been created so that Americans could send out missionaries and hasten the End of Days.[11]

The aim of the missionaries was to convert all the inhabitants of the Middle East, but this almost immediately proved to be impossible. Jews, who were at first to be the primary beneficiaries of conversion to Protestant Christianity, turned out to be remarkably resistant to conversion. Muslims, too, were so resistant that their conversion was virtually unknown throughout the nineteenth century. The missionaries blamed this obstinacy on the allegation that Jewish converts would be punished by the other Jews, Muslims who converted would be made to suffer by the Turkish government, and native Christians would be punished by their own communities and clergy if they converted to "true Christianity."[12]

The other reason advanced by the missionaries for the difficulty in converting Muslims was the low esteem in which Muslims held Christianity in general. They attributed this to the state of native Christianity. The missionaries were forced to acknowledge that there were already Christians in the Middle East—ancient churches that claimed direct descendance from the teachings of the apostles. This, the Americans felt, was not a positive factor. They believed that the Eastern churches were so debased that the image of Christianity they presented was rejected outright by Muslims and Jews. As long as this was the image of Christianity in the mind of infidels, real Christianity could never triumph. Two of the first missionaries to the Ottoman Empire, Eli Smith and Harrison Dwight, wrote:

> The Moslem has hitherto known Christianity only as the religion of the Christians around him...Never in the course of their history have Mohammedans been brought in contact with any form of Christianity that was not too degenerate in its rites, its doctrines, and its effects to be worthy of their esteem. Preach to him Christianity, therefore, and the Moslem understands you to invite him to embrace a religion which he has always regarded as beneath him, and less beneficial than his own.[13]

The native Christians had at least persevered in believing themselves to be Christians, however, so the missionaries had reason for hope. If only true Christianity could supplant the Eastern Christian beliefs, then the Muslims would themselves see the light and convert.

> Let every missionary station raise up from the corrupt mass of nominal Christians around it, a goodly number of true followers of the Lamb, and it will be a city set on a hill which cannot be hid, a light to lighten the gentiles also. Had the churches of the East remained as when the apostles planted them, how long since would Mohammedanism have shrunk away from their holy contact? Or, rather, would it have ever existed? Restore to them their primitive purity, therefore, and the prop upon which Mohammedanism has so long stayed itself is gone, and it must fall. Remove it from the darkness, where like an unsightly weed, it has grown so rankly, into the noble blaze of true religion, and it must wither and die.[14]

The missionary purpose was clear, set in the 1830s by Smith and Dwight and carried out thereafter: convert the native Christians and the conversion of the Muslims and Jews would surely follow. The mission was thus changed very early from a Mission to the Infidels to a Mission to the Eastern Christians. Conversion now meant not conversion to Christianity but conversion from one Christian sect to another or, where this was not practicable, the transformation of the native churches to fit Protestant ideals. In the words of Smith and Dwight, it was necessary to bring the native Christians back to "primitive purity"—that is, to the Christianity of the missionaries. The purpose of the mission became leading the Greeks, Armenians, and other Middle Eastern Christians through the Reformation. Although minor efforts were later made to convert Muslims and Jews directly, the conversion of Christians remained the purpose of the mission.

The missionaries also were greatly concerned with battling the ongoing conversions of Middle Eastern Christians to Catholicism. They felt, with justification, that Middle Eastern and Balkan Christians had for some time been converting to Catholicism largely because that was a route to contact with and profit from acquaintance with Europeans. Even Protestant Europeans, they found, were in the practice of hiring Catholic Armenians and Greeks for their service as translators and local representatives. The missionaries wished to offer another avenue of conversion, away from the wiles of Rome, so that the Europeans would "withdraw the contribution of their influence from the pope, and direct it to a quarter where it would effectually weaken his antichristian power."[15]

Of the Near Eastern Christians, the Greek Orthodox proved to be most resistant to Protestant appeals. Few Greeks were willing to convert or even to admit encroachment of Protestant theology into their beliefs. The Greek establishment was both tied into the Ottoman power structure and favored by European Christians. It had well-developed schools and religious institutions. Greeks were interested in Western ways, books, language, and education but not in the American religion. Their resistance was perhaps partly the result of Greek ecclesiastical pressure. The Orthodox Church, which held considerable power in the Ottoman Empire, was a formidable opponent that stood resolutely against theological innovation. Greek bishops opposed Protestant evangelism in every way possible, and to leave the Greek Church was to divorce oneself from the Greek community, in effect to lose one's cultural identity. Most likely the main reason for Greek resistance to the appeal of Protestantism was simply that the Greeks were satisfied with their own church. Like the Muslims and Jews, the Greek Orthodox saw little corporal or spiritual benefit in welcoming Protestant ways. The missionaries were forced to look elsewhere for their converts. Those who welcomed them most readily were the Armenians.

Like other Christians and Jews in the empire, Ottoman Armenians were defined by their membership in the Armenian Gregorian (or Apostolic) Church. The church was Monophysite in its beliefs, holding that Christ had only one divine nature, not both divine and human natures, and was considered heretical by Catholics and Orthodox. Its primary see was at Echmiadzin in the Russian South Caucasus, but members of the Ottoman Armenian community were led by the Armenian Patriarch of Constantinople. As was true with the other non-Muslim groups, the Armenian community was in many ways autonomous, with its own schools, courts, and welfare system. Although Armenians had been migrating from their impoverished homeland for hundreds of years, the center of Armenian population still lay in Eastern Anatolia and the South Caucasus. In the early nineteenth century the wealth and status of the Armenian *millet* could not compare to that of the Greek *millet,* reflecting the poverty of its homeland. Its clergy was far less educated, as were community members. The Armenian merchant population, however, was sizable, growing, and often dissatisfied with the old ways and the rule of the clergy.

Missionaries of the American Board first made contact with Ottoman Armenians in Istanbul and İzmir but soon extended their mission field to the Armenian homeland in Eastern Anatolia. Interest in the Armenians was specifically heightened by the journey of Eli Smith and Harrison Dwight to Eastern Anatolia and the Caucasus in 1830. Smith and Dwight had been sent to ascertain the possibilities of the region as a mission field. Their account, part travelogue, part analysis of Armenian Christianity, attracted further American interest in the Armenians.[16] As they toured from Istanbul to Tiflis, Smith and Dwight observed the Armenian clergy and laity and studied the practices and doctrines of the Armenian Gregorian Church. They were not pleased with what they saw. The worship and belief they observed had many of the elements that Calvinists detested in the Catholic Church—saints, fasts, feast days, a priesthood, complicated liturgies, and especially the belief that all of these were essential components of the way to salvation. They felt that the Armenians were not true Christians—they were a people who substituted "a system of salvation by external ceremonies for faith in the atoning blood of Christ," which led to "the hireling character and debasement of the clergy" and "want of moral principle universally manifested in conduct immoral or vicious." They acknowledged the depth of belief of the Armenians, but this would not save them from damnation: "They are sincere in believing that their superstitious rites and ceremonies will cancel their sins. But can such sincerity save them? It is the very thing that encourages them to indulge in sin. It makes them feel secure in courses which they know to be wicked. It leads them blindfold to perdition." The Armenians would not be saved without assistance and change. Salvation was to be delivered by the missionaries.[17]

> But, though they [the Armenians] are in a perishing state, their rescue is not to be despaired of. For, another consideration we would suggest respecting them is, *that their reformation is practicable.* It is so because the truth can be brought to bear upon their minds. Christians in Mohammedan lands are accessible to missionaries—in the Turkish empire may the missionary enter at every point and labour among them, with no Turkish ruler disposed, *of himself,* to hinder or make him afraid in so doing. Wherever he finds them, may he plant the standard of the Cross, and Moslems, if left to themselves, will look on with indifference.[18]

The Armenians were to be converted. Then, Smith and Dwight believed, the Muslims would surely follow and themselves become Christians. Muslims had not converted in the past because they had only seen the Middle Eastern churches as the representatives of Christianity, little better than Islam. Once the Armenians had been converted, the Muslims would see the truth of real Christianity and be drawn to it.

Thus did the American missionary enterprise among the Armenians begin. Smith and Dwight correctly believed that the attitude of the Ottoman government and the Muslims toward Christian missionaries would be noninvolvement. The Ottomans kept to a long tradition of noninterference with Christian religion. The faith of the missionaries and the tolerance of the Muslims were to be the foundations of a great missionary venture among the Armenians. Mission stations and schools supported by the American Board soon spread out across Anatolia, ministering primarily to Armenians. Other missions were sent to the Nestorian Christians in southeastern Anatolia and western Iran. The numbers of American missionaries grew significantly. The number of missionaries of the American Board and the Presbyterian Board of Foreign Missions in the Ottoman Empire increased from 34 in 1845 to 359 by 1914. An additional 75 Presbyterian missionaries served in Iran. When missionaries from other Christian denominations are added, 535 missionaries were serving in the Ottoman Empire and Iran.[19] At the beginning of World War I, 36,004 students were studying at American mission schools and colleges in both empires.[20] Four missionary colleges educated Christians—Robert College and Constantinople Women's College in Istanbul, Anatolia College in Merzifon, and Syrian Protestant College in Beirut. The schools provided the best education available in the Ottoman Empire.

The Missionary Establishment
and the Image of Turks in America

The American missionary enterprise in the Middle East and the Balkans was one of the greatest such endeavors in history. Its benefits for the Christians of the Ottoman Empire were significant and have been extensively described elsewhere.[21] My purpose here is not to describe the mission itself in detail but to assess the impact of the missionaries and their writings on the American image of the Turks and other Muslim peoples of the Middle East. There the missionary effect was not so salutary. The American missionaries were the primary source of a negative image that has persisted long after the missions had closed and the churches that sent the missionaries had evolved into advocates of an unprejudiced acceptance of other cultures.

The minds of the missionaries were formed by the universally negative image of Turks and Islam prevalent in America. The missionaries in turn widened and deepened the prejudice of Americans. For most of the nineteenth century missionaries were virtually the only Americans who lived in the Ottoman Empire and reported on it to Americans back home. With a few exceptions, the only other Americans to see the Middle East and Balkans were merchants, who seldom stayed there long and even more seldom recorded their impressions in books. The image of the Turks that the missionaries portrayed was deeply flawed by their prejudices, but as clergy they were trusted by a believing nation that expected to hear the worst of "infidels" and was not to be disappointed.

The missionary establishment that began with the first efforts of the American Board was to become a great force in American life. The term "establishment" would not have been used at the time, but it describes those in authority, religious and political, who supported the American missions in the Ottoman Empire. It was made up of the missionaries themselves, missionary organizations such as the American Board and the Presbyterian Foreign Mission Board, and a multitude of clergy and lay members of churches and religious societies. Supporters included American presidents and members of Congress, newspaper editors, industrialists, college presidents, and, in general, those in a position to affect American public opinion. Members of the missionary establishment had different religious views, but until the 1920s they spoke with one voice on the Turks and on Islam. That voice was overwhelmingly negative and uniformly unjust.

2

Turks and Muslims in Early America

The image of Turks began with a historical disadvantage in early America.[1] The new American Republic, despite the secularism of its Constitution, was a resolutely Christian state. Little was known of Islam, except as a supposed enemy of Christianity. The Americans were justly proud of their new democracy, and the Turks were anything but democratic. Again, based on scant knowledge, the Turks were viewed as the epitome of the despotic. Like the Europeans of the time, the Americans looked back to the classical traditions of Greece and Rome as their ancestry, the founts of democracy, naming their children Cassius, Augustus, and Pericles and building their civic monuments based on somewhat fanciful ancient models. The Turks were not descended from that tradition. Indeed they had destroyed the last vestige of the classical world, the Byzantine Empire. In the minds of Americans the Turks appeared to be the opponents of both religious and secular good. They were not Christians. They had defeated the armies of Christendom. They were infidels who controlled the Holy Land. From the perspective of early Americans, Turkish history could be viewed as a long campaign against that which Americans held most dear.

Early Americans knew little about the Turks or Muslims. What they thought they knew was heard in church, learned in school, or read in the occasional newspaper. All presented only a negative image of the Turks.

The Turks from the Pulpit

Religion was an intrinsic part of the formation of the American image of the Turks. It both reflected and formed the views of Americans. It is of course impossible to know what local ministers such as circuit-riding preachers in the West taught their congregations of the Turks or Islam—probably very little. Published sermons (mainly from New England), however, do reveal that a stereotype of the Turks was imbedded in the minds of early Americans by the clergy. Early Americans were proud of their preachers and published a great number of their sermons.[2] Preachers declared the Turks to be the natural enemy of Christianity, "the greatest obstacle in the way of spreading the Gospel."[3] Reading these sermons affords an idea of what congregations heard in the churches.

A common negative view of the Turks suffused the sermons. Preachers vilified Turks and Islam whenever they were mentioned, often in the same phrase as others who were despised—"Turks, Jews, Papists, and heathens."[4] The Turks were seen as creatures of the spiritual darkness, unable to recognize "the falsity of their dark religion."[5] No language was too intemperate to describe "that great Dog the Turk" or rule by "vicious and vile" sultans.[6] One sermon characterized the Turk and the pope as Gog and Magog.[7] Ministers never described Muhammad without adding "the Imposter" or "the Arch-Imposter" after his name; and they usually simply said "the Imposter," assuming the congregation would know to whom they referred.

When preachers gave accounts of Turkish life, most alluded to Turkish "brutality" and "viciousness" but gave no details. Occasional descriptions were less than edifying, such as those of the Reverend Elijah Parish, who claimed that the Turks murdered with impunity and drank the blood from corpses.[8] The condition of Christians in the Ottoman Empire was routinely called slavery. The glorified state of the Middle East in biblical times—which had no historical reality—was compared to the contemporary state of the region. All the sermons depicted depopulation and disintegration—poor and miserable people living in ramshackle huts, plagued by filth and disease. The physical degradation was held to be God's judgment on the local Christians, who had abandoned true belief and thus were punished through the agency of the Turks.[9] Echoing the portrait of Turks in the popular literature, preachers saw Turks as essentially indolent: "Time was, when there were seven churches in Asia, and pure religion beamed, where now ignorance and superstition brood, and where the Turk, dreaming of a Mahometan paradise, sleeps his life away."[10]

To the ministers Turks were the universal bad example, cited when a negative model was needed, such as in Cotton Mather's call for families to pray together: "The very Turks themselves at this day uphold a family-worship among themselves; God forbid that any styled Christians here should be worse than they."[11] Mather also condemned those who had persecuted Christian Dissenters in the worst words possible: "They would as soon be Turks or Papists."[12] In the rhetoric of the American Revolution, the British were described as bringing to America "barbarity unknown to Turks and Mahometan infidels."[13] Only one was worse than "the Turk"; as Increase Mather noted, "The devil is more cruel than any Turk."[14]

Aside from the devil, the only others to be pilloried like the Turks were Catholics and "loose Protestants": Protestant sinners who should have known better. The fate of the latter was to be associated in the hereafter with Turks and "idolatrous Papists." They were to be placed, along with the Catholics and Turks, in the left hand of God, from which they would be cast into the fiery pit of hell.[15] Associating Christians who had lapsed or, despite outward piety, had not experienced a true conversion of the soul with the Muslims was an old trans-Atlantic tradition. The great preacher and reformer John Wesley also made the comparison.[16]

The image of the Turks in the colonial and early American mind was bound up in the Americans' interpretation of the biblical Book of Revelation (also known as Revelations or the Apocalypse). The Book of Revelation was very much alive in the minds of the ministers and congregations of America. They believed that the end of the world as they knew it was approaching and the reign of Christ was imminent. The events of the Last Days were held to be foretold in Revelation, in which Turks would play a prominent part.

Like Nonconformist beliefs in general, the American view of the Last Days was shared by their English brethren. English sermons on the Apocalypse were reprinted in America. Their theology was the same as in the American sermons, but the American preachers gave less detail.[17] The British divine Elhanan Winchester gave the most complete surviving description of the accepted place of the Turks in God's plan in a book reprinted in Boston.[18] Winchester described the destruction brought upon the earth as angels sounded the trumpets given them by God (Revelation 8–10): the Turks were the agents of the Destruction of the Sixth Trumpet, "another dreadful plague, or woe, was about to come upon the world," as a punishment for their sins.[19] Revelation said that the sounding of the trumpet would loose upon the world devastation that would destroy "the third part of men" (Revelation 9:15). So Winchester wrote the abundant absurdity that the Turks were prepared to kill one-third of humanity, although the expression might be taken to mean a great part of the whole of humanity. Nevertheless, "We may reckon the Turks as the greatest destroyers of the human race that were ever raised up; and it is likely that in the course of their wars they may have actually slain as many persons as would amount to nearly one third of all the people now living upon the earth."[20] But Winchester was not sure that the Turks had killed enough to make up the one-third. They still had work to do and would return to fill their quota: "I am persuaded that they will be the principal leaders in the army that shall come against the children of Israel, after their return to their own land, as shall be destroyed at the coming of the Lord, as mentioned by the Prophets Ezekiel and Zachariah."[21] Winchester went on to devote much description to the role of the Turks as evil agents of the Antichrist who would eventually be brought down by God. Despite the assertion that the Turks were hated by God, they were working according to God's plan. God had always used the Turks to punish the wicked, particularly the Greek Church, chastised for its "idolatry."

American preachers used the same terms and analysis as Winchester, sometimes adding that the Turks were also described in another part of Revelation: the Turks were ultimately to be punished for their sins when God directed that the "seven vials" of destruction be poured out on the followers of the Antichrist (Revelation 16). Jonathan Edwards, the greatest of the New England preachers, felt that the vials were "God's wrath on the Antichrist: one is poured out on the Jews, another on the Turks, another on the Pagans, another on the church of Rome; but they all signify God's successive judgements or plagues on the beast and his kingdom." Edwards was convinced that that the Turks were agents of the Antichrist "let loose on Christendom."[22] Others agreed that the vials were to be poured out "upon the western and eastern Antichrist, the pope and the Turk; who must be removed for the spiritual reign of Christ."[23]

Opinions on the seven vials differed somewhat, but all believed the Turks to be either agents of the Antichrist or the Antichrist himself. In any case, the Turks would have to be removed if Christ was to reign: "The Day is at the Door (Lord Hasten It!) when the Papal and the Turkish Power being extinguished, and the Divel [sic] also having no power to deceive the Nations, it will be proclaimed, *The Kingdoms of the world are become the Kingdoms of our Lord and of His Church, and He shall Reign for ever and ever.*"[24]

Educating Early Americans about the Turks

Early Americans who wished to learn of foreign cultures at first depended on British books, which were costly and difficult to obtain. The first organized description of Turks and Muslims in America came in geographies and later in brief histories, usually written by clergymen. The religious orientation of the authors deeply affected their portrayal of Middle Easterners, as did a general lack of information on the Middle East. Two dominant themes were evident in the early American publications: the exotic nature of the Turks and their brutality. The theme of sexuality and sensuality (much in evidence later) was only hinted at in these publications. The American geographers portrayed the Turks as indolent, only arousing themselves to be brutal, especially to Christians. The Turks were exotic, dressed in strange clothes, with exceedingly odd social habits. They were sensuous and sexually immoral. This picture of Turks as lazy, brutal, and ignorant would become the basis of the American vision of "the Turk," a myth that was to last and become engrained in the American consciousness.[25]

Little evidence has survived on the teachings on Turks and Islam in the religious schools that were ubiquitous in early America. The titles of the books used in Sunday schools demonstrate that children were taught to detest Islam and its Prophet, such as *The False Prophet; or, an Account of the Rise and Progress of the Mohammedan Religion*,[26] published by the Massachusetts Sabbath Sunday School Society. The book used the conceit of a Christian mother who explained Islam to her children. She was approximately as successful in the endeavor as a Turkish mother of the time who explained New England Protestantism to her children would be. The American mother taught her children that Muhammad was a robber, a murderer, morally "polluted," and "the most successful Imposter that ever lived." The children asked why God would have allowed such a monster to be so successful and were told not to question Providence. Mother said that Muhammad had been allowed to flourish because of God's mysterious plans, which could not be questioned, but conjectured that God allowed Muhammad to deceive the Arabs as punishment for their many sins. Other books, such as *An Entertaining History of Two Pious Twin Children Who Were Stolen from Their Christian Parents by a Jew, and Sold to the Turks as Slaves and with Their Father Were Marvelously Saved from Death, to Which Is Added, Little Charles, or, the Good Son*, must have found an interested readership among adults as well as children.[27]

Jedidiah Morse, a Congregational minister in Charlestown, Massachusetts, near Boston, was the author of the first geography of America, *Geography Made*

Easy (1784). He extended his efforts to world geography, publishing *The American Universal Geography* in 1793, expanded in 1813. *The American Universal Geography* and other Morse books on world geography went through dozens of editions up to 1828.[28] Some of these, such as *Geography Made Easy*, gave Turks and Muslims only a few pages, all with negative stereotypes. *The American Universal Geography*, however, included extensive descriptions of the pre-Islamic Middle East and Balkans, stressing the historic and Christian background of the region, obviously drawn completely from British works. Morse obviously knew nothing of the Middle East himself, as evidenced by his statement that "the Turkish dominions [a list of Asian Ottoman provinces follows] belong to those parts of the world which enjoy the most delightful climate and the happiest situation for commerce and the acquisition of opulence."[29] Morse had almost nothing good to say about the Turks. "The morals of the Turks are loose in the extreme, and lewdness, in its worst forms, is common throughout Turkey. Both sexes are distinguished for cleanliness, and bathing is one of their stated amusements."[30] He called Islam "the contagion,"[31] but his works were still less obviously prejudiced than many later publications. He stressed and exaggerated the negative, such as governmental corruption, but usually was content to describe government and geography (with numerous errors).

Those who followed Morse were even less kind to the Turks. Clergymen were the foremost educated class in the colonies and early United States, so they naturally were the authors of the uplifting and educating books found in the schools and in the homes of the literate. Their books and presumably their teachings reflected a definitely negative view of the Turks. The Reverend Nathaniel Dwight wrote: "The Turks are indolent and superstitious, but commonly temperate. They are heavy, morose, treacherous, furiously passionate, unsocial, and unfriendly to people of all other nations."[32] The Reverend Royal Robbins was undaunted by the task of portraying everything in *The World Displayed in Its History and Geography; Embracing a History of the World from the Creation to the Present Day, with General Views of the Politics, Religion, Military and Naval Affairs, Arts, Literature, Manners, Customs, and Society, of Ancient as Well as Modern Nations, by the Rev. Royal Robbins; To Which Is Added an Outline of Modern Geography.* Robbins did not hide his feelings about those he called the "barbarous Turk" and the "vindictive Turk." He thought a page and a half was sufficient to describe the Ottoman Empire. Muhammad was given one page. Robbins described him, as did most others, as "the Imposter," a man who brought "daring impiety and wickedness" to the world by deliberate deception.[33] Other books by Robbins repeated the depictions of Turks and Islam, often in the same words.[34]

Early American geography and history texts devoted very little attention to the Ottoman Empire or Islam beyond a few pages of insults and questionable history. The portrayal was mainly negative but brief. Descriptions of the Middle East and the Balkans stressed their Christian and classical heritage. The texts cited regions, rivers, and mountains with names that had not been used in more than a thousand years. They devoted more print to interesting and colorful "facts" on the Middle East than to actual history: the monks on Mount Athos lived to a great age; the

Arabians were all thieves; the Arabs, descendants of Ishmael, had been eternally blasted by God. The books often gave more space to camels than to the Ottoman government and always paid more attention to ancient ruins. They usually dedicated a paragraph or two to the present government, in which the words "cruel," "despotic," "arbitrary," and "brutal" featured prominently:

> The government of Turkey is a cruel and debasing despotism. The inhabitants are indolent and sensual. They keep many wives, and are much addicted to smoking.[35]

> This country was formerly one of the finest in Europe, but owing to the despotism and wretched policy of the Turks, it is now one of the most miserable.[36]

> The Turks are grave and sedate in their manners, but ignorant and bigoted; and so indolent that nothing short of the strongest excitement will rouse them to activity.[37]

> The people of Turkey are chiefly Mahometans, who are generally ignorant, indolent, and unskillful in arts and manufactures.[38]

> The Turks are grave, honest, and hospitable in their intercourse with strangers, yet haughty, superstitious, revengeful, and vicious in their habits. Indolence is their most striking trait.[39]

The entire consideration in Robert Davidson's *Geography Epitomized* was a short ditty:

> To Asia Minor more north we proceed,
> Where flourishing Cities in ruin are laid.
> Rich provinces here are said to have been,
> But indolent Turks have quite altered the scene.[40]

The exotic was prominent in American books, usually taking more space than the political or religious elements. The standard of accuracy was not great, although the life portrayed would surely have been of interest to an American audience. Most Turks supposedly had auburn or chestnut hair. Turks usually woke in the middle of the night, smoked pipes, drank coffee, and ate sweets. They did not drink alcohol but smoked opium instead. Turkish women's clothes were ringed with pearls and lined with ermine or sable; their shoes were made of white kid leather embroidered with gold. They wore a large silver or gold ring through their right nostril.[41] When the sultan passed in the street all the people prostrated themselves in the dirt.[42] Almost none of this was true, but it was interesting.

If the exotic dress and strange customs of the Turks might attract American schoolchildren, the alleged character traits would surely repel them:

Their character is a curious mixture of good and bad. They are hospitable and courageous. When provoked their passions are furious and ungovernable; they are vindictive, jealous, haughty, intolerant, and full of dissimulation. Their religion inspires them with contempt and hatred for those of a different creed; their despotic government makes them blindly submissive to their superiors, and oppressive to their inferiors.[43]

The Reverend George Bush wrote a standard American history of Muhammad for his time.[44] It was not an age that attempted objective consideration of religions as understood by their believers. Even in the table of contents Bush wrote of Muhammad's deceptions with the intention of "palming a new religion upon the world." "The Imposter" was of course used almost as if it was the Prophet's title. Bush spared no invective in describing Muhammad, a man of "the most unbounded ambition and the vilest sensuality," allegedly full of "delinquencies," "corrupt propensities," and "personal degeneracy": "Fanaticism, ambition, and lust were his master-passions."[45] Bush respected Muhammad's innate political abilities but felt that he only succeeded because "the mysterious wisdom of Jehovah" had decreed that the divine plan would somehow be carried out by him. Bush offered quotations from Revelation and the Book of Daniel, with explications, to show how Muhammad and Islam fit into that plan.[46] Muhammad's conquests and his life were portrayed as the evil actions of an evil man, but he was still doing God's work.[47]

In a study considerably more scholarly than Bush's, Washington Irving showed more respect for the Prophet of Islam.[48] He portrayed Muhammad as a good man who tried to reform the corrupt religion of his fellows. Irving could not, however, countenance the possibility that Muhammad's vision was truly spiritual. Instead, Muhammad's summons from God was put down to fatigue, self-delusion, or some type of mental illness or epilepsy (an analysis that became common in later years).[49] Nevertheless, Irving, unlike his contemporary religious writers, held that Muhammad believed in his visions and his faith and asserted that Muhammad was a great man.[50] Although Irving believed that Muhammad had been deluded, he treated him more sympathetically than any Americans had done before or were to do for generations to come. It is instructive that Irving's book was published in 1850 but did not appear in an American edition until it found its way into his collected works. Bush's book was printed in both American and Canadian editions in 1830, reprinted every year until 1839, and reprinted again in 1842, 1847, 1852, 1854, 1864, and 1900.[51] It was also included in the popular Harper's Family Library.

The most prolific of the American textbook writers was Samuel Goodrich, who wrote both under his own name and under the pseudonym "Peter Parley." The son of a minister, Goodrich began an incredible writing career after serving in the War of 1812. Editions of his various educational books of literature, history, geography, and natural sciences numbered approximately 170 volumes from 1827 to 1859. A third of them (geographies and histories) included some information on the Turks.[52] Goodrich's books can be considered the main source of information on the world for American schoolchildren. Thus it is instructive to see what American youth learned of the Turks from Peter Parley:

> The chief ruler or king of the Turks is called the Sultan. He lives at Constantinople, in a splendid palace. Like most eastern princes, he has two or three hundred wives, which he keeps shut up in a place called the harem.

> The Turks have long beards, wear turbans on their heads, and a loose flowing robe over their under dress. They sit on cushions instead of chairs, and take their food with fingers, instead of forks.

> The Sultan rules over his country, not according to certain established laws, but according to his own will. The people generally do exactly what he requires; if they refuse to obey him, they are sure to lose their property and their heads.

> If you were to go to Turkey, you would discover that the climate is warm, and the country naturally fertile; you would see that the people are indolent and cruel. You would see that they have not many manufactures, and but little commerce. You would see that the lands are poorly cultivated, and that many tracts naturally fruitful are barren and desolate for want of tillage.

> You will discover that the people dislike the Christians, and worship according to the faith of Mahomet. You will discover that they have mosques instead of churches. At Constantinople, you will see a very splendid edifice, called St. Sophia. This was formerly a Greek church, but is now converted into a Mahometan mosque.[53]

In order to entertain his young readers, Goodrich included wholly fictitious stories of murderous sultans, including Murat IV: "The sport that pleased him best, was to run about the streets at night, with a drawn sword, cutting and slashing at every body whom he met."[54]

Like many others of his time, Goodrich was a racialist. He described what he considered to be the various human races by their supposed racial characteristics, grading them by their moral qualities, industriousness, and achievements. Caucasians, as might be expected, were first on the list. The Turks were not highly placed: "Accustomed to a roving and predatory life in the vast steppes of Asia, these wandering tribes have left them only to devastate the inheritance, and subvert the civil institutions, of their more polished brethren."[55]

It is obvious from Goodrich's texts that by the 1850s the Myth of the Turk had become firmly planted in America. Goodrich described the Turks as essentially exotic and strange:

> The Turks are the same in Asia as in Europe. They are an Oriental people, and form a complete contrast in all the external forms of life to Europeans. The

men, instead of our dresses [*sic*] fitted tight to the body, wear long, flowing robes, which conceal the limbs; and instead of standing, or sitting on chairs, they remain stretched on sofas in luxurious indolence, considering it madness to stir or walk, unless for special purposes or for business. They sit cross-legged, and recline at meals. On entering a house, they take off, not their hat, but their shoes. In eating, they use the fingers only, without knife or fork; they sleep, not on beds, but on couches upon the ground or floor. The females, excluded from all society, remain shut up in the harem, and must not be seen or named by any person of the opposite sex.[56]

To demonstrate his points, Goodrich included what seem today to be humorous drawings. An illustration of Turkish eating habits showed two men (who appeared to be Noble Romans but with muttonchop whiskers) reclining on a raised Roman couch. Despite the talk of completely covered and secluded women in the text, women in the pictures were unveiled.

Goodrich's Turk was basically an indolent man from whom very little was required. "The amusements of the Turk are chiefly domestic. His delight is to give himself up to continued and unvaried revery; to glide down the streams of time without thought or anxiety; to retire under the shade of trees, there to muse without any fixed object, and to inhale through the pipe a gentle, inebriating vapor"— a wonderful poetic description, even if completely ridiculous. Though perhaps not as seduced by the pleasures of indolence as Goodrich asserted, Turks would surely have loved to have lived in the environment he described: "The apartments of the harem, which are devoted to the women, are spacious and gorgeously decorated. The center room has a marble fountain, whose falling waters lull the indolent to repose, or amuse the thoughtless with its murmurs; the air is at the same time filled with perfumes."[57]

As might be expected, Goodrich related a remarkable history of the Turks. Some of his accounts were so strange that it is difficult to imagine where he might have found them. They were not particularly negative, however, stressing interesting if apocryphal stories rather than derogatory statements. Turks were even praised for their tolerance toward conquered Christians. He described Persians and Arabs in less detail and less fancifully. The obvious intent was to tell intriguing stories. Thus "interesting Muslims" such as the Assassins were given considerable space, interweaving fanciful stories with real history. Like other authors, Goodrich was sympathetic to the early Arabs, the "Saracens." Armenians, in a time when the missionaries' preferences had not yet taken hold in America, were sometimes described in negative terms, such as speaking of "degraded" females, "addicted to excess in liquor."[58]

What was wrong with Goodrich's depictions was not only the false image of indolent Turks and slashing sultans but the lack of any positive image. Turks, of course, had laws: a complicated and long established set of Islamic laws, the Sharia, and administrative laws codified by Süleyman the Magnificent and updated. The laws were not the same as those in use in Connecticut, but the Turks were not lawless. As for dislike of Christians, many Muslims undoubtedly did dislike Christians, just as many Christians disliked Muslims. Some mention should have been made, however, of the long tradition of religious tolerance, which meant that those Christians still existed in the Ottoman Empire and practiced their faith 700 years after the appearance of the Turks in Anatolia. Goodrich surely knew no better. He was simply repeating and reinforcing a long heritage of ignorance.

The Constant Image

As the following chapters demonstrate, seventy years after the early American geographers described the Turks as "vindictive, jealous, haughty, intolerant, and full of dissimulation," American newspapers and magazines were still depicting the Turks in the same way, using virtually the same terms. They still portrayed the Turks as people of violent and ungovernable passions, indolent until they roused themselves to become brutal. Islam fared little better. Muhammad was as much "the Imposter" in 1900 as he was to the early American ministers. Writers still blamed Islam for the destruction of industry and agriculture. The suffering caused by Turks was much exaggerated, while the suffering of Turks went unmentioned.

3

THE GREEK REBELLION

*The Turk is a barbarian. All his vices are thoroughly and incurably bar-
barian. He is habitually tyrannical, passionate for plunder, and a lover of
blood—his tastes are barbarian, extravagant splendor, gross indulgence,
savage indolence of mind and body—he enjoys none of the resources of civilization—he has no national literature—he cultivates no language—he
produces no picture, no statue, no music.[1]*

In America, the Greek War of Independence began a cycle of biased public information that was to continue for a century. Newspapers and magazines both
reflected and shaped American prejudices; preexisting bias and the media reinforced each other. Readers expected to see that the Turks were evil, and the press
gave them what they wanted.

The Greek revolution began in March 1821. At first Ottoman officials, especially tax collectors, were the targets of the rebels; but by April they had advanced
to a slaughter of Turks in the Morea (Peloponnesus). The only Turks who escaped
were those who were able to make their way to Ottoman fortifications. Many of
these were ultimately killed when the strongholds were overrun or starved out.
As the rebels advanced out of the Morea, more Turks were massacred or forced
to flee. Some Turkish women and children were taken as slaves and thus escaped
death, but most women and children were killed. Torture was common. The rebels admitted and reveled in their killings. At the same time, rebels in Galatz and
Yassy (today in Romania) exterminated all the Turks in the cities and villages that
came under their control. Estimates vary, but it seems that 25,000 Turks were
killed in Greece alone, as well as an unknown number of Jews.[2]

Ottoman soldiers responded with tactics as brutal as those of the Greeks. The
Greek Orthodox patriarch of Constantinople, suspected of supporting the rebels, was hanged in Istanbul. An attempted uprising in the Aydın Province of Western Anatolia was put down ferociously, with much Greek mortality. Nearly 5,000
Greeks were killed after a failed revolt on the island of Chios. More were killed as
Ottoman forces attempted to retake territory from the rebels. In fact, the rebellion quickly became a war in which no quarter was given on either side.

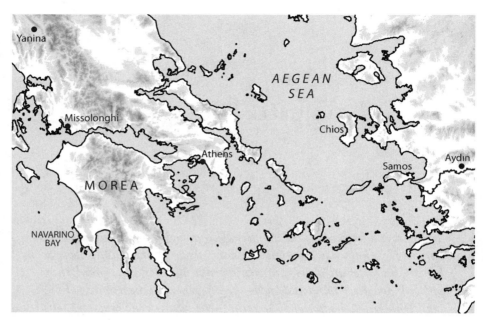

3.1. Ottoman Greece and the Aegean Islands

The rebels were initially successful in holding their own against Ottoman forces. In 1822 and 1823 Ottoman armies were forced to withdraw when they could not dislodge the Greeks from fortified positions such as the city of Missolonghi before winter set in. The Greeks fought among themselves for control of central and southern Greece, but the Ottomans failed to capitalize on the disunity. In 1825 the sultan called on his nominal vassal and governor of Egypt, Mehmet (Moham- med) Ali, promising him governorships in Crete and Greece if he put down the rebels. Mehmet Ali's son İbrahim quickly took Crete from the rebels then slowly advanced into Greece proper. Joined by an Ottoman army, the Egyptians and Turks had retaken almost all of Greece by June 1827. Their victory was short-lived. England, France, and Russia intervened, burned the Ottoman and Egyptian fleets at Navarino, and forced the Ottomans to grant Greece independence.

The News

The news that reached America from the Ottoman Empire was at least a month old. It came from British and occasionally other European newspapers and in let- ters from the Middle East and Balkans. No American journalists were stationed in the region. Articles from the same sources often appeared many times in different newspapers and magazines,[3] and the newspapers copied freely from each other.

The reports of the Greek revolt were often confused and their details often wrong. In the beginning most newspapers showed little awareness of exactly who was revolting. The papers did not realize that most of the Christians of the Otto- man Europe were Orthodox in religion but not ethnic Greeks, so they wrote of the rebellion as a revolt of all the Ottoman Christians. They also did not realize that ethnic divisiveness meant that other Orthodox ethnic groups might not welcome

Greek rule.[4] Much was invented. Improbable alliances that never existed were created on paper.[5] Echoing the British newspapers that were their usual sources, the American papers tended to print what they hoped to be the facts rather than what actually occurred. The newspapers made no attempt to hide their desire for a Greek triumph and printed whatever news they could to prove that the triumph was imminent: Greeks supposedly defeated Turks in battles in which the Greeks were outnumbered by more than ten to one. Reports claimed that the Dardanelles were seized by the Greeks.[6] The Ottoman ruling family was "nearly extinct."[7] The Turks were so belabored by the Greeks that they were starving and had begun to eat each other.[8] Sixty thousand or two hundred thousand Greek men, depending on the source, were fighting the Turks, and the Greek women had taken up arms.[9] Fanciful accounts from the battlefield reported that in each engagement the Turks lost many more men than the Greeks.[10] One article reprinted in many newspapers reported that the Greek rebels had seized the city of Edirne (Adrianople), the entire Christian population of Anatolia had taken to the mountains, all of Bulgaria was in revolt, and "a corps of 5,000 Janissaries, in ascending the Bosphorus, burnt and pillaged all the houses, without distinction, belonging to the Turks and the Greeks."[11] None of this was true.

Newspapers wrote as if they had intimate knowledge of the secret deliberations of the European powers, including wholly fictitious plans to dismember the Ottoman Empire.[12] And it was not only the secrets of Britain, France, and Russia that were supposedly known to the Americans. Newspapers described the sultan's evil intentions and the inner workings of the Ottoman government: the *Boston Daily Advertiser* wrote that the sultan had ordered that every Greek in Istanbul be destroyed, but the "Captain Pacha and the Mafti [mufti]" prevented the order from being carried out.[13] The *Christian Repository* felt the sultan's sanguinary wishes were more inclusive: "On more occasions than one, the Sultan has proposed to put to death all the Christians in the empire, and has been dissuaded from the purpose, only by the consideration that such destruction would reduce the amount of the capitation [tax paid by Christians]."[14] The *Boston Commercial Gazette* wrote that the Turkish Imperial Council had entertained proposals in 1790, 1807, and again in 1821 "to massacre all the Christians in the Ottoman Empire." According to the *Commercial Gazette,* the 1821 proposal had been opposed by the grand vezir; but when he was replaced massacres had begun, including hundreds in Istanbul.[15] These articles, like other distressing ones, did not attempt to name their sources and may have had no source other than the editors' imagination.

At the beginning of the revolt, statements that the Greeks were victorious were accurate, if overblown. The Ottomans were indeed losing.[16] The situation changed, however, when Mohammed Ali's son İbrahim led his Egyptian troops against the rebels. Readers of the American media would not have known it. It took some time after Mohammed Ali's forces entered the war for the American newspapers to accept that the Greeks were being defeated. They printed entirely spurious accounts of Greek victories over the Egyptians.[17] The *Saturday Evening*

Post declared that "the Greeks are going on triumphantly," easily defeating their opponents.[18] The *Western Luminary* reported that the Egyptian and Turkish forces were soundly defeated. Concerning the Egyptian army in the Morea, the *Luminary* added that "the next arrivals [of news] will probably bring us intelligence of its capture or entire destruction."[19]

In fact, the Greeks were being defeated. Missolonghi fell to the Egyptians on April 24, 1826. More than two months after the city's fall, the *New Harmony Gazette* was still reporting that the Greeks had been successful at Missolonghi and that İbrahim Paşa had been killed there.[20] Other papers also printed news of İbrahim's death, even providing details of his demise.[21] The *Escritoir* wrote that İbrahim Paşa had taken Missolonghi and lived but was being besieged there by Greek forces.[22] İbrahim Paşa had actually taken Missolonghi and had not been besieged by any Greek force. He died in 1848, not 1826.

By late summer of 1826 most newspapers finally began to admit ruefully that the Egyptians and Turks had defeated the Greeks—"Missolonghi Fallen!"[23] The papers turned to printing articles on the sufferings of the Greeks in the city before and after its capture. Some began to despair of the Greek cause, but more printed whatever good news could be found or manufactured, always with calls for European intervention to save the Greeks.[24] In their safe homes thousands of miles away, the Americans called for the Europeans to go to war. The imminent demise of the Ottoman Empire in Europe was confidently expected, if only the Europeans would take action. Americans felt that the best solution to the "Turkish problem" was British intervention on the side of the Greeks. American newspapers and preachers did not hesitate to recommend that action to the British or to complain that the British were not acting quickly enough.[25] Many feared that Russia would take over, rather than allowing the Greeks to create a new Greek empire or republic in the Balkans, but they were willing to accept such an outcome. Some, indeed, actively campaigned for Russian conquest.[26] For most, however, Russian conquest was held to be undesirable but acceptable because it would be an improvement: "Humanity will not drop many tears over the extinction of the Turkish power. It can hardly pass into worse hands. The Turks seem incorrigibly barbarous."[27]

When things looked bleakest for the Greeks the Americans offered advice. The Greeks were told, assuming they read the American press, to take courage by looking to the spirit of their noble ancestors, by remembering Alexander the Great and Leonides and by emulating the Greeks at Marathon; then they would be saved.[28] Whether or not the Greeks took the American advice to emulate their forefathers is unknown. They were ultimately saved by the European powers. The Battle of Navarino, in which European navies destroyed the Egyptian fleet, was the cause of general rejoicing in the American newspapers, with headlines such as "Good News from Greece!" The newspapers almost gleefully described the loss of thousands of Turkish and Egyptian troops and sailors: "If that can be called *good news* which relates the account of human blood lost in battle, this may indeed be called such by all the friends of suffering Greece—all the friends of humanity."[29]

The press began a campaign that was to be mainstay of American articles and editorials for the next century: evicting the Turks from Europe. Despite four hundred years of residence in the Balkans, Turks, it was believed, could never be true Europeans; they were not like other Europeans. Indeed, they had destroyed what was best in Europe:

> The Turks, being heterogeneous in their laws and politics, as well as in religion, from the rest of Europe, who do not even acknowledge the law of nations, can never be looked upon as rightful dwellers on European soil; they are interlopers upon the conquered, whom their barbarities have never been able to destroy; and ought therefore to be swept from the face of Europe, and driven back to the mountains and deserts of Asia, whence their ancestors spread like a torrent over the finest parts of the world, and fixed the seat of their government in the noblest and most delightful city at that time in the universe. The Greek nation became a non-entity; the good, the learned, and the wise, fled from the Goths of the east, and sought a refuge in Italy, whither they carried the fine arts, and rekindled the flame of learning and genius, which had so long laid smothered in the embers of barbarism and Gothic darkness.[30]

Massacre

The Greek rebellion began another pattern of reporting on Turks that was to continue through World War I. Christian deaths were reported and usually exaggerated in number. Christian mortality, whether in battle, from disease and starvation, or truly from a massacre, was reported as "massacre by the Turks." Turkish mortality was seldom reported and was greatly minimized in the few papers that reported it at all. Only very occasionally did the American press admit that Greeks massacred Turks, but this was excused as understandable revenge. When Turks killed Greeks, it was an outrage—not so when Greeks killed Turks.[31] Some of the reports were not simply omissions of Turkish dead but outright falsehoods. According to the *National Intelligencer,* the rebels took Athens, with "not a Turk being injured in his person or that of his property."[32] In fact, the Turkish men were massacred immediately when Athens was taken by the Greeks, along with many of the women. The rest of the women were enslaved. The only Turks who escaped were some women ransomed by Europeans.[33]

Many of the stories told of the Turks can never be corroborated but seem more than unlikely. For example, one story reported that the Turks "disposed of 1,000 children (too young for their brutal purposes) by tying them two by two, and hanging them up to trees, when they amused themselves by shooting at them. They afterwards cut them to pieces, in the manner in which butchers cut up their meat."[34] Fed on such stuff, readers would have no way to know that the bloody tales they were told were untrue. Headless corpses were not to be found in every Istanbul street, as alleged by the *Boston Recorder, Mount Zion Missionary, Religious Intelligencer,* and other newspapers and magazines.[35]

The most prominent reports in American newspapers were of the massacre at Chios (Scio, Sakız). The details of the events on the island of Chios are imperfectly known. On the night of March 22–23, 1822, a force of an estimated 1,500–2,500 Greek rebels from Samos landed on Chios. They were joined by a great number of the island's inhabitants. They sacked the main town, also called Chios, and besieged the Turkish garrison in the Citadel but soon divided into two parties that could not agree upon united action against the Ottomans. Upon hearing of the imminent arrival of a Turkish fleet, the rebels from Samos escaped, leaving behind the Chios rebels as well as inhabitants who had taken no part in the rebellion. The Ottomans punished the innocent and guilty alike, destroying buildings and killing many Chiotes and taking a large number away as slaves. Greek forces once again invaded the island in June, bringing more battle and loss of life.

Limited Ottoman population figures indicate that 25,000 people were on the island before the troubles.[36] This may have been an undercount, but American newspapers, magazines, and politicians routinely gave figures as high as 120,000 Greeks. Given the size of the island, the figure was ridiculous.[37] Exaggerating the population, however, allowed even greater overstatements of mortality. Forty thousand "killed or enslaved" was a common estimate.[38] The missionary establishment gave by far the highest number. The *Missionary Herald* stated that only 800 to 1,000 remained out of an island population of 150,000.[39] The *Christian Watchman* was not far behind: "Nearly 100,000 persons at Scio had fallen victims to the barbarity of these Mahometans."[40] The actual number who died of all causes was less than 5,000.[41]

In what was to become a common claim in later years—that Turks simply massacred without any cause—many articles alleged that the Greeks on Chios had never rebelled but were set upon wantonly by the Turks.[42] Others invented massacres on nearby islands that actually had experienced no mortality.[43]

As always, few articles offered sources for their information. "On good authority" was a common informant. Those that did give sources quoted anonymous writers from Smyrna (İzmir) or Constantinople (Istanbul), including "private letters," unidentified by author or recipient or using only pseudonyms: "A young Greek," "An American gentleman in the Mediterranean," "An American Gentleman to his friend in Boston," "A Friend to Greece." No article cited any source that allegedly had seen the events at Chios, not even an anonymous source. Newspapers printed letters from the Greek rebels, describing their exploits and the evils of the Turks.[44] Obviously spurious letters from the Middle East were common. For example, "part of a letter from a European in Egypt to his countryman in Greece," which appeared without provenance in the *Christian Watchman*, described how easily the Greeks would defeat the Egyptians.[45] The paper gave no information on how it had obtained a copy of the letter.

When only one side's mortality is reported, warfare will always appear to be massacre or, worse, genocide. The Greek rebellion had begun with the slaughter of innocent Turks. The American press, however, created a very different image: "The first care of the Provisional [Greek] Government was to distribute through all the towns of the Peninsula a Proclamation addressed to the Turks, by which they guaranteed them the safety of their persons and properties, the liberty of their religion, and equality of civil rights. But the Mussulmen only replied to this generous act by the massacre of the Christian women, children, and old men. The Greeks had then recourse to reprisal."[46] Although bloody revenge is always morally questionable, it would indeed be expected in the 1820s in southeastern Europe if the Turks had acted as described. In fact, however, it was the Greeks who began the cycle of massacres, to which the Turks responded. This excuses neither the Greeks nor the Turks, but it is an honest assessment.

American reporting on the Greek rebellion set a pattern that was to continue through all the upheavals of the next century. No matter who struck the first blow in a war or rebellion, no matter who started a cycle of massacre and countermassacre, the Turks were blamed. If Christians began the killing, Americans would never hear of it. Turkish reprisals would be portrayed as irrational attacks on Christians. The consequence was an image of Turks as murderous barbarians.

THE PUBLIC OUTCRY

Newspapers reported widespread fund-raising efforts to support the Greek cause:

> The exertions in favor of the Greeks have become so universal, that it is difficult to detail the numerous meetings that have been held to aid them in their sanguinary struggle with the Turks. The instances of active philanthropy are not confined to any one age, sex or circumstance. Children of tender age are contributing to funds—meetings of adults in all directions around us have been called to raise subscriptions—females are actively engaged in the benevolent cause— the products of the stage are voluntarily offered, Mr. Booth having given one evening's proceeds of a benefit night—our temples of worship resound with the complaints of the Christian Greek, groaning under Turkish cruelty—and the Clergy of many cities are taking up contributions for their benefit. In Philadelphia, the ward committees are calling at every house to receive donations in money, in no case to exceed one dollar for an individual, and in this manner it is confidently expected a large fund will be raised, as those who are opulent will probably subscribe that sum for each of the members of their family, and thus give their children an opportunity to participate in this glorious work of benevolence. One mariner has tendered his services to navigate a vessel that may be sent to their relief; and there seems to be but one opinion and one voice in this country—and that is that GREECE *shall be succoured—shall be* FREE.[47]

The democratic ideals of the young republic were moved by what seemed to be a new revolution sparked by the same sentiments that had led to American independence.[48] President James Monroe praised the Greeks in his 1824 Message to Congress. Daniel Webster delivered a much-praised oration in favor of the Greeks in Congress.[49] Thomas Jefferson, James Madison, and John Adams wrote in praise of the Greeks, and Jefferson suggested the American Constitution as a model for their new state.[50] "Greek Committees" sprang up all over America, but especially in the New England and the Middle Atlantic states. They mounted extremely successful fund-raising campaigns for the Greek rebels. The campaigns featured printed circulars, reports in newspapers and magazines, and "orations." The appeals were filled with emotion, depicting both the sufferings of the Greeks and the wickedness of the Turks. Greeks were murdered by impalement and other exotic tortures or had their noses and tongues cut off before they were enslaved. Women were taken to the harems of rich Turks, where they were cast out to die after they lost their beauty. In all, the campaigns presented a terrible picture intended to draw maximum contributions. Religious kinship between the Greeks and Americans was a constant theme, as was comparison between the freedom fighters of the late American Revolution and the rebellion of the Greeks. "They have taken the liberty, as we did in 1776, of declaring themselves free."[51]

The Greek Committees collected what were major sums in the 1820s as well as collecting and forwarding arms and supplies. Charles King, secretary of the New York Greek Fund, reported that $32,000 had been sent to the Greeks by May 1824 from New York alone and stated that more would be sent later. It was also noted that "the various swords, pistols, and munitions which have been received by the committee, will be forwarded to Leghorn, by the first convenient opportunity, and placed in safe hands at the disposition of the Greek chiefs."[52] Yale students gave $500 to the Greek Committee in New York.[53] In thanks for the efforts of the Greek Committees, the Greeks sent three camels, captured from the Turks, to their supporters in America.[54]

In his capacity as chairman of the New Haven Greek Committee, the famous lexicographer Noah Webster signed an "Address to the Citizens of New Haven, asking for funds to support the cause." He did not spare the Turks: "That ferocious tyranny which tramples on the common laws of humanity, and treats men as brutes, can never gain right by prescription. To the native brutality and ferocity of the Turks, is added a bigoted intolerant spirit." The Turks, in their supposed hatred of Christianity, intended to force all the people of the earth to become Muslim by the sword then rule by brutality. "The despotism of the Turks is of a peculiar nature, and without a parallel in the history of man." The sultans so hated Christians that they had on many occasions planned to kill all of them in their empire but were only stopped by the loss of tax revenue that this would entail. The Turks were enemies of the arts and sciences. All this, Webster declared, was the reason the Turks fought the Greeks, who were heroically defending Christianity.[55]

THE TERRIBLE TURK: THE EMOTIONAL APPEAL

The factual errors about the Greek rebellion printed in the American press lived on and are still often repeated today. It is doubtful, however, that the details that were printed in the 1820s survived long in the memories of most Americans. They would have lingered only as a myth of Turkish cruelty and Greek suffering, unsupported by facts and without any idea that facts were needed or that there was any doubt of Turkish barbarity and Greek innocence. What remained was an emotional antipathy toward the Turks. The newspapers and the preachers had done much to create that antipathy. Given the sentiment of the time, little sympathy for the Turks would be expected, and little sympathy was shown. Americans had read the Ottoman Empire described as the "yoke of Mahomet," "tyranny and rapine"—an image that was to remain in the American consciousness.

Descriptions of the Greeks and Turks and appeals for the Greek cause were often melodramatic. American newspapers and magazines featured laudatory articles and even epic poems on Greek rebel heroes.[56] They printed thrilling stories of Greek prisoners of the Turks who escaped.[57] One article provided supposed details of monks and priests martyred by the Turks.[58] The image of Greek women carried off to satisfy "Turkish lusts" was everywhere: "What heart is so adamantine as not to feel, at seeing thousands of beautiful damsels, with tears in their eyes, bidding farewell to their native land, wet with the blood of their fathers and brothers, going to drag out a wretched life in a Mussulman haram?"[59] But the image of Greek women included not only suffering and outrage. Romantic tales of their patriotism were also prominent.[60] Plucky, courageous Greek women were willing to give their lives for the cause.[61] A young Greek girl raised eight hundred men for the cause "by her activity and enthusiastic eloquence."[62] The press told stories of pure Greek women and their love for Greek rebel heroes.[63] A Greek woman killed a Turk who had abducted her.[64] None of these stories had any source or provenance, but they undoubtedly stirred the hearts of the readers.

The separation between news and opinion was never strict in the American newspapers, but the feelings of the press were most evident in commentary articles. The following excerpt, from an article reprinted in the *Essex Patriot,* is an almost perfect summary of the emotional appeals that inundated the American people:

> We cannot be persuaded (says the *Democratic Press,*) but that *all* the civilized world sympathise with the Greeks. There are associations and recollections connected with *ancient* Greece familiar to all the reading world, which must operate greatly in their favor. Theirs is the page of history on which we dwell with most delight. Their arts and their arms irradiate their name, and their patriotism makes them estimable in our eyes. But with modern Greece we have bands and ties and common principles which entwine it around our hearts and connect it with our dearest wishes, our holiest hopes. They adore the same God, they acknowledge the same Redeemer. They believe in a state of future rewards and punishments founded on the same evidence as we do; in one word they are *Christians.* They are humble believers in that system of religion and morality which is believed by all that portion of the world which do honor to Humanity. Can we then be indifferent as to their success? assuredly not—but if the causes we have relied upon were not enough to enlist us in their behalf, let us ask who are their opponents?

They are furious, bigoted, and persecuting enemies of Christianity. How often, and for how many centuries, have their swords been red with Christian blood! How often have the Turks persecuted unto the death, all who acknowledged Christ and him crucified. Did they not for ages raise the Crescent against the Cross and advance against Christendom? Has not all Christendom been in self-defence, compelled to league against the Turks? Have they not always made war against knowledge and burned with a red hot furnace all the books which centuries had gathered together. These Musselmen, *even now,* break into the sanctuary of an Ambassador's Palace, and seize upon and put to death the Christian Greeks. Neither age, sex nor condition, is a protection against their inhumanity. The Venerable Patriarch, and the Infant but newly born, are alike food for the appetites of the savage Turks. If the Turks now triumph, they will, within their dominions, prohibit the exercise of the Christian religion.

Can we then but rejoice and be exceedingly glad even when there is a *prospect* that Truth and the Greeks shall triumph over Imposture & the Turks.[65]

Readers in Massachusetts cannot be expected to have known that Muslims in fact were instrumental in preserving ancient knowledge, not burning it in red-hot furnaces, or that Turks never prohibited the exercise of the Christian religion.

The *Essex Patriot* included all the emotional elements of the Myth of the Terrible Turks: the "imposture" of Muhammad, the persecutors of Christianity, barbaric murder of newborn infants and men of God, swords red with Christian blood. The Greeks, whose actions go unmentioned, were inheritors of ancient Greece and, most important, were Christians—the necessary prerequisite for inclusion in humanity. This was heady stuff to Americans who named their cities after those of ancient Greece, had a worshipful belief in what they thought was Greek democracy, and thought of themselves as heirs of ancient Greece. The only virtue lacking in the classical Greeks was Christianity, and this lack had been remedied.

Descriptions such as those of the *Essex Patriot* and the quotation at the beginning of the chapter were in no way unusual. This was the typical method of describing the Turks. Perhaps most telling of the image presented to Americans by the press, the preachers, and the orators were the terms used to describe Turks (see table 3.1). This list of epithets, drawn from newspapers and speeches, is not complete. It must be stressed that they were the usual terms applied to the Turks. There were no positive images or even neutral images of them.

The Greeks enjoyed nothing but positive images. Much could have been written of the unsavory side of the Greek rebellion, but the American newspapers did not do so. It is likely that editors knew little of it. The newspapers and magazines do not mention the banditry of many of the Greek heroes, the internecine fighting of the various Greek factions, or the greed and personal aggrandizement that contributed to Greek losses. Much was made of Turkish enslavement of Greeks, but nothing was said of Greek enslavement of Turks, which also occurred.[66] And, of course, almost no paper printed news of the bloody massacres of Turks.

TABLE 3.1. LIST OF EPITHETS APPLIED TO TURKS

Barbarians	Cruel and barbarous tyranny
Monsters	The barbarous disciples of Mahomet
Tyrants	Stupid ferocity of the Turk
Assassins	High-handed and barbarous Turks
Fiends incarnate	Merciless and unrelenting tyranny
The barbarous Ottoman	Native brutality and ferocity of the Turks
Perfidious Musselmen	Ignorant, superstitious, vain, and bigoted
Anti-Christian empire	Turkish Mahometan tyranny
Despicable horde of Tatars	Lustful passions of a bestial soldiery
Merciless and unrelenting tyranny	Ignorant and bigoted believers in that gross imposter Mahomet
Barbarian oppressors	Tigers, a thousand times more cruel than those of the forest
Ghastly despotism	The turbaned Turk tramples upon the cross of the Saviour
The prince of bigots	

> They perceive that it [the Greek revolt] is not, what some would represent it, a bloody struggle between barbarous masters and not less barbarous slaves, in which it is difficult to take a lively interest. It is, on the contrary, a struggle between cruel and barbarous masters, and a people whose hard earned wealth is devoted to the collection of libraries, to the printing and circulation of books, and to the improvement of the means of education.[67]

The Turks were depicted as cruel and barbarous, but "the Greeks are a Christian, civilized, enterprising people." They were fighting for Christianity. "The war is emphatically a war of the crescent against the cross," in which "the village churches are leveled with the dust or polluted with the abominations of mahometanism." Christians must intervene "to effect the banishment of the crescent to the deserts of Tartary."[68]

Although appeals to memories of classical Greece were ubiquitous, the foremost calls to American sympathies were religious. The Greeks were Christians—not proper Protestant Christians but Christians nonetheless. Men of religion took up defense of the Greeks in what was seen as the Battle between the Cross and the Crescent. The best extant example of this religious feeling is an address by the Reverend Sereno Edwards Dwight, a leader of the Congregationalists.[69] Dwight defined what he perceived as the battle between Muslim and Christian. Addressing a meeting of supporters of the Greeks at the Old South Church in Boston, he alluded to the classical and religious tradition of Greece, mentioning Paul, Luke, Timothy, and other early Christians: "Greece is consecrated ground." He appealed to the American ethos by extolling Greece's mercantile advantages and the Greeks' industry and love of education. The address dwelled especially on the evils of the Turk, who had placed the crescent over the churches of God, supplanted the Bible with the Quran, and driven out ministers "to make room for the imams of Mohammed." If the Greeks did not succeed, Edwards stated, "the Mohammedan religion will gain new strength, and the churches of the east will cease to hope for the termination of their long and abject servitude." If the Greeks succeeded, "in proportion as Turkey, the bulwark of the Mohammedan faith, is humbled or subdued, will that faith be weakened or destroyed." Missionaries would then be able to spread throughout the Ottoman Empire, bringing true religion: "In Arabia and Persia, in Chaldea and Tartary, the tidings of salvation will be proclaimed." Dwight called on Americans, in the spirit of both religion and American independence, to support the Greeks.[70]

To the American religious leaders and their followers, Dwight's assertion of upcoming missionary activity was most important. The only American complaint about the Greeks was religious. Their Orthodox Christianity was described as "superstitious." In its formal worship, theology, and invocation of saintly intervention it was likened to the hated Roman Catholics. That would have to be remedied, but American and British missionaries would perform that task once the Turks were banished from Europe.[71] When Sereno Dwight delivered his address there were only four American missionaries in the Ottoman Empire, but American men of religion were always confident.

Poetry had a prominent place in the cultural life of 1820s America.[72] Well-known poets wrote in praise of the Greeks and condemnation of the Turks. The amount of awful poetry on Greece printed in American newspapers and journals is stupefying. Quoting much of it would be cruel, but this first stanza from a much longer poem is representative:

> The flag of freedom floats once more
> Around the lofty Parthenon;
> It waves as waved the palm of yore;
> In days departed long and gone:
> As bright as glory from the skies
> Pours down its light around those tow'rs,
> And once again the Greeks arise,
> As in their country's noblest hours;
> Their swords are girt in virtue's cause,
> Minerva's sacred hill is free—
> Oh! may she keep her equal laws,
> While men shall live and time shall be.[73]

THE IMAGE

The public outcry in favor of the Greeks was a foreshadowing of an American reaction against the Turks that was to continue through World War I. After the Greek Revolution, Americans were not to be so intensely involved with events in the Ottoman Empire for the next seventy years. When Americans did once again take up the call of the Ottoman Christians it was with the same fervor, and the same sort of misinformation, manifested during the Greek rebellion. Fed by religious sentiment and the popular press, Americans were to see only one distorted picture of many-faceted events. All the evils done by Turks were to be exaggerated, evils done to the Turks to be ignored. The pattern of prejudice set in the Greek rebellion was to continue.

4

THE RELIGION OF THE TURKS

The Americans of the nineteenth and early twentieth centuries knew little of Islam or of Muslims. Those who wished to learn would have been able to find very few sources that treated Islam sympathetically or even fairly. Many books and articles written by missionaries and other Christian apologists described Islam and Muslims, but they were neither sympathetic nor fair.[1] Americans did not have access to analyses of Islam by Muslims, by those who might be sympathetic to Islam, or even by neutral critics. What was available to them was not Turkish history, culture, and politics as seen by the Turks themselves or by neutral observers. It was the analyses of those who viewed the Turks and Islam as enemies.[2]

It is of course not possible to discover the exact effect of these writings on the opinions of Americans. It is accurate to state, however, that the missionary writings must have had their effect, because they were virtually the only studies available to Americans. A high school or college student who wished to do research on Islam would find only missionary books. A journalist who needed a quick bit of information on Turks, Arabs, Muhammad, or Muslim customs and law would find books by the clergy in the city's library. Teachers, insofar as teachers were trained in non-Christian religions or peoples at all, would be trained using the books written by Protestant apologists. Based on analysis of American library holdings, 88 percent of the books on Islam printed from 1790 to 1929 were written by missionaries, other Protestant clergymen, and members of mission groups—constituents of what can be called the missionary establishment.[3] It was these writers who taught Islam to Americans. What they taught was often factually wrong, frequently filled with prejudice, and always distorted. What little was known in America of Islam and Muslims was based on the witness of exactly those critics who were most likely to treat it unsympathetically. The missionary view of Islam and Muslims that was transmitted to the American people was so negative that it fed and enlarged a deep prejudice that has lasted until the present day.[4]

The other important factor in the American Protestant vision of Islam and Muslims was the effect it had on those who reported on events in the Middle East. Missionaries were the main source of information that Americans received on those events. Prejudiced by their education and steeped in an almost completely negative view of Islam and Muslims, the missionaries found it impossible to report accurately. The negative actions of Middle Eastern Muslims were magnified, sometimes invented, whereas the negative actions of Christians were ignored. The same was true to a slightly lesser extent for journalists. Like the missionaries, journalists and editors were products of a culture that denigrated Islam and the Turks. They also felt the necessity of giving their readers what they expected, and the readers, also products of the culture, expected to hear only bad of the Turks.

ISLAM

O Lord God, to whom the sceptre of right belongeth, lift up Thyself, and travel in the greatness of Thy strength throughout the Mohammedan lands of the East; because of the anointing of Thy Son, Jesus Christ, as Thy true Prophet, Priest, and King, destroy the sword of Islam, and break the yoke of the false prophet Mohammed from off the lands of Egypt, Arabia, Turkey, Persia, and other Moslem lands, that so there may be opened throughout these lands a great door and effectual for the Gospel, that the Word of the Lord may have free course and be glorified, and the veil upon so many hearts may be removed, through Jesus Christ, our Lord. Amen.[5]

—Church Missionary Society Cycle of Prayer

This prayer, drawn from a 1906 missionary report on attempts at converting Muslims, summarizes the missionary attitude toward Islam. It was a view born long before 1906. The seeds of what was to come can be seen in the beliefs of early Congregationalists such as Pliny Fisk and Levi Parsons at the very beginning of the missionary enterprise. Their belief, although later stated less boldly, was to last: only Protestant Christianity was acceptable and was destined to triumph. Muslims were a bloody and cruel people who kept others from true salvation. Islam (like Roman Catholicism) was an eternal enemy to true Christianity.

The principles of the Protestant missionaries to the Middle East in the nineteenth century were heavily affected by the natural human propensity to suppose that what is different must be wrong. Their religious beliefs were founded in a Calvinism transformed into a distinctly American religion. John Calvin himself had felt that God would arrange matters such as the conversion of the world according to His own timetable. The American Calvinists felt a strong sense of duty to the world that transcended the older Calvinist ideas of predestination. They believed that people could do something to save the world, a radical departure from their theological origins. Human beings could be saved if they were given the chance to know God's will. The concept of religious duty also spread to the worldly lives of non-Christians. Preaching the Gospel was the main end, but improving the education, economy, and health of the world's people was also a desirable goal.[6]

Despite their innovations, the missionaries remained distinctly Protestant in most of their views and Calvinist in their religious practice. They held very forcibly to the Reformation ideas of salvation. Accepting Jesus as personal savior, a process brought about by personal cognizance of the Bible, was the path to salvation.

Salvation was not to be achieved by good works, no matter how noble or ethical the individual. This naturally kept the missionaries in traditional opposition to Catholicism and Eastern Orthodoxy, both of which stressed the necessity of good works for salvation. The missionaries' Calvinist liturgical traditions also led to abhorrence of Catholic and Orthodox worship. They routinely interpreted such worship as reflecting a belief that the worshipper would be saved if only the formulas of the liturgies were correctly carried out, something akin to magic. William Goodell, long a missionary in the Ottoman Empire, wrote:

> There is an abundance of religion in the East, but it is all ceremonial. The Jews, Greeks, Armenians, Catholics, and others, are, all of them, as Paul said to the Athenians, *most superabundantly religious*. But this religion of theirs has little or nothing to do either with the heart or with the life; that is, it is not necessarily supposed to exert any influence on a man's moral character. It has little or nothing to do with the religion of the Bible—it is a thing of their own manufacture. And, according to their practice, a man may be most highly religious, and at the same time most grossly immoral. The two things, viz., religion and morality, have, in their practice, if not in their apprehension, no necessary connection, but are entirely divorced from each other.[7]

Although none of the practitioners of such liturgies would agree with that analysis, the missionaries considered it accurate. It is no exaggeration to say that they looked upon the Catholics, the Orthodox, the Armenian Gregorians, and the Nestorians that they met in the Middle East as religiously degenerate and damned.

The missionary attitudes also necessarily applied to Islam. Its theology was far different from that of Orthodox and Catholic Christianity, but it too stressed conformity to rules of behavior, "good works," as the path to salvation. Like the Catholics and the Orthodox, Muslims believed in the benefits of religious asceticism, which the missionaries held to be against the ideals of Jesus.[8] Muslims also took part in worship that was formulaic, saying the same prayers five times each day as they had for centuries. As in the case of the Catholics and Orthodox, the missionaries saw this as an iniquitous attempt at buying passage into heaven by performing ceremonies rather than by changing one's heart. Indeed, the ritual of Islam was actually held to deaden true religious impulse:

> Spiritual hunger and thirst after righteousness are almost unknown [in Islam]. They regard their ceremonial righteousness as complete, and they are satisfied. Even where spiritual longing for peace with God is felt, there is nothing in Islam to satisfy it.[9]

Thus, in reference to prayer as well as to almost everything else, Islam gives man a stone when his heart hungers for the bread of life, and too often chokes the aspiration after God which has been implanted in the heart of every man in order to lead him to feel after his Creator till he find him, and in him attain to life and peace.[10]

The possibility of changing one's heart and worshipping in set liturgies was not accepted.

As the nineteenth century came to a close, the American churches slowly began to change into what is called Liberal Protestantism today.[11] The Protestant attitude toward Islam and the Middle East altered and became more sophisticated, with fewer outright insults. Muhammad was no longer routinely called "the Imposter." The tools of the new science of sociology began to be applied to Muslim peoples, although with a determination to find what was wrong with Muslim societies. What did not change was a general view of Islam and its faithful as the enemies of the Christian endeavor. While they were sure that the advance of Western technological civilization would eventually overcome Islam, the missionaries could not close their eyes to the advances that Islam was making among the people of Africa and Asia. In their world, conversion to Islam was the only force that could numerically equal or better conversion to Christianity. Missionaries were thwarted not only by the general failure to convert Muslims to Christianity but by "the peril of Islam in certain parts of Asia and Africa."[12] Muslims were thought to be fellow humans who needed to be brought to Christian belief, but missionaries had no hesitancy in calling Islam "the enemy."

Missionary feelings were not only theological. They were as confident in the superiority of the economic and political system of America as they were of their religious convictions. When they arrived in the Middle East and other foreign lands, they saw cultures that had not benefited from the long Western development that began in the Renaissance and extended through the scientific and industrial revolutions. The missionaries could not help but see that European and American Christians were richer and better fed, lived longer, and were better educated than the non-Christians of Asia and Africa. In their minds, worldly success and moral character were tied together. Explanations of varying levels of development based on differing environments and plain luck were to be the analyses of a later age. To the missionaries, as to Westerners in general, the reasons for riches were innate ability and character—and good character was necessarily Christian. The primary reason for lack of material wealth was spiritual degradation. The remedy was conversion to Christianity.

Missionary and other Christian writers seemed to view the existence of Islam as an affront to Christianity. They surely were not content to state their assumption that Islam was wrong and leave it at that. They felt the need to attack. Every possible negative factor in Islam was to be laid before the American public to make clear the superiority of Christianity. This was a fairly simple task, because the Americans already believed their own religion was superior (why else hold to it?). To ensure success, Islam was seldom portrayed in an accurate fashion; Muslims would not have recognized their religion after its translation by its Christian critics.

Missionary opposition to Islam and adverse reaction to the conditions of life and morality in the Middle East stood behind the picture of the region and its peoples that the missionaries transmitted to the Americans.[13] The picture was extremely negative, and it was well received. Schooled in centuries of anti-Muslim and in particular anti-Turkish prejudice, Americans expected to hear the worst. The writings and speeches of the missionaries conformed to popular expectations.

For most people, theology is not the most interesting of topics. If they are religious, they are content to believe the basic principles of their religions, to perform whatever actions and prayers are required, and to try to live a good life. Nevertheless, theology must be studied in order to understand the mind-set of the missionaries and the message they carried to Americans. This theology lay behind the image of Turks and other Muslims that was presented to the American people and created the mind-set through which the missionaries saw the Middle East and Islam. The theology was so prejudiced that neither the missionaries nor the American public could possibly have gained a truthful view of Islam.

God

Theologically, the Protestant critics' first objection to Islam was the Islamic conception of God. They felt that God in Islam was a remote authority rather than a loving friend. "Of any kinship between God and Man, of the very possibility of any genuine sympathy between the Creator and His creatures, Muhammad had not the slightest idea."[14] The writers believed that the only attribute that counted for Muslims was God's power: "Thus the God of Muhammad leaves upon us the impression of an arbitrary Oriental despot, who makes His enemies experience His wrath in a terrible manner and loads His faithful servants with benefits, besides winking at their misdeeds."[15]

Though the writers would surely deny it, the similarities of the power of God in the Quran and in the Old Testament appear obvious to most modern students of the two religions.[16] It was not within the scope of the Christian commentators' faith, however, to consider the possibility that descriptions of God might be contingent on the environment in which they arose. More problematic for anyone who has discussed religious matters with Muslims is the Christian commentators' complete misrepresentation of power as the only divine attribute that mattered to Muslims. Muslims, after all, began all their serious endeavors with the saying "In the Name of God, the Compassionate, the Merciful." The Quran itself, in sections that never seem to have appeared in the commentators' writings, spoke of God as a loving father, as described by Caesar Farah:

> God rewards and punishes, yet He is also the Merciful, Guardian of His servants, Defender of the orphan, Guide of the wrong-doer, Liberator from pain, Friend of the poor, generous and ready-to-forgive Master. "And, O my people! Ask forgiveness of your Lord, then turn onto Him repentant; He will cause the sky to rain abundance on you and will add unto you strength to your strength. Turn not away, guilty!" God is the Merciful (al-Rahman) and the Compassionate

(al-Rahim); these are basic to His attributes, as attests the Quran in every surah [chapter]. He is forgiving and reassuring to the sinner who repents; and, although God can overtake with his punishment anyone He wishes, His mercy "encompasses everything," because He Himself has commanded that mercy shall be an unbreakable law.[17]

So many of those who complained of the harsh power of God in Islam were from religions with a Calvinist background that they seem to have been exorcising their own religious demons, rather than those of Islam. Nineteenth-century Muslims, had they so desired, could have written a commentary on the harsh and vengeful God of Calvinism by exaggerating some parts of Calvinism and ignoring those parts that would soften this verdict—exactly what the Christian critics did with Islam.

One of the proofs offered that the Muslim God could not be the same as the Christian God was that no true God could promise his followers the type of paradise promised by Allah. The Quran described paradise as a place where sensual pleasures were not absent. Sexual intercourse, wine-drinking, and other activities were freely available to the blessed. This was the sort of thing that could have been expressly designed to bring down the wrath of Christians of the Victorian age.[18]

> There are some few indications that Muhammad deemed a *very* great excess of unchastity a sin on earth [fornication and adultery are forbidden in the Quran, but Muhammad's idea of what constituted these sins was very different from ours], but he nevertheless in the Quran encouraged his followers to contend for their faith by promising them a practically unlimited indulgence in that vileness before the very Throne of God in heaven.[19]

While "vileness" is surely not a proper term, it is true that the Quran does promise earthy delights in paradise. Muslim thinkers of their own and much earlier times had a much more sophisticated concept of humanity's ultimate end, which went unmentioned. The Islam described by the critics was "textual": not the religion as practiced but the religion of the books, and even then only a selection of quotations chosen to portray Islam badly. Had this criticism been done accurately, it would have been fair as far as it went—as an analysis of certain parts of certain books, not of faith. Protestant writers were mightily and negatively impressed by the place of Holy Law in Islam, which was very different from the relative lack of formal rules in Christianity. It is true that what is called Orthodox Islam stressed Holy Law more than feeling. But the Protestant critics did not describe Islam as it was among its believers. Their diatribe against God as powerful monarch, as opposed to loving father, did not describe mystical Islam, particularly in Turkey, or folk religion. Muslim mystics stressed the very attribute of God—loving communion with His subjects—that the critics alleged was nonexistent in Islam. Muslim mystics wrote of a God of love, to whom humans would return and with whom humans would be joined.[20] The Protestant critics themselves had no truck with mysticism, and that may explain their lack of knowledge of the vibrant mystical tradition in Islam.

MUHAMMAD

The missionary position on Muhammad, indeed the position of American Christianity in general, was that he was either an imposter or a madman.

> His [Muhammad's] whole history makes it evident, that fanaticism, ambition, and lust were his major passions; of which the former seems to have been gradually eradicated by the growing strength of the two last. An enthusiast by nature, he came to be a hypocrite by policy; and as the violence of his corrupt propensities increased, he scrupled not to gratify them at the expense of truth, justice, friendship, and humanity.[21]

The view of Muhammad as an "imposter," a false prophet who desired to lead people astray, was the unquestioned belief of the early American Protestant Church. Muhammad was an evil man who was allowed to play his part because of divine plan, both to humble the Christians of the time who had fallen from true belief and to act in concert with "popery" in the reign of the Antichrist. Muhammad was assumed to be not simply wrong but an incarnation of evil, sent to tempt people in the long darkness that preceded the Second Coming of Christ. As such, he played a major part in the Protestant, particularly the Calvinist, concept of salvation history.

The view of Muhammad as evil had moderated somewhat by the end of the nineteenth century.[22] By then the majority view among Protestant scholars had shifted to the belief that Muhammad was in error, although not really evil, in the first years of his preaching but that he "degenerated" in his latter years. The "degeneration" was primarily sexual, as evidenced by his many wives. This was the standard belief.[23] George Herrick, a missionary of the American Board in the Ottoman Empire, took a very informative survey of the opinions on Islam held by leading missionaries in Muslim lands.[24] Their responses on the life of Muhammad universally condemned his later years. They particularly compared "Christ's sinlessness and Mohammed's moral degeneracy." Indeed, "degeneracy" was the word most used to describe the Prophet of the Muslims. Writers constantly complained that Muslims did not accept Muhammad's moral failings. Once Muhammad's sinful character was accepted, the missionaries believed, Muslims would have to admit that Christianity was superior, something they obstinately refused to do: "for if they acknowledged this one great fact, they would be obliged to go on and to accept the absolute claims of Christ on their conscience and faith."[25]

The missionaries were surprised that some Muslims even became angry at imputations of Muhammad's moral degeneracy, which they considered indisputable. (How would New England Calvinists have accepted imputations of immoral behavior to Jesus?) Nevertheless, they felt that they must continue to bring up the point. It was necessary for Christians to attack the life and personality of

Muhammad, for they rightly believed that imitation of Muhammad's life was a core tenet of Islam. Islam depended on belief in the uprightness of Muhammad's life as well as belief in his message. As the Prophet, Muhammad was the base of the religion: destroying the foundation would in theory bring down the edifice. Thus the Christian critics blamed all the evils they cited on the essential nature of Islam as preached by Muhammad.

> In Mohammedanism, in spite of its greater pretensions, almost every apparent truth crumbles into mere truism or actual falsity the moment you try to make it the base of anything practical. Also, the more I read of the life of Mohammed, the more convinced I am that the radical rottenness of the system is due to his original teaching. I firmly believe that the difficulties in the Islam of today are due rather to the essential wrongness of the system than to its corruption by the masses.[26]

Therefore, the missionaries felt, Muhammad must be condemned. Many of the Middle Eastern practices that they abhorred were laid at Muhammad's door. For example, the Middle Eastern custom of the veiling and relative seclusion of women long predated Islam but was portrayed as an evil or mad Muslim concept dictated by Muhammad. Missionary writings did not hesitate to state that women's condition before Muhammad's message was better than afterward, a complete historical inaccuracy. George Herrick wrote that "the whole system of mechanical defenses of chastity in women" among Muslims was the result of Muhammad's need to guard his harem.[27] Stressing the psychological, writers spoke of "the insane jealousy of Muhammad" that led him to veil his wives, a practice that later Muslims followed, like polygamy.

The description of Muhammad as fundamentally mad was best exemplified by Duncan Black Macdonald, a minister and professor at Hartford Theological Seminary, one of the main centers of missionary education. Macdonald's *Aspects of Islam* was a basic text used by seminaries in training ministers and missionaries.[28] Macdonald was a modernizer who rejected the traditional view of Muhammad as an imposter. He was willing to accept that Muhammad was sincere, though misguided: "the fundamental thing in him was that he was a pathological case."[29] Macdonald and those who followed his ideas believed that Muhammad was in essence a madman who heard voices and thought they were the voices of an angel or God. The periods that Muhammad spent in the desert praying and fasting and receiving visions were cited as examples of abnormal behavior. It was this mental abnormality that led Muhammad to preach the lies that became Islam. "*He was a pathological case* [Macdonald's emphasis]. His revelations came to him in trance and, like all trance-mediums, he had strangely perverted ideas."[30]

Views such as these were surely an improvement over those of the critics who saw Muhammad as a deliberate enemy of God. But how much of an improvement? Christians were still enjoined to see Muslims as the followers of a madman, zealots who could not see that the religion they treasured was the product of pathology. What is intellectually astounding, however, is the assertion by a Christian that Muhammad must have been mad because of his visions and fasting and prayer in the desert. Was St. Paul to be considered mad by the same standard? And Jesus went into the desert to fast and pray. Of course, they did not entertain such questions. St. Paul was not mad because he saw a real vision. Jesus was, well, Jesus, and what he did could never have been a sign of madness. Belief led to certainty about Muhammad just as much as about Jesus or St. Paul.

The critics' lack of understanding of the Middle Eastern social, economic, and political environment naturally extended to the life and laws of Muhammad. Most scholars today mention the traditions of marrying wives of fallen comrades or relatives to provide security for them as one of the main reasons (although not the only one) that Muhammad took many wives, but the Christian writers wanted none of that. To them, it was only degeneracy. Polygamy, especially polygamy in modern societies, is justly condemned for the harm it does to the position of women. The Christian critics gave no consideration, however, to the great changes for the better that Muhammad's laws brought to the position of women in his time, including limitations on polygamy. Likewise, the improvements that Muhammad and later Muslim jurists brought to women's inheritance rights, the creation of formal law in the place of blood feuds, fair market practices, and the idea of justice as a necessity for political rule were never mentioned. Even if the critics had considered them, they probably would not have found the improvements acceptable. What was called for was perfection, in the sense understood by the missionaries.

Perhaps the most unbelievable criticism of Islam was stated succinctly by the Reverend W. St. Clair Tisdall: "Islam—like all other false religions—is entirely destitute of proof. In spite of Muhammadan arguments to the contrary, it has neither previous prophecies nor attendant miracles to confirm the lofty claims of Muhammad to be considered as the Seal of the Prophets and the bearer of God's final and perfect Revelation to Mankind."[31] Muhammad performed no miracles; therefore he was wrong. The dependence of their own miracles on belief in the literal truth of the Bible seems not to have troubled the critics of Islam.

Sin

Mohammedanism is held, by many who have lived under its shadow, to be the most degraded religion, morally, in the world.[32]

—Robert E. Speer, secretary (chief executive)
of the Presbyterian missions

The doctrinal differences between Muslims and missionaries were real and important in the missionary view of Islam. Of far more importance, however, was the difference in practical ethics, particularly sexual ethics. Indecisiveness and lack of moral certainty were not in the missionaries' character. Their sense of sin was rigid and absolute. They knew what was right and what was wrong, and what they saw in Islam was to them distinctly wrong. Missionaries viewed moral practice in Islam and found it wanting, because it was not American Calvinist moral practice.

The ethics of Islam were unquestionably different from those of the Protestant Christianity that was dominant in nineteenth-century America. It was not an age of tolerance for different ethical systems. Thus Islam was condemned for being Islam, not Protestantism. A common complaint was what was viewed as the lax Muslim concept of sin, guilt, and punishment: "[In Islam] unpremeditated lapses from virtue are leniently judged. In short, Allah makes it no onerous task to serve him."[33] Islam made too many allowances for the failings of human nature. This was not acceptable. To Calvinists, Islam was too easy, especially in the area of sexual ethics. It did not take sin seriously enough and allowed far too many into heaven. One missionary complaint was the lack of consciousness of original sin in Islam. Islam only recognized guilt if the sinner had committed a conscious offense; it had no concept of inherent sin and guilt. Muslims depended on God's mercy and forgiveness even for the sins they committed. The missionary writers doubted whether Muslims had any proper idea of sin and repentance.[34] Some said that real purity, even the knowledge of the concept of purity, was beyond Muslims: "It will be evident that purity of the heart is neither considered necessary nor desirable; in fact it would be hardly too much to say that it is *impossible* for a Muslim."[35] To the missionaries, Muslims seemed to be concerned only with following the rules, and even when Muslims broke the rules God would easily forgive them. It was a short step for the missionaries to assert as true what Muslims would view as a lie and a horrible blasphemy: "It is true that Mohammedanism declares God to be 'compassionate and merciful,' but it is to sin as well as to the sinner that He offers his condoning grace. Herein is the fatal defect in the ethics of Islam. God was made to forget Himself and to become in certain respects a participator by law and by sanction in the iniquities of Islamic practice."[36]

Another difficulty with Islam as seen by the missionaries was its violation of some of the most basic concepts of Protestant Christian ethics. The Calvinist ideals of the Congregationalists and Presbyterians who provided most of the missionaries to the Middle East did not admit anything but divine grace as a source of goodness. The two major philosophical enemies of the missionaries—Catholicism and Islam—had similar ideas of faith and good works. Islam and Catholicism both believed that people should do good and avoid doing evil first because of love of God but also out of fear of God's punishment and desire for God's reward in paradise; someone who lived a good life only out of fear would still be saved. The missionary Calvinists held a different view: "The faithful Christian does right, speaks the truth, keeps himself socially pure, because it is the right thing to do.... It is enough that he is obedient to God out of love to Him, that he serves men and seeks their welfare because brotherly love impels him."[37] Lesser motives fell outside the path of righteousness. Whether or not such a philosophy contained a liberal dose of self-deception is not a question here; if, deep inside their psyches, missionaries did good because they feared hellfire or wanted paradise, they would have condemned such lapses in themselves, just as they condemned them in Muslims. The justification for goodness was an unbridgeable gulf between Calvinists and Muslims, just as it was between Calvinists and Catholics.

THE SINFUL MUSLIM

The missionary view of the Muslims was drawn in part from the same sources as their views on Islam, for they felt that the followers of "the Imposter" Muhammad could not help but be adversely affected by their religion. The critics also drew on the prejudices of their time. Like others in Europe and America, they effortlessly assumed the natural superiority of the West, which they believed was based on Christianity. They saw proof of their assumptions in the relative poverty and disorganization of the Middle East. Their writings reinforced these prejudices in themselves and in the Americans they affected.

To the American Protestants of the missionary establishment, Muslims were naturally seen as sinners. Indeed, in the prevailing theology those who were not Christians could not help but be sinners to one degree or another—no other option was available to non-Christians. Muslim sinfulness as reported to Americans, however, was no abstract fault attached to noble but mistaken humans who attempted to be good but could not succeed without God's grace. It was hot-blooded sin, full of sex and violence. It is tempting to say that it was the sort of sin that made for interesting reading.

When writing on Islam and Muslims the missionary establishment stressed sins of the flesh. To anyone who has lived among Muslims or read anthropological and sociological literature, the image of Muslims as especially licentious will appear ludicrous. Yet the American impression of Muslim sensuousness was a staple of art and literature from newspapers to pornography and obviously caught the popular imagination. "Oriental" art of fanciful harems and female slave markets obviously fed this impression. Illustrations were available in American books, but it is doubtful that most Americans saw the paintings of Eugène Delacroix, Jean-Léon Gérôme, or Jean-Auguste-Dominique Ingres.[38] They did see the writings of missionaries and other Christian critics, who portrayed a sordid and debased Muslim sexuality and family life.

Sexual crimes as defined by the missionaries were held to be accepted and even promoted by Islam. Many missionary critics could not bring themselves to mention the nature of the sins they felt to be routinely committed by Muslims: "There are aspects of vice in Mohammedan lands, and indeed throughout the Eastern world, which can only be referred to in veiled phrases as veritable mysteries of iniquity."[39] Others were willing to name at least some of the sins: "The *sin of sodomy* is so common among them [the Muslims] as to make them in many places objects of dread to their neighbors...A crime so abominable, unspeakable and incredible, instead of being checked by Mohammedanism, is fostered by it, and it is one of the scourges of Mohammedan society."[40]

It is no exaggeration to say that the missionary literature contains almost no accurate representations of Muslim sexuality. The missionaries never wrote of the large majority of Muslim men who prized faithfulness to one spouse; and, to the Christian critics, all women in polygamous marriages were unhappy. They wrote that no Muslim marriages of any sort were truly happy and love between spouses and between parents and children was nonexistent. Husbands supposedly never viewed their wives as anything but objects of sexual gratification; nor did they have any affection for their children.[41] For example, the affection between Turkish fathers and their daughters is a commonplace of the anthropological literature of today and is obvious in Turkish families.[42] Yet the critics of Islam baldly stated that Muslim girls often did not even see their fathers or converse with them.[43] Some missionary writers asserted that Muslim children were uniformly unhappy. Others, who presumably had seen the children laugh, held that this was the false happiness of ignorance, not the real joy of knowing the truth. "Where there is love between the parents and the children there is still unhappiness, for, as Dr. Cantine of Arabia remarks, 'Moslem children are unhappy not because of lack of love, but from lack of knowledge of what is best for them.'"[44]

As might be expected, missionary writings on Islam made prominent mention of polygamy. The moral philosophy behind it was roundly condemned. That is to be expected; in the nineteenth century some Muslim thinkers had themselves begun to question it. It is also understandable that the relatively great separation between the sexes would be unacceptable to nineteenth- and twentieth-century Westerners. Other conclusions on Muslim sexual life are less understandable. The picture of Islamic life in the writings of many missionaries and their apologists is unrecognizable to those who have lived among Muslims. The writers once again made the assumption that a system with which they disagreed and which opposed some Christian values must necessarily be evil and that all parts of the system must necessarily share in the evil. Thus all aspects of Muslim sexuality and family life were condemned.

Readers naturally must have abhorred the image of Muslim family life that the missionaries portrayed: "Every man may have a private brothel under the forms of law as in Mohammedan lands, and call it his family."[45] "Sound family life is impossible. The children grow up in the poisonous atmosphere of intrigue, fleshly lust, bad language, and shameless licentiousness. They are polluted from youth up."[46] Muslim mothers supposedly taught licentiousness and immorality to their children: "It is no wonder the children have foul minds and fouler tongues. It was not shame for a Moslem mother to engage in the most filthy and polluting conversation before her young children, and when she has taught them to curse their own father, she praises them for their cleverness." This statement from an unnamed "correspondent from Nablus, Palestine," quoted by the missionary and prolific author Samuel Zwemer,[47] leads to the question of how many Christian missionaries had been welcomed into Muslim homes to listen to mothers teaching their children to curse their fathers. Modern reporters who have lived in Muslim homes have never heard of this strange custom, of course, and it seems unlikely that Muslim standards of child-rearing have changed so drastically. It is hard to imagine a further departure from Islamic customs than teaching children to curse their fathers, which would be a grave offense against the most sacred traditions of the Muslim family. The important point is not where the writers got such harebrained ideas but that American readers would have no way of knowing that they were completely untrue.

Muslim mothers also supposedly inculcated sexual immorality in their children by their speech and example. The writers averred that as men and women of religion they did not feel they should describe the sexual wickedness learned by children. They left the details to their readers' imaginations. Words such as "degrading and polluting," "immoral training," and "nameless vices" were felt to be sufficient. In one example, the missionary Mary Schauffler Labaree wrote of Muslim women, supposedly from upper-class Persian homes, who invited their friends over to engage in conversations on sexual matters: "The conversation—no, it cannot be repeated here, for it is not fit for the printed page."[48] The children supposedly listened eagerly and thus learned evil. Missionaries frequently mentioned polygamy, though polygamous households were seldom described, except in anecdotes: "A splendid Christian teacher was talking with one of the boys of our Moslem school about personal purity. 'That is all very well,' responded the boy, 'but what do you really expect of me with my training and home life when my father has had one hundred and five wives?'"[49]

Again inferences were left to the reader, who would have no way to learn that Muslims never had 105 wives (those who would treat wives equally being restricted to 4) or that the large majority of Muslim marriages were not polygamous.[50] In condemning polygamy, the missionaries gave no thought to its possible social function in Middle Eastern lands, where high male mortality in warfare (especially wars with Christian Russia) would otherwise have left women without a chance of marriage or childbearing. The questions asked were purely religious, divorced from any consideration of the environment.

The comments reveal as much about the authors as about the subjects. One of the major complaints was that Muslim children were taught evil by their parents and their religion. Describing a book on Islam for children, Zwemer stated: "The first part of the book also treats of Moslem theology, but includes a chapter on purification which is utterly unfit for the mind of any child, giving, as it does, all the disgusting details of the Moslem ritual for married folk, as well as a special section on menstruation and childbirth."[51]

The missionary accounts of Muslim home life cannot help but have left negative impressions on Americans. They depicted a people who could not be liked. The spiritual life of Muslims was degraded by false descriptions. For example:

> Other examples of the Islam cult [sic] are things on which the devotees of that faith pride themselves, in comparison with Christians. We are, however, bound to think their ground for self-congratulation very insecure. They give a whole month to fasting by day,—yes, and to feasting and other self-indulgence by night. It is difficult to see how any spiritual value can be assigned to such debauchery.[52]

This passage supposedly describes the month of Ramadan, in which all good Muslims fast: no food or liquid crosses their lips from sunup to sundown. At dusk Muslims gather with family and friends, pray together, then eat a large meal after the sun has set. It is impossible to guess what the other "self-indulgence" could have been. Alcohol is forbidden. Sex in such a setting is against all Muslim rule and practice. The debauchery was in the mind of the writer, not an activity of those having a family dinner after a session of prayer. This quotation from a book on missions to Muslims written by a missionary to the Ottoman Empire, George Herrick, is simply a lie, and it is hard to believe that the author did not know that it was a lie. Yet it was a lie that fit perfectly into the image of Muslims in the minds of Americans.

The "proofs" offered by the missionary writers were always anecdotal—one or two examples of evil practices that were supposed to represent entire nations and an entire religion. As an example, take this comment on Muslim sexuality written by a missionary in Egypt:

> The element of love was left out of both the religion and morality of Islam. Marriage was not founded upon love but upon sensuality. A mother was rebuked for arranging a marriage for her fourteen-year-old son. Her excuse was, "I do it to keep him from learning the bad habit of visiting prostitutes." The sensual nature has been trained in the Egyptian to an indescribable degree of disgusting perfection. As some one has said, "Mohammedans have added a refinement of sensuousness to pagan sensuality." As a result of this training men and women have sunk to depths of degradation unconsciously manifested in their customs, in their speech, and in their life.[53]

How much does the story of the woman with a fourteen-year-old son, even if true, represent Egyptians or Muslims? What does "depths of degradation" mean? This quotation is typical of the evidence used by the missionaries to prove the Muslims' sins. Missionary writings foisted anecdotes as examples of Islamic life: women were divorced or beaten in the ones or twos. The occasional European was set upon, in one case as the subject of an unsuccessful homosexual attack. Various Muslims were quoted either as being proud of the sins or as bemoaning the sins of other Muslims. With the rarest of exceptions, the authors gave no names; the supposed perpetrators and commentators were anonymous.

The article from which the "refinement of sensuousness" quotation above was taken provides a good example of the anecdotal attack on Muslims.[54] In order to prove the errors of Islam, the missionary author told stories of Egyptian women who were wronged: a man divorced his wife to marry a richer woman; a divorced woman told a missionary that she must marry again or she was afraid she would "live in sin"; a man slept with different women; a woman was abandoned while she was pregnant; a child was abused by her parents. The anecdotes of evil Muslim marriages and couplings were accompanied by stories of the blameless lives of pious Christians. Other chapters in the same volume *(Our Moslem Sisters: A Cry from Lands of Darkness Interpreted by Those Who Heard It)* and in countless other books made use of the same technique to castigate Muslim morals. The author of the book mentioned above in which the Muslim women gather to talk pornographically, a missionary to Persia, went on to describe the rest of the family's day: children were encouraged to fight each other, egged on by the women. The friends left before the men came home. Later that night the father was angry at dinner time and divorced his wife on the spot because the rice was not properly cooked. This was portrayed as typical of Muslim households.[55]

Many of the missionary tales of evils in Islamic lands were perhaps true, even if embroidered and exaggerated. They were examples of individual behavior, however, that could not rightly be taken as representing Muslim society. Nor would the missionaries have accepted similar analyses of their own culture. For example, Henry Jessup, a Presbyterian missionary in Syria, made much of Arab husbands who had physically abused their wives.[56] Did this never occur in Christian lands? Jessup also quoted a case in which Ottoman authorities arrested and imprisoned an attempted homosexual rapist. He did not use the incident as an example of the efficiency of the Ottoman police but as an example of the depravity of (in this case) Ottoman Muslim Syrians.[57] Were such things completely unknown in the United States? Missionary authors who used anecdotes of sexual depravity to prove Muslim deficiencies seemed oblivious to the possibility that exactly the same technique could be used to "prove" that American Christianity was evil or at least a failure. Evils of the type described by the missionaries were surely not lacking in New York, Philadelphia, or Boston. Certainly American authors of the same period were writing novels and social criticism describing such evils. The differential effect on the readers, however, would have been great. Americans who read of evils in their country would have been able to compare them to myriad examples of happy home life around them. Readers of the missionaries' writings would only have seen the evils, never the good, in Islamic society. No American missionary was anxious to write of happy Muslim homes and marriages, and none did. The only examples of Islamic sexuality and family life available to their readers were negative.

The Violent Muslim

It was essential to the missionary argument against Islam that it be seen as a violent religion whose main support was military. Thus when they discussed why so many of the world's people were Muslims, they blamed it all on military force:

> The extension of Islam, depending on military success, stopped wherever that was checked. The religion advanced or retired, speaking broadly, as the armed predominances made head or retroceded... It is true that when once long and firmly rooted, as in India and China, Islam may survive the loss of military power, and even flourish. But it is equally true that in no single country has Islam been planted, nor has it anywhere materially spread, saving under the banner of the Crescent or the political ascendancy of some neighboring state.[58]

The authors were "speaking broadly" indeed. The Turks had been converted to Islam in Central Asia not by the sword but by missionaries and the example of Muslims. The same can be said of large tracts of Africa and Southeast Asia. Perhaps naturally, the same missionaries contended that "Christianity was not propagated by force"[59]—an equally astounding assertion, given, for example, the treatment of Jews and Moors in Spain.

Some Christian critics of Islam did not scruple at falsifying the record to make their point. Take the issue of Muslim treatment of Christians. It is no exaggeration to state that the historical record of Islam regarding the religious liberty of Christians and Jews, while far from perfect, was a vast improvement over the treatment of Muslims and Jews by Christians. The laws of Islam distinctly commanded that Christians and Jews were to be allowed to keep their religion. They were to be exempted from military service but were to pay a special tax. Yet the truth of Muslim-Christian relations was seldom seen by Americans who read missionary writings or heard sermons. It was instead often submerged in inventions such as the following:

> The sword is consecrated to the cause of Islam. It may be unsheathed to repel an enemy or to make a convert. All Christians are regarded as idolaters, who may be destroyed at any time without sin whenever the interests of Islam require their removal. "Kill the idolaters," said the prophet, "wheresoever ye shall find them, and take them prisoners, and besiege them, and lay wait for them in every convenient place. But if they shall repent, and observe the appointed times of prayers, and pay the legal alms, dismiss them freely." Quran, chap. IX, 5.[60]

This analysis of Muslim fanaticism was presented by the Reverend E. M. Wherry, sometime lecturer at Princeton Theological Seminary, missionary in India, president of the Missionaries to Moslems League, official of the World's Congress of Missions, and an author whose books were used in seminaries and recommended to seminarians.[61] It appeared in a religious tract, a short work intended for a popular audience and distributed by church groups. The analysis was a complete fabrication. Christians were never regarded as idolaters by Muslims, who knew them as "People of the Book" (the Bible) and believers in the same God that the Muslims believed in. Muhammad specifically enjoined that Christians were to be allowed to keep their faith, not forcibly converted. Christians were surely not to be "destroyed at any time without sin." The quotation from the Quran did not refer to Christians at all but to pagans in Arabia. It is impossible to believe that Wherry did not know that what he had written was a lie. His readers would not have known that to be the case.

Wherry's opinion of Islam was unambiguous:

> The difference between the immoral Christian and the immoral Moslem may be thus described: The Christian is immoral in spite of his religion; the Moslem is immoral because of his religion. It is, indeed, chiefly owing to this cause that

> Moslem empires are not enduring. The social and national life is undermined by
> a fatal disease, which, like leprosy, festers and rots, though the life may be long
> continued.[62]

When Wherry wrote, the Muslim Ottoman Empire had already lasted nearly six hundred years, quite an extended "festering." His sense of immorality speaks for itself.

The image of Islam and of Arabs and Turks that appeared in missionary writings could only have made a negative impression. Ottoman history, in particular, was presented in "history by anecdote," with no attempt to check the veracity of the tales told. An official publication of the American Board stated that janissaries routinely cut off the heads of Christians in the street in order to test the edges of their swords and used Christians as targets for rifle practice.[63] Naturally, no such practices appear in the diplomatic literature or contemporary accounts of even the most biased travelers in the Ottoman Empire, but how would American readers have known?

Most missionary writers did not attempt detailed comparisons of the history of Islam and the history of Christianity. This was philosophically consistent. They did not hold that the history of the Catholic Church before the Reformation could in any way be their history. Thus they were spared comparisons between the relative religious tolerance of the conquering Muslims and the conversion by the sword that had spread Christianity through much of Europe. In fact, they seldom mentioned even early Protestant beliefs in this context (Calvin's policies in Geneva would have made an interesting comparison). The Thirty Years' War was conveniently forgotten. Instead they compared Islam to the religious and social position of religions in America. Even then, some examples of Christian intolerance, such as the puritan legal system of early New England and riots against Catholic immigrants, went unmentioned.

Some writers, however, essayed comparisons between the entire history of Christianity and that of Islam, with some incredible results. The missionary Frederick Greene somewhat astoundingly believed that the history of Christianity was superior to that of Islam when it came to dealing with subject peoples and their religions. Did he not know of the expulsion of the Muslims and Jews of Spain, the bloody history of the Crusaders, or the treatment of Jews in general in Christendom? Greene felt that the Quranic injunction to fight infidels until they submitted to Islam and paid a tax proved the superiority of Christianity.[64] He was right in stating that Christianity had no such law. Indeed, Christianity was not fundamentally a religion of laws. But Christian practice surely should have been considered.

The Backward Muslim

The Protestant writers were quite cognizant of the economic gap between the West and the rest of the world, just as we are today. But their explanations were different from ours. It is most common today for historians to view the non-Western world as underdeveloped due to a myriad of factors, including chance working through the complicated machinations of history. Only those who had undergone the Renaissance and the scientific and industrial revolutions that followed could have reached a high level of economic development, and the non-Western world did not have the luck to host the Renaissance. The power and riches of non-European peoples remained approximately as they had been, while Europe improved. Once the educational and technological causes of Western development were understood, the non-West began to try to catch up. The West was continuing to advance at the same time, so the non-West remained behind. In the main, it remains economically behind today.

To nineteenth-century Americans and other Westerners the answer seemed less complicated: the West was in front because it was inherently superior. Some ascribed this superiority to "racial qualities," the superior "blood" that was the European inheritance.[65] Others ascribed the inferiority of non-Westerners to religion: Christianity and to a lesser extent Judaism were thought to be the basis for advancement; or, more radically, economic advancement was believed to be God's reward to Christians.[66] The latter view fit nicely into traditional Calvinistic doctrine, in which earthly success was seen as a sign of God's grace, and into the Social Darwinism of the age. Most Westerners, of course, simply assumed the inherent superiority of Europeans and Americans, without thinking overly much on causes.[67]

In general, missionaries seemed unwilling to consider that the condition of Muslims—often poor and often engaged in deeds of which the missionaries disapproved—was due to forces other than their religion: "Conditions in Christian lands are not what they should be, but they are infinitely superior to the conditions in other lands, and in proportion as they are Christian, famine and disease and want are overcome."[68] Missionaries firmly believed that acceptance of Christianity was necessary for a people to progress not only morally but economically. The evidence seemed to be before them. After all, was not all modern development a product of Christian lands? Did it not therefore follow that development must be tied to acceptance of Christianity? Those who today view Japan or Singapore know the answer, but the missionaries had no such examples.[69] They attributed what they saw as the low economic and social condition of the world's Muslims exclusively to Islam. Just as Christianity had been the cause of Western advancement, Islam was the cause of the backwardness of its adherents.[70] Writers made the logical leap: if Christianity was good for economic progress, other religions must be bad. The ahistorical nature of such a view did not trouble them: "Islam has wrought the material ruin of every people she has conquered."[71] Lack of European-style sanitary facilities was blamed on "Islamic fatalism."[72] Warfare was based on "the spirit of the Jihad." Islam was the cause of poverty and illiteracy in the Muslim world.[73] Even infant mortality was allegedly the fault of Islam.[74] Environmental and historical factors that might have been the main cause of these conditions were not considered. They did not, of course, take the corresponding opportunity to blame the excesses of Christian nations on Christianity.

Perhaps the most noteworthy effect of Islam was its negative influence on the climate and physical environment, according to Robert Speer, the leader of the Board of Foreign Missions of the Presbyterian Church in the United States: "Is it not a significant fact that the great wastes of the world are under the faith of Islam? Wherever Mohammedanism has gone it has either found a desert or has made one."[75] He conveniently forgot to mention which deserts had supposedly been created by Muslims.[76]

To the missionaries, Islam by definition could not have produced anything that was worthwhile. Indeed, they believed that Islam had blighted the civilizations it had touched.[77] Presented with the obvious historical successes of Muslims in the arts, politics, and the sciences, the missionary response was either simply to deny that they had ever really occurred or to contend that all successes in Muslim lands were really the products of non-Muslims. The Muslims themselves had produced nothing: "No great civilization, no scientist of note, no renowned school of philosophy has ever arisen upon purely Muhammadan ground."[78] How then had all those poems, medical treatises, and architectural wonders come to be? According to the missionaries, Muslims had borrowed them from other civilizations. Philosophy came from the Greeks, medicine from Galen, and so forth. The missionaries never considered the possibility that intellectual greatness might be demonstrated by taking the work of others, improving it, and going on to new conclusions, even though this might be considered the American genius. Perhaps they did not accept that Muslims could ever improve anything.

The critics of Islam went to incredible lengths to prove that Muslims had produced nothing. The glories of Islam were turned into liabilities. They viewed Islamic art and architecture, for example, as the work of "craftsmen" not "artists." This meant that "there were no fine arts in our [i.e., the American] sense."[79] They never considered that the American and European idea of art might not be the only possibility or that the marriage of art and craft was perhaps desirable. In any case, true art was supposedly beyond Muslims: "And down to the Turkish period it may be said broadly that these architect-builders were not Muslims. There was never any such thing as Arab architecture, and when we speak of Muslim architecture, all that can be meant under that phrase is the architecture developed in Muslim countries by non-Muslim builders on Byzantine, Roman, or Persian models."[80] Any book on Islamic architecture will put the lie to the statement that no Muslim architects existed, but equally troubling is the idea that development of past architectural forms shows limited ability and limited culture. How would the Renaissance be viewed by such standards? Turks in particular came in for what might be called aesthetic condemnation. The Reverend Henry Northrop was willing to admit that what he called Saracens or Persians had made a small contribution to art, but he was confident that the Ottoman Turks had made none at all.[81]

The aesthetic critics probably had little or no knowledge of the glories of Ottoman poetry, calligraphy, ceramics, textiles, or miniature painting, but how could they not have noticed Ottoman architecture or the tiles and carpets that had been so much admired in the West? Those who had seen Istanbul could not have missed the great mosques and palaces, and Ottoman architecture was undergoing a florescence at the very time when the most condemnatory missionary publications were being composed, in the late nineteenth and early twentieth centuries. Some analyses can be excused as the blindness of prejudice, but these statements can only be deceptions. American readers would seldom have known any better.

If Islamic excellence could not be accepted in the arts and sciences, how could it be accepted in politics? American Christian critics of Islam seldom studied or wrote on the history of the great Islamic empires. When they did so, they showed only partial understanding of the Islamic empire that was in their midst, the Ottoman Empire. Its past greatness was explained by the presence of Christians in the government, presumably meaning Christian converts to Islam. To the polemicists, all Ottoman greatness was due to wise Christians who guided Ottoman affairs. The critics then applied this incredible assumption to other Islamic empires. If, as they alleged, it was true for the Ottomans, it must have been true for earlier empires as well: "No Muslim government has ever long been able to carry on its affairs without the assistance of Christian or Jewish officials, and these have sometimes risen to the highest positions under the state. Naturally, then, oppressive regulations upon their fellow believers would not be enforced."[82]

Absurd as such statements were for the Ottomans, of course, they were even more absurd for the other Islamic empires. Did the Abbasids, Umayyads, Ghaznavids, and Moguls all owe their success to Christians, or perhaps to Jews? Who were these Christians and Jews? Such questions were not asked. The Ottomans did make use of many talented Christians, especially in their early days and in the late nineteenth and twentieth centuries. The Ottoman governmental and even military systems did owe much to the Christian systems that had flourished in earlier years in the lands taken by the Ottomans. But was this not a mark of wise statecraft? Who made the decisions to use these talented Christians? The critics' assertion that the Ottoman government was populated by Christians was nothing short of racist, for these so-called Christians in most cases had never been Christians themselves but were the descendants of Christians. The critics stated that the greatest sultans were born of Christian mothers, which was partially although not completely true. Those sultans spoke Turkish and often Arabic and Persian as well, were believing Muslims, and were thoroughly immersed in Muslim culture. Was their glory the product of "Christian blood"? Such assertions not only were intellectually untenable but were sad reflections on the minds of the authors.

Occasionally the missionaries were forced to concede that some good points could be found in Muslims. They often acknowledged that Turks in particular were truthful and honest in their dealings. For the missionaries, however, Turkish honesty did not arise from the proper fount: "His [the Turk's] truthfulness and honesty were purely a matter of natural dignity of character, and have no moral quality," according to the missionary E. M. Bliss.[83] Those words can only be understood to mean that the Turks' honesty was not moral because honesty came naturally to them. Bliss and his fellows believed that honesty did have a moral quality for real Christians, so was dishonesty therefore the natural state of Christians? In any case, Bliss went on to state that the natural honesty of Turks did not apply to dealings with Christians, because Islamic Law allegedly told Turks that they did not have to deal honestly with infidels. (It should be added that this is the direct opposite of the truth.) Therefore Turks were naturally honest and good people, but they did all sorts of evils because they were also Muslims. Islam, according to Bliss, had conquered the native goodness of the Turks.

Imperialism

Islam must be put under external restraint, and must be brought into providential subjection to civilized Christian governments, before its inaccessible fields will be fully opened to the entrance of the Christian missionary. God can do this, and he will do it in answer to prayer.[84]

—James S. Dennis, D.D., "22 years a Missionary in Syria"

Missionaries saw two solutions to what they portrayed as the evil of Islam and other non-Christian religions: imperialism and Christianity. The Christian apologists took great joy and comfort in the spread of European rule over Muslims. Soon, they felt, Christianity would triumph over Islam. Missionaries evinced nothing but praise for European imperialism.

First, the success of Western imperialism, British imperialism in particular, was viewed as evidence that God's plan was at work in the world. Christian nations had shown themselves to be superior, an outcome of their Christianity. Protestant England's expansion was naturally seen as the greatest success. Imperial triumph was thus a vindication of belief. Although the missionaries no longer completely adhered to early Calvinist doctrines on the saintliness of achievement, missionary writings still evidenced a belief that spiritual success was reflected in worldly success.

Naturally, most praise was reserved for Protestant imperialism, in particular that of England and the United States.[85] Missionaries did not conceal their feelings that the spread of the British Empire was God's will and thus was necessarily beneficial. Missionary publications described in some detail all the blessings that would flow from British imperial rule in the Middle East.[86] They did not notice any contradiction between their praise of European conquest and their complaint that Islam had been "spread by the sword."[87] Speaking of the Sepoy Mutiny of 1857, Robert Speer, secretary of the Presbyterian Foreign Mission Board, described it as "an incipient revolt of a great body of the Indian people against the British Power and the whole movement of civilization, enlightenment, and uprightness for which it stood."[88] That statement summarized the missionary attitude toward imperialism—those who opposed it also stood against "civilization, enlightenment, and uprightness."

More importantly, the missionaries believed that imperialism gave them the chance to convert Muslims.[89] When Muslim lands were in the hands of Christian rulers there would be no hindrance to missionary activities among Muslims, which the missionaries believed would then necessarily be successful. They felt the need to explain why Muslims almost never seemed to be attracted to the Christianity offered by the missionaries, who often went through entire lives in the mission fields without a single Muslim (or Jewish) convert. Missionaries were constrained by their beliefs to insist, to themselves as much as to others, that the paucity of Muslim converts must have a reason. They could not, of course, consider that Islam might have a greater religious attraction for its adherents, who might judge Islam to be superior to what the missionaries had to offer. Arguments that Muslims were incapable of accepting the truth, while mentioned, were seen to contradict not only the essence of evangelical Christianity but the rationale for missionary work. Thus the reason had to be found in something neither philosophical nor theological. The answer arrived at was fear: Muslims were said to be too afraid to convert.[90] The primary cause was Islamic Law, which specified death as the punishment for apostasy. Additionally, the apparatus of state in Muslim countries favored Muslims.[91] If Christians ruled, the state would be a help not a hindrance to the missions, and apostasy from Islam would be welcomed.

Although they perhaps would not have recognized it, the missionaries were imbued with the philosophy of Western imperialism. To them the advancement of European control over the world was a natural and proper development of history. They did view imperialism through a Christian prism, seeing the advance of the West as the advance of Christendom. These writers did not mention the excesses of imperialism and glorified its advances. They saw even the more unsavory aspects, such as the expulsion of the Muslims and Jews of Spain, as only another benefit of Christian advance.[92] Missionaries were especially enthusiastic as the Europeans expanded their empires in the Middle East immediately after World War I. The whole world seemed open to them as it had never been before: "perhaps four-fifths of the 235,000,000 who constitute the population of the Muslim World are now increasingly accessible to every method of missionary approach."[93] Not only were the rulers and the law now on their side, but roads and railroads were being built that would allow missionaries to reach new territories quickly.

With the benefit of knowledge gained from post–World War I imperialism, when 90 percent of the world's Muslims were under Christian rule, we can now see that fear of reprisal was not the cause for lack of conversions to Christianity. Even under European imperial rule, when Islamic retribution for apostasy was forbidden everywhere, only an infinitesimal number of Muslims ever became Christians. The missionaries could not foresee this, however; they were sure that mass conversion would eventually follow European or American rule over Muslims. Evidence to contradict this that existed even in the missionaries' time was ignored or explained away. The lack of conversions in Dutch Indonesia was blamed on Dutch policies that did not do enough to favor Christianity. The lack of conversions in India or later in British-ruled Egypt was put down to the need to be patient; potential Muslim converts still felt threatened until imperial control became more effective.[94]

Given their beliefs, it was impossible for the missionaries to see why inhabitants of other lands would refuse the blessings of European control, unless the real reason was that the debilitating effect of non-Christian religions kept them from seeing the truth. Missionary George Herrick wrote: "I once asked a Turk of intelligence and an officer of state, after a prolonged and friendly conversation, if he intended, in what he had said to me, to imply that he would prefer to have the Ottoman state perish rather than have it come under Christian control, with the condition that it should retain its integrity. He replied solemnly but unhesitatingly, 'Yes, that is my meaning.'"[95] Could Herrick not understand that a Turk might resent and resist occupation by any foreign power, especially when that power would almost certainly be the ancient enemy of the Turks: Russia? For Turks, the real concern was not religion but imperialism. The true question was whether Europeans would become their unwanted masters.

An unbridgeable political gulf existed between the missionaries and the Middle Eastern Muslims. The missionaries, as might be expected from the fervor of their belief, saw politics through the light of religion. Anything that advanced the conversion of the world was proper, and European imperialism seemed to favor conversion. The missionaries, like most Europeans and Americans of their age, actually saw the European rule over "lesser races" as foreordained by nature, by God, or by both.[96] Robert Speer stated the belief in a sentence: "In pressing out over the world, the Western nations are discharging a great duty."[97]

Missionaries wrote often of the many benefits that would come to Muslims if they became members of European empires. The main benefit, of course, was increased access to Christian missions, along with undoubted material benefits from increased education to dams built on the Nile. The missionaries nowhere mentioned the desire of people to be ruled by their own leaders, not by Europeans. Instead, they painted a picture of imperialism that might not have found complete agreement among subject peoples. Under the title of the benefit of "Just and Impartial Government" under imperialism, Herrick remarked:

> It should be observed that, whether in India and in Africa, or in Sumatra and Java, the governments which these Christian rulers displaced were unjust, oppressive and inhumane. From war and fear of war, from poverty and anarchy, from ignorance and moral night, those very populations have been brought out into the enjoyment of personal peace and safety; have been taught that only right is might, and that property as well as life is secure under the aegis of their new rulers.[98]

The history described above does not seem to have taken place on this planet. Was European rule in India, Africa, and Indonesia such a paragon that the subjects would want it to continue forever? It is true that imperialism had brought railroads, improved government bureaucracy, and a new justice system to India, but it had also brought the massacres of the Sepoy Mutiny. The opium trade and the Opium Wars in China and the atrocities of the Belgian Congo indicate that European imperialism had at least a mixed record. And how could anyone allege that imperialism, by nature military conquest over subject peoples, taught that "only right is might"? They forgot that America was founded on repudiation of foreign rule and self-determination. The spirit that spoke here was the belief that the expansion of Christian rule, and only Christian rule, was of itself naturally good.

Nowhere was the missionary point of view as clear as when they considered the Russians. The adverse effect of Russian imperialism on the history of Anatolia and the Caucasus is difficult to ignore. Beginning at the end of the eighteenth century, the Russians actively pursued a policy of forced expulsion of Muslim peoples from the lands they conquered. In the 1850s at least 300,000 Crimean Tatars were driven from their lands by the Russians. In the 1860s the Russians killed or expelled from the western coast of the Black Sea 1.2 million Circassians and Abkhazian Muslims, of whom one-third died. During and after the 1877–78 Russo-Turkish War in Bulgaria, 17 percent of the Muslim, mainly Turkish, inhabitants died and a further 34 percent were driven from the country. The Russians supported by armed force the expulsion of Muslims from Serbia and lands taken by Serbia. In short, the Russians were the force behind the expulsion and death of millions of Muslims during the nineteenth century.[99] They can also be seen as a primary force behind the animosity between Muslims and Armenians. It was the Russians who forced Turks from their lands in the Caucasian regions they conquered and gave the lands to Armenians from the Ottoman Empire and Iran.

The effect of Russian imperialism on the Ottoman Empire was immense. From the 1850s to the 1880s the millions of Muslims driven out by the Russians had nowhere to go but the Ottoman Empire. The empire was poor, an economically underdeveloped state made all poorer by Russian attacks. It nevertheless accepted the refugees, but it had little to give them in support. One result was civil disorder: starving refugees stole from those around them. Another result was animosity between Muslims and Armenians. Armenians had aided the Russians in their conquests in the South Caucasus. The newcomers and other Muslims saw Armenians as allies of the Russians, who were their enemies; in many cases this was true, just as the remaining Muslims in the Russian Caucasus could be viewed as potential allies of the Ottomans. Russian imperialism had brought a new suspicion among religious groups in Ottoman Anatolia and exacerbated divisions along sectarian lines.

None of this appeared in missionary writings. They castigated the Circassians, driven from their homes in abject poverty by the Russians, as a disorderly element, with no mention of the reasons why the Circassians were disorderly. The missionaries could not have overlooked the hundreds of thousands of Muslim refugees in the Ottoman Empire at any one time, but they made no mention of them. Instead they generally praised Russia as a Christian power that would bring benefits to the Christians, particularly the Armenians, of the Ottoman Empire. Speer praised the Russians as the "avengers of the Bulgarians,"[100] without any mention of the slaughter of Turks that accompanied the "avenging." In fact, Speer, the leader of the Presbyterian Missions, included an entire long chapter in his *Missions and Modern History* (volume 2, chapter 12) that praised the Russians unstintingly, calling their expansion the "natural" and proper development of a great people. Nowhere in fifty-nine closely printed pages did he allude to the methods that the Russians used in their "natural" expansion over the lands of Muslim peoples. His only complaint was that the Russian political and religious system was inferior to the American system, although much better than the systems of the indigenous Muslims conquered by the Russians.

For the missionaries, the one problem with Russia was its general dislike of Protestantism. Russia, an Orthodox power, preferred its own belief, which the missionaries often compared to Roman Catholicism, to the detriment of both ("The Russian Church rests neither on truth nor on righteousness, but on superstition").[101] Yet even this did not make the Russians an enemy. Russia, after all, was a Christian power that advanced Christian rule. Russian rule was to be preferred to any Muslim self-government. To the missionaries, the reason was evident: Muslims were incapable of proper self-rule.[102] Russians were praised for their steadfast opposition to the Ottoman Turks. Russian imperialism was described as a fight for the freedom of Christian peoples. Readers of missionary literature, in fact, would learn of Russian imperialism as a constant advance of civilization and Christianity.[103] What readers would not learn was that in their advance the Russians had killed or forced into exile millions of Muslims who lived in the lands they coveted. They would not find out that, until the later world wars usurped the opprobrium, Russian imperialism was the most murderous advance since ancient times.[104]

Missionaries did not endorse the imperialism of their day completely. Too often, they recognized, it brought a purely capitalistic orientation toward life and neglected religion. Most importantly, the imperialist powers did not give enough support to the missionary enterprise. According to the missionaries, the two most evident duties of imperial powers were to stop Islamic government and law and to assist the missionary enterprise. They felt that the European conquerors should have abolished Islamic marriage and family law and Muslim commercial law, and this was seldom done.[105] Too often, they felt, the Europeans were content to abolish Muslim rule, without ending Muslim social and religious customs. The missionaries complained that the imperial powers, particularly the British, often gave too much benefit to Muslims and did not show enough diligence in advancing Christianity. These complaints extended to the absurd, such as the failure of the British to declare Sunday the day of rest in Egypt. Nevertheless, it was an unquestioned truth among the missionaries that European imperialism was necessarily better than "native" rule. Despite the unfortunate contradictions between such a view and the tenets of American democracy, their view was that the native peoples must first become like the Christian Americans, for whom democracy worked—then they could be independent.

On a practical level, missionaries were proud of their cooperation with the mission of imperialism. Both American and British missionaries openly and proudly stated that they had been essential parts of imperial expansion. They had taken part as translators and advisors in the treaties that "opened" China after the Opium Wars, although they did not mention the actual purpose of the wars and treaties—the opening of China to free trade in opium.[106] Not coincidentally, the treaties contained articles opening China to American missionaries and guaranteeing them special extraterritorial privileges, putting them outside of Chinese law.[107] The missionaries were proud that freedom to preach Christianity was included in the treaties. Missionaries served both the commerce and diplomacy of the United States, especially in China and the Ottoman Empire, and the imperial ambitions of Great Britain. The British and Dutch governments, for example, lauded them for their help in the "peaceful occupation" of New Guinea and Indonesia.[108] American missionaries praised their British missionary colleagues for their success as agents of British imperial expansion. The Americans held up British missionaries as examples because they had been the main force behind the British takeover of Uganda and Nyasaland.[109]

Racism

Chapter 5 considers in depth the effect of racism and racialism on the image of the Turks: the categorization of humankind into various races and subraces based on supposedly inherited traits. The racialism of the missionaries is briefly discussed here.

It is tempting to say that the missionaries were racists, or at least racialists, who believed in inherited characteristics of "races," their own being at the top of the list. The statement is true but incomplete and unfair. The racism shown by the missionaries was more than anything else the result of the beliefs of their times, not any specific missionary failing. The racialist sentiments of most missionaries seem to have been part of a common heritage of racism in the America of their time, which not even the well-meaning could escape. To the missionaries and their supporters the most important classification within humanity was religious, not ethnic, linguistic, or "racial." All were children of God. Even those missionaries who adopted racial stereotypes or most believed in imperialism and the political subjection of non-Western peoples to Europeans strongly asserted the potential spiritual equality of all peoples. Indeed, missionaries often spoke against those who thought other peoples were unfit for Christianity or too racially inferior to accept it.[110] It should also be remembered to their great credit that the same men and women who supported the missionary movement were at the forefront of first abolitionism then racial equality in America.

That being stated, the missionaries undoubtedly did feed and amplify common American racist beliefs about Turks and other Muslim peoples. Missionary leaders such as Arthur Judson Brown, the leader of the Presbyterian Board of Foreign Missions, did not hesitate to quote Rudyard Kipling on the deficiencies of the "native races."[111] Nor did they hesitate to use the racial analysis that was common in their time, which divided peoples into putative racial groups and assigned "racial characteristics."[112] They portrayed the characteristics of Turks, in particular, as exceedingly negative. Their racial hierarchy listed Turks as Mongols or close relations of Mongols, with all the stigma that attached to Mongols in the European and

American mind. They only gave Turks high marks for undesirable characteristics: "The Turks have sensual and truculent possibilities that have never been equaled by any other race."[113] When a missionary such as Samuel Zwemer avowed that "the whole Moslem system, as based upon the practice and teaching of the prophet, is utterly opposed to eugenics,"[114] he was assuming an audience that believed in eugenics, not a modern audience that has learned to abhor the concept of selective breeding of humans. But he was also reinforcing the racialist beliefs of his time.

Religion mixed with racialism, and missionaries often wrote of Muslims as if they were a racial group adversely affected by Islamic practice. Muslim customs such as polygamy had supposedly led to racial degradation, which was one reason why the people were poor and uneducable.[115] The cause may have been heredity or environment, but Turks were held to be distinctly inferior:

> One who has traveled widely among them [the Turks] has said that the Turk possesses a childlike mind, a curious blending of strong and weak qualities, and that in his travels he has never seen a Turkish mullah much less a common citizen whose mental process could be sympathetically understood and valued by an Anglo Saxon, or who gave the impression of thorough scholarship and logical grasp of the subjects under discussion.[116]

In comparison to the Muslim peoples, the Christians of the Middle East were held to be intelligent and capable of dealing with the modern world, because they had been genetically improved through contact with Europeans. "Moslems, as a rule, are inferior in mental equipment to the Christians [of the Middle East] who at the Crusades and later have gained new vigor from intermarriage with Europeans and are naturally bright and commercially keen."[117] These sentiments would have fit well with the preconceptions of American readers, who would not have known that such intermarriage was historically insignificant. In general, through allusion if not outright assertion, missionaries portrayed Middle Eastern Christians as being of a higher racial quality than Muslims. They described Armenians, in particular, as "Aryans" whose native abilities had been submerged by Turkish overlordship but who were essentially like the English or Americans: "above all they are a race which can be raised in all respects to our own level, neither religion, color, customs, nor inferiority in intellect or force constituting a barrier between us."[118] Positive comparison to Americans was the highest praise that could be offered: "The Armenians are the Yankees of the Orient. They are the brightest, brainiest, and smartest of all the people of Asia Minor."[119]

These were isolated examples. Outright racist depictions of Turks and Muslims were not a main feature of missionary literature. This was not true, however, of the racial descriptions that the missionaries often gave of themselves. It was not coincidental that missionary praise of Armenians took the form of comparison to Americans. Americans, strangely considered a racial group, were believed to be at the pinnacle of the racial pyramid, members of the "Anglo-Saxon races." Perhaps the deepest racialism of the missionaries dwelt in their praise of Anglo-Saxons:

"The Growth of Christian Civilization. In contrast to the impotence of Moslem rule has been the spreading power of the Anglo Saxon races as they have claimed every element of civilized life for their own, bringing education, justice and industrial development to every land over which the flags of Christian peoples wave."[120]

This was racialism tied to religion, a religious and racial Manifest Destiny and the survival of the early American belief in the divine purpose in creating America, now brought up to date by including the British in the plan. The conversion of the world to Christianity was in the hands of the "Anglo-Saxon races": Britain and America. American missionaries would follow British imperialists. That was God's plan: "Great Britain not only has political leadership but a moral and spiritual leadership among the nations of Europe which no one can question. No believer in God doubts that there is a definite purpose in all this."[121] One missionary, Henry Jessup, openly stated that God had raised up the Anglo-Saxons to convert the Muslims:

> He is already preparing the way [to convert the Muslims]; and it is our purpose to notice the remarkable interposition of the divine providence in raising up in the two great branches of the Anglo-Saxon Christian family, in Great Britain and the United States of America, the political, religious, and educational means and appliances which are tending to bring the Mohammedan world to Christ.[122]

THE FORMATION OF THE MISSIONARY MIND

American missionaries were educated men. Those among them who had the most effect on the American public were authors and preachers. They were well trained in Christian doctrine in the theological seminaries of America, such as Andover, Hartford. Princeton, and Yale. There they were presented with a certain portrait of Turks and Islam before they entered the mission fields. The same seminaries educated seminarians not destined for the mission fields in courses on World Religions and Christian Apologetics. Class lectures or syllabi from the seminaries have not survived, but the names of many of the professors, instructors, and lecturers are known.

Congregationalist missionaries were mainly educated at the Andover and Hartford seminaries. Their instructors included Duncan B. Macdonald, W. Douglas Mackenzie, Robert Speer, James L. Barton, and William Rockwell—all prominent in the missionary establishment's attack on the Turks and Islam. The courses cannot have given a balanced view of the Middle East: future missionaries at Hartford, for example, were taught Turkish history by an Armenian. In addition to theology, courses were provided on Racial Psychology ("This course is a study of the different ethnic stocks in the light of their culture-level and the more significant mental traits"), on "the practical benefits Christianity has brought to the West and how to apply them to the rest of the world," and on Sociological Progress in Mission Lands.[123]

The Princeton Seminary was the premier American college for the education of Presbyterian clergymen and missionaries.[124] E. M. Wherry and James Dennis offered lectures at the seminary. Two of Dennis's books attacking Islam were based on his lectures there. Samuel Zwemer, the most prolific missionary antagonist of Islam, first lectured at Princeton Seminary then took a position as professor of the History of Religion and Christian Missions there. Like Hartford Seminary, Princeton Seminary was at the forefront of attacks on Islam.

Published bibliographies list the books used in seminaries and recommended to missionary students.[125] What professors wrote in their published works was presumably the same information that they gave to their students. We can learn much about seminary education from the books.

The orientation toward Islam in the seminaries was naturally to prove it wrong. At its founding, all professors at Andover Seminary took an oath "in opposition not only to Atheists and Infidels, but to Jews, Mahommetans, [a list of Christian heresies followed]."[126] Opposition to non-Christian beliefs was a part of the constitution of seminaries. They taught that Islam was fundamentally wrong because it was not Christianity—the same approach used at the time in Protestant seminaries toward Catholics or in Catholic seminaries toward Protestants. It was in the attempt to show what evils grew out of Islamic error that the seminaries descended to prejudice and did the most damage to their students.

The basic seminary texts on Islam were those written by Christian religious writers (some of which, such as Macdonald's, have been discussed above). Some of the works most often seen in reading lists were those of Sir William Muir.[127] He taught, sometimes originated, what can be called the "canonical" Christian view of Islam: Islam was an imperfect reflection of Judaism and Christianity. Anything good in Islam came from those sources, and all else in Islam was perversion. Muir quoted the Quran and Sayings of the Prophet selectively, choosing what would appear most ridiculous to English or American readers or passages that would appear inconsistent. The sex life of the Prophet was a constant topic. Muir, for example, described one of Muhammad's marriages: "By this alliance he not only gratified his passion for the sex (a whole year had passed since his last espousals), but no doubt also hoped to make Abu Sofiân [his wife-to-be's father] more favourable to his cause."[128] Muir generally devoted far more time to Muhammad's marital relations than to any other aspect of Muslim history.

In points of theology it is often difficult to see how Muir and other Christian commentators could avoid charges of hypocrisy. They complained of Muhammad's acceptance of slavery, which Christianity at the time of Muhammad and long after accepted as well. They looked askance at the "many points of doctrine and fine casuistry which have been fiercely contested by the different [Muslim theological] schools,"[129] as if such arguments have been unknown to Christianity. Islam was held to be a matter of "cold and formal round of Moslem ordinances, altogether wanting the genial and motive power of the Heavenly Father's love,"[130] again a claim that might have been made of certain Christian sects. Muir contrasted Christianity and Islam, to the latter's detriment, in most areas of societal relations, but he ultimately blamed all on the Prophet, whom he compared to Jesus:

> To put the matter shortly, each religion [Islam and Christianity] is an embodiment of its Founder. Mahomet sought power; he fought against those who denied his claims; he put a whole tribe to the sword; he filled his harem with women, bond and free; he cast aside, when they had served his purpose, the Jewish and Christian Scriptures, and he grafted his faith on the local superstition of his birthplace. He did all these things under cover of an alleged divine authority, but he did no miracle.
>
> The life of Jesus is all in contrast.[131]

Muir's prejudice is evident in his choice of words but especially in the selection of events and writings, which avoids all Muhammad's graces and benefits. Following Muir's principles of description, King David, for example, could be described as "voyeur, lustful coveter of another's wife, killer of a friend," and so forth. Something would be missing with David, as it was with Muhammad.

Other books used in seminaries or recommended for the formation of missionaries' minds and presented to the general public as textbooks on religion also carried the message of Muslim confusion and inferiority. The thrust of all the books was proving Islam's supposed deficiencies. The writers stressed whatever points they felt to be most representative of the religion of Islam. What seemed representative to them was almost always negative. Most of the authors were willing to concede that Islam was better than "heathenism," while considerably worse than Christianity. In *History of Religions,* Allan Menzies stressed violence in Islam, wrote that the Quran was virtually unreadable, and made other such comments but at least did not have much to say on Muhammad's sexuality.[132] His primary criticism was that in Islamic belief God was withdrawn and had not come down to earth. G. M. Grant's *The Religions of the World in Relation to Christianity* facilely summed up the problem with Muhammad: "he could not distinguish what was true from what was false."[133] To Grant, all that was good in Islam was borrowed from Christianity or, to a lesser extent, from Judaism.[134] Though Grant questioned the impact of madness, epilepsy, and other such factors on Muhammad, he repeated all the standard claims of sexual obsession: "when tested by the possession of absolute power, [Muhammad was] unable to keep himself pure."[135] Nor, according to Grant, was Muhammad able to remain either just or merciful as a leader. The real problem with Islam in Grant's appraisal was a simple one: Muhammad and the Muslims who followed knew only of God the Father, not God the Son. Grant stated quite openly that Islam was wrong because it was not Christianity, and this was a battle Muslims could not win. When judged by the principles of Christianity, Islam would perforce be wrong.

Grant was actually one of the least offensive of the commentators recommended to missionaries. While he could not refrain from bringing up the old canards of sexual obsession and lack or religious originality, Grant did accurately portray contemporary Muslim practice.[136] Would that other books that formed the missionary mind were nearly as objective. Another book used in classes and recommended for missionaries, Dean Frederick William Farrar's *The Witness of History to Christ*, was more typical, reflecting the romantic sensibility of its age:

> Strong only as a military theocracy, Islam as a creed was a mixture of fatal apathy with sensual hopes, and did but repeat the same mechanical formulas with lips of death....It now acts only as a gradual decay in every nation over which it dominates. The traveler in Palestine may be shocked to see even the fair hill of Nazareth surmounted by the white-domed wely of an obscure Mohammaden saint, but he will be reassured when he notices that in every town and village where Christians are there is activity and vigour, while all the places that are purely Islamite look as though they had been smitten, as with the palsy, by some withering and irreparable curse.[137]

By no means were Turkish, Arab, or Persian Muslims the only ones to be denigrated in missionary publications and in the missionary mind. All parts of the non-Western, non-Christian world were subjects of intense analysis and ethical criticism. Traditionally, Roman Catholic peoples were often held up to the harsh scrutiny of the missionary analysis, but non-Christians were the primary subjects. The basic approach was an investigation into all that was wrong, and little that was right, with foreign cultures. The Reverend James Dennis, formerly a missionary in Beirut, wrote the basic seminary text on the sociology of the missionary undertaking, *Christian Missions and Social Progress: A Sociological Study of Foreign Missions*.[138] The book originated in the author's lectures on the subject at Princeton Theological Seminary. It was often quoted by others and was recommended as a valuable source to be included in missionaries' libraries.[139] This rather long book (three volumes) is full of interesting detail, devoting 468 pages to one chapter: "The Social Evils of the Non-Christian World." The evils ranged from the horrific (burning of widows in India) to the titillating ("promiscuous bathing" in Japan and "abominable dances" in Polynesia). The illustrations included photographs of healthy non-Christian bare-breasted women and starving non-Christian famine victims.

The purpose of the book and of others like it was obviously the arousal of moral indignation among the missionaries themselves and the public in general. The effect was to paint all the world's non-Christian inhabitants as strange people with evil customs. Dennis gave no consideration to the effects of environment on poverty. Indeed, he stated that poverty was the result of a lack of Christianity and that adoption of Christianity would cure it. Religious but poor sharecroppers in the American South might have been amazed by his words.

The chapter titles in *Christian Missions and Social Progress* indicate the thrust of the book, especially chapters whose headings contain the word "evil," such as "Evils Affecting Primarily the Individual," "Evils Affecting Primarily the Family," and "Evils Which Afflict Society." The chapter subheadings all illustrated individual evils, including "Ignorance," "Quackery," "Neglect of the Poor and the Sick," "Uncivilized and Cruel Customs," and "Lack of Public Spirit"—a catalog of everything that could possibly be wrong in the non-Christian world. Islam was by no means taught as the only religion that led to evils. The whole gamut of non-Christian religion was represented. But Islam was represented as a primary cause of societal evil. The Ottoman government was described as "little less than organized brigandage in the name of government." Every traditional missionary criticism of Islam and the Ottomans was brought forward in capsule form. This is scarcely odd, because the sources that Dennis quoted were all anti-Turkish missionaries. Not one sentence treated Turks or Muslims sympathetically, including complaints about Muhammad's "debauchery," Islam being "spread by the sword," Turkish hatred of Christians, the low level of Islamic sexual ethics, and all the others noted above.

Yet not only was Dennis a teacher of seminarians, but his works were a staple of the missionary literature. The Student Volunteer Movement for Foreign Missions was a missionary support group spread across the United States and Canada.[140] The group's bibliography on missions described *Christian Missions and Social Progress* as a "monumental work, superior to anything ever published on the social problems confronting missions and the Christian solutions confronting missionaries."[141]

A selection of the material in *Christian Missions and Social Progress* was excerpted and published for easier study by seminarians and for "Mission Study Classes in institutions of higher education."[142] The headings of the "Analytical Index" provided for teachers are shown in table 4.1. In the Dennis book and others like it Muslims were treated differently than many others. For one thing, they had few of the sorts of customs that were most interesting. They did not bind women's feet or burn widows or bathe naked with members of the opposite sex. Had they been described accurately, they might have appeared as puritanical as the missionaries in their outward demeanor. Muslims were therefore depicted in more general terms. Polygamous households were described as "licentious," but without any details, because, presumably, the Muslims would not let anyone in to see their supposed debaucheries. General statements of evil were the rule. As Dennis stated in describing the licentiousness of Muslim males, "The Muslim soldier for centuries has marched to his victories, not alone over the dead bodies of men, but over the dishonored forms of women. He even departs for his paradise with the gleam of expectant passion in his glazing eyes. The family life of Islam is a nursery of ideas which are necessarily fatal to social purity."[143]

An early formulation of the basis of the missionary critique of Islam was written by a British professor of divinity at King's College, London, Frederick Maurice. His book was used in American seminaries and was recommended to American missionaries as a source on Islam. Maurice was mightily concerned with the undeniable fact that Islam had prevailed over Christianity in the Middle East. To him, "the propensity of man to believe impostures" was only part of Islam's appeal. Not even the assertion that the best portion of Islamic belief was taken

TABLE 4.1. DENNIS'S INDEX OF TRAITS OF NON-CHRISTIANS

Intemperance	Human sacrifices
The opium habit	Cruel ordeals
The gambling habit	Cruel punishments and torture
Immoral vices	Brutality in war
Self-torture	Blood feuds
Suicide	Lawlessness
Idleness and improvidence	Ignorance
Excessive pride and self-exaltation	Quackery
Moral delinquencies	Witchcraft
Degradation of women	Neglect of the poor and sick
Polygamy and concubinage	Uncivilized and cruel customs
Adultery and divorce	Insanitary conditions
Child marriage and widowhood	Lack of public spirit
Defective family training	Poverty
Infanticide	The tyranny of custom
The traffic in human flesh	Caste
Slavery	

from Judaism and Christianity or that what was noble and correct in Islam was basically Christian was enough to explain Islam's power. It was also not sufficient to note that Muhammad truly stated many eternal verities: "We cannot believe that mere phrases and sentiments, be they ever so good, nay, even if they did not occur in the midst of any that are fond or trivial and contradictory in themselves, could have wrought a deep conviction into the minds of men previously indisposed to them." In other words, precepts themselves were not enough to generate righteousness. What accounted for Islam's success in the world was simply that it was part of God's plan. God had foreordained Muhammad's mission and Islam itself for various purposes—to test Christianity, to bring low haughty and heretical Christian princes, and to bring the message of monotheism to heathens who would later learn a greater truth.[144]

To Maurice, the essential internal strength of Islam was its monotheism and its assertion of the power of the Great God. But this was also Islam's downfall. All that Islam knew was God's power, not his love. Islam had become a stale religion of rules that allowed all sorts of transgressions against true personal and social morality, because it knew nothing of God but laws and power.

> The grandeur of the Crescent can be understood only by the light that falls upon it from the Cross. Because the Mahometan recognizes a mere Will governing all things, and that Will not a loving Will, he is converted, as we saw that he had

been in the course of his history, from a noble witness of a Personal Being into a worshipper of a dead necessity. Because he will not admit that there has been a Man in the world who was one with God—a Man who exercised power over nature, and yet whose main glory consisted in giving up Himself—therefore he cannot really assert the victory of man over visible things when he tries most to do so. He glorifies the might of arms, when he most talks of submission. Because he does not acknowledge a loving will acting upon men's wills, to humble them in themselves, and to raise them to God, therefore he becomes the enslavers of his fellows, therefore cheerful obedience to a master, which for a while distinguished him, becomes servitude to a tyrant.

Maurice held that Muslims, seduced by this idea of God as only ruler and lawgiver, did not accept that "His glory is ever anything but the glory of purity, and goodness, and truth."[145] Thus they set themselves against those things. Yet Maurice had great hope, because Islam, after all, existed as part of God's plan, which ultimately would lead to the conversion of the world to Christianity.

Another standard work on Islam recommended to theological students and missionaries was S. W. Koelle's *Mohammed and Mohammedanism*. Koelle, a missionary himself, included all the standard missionary misstatements on Muslim history, Turkish rule, and the life of Muhammad. He summarized his analysis with an assertion of the reason for the existence of Islam: it had come from the devil. It was "a reaction and aggression of the Kingdom of Darkness against the Kingdom of Light." To Koelle the necessary Christian response was easily understood: because Islam was spawned by Satan, Islam must be destroyed.[146]

This was the type of education for both those who went out to the mission fields and those who went as ministers to American churches. For the missionaries, such an education can only have predisposed them to see evil in the Muslims they encountered. The ministers could draw on their education when they, in turn, educated their flocks.

The Protagonists

Many of the opinions described above may seem to modern readers to be too absurd to be attributed to mainstream churchmen.[147] Readers might prefer to think that these must be the beliefs of a fringe group or perhaps that the beliefs look odd because they are taken out of context. This is not the case. The missionaries and mission supporters quoted above were the leaders of the missionary establishment, prominent in religion and society.

Robert Speer, the apologist for imperialism who felt that Islam was the most degraded religion in the world, was a member of the boards of Princeton Seminary and the Student Volunteer Movement for Foreign Missions and one of the secretaries (directors) of the Presbyterian Board of Foreign Missions.[148] In 1927 he was elected moderator of the Presbyterian Church. He was also an influential leader of American Protestantism as a whole. He served as chairman of the General War Time Commission of the Churches, the organizing body for Protestant church war efforts during World War I, and as president of the Federal Council of Churches from 1920 to 1924. Speer Library at Princeton Seminary was named after him.

Arthur Judson Brown, who cataloged all the supposed evils of the Muslim world, was a secretary of the Presbyterian Board of Foreign Missions, a member of boards of missionary colleges, and an executive or board member of most of the important religious conferences of his time, including the World Missionary Conference, the Foreign Missionary Conference of America, and the Council on Religion and International Affairs. Brown was a prolific author. He served as a member of Herbert Hoover's World War I relief committee and was decorated by Greece and Siam.

Henry Jessup, who asserted that God had created the "Anglo-Saxon races" for his purposes and was mightily concerned with homosexuality among Muslims, was a Presbyterian missionary in Beirut who wrote six books on Islam.

Like Jessup, James Shepard Dennis was also concerned with sexual immorality in Islam and was an apologist for European imperialism. He was a prominent leader of the missionary establishment, offering courses at Princeton Theological Seminary and serving on the Presbyterian Board of Foreign Missions and the board of the Syrian Protestant College (AUB). He was the principal of the Presbyterian Theological Seminary in Beirut.

Mary Schauffler Labaree, who wrote with distaste of Muslim family life and Muslim sexuality, was a missionary. After returning from the Middle East, she became traveling secretary of the Student Volunteer Movement for Foreign Missions and lectured across America. She was an instructor at the School of Missions at Hartford Seminary.

E. M. Wherry, who falsified Muhammad's message in the Quran and Middle Eastern history, applauded imperialism, and damned Muslim morality, was the author of seven books on Islam as well as editor and translator of many others. He was corresponding secretary of the World's Congress of Missions, president of the Missionaries to Moslems League, official of the American Tract Society, and moderator (head) of the Indian Presbyterian Church. Wherry was a lecturer at Princeton Theological Seminary.

Samuel M. Zwemer was the most prolific of the missionary establishment writers against Islam, with more than thirty books. His output included works for children, studies of Islamic theology, biographies of missionaries, and studies of Islamic life, all of them extremely negative. His works covered most of the attacks described above, including sexuality and home life, the glories of imperialism, and backward Muslims. For many years a missionary in Arabia and Egypt, he was a prolific speaker in America, traveling widely and becoming a professor at Princeton Theological Seminary, where he trained a new generation of missionaries.

THE IMAGE

Understanding the missionary establishment's view of Muslim peoples is essential to understanding the image of the Turks that developed in America. The

Turks were the most prominent Muslim people. They were naturally included in, and took the brunt of, prejudices against Muslims. The missionary establishment's image of Turks and Muslims in general was virtually the only one to reach Americans. Where else would a nineteenth- or early twentieth-century American have found information on Islam? A small number of books attempted a nonadversarial view of the religion.[149] These might have been found in great university libraries, essentially unavailable to all but a few. The books that might have been seen by most Americans were the missionary works. As noted above, 88 percent of the books on Islam in American libraries were written by members of the missionary establishment. Missionary societies and churches all over America kept lists of the books for readers, and some kept libraries for their congregations. Those were the books that taught Islam to Americans.

The effect that the missionary establishment had on those who were important in shaping American public opinion was exceedingly significant. The greatest American universities (such as Harvard, Yale, and Princeton), where a large number of American leaders were formed, were in the hands of missionary supporters. Indeed Princeton lecturers, professors, and graduates were the source of many of the missionary tracts on Islam. But most important for the negative image of the Turks was the formation of the missionaries' minds. Their prejudices were to have a great impact on what Americans learned of the Turks, especially their reporting on the Armenian-Turkish conflicts of the 1890s and World War I. Those who reported on those conflicts were the products of what had become the standard American view of Islam and the Turks. With few exceptions, they proved incapable of rising above their prejudices to report fairly. This was especially true of the missionaries who were to provide the bulk of what Americans learned of troubles in the Middle East. Can the word of the missionaries be trusted? How reliable can witnesses be when they are fully committed to one side before the battle begins, when they have a tradition of viewing one side as the devil, when they have been avoiding the truth or telling lies about one side for decades?

5

EDUCATION

Nothing identifies the beliefs of a country and its cultural traditions better than its schools. In an age before television or radio, it was very possible to avoid knowledge of current events simply by not reading newspapers and magazines. High art, literature, and history could easily be ignored. But two avenues conveyed cultural beliefs to nearly all Americans: churches and schools. While most nineteenth- and early twentieth-century Americans had only limited schooling,[1] the educated shaped the culture: training the ministers and politicians and writing the newspaper articles that reached the masses. Because very few records of actual class lectures exist, textbooks offer the best picture of what the Americans learned in their schools. The textbooks also reflected the culture and beliefs of their time.

The geographies and histories of early America have been described above. This chapter concentrates on education in the late nineteenth and early twentieth centuries. The coverage of the Turks and Islam in the period between the early Republic and the late nineteenth century can be seen as continuing the earlier American tradition. The prejudices and lack of accurate information on the Turks seen in the early books were repeated in the texts of the middle nineteenth century. Indeed, some of the most prominent textbooks of mid-century were largely unchanged editions of early American books. Jesse Olney's *A Practical System of Modern Geography; or, a View of the Present State of the World*, for example, was in its ninety-second edition in 1855.[2] Olney repeated the "ignorant, indolent, intolerant, and brutal" view of the Turks that was universal in the textbooks. Textbooks that were new at mid-century also repeated the old stereotypes. Frederick Emerson's geographies portrayed the Turks as "idle, ignorant, and treacherous" and the Greeks as "having submitted to the cruelty and oppression of the rapacious Turks."[3] Students who used Roswell Smith's *A Concise and Practical System of Geography for Common Schools* (1850) learned nothing about Turks except that "the people [Turks] who form the only Mohammedan nation in Europe are indolent and ignorant, descendants of an Asiatic race, who acquired their present position through conquest."[4] J. H. Colton's *American School Geography*, an 1863 text with a distinctly religious bias, blamed Islam for what it portrayed as Turkish deficiencies and cruelty.[5] Mothers who wished to instruct their children were told by *The Mother's Geography:* "The Turks are generally ignorant, but honourable in

68

their dealings. They are sedate and polite, but when excited they become violent and cruel."[6] Other books for children, such as Mary L. Hall's *Our World: First Lessons in Geography for Children*, stressed the exotic, with stories of strange clothing, an addiction to bathing, dancing slave girls, and so forth, with no mention of any other aspect of Turkish life or governance.[7]

A direct continuity existed between the textbooks of early America, the middle of the nineteenth century, and the end of the century. The later texts often contained more material, but the negative image of the Turks was the same.

Textbooks and Authors

The textbooks described below were the standard books found in American schools. Like today's most popular texts, they went through many editions and were used for decades throughout the country. For example, Charles Downer Hazen's history textbooks went through twelve editions; James Harvey Robinson's histories, thirty editions, including an influential textbook written with Charles Beard; Richard Dodge's various school and home geographies, fifty-three editions; and Willis Mason West's elementary and secondary school histories, thirty-nine editions.[8] The textbook authors were at the center of American academic life and pedagogy. James Harvey Robinson and Charles Beard were professors at Columbia University, founders of the New School for Social Research, and among the most influential scholars of their time. Robinson was president of the American Historical Association. Carlton H. H. Hayes, Parker Thomas Moon, and Charles Downer Hazen were also professors at Columbia University. Hazen was a fellow of the National Academy of Arts and Letters and a chevalier of the Légion d'Honneur; Hayes was the recipient of many awards, including a knighthood. George Burton Adams and Daniel C. Knowlton were professors at Yale, Merrick Whitcomb at the University of Pennsylvania, and Ferdinand Schevill at the University of Chicago. Henry E. Bourne, a professor at Western Reserve University, was a member of the board of editors and managing editor of the *American Historical Review*, the premier historical journal in the United States. Albert Bushnell Hart, a professor at Harvard, was editor of the *American Historical Review*. Henry William Elson, a Lutheran minister, lecturer at New York University, and professor at Ohio University, was not as academically renowned, but his *Who's Who* entry states that one of his many books sold more than a million copies.[9]

The image of Europeans in American textbooks, particularly northern Europeans, was fairly well rounded. American students learned of the culture as well as the politics of Europe. Indeed, they often learned of no culture but European culture and its offshoot, American Anglo-Saxon culture. History and geography books most often mentioned non-European cultures only when pointing out their inferiority to those of Europe and America. They painted a rosy picture of European history. The books extolled ancient Greek culture but did not mention Greek slave holding. England's Magna Carta was prominently featured, but not the Irish potato famine or the Opium Wars. The opposite was true of the

Ottoman Empire and the Turks. Like the news media and the churches, text-books both reflected and shaped the negative image of the Turks by excluding Turkish achievements and maximizing, often inventing, Turkish failures.

WHAT WAS WRITTEN AND WHAT MIGHT HAVE BEEN WRITTEN

History textbooks should present both the good and the bad. True impartiality is as impossible for textbook writers as it is for anyone else. Writers should try, however, to portray the varied facets of any people, government, or religion. At the very least, they should attempt to get their facts right. Histories should encompass the successes as well as the failures of governments and cultures. A history of European civilization that dwelled solely on English culture and neglected to say anything of French or German art or literature would be worse than incomplete. An account of losses in the American Civil War should not include only dead Southerners. A World War I history that only tells of brave Germans would be less than complete. Yet that is exactly the sort of incomplete and highly prejudiced history of Muslims, especially Ottoman Turks, that was presented to American schoolchildren in their schoolbooks.

Certain elements of Middle Eastern and Balkan history should have been present in any textbook that considered the region's history. A search for some of these elements in textbooks can serve as a guide to the author's intentions, prejudices, and knowledge. Omission equals prejudice. Books should discuss the following elements

1. The facts: most important was the presentation of the facts of history. Did the events portrayed in textbooks actually occur? Were important facts omitted, especially those that might balance an otherwise negative portrayal of the Turks?

2. Ottoman government: assuming that a governmental system that lasted more than six hundred years must have had some good to it, did textbooks mention anything but negative features of the Ottoman governing system? Indeed, did they mention anything at all about the Ottoman system, as they mentioned the governmental systems of other countries?

3. Turkish life and culture: would readers have learned anything about the glories of Ottoman art and architecture or the great Ottoman poetic tradition? Even if authors were unwilling or unable to evaluate Islamic culture, did they at least give some consideration to the Ottomans as inheritors of the cultures of the Roman Empire and Byzantine Empire? Did they say anything good about the Turks, their lives, and their culture? Or were the Turks considered to be so benighted that nothing good could be said of them?

4. Islam and other religions: was the consideration of Islam unbiased (if Islam was considered at all)? Did the textbooks note that the Ottoman tradition of religious tolerance stands out, despite its faults, in comparison to the history of Christian relations with other religions (as seen in the continued existence of Christianity in the Ottoman Balkans versus the fate of Islam and Judaism in Spain)?

5. Ottoman reform: did the books report the great efforts to reform politics and economy that the Ottoman Empire made in the nineteenth and twentieth centuries? Or did they portray the Ottoman Empire as being in a permanent and irreversible state of "decline"?

6. Muslim wartime suffering: did the authors note that millions of Muslims, especially Turks, died or were evicted from their homes by Russian conquerors and by emerging Balkan nations? Specifically, did they describe Muslim as well as Christian losses in the conflicts of the nineteenth and twentieth centuries or only report Christian losses, leaving half the story and a very false impression of history?

7. General portrayal: did the books treat the Turks even remotely as sympathetically as they treated the Christians of Europe or the Ottoman Empire? Did the authors make any attempt to understand the actions of the Turks or any presentation of their justifications?

In fact, none of these points appeared in American textbooks. From what they learned in school, children and the adults they would become could only assume that the Turks had no art or literature, no effective government, and no caring religion. They would only know what they were taught, much of which was erroneous and all of which was one-sided. The textbooks had nothing good to say of the Turks. Some texts wrote as if the Turks existed only as a negative force in European history—ruthless and uncivilized but not very important. These were the texts most "favorable" to the Turks. Most texts, however, presented distinctly negative images of them. None referred to the considerable Turkish political achievements in administering an empire for more than six hundred years. It would probably be too much to expect that authors might have known much of Turkish art, architecture, or poetry, but they gave no indication that the Turks had any culture. The texts suggested that the only Turkish skill had been military.

In the general histories of Europe as a whole, the Ottoman Empire seemed to exist only as a foil to the European powers and the Balkan nationalist movements, even though the empire was definitely a European state and part of European history. For example, the college textbook *A History of Europe* by University of Chicago historian Ferdinand Schevill devoted considerably more words to the Greek Independence War than to all mentions of the Ottoman government.[10] While the book described the governments of all other major European states (and most minor states) in detail, the only description of the Ottoman government until the nineteenth century was that it was "decaying" after Lepanto. Ottoman military reforms were supposedly "largely due to British pressure." Schevill stated that reform in general was a failure, however, and "the old evils were ineradicable."[11] Another Schevill textbook, *History of Modern Europe*, mentioned the Ottomans in only a few words in a few sentences, always noting that they were at war with a European country, with no details, until the Greek rebellion. Then Schevill devoted pages to "Turkish tyranny" and massacres of Christians, followed by a section on the "Bulgarian Horrors."[12] The book contained nothing on Muslim suffering or, indeed, on anything else Turkish. A reader would believe that the Ottomans existed only to fight wars and kill Christians.

History texts did not attempt any description of the lives and customs of the Turks, although their depictions of what the Turks did could only have created an extremely negative image. Some geographies barely mentioned the Turks, or most other peoples, at all, concentrating on mountains, rivers, farming, and industry; but most gave short, disapproving descriptions of the Turks (usually a few sentences). Although the authors sometimes cited Turkish honesty, courage, and hospitality, the alleged Turkish traits most portrayed were ignorance, indolence, and religious fanaticism. The books depicted Turks as a fundamentally slothful people who sometimes bestirred themselves to commit violent acts against Christians.[13]

Most history textbooks treated the Ottoman Empire only as a scene of European diplomacy and military action, not as an intrinsic part of European history. The "Eastern Question" was considered from the standpoint of the British, French, Austrians, Russians, and, to a lesser extent, the Ottoman Christians. Daniel C. Knowlton and Samuel B. Howell's *Essentials in Modern European History*, for example, described the Turks' history in the Balkans in two sentences: "It [the Eastern Question] early manifested itself in a series of successful efforts to reclaim a large part of Europe from the sway of an Asiatic people, who had long menaced its institutions and culture. These were the Turks, who had captured Constantinople in 1453 and for the following two centuries had hovered like a black cloud over southeastern Europe."[14] Knowlton and Howell considered the Slavs to be a "race" pitted against the "Asiatic" race of the Turks and aided in their crusade by the European Christians.

The later nineteenth-century geographies showed the same prejudices against the Turks that had appeared in early America. The two dominant images in the American mythology of the Turks were barbarism/religious fanaticism and indolence. "Turkey is as well adapted by Nature as any other country in Europe to the uses of man. It would be flourishing and prosperous, were it not that the inhabitants are naturally indolent and bigoted to an extent which prevents intelligent enterprise."[15] This description was published in a 1901 geography text. Nathaniel Dwight and Jedidiah Morse had evinced the same sentiment, in nearly the same words, almost a hundred years before. The geographies of the middle of the century likewise had written of the indolent and bigoted Turks, again in nearly the same words. The geographers, knowing little of the people of whom they wrote, presumably repeated for generations what had been first written in colonial times. What is most instructive is that no one thought to correct them, almost surely because all shared the same prejudices and ignorance of the true lives of the Turks.

The textbooks gave much play to "barbarism." One book devoted only one paragraph (a total of 122 words) to the entire history of the Turks but managed to include their "barbaric characteristics."[16] Given the image of Turks in Europe since the Crusades, this was perhaps understandable. The stress on the avowed indolence of the Turks is harder to comprehend. It surely was not based on any analysis of Turkish work patterns. Perhaps the answer lies in the prevalent image of the Turkish lord lying by a pool while a female slave danced, which had long fascinated artists and writers. The American elevation of "enterprise" and hard work certainly contributed to the picture. Mediterranean and South American peoples suffered from the same stereotype.

The worst feature of the texts was not what they had to say of the Turks, bad as it was. The authors' omissions were even worse: no examples of Turkish art, literature, or architecture were included, which made it easy to state, as many did, that the Turks had no "civilization." No Turk ever died in the warfare and rebellion discussed in the texts, or at least no Turkish civilian deaths were ever mentioned. The only deaths reported were deaths of Christians, which made it all the easier to portray Turkish actions as atrocities. Even when the dead had been overwhelmingly Turkish, as in the 1877–78 Russo-Turkish War or the Balkan Wars, dead Turks did not appear. Russian imperial expansion had resulted in the exile or death of millions of Muslims in the Caucasus and the Balkans, but no text mentioned the millions expelled or killed by the Russians. This of course made it simple to portray Russian expansion only as a triumph for Christian peoples. According to the texts, the only loss to the Turks was loss of land where, in the authors' view, the Turks did not belong anyway.

Ottoman Rule

High school and college students either read nothing of the Ottoman government in their textbooks or, more commonly, read short negative sentences. *A History of Medieval and Modern Europe for Secondary Schools* by William Stearns Davis was typical. Its only description of the Ottoman government was the word "decay."[17] Other texts also gave only a few words to the Ottoman system: "despotic, corrupt, and inefficient" in one book;[18] "oppression, heavy taxation, and consequently discontent" in another.[19] Ottoman Christians were depicted as cruelly dominated and always oppressed. They never described the Christian officials serving in the Ottoman government at the time or the relatively high economic state of Ottoman Christians.

Nineteenth- and early twentieth-century American textbooks reflected what might be called the assumptions of the age. Nationalism was good, a necessary and progressive force. Authors gloried in nationalism and considered it a necessary and progressive force, especially as seen in the Balkans. This naturally cast the Ottoman Empire in a bad light. As a multiethnic empire, it could be portrayed as standing in the way of national aspirations. It should be noted, however, that the textbook authors very seldom applied the principle of nationality to the Christian empires, such as Russia and Austria-Hungary, and never applied it to the European colonial empires. The principle of dissolving empires for the sake of nationality was only applied to non-Christian empires.

The most important factor in the misunderstanding of Ottoman rule was the lack of analysis of the factors behind the political situation. The texts described European governments, especially the government of Britain, in detail. Students could see that the British system was the result of the actions of individuals, economic factors such as enclosure and the Corn Laws, and external factors such as wars and European alliances. The French Revolution was properly put in the context of the failure of a government system to adapt to new situations, economic depression, and new philosophies of human rights and government. The authors never presented such analyses for the Ottoman Empire. They never considered important factors such as the Capitulations (low Ottoman customs duties and other economic disabilities enforced by European power), European economic imperialism, and the horrible economic, political, and demographic effects of Russian imperialism. Students would have no way of knowing of the successes of nineteenth-century Ottoman political reform. Instead they read that the Ottoman system was unchanged, corrupt, and doomed. In the words of Hayes and Moon's secondary school text (written in 1923, almost a century after the beginning of Ottoman political reform): "In short, the Turkish government in the nineteenth century was rotten through and through."[20]

Much of the lack of accurate information on the Ottoman Empire was surely the result of simple ignorance. Textbook authors seem to have made no great efforts to enlighten themselves on Ottoman history. Fairly accurate political histories of the Ottoman Empire did exist.[21] The American textbook authors seem not to have read them.

The Turks and Civilization

"Civilization" is an indefinable word, although dictionaries perforce attempt to define it. *Merriam-Webster* identifies civilization as "a relatively high level of cultural and technological development" or "the culture characteristic of a particular time or place."[22] Ignoring the problem that "culture" is just as difficult to define, modern textbooks for World Civilizations or Western Civilization courses take the second meaning. That is not what textbooks of the late nineteenth and early twentieth centuries meant by the word. To them, civilization primarily meant "being like us." It is not too much to say that American and British authors felt that they had reached the height of civilization. In terms of technological achievement, which was often confused with civilization, Americans and Western Europeans had surely reached a higher level than the Turks. The question was whether the Turks were even capable of becoming civilized. Those authors who considered the question answered no.

The textbooks portrayed Turks as the enemies of civilization. They had supposedly destroyed the once great Arab civilization and had done their best to destroy Christian civilization in the Balkans.[23] On Serbia, a high-school text by Willis Mason West and Ruth West stated: "As in all Christian lands ruled by the Turk, oppression and cruelty dwarfed their civilization." The Turks had "small part in European civilization."[24]

Echoing the early American textbooks, the texts alleged that the Turks had damaged or destroyed what should have been a prosperous region. Here is one prejudiced and erroneous example from a high-school text:

Then in 1453 a savage race of Turks, known as the Ottomans, captured Constantinople, overran the surrounding country, and began to interfere with trade. They seized goods, robbed and killed the traders, and burned what they could carry away. No caravan was safe. Trade fell off. The people of Europe could no longer get the goods from Asia that they were coming to need more and more all the time. A new route to the East must be found.[25]

It is hard to know where to begin in analyzing this short paragraph. The Turks took Istanbul's surroundings before, not after, the city's conquest. They did not seize goods, rob, kill, and burn. In fact, the Turkish conquest of what had been warring states facilitated trade. As for the trade from the East, the Ottomans so depended on it that they built whole fleets in the Persian Gulf and Arabian Sea to try to protect it, only to be ultimately defeated by Western Europeans. The Ottomans also used every technique possible—including posting soldiers as guards, bribing bedouin raiders not to raid caravans, and building caravansarays—to protect the caravans. The phrase "savage race" describes the author's mind, not the Turks.

The texts most often praised medieval Arabs, frequently called Saracens in the texts, for their achievements. The books recognized the relatively superiority of medieval Islamic science over that found in Christendom. They admired the Arabs for their medieval accomplishments then forgot them. All but a few texts never mentioned Arabs after the Turkish conquest. Textually, the Arabs ceased to exist. Their place on the stage was taken by the Turks, who were treated with far less charity. The textbooks blamed the Turks, with no historical accuracy, for all the troubles that beset the Middle East. The following description comes from what was probably the most popular secondary-school history text of the immediate post–World War I period, *The Story of Modern Progress* by the Wests:

> The Turks were a Tatar people who had migrated westward from beyond the Oxus. They adopted Mohammedanism and swiftly won military and political leadership away from the Arabs. Then followed for the Mohammedan world its period of "Dark Ages." For some centuries the Turks seemed impervious to either Saracenic or European civilization, and, under their ignorant rule, the old Saracenic culture fell to decay.[26]

The Turks were held to be fundamentally incapable of high civilization. Samuel Banister Harding and Alfred Bushnell Hart's *New Medieval and Modern History* taught American high school students that "[the Turks] cared little for Arabian art and learning; for they were far below the Arabs both in the culture which they possessed, and in their capacity for civilization."[27] The most effective way to deny the existence of Turkish culture was simply to include no information on Turkish art, architecture, or literature. Of course, it is likely that the textbook authors knew little of Turkish culture and its connections to and refinements of past cultures, including that of the Arabs. Nevertheless, they felt capable of making judgments on Turkish culture's supposed deficiencies.

The actual treatment of religion in the Ottoman Empire provides a good example of the distortion of the image of Turks in textbooks. Under the Islamic Law followed by the Ottomans, Christians and Jews were allowed to retain and practice their religions. Because of this, Christian communities such as the Greeks and Armenians remained in the empire. In Europe, in contrast, such religious tolerance was unknown until modern times. From the later Roman Empire through the Middle Ages religious intolerance and often forced conversion were the rule in Christendom. The Ottoman record was imperfect: non-Muslims were forced to pay a special tax in lieu of military conscription and in most periods were not part of the governing system. Muslim prejudice against Christians and Jews surely existed. Despite this, the Ottoman record of religious toleration stood well above the European record. The Jews expelled by Spain in 1492 were welcomed by the Ottomans. Christian churches were common in Ottoman cities. Christian processions marched through Ottoman streets. Readers of American textbooks would not have known any of this. None of the textbooks included Ottoman religious tolerance, much less compared it to the Christian record. Those that referred to it at all turned it into an indictment. Charles Downer Hazen felt that the Turks had shown contempt, not tolerance, by allowing non-Muslims to retain their religions:

> Full of contempt for those whom they had conquered, the Turks made no attempt to assimilate them or to fuse them into one body politic. They were satisfied with reducing them to subjection, and with exploiting them. These Christian peoples were effaced for several centuries beneath Mohammedan oppression, their property likely to be confiscated, their lives taken, whenever it suited their rulers. They bore their ills with resignation as long as they thought it impossible to resist oppression, yet they never acquiesced in their position. Hating their oppressors with a deathless hatred they only waited for their hour of liberation.[28]

It was common to assert that Muslims held all Ottoman government offices in the early twentieth century. That had never been completely true and had long since ceased to be the case in both the central and provincial governments.[29] One book asserted that Christians were few in Ottoman Asia,[30] but most at least doubled the actual number of Christians. Robinson and Beard felt that, rather than enjoining tolerance, Islam's acceptance of non-Muslims was actually a license for oppression: "The Koran commands them [the Turks] to regard 'the people of the book,' as they call the Christians, as distinctly inferior, and therefore they despise the Christian peasants and have no hesitancy in robbing and maltreating them."[31]

Vilification of Islam in the American textbooks never reached the level seen in the writings of Christian missionaries and their supporters. Muhammad and Islam were usually described as objective historical forces. The books seldom considered matters of belief and truth and falsehood, although they routinely described Christianity as a more highly developed, more "spiritual" belief than Islam.[32] The worst said about Islam was that it was incapable of developing into a modern cultural force. Only occasionally did the canards about Islam appealing to the "lower passions of man" or Islam borrowing all its good points from Christianity, staples of the missionary literature, appear. The authors' feelings about Islam were seen in their language but seldom in purely negative descriptions. For example, in his important text *Modern European History* Charles Hazen repeatedly wrote of "the infidel Turk,"[33] but he said nothing bad about Islam per se.

WARS AND REBELLIONS

The depiction of the Greek rebellion in almost all the textbooks simply repeated the errors that had been common in the press at the time of the revolt. Turks slaughtered Greeks, but no Turk died.[34] The section on the Greek rebellion in Schevill's *History of Europe* is an example. He portrayed the Greeks as a group of prosperous merchants (mentioning no bandits and peasants); Western ideas had been disseminated among them, but they were stifled by the "progressive decadence of the Ottoman Empire."[35] Schevill described the slaughter of the rebellion as Turkish massacres of Greeks for which the Greeks took revenge in countermassacres, when in fact the truth was exactly the opposite, as accounts written during and immediately after the war stated.[36] Very unusually, two texts included statements that both the Greeks and Turks had committed atrocities, although Greek atrocities had occurred because the Greeks had been "made brutal by long centuries of Turkish oppression."[37]

Almost all textbooks included what were called the "Bulgarian Horrors" (considered in the next chapter). What had actually happened in Bulgaria was the result of an abortive revolution against the Ottomans in central Bulgaria in 1876. The main revolutionary act of the rebels was the slaughter of 1,000 Turkish peasants. The Ottomans responded with severity. The main army was occupied with a revolt among the Serbs of Bosnia, followed by a war with Serbia. Pressed for manpower, the government enlisted irregular forces made up of local Turks and Circassians against the rebels. In putting down the revolt and in revenge for the deaths of their fellow Muslims they killed between 3,000 and 12,000 Bulgarian Christians. The Russians then invaded Bulgaria and, in concert with many Bulgarians, eventually caused the deaths of 288,000 Turks and other Muslims of Bulgaria.[38]

The American college textbooks reported a uniform and false tale of the events of 1876–78. According to the authors, Turks had killed Bulgarian and Bosnian Christians. That was the end of their story; they did not mention Turkish mortality. On Bosnia-Herzegovina, Hazen's *Modern European History* stated: "The oppression of the Turks became so grinding and was accompanied by acts so barbarous and inhuman that the peasants finally rebelled. These peasants [in Herzegovina] were Slavs, and as such were aided by Slavs from neighboring regions, Bosnia, Servia, and Bulgaria."[39] In fact, half the population of Bosnia-Herzegovina had been Muslim. As in Bulgaria, the Bosnian revolt had begun with the slaughter of Muslim peasants, a fact unmentioned in the American histories.[40] Harding and Hart's *New Medieval and Modern History* not only failed to mention any Turkish dead in Bosnia or Bulgaria but lamented that the Ottomans had been left with any land in Europe to continue their "oppression" of Christians.[41] Other college texts were similar. Some devoted a few negative paragraphs to the Turks, most only a sentence or two to the war.[42] All told a completely one-sided story.

The high-school texts were no different. In a popular secondary-school history that went through many editions: "Turkish soldiers destroyed a hundred villages, with every form of torture and cruelty, and massacred thirty thousand people, carrying off also thousands of Christian women into terrible slavery."[43] Another wrote of Turkish "unusual cruelty and atrocities" and "barbarity."[44] Neither included Bulgarian and Russian cruelty and barbarity toward Turks, even though many times more Turks than Christians had been killed.

The Armenian Troubles of the 1890s (considered in chapter 7) were a complicated history of rebellion, massacre, and countermassacre. Their coverage in American textbooks was exactly what might be expected: Armenians were always innocent; Turks were always guilty. The only difference among the various texts was the number of Armenians supposedly killed, ranging from 25,000 to 100,000. None mentioned any revolt or any Muslim dead. Some only stated that Turks had killed Armenians;[45] others stated that the sultan had ordered the massacre of Armenians.[46] Some portrayed the Turkish-Armenian conflict as a "racial" contest: "Turkish passion—the passion of a dying race taking vengeance upon any of the races that are supplanting it which it still has in its power—broke out in fearful atrocities against the Christian Armenians of Asia."[47] As in the case of every other war and rebellion, Muslim mortality was omitted.

The troubles that began in Macedonia early in the twentieth century were primarily a conflict of Macedonian, Bulgarian, Greek, and Serbian rebels to take control of a region that was predominantly Muslim in population.[48] The Ottomans attempted, with limited success, to keep order and oppose the various guerrilla groups that were attacking each other and civilians. American textbooks gave students a quite different story: battles between different groups of rebels went unreported. It appeared that the fight was solely one of Christians against Ottoman rulers, as indicated by Hazen's *Modern European History*: "Owing to the rival ambitions of the great powers, Macedonia's Christians were destined long to suffer an odious oppression from which more fortunate Balkan Christians were free."[49] Hazen gave no indication that any Muslims, other than soldiers and officials, lived in the Ottoman Balkans, much less admit that they were a majority. Robinson and Beard listed the inhabitants of the Ottoman Empire in Europe as "Greeks, Bulgarians, Servians, Romanians, and Albanians"[50]—no Turks.

The textbooks' single-minded concentration on Christian suffering continued in coverage of the Balkan Wars of 1912–13. This was the best example of the condemnation of Turks by omission of Turkish suffering. In the Balkan Wars, the Ottomans had been attacked by their Balkan neighbors (Greece, Bulgaria, Serbia, and Montenegro), each intent on gaining land at the Ottomans' expense. Ottoman Europe then was a great admixture of peoples, with Muslims making up slightly more than 50 percent of the population. At first the allies held together and defeated the Ottomans. Ottoman forces were driven back almost to the gates of Istanbul. But the Balkan alliance disintegrated over division of the spoils of war. The other erstwhile allies, along with Romania, joined forces against Bulgaria, the main territorial beneficiary of the first war, in the second Balkan War. Bulgaria was defeated, and the Ottomans took advantage of the conflict to retake the city of Edirne and some territory in Europe, coming to approximately the same European borders as those of today's Turkish Republic. The wars were a disaster for the Muslim population of Europe, primarily Muslim Turks and Albanians. About 27 percent of the Muslim population of the conquered territories died in circumstances as horrible as any in European history. An additional 35 percent ultimately became refugees in what remained of the Ottoman Empire.[51] It was one of the worst disasters ever to strike a population.

As was the case with the "Bulgarian Horrors," the American textbooks included nothing on Turkish suffering in the Balkan Wars, even though, as in Bulgaria in 1876–78, the Turks suffered by far the worst casualties. No American textbook mentioned the inhuman treatment of Turks and Albanians. Students would have no way of knowing that Turks had suffered in any way; indeed, the texts never mentioned Muslims or Turkish residents in Ottoman Europe during the period when the Balkan armies advanced.[52] This was important, because the authors wrote that the Turks had denied the legitimate national aspirations of the Balkan Christians, when in fact Turks were a plurality and Muslims a majority of the population of Ottoman Europe.[53] The Balkan Wars were treated simply as wars of national liberation, when they were actually wars intended to create rule by minorities over a majority. The authors lamented only that the Christians had fought among themselves rather than uniting against the Turks.[54]

REPEATING THE OLD ERRORS

Why were the school and university textbooks so deficient, so dreadfully biased in their treatment of the Turks? One of the most basic reasons is a generic fault: textbook writers copy from other textbooks. If a good story appears in a book, it will surely appear in later books written by others. Textbook authors cannot be experts in all areas, and none of the American authors knew much about Turkish or Islamic history. They depended on those who had gone before. Unfortunately, those early authors knew as little as they did.[55]

A classic example of the problem of perpetually repeated error was the history of the Crusades, a prominent feature in all history textbooks. Pope Urban II had preached the Crusade at the Council of Clermont in 1095, asserting in his sermon that conditions in Palestine had been satisfactory for pilgrims until the advent of the Seljuk Turks. He claimed that the Turks had persecuted pilgrims, closing the Holy Land to European Christians. The truth was quite different (see the discussion below), but textbook authors seem to have taken Pope Urban as their only source. George Burton Adams, a professor at Yale, wrote in his college textbook *Medieval and Modern History* that when the Turks took Jerusalem, "the pilgrims from the west began at once to suffer grievously from their more barbarous [than the Arabs] disposition."[56] Writers of secondary-school textbooks all blamed the Turks for the Crusades. Willis Mason West wrote of "the abuse of pilgrims by the Turks" and called the Crusades a noble pilgrimage.[57] William Stearns Davis stated in his high-school text: "The relatively refined and tolerant Arab rulers of Palestine had been supplanted by the barbarous and intolerant Turks."[58] Henry William Elson and Cornelia E. MacMullan's high-school text claimed: "The Arabs, however, were kind to the Christians when they came to Jerusalem, and gave them protection when they made pilgrimages to the sepulcher of their Lord. But there came a time when the Turks, who were also Mohammedans, conquered the Arabs and obtained possession of Jerusalem. They were fierce and cruel, and they either put the Christian pilgrims to death or made them endure terrible torture."[59]

The actual history is that the rule of the Fatimid dynasty of Egypt in Palestine was breaking down in the eleventh century. The Fatimids, never named in the textbooks, were the "Saracens" who had supposedly welcomed Christian pilgrims to the Holy Lands. An independent Turkish chief seized Jerusalem in 1071. Turkish and Arab chieftains fought over the area, usually accepting some form of Seljuk overlordship. The Fatimids regained Jerusalem, however, in 1098. General confusion reigned over the entire region, with local lords fighting each other. It was indeed a bad time for pilgrims, or anyone else, but the Fatimids were attempting to reassert their control—the very factor that those who preached the Crusade said had allowed safe pilgrimage. When the Crusaders arrived, the Fatimids attempted to deal with them, offering free access and European establishments in all the Holy Lands. The Crusaders refused. Instead they conquered Jerusalem, where they killed nearly every Muslim and Jewish man, woman, and child as well as many Orthodox Christians. When the first Crusaders arrived at Jerusalem, Turks were neither in charge of the city nor significantly involved in any of the events in Palestine.[60] Furthermore, the historical record shows no evidence that the Seljuks deliberately hampered or persecuted Christian pilgrims, much less torturing them. Nevertheless, the Turks were blamed.[61]

Racism

Nineteenth- and early twentieth-century Americans, as well as most Western Europeans, were infected by a belief in "scientific racism." Like other peoples, Turks were considered to be a "race" or "subrace" with nearly unalterable racial characteristics that were etched into their "blood" or their "national soul." The scientific racists did not believe in the necessity of rigorous investigation to support their absurdities. The essence of the racial image ascribed to the Turks was conflict and brutality, exactly the image found in the popular culture. It was the Turks' misfortune to be compared adversely to another racial image: that of the "Caucasic" peoples who were reputedly oppressed by the Turks. The American image of the Greeks and Armenians benefited greatly from their presumed membership

Table 5.1. Putative "Racial" Qualities of Turks, Greeks, and Armenians

	Turks	Greeks and Armenians
Temperament	"dull, reserved, somewhat sullen and apathetic . . . nearly all brave, warlike, even fierce, and capable of great atrocities, though not normally cruel"	"brilliant, quick-witted, excitable, and impulsive; sociable and courteous . . . aesthetic sense highly, ethic sense slightly developed. All brave, imaginative, musical, and richly endowed intellectually"
Culture	"settled agriculturalists, with scarcely any arts and letters and no science"	"generally high—all arts, industries, science, philosophy, and letters in a flourishing state now almost everywhere"

Source: A. H. Keane, *Man Past and Present,* pp. 266, 267, 442, 443. See also A. H. Keane, *Ethnology.*

in the "Caucasic race." They were thus members of the same group as Europeans and white Americans. By association, this provided them with an excellent set of racial credentials. The Turks, in contrast, were definitely considered to be non-Caucasians, belonging to what was sometimes called the Turki or Tatar branch of the "Mongol race" (the "yellow race"). In terms of intelligence and culture, they were placed a distant second behind the Caucasians. In terms of ferocity, they were put first.

The British anthropologist and geographer Augustus Keane summarized the standard academic racial view of Turks, Greeks, and Armenians (see table 5.1). His views were more charitable than many. The Greeks and Armenians were placed in the second rank of the "Caucasic" peoples ("homo mediterranensis"). Had they been in the first rank, their qualities would have been even more superior ("homo europaeus": "earnest, energetic, and enterprising; steadfast, stolid, and solid; outwardly reserved, thoughtful, and deeply religious; humane, firm, but not wantonly cruel"). Nevertheless, "homo mediterranensis" was obviously considered to be racially superior to the Turks. Indeed, in terms of human cruelty only the "South Mongols," considered racial brothers to the "North Mongol" Turks, were depicted as worse.

The depiction of the Turks as an essentially indolent people who occasionally rose to ferocity (a staple of the geographies described in chapter 2 and below) was also present in the racialist literature.[62] Louis Giguier depicted the Turks in *The Human Race* as lazy members of the "yellow race": "Lazily reclining on his cushions, he [the Turk] smokes his Syrian tobacco, sips his Arabian coffee, and seeks from a few grains of opium an introduction into the land of dreams."[63] Giguier stated that Turkish women "of all classes" lived a life of "total and complete idleness,"[64] showing that he had no idea of the labors of Turkish women. Friedrich Ratzel, a German racialist published in America, felt that the Turks had no desire to work and were only suited for "the lower walks—as cattle-breeder, husbandman, small artisan, caravan-attendant."[65] He gave no consideration to what would seem to be the obvious question—how could such lazy cattle-breeders have ruled an empire for centuries? To the racialists, nothing good had ever come from the Turks. Robert Brown wrote in his multivolume consideration of every race on earth that "the Turks have never been a civilizing power. Since the day when, two centuries BC, they invaded Bactria, they have done nothing for civilizations."[66] The eminent scientists who wrote *The Standard Library of Natural History, Embracing Living Animals of the World and Living Races of Mankind* stated that the Turks' only prowess was on the battlefield and that they had no other achievements. They did nothing but live off the labor of Greeks and Armenians, whom they exploited and subjugated.[67]

A particularly odd example of the feeling toward Turks was the common practice of placing them among the "colored races." The common prejudices of nineteenth-century Americans toward those of African and Asian descent is well known and needs no elucidation here. Inclusion of Turks within the general non-white category began very early. Already in 1848 Charles Hamilton Smith had so placed them in *The Natural History of the Human Species*,[68] in which he obligingly included illustrations of the various racial types. His illustration of a Turk was a fanciful drawing of Sultan Mehmet II, whose skin was tinted in a dark coffee color, as dark as the corresponding portrait of a Nubian. At a later date the Turks were described as part of the "Yellow Peril" that allegedly threatened Europeans and Americans.[69]

Even after World War I those who worried that America's "racial stock" was being diluted by immigrants of "lesser races" included Turks in the groups of "colored peoples" who should be excluded.[70] By that time the difficult fact that Turks did not look "colored" had to be approached. Newspapers, magazines, and even newsreels had shown Turkish faces to the public. The widely held view was that the lightness of Turkish skin arose from their lust: "The mania of the Turks for white women, which is said to be one of the motives that led to the conquest of the Byzantine Empire, has unconsciously resulted in the obliteration of the Mongoloid type of the original Asiatic invaders."[71] Joseph Deniker, a Frenchman whose work was translated and issued in a number of editions in America, felt that this mixing with other races was the only thing that had allowed the Turks to create an empire.[72] John Ridpath, author of a very popular history of the world, wrote that any Turkish success was largely the result of the infusion of "Aryan blood" through the taking of foreign slave women: "The result of this gathering of foreign and beautiful women into the harems was the improvement of the race." The Turks were thus infused with "superior blood."[73] This belief had a long European and American tradition. The high priest of racialism, Comte Arthur de Gobineau, devoted much space in *The Inequality of Human Races* to the idea that Turkish successes were due to "the admixture with Aryan blood."[74]

Even though Turks were included among the "lesser races," they occupied a distinct place within the hierarchy of racism. They were considered *Untermenschen*, but dangerous *Untermenschen*. It could not be denied that Turks had at one time or other defeated many Caucasians and indeed ruled over them for centuries. The same could not be said about most of the other "races" that were looked down upon. Whereas other groups were described as weak, the Turks were characterized as brutal and cruel. Such characterization was especially important during and immediately after World War I, when racist thinkers, awed by the "suicide of the white race" in the war, began to fear that the "brown and yellow races" might rise up and overwhelm the whites. The same American writers who led the eugenics movement and the drive to exclude Asian immigrants warned of the Caucasians' need to unite and defeat the other races. Lothrop Stoddard was perhaps the most prominent American spokesman for the movement. He wrote of the "bigoted, brutal Turk" as "a race of dull-witted bigots under which enlightened progress was impossible."[75] Yet, because of their brute force, Stoddard assigned the Turks a high place in the potential ascendancy of the "brown race," whose organizing principle of upcoming conquest was to be Islam.[76]

With more modern racist beliefs in mind, it would be easy to assume that the racial stereotyping of the Turks was the product of a fringe group of bigots, but this was not the case. Augustus Keane, the author of the descriptions of racial qualities quoted above, was a lecturer in geography at Cambridge whose work was well reviewed in the scholarly press in England and the United States and routinely cited in anthropology texts.[77] Friedrich Ratzel was a well-respected professor at Leipzig (and one of the founders of Social Darwinism) and is often considered one of the founders of modern geography and anthropology. Similar beliefs abounded in American academic circles. Joseph Deniker was chief librarian of the Natural History Museum in Paris and one of the editors of the *Dictionnaire de géographie universelle*. Lothrop Stoddard's works were published by a notable publisher (Scribner's) and were favorably reviewed in the press. He was a frequent contributor to the celebrated journals of the time, such as the *New Republic, Current Opinion*, and *Saturday Evening Post*. This absurd racist belief was common even in high circles, as exemplified by Henry Morgenthau, American ambassador to the Ottoman Empire, who explained the troubles between Turks and Armenians by transferring his own racist beliefs to the Turks. He asserted that Turks wished to rape Armenian women and then take the resulting children because the Turks, "in their crude intuitive way, recognized that the mingling of their [Armenian] blood with the Turkish population would exert a eugenic influence on the whole."[78]

Scientific racism was a general and completely accepted feature of American textbooks. History texts referred to race, but it was most important in geographies.[79] In geography texts humanity was divided into five races, described as "the Negro or Black Race, the American or Red Race, the Malay or Brown Race, the Mongolian or Yellow Race, and the Caucasian or White Race."[80] These groups were sometimes divided into "subraces," each with differing characteristics. Only in the "white race" was civilization properly advanced, according to this view, although some groups, such as the Japanese, prospered because they "have been wise enough to adopt many of the customs of the leading white nations."[81] Geography textbooks unblushingly praised the Caucasian: "He is the tallest of the five races of men, and has always been foremost in intelligence, the arts, and in all intellectual pursuits. The principal nations of ancient and modern times have been of this race."[82] Statements such as this were made possible by the simple expedient of not mentioning the Indian and Chinese empires. The American geographers did not highly esteem the "yellow race," in which, against observation and genetics, the Turks were usually included: "Most of the people of this race are barbarians, having developed few of the arts of civilization."[83] Most felt that the "yellow race" was dangerous, but some felt it to be insignificant. The *School Geography* of A. von Steinwehr asserted that the Turks were of the Mongolian race: "In Europe, the Mongolian race is represented by the Turks, the Magyars in Hungary, and other unimportant nationalities."[84]

Recommended Readings

Textbooks at the turn of the twentieth century recognized, as textbooks do today, that students should be given "recommended readings" that would add to their store of historical knowledge. Most of the books recommended were other textbooks. High-school textbooks recommended college textbooks for further study, and college-textbook writers recommended each other's works, which was understandable, because the authors had freely borrowed from each other. Only a small number of books on specific regions or subjects were usually included in the recommended readings. Information on the Turks in these lists was especially limited (usually only one or two books on the Middle East, if any), but the recommended works were even more prejudiced than the original textbooks.[85] The recommended readings are instructive not only because they would have been the first recourse for students who wanted more information but also because they were surely books from which the textbook authors took their own information.

As in many areas of scholarship, American histories that considered the Middle East owed much to the British.[86] As is the common practice of textbook writers, they usually did not cite the sources from which they drew their material; but American works often quoted or referred to one British scholar in particular, Edward Freeman. Freeman was a fellow of Trinity College, Oxford, and the author of a short book (ninety-eight pages) called *The Turks in Europe*,[87] which was widely circulated in America as part of the popular Harper's Half Hour Series, intended for a mass audience. Moreover, textbooks recommended *The Turks in Europe* to students who wished to know more on the subject. Freeman is an excellent example of both the ideas that formulated textbook writers' own ideas and the type of book that reached the educated American public.

Freeman was a Grecophile, a knight commander of the Greek Order of the Savior. His thesis was that Turks did not belong in Europe, because they did not share in the essential traits that were common to Europeans: Christianity and their inheritance from the Roman Empire. Europeans were racially united, a "real original kindred." Freeman also held, against much evidence, that this common heritage had resulted in "fairly good governments."[88]

Freeman felt that the Turks were not historically, culturally, or "racially" Europeans. By itself, this is not an unusual sentiment, even today. Freeman, however, carried it considerably further. He wrote that the Turks should be expelled from the European continent because they had not become "Europeans" in either language or customs. He compared the Turks to two other peoples who had come into Europe from Asia: Magyars, who had adopted European customs, and Bulgars, who had adopted a Slavic language. He considered it a fault that the Turks had not done either. It was also a fault that the Turks had not chosen to partake of Roman-based culture: "As the Turks are alien in blood and language, they have no share in the history and memories which are common to Europe." Unlike the Magyars and Bulgars, who were praised for adopting Christianity, the Turks had remained "Mohammedans with a kind of half civilization." "It is therefore impossible for the Turks or for any other Mohammedan people, so long as they remain Mohammedan, to establish what we in Western Europe should call free and just government." Because of their religion and their Eastern traditions, Freeman asserted, it was impossible for the Turks ever to have a government that was anything but "subjection and degradation." He held that no one, including Turks, could ever have allegiance to a Turkish government; they could only be subjected through violence. This could never change. "The Turk cannot reform, because the principles of his religion forbid him to reform."[89]

After establishing to his satisfaction that Turks had no place in Europe, Freeman proceeded to give a synopsis of Turkish history. He mentioned nothing of Turkish art or culture, of course, or any examples of good government. The only Turkish virtues were those of "hardy warriors." Whatever good government existed was the product of Europeans pressed into Ottoman service, but all else was bad. Freeman was forced to admit that the Ottomans had begun to attempt reform in the nineteenth century, which might have gone some way to disproving his assertions on the impossibility of change among the Turks. He explained this, however, as purely a Turkish deception: "No doubt all this time the Turks were learning to ape European ways, and to put on a varnish of European civilization, which has deceived many people."[90] Freeman stated that the reforms were in reality promises that were never kept. Indeed, they could not be kept, because Muslims could never reform. They could act like Europeans but could never be anything but despotic. Thus, with absolutely no evidence, did Freeman deal with all the nineteenth-century Ottoman reforms.

Freeman's "history" was full of gross inaccuracies. For example, he portrayed Bosnia purely as a place where Christians revolted against what he called a small number of unjust Muslim Turkish rulers, neglecting to mention that the largest population group in Bosnia was Muslim.[91] He made no reference whatever to the Muslim populations of Europe or their suffering when Greece or Serbia became independent. Freeman may not have known they existed. His book creates the impression that the only Muslims in Europe were a small veneer of Turkish rulers and a great mass of subject Christians, with a small sprinkling of Muslims. When Freeman's book was published in 1877, the Muslim population in Ottoman Europe (most of it Turkish) was actually more than 4 million, 38 percent of the total population.[92] Their numbers were to be considerably diminished by the deaths and exile that accompanied the creation of new Christian states in the

Balkans.[93] Freeman assured his readers, however, that Muslims had nothing to fear from Christian rule, because the danger of bad government existed only under Islam.

Freeman's recommendation for the Ottomans in Europe was to drive them out. Western Europeans, in league with Russia if necessary, should remove the Ottomans by force. He admitted that some might complain that to drive the Turks from Europe would be to open the way to Russian conquest but asserted that Russia had no desire for such conquest: "We may be quite sure that Russia does not want Constantinople."[94] That analysis was not shared by Freeman's own British government or other Europeans, who feared exactly that.

The only books that could compare to Freeman in sheer prejudice were the missionary accounts of the Armenian troubles. Yet Freeman's book was often recommended to the high-school students of America.

Histories of the Middle East

The two books on Ottoman history and politics that were most commonly included in textbooks' suggested readings were both written by members of the missionary establishment, William Stearns Davis and Herbert Adams Gibbons.[95] Davis, a professor at the University of Minnesota, was the son of a missionary minister who had taught at Robert College in Istanbul. He made little attempt to hide his feelings about the Turks. His book *A Short History of the Near East* was the only general textbook on Middle Eastern history recommended in the general textbooks.[96] It enjoyed very wide circulation, as did his other textbooks.[97]

Davis considered most of Turkish history too boring for consideration: "[The Turkish dynasties] are inevitably monotonous and bloody—change without progress."[98] He did mention the Great Seljuk dynasty (in four pages), although he had nothing but bad to say of it. He styled the Seljuk sultan a "noble savage." The Rum Seljuks, who had reigned in Anatolia for 225 years, were given one short paragraph. To put this into perspective, Davis devoted as many pages to Byzantine court ceremonial as to the more than 250-year history of the Seljuk Empires, but of course he much preferred the Christian Byzantines to the Turks.

Only a small amount of negative sentiment could be fit into the few pages allocated to the Seljuks. His much more extensive treatment on the Ottomans gave Davis more scope for vilification. His incredible description of the great sultan Mehmet II is typical of his depictions: "Few among the world's bloodstained empire builders command less sympathy than Mohammed 'the Conqueror.' Pitiless, faithless when it pleased his policy, remorseless, delighting in refined tortures and unspeakable immoralities, we can hardly find in him even those flashes of high magnanimity which redeemed the characters of Jenghiz Khan and Timur the Tatar."[99]

The treatment of Ottoman history by Davis could well have been written by the missionaries, who were very likely his unnamed sources. The Turks were always wrong, always the oppressors of others. He said nothing of Turkish administrative abilities and gave Turkish culture and art one very negative page.[100] Davis never mentioned Turkish dead or massacres of Muslims in the great conflagrations of the later empire: the 1877–78 War, the Balkan Wars, and World War I. Readers of the section on the Turkish War of Independence, for example, would never know that many more Turks were killed by Greeks than Greeks killed by Turks. He described the Turks only as "barbarians" who engaged in "the now standard-ized Ottoman massacres of conquered populations."[101] The Greeks were innocents who were trying to set the Greeks of Anatolia free, not, as was the case, invaders of a region where more than three-fourths of the population was Turkish. In any conflict, the Christians were always right, the Turks always wrong. Davis exulted whenever the Turks were defeated, lamented whenever the Turks won.

Islam fared somewhat better than the Turks, although not much better. Davis adopted the "madman" thesis on Muhammad, stating that if the Prophet had been alive in the twentieth century he would be considered a "harmless, well-intentioned crank." But he considered Muhammad to have been sane enough to understand "the enormous value of an appeal made simultaneously to religion and cupidity," which was the basis of Islam's early triumph. Islam was not bad, only deficient. Davis's judgment was summarized in the heading of one section: "Non-Originality of Islam. Its Suitability for Partially Civilized People."[102] The section was a straightforward declaration of the superiority of Christianity that would have fit easily into a religious tract.[103]

One book by Herbert Adams Gibbons was cited as a source and recommended reading by a number of textbook authors: *The New Map of Europe (1911–1914)*.[104] Gibbons, a Presbyterian minister and graduate of Princeton Theological seminary, was a pillar of the missionary establishment. He had been a missionary in Anato-lia and a professor at Robert College, the missionary college in Istanbul. Gibbons had a definite bias against the non-Christians of the Ottoman Empire, which included opposition to Jewish as well as Muslim groups. He was a confirmed anti-Zionist who believed that the Jews should remain a spiritual, not a political, com-munity.[105]

Gibbons repeated the usual attacks on the Turks—accusing them of over-whelming corruption, barbarity, and indolence—and went so far as to say that the Turks were disappearing: "The Turkish population has actually decreased, and the ravages of garrison life, due to dyspepsia and syphilis, have diminished fearfully the physical vigour of the race."[106] The Turkish population was actually increas-ing.[107]

Gibbons was not above changing history to fit his mold: he wrote that the Turks had settled Bosnians and Circassians in Macedonia after 1908 as part of their plan to keep control of Macedonia and that these had caused the troubles in Macedonia. This never happened. Muslims had come to Macedonia from Bul-garia and Bosnia in 1878 and immediately after, long before there was a Macedo-nian problem. Gibbons invented massacres of Christians but mentioned none of the massacres of Turks and Albanians in the era of the Macedonian Problem and the Balkan Wars. In attempting to prove that the Arabs hated the Turks, Gibbons fabricated unending Arab rebellions against the Ottoman government after 1908:

"We cannot even enumerate these rebellions." This was true: it is impossible to enumerate rebellions that never occurred. Gibbons was a great believer in conspiracies. According to him, the Balkan Wars and ultimately their upshot, World War I, were the result of a conspiracy between Austria and the Ottoman Empire: "It is the direct, immediate cause of the European War of 1914." The Ottomans and Austria-Hungary conspired to create the Macedonian Problem, although his only explanation for the Ottomans doing something that was completely against their own interest was their desire to stir "racial hatred."[108]

In this entire very lengthy treatment of the Balkan Wars Gibbons did not note a single Turkish civilian death. He unstintingly praised the actions of Serbia, Greece, and Bulgaria against the Turks. Politically, the Turks were portrayed as constant failures, incapable of reform or surviving in the modern world. Gibbons never wrote of the Turkish successes in education, civil administration, or any other area of politics or life. The reader was left with the impression of an impotent but cruel people who were justly doomed.

THE EDUCATION OF YOUNG CHILDREN

Primary-school textbooks contained almost nothing about the Turks or Islam except for a few negative statements. American Protestantism transmitted its values and beliefs to its children in Sunday schools, which offered more fertile ground for the teaching of prejudice. Children in Sunday schools were taught simplified theology, Bible studies, and virtuous living, all with the best intentions. The method of instruction, however, was often negative. The positive religious values of their own tradition were contrasted with the supposedly negative values and moral deficiency of other traditions. Sunday schools were ubiquitous and laid claim to young minds in their most formative stage. For this reason, they were instrumental in creating a negative image of Turks and Islam among Americans.

Sunday-school curricula devoted time not only to religion but to the lives of peoples around the world. Students were given a picture of the pleasant lives of European Christian children, somewhat different than their own but morally good and basically prosperous. This was accomplished by ignoring any evils that might touch these children's lives. The Irish potato famine, atrocities against Africans in the Belgian Congo, pogroms against Jews, and the like were not mentioned. This is understandable. Children would learn of the evils of the world soon enough, and it was perhaps better to stress the positive in the hope that children would see the good in others. Unfortunately, this optimistic view did not extend to Muslims. For Muslims, the formula was reversed—the schools chose to portray the evil and ignore the good.

The treatment of Islam and Muslim peoples in Sunday-school classes was based on manuals for the teachers and stories for the pupils. The manuals assigned lessons and readings as well as question-and-answer sessions for the teachers, who were supposed to ask children questions such as "Why, if the Turks believe Allah is merciful, are they cruel to Christians, and glad to be rid of them?"[109] The American Board, the Student Volunteer Movement for Foreign Missions, and other missionary agencies provided local churches with organized Sunday-school classes for children and education programs for adults. The American Board–suggested curricula outlined that students in the Sunday schools were to study the decline of Islam and the triumph of Christendom in the Balkan Wars. One class was devoted to "The Evils of Islam." Students were to be actively involved: "Show the weakness of Islam as compared with the lofty morals of the New Testament." "Have six older boys and girls each mention one of the great evils of Islam."[110]

The image of Islam in the Sunday-school classroom is best exemplified by the books on Islam used in the classes and recommended for reading by students, teachers, and parents. With extremely rare exceptions, the children's literature said nothing good about Muslims. The exceptions were those Muslims who became Christians or allowed their children to become Christians. Some writers depicted Muslims as at best morally neutral, damaged by their religion through no fault of their own, but nonetheless morally damaged. Some writers included brief descriptions of alleged Muslim evils in their stories. Others went into vituperative detail, describing Muslims as inveterate liars and cheats, wife-beaters, enslavers of women, bigots, fanatics, and committers of other sins.[111] Children who read such material, given them by ministers and teachers, can only be expected to have developed a wholly pejorative view of Muslims.

Books written for Sunday-school children included stories of heroic missionaries or tales of the lives of children in other lands.[112] Stories on Muslim children stressed the difficulty of their lives, being forced to do hard work weaving carpets or minding flocks. The children were not able to go to "real" schools, although they sometimes did attend Muslim schools, where they memorized the Quran and were beaten by their teachers.[113] Their parents were well meaning but invincibly ignorant. Muslim parents stressed what must have appeared to American children to be the meaningless rituals of Islam, because the reasons for the rituals were never explained. When their children became ill, Muslim parents denied them the chance to be cured by missionary doctors. The one exception to a hard life came to the few lucky children who were able to come into contact with missionaries and thus achieve a better life, including the opportunity to become Christians. Muslim religious forces, however, stood in the way of children's advancement. Some authors went so far as to state that many Muslims realized that Christianity was a superior religion and wanted their children to be educated in it but were stopped by Muslim leaders, who also supposedly realized the superiority of Christianity and were afraid to let anyone learn of it.[114]

Children's books seldom dealt with the more gruesome aspects of life as portrayed in missionary books for adults. They did occasionally depict these elements, however, usually in stories about Armenian children, who were almost always described as victims of the Turks. More often the children's books stressed the poverty of the people, implying or sometimes stating outright that this was a result of Islam. The books offered no positive images of the lives of Muslim children. Sometimes they even blamed Islam for conditions such as the lack of water for washing and poor harvests. Few social customs were described sympathetically: the

authors portrayed the Holy Month of Ramadan not as a time of family together-
ness, as Muslims would have described it, but only as a time when people became
ill from fasting. They depicted Muslims as superstitious and Muslim prayers as
peculiar formularies. Naturally, not every religious book for children went into
detail on many aspects of Muslim life, but the descriptions were uniformly unsym-
pathetic.[115]

American children were taught that the supposed deficiencies in the lives of
Muslim children were due to their religion, its customs, and its Prophet. For
example, in describing Persian children who were forced to work at an early age,
the missionary Mrs. Napier Malcolm offered a lesson to her child readers:

> You will find, roughly speaking, if you look at the animals that the higher the
> animal, the longer its childhood lasts, because it has more growing up to do.
> Caterpillars and tadpoles look after themselves from the time of coming out of
> the egg, mice grow up in a few weeks, horses in a few years, and man takes lon-
> ger to grow up than any animal.
>   Now Muhammad, the false prophet whom the Persians believe in and obey,
> had no such high standard to set before them, no such high ideal for them to
> grow up to, as our Lord Jesus Christ set before His followers and enables them
> to grow up to; and so his religion provides only a short time for growing up, and
> stunts instead of assisting the growth both of individual Muhammadans and of
> Muhammadan nations.[116]

Students would not have known that Muhammad had nothing to say on the subject of duration of childhood education (nor, for that matter, did Jesus).

The writings of Samuel M. Zwemer, the foremost and most prolific American
writer against Islam, extended to children's literature. He and his wife, Amy E.
Zwemer, wrote a number of books and articles for children. The depictions of the
books were the usual ones, distilled for children: Muslims were poor, both economically and intellectually, and lived lives of moral evil. Their sinfulness, poverty, and backwardness were the outcome of their religion, but there was hope,
through conversion to Christianity. In *Two Young Arabs,* a traveling Muslim family saw a multitude of evils (including child marriage, bloody vengeance, superstition, and ritual mutilation) in the Islamic world.[117] These were contrasted with
the ways of the missionaries that the children met. The young Arabs were saved by
becoming Christians. In *Zigzag Journeys in the Camel Country*, the Zwemers told
American children of Muslim education: "They [boys] are also taught the ceremonial washings and correct postures for devotions. But purity of conversation
and truth are seldom taught by precept, and never by example."[118] They described
the hard lives of bedouin and villager alike, imputing the difficulty of their lives
to Islam. The Zwemers baldly presented what they viewed as the essential problem: Islam had made the people of Arabia evil, or at least made Muslims into those
who did evil daily. An example: "Another sad thing in this topsy-turvy land [Ara-
bia] is that there are no Sunday schools—they do not observe our Sabbath—and

the boys and girls do not have bright Sunday-school lesson leaves or a picture-roll. They spend Sunday and every day in learning all the evil they see in those that are grown up. Poor children!"[119]

It must be stated that not all the tales written for schoolchildren were as distasteful as these. Although *Everyland* (a "missionary magazine for children" published between 1909 and 1928) did feature stories on negative aspects of Islamic life, such as child brides, it mainly printed stories on the missions themselves or on the lives of Protestant converts as well as tales of the "true adventure" sort. The stories featured Armenians rescued from the hands of Turks and Kurds or missionaries who saved Allied soldiers from Arab tribesmen. These would surely leave a poor impression of Turks and Kurds, but the stories were far better than those that spoke of lying, cheating Muslims who had no concern for their children's welfare. Affectionate stories of the lives of Middle Eastern Christians that said little negative about Muslims also appeared.[120]

Books on Islam and the Near East were recommended to Sunday-school teachers for their own intellectual development. For example, *Missionary Education in Home and School* (one of the "Manuals of Religious Education for Parents and Teachers") specified two books on Islam for parents and teachers: *Aspects of Islam* by Duncan Black Macdonald and *Christian Missions and Social Progress* by James Dennis.[121] Both books, Dennis's in particular, were filled with prejudice about Islam and Muslims (see chapter 4). No other works on Islam were recommended. Another book, *Missionary Programs for Schoolboys*, offered Samuel Zwemer's *Islam: A Challenge to Faith* as the only source on Islam for teachers.[122] In fact, Zwemer was the author most often recommended; *Islam: A Challenge to Faith* and *Childhood in the Moslem World* were both popular recommendations for Sunday-school reading.[123]

Zwemer's *The Moslem World* was surely the most widely distributed textbook on Islam.[124] It was published in 1908 by commercial publishers and separately by the main missionary organizations and was distributed in churches in the tens of thousands of copies. It came complete with study guides, bibliographies, and questions for classes. Zwemer repeated all the standard Christian analyses of Muhammad's supposed "sinfulness," "treachery," and "lust" and statements on the purely formulaic nature of Islamic worship, Islamic violence, and so forth. He praised imperialism but called for more Western action against Islam and favoring Christian missions. Islam was characterized as "the Problem." Zwemer's chapter on "The Social and Moral Evils of Islam" was exactly what the title implied—a detailed list of real and imagined social problems in Muslim countries. He blamed them all on Islam without considering the environment or history, let alone discussing the corresponding evils in Christian lands. Half the book was devoted to Christian missions in Muslim lands.

Some books were aimed at the parents of schoolchildren as well as Sunday-school teachers. Parents were told what children should be taught of the world. The Central Committee on the United Study of Missions, which also published texts for schoolchildren, brought out *The Child in the Midst* by the missionary

Mary Schauffler Labaree. It evoked all the evil that could be seen in the non-Christian world, and none of the good, praised imperialism and Christian rule, and imparted to parents an appreciation of the "eugenic" benefits of Christianity—all with Bible readings, prayers, and questions for parents and children

> How would you go to work to eradicate harmful superstitions in a Mohammedan land?

> What do you consider the greatest sorrow of Mohammedan motherhood?

> If you were facing a school of fifty little [Muslim] children who had absolutely no idea of education, cleanliness, manners, morals, or Christianity, what would you try to teach them in the first week?[125]

Needless to say, the little children portrayed in the book were without education, cleanliness, manners, or morals.

The Image Portrayed

American students learned little of the Turks from their textbooks. It is doubtful that their instructors, who had themselves learned from the textbooks, added much to their knowledge. None of the points that should have been taught (listed at the beginning of this chapter) were treated. The books never portrayed the Ottoman government accurately; it was the only European governmental system that they omitted. A few negative epithets sufficed to describe a system that had lasted and evolved for centuries. Far from adequately describing Ottoman reform, the textbooks most often indicated that the Ottomans were incapable of reform. No textbook included Turkish literature, art, and architecture, leaving students to believe that Turkish high culture did not exist and adding to the image of Turks as barbarians. The authors showed no sympathy for the Turks. They never wrote of the one thing most likely to have made students sympathetic: the mortality and forced exile of millions of Turks and other Muslims (discussed in the following chapters).

It is probably correct to say that most of the textbook writers did not set about their task with the intention to vilify Turks. They simply reflected their own culture, in which Turks were little known but disliked.

6

The Bulgarian Horrors

The period described in the West as the "Bulgarian Horrors" actually began in the Ottoman province of Bosnia (Bosnia and Herzegovina). In 1875 Serbs in Bosnia and Herzegovina rebelled, aided by the governments of Serbia and Montenegro, both of which sent supplies and "volunteers" to the province. Pan-Slavic elements in Russia added their support. The rebellion began with attacks on Muslim villages and soon degenerated into a bloody intercommunal war between the Bosnian Muslims and the Serbs. An Ottoman army put down the revolt. Serbia and Montenegro then attempted to intervene, declaring war on the Ottoman Empire in 1876. By August of 1876 the Ottomans had defeated them, although the European powers (especially Russia) that supported the Serbs did not allow the Ottomans any territorial gains or compensation.

Events in Bulgaria in 1876 eclipsed the battle over Bosnia. On May 2, 1876, rebels took advantage of the Ottoman army's preoccupation with Bosnia, Serbia, and Montenegro to revolt in central Bulgaria. From the start the revolt was accompanied by a slaughter of Turks: "The excited populace [of Panagiurishte] assembled in the square, sang revolutionary songs, heard flaming speeches from [rebel leader] Benkovski, and then scattered to kill peaceable Turks wherever they could be found."[1] Approximately a thousand Turks were killed.[2] Because most regular troops were occupied elsewhere, the Ottoman government mainly resorted to local irregulars (*başı bozuk*s) and Circassian tribesmen, who had been exiled from their homeland by the Russians, to put down the revolt. They did so brutally, plundering Bulgarian villages and killing many. For example, near Burgas irregulars defeated two thousand to three thousand rebels then plundered five Bulgarian villages.[3] The Ottoman government's reaction to events was confused. Regular soldiers were sent out to protect Bulgarian Christians and Muslims alike, but in at least one instance regulars killed 186 Bulgarians as an "example" to rebels. Not until the Serbians were defeated and large numbers of regulars were sent to Bulgaria was peace restored. Three thousand to twelve thousand Bulgarians had died.[4]

Peace in Bulgaria came too late for the Ottomans. Using the upheavals in Bosnia and Bulgaria as an excuse, Russia prepared for a war that would drive the Ottomans from Europe. In other circumstances, the Ottomans could have depended on allies, particularly Britain, to stand with them against the Russians, as they had in the Crimean War. Benjamin Disraeli's government was disposed to do so. Popular agitation over the Bulgarian Horrors made that impossible. Disraeli's political enemies, the Liberals, led by William Gladstone, had mounted a campaign against the Turks and, by association, against Disraeli and the Conservatives.[5] The campaign was fueled by the Liberal press,[6] especially the *London Daily News,* which trumpeted, exaggerated, and often invented atrocities committed by Turks and ignored those committed against Turks. Graphic reports of massacres so stirred British public opinion that Disraeli could not act. The Russians had a free hand to attack Turkey, declaring war on April 24, 1877.

The cycle of massacre and countermassacre in the Balkans had begun with attacks on Muslims in Bosnia and Bulgaria then escalated in attacks on Bulgarians. With the advent of Russian invaders it was once again the turn of the Muslims to suffer. Their mortality was much worse than anything seen before. European consuls reported the slaughter of Turks all over Bulgaria as the Russians advanced. Although Russian regular soldiers sometimes took part in the murder and pillage, those who most persecuted the Turks were Bulgarians and Cossacks. European reporters also attested to the attacks on the Turks (although these reports were not seen in American newspapers, which preferred the British Liberal press).[7] The stories of atrocities against the Turks were fully as horrible as those that had been told of atrocities against the Bulgarians and were on a much greater scale.

As a result of the Russian invasion 288,000 Muslims of Bulgaria (19 percent), mainly Turks, died and 515,000 were exiled, never to return. More than half the Muslims had been either killed or forced from Bulgaria.[8]

Americans did not read of Turkish suffering. What they read in their newspapers and magazines was a tale of the suffering of innocent Christians at the hands of evil Muslims.

NEWSPAPERS

The American press had no news sources of its own on events in the Ottoman Empire. With a few exceptions (described below), the information on Bulgaria came from the British Liberal press, much of it forwarded, excerpted, or paraphrased by the Associated Press.[9] The information in different newspapers was thus usually the same. Some printed one article from the *London Daily News* or the *Times*, others another. Often they printed the same story, the only difference being an introductory sentence.[10] This was as true for the newspapers in smaller towns as for those in major cities—the source was the Associated Press, which distributed the London news.[11] The smaller-town newspapers, however, usually printed only excerpts of stories that were to be found at greater length in the larger city papers.

The articles were uniformly anti-Turkish, varying from the merely prejudiced to the scurrilous: Islam was reported to be the only religion tolerated in the Ottoman Empire, all Muslims looked on Christians only as "appropriate victims," no

Christian woman was safe from the Muslims.[12] Turks were depicted as "blood-sucking Turks," "the turbaned tyrants of the Golden Horne," or "an Asiatic horde encamped in Europe," the Ottoman government as "venal, capricious, and ferocious" and "the cruel yoke." The staples of yellow journalism abounded: babies on bayonets, fetuses torn from their mothers' wombs, bodies left to decompose or to be eaten by dogs, hideous tortures.[13] Of course, none of these stories could be verified. Many were fiction. For example, the *Boston Globe* and other newspapers reported: "At Jambull [Yambol] a bag full of human heads was emptied in the streets before the house of the Italian consul."[14] Yambol, a town in the Burgas district, had no Italian consulate.

Perhaps the *Boston Globe* accepted such tales because of a certain predisposition against the Turks. In another article the *Globe* described the Turks as "alien in race, in language, and in religion from all others in Europe, with institutions repugnant not only to the morality but to the economic conditions of modern civilization."[15] The *Chicago Tribune* echoed the sentiment: "The Turk is an alien in Europe, an enemy of Western civilization, a sanguinary fanatic by nature, a ruler whose Government is not a Government of law but of plunder."[16] Readers in Chicago were told that Turks did not actually live in Bulgaria: "In Bulgaria, Turkish occupation is simply that of garrison. The Turks are not the people. They have, as a rule, no homes there. They are the rulers, and they have ruled with a fierceness and cruelty unparalleled in national records."[17] This was complete nonsense. The Turks of Bulgaria, mainly farmers, in fact were more than one-third of the population before the war, quite a garrison.[18]

The standard of evidence was weak. For example, one Ahmet Ağa was reported to have "destroyed the [Bulgarian] houses and then slaughtered the inhabitants, reserving for a fate worse than death one hundred fair young creatures whom he afterwards butchered in cold blood." This was supposedly ascertained by examining bodies three months after the event.[19] Even the examination of the remnants of months-old battles was a rare exception, because reporters had actually seen bodies. It is obvious from reading the press reports that the authors, remaining in Istanbul or London, had seen nothing themselves. The reports reaching the American reader gave no indication of the sources or how the unnamed reporters could have reported so infallibly on events they had not seen.[20]

Most of the press stories of atrocities came in the form of short paragraphs or sentences stating that the Turks had committed horrid atrocities, without evidence.[21] Articles that dwelled on the suffering of individuals, sometimes described at length, were taken from the unverifiable accounts of individual Bulgarians. Some reports of burned villages and bodies seen by correspondents were most likely true, at least insofar as the reporters only wrote of what they had actually seen. But reporters, usually from London papers, generally relied on the testimony of Bulgarians to report the overall picture of the massacres.[22] A representative article copied from the *London Daily News* named its sources as "an intelligent Turk," "an intelligent Pole," "Bulgarian sources," and that staple "trustworthy information."[23] While some reports said the Turkish regular soldiers were acting well, protecting Christians and Muslims alike, most allowed the Turks no mitigation. Some, especially articles from the *London Daily News*, stated that Turkish soldiers had been ordered to shoot all escaping Bulgarians. It gave no authority or sources, only the allegation.[24] Echoing the allegations made during the Greek rebellion, articles reported that Ottoman authorities had sanctioned the massacre of Bulgarians. As was the case in Greece, they gave no evidence.[25] As a rule, the papers printed greatly exaggerated statistics of Bulgarian mortality. In one article reprinted in America, the *London Daily News* stated that 25,000 to 100,000 had been killed.[26] In another reprinted piece, the *London Times* described 25,000 to 40,000 "massacred in cold blood," along with 10,000 Bulgarians in prison, where they were being tortured, and 1,000 Bulgarian children sold as slaves.[27] Of course, the Ottoman Empire had no prisons large enough to hold 10,000, and the dispatches of European consuls did not refer to the enslaved children, which they presumably would have noticed. It was all invented.

In the Ottoman war with Serbia and Montenegro, newspapers often printed as fact atrocity stories and press releases on the war from the Serbian and Montenegrin governments.[28] This had the effect of indicating that the Serbs were winning, until they lost. In the Russo-Turkish War, reports of atrocities against Christians from the Romanian government, then fighting the Ottomans, were similarly accepted and printed.[29] The newspapers printed press releases from the Serbian government on the atrocities in Bulgaria, filled with incredible stories of horrors that were found in no other sources, such as consular reports, and that undoubtedly did not occur.[30]

Russia was praised and England damned. American editorials and magazine articles called on England to intervene against the Ottomans. England was blamed for allying itself with the Ottomans in the past, thus neglecting its Christian obligation to rid Europe of the Turks.[31] It was alleged, quite falsely, that Russia had fought the Crimean War "to mitigate the barbarities inflicted upon the Christian subjects of the Turkish Empire" and would have done so if not stopped by England.[32] The newspapers printed dire predictions, often on the basis of reports in the *London Daily News:* all Christians in the Ottoman Empire were to be attacked and massacred, including those in Istanbul.[33]

The Turks were given no credit for reform;[34] indeed, Ottoman reforms were supposedly not possible. When the Ottoman nineteenth-century reforms were cited, which was seldom, it was only to say that they were a sham. The only remedy was to abolish the Ottoman Empire or at least to expel it from Europe.[35] Nowhere was this sentiment more evident than in the single source most often quoted in the press, the British Liberal leader William Gladstone.[36] Out of power as prime minister, Gladstone had taken up the cause of the Bulgarians, writing pamphlets and articles and organizing rallies. These touched a sympathetic chord in the British public, and the Liberal press, quoted in America, gave his campaign great publicity. Gladstone was an eloquent enemy of all things Turkish:

Let the Turks now carry away their abuses in the only possible manner, namely, by carrying off themselves. Their Zaptiehs and their Mudirs, their Bimbashis and their Yuzbachis, their Kaimakams and their Pachas, one and all, bag and baggage, shall, I hope, clear out from the province they have desolated and profaned. This thorough riddance, this most blessed deliverance, is the only reparation we can make to the memory of those heaps on heaps of dead: to the violated purity alike of matron, of maiden, and of child; to the civilization which has been affronted and shamed; to the laws of God, or, if you like, of Allah; to the moral sense of mankind at large. There is not a criminal in a European jail, there is not a cannibal in the South Sea Islands, whose indignation would not rise and overboil at the recital of that which has been done, which has too late been examined, but which remains unavenged; which has left behind all the foul and all the fierce passions that produced it, and which may again spring up, in another murderous harvest, from the soil soaked and reeking with blood, and in the air tainted with every imaginable deed of crime and shame.[37]

MAGAZINES

The greater length of magazine articles gave authors more scope to attack the Turks and Islam.[38] A long article in the *North American Review* brought up deficiencies of the Turks and other Muslims throughout much of history, some accurate, most imagined. The problem, the author believed, was religious. Reform was impossible, because Muslims could not reform. Nor could the Ottoman Christians better their lot, because they were too cowed by the Turks. The answer was imperialism, which would ensure that Islam was "to be set aside, if not destroyed, with as little ceremony as possible."[39] Magazines continued the long American tradition of misinformation on the Turks. Readers of the *International Review* were told that the sultan changed the government every month to please the whims of his wives or his eunuchs, that the Ottoman Empire had hardly any schools except traditional Muslim Quran schools, that Ottoman Christian religions were "pagan in form," and that Turks were "too stupid and too lazy for even the rudiments of civilization."[40] The *Princeton Review* described the Turk as "brutal, sensual, savage, deceitful at the core of his nature, reckless in physical courage, a born robber and tyrant ... His religion has not improved him; rather it has developed the worst parts of his nature."[41]

All the supposed negative traits of the Turks seen in American writing for decades were repeated. The Turks were lazy, indeed incapable of modern industry or agriculture. The Turks were ignorant and would remain so, incapable of modern civilization. The Christians of the Ottoman Empire, however, were potentially capable of great things, if only they were not ruled by Turks: "The natural apathy of the Turks is a constant and irremediable hindrance to the national advancement [of Christians]. While everything is going to ruin around him, and even while the iron hand of tyranny is crushing out his life, the Turk will sit in luxurious stupidity, devoting his enfeebled energies to his scented pipe and his harem."[42] Indeed, the Turks had purportedly kept the Christians from developing even the most ordinary agricultural pursuits. The plains of Ottoman Europe were described, completely falsely, as deserted, because all the people lived in the mountains out of fear of massacre and of the tax collector.[43]

American popular magazines, like the newspapers, took their material from British Liberal sources, reprinting British articles in America.[44] Among the worst were articles by Edward Freeman, the vehemently anti-Turkish author described in chapter 5, which were reprinted in *Littell's Living Age* and other magazines.[45] Freeman did not hesitate to identify the Turks as evil, as were those who sympathized with the Turks:

> The Turks as a Turk, the Turks as a body or gang, simply fought for the right—at least for the power—to do evil. Their courage therefore had nothing honourable about it, any more than the courage which the murderer or burglar may show in withstanding the policeman. The Russian, in short, fought that he might save his brethren from the foul and bloody passions of the Turk. The Turks fought to keep for himself full power of gratifying those foul and bloody passions.[46]

Thus Turks could not act honorably or fight in an honorable cause, as could Russians, Freeman declared, because Turks had no honor. He described Turks as "barbarian despots," "immoral," "Mahometan oppressors," and "Moslem barbarians," among other insults. The Turks were "a mere horde of invaders," "an Asiatic horde encamped in Europe," their "hands reeking with Christian blood." Turks were rapists who carried off every pretty young woman. Christians, including bandits and rebels, were chivalrous to captives and civilians, but Turks killed all their captives and laid waste to entire provinces. Each of Freeman's articles was a long series of invectives, wholly or largely untrue.

The general sentiment of the magazines, like that of the newspapers, was pro-Russian and anti-British. The British were castigated for not doing "their duty to Christendom." It was generally agreed that the Ottomans must be expelled from Europe. Many writers did not like the idea of Russia taking over the Balkans but accepted it as a necessary evil.[47] Others saw the Russians as agents of Christianity:

> [On the presence of the Turk in Europe:] He came on an evil errand and is now an anomaly and an anachronism in the civilization of the age; a tyrannical oppressor, whose interests are in the most direct antagonism with all the races that inhabit these provinces. He is an interloper, he came unbidden, and has dealt in blood and carnage since he came, reaping no other harvest than gold through the wails of women, the tears of children, and the curses of slaughtered men. Every duty and every interest of Christendom seems to demand that the Turk be driven out of Europe.[48]

It was up to the European powers, especially Russia, to do the deed in the name of "Christendom." The number of Turks and other Muslims in Bulgaria was grossly underestimated, the number of Christians grossly overestimated, thus "proving" the case that the Turks were simply a small occupying force in Ottoman Europe. The people of Bosnia-Herzegovina, for example, were characterized as "genuine Serbs" and were said to be more than half Orthodox and nearly 20 percent Catholic,[49] when in fact in Bosnia the Serbs (Orthodox) were 36 percent of the population, the Croatians (Catholic) 13 percent, and the Bosnian Muslims 50 percent.[50] One author adopted the dubious statistical practice of asserting that all non-Turks in Ottoman Europe hated the Turks and thus "[the Turks] are but a handful as compared with the Christian races [15 million to 2 million]."[51] The idea that Muslims such as the Bosnians and Albanians would prefer Christian rule was, to say the least, an indefensible leap of logic.

AGGRESSION AGAINST THE TURKS

The primary difficulty with American reporting on Bulgaria was not the falsehoods and exaggerations, bad as these were. After all, following attacks on Turks, Turks had indeed attacked Bulgarians in 1876. Nor was the blatant racism that described the "Asiatic hordes" bent only on doing evil the worst element. The worst journalistic crime was the almost total lack of reporting on the sufferings of the Turks. No newspaper or magazine chronicled the massacre of Turks that had been the beginning of the "Bulgarian Horrors." Worse, almost none reported the horrific mortality among the Turks during and immediately after the 1877–78 war, who endured suffering that was much worse than anything experienced by the Bulgarians. Even those very few news articles that referred to Turkish deaths only stated that some Turks were being killed, without details. Articles on the suffering of Bulgarians, however, often went into gruesome detail—murdered priests, babies on bayonets, raped young girls, piles of skulls, and similar graphic images. Americans learned no such horrors about the agony of the Turks.

This was in keeping with the reporting in the American press both before and after the events in Bulgaria. It said nothing of Turkish suffering in the Greek rebellion and the Russian treatment of Muslims before 1876: the mortality and forced migration of the Turks and other Muslims of the Caucasus and Crimea. The Russians had evicted 30 percent of the Turks from regions in the South Caucasus that they conquered in 1829. They had forced 300,000 Crimean Tatars from their lands in the 1850s, with attendant massive mortality. They had killed or exiled 1.2 million Caucasian Muslims (Circassians and others) in the 1860s, and one-third of these had died.[52] The deaths of three thousand to twelve thousand Bulgarians were a horrible crime, but were the deaths of hundreds of thousands of Turks and other Muslims not a far worse crime? Yet the newspapers ignored the Muslim deaths. If they had reported the Muslim suffering, including the deaths in Bulgaria, they would have given Americans a perspective on what was actually occurring as the Russians conquered. Americans received no such information. Indeed, analysis of the Turkish losses in the nineteenth century was not printed in America for a century, and then only in scholarly works with little public circulation.

The few articles that did mention Turkish suffering were short, with none of the ghastly descriptions that accompanied notices of Bulgarian suffering. For example, an entire entry on the Muslims in the *Boston Globe* read: "Official dispatches received at the [British] Foreign Office expose the fearful outrages committed upon the Mohammedans by the Bulgarians."[53] The *Boston Globe* also printed an article from *Lloyd's Weekly* in Britain stating that Turks and Jews had been massacred by Cossacks and Bulgarians.[54] The *New York Times* offered this sentence: "From other letters which have reached me, I have little doubt that the Bulgarians are behaving much in the way as the Bashi-Bazouks."[55] The *New York Times* also printed one short statement that "various correspondents at Shumla concur in stating that they had personally witnessed the results of the Russian attacks on the unarmed Turkish populations, in the shape of wounded old men, women, and children." This was followed immediately by a much longer statement from a *London Daily News* correspondent that concluded: "I do not believe that in Bulgaria there has been a single instance of personal maltreatment of a Turkish civilian at the hands of Russian soldiers."[56] *Littell's Living Age* printed one article by a British reporter, Archibald Forbes, that exonerated the Turks. It stated that they had not treated the Bulgarians badly as the Ottoman forces retreated but that the Bulgarians had persecuted the Muslims, killed Turks and Jews, and stolen their property.[57] Two articles from the one American correspondent who was actually on the scene, the reporter from the *New York Times* in Bulgaria in 1877, gave surprisingly evenhanded accounts of atrocities committed by both sides.[58] It is instructive that he did not write from far afield in Romania, Serbia, or Istanbul and that he actually interviewed both Turks and Bulgarians.

Such articles were very rare exceptions. Most of the American media included nothing on the sufferings of Turks. Some that did comment on it were less than sympathetic. A fairly long *Chicago Tribune* piece acknowledged massacres of Turks (although it stated that they "may be exaggerated for political effect"). Most of the article, however, was given over to the *Tribune's* solution to the problem: all of the Muslims were to be evicted from Bulgaria, unless of course they became Christians, in which case they could remain.[59] In 1877, as the Russo-Turkish War raged, the *Chicago Tribune* editor predicted correctly that if the Russians won the Turks of Bulgaria would be attacked by the Bulgarians and finally killed or driven out of the country. The editor's opinion was that this was a good thing—justifiable revenge for Turkish "enslavement" of the Bulgarians.[60] A *New York Times* editorial expressed much the same sentiment, with no sympathy for the suffering of the expelled Turks.[61] Another *New York Times* editorial admitted that Russian methods were "harsh," but stated that "the service which Russia has done to the cause of human progress [in evicting the Turks] will turn the edge of any very harsh criticism of her methods."[62] An article reprinted from the *London Spectator* in *Littell's Living Age* purported to demonstrate that the Turkish exodus from Bulgaria was a natural phenomenon for "Asiatics," who tended to wander.[63]

THE MISSIONARIES AND THE BULGARIANS

The reporting on Bulgaria in the American press fit the pattern set in the Greek rebellion. The standard of reporting was essentially the same: exaggeration of Christian suffering, little mention of Muslim suffering, many references to the purported evils of Ottoman governance, intemperate language, bloody descriptions of massacres. The reports were less religious in tone than they had been in the extremely religious 1820s, but the battle was still portrayed as one of Christianity against its archenemy, Islam. Writers were more sophisticated in the 1870s and technology had improved greatly, bringing the news from British papers to America by cable overnight. The essence of reporting, however, had not changed. It was still bigoted and unfair.

Americans of the 1870s had no more access to accurate information on the Turks than they had in the 1820s. They could only have believed that the Turks were guilty of all the crimes attributed to them in the press. But the main difference between the 1820s and the 1870s was that Americans simply did not care as much about the Bulgarians as they had about the Greeks. Bulgaria was not seen as the founder of democracy or the home of ancient philosophers still important to Americans. No American public buildings were designed to mimic Bulgarian monuments, no American cities were named after Plovdiv or Sofia as they were after Athens or Ithaca. Very few public meetings were held to elicit popular sympathy for the Bulgarians. The New York press, for example, mentioned only one such meeting (held on January 30, 1877). The speakers were not well-known public figures but two missionaries and William H. Thompson, M.D., whose only qualification seems to have been that he was the son of a missionary who had written a book on Palestine.[64] Whereas newspapers of the 1820s gave prominent mention to collections for relief of the Greeks and for arms, no one began a major campaign to collect funds for the Bulgarians.

If the difference between popular support for the Greeks and the Bulgarians was great, the gap between popular support for the Bulgarians and for the Armenians in the 1890s was even greater. Newspapers and magazines published more than ten times the number of articles on the Armenians as on the Bulgarians.[65] No American books called attention to the plight of the Bulgarians, but many were written on the Armenians.[66] Public meetings and collection campaigns took place all over America for the Armenians but not for the Bulgarians. Yet it would seem that in many ways Bulgarians should have been at least as important as Armenians, perhaps more important. Ottoman Bulgarians in the 1870s were more than twice as numerous as Ottoman Armenians in the 1890s. The Bulgarians were Europeans, for whom Americans might have felt a distant kinship. Why would the Armenians become so much more important? The answer is the missionaries.

It was the missionaries who began and sustained the American campaign to support the Armenians (see chapter 7). They did not, or perhaps could not, do the same for the Bulgarians. Surprisingly few articles on the Bulgarians originated with or contained quotations from missionaries.[67] The missionaries and their domestic supporters were not as organized as they were two decades later when they pleaded the Armenian cause. They also had far less invested in Bulgaria than they did in the Armenians. In 1876 the American Board had little presence in Bulgaria. It had agreed to leave all missions north of the Balkan Mountains to the missionaries of the Methodist Episcopal Church, who operated a small and largely unsuccessful mission.[68] The American Board first came to Bulgaria only in 1858. By 1870 it had three mission stations in Bulgaria: Eski Zagra, Filibe, and Samokov.[69] Six "ordained ministers" were attached to the stations. In contrast, thirty-seven ordained ministers and four missionary doctors were already attached to the Mission to the Armenians in 1870. In 1876 the American Board operated only one missionary school, in Samokov, although many Bulgarians attended the missionary college in Istanbul (Robert College). When the missionary agitation in favor of the Armenians took place in the 1890s, Anatolia had 48 ordained missionaries, missionary teachers, and physicians and 94 "female assistant missionaries." The missionaries supervised 106 churches led by 732 "pastors, preachers, teachers, and other helpers." The mission included 3 colleges with 451 students, 3 theological seminaries, and 418 schools with 16,203 students.[70] The incentive to protect the mission that was to be so much a part of the missionary agitation for the Armenians was thus not present for the Bulgarians.

This is not to say that the Bulgarians did not enjoy the support of the Christian establishment in the United States, only that this support did rise to the heights seen later. Christian magazines wrote on the Bulgarian atrocities at length and with anti-Turkish venom. To the religious writers, nothing good had ever happened in the Ottoman Empire. "The Turk" ("brutal," "savage," "ignorant," "intolerant") was described as unredeemably hostile to all ideas of liberty and proper government, which could only be attained through Christianity.[71] Supposedly only Turkish tyranny had stood in the way of Christian advancement in the Ottoman Empire: "The Turk regards every Christian as his slave."[72] Those Christian slaves longed to be free: "The Christian populations of European Turkey, like the souls beneath the altar in the Apocalypse, raise forever the cry, 'How long, O Lord, how long?'"[73] The only answer was the complete eviction of the Ottoman Empire from Europe.[74] One article hailed the Turkish defeat by the Russians as a "victory in the interests of Christianity and civilization."[75]

Like the secular press, the Christian press reprinted reports from the London Liberal press, especially the *Times* and the *Daily News*. Unlike the regular newspapers, which usually printed summaries or short statements, the Christian media printed extended descriptions of massacres, with details of piles of skulls and decaying corpses. Exaggeration was the rule: Bulgarian villages had many thousands of inhabitants, mostly killed; one churchyard, which must have been incredibly large, held three thousand corpses.[76]

As was to be the case in the Armenian Troubles of the 1890s, the Christian media published reports that were purportedly letters from the scene of massacres. These contained the most damning stories of Turkish atrocities—babies on bayonets, children hacked to pieces, eyes gouged out, Turks herding Christians ahead of them in battle to draw the enemy's fire, pretty women taken for harems or sent to slave markets in Istanbul to be sold (these supposed events, it should be added, were never noticed by diplomats or even by the secular press).[77] Reports from sources such as the Evangelical Alliance of Athens ("whole plains strewn with human heads") were printed as fact.[78] In general, no sources were offered for reports that thousands had been slaughtered in each of many (unnamed) "villages."[79]

The Christian critics of the Ottomans could be surprisingly naïve, given past history, much more so than the secular writers. Christian writers praised Russia as a disinterested proponent of reforms in the Ottoman Empire. According to them, Russia had no desire to dismember the Ottoman Empire or to drive the Turks from Europe.[80] Under tolerant Russian rule all people, including the Muslims, would be free and better off, because they would be able to convert to Christianity. The Christian critics welcomed Russian defeat and occupation of Ottoman Europe and described it as God's will.[81] They were also not above using events to advance their own religious agenda: one article even declared that the pope was on the side of the Turks and that he hoped the Turks would wipe out all the Orthodox Christians.[82] The demise of the Turks in Bulgaria, these writers confidently anticipated, would result in the conversion of the Bulgarians to proper Protestant Christianity over time.[83] As might be expected, religious attacks on Islam continued in the religious press, given new force by current events. All the old attacks continued: Muhammad's "imposture" and "sexual impurity," the bloodthirstiness of Islam, the sensuality of Islam, the lack of real humanity and charity in Islam, the universal negative effect of Islam on human industry, and all the other calumnies.[84]

Some Christian publications briefly mentioned Bulgarian crimes (juxtaposed with their lengthy catalogs of Turkish atrocities) but largely excused them: "The Bulgarians have been guilty of massacres and outrage. We do not defend them, but at least we cannot forget that this mad outburst is against members of a race and creed who have crushed them for generations, and that those who have taken part in it cannot yet have dismissed from their recollection the infernal outrages of last year." The Ottoman Empire, however, had "enlisted the legions of hell upon its side."[85] One Methodist missionary did mention in one sentence that the Turkish families of Tirnova had fled but wrote that the Turks planned to return and massacre the Bulgarians.[86]

The article "Turkish Barbarity" by the retired missionary H. J. Van Lennep summarized the religious position: he cataloged instances of supposed Turkish inhumanity throughout Ottoman times, with all the usual exaggerations and outright falsehoods, and blamed everything on Islam. In an interesting slant on history, he held that the Turks in Central Asia had been "a people of mild character" until "the adoption of Islam turned them into bloodthirsty tigers."[87]

Although Islam was more usually blamed for the supposed Turkish faults, outright racism was not absent. The Turks were "an inferior race":

In its [the Aryan race's] irrepressible progress, this family of nations has now obtained control of the government of nearly all Europe, America, and Australia, and the larger portion of Asia, and it is still advancing. The Turks do not belong to it, but to an entirely different race, which, in the progress of civilization, has thus far lagged behind, and, on account of its obvious inferiority, has been steadily losing ground for centuries. The inference has been drawn from this historical argument that the Turks have not only been unsuccessful in the past, but that as an inferior race they will also be constitutionally unfit in future to raise the countries over which they rule to a level with the Aryan nations of Europe and America.[88]

One Christian magazine, the *Messenger*, went so far as to call for the total destruction of Islam, holding that all Christian peoples conquered and ruled by Muslims were either killed or enslaved and thus Christianity would only be safe if Islam no longer existed.[89]

Christian leaders obviously had a deep antipathy to the Turks, but it remained literary. Missionaries and their supporters felt strongly about the Bulgarians, but the American Board and Protestant leaders organized no anti-Turkish campaign. Although some preachers undoubtedly spoke against the Turks from the pulpit, newspapers made no mention of church sermons about Bulgarian atrocities. All this was to change when the churches and the missionaries took the lead in organizing America in a new cause, the "Armenian Atrocities."

7

AMERICANS AND ARMENIANS

Readers may experience a sense of déjà vu as they go through this chapter. Islam is again accused of mandating the deaths of all Christians, just as it was in earlier times. Turks are accused of being lazy and incompetent, skilled only at massacre, just as they were as far back as colonial America and as they were portrayed in American textbooks. Like the newspaper articles of the Greek rebellion and the Bulgarian Horrors, the articles of the 1890s wrote only of murdered Christian dead, never of murdered Muslims. The descriptions of Turks in the 1890s were the same caricatures seen in American colonial days and were scarcely more temperate. The temptation is simply to write "more of the same," but that would not describe the great increase and development of anti-Turkish prejudice during the Armenian Troubles of the 1890s. In earlier periods schoolchildren and university students learned only bad things about the Turks, but Turks made up only a small part of the curriculum. Newspapers and magazines did tell horrible stories of the Turks during the Greek rebellion, but they reached a limited reading public. During the Armenian Troubles of the 1890s books and newspapers kept the image of the Terrible Turk constantly before American eyes. Few weeks went by in which newspapers did not print anti-Turkish articles, most of them either false or, if true, deceptive because they ignored the actions of Armenian rebels and the suffering of Turks.[1] The Turks were seen everywhere, and their image was not good.

THE ARMENIAN QUESTION

The history of what came to be called the Armenian Question is hotly contested. It is not my intention here to become embroiled in that debate but to relate how the Turks were portrayed to Americans as the conflicts between Muslims and Armenians and the Ottoman government and Armenian rebels developed. It is necessary, however, to state that many different versions of the history of the conflict existed.

The Ottomans at the time contended that in the 1890s Armenian insurgents had rebelled against their government and killed soldiers, police, officials, and civilians. Undoubtedly, Armenian insurgents were sometimes purely local rebels, but the rebellions were usually led by the two main Armenian revolutionary parties—the Hunchaks and the Dashnaks.[2]

The Hunchakian Revolutionary Party (the Hunchaks), which staged major rebellions in the Sasun and Zeytun regions, had been founded in Geneva, Switzerland, in 1887 by Armenians from the Russian Empire. The party's objective was to foment Armenian revolution in the Ottoman Empire. Louise Nalbandian, the primary historian of the Armenian revolutionaries, has described the Hunchak methods as "Propaganda, Agitation, Terror, Organization, and Peasant and Worker Activities."[3] The aim was Armenian revolution. The party manifesto proclaimed: "It is necessary to forcefully reshape, revolutionize the present social organization in Turkish Armenia, inciting popular revolt."[4] In the 1890s the Hunchaks engaged in a large number of terror attacks and assassinations against both Ottoman officials and Armenians loyal to the state,[5] but their most prominent actions were the rebellions of 1894–96.

The second major revolutionary organization, the Armenian Revolutionary Federation, called the Dashnaks (from the title Dashnaktsutiun, "federation" in Armenian), was founded in 1890 in Russian Transcaucasia.[6] The "Program and Rules" of the party stated its purpose clearly: "The aim of the ARF Dashnaktsutiun is to achieve political and economic liberty in Turkish Armenia by means of insurrection." The program went on to describe the means to achieve this end, which included arming "the people," sabotage, and execution of government officials and Armenian "traitors."[7] In their founding meetings in 1890 the Dashnaks had declared a "people's war against the Turkish government."[8] Although they were to become the main party of Armenian rebellion in the early twentieth century, the Dashnaks were not prominent in the 1890s rebellions. They were only involved directly in the abortive 1896 rebellion in Van,[9] in various small-scale actions, and in assassinations.

The aim of the Armenian revolutionaries was to pattern their revolution on the successful revolution of the Bulgarians in 1876. In Bulgaria the revolution, even though initially completely crushed by the Ottomans, was saved by Russian intervention. A new Bulgaria was born. This was not to be the case in the Armenian rebellions of 1894–96. Whether out of fear of ramifications in Europe if they committed troops to Anatolia or fear that they could not control the Armenian revolution, the Russians did not intervene. The Bulgarian intervention had not produced the Bulgarian client state that the Russians wanted, and they desired Eastern Anatolia for themselves, not for the Armenians (as they would demonstrate during World War I). Even though the British government was supportive of the Armenians, the British were daunted by European politics and the immense difficulties of sending an army to Eastern Anatolia (see map 7.1). No Europeans intervened to support the Armenian revolution. What transpired was a bloody intercommunal battle between Muslims and Armenians that the Armenians lost.

Armenian revolution broke out in the Sasun region of the Bitlis Province in 1894 with a refusal to pay taxes. Armenian villagers led by Hunchak organizers at first drove Ottoman forces from their villages and attacked nearby Muslim villages then fled to the mountains, where they initially fought off the forces sent to

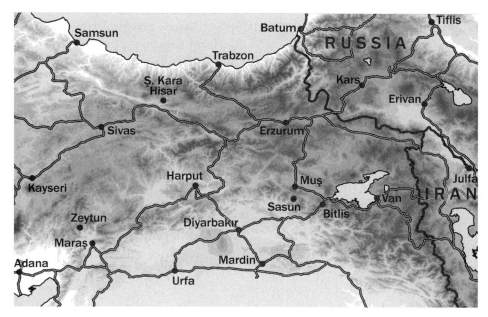

7.1. Eastern Anatolia, 1878

subdue them. When Kurdish tribes intervened, battles between the Kurds and Armenians began, including a fierce twelve-day battle at the village of Geligü-zan. Kurdish cavalry units (known as Hamidiye Tribal Cavalry) were sent from Erzincan. They defeated the Armenians, who fled, slaughtering Muslim villagers and destroying the villages in their path. In turn, the Hamidiye units that pursued the Armenians slaughtered Armenians and destroyed Armenian villages. Neither side spared women and children; most of those who died were innocent. The Armenians undoubtedly suffered the worst of it. Many died of starvation or exposure in the mountains.

In 1895 Hunchak organizers arrived in the region of the town of Zeytun (northwest of Maraş) led by a rebel known only as Aghassi. Zeytun's Armenians often had rebelled against the government before, based on the desire not to pay taxes. Aghassi and his men built up defenses and organized a rebellion. On October 10, 1895, they began their revolt by burning two gendarmes alive. The Ottoman garrison in Zeytun does not seem to have believed that a real rebellion was in the offing. On October 20 the 650-man garrison was surprised and captured. All but 57 of the soldiers were killed after they had surrendered. The rebels then attacked surrounding Muslim villages, killing the villagers. The Ottoman government delayed taking action because of European diplomatic efforts to save the Zeytun Armenians. But eventually, on December 24, they attacked and defeated the rebels, most of whom fled to the south. The Europeans forced the Ottomans to grant clemency to the rebel leaders, including Aghassi, who later wrote a book on his experiences. He claimed that in the revolt 125 Armenians and 20,000 Muslims had been killed, a great exaggeration of Muslim dead and diminution of Armenian mortality, but an indication that Muslims had died in great numbers.[10]

Assassinations, demonstrations, and outright battles between Armenian rebels and Ottoman forces and between Muslims and Armenians took place in eastern and central Anatolia in 1895 and 1896. At least twenty-three separate incidents resulted from provocations by Hunchaks.[11] In September 1896 in Istanbul an estimated one thousand to two thousand Armenians, led by Hunchak organizers, marched from the Armenian Patriarchate to the Bab-ı Ali, seat of the government. While the organizers claimed that the intent of the march was peaceful, even European observers friendly to the Armenian cause felt it was intended as a provocation. British ambassador Philip Currie, who definitely favored the Armenians, nevertheless wrote: "There is good reason to suppose that the object of the 'Hindchag' [Hunchaks] was to cause disorder and bloodshed with a view to inducing the Powers of Europe to intervene on behalf of the Armenians."[12] Some facts are certain. Many of the demonstrators were armed with revolvers and knives. When the Armenians reached the Bab-ı Ali, an Armenian shot and killed the head of the police force that was trying to restrain the crowd. Fifteen policemen and sixty Armenians were killed in the subsequent riot.

Worse events occurred on August 26, 1896, when Armenian revolutionaries seized the Ottoman Bank in Istanbul, killing two porters and shooting and throwing bombs from the bank's windows. They remained in control of the bank until European diplomats intervened, promised the attackers immunity, and took them away on a yacht.[13] The attack was to have been part of a number of concerted rebel actions throughout the city, most of which were foiled. The rebels attempted to occupy the law courts and central police department and threw bombs at Muslim targets, however, causing panic and reaction from the Muslim mob.[14] Anarchy reigned. Armenian bombs were still being thrown on August 30;[15] according to what was probably an overestimate by the British, 5,000–6,000 Armenians were killed.[16] No one counted the Muslim dead, except for dead soldiers: 120 were killed and 250 wounded. If 120 soldiers were killed, the mortality among Muslim civilians must also have been high.

The final rebellion of the 1890s took place in Van, in southeastern Anatolia, in June 1896. Armenians erected barricades in one section of the city and began to fire on Ottoman troops and gendarmes. The plan of revolt called for the Armenians to hold off Ottoman forces until they could be relieved by a rebel column sent by Armenians in western Iran. The column, intercepted by Kurdish tribesmen, never arrived, and the revolt failed ignominiously. The Van rebels escaped, slaughtering Muslim villagers during their retreat. Most of the rebels subsequently fell into the hands of Kurdish tribes and were killed, along with many innocent Armenian villagers. The Ottoman commander in Van counted 418 Muslim and 1,713 Armenian dead in the province and 363 Muslim and 71 Armenian wounded.[17] The actual mortality for both was surely higher.

While admitting failures of governance and failures to protect the populace, the Ottomans essentially blamed the rebels for the Armenian Troubles. Supporters contended that Armenians were innocents, attacked by the government and by local Muslims for a variety of reasons. Some cited "racial hatred," bred by religious differences or envy of Armenian economic success. Others held that leaders of the Ottoman government, in particular Sultan Abdülhamit II, deliberately targeted the Armenians because they feared the Armenians would break away from the Ottoman state and form their own country. Armenian apologists denied that the rebels had been an important factor in the Troubles.

Later historians have adopted various positions.[18] It seems likely that both sides were at fault. Led by revolutionaries, Armenians did indeed revolt in many places in Anatolia, most notably in Sasun, Zeytun, and Van. Their intention, in their own words, was to spark reprisals that would result in European intervention that would create an Armenian state,[19] as had happened in the creation of independent Bulgaria in 1876–78. The revolts did result in great mortality in the Muslim population, particularly among Kurds. The Ottoman government proved incapable of controlling the ensuing Muslim reaction. Kurdish tribes, never under effective government control, attacked Armenians, sometimes engaging in massacres but more usually stealing animals and property that were necessary for the Armenians' survival. Some government officials even joined in the attacks on those they considered rebels, but no evidence has ever appeared that implicates the Ottoman central government or the sultan in massacres. Both Muslims and Armenians suffered heavy losses, although the losses were not nearly as great as portrayed at the time.

No accurate statistics of mortality in the Troubles were ever compiled. The one detailed European examination of Armenian dead, by the Sasun Investigation Commission,[20] demonstrated that the figures given in missionary and newspaper accounts were greatly exaggerated. The American Board of Commissioners for Foreign Missions stated that 6,000–10,000 Armenians had died in Sasun. Newspapers printed estimates of up to 25,000 Armenian dead there. European delegates to the Investigation Commission, who investigated on the scene and surely had no desire to exonerate the Turks, counted 265 Armenian victims and estimated that 500 Armenians had died of all causes, including starvation. For the entire period of the 1890s Troubles, the missionary establishment and the newspapers alleged at various times that 100,000, 500,000, and even 1 million Armenians had died. More rational voices put the Armenian death toll much lower: the German ambassador estimated 60,000–80,000;[21] the Ottoman government, 20,000, a number accepted by some European sources.[22]

Muslim deaths were never estimated, and almost never even mentioned, by missionaries or newspapers. Both the Sasun and Zeytun troubles had begun with the massacre of Muslim villagers, followed by battles between Muslims and Armenians in which both sides suffered high casualties. The Ottoman government counted 1,433 Muslim and 2,238 Christian dead in 1895, surely an undercount of both. The number does not include the Zeytun rebellion, in which (according to the Armenian leader of the rebels) many times more Muslims than Armenians died; the Van rebellion, in which more than 500 Muslims and 2,000 Armenians surely died; or other massacres in 1896, in which the death toll was largely Armenian. It is obvious that Armenians suffered greater mortality than Muslims; but a significant number of murders of Muslims as well as Armenians occurred. That, after all, had been the plan of the rebels, who started the rebellions by killing Kurds, confident in the knowledge that Westerners would only count Christian dead.

Many American voices were raised in support of the Armenians (see the discussion below). The Ottoman side suffered because it had no American advocates. Extremely few Turks lived in America in the 1890s, just as few lived in Western Europe. In any case, it is doubtful that their voices would have been heard, given the prejudices of the day. The only voice in America for the Ottoman view was the Ottoman Embassy in Washington. Today, in the light of historical studies, the embassy's press releases appear to have been mainly accurate, although surely flawed. That made no difference at the time, because most American newspapers assumed that anything released by the Turks was not to be trusted. Of the many American newspapers surveyed for this study, only one, the *Washington Post,* attempted anything like evenhanded reporting.

The Missionaries and the Armenians

What Americans knew of the conflict between the Armenians and the Muslim Turks and Kurds (as well as what they knew of the Ottoman Empire in general) came primarily from the missionary establishment. While a few clergy and congregants may have supported the Turks or at least been neutral, they were silent.

The American missionary endeavor in the Ottoman Empire had been a failure as an evangelistic enterprise. The original intent to convert the Jews and Muslims was very early seen to be impossible. Neither Jews nor Muslims would convert. Orthodox Christians also proved resistant to the calls to Protestantism. The only ones who had listened were Armenians. The missionaries did not approve of the Armenian Gregorian Church, which seemed to them to be similar in belief to the despised Roman Catholic Church;[23] but they did find Armenians who were willing to convert to Protestantism, and they hoped that their message would gradually turn the Armenian Church in a Protestant direction. A relatively small proportion of Armenians actually became Protestants, but they were the only sizable group of Ottoman Christians to do so.[24] The imminent success of the missionaries in converting first the native Christians then the Muslims and Jews had been confidently predicted for generations,[25] until it quietly disappeared in the late nineteenth century, to be replaced by more secular goals for the mission.

The American mission took on a life of its own that had little to do with religious conversion. The missionaries sent letters to the congregations at home saying that the work of conversion was advancing. Missionaries wrote books telling touching and elevating stories of Bible-readings, conversions of the spirit, and individuals who had become Protestants. Certainly the publications and meetings of the American Board and the Presbyterian Board portrayed the missionaries as mainly involved with preaching the gospel. The reality, however, was that a vast missionary corporation whose activities were primarily educational had been created in the Ottoman Empire. By 1890 the American Board was operating more than 400 schools and colleges in the Ottoman Empire, with more than 17,000 students (25,000 students by 1913).[26] The Presbyterian Board was educating 9,700 students in 234 schools and colleges in Ottoman Syria and in Iran.[27] As happens with all corporations, the organization itself and its continuance and growth became the missionaries' primary concern.

As the Mission to the Armenians developed, American missionaries increasingly became advocates for all things Armenian. The increased presence of American missionaries among the Armenians coincided with the rise of Armenian nationalism. The place of the missionaries in the creation and fostering of this nationalism has been argued for years. Turks and many Europeans at the time, the French in particular, felt that the missionaries were solidly behind Armenian revolution. But both the French and the Ottoman government had other reasons to oppose the missionaries. The missionaries themselves denied that they took sides in domestic politics. The concern here is not whether the missionaries were active in the Armenian revolution but that they actively supported it in America. Indeed, by the later part of the nineteenth century missionaries and missionary publicity organs had become veritable propaganda machines for the Armenian cause.

The reasons for the missionary support of the Armenian cause were both religious and personal. Given the American milieu in which they were raised and their education in seminaries, the missionaries were unlikely to come to the Ottoman Empire with anything but an overwhelmingly negative image of Islam and the Turks. The missionaries were firm in their belief in the superiority of Christianity and Christians. As shown above, missionaries and their supporters were willing to accept even the excesses of the Russian conquests of non-Christian peoples for the ultimate benefit of Christianity. They especially praised the Russian and British empires, which grew on the principle of a Christian minority ruling over non-Christian majorities. On the personal level, Armenians were the people closest to the missionaries. Missionaries lived among the Armenians, taught them, ministered to them, and saw in them the best opportunity for the ultimate success of their mission. Members of the Armenian revolutionary movements were students and occasionally teachers in the missionary high schools and colleges. When Armenian revolutionary sentiments led to bloody conflict, it was natural that the missionaries would take the Armenians' side.

The 1890s conflicts saw the beginning of a campaign of "charitable propaganda" that was to reach a crescendo during World War I. The impetus of this campaign was the worthy cause of providing relief to the Armenians who had suffered in the conflict. It perhaps need not be said that the only beneficiaries of American charity were Christians, not all those who suffered. The method was effective. Readers, audiences, and congregations all over the United States were flooded with stories of Muslim atrocities against the Armenians. The campaign built righteous indignation to a fever pitch then collected relief funds. Missionaries and missionary organizations, especially the American Board and the Presbyterian Foreign Mission Board, were at the forefront of the campaign.

The American Board began its official propaganda in December 1894 with the press release of an official statement describing its view of events in Sasun, ostensibly drawn from missionary reports. This was odd, because the board report noted that no missionaries were stationed in the Sasun region. Nevertheless, the board stated that the Troubles had begun when Armenians pursued Kurds who had stolen their sheep and Turkish soldiers intervened on the side of the Kurds, allegedly massacring six thousand to ten thousand Armenians. The only solution, according to the board, was European intervention.[28]

Other Protestant organizations joined the American Board in its condemnation of the Turks. The Evangelical Alliance for the United States, which claimed 15 million Americans as "unofficial" members, petitioned the U.S. secretary of state to support the Armenian cause and provided information to the media.[29] The American Baptist Missionary Union unanimously passed a "resolution condemning the Armenian outrage."[30] Local ministerial associations in cities all over America and groups of missionary societies in the United States and Canada passed resolutions in favor of the Armenians and against the Turks.[31] Nearly all the Protestant Episcopal bishops signed a memorial to the president demanding that the United States take action on the Armenian issue.[32] The Congregational, Episcopalian, Methodist, Presbyterian, Baptist, Evangelical Alliance, and other churches and church organizations all passed anti-Turkish resolutions at their annual meetings.

Newspapers and Magazines

Americans knew almost nothing of the Middle East. What they learned of the region in school was always very limited and often very wrong (see chapter 5). The newspapers did little to educate the public. A search through years of newspaper issues in smaller cities reveals only the occasional short paragraph on the Middle East or Turks in most years. Major events such as the Crimean War increased the coverage to some degree, but even then stories were usually short. Big city newspapers offered somewhat more complete reporting than newspapers in smaller cities. Even the newspapers of New York, Philadelphia, and Chicago, however, did not cover the Middle East comprehensively. Unless America was directly involved, reporting from any part of the world other than Europe was slight, in general simply short reports such as "Turkish Prime Minister Resigns," "New Turkish Sultan," and the like. The occasional nonpolitical reports usually focused on Muslim relations with local Christians and were heavily affected by missionaries. Indeed, these matters most likely were considered to be of interest primarily because of American (i.e., missionary) involvement. This holds true for other areas of the world as well. Reporting on China, for example, was also predominantly on missionaries and their labors. The American media only became truly interested in the Middle East and the Balkans at times of civil disturbances involving Christians, such as the Greek revolt and, to a lesser extent, the Bulgarian revolt. In the 1890s reporting on the Middle East once again swelled dramatically.

The American public that read reports of "Turkish atrocities" in the 1890s knew little more of the Middle East than had their forebears in the 1820s. The effect of a sudden onslaught of prejudice and vilification against the Turks must have been tremendous. Most Americans knew only what they read in the newspapers, heard from the pulpit, or learned from the missionary establishment, and the image of the Turks presented in these sources was not good.

The Sources

The basic sources of reports on events in Eastern Anatolia were missionaries and Armenians. Newspapers had no reporters at the events in Sasun and Zeytun. News from Western journalists was sent to London or New York from Istanbul or even farther from the scenes of the Armenian Troubles. The journalists gave little credence to official Ottoman reports and very seldom had access to European consular reports. Instead their news came from missionaries and Armenian nationalists.

Newspaper accounts of the Armenian Troubles began with the 1894 American Board report. The original press release condemning the Turks and stating that everything was done with the sultan's approval appeared in newspapers across America, either quoted in its entirety or summarized.[33] Following the American Board's lead, the newspapers laid all blame for the Sasun troubles on the Turks and the sultan. In the newspaper pages no Armenian was guilty of anything but self-defense.[34]

The pattern continued throughout the Troubles. Newspapers printed press releases from the American Board verbatim or in part.[35] Some board releases were identified as such: pieces on troubles in Maraş, quoting Judson Smith, foreign secretary (chief executive) of the American Board, appeared verbatim in the *Trenton [N.J.] Evening Times, Lowell [Mass.] Daily Sun, Williamsport [Pa.] Daily Gazette and Bulletin, Fort Wayne [Ind.] Gazette,* and *Salem [Mass.] Daily News,* among many others.[36] Identical articles quoting American Board missionary the Reverend H. O. Dwight appeared in many papers, as did identical articles quoting the Reverend H. H. Van Meter.[37] Although the stories did not give the original sources of most of the missionary reports (omitted either by the missionary headquarters in Boston or by journalists), they were American missionaries. The *Dallas News, New York Times,* and many other newspapers, for example, all contained the same article on December 17, 1894, extolling the work of the American Board and condemning the Turks.[38] Although the article did not identify the source, it exhibited all the marks of a press release from the American Board, which was never hesitant to praise its own work. Reports often originated in Boston, headquarters of the American Board; indeed, in the early days of reporting on the Armenian Troubles many more newspaper reports on events in the Ottoman Empire were datelined Boston than were datelined Constantinople.[39] The reports contained information and descriptions of activities that could only have been sent by missionaries. What other English speakers in Bitlis, for example, would cite the letters they were receiving from other Eastern Anatolian cities that were all sites of mission stations?[40]

While the writers were not identified, many "letters received from" or "reports from" can only have come from missionaries and probably were distributed by officials of the American Board. For example, sources identified only as "persons engaged in relief work" must have been missionaries, who were the only ones engaged in such work.[41] "The Rev. Dr. James Chambers of this city has just received a letter from a friend who has lived in Turkey for fifteen years" is typical of the sort of provenance found in most articles. The letter gave much information that, if true, would indicate that the author had carefully observed a massacre (accounts of the actions of individuals, exact descriptions of movements of soldiers, reports of the intentions of officers, and so forth), although it never stated that the correspondent was at the scene. Indeed, any correspondent who had been at the scene described could not have survived. It is unlikely that the writer "resident in Turkey for 15 years" who sent the letter to Reverend Chambers, moderator of the Presbytery of New York, was anyone but a missionary.[42] "An American who was for a long time resident at Constantinople writes from Harpoot" was quoted as writing that "the sultan is reported to have said that he will feed these unfortunates [Armenians] if they will become Mohammedans." The only American at Harput who had long resided in Istanbul would have been a missionary, assuming that such a letter from the unnamed American ever existed. How the unlikely story of the sultan reached him was not explained.[43] The *Atlanta Constitution* featured on its front page a story titled "A Bath of Blood." The article was a long quotation from an anonymous person "who has spent several months of this year in Armenia," whose letter was forwarded to American newspapers by the British clergyman who edited *Review of the Churches*. Not unusually for documents of the type, it refers to rivers choked with corpses, Armenians buried alive, "roasted infants by their mangled mother's corpses," and other horrific sights.[44]

Sometimes identifying the missionary sources and sometimes not made all the stories appear more believable. The same information was paraphrased in newspapers that cited missionary sources and those that neglected to do so. The effect was to show that various sources agreed, when in fact they were the same source. For example, the reports from American consuls that appeared in American newspapers were drawn from missionary sources. They naturally corroborated the reports sent to America by the missionaries themselves.[45]

Other than ascertaining that many of the unnamed sources were missionaries, it is almost always impossible to identify the sources of most of the accounts printed in American newspapers. Standards of journalism at the end of the nineteenth century did not include verification of sources. "Advices from Trebizond," "reliable correspondence received in Boston," "an eye witness," "it is rumored that," "reports received from the interior," "a letter received in this city by a correspondent in Constantinople," "an American woman at Constantinople," "a reliable correspondent," "a trustworthy correspondent," "a letter received by a citizen in Boston from an American resident in Turkey"—those were the sources of the news that reached America.

Long articles describing "outrages" were based on "[a] letter referring to the massacre of Armenians just received in this city [Boston]."[46] Articles originating in Varna, Bulgaria, without named sources told of slaughter in Sasun (more than 800 miles away by road) and of impending massacres of Armenians in Antioch (more than 900 miles away by road);[47] they were printed as true stories.[48] A fairly typical article in the *Chicago Tribune* cited a *London Times* dispatch from Vienna.[49] The dispatch reported that Turkish soldiers had killed 2,000 Armenians in Sasun, based on "a letter received there [Vienna] from Smyrna." Smyrna (İzmir), of course, was slightly more than 1,000 miles from Sasun by road; the report did not indicate the source of information of the Smyrna letter writer, who also was never identified. Articles such as one that began: "Boston, Dec. 5. A letter descriptive of recent events in Erzurum, Asiatic Turkey, has been received in Boston" may have been from anyone, anywhere—and sources were often given in that form.[50] It was not uncommon for the only source offered to be someone in Boston, with no information on how the Bostonian knew what was occurring in Anatolia. The identifications given usually were so vague as to be useless: "A prominent Armenian in this city has received a letter from a friend in Harpot [Harput]."[51] "Letters have been received by well-known parties in this city [Boston] from reliable sources in Turkey giving still further testimony regarding the outrages in Eastern Turkey. The following letter comes from a city not a great distance from the scene of the outrages."[52] Allegations were printed as fact when the only source was a clergyman living in America, often an Armenian Protestant clergyman.[53] The rebel Hunchak Party, which was leading the revolt, was even taken as an authoritative source when the Hunchaks claimed that the Turks were planning to massacre all Armenians in various places.[54]

Armenians were the other main source of information on the Troubles that appeared in the American press. The Armenians who provided information were seldom at the scene themselves.[55] They were usually representatives of Armenian organizations who stated that they had secret sources in Anatolia. Newspapers occasionally printed interviews with Armenians who had come to America, full of heart-rending stories and accusations of murder and brutality. While the papers had no way to ascertain whether the stories were true, they printed them as fact.[56] Although American readers would not know it, the Armenian sources often spread errors that could not be made by anyone who knew Eastern Anatolia. J. S. Donian (president of the Philarmenic Society), whose anti-Turkish opinions are described below, told the *New York Times* that 4 million people lived in "Armenia," half of them Armenians (both statistics wildly wrong) and that the government prevented Armenian youth from going to school—the opposite of the truth.[57] A very few articles supposedly cited letters identified as coming from Armenians on the scene in Sasun and Zeytun, but they did not name the Armenians or disclose the provenance of the letters. They naturally described only

Muslim attacks on Armenians, never Armenian attacks on Muslims.[58] Armenians provided numerous spurious quotations from Turkish officials in which they publicly called for atrocities against Armenians.[59] The false quotations were printed with no consideration of the unlikelihood that the officials would make any such pronouncements.

THE ASSOCIATED PRESS

The conduit for stories on the Ottoman Empire that reached the American public was usually the Associated Press (AP).[60] For the larger city papers it was the main source. For the smaller city papers it was almost always the only source. (In all the articles read for this study the United Press [UP] was mentioned in a few pieces in 1895, primarily from London.[61] The *New York Times* began to run a number of stories from a United Press correspondent in Istanbul in 1896.) The one difference was that the smaller city papers sometimes printed extremely scurrilous Associated Press stories that obviously were too much for the main dailies.[62] The small newspapers also tended to excerpt the "juicy" stories of massacres from the AP accounts and publish them in one- or two-paragraph articles. The larger city newspapers seldom acknowledged that their stories originated with the Associated Press.[63] The same stories printed in larger cities' newspapers often appeared verbatim in the smaller newspapers, however, which often cited the AP, so it was obviously also the source for the larger papers. Newspapers, small and large, occasionally published information from Armenians and ministers in their own towns and cities, but the Associated Press was the source of information from Europe and the Ottoman Empire.

The Associated Press distributed articles on the Armenian Crisis by both Armenians and missionaries (not by Turks or their supporters, perhaps needless to say). It was the distributor of press releases from the American Board and other missionary sources, such as the articles from Secretary Judson and others cited above. The AP also took entire articles or excerpts from articles from some London newspapers and distributed them across America.

The only regular American news correspondent in Istanbul whose articles reached the American newspapers in 1894–95, who was the representative of the Associated Press,[64] seems seldom to have noticed any official statements from the government. Most of his reporting from Istanbul recounted political rumors— the Russians would intervene against the Turks or the Russians had allied with the Turks, the British were in agreement with the Russians or the British opposed Russian plans, the sultan would be deposed or he would not. The Associated Press representative was often simply wrong, such as in his assertion that the Armenians at Zeytun had freed their Turkish prisoners, when in fact they had killed them.[65] The accounts of Armenian massacres were similar to those described above—citing unidentified sources and individual Armenians with no evidence that they had seen what they described. On the rare occasions when the Associated Press representative identified his sources on massacres, they were sometimes missionaries and more often Armenians. The Armenian sources almost never alleged that they had seen the events themselves. They relayed what they said they had heard or read in letters. Thus the AP reports printed in American newspapers were at best second- or third-hand reports from those who had cause to blacken the image of the Turks.

The news reported by the Associated Press representative in Istanbul does not inspire confidence in his grasp of politics or geography. He reported on Armenian troubles in "Caesarea, Palestine, fifty-five miles from Jerusalem."[66] Although such a place indeed existed, the Armenian Troubles were in Caeserea (Kayseri) in Anatolia, not Palestine, more than 600 miles from Jerusalem by road. The correspondent was also confused by Turkish names, thinking for a time that "Pasha" was a last name rather than a title.[67] He also wrote of an attack on "the house of the leading [Istanbul] Armenian, Kassim Pasha."[68] Kassim Pasha (Kasimpaşa) was a neighborhood in Istanbul, not a person. Perhaps a "leading Armenian" lived there, although at the time it was an unsavory area. How could someone living in Istanbul have made such a mistake? Such errors might seem trivial if they did not call into question the reporter's understanding.

Early in 1895 the Associated Press also sent an unnamed correspondent to "Armenia," with no more specific location stated. He reported what he had heard in whatever region he visited, and his accounts of what he actually saw were good. Someone had reported, for example, that fourteen Armenian villages in far Eastern Anatolia had been raided by Kurdish tribesmen, who massacred the men and carried off the women and children. The intrepid representative of the Associated Press, however, visited the scene and found that the fourteen villages were actually Kurdish. Kurds had been fighting Kurds.[69] The AP correspondent actually saw the guns and spoke to the Armenian leaders who were importing them to fight in Van.[70] Although he obviously did not often speak to Ottoman officials or local Muslims, or at least did not write of any meetings, he was one of the very few to admit that Armenians had killed Turks. This correspondent also surmised that Armenians had killed Turks in order to bring reprisals that would cause European intervention and that the Ottoman Palace had poor intelligence on what was occurring. Unfortunately, he also reported rumors as fact. He admitted that his reporting on Armenian suffering was based on "stories," which he nevertheless repeated.[71] Much of his reporting was based on what he had heard in cities far from the scenes of the Troubles.[72] For example, his report on the Sasun violence, estimating 11,000 killed, was entirely drawn from an interview with the Armenian patriarch at Echmiadzin in Russian Armenia, far from the Troubles.[73] Interestingly, many newspapers quoted his stories about Turkish atrocities but not his statements on Armenian actions against Muslims.[74] Other reports from the correspondent, such as his somewhat overblown assertion that a major Armenian revolt would soon take place "all over Anatolia,"[75] seem not to have fit editors' ideas and were printed only in the *Chicago Tribune* and some smaller city newspapers.

Nearly all of the Associated Press articles were anti-Turkish, sometimes violently and irrationally so. The best example may be a long article from H. H. Van Meter, a missionary who had previously written in support of missionaries and European imperialism in China. Van Meter began his polemic with a ridiculous short history of Islam, in which Muslims intended to kill or forcibly convert all non-Muslims, falling short of their goal because there were simply too many non-Muslims. Passing to contemporary events, he told horrible stories of rape and murder of individual Armenians. In his telling, any Armenian girl ("blooming into the beauty of a pure Christian womanhood") could be, and usually was, raped by Muslims. The article was replete with "gleaming scimitars" cutting off heads, babies killed in front of their mothers, and horrible tortures, the staples of yellow journalism. By November 1895, he wrote, 300,000 Armenians had been killed and more than 400,000 were starving. Van Meter asserted that this was a continuation of a persecution of the Armenians in which 20 million had been lost over the years—one of the most absurd assertions even by the standards of gross exaggeration of the time. The Europeans had failed them, even though, according to Van Meter, the Armenians were "direct descendents of Japhet, and therefore belong to the Caucasian family, and so kin, both by blood and belief, to the great Christian nations of the earth." Among the Christian powers, only Russia had tried to do its duty to its fellow Christians. Assertively Christian, Van Meter assured his readers that the Turks were going to hell, followed by the Europeans who had abandoned them.[76]

THE BRITISH LIBERAL PRESS

As they had during the Bulgarian Troubles, American newspapers relied heavily on the London Liberal press. American press representatives in London sometimes forwarded articles (taken especially from the *London Times* and the *Daily News*) to the major American city newspapers, where they were copied or excerpted. More often the articles were forwarded by the Associated Press. American papers so much relied upon news from London that both the *New York World* and the *Chicago Tribune* printed articles from London detailing the supposed plans of the American administration in Washington to deal with the Armenian problem.[77] Most commonly quoted was the *London Daily News,* which had served for two generations as spokesperson for Gladstone's anti-Turkish campaigns.[78] The *Daily News,* in turn, often drew its material from sources within the Russian Empire.[79]

It is evident from the London newspapers' datelines that they had little actual information from the scenes of conflict. Many Liberal press reports originated in Istanbul and in Kars, part of the Russian Empire. These reports from the British Liberal press not only were usually impossible to prove, and frequently later proven to have been false, but were often simply impossible. The reporters could not have seen what they said they had seen or forwarded their reports to London so soon after the supposed events. The material sent from Kars allegedly told of events in Sasun and other regions, hundreds of miles away. The stories were sent to London's Liberal press immediately after the alleged events or even on the same day. It seems exceedingly unlikely that the correspondents in Kars could have received any accurate information from the places they described. In one report, for example, readers were apprised of hair-raising events in both Kemah (280 miles from Kars by road) and Muş (230 miles from Kars by road). And the roads were very bad.[80] The report supposedly related events as they happened, when in fact any news would have taken weeks to reach Kars.

The probability that the Liberal news was invented was not lost on their competitors in London, who noted that it was impossible for the news to have reached Kars so quickly. They wrote that the reporters who datelined their articles "Moosh, Bitlis, Van, and Erzeroum" had never been near those places and that the news they reported from Sasun could never have reached them as quickly as they alleged. The speed of the arrival of the news (in one case a message traveling from Muş to Kars in three days; in another an article that came from Muş to London in one day) was completely impossible.[81] The *St. James Gazette* and the *Globe* came as close as British diffidence would allow to declaring that the articles in the *Telegraph*, *Daily News*, and *Times* were lies.[82]

The *Daily News* material was always from unverifiable sources and was often simply wrong. The newspaper alleged, for example, that the truth of the situation of Armenians could not be sent to foreign countries from the Ottoman Empire because "all the post offices are in Turkish hands and no scruple is made of opening letters. This is so well known that nobody dares to describe the affairs except in general terms." In fact, European countries were allowed to operate their own sovereign post offices in the Ottoman Empire. Uncensored letters on any matter could be sent to Europe for the price of a stamp. Oddly enough, the same *Daily News* article, reprinted in America, cited a long letter from Istanbul (no author listed) that would never have passed any Ottoman censor.[83]

It is most likely that the representatives of the Liberal press simply invented much of their news or heard it from local Armenians.[84] For example, in an article copied in America the *Daily News* reported that Turks had burned down the city of Harput,[85] an event that never happened. British diplomats commented that the *Daily News* invented news and spurious quotations, even false quotations from British diplomats.[86] In one particularly egregious example the *Daily News* wrote that the British consul at Van had reported that "thousands of women and girls are wandering through the snow piled streets without shelter or food, and barefooted, their ravishers having only left them a chemise and some of them only a cloth to cover their nakedness."[87] In fact, the British consul in Van never made such an observation, because it was untrue, as can be seen in his reports to the Foreign Office.[88]

Ottoman Sources

In the beginning of the Troubles, some newspapers, including the *New York Times* and the *Chicago Tribune*,[89] printed brief excerpts from press releases by the Ottoman Embassy in Washington or, very rarely, excerpts from statements made by Ottoman officials in Istanbul. These were vastly outnumbered by anti-Ottoman articles, however: they were given little space and no large headlines and were often accompanied by much longer anti-Ottoman articles on the same page. Nevertheless, some newspapers did occasionally attempt to print the other side.[90]

Turkish justifications, however, were presented with a significant difference. They were always published as governmental assertions ("Tevfiq Pasha states" or "The Turkish ambassador stated"), whereas anti-Turkish articles usually were presented as assertions of fact, even when they were based on no evidence or were completely false. As the journalistic frenzy on the Armenian issue took hold, the papers cited fewer and fewer of the Ottoman press releases and usually accompanied the few that were mentioned with headlines and comments indicating that whatever the Turks said was a lie.[91]

The *Washington Post* was the one exception to the general anti-Turkish line. The *Post* printed the same sort of Associated Press releases on Turkish atrocities seen elsewhere ("Islamism or the Sword," "Slaughtered with Axes," "Porte Orders the Massacre"), but it also printed some articles and many editorials that portrayed the Turks in a different light.[92] More Turkish embassy press releases appeared in the *Post* than in any other major newspaper.[93] The Turkish embassy articles most often appeared on interior pages, less prominently than the massacre articles, but at least they were printed. The *Post* was also one of the few newspapers that admitted that the Ottoman government had tried and convicted Muslims for murders of Armenians.[94] It was willing to print news from British sources other than the British Liberal newspapers and in general to print reports from Istanbul and London that did not find their way into other papers.[95] The *Post* printed news of bombs and other explosives of Armenian revolutionaries being discovered in Istanbul and of attacks on Armenians by Armenian revolutionaries; other papers did not.[96] It reported when information on massacres taken from the *London Daily News* later proved to be false, whereas other newspapers only printed the initial articles, without retractions. The *Post* was the only major newspaper to contend in editorials that the origins of the Troubles were political, not religious, and to lay the blame on Armenian rebels.[97]

A search through thousands of articles reveals extremely few that were as even-handed as those in the *Washington Post*.[98] This does not mean that newspapers did not pretend to quote Ottoman sources. In fact, Ottoman statistics and quotations from Ottoman officials appeared frequently. Unfortunately, they were most often counterfeit or at best deceptive selections out of context. "Official reports" turned up in unlikely places. For example, an article from Athens quoted "an official report" stating that a band of Kurds had killed British, French, and German employees near İzmir, but the Ottoman government would surely have known that any Kurdish bands were hundreds of miles away from İzmir.[99] The *New York Times* reprinted an article from the *Independent* (a publication with ties to the Congregational Church), which denied that any conflict between Muslims and Armenians had occurred. According to the *Independent,* it was all a plot to kill Armenians. The central government had allegedly planned it in order to kill Christians. "An unnamed Turkish Governor" was "quoted" as saying that the Christians were being goaded to rebel so that they could be killed in reprisal. It may seem unlikely that a Turkish governor would make such a statement, even had it been true, but most readers would not make such an analysis.[100] Nor were readers likely to consider that encouraging disorder was the last thing a government that depended on taxes, and thus on civil order, would do. The Ottoman government was simply assumed to act irrationally.

Articles cited wholly invented "Turkish official statistics." For example, a report of "untrustworthy Turkish statistics," allegedly from the Ottoman government, stated that 1.5 million Kurds lived in Turkey.[101] The Ottoman government never said any such thing, because all Ottoman population statistics were recorded only by religion: the government had no idea of the ethnic composition of the empire's Muslim population. Ottoman statistics listed "Muslims," not Turks, Kurds, or Arabs. Americans read that in the riots following the Armenian takeover of the Ottoman Bank and other assaults in Istanbul what were called "official Turkish estimates" counted 1,100 Armenian dead, 3 soldiers killed, and 30 wounded.[102] The actual Ottoman statistic on dead soldiers was 120: sixty times what Americans read. In an article headlined "Turkish Crimes: A Tabulated Statement by an Official of the Government," the *New York Times* offered a table that appeared damning in its very specific list of murders and forced destitution.[103] It is difficult to see how anyone in the government could have made such a list or even gathered the information in such times. The article itself, however, said the table came from a "local Moslem in a high extra-governmental position" (note "extra-governmental," not the governmental official cited in the headline). Naturally, the supposed Muslim informant was not further identified. It is doubtful that he existed.

Editors made use of headlines to condemn the Turks even when the news in the articles themselves might cast doubt on the universal condemnation of the Turks.[104] Headlines sometimes flatly contradicted their stories. A headline in the *Dallas Morning News,* for example, stated of the Ottoman Empire: "Disorder Is Universal: Army and Navy on the Point of Rebellion." The article, by the Associated Press, mentioned no disorder and no rebellion. An article headlined "More Bloodletting: Massacre Treads Hard upon Massacre in the Sultan's Dominion" in fact stated that Turkish soldiers were protecting Armenians and that "the Armenians of Constantinople are now reassured" by government actions.[105] It did not mention "bloodletting." Those who did not read past the headlines would form a far worse opinion of the Turks than those who read the articles. In general, headlines were more emotive than articles. Some of the headlines from the *San Francisco Chronicle* serve to indicate the sorts of headlines that were ubiquitous: "Ten Thousand Slain in Armenia," "No Mercy Shown by the Turks," "Lawless Deeds of Brutal Turks," "Horrors of a Turkish Massacre," "Slaughter of the Armenians," "More Victims of the Turks," "The Armenians Doomed to Death."[106]

THE HAZARDS OF DISSENT

Undoubtedly the absence of those who would stand up for the Turks was primarily due to the general belief that the Turks were indeed as they were portrayed. But it was also hazardous to anyone's personal standing to go against popular beliefs. Admiral William Kirkland, head of the American naval forces in Europe and commander of the American squadron sent to the Ottoman Empire to protect American (i.e., missionary) lives, reported that he had spoken to alleged victims and tried to discover the facts of the Armenian Troubles. He said he had been unable to substantiate the atrocities, was sure they were exaggerated, and was absolutely convinced that the sultan was not responsible for whatever had occurred.[107] The *New York Times* editorialized that the judgment of Kirkland and others who denied the standard accounts was not to be trusted, because Armenians had declared the sultan to be responsible: "Whom are we to believe? The men who have suffered at the hands of the Turkish Government, or the men who have been fêted, dined, and decorated by the Sultan?"[108] Kirkland in fact had not been fêted or decorated by the sultan and surely had not dined with him, but such facts were not a problem for the editorial writer. Soon after, Kirkland was relieved of his command, "because of certain indiscretions."[109]

REMARKABLE PORTRAYALS

It is not an exaggeration to say that nearly all of the American reporting on the Armenian Troubles was simply wrong: wrong on the details of events, on estimates of mortality, on the intentions and actions of the Ottoman government, and often even on geography. Worst was the omission of any but Armenian suffering. As was almost always the case, American journals and magazines uniformly neglected to write of any sufferings or deaths among Muslims. They seldom mentioned Armenians killing Turks or Kurds, although the 1890s Troubles had begun with the murder of Muslims. The claims of Armenians and Armenian revolutionary organizations accused of crimes by the Ottomans were unquestioned, unless, as in the Ottoman Bank raid in Istanbul, the revolutionaries fired their revolvers and threw their bombs under the noses of journalists. Even then, the papers usually portrayed the Armenians' actions as justified or completely falsified them. Most American newspapers presented the Istanbul riots as purely massacres of Armenians, concealing the Armenian attacks that initiated the Muslim reaction and the Turkish killed and wounded by Armenian bullets and bombs.[110] The writers gave little consideration to the possibility that the accused had been guilty. They trusted accounts of the sufferings of individual Armenians told by those individuals themselves. Many articles were not actual news but rather collections of individual stories, attacks by anecdote. It is impossible to do a proper analysis of the myriad printed stories of individual suffering, because the articles provided no verification, except the word of the individuals. Surely some of them had suffered, and just as surely some had not.[111] Only one side presented its case in the court of American public opinion—the definition of a kangaroo court.

The reporting of events was confused. Editors obviously printed whatever came across their desks, without even a cursory examination of the allegations. Armenian sections of towns were reported to have been destroyed once then to have been destroyed again a month later. In one article, Russia would be backing the Armenians completely; in another article in the same paper, Russia was "anxious to get rid of the Armenians."[112] A paper would one day report that the sultan was in complete control of the situation, ordering the murder of Armenians; a week later the same paper would report that the sultan had no control over anything; a few days later it would report that the sultan had ordered some massacres but had later lost control of his followers. At various times, most of the European powers were reportedly about to go to war with the Ottomans. Even the Americans were supposedly preparing for war.[113] Concerning the incidents at Zeytun, for example, the newspapers reported one day that the Turks had been thrown back by the Armenian rebels then, a few days later, that the Armenians had been defeated and slaughtered. A few days after that, the rebels were still alive and holding their own. One newspaper reported that missionaries were in grave danger and printed on the same page another article stating that the missionaries were all safe.[114] The conflict of information was not odd, because journalists were not on the scene of the events. They depended on the stories they were told, which differed. The remarkable thing was the ability of journalists to believe, and print, conflicting stories as if they were all true.

American reporting of the 1890s Troubles contained so many factual errors that we can only assume that editors had no real sources or simply did not care about the facts. Cities that in reality saw no disturbances were listed as the sites of massacres. The Russian tsar was alleged to be the head of the Greek Orthodox Church,[115] and even in 1890s America it should not have been difficult to find out that this was untrue. In 1896 Russia and the Ottoman Empire were falsely and improbably reported to have signed an "offensive and defensive alliance," which would soon be joined by France.[116] Kurds were supposedly flooding Istanbul to sell plunder stolen from Armenians and were staying to attack the Istanbul Armenians when allowed to do so by the sultan.[117] Any source in Istanbul itself could have testified that no Kurdish influx had occurred. Kurds were reported to be preparing to kill the Christians in Smyrna (İzmir),[118] an amazing feat involving a march of Kurdish tribesmen across the entire length of Anatolia. The Ottoman government was supposedly making a list of all places in which Armenians lived, in order to plan massacres better, and even marking Christian doors in cities such as Istanbul and İzmir as a prelude to massacre.[119] No diplomatic records mention any such activity, although soldiers going through the streets marking doors would have been fairly obvious. Alternatively, the Armenians of Istanbul were supposedly all being moved from the city.[120] Again, any local source would have known that such assertions were ridiculous. Many editors could not fathom the difference between Turks and Kurds, so Turks were often described as conducting massacres in places devoid of Turks.[121] The *New York Times* wrote that all Armenians who were seen talking with foreigners were thrown into prison.[122] This would have meant that all of the many Armenians working for European and American businesses, as well as the thousands of Armenians in missionary schools, would have been incarcerated, which clearly did not happen and surely would have been mentioned in the correspondence of European diplomats if it had.

Some of the assertions in American publications were fantastic fiction: for example, the report that 600 Armenian boys in Zeytun were deliberately killed with "impure vaccine" by Turkish doctors under government orders. Armenian

notables were supposedly being murdered all over the empire.[123] The first assertion was preposterous and reported nowhere else; the second was simply a lie.
The Associated Press reported that the events in Anatolia had been caused by a
Russian plot, the sultan being so afraid that he allied himself with the Russians.
The Russians supposedly planned to force all Catholic and Protestant missionaries from the Ottoman Empire, substituting Russian priests in their place and
thus beginning "the Russianizing of Asiatic Turkey."[124] Armenians of Istanbul had
reportedly been taken away in specially constructed ships, "having chutes from
which the victims were shot into the water and drowned in batches."[125] Some articles were stirring but unlikely. One told of an elderly man who killed twenty-one
Turks with his bare hands before they overpowered him. As he died a bright light
was seen in the sky three times, indicating that heaven would avenge his death.[126]

It is obvious that many writers and editors had no idea of the geography of
the Ottoman Empire or its religions. The *Chicago Tribune* listed Erzurum as "in
the province of Sassoun";[127] in fact, Sasun was a town in the Bitlis Province and
Erzurum was itself a much larger province—similar to stating that California was
in the state of Las Vegas. Newspapers in smaller cities ran an article that asserted
Turkish forces were "overrunning Syria" in 1896, which was odd, because Syria was
already under Ottoman control. The article also declared that Muslims were planning to exterminate Buddhists in Syria.[128] An Associated Press article declared that
"the missionaries in Khartoom, eastern Turkey, are in danger" (perhaps it meant
Harput, but a copy editor might be expected to know that "Khartoom" was in the
Sudan in Africa, on a different continent).[129] Another Associated Press article gave
a report from "Hadjin, Serbia," when Hadjin was in fact in southern Anatolia,
again on a different continent.[130] Yet another Associated Press article on November 16, 1895, stated that all the Armenians of Gürün had been killed.[131] In fact, the
Gürün Armenian community continued to exist until World War I. An article in
the magazine *Outlook* stated: "While this is probably an exaggeration, we know
that failure to pay a tax is regarded by Turkish law as rebellion [and thus the non-
payer can be killed]."[132] "Probably an exaggeration" indeed: if nonpayment of taxes
was a cause for death, a large portion of the population of the Ottoman Empire
would have been awaiting the hangman. One *New York Times* article alleged that
2,000 of 17,000 Armenians of Arapkır had been killed and that the remaining
Armenians were "crowded into less than 200 houses."[133] That would make 75 per
house, hardly possible in small Anatolian houses. Readers, of course, would not
have known this. Nor would they have known that Arapkır was a small town with
a total population (Muslims and Armenians combined) of far less than 10,000.[134]

Some mistakes may be called the product of wishful thinking. One frequent
fancy was that Armenians were a numerically mighty people, a majority in the
ill-defined region called Armenia. Articles alleged that there were more Armenians than Kurds.[135] Some papers claimed that 4–5 million Armenians lived in
the Ottoman Empire and another 1 million in the Russian Empire.[136] In fact,
fewer than 1.5 million Armenians lived in Ottoman Anatolia. Armenians con-
stituted less than 20 percent of the population of the region usually described

as Armenia—the provinces of Erzurum, Sivas, Mamuretülaziz, Diyarbakır, Bitlis, and Van.[137] Some newspapers avoided demographic considerations by simply stating or implying that all the Armenians lived in Armenia or all the inhabitants of "Armenia" were Armenian.[138] Other publications provided a great number of imaginary statistics on Armenian mortality, while never alluding to corresponding Muslim deaths. The *Chicago Tribune* editorialized: "The whole number of victims reaches 100,000, and 500,000 are in the mountains living upon roots and herbs."[139] Many newspapers alleged that 200,000 Armenians had died between 1895 and 1897.[140] The September 1896 issue of the *Chautauquan* estimated that "a million of the Christians of Armenia had perished by violence or want since the persecution began last year."[141] A million deaths would represent two-thirds of the Anatolian Armenians and is about fifty times the real number of Armenians who did die. All of these calculations pale, however, before that of the Reverend H. H. Van Meter (the missionary author whose excessive views are discussed above). Van Meter stated that the Armenians had once numbered 25 million but had been cut down to 4 million by the Turks.[142]

Both Ottoman history and Armenian history were invented for the American reader. Recent history was the most likely to be created out of whole cloth, of course, but journalists did not hesitate to create entire millennia of history. Armenia was said to have been governed by its own kings and rulers for nearly thirty-five centuries until it was conquered by the "Turkish Empire" in the thirteenth century. This would start Armenian self-rule in approximately 2300 BC, 1,400 years before even the most optimistic Armenian historians believe the first Armenian kingdoms began. That history was found in a small Wisconsin newspaper,[143] but newspapers in large cities such as New York also provided their own versions of history. An entire page in the *New York Commercial Advertiser,* copied in other papers, stated that "bondage and degradation" of all peoples was the essence of the Ottoman system, which only retained its rule through "fanaticism and bloodthirstiness" that had killed millions.[144] In its efforts to paint the Ottomans as black as possible the article stated that the depredations of the Ottomans had brought on the Crusades: "There had been no crusades until the Ottomans got into power" (in reality, the Crusades had begun more than two hundred years before the Ottomans came into power). In a long history lesson in the *New York Times,* as in other *Times* stories, readers were told that the Russian emperor was "head of the Greek Church." They read that the Greek rebellion had begun when the Turks slaughtered the Greeks, when in fact the Greek rebellion began with the slaughter of the Turks in the Morea. The *Times* described the 1875 insurrection in Bosnia and 1876–78 insurrection and war in Bulgaria as massacres of Christians, when in reality many more Muslims had died in each. It declared that the Ottomans had begun the so-called Bulgarian Atrocities in 1876 by killing Bulgarians in order to stifle reform and that Circassians and Tatars were imported to carry out the task.[145] In fact, the "horrors" had been a reaction to the Bulgarian revolt and the Russians had evicted the Circassians and Tatars to Bulgaria in the 1850s and 1860s. The *Times* claimed that the

Russians had always looked for peace, neglecting a centuries-long history of Russian conquest. It made no mention of the dead and exiled Muslims who were the victims of the Russians.[146]

According to the American media, Islam had always allowed Muslims indiscriminately to attack, rob, and even kill Christians: "The Bulgarians were Christians, and the Circassians were Mohammedans, and the latter was consequently allowed to pillage and ravish at leisure.... Now the Kurds were good Muslims, and on that ground were entitled, according to the general principles of Turkish rule, to harass and abuse their Christian neighbors."[147] The *Chicago Tribune* wrote that the entire problem of the Armenians came about because they would not renounce their faith.[148] The fight with the Armenians was portrayed as the first step in a general religious war: "It is a crusade against Christ and Christianity."[149] Given the chance, the Turks would massacre all peoples who were not Muslim.[150] Islam, of course, sanctions no such activity. As a practical matter, could the Christian communities have survived for centuries under Islamic rule if this had been the case? The missionaries and editors never considered this basic point. Instead, they appealed to Americans with horror stories and analogies. The Reverend James Dennis (the missionary and writer discussed in chapter 4) wrote of the situation in Anatolia in the *New York Times:* "It is as if 100,000 wild Indians had New York City at their mercy, and knew that they could do what they liked with impunity. It is as if they could cut down women, old men, and children in the street and enter houses at their pleasure, with no police to interfere and no authority to prevent any atrocity they wished to perpetrate. The state of horror which must now prevail throughout Armenia and Asia Minor is too terrible for us to understand."[151] To Dennis and his fellows, Muslims were the "wild Indians" who threatened the peaceful settlers.

Descriptions of the Armenians, in contrast, stressed their Christianity, entrepreneurial spirit, and peaceableness. Very few Armenians in these histories ever committed an evil act.[152] The American press portrayed Armenians and Turks quite differently. Following the established myth, they depicted Turks as lethargic and apathetic, until they roused themselves to attack Christians. The terms used to describe Turks had been standard since the Greek rebellion: "Turkish rapacity," "Turkish bribery, corruption, and dishonesty," "horrible Turks," "barbarous Turks," "butchers," "corrupt, vile, and depraved."[153] Muslims in general were "fanatically ill-disposed to the Christians."[154] The papers reported and amplified anything bad that could be said against Turks. Individual criminal assaults in Istanbul, slight in comparison with the state of crime in America, were reported as "Mob Law in Constantinople."[155] The *Chicago Tribune* outdid itself with invective: "The unspeakable Turk[s]" had been "a curse to every country they govern," engaging in "cruelty and barbarity" and "Turkish tyranny."[156] In contrast to the Turks, according to the *Tribune:* "The Armenians are a civilized people, a people of great natural gifts, and a people who have played a considerable part in history."[157] To most of the American press, Armenians had always suffered and had never done any wrong. They were "a most affectionate and home-loving people," "a civilized people," "a people of great natural gifts," "naturally a moral people," "pure," with a "beautiful family life," "superior to their neighbors." Some of the arguments were outright racism: Armenians were Aryans, Turks Turanians. Armenians were of the "white race," Turks were of the "yellow race," and these differences "provoke riot and war."[158] Newspapers made both moral and biological assertions. The Armenians, in contrast to the Turks, were supposedly "not equaled in the world for purity of thought and sincere Christianity."[159] Against common sense and demographic evidence, the Turkish population was said to be diminishing, "sapped by polygamy." The Armenians were supposedly increasing faster than the Turks because of their moral superiority.[160]

Most of the allegations made about conditions in the Ottoman countryside cannot be judged, because only the protagonists—Armenian farmers, Armenian revolutionaries, Muslim farmers, Kurdish tribes, and soldiers—were there, and they told very different stories. Some of the stories about cities, however, can be scrutinized. Many of these were fanciful, such as the assertion that Armenians in the cities of Eastern Anatolia were taken nightly to "the Government Mansion," where they were tortured.[161] If such things happened, the European consuls in the cities would surely have noticed, and they did not mention them in their reports.

It was an age of what later would be called yellow journalism. The Turks bore the full brunt of the emotional attack. Stories of gruesome tortures were a staple of newspapers, which reported that Armenians had been boiled alive and crucified, burned alive, forced to eat the flesh of their relatives, slowly suffocated, put on the rack (as in medieval dungeons), burned with hot rods, bound to stakes and had their limbs cut off, or had their eyes gouged out and their hairs plucked out one at a time. The Turks allegedly impaled babies on bayonets or beheaded them, ripped fetuses from their mothers' wombs, hung wounded men from trees to be eaten by birds, threw children thrown into boiling oil, buried men up to their necks in earth or snow to be eaten by wild animals, and cut off ears to take the earrings and sell them, ears attached.[162]

One English commentator, reprinted in America, wrote of "roasting alive, flaying, disemboweling, impaling, and all that elaborate and ingenious aggravation of savage pain on which the souls of these human fiends seem to feast and flourish." He added a religious motive, stating that "the murdered of Sassoon, of Van, of Erzeroum were also Christian martyrs; and any and all of those whose eyes were lately gouged out, whose limbs were wrenched asunder, and whose quivering flesh was torn from their bodies might have obtained life and comparative prosperity by merely pronouncing the formula of Islam and abjuring Christ."[163] The author went on to describe various tortures in even more bloody detail. Calls for European intervention drew on the emotions. The level of appeal can best be understood from a short article in the *New York Times:* "The following telegram from Constantinople, dated December 9, and signed by a number of Armenians in that city, has reached London: 'Armenia is in her last gasp. The work of extermination continues. The massacred people number 100,000. Half a million survivors have taken refuge in the forests and mountains, where they are feeding upon herbs and roots. Hunger and cold have begun to ravage greatly. In the name of humanity and Christianity, save us.'"[164]

Sexual violence was a constant theme. Most of the articles that described Armenian suffering stressed "outraged" and "dishonored" women, depicting "young maidens carried into the pasha's harem."[165] A Dallas paper described naked women attacked in public baths.[166] One article even alleged that nearly all of the Christian women in Eastern Anatolia had been raped, which was a physical impossibility.[167] The sultan was supposedly expecting a delivery of "four of the fairest maidens of Sassoun."[168]

The newspapers faced one difficulty that existed from the Greek rebellion to World War I and the Turkish War of Independence. They wished to show that the victims of "Turkish barbarism" were completely innocent, yet they also reveled in the military successes of the enemies of the Turks. This led to contradictions, often in the same issue of a newspaper. Articles frequently alleged that the Armenians were unarmed. The newspapers that printed the claim, however, could not completely ignore the Armenians in various places who were battling Ottoman troops and in some places succeeding—battles that the newspapers called self-defense. They seemed to have no problem in reconciling the claim that Armenians were unarmed with the claim that Armenians did battle. Some newspapers, however, so wanted the Armenians to triumph that they greatly inflated Armenian strength, even to the point of claiming that Armenians would soon be bringing their war to Istanbul itself.[169]

REPORTING THE FACTS

Although this chapter cites many factual errors in American reporting, it would be impossible to include even a small sample of the thousands of examples of false reporting. In general, the largest journalistic crime was one of omission: the press reported only Armenian deaths, almost no Turkish deaths. The troubles in Zeytun are an example of this.

The quality of evidence was the same as elsewhere. For example, "a letter written by a priest who represents the [Zeytun] community" stated: "Thousands of men, women, and children from the Geoksoon and Alabash villages have poured into Zeitoun." "It is reported here in Hadjin that an imperial irade has been issued to the effect that Zeitoun must be annihilated."[170] The press so wished the Armenian rebels to triumph that it fantasized victories. For example: "A battalion of regular troops has surrendered to Armenians at Chikour Hissar, near Zeitoun," an event that never happened.[171]

The standard and much-repeated report on losses at Zeytun stated that 2,500 Armenians were killed and only 250 Turks.[172] It would be military madness for those in a defensive position to lose ten times as many as the attackers; but it is even more egregiously false because everyone, even the Armenians, admitted to much greater Turkish losses. More than 400 soldiers were slaughtered in the Zeytun barracks alone. The newspapers knew of this murder and approved of it. The *Chicago Tribune* and other papers quoted a *London Daily News* story justifying attacks on the Turkish soldiers, because "they were preparing to do mischief." The article stated that the Turks had been killed by the Armenian women of Zeytun and praised the women for their "bravery."[173] The event it was describing was the cold-blooded murder of soldiers who had surrendered.

The Ottoman government actually published an account of the Zeytun rebellion, which appears to be largely accurate. The Ottoman Embassy distributed it to American newspapers, but they seldom printed it. Even when papers cited part of the Ottoman report, its force was minimal. The *New York Times* gave it fourteen lines on page 5 one day and twenty lines on page 5 another day.[174] This contrasts to the hundreds of lines of print given on an almost daily basis to the other side, but it was still considerably more than other newspapers did: most of them did not mention the Turkish report at all. The article on the Ottoman report in the *Newark [N.J.] Daily Advocate* offers an excellent illustration of the impossibility of a neutral hearing for the Turks. It began with a letter from an Armenian accusing the Turks of all sorts of crimes and ended with a letter to "the Christians of America" from the wife of an Armenian Protestant pastor, also describing Turkish evils. Sandwiched in between was a small selection from the Turkish report. The headline read: "Huge Fish Story: That's about the Size of the Turkish Report Sent Out: Gross Insult to Intelligence."[175]

Reporting on the province of Van provides another good example of the reliability of American newspaper stories.[176] The *New York Times* began its reporting on Van by alleging, as it often did, that missionaries were in danger.[177] This was printed many months before any trouble began in Van City, where the missionaries resided. Throughout all the turmoil in Van the missionaries were never in any danger. In contradiction to the public missionary reports, the Van missionaries reported privately to the American Board (but never publicly) that they had been well protected by government officials and soldiers. They particularly praised the governor, Bahri Paşa, whom the *Times* had blamed for troubles in Van.[178] None of their honest reports reached the American press. Before any troubles started, the *Chicago Tribune* had written that massacres were expected in Van City, along with incredible statements of what was occurring in Van Province: the Turks were training cannons on Armenian quarters, cutting down trees to allow free fire for the cannons, and so forth.[179] Consular reports do not mention this, and Van's few trees would never have been a problem for cannons. On November 29, 1895, the *Dallas News* reported that 1,000 Armenians had been killed at Maraş and "a similar story from the Van Colony."[180] The use of the word "colony" and the gross exaggeration of mortality in Maraş are instructive in themselves, but it is even more noteworthy that the disturbances in Van began in June 1896, six months later than the *Dallas News* alleged they had begun.[181]

The American newspapers created an entirely fabricated set of atrocities in Van. Many newspapers printed in whole or excerpted form an Associated Press report that "40 villages of Armenians in vicinity of Van destroyed and every male over eight years has been killed, 12,800 killed in all." It quoted an unnamed missionary who stated that Kurds were wandering the streets of Van City, carrying out burnings by order of the government and attacking Armenians: "'I fear most of the villages will be utterly destroyed.' A few days later the writer's fears were realized."[182] According to both Ottoman records and British diplomatic reports, none of this happened.[183] Newspapers also printed entirely fanciful tales from Van of forced conversions to Islam, women being forced into the governor's harem, and so forth—once again, events not found in the diplomatic literature.[184] The reports had been forwarded by Armenian organizations and the missionary boards.

The *New York Times* quoted the "Constantinople correspondent of *The [London] Chronicle*," who reported rioting at Van in which 1,500 Armenians and 200 Turks were killed and said that "the Kurds are gathering from all directions to pillage Van."[185] It was indeed true that Kurdish tribes did ride to Van City to oppose the Armenian rebels. The *Times*, however, neglected to note that the military commander in Van, Sadettin Paşa, had told the Kurds that the authorities had the matter in hand and sent them all home. "Reliable advices" stated that 10,000 Armenians in the Province of Van had been forcibly converted to Islam.[186] Not to be outdone, the *London Daily News* (quoted in the American press) reported that no Armenians were left in Van; all had been killed or fled.[187] The Ottoman commander, however, reported that 340 Muslims and 219 Armenians were killed in the brief rebellion in the city. The British consul estimated 300 Muslim and 200 Armenian deaths.[188] The *New York Times* printed news from St. Petersburg, supposedly drawn from statements by Armenian refugees from Van at Echmiadzin: "The Kurds butchered the men in cold blood, kidnapped the prettiest women, buried children alive, outraged the priests, and desecrated the churches. The work of the murderers was thoroughly done, and there now remain no Armenian peasants in the vicinity of Van." In reality, nearly 40,000 Armenians lived in the Van district (*kaza*) in 1912. The *Times* wrote that the Kurds did it all "at the will of the sultan."[189] "Advices received from Van" reported that "the massacre is ascribed to agents of the Porte, who were paid to provoke a demonstration on the part of the Armenians which might serve as a pretext for a general slaughter of Christians."[190]

On August 22, 1897, long after the revolt in Van, the *New York Times* did print two short paragraphs on page 5 declaring that the Dashnaks admitted that they had been behind the events there. This was its only admission that the Van troubles had been an insurrection and not a planned massacre of Armenians.[191]

SASUN

The events at Sasun, which began the campaign against the Turks, also were the focus of its worst attacks. A detailed examination of the coverage of events in Sasun illustrates the force of the campaign against the Turks as a whole.

Most of the newspapers were content to allege that Turks had massacred Armenians at Sasun. They gave no information on the cause, simply portraying the deaths as wholly the result of Turkish blood lust: "It was an absolutely unprovoked massacre, and has all the appearance of having been deliberately planned in order to exterminate the Christian population."[192] Many of the few papers that did cite a cause offered the standard story given out by the American Board: the affray had begun when Armenians defended themselves or tried to take back their flocks from Kurds who had stolen them.[193] Turkish troops were supposedly sent to take the side of the Kurds.[194]

Others stated that the Armenians refused to pay taxes because the Kurds had robbed them of what they needed to pay. The Turkish troops that were sent were beaten back by the Armenians. The governor of Bitlis then sent a large contingent. Supposedly the Sasun Armenians surrendered after they had been promised that no harm would come to them. Once they had given up their weapons, they were slaughtered.[195] The only opinion that the stories entertained was that the Turks were guilty of a horrible planned massacre. The *New York Times* editorialized that "in not one single instance" were the disturbances in Sasun and elsewhere caused by Armenian actions. The Hunchaks, the *Times* wrote, were organized in Athens, Marseilles, and London but not in Turkey. Instead, "the Turkish Government either directed the murder of its own subjects, or stood by and lifted not a finger to protect them."[196]

The reports of the Armenian losses at Sasun varied, but all were vast overestimates. The *Washington Post* reported 27 villages destroyed and 6,000 massacred,[197] but another article on the same page claimed that 10,000 had been massacred.[198] The *Congregationalist* reported that 12,000 people had been massacred,[199] while other papers gave the number 16,000.[200] Some articles even included very precise details: the Reverend Dr. Newman Smith of the Central Church in New Haven, Connecticut, stated that he had received letters that allowed him to provide "carefully prepared statistics" and cited very specific numbers: "burned to death 1436, preachers and priests killed 51, women and girls abducted 5546."[201]

The stories supposedly coming out of Sasun, usually attested by letters from unknown writers, were often extremely improbable. One author added a unique twist. According to the *Outlook,* the Turks did not want to kill all the Armenians, in order to leave some to pay taxes. So the Turks only allowed killing from 10 to 4 o'clock in the afternoon, after which it was forbidden.[202] The Associated Press alleged that "enormous quantities of petroleum were shipped from Erzurum to Moush [the largest city close to Sasun]." The petroleum supposedly came from Russia through Erzurum. The government allegedly planned to use it to burn Armenian bodies in Sasun and did so. The AP contended that this proved that the Sasun events were premeditated.[203] None of the diplomats who investigated Sasun mentioned the unlikely event of large numbers of camels and donkeys, loaded down with petroleum, passing to Muş in caravans, which was the only way to transport goods there.

All of the usual types of stories appeared, and many of the horror stories mentioned above referred to Sasun. The stories were full of eye-gouging, burning alive, torturing priests, flinging bodies into pits, cutting out tongues, cutting off fingers and hands, impaling babies or bashing their heads against walls, forcing victims to dig pits before they were killed and thrown into them, crucifixions, and other alleged atrocities. Articles asserted that 400 women were repeatedly raped then hacked to pieces.[204] One report spoke of all the women in villages being raped, tortured, then killed. It contended that "there was hardly a man alive."[205]

The sources were obviously Armenians or missionaries. Most articles did not mention their sources, but many of those that did stated that they had learned of the events in Sasun from Armenians sometimes avowed refugees from Sasun, usually Armenians who said they had heard the accounts from others.[206] Although missionary sources were seldom identified as such,[207] it is obvious that the stories came from missionaries. The information was described as emanating "from the highest authorities in such matters—not from Armenians" and came to Boston (the American Board headquarters) from Bitlis (a mission station), a place from which only a missionary or an Armenian would be writing to someone in Massachusetts.[208] Allegedly personal stories from Sasun refugees relayed to Americans also seemed to arrive primarily in Boston and were probably transmitted to the media by the missionary establishment.[209]

Bolstering its own case that the Turks should be punished, the *Chicago Tribune* printed a list of the comments of various newspapers' opinions on the Sasun events that conveniently summarized newspaper assertions:

Armenian Horrors

Pittsburgh Dispatch: It would be a blot upon civilization to allow such atrocities to go unpunished.

New York Tribune: One of the most appalling chapters of inhuman massacre and Pasha despotism has been added to the revolting history of Turkish rule in the East.

New York Herald: There seems to be every evidence that such atrocities will occur until the Armenian population throughout Asia Minor is exterminated, according to the desires of the authorities at Constantinople.

Philadelphia Press: The unspeakable Turk has, it seems, been committing unspeakable outrages on the Christians in Armenia. What the Turk needs is a thrashing of unspeakable severity, and he needs it very badly.

Troy Times: The Porte tries to avoid responsibility for the massacre, charging the slaughter to Kurdish brigands. By whomsoever committed, the atrocities form a blot upon the Turkish Government which years cannot efface. In cruelty and brutishness the massacre rarely has been equaled.

New York World: Civilized powers cannot and should not maintain friendly relations with a power whose methods of repression, according to its own showing, are the murder of men, the violation of women and the slaughter of innocent children. This fact should be forcibly and promptly made known at Constantinople.

New York Recorder: The world had hoped that atrocities of this character under the rule of Turkey had come to an end, that the volume of brutality had been closed with the crimson record in Bulgaria, but if the Armenian dispatches are correct the Moslem monster is as insatiable as ever. The Turk cannot outrage humanity in this way and remain in Europe. He is in the wrong century for this kind of business.

Philadelphia Record: The time has come when the existing administration of Armenian affairs should be abolished and replaced by a government more consistent with the civilization of the nineteenth century. The powers have a duty to perform in this matter, even if it be inexpedient to insist upon the creation of an independent Armenian kingdom. A repetition of the awful massacres of the subject races in Turkey should be made absolutely impossible.

New York Press: The blood of the innocent mothers and babies, put to death by the half savage troops of the Sultan, cries for vengeance upon the murderers, and every country worthy of being called Christian and civilized should join in demanding justice. The unspeakable Turk should go from Armenia as the unspeakable Chinese have gone from Corea, and the country which deprives the Turk of his Christian prey will be doing a signal service to humanity.

New York Advertiser: That Great Britain, which claims to be the supreme Christian nation of the earth, will attempt to defend and shield the Turk for purely political purposes is beyond doubt. For such purposes the Turk and others of his kind have been allowed not only to oppress Christians, but to nourish the seeds of cholera to be scattered over the civilized world at the cost of millions of valuable lives. Every effort of other people to enforce a protective system has been defeated by Great Britain. The appalling record of Turkish barbarity has now this added atrocity of the outrage of Christian women, the pillage of Christian communities, and the ruthless slaughter of 6,000 human beings. It is time for civilization to arise and crush the Turk—to bring him to rational conditions of living for the just protection of those unhappy peoples whom he has been allowed to oppress.

The *Tribune* itself added: "The unspeakable Turk has been at his horrible work again." It declared that the Kurds had been given orders "to cut the Armenians up, root and branch." Its source seems to have been primarily the Armenian Patriotic Association in London, which was quoted as alleging that 6,000 to 10,000 Armenians had been killed. The article did not mention the Armenian revolt.[210]

The Europeans who actually investigated the events in Sasun, the Sasun Commission of Investigation, demonstrated that all of this was false.

THE COMMISSION OF INVESTIGATION

The Sasun rebellion was the only incident in the 1890s Armenian Troubles that was actually thoroughly investigated by an Ottoman commission to which European consular delegates were attached. The European delegates prepared their own report.[211] No one could accuse the European delegates to the commission of pro-Turkish sympathies. The transcripts of the commission meetings show that the standard of evidence for Armenian witnesses was much more lax than the standard for Muslims. Nevertheless, the European commissioners were forced to admit that the real story of Sasun was not the story that had been accepted. They put the lie to the atrocity tales (priests were not spitted on bayonets, and so forth). The commissioners concluded that the Troubles had begun when the Hunchak revolutionaries led an attack on Kurds, not the fanciful tales of attacks on innocent Armenians that were to be found in the newspapers. The Kurds were not exonerated, but their actions were seen to be retaliation for Armenian actions. Of greatest importance, the European commissioners found that 265 Armenians had been killed and 500 had died from all causes, including starvation and disease.[212] The commissioners did not like the Turks very much, and especially did not like the Kurds, but they were honest men who reported what they saw. In keeping with European prejudices, however, they gave detailed accounts and statistics of Armenian dead, not Muslim dead.

Only occasionally was the commission's report quoted accurately in the press. The few accounts that did mention the actual Armenian death toll were duplicitous or contradictory. For example, the *Dallas News* reported that the commission stated that all the Armenians that fell into the hands of the soldiers or the Kurds were either killed or wounded then wrote that the Armenian death toll was only 265, a major contradiction. It never mentioned Muslim deaths, of course.[213] Newspaper articles did not report the commission's findings that the Armenians under their revolutionary leader Murad had first attacked Kurds, who then retaliated.[214] Instead they reported at length on some of the letters printed in the *Parliamentary Blue Books* that took missionary accounts as their basis for stating that great massacres had occurred, a minority view that the European commissioners had stated was not their conclusion.[215] The papers left the impression that a wholesale massacre had indeed taken place, which completely contradicted the European commissioners' report.

While the commission was meeting, newspapers printed stories of the testimony of Armenian witnesses before the commission, never Muslim witnesses (usually drawn from the London Liberal press). One article remarked that the evidence given "fully corroborates the worst details already published."[216] Another article spoke (without specifics) of overwhelming evidence against the Turks that was presented to the commission and offered its readers tales of torture.[217] Some newspapers stated that the commission's findings would fully support a set of dubious horror stories, which they proceeded to relate. The stories were nowhere to be found in the commissioners' report.[218] The commission actually specifically denied that these tales were true. A *Pall Mall Gazette* correspondent interviewed European members of the Commission of Inquiry and reported that the stories of mutilations, torture, and massacre were completely false, that Armenians had been well armed, and that statements of Armenian mortality were greatly exaggerated.[219]

The *New York Times* printed a report from an "unnamed correspondent in Constantinople" who supposedly had access to consular reports and to the commission's deliberations. The article stated that unnamed Turkish soldiers had admitted the massacres and believed the order had come from the government, which was not in fact in the consular or commission reports. It was all fabricated.[220] The

Times and other papers printed a number of supposed "leaks" from the meetings of the commission that in reality do not appear in the record of the commission.[221] A *Chicago Tribune* report on commission deliberations stated that 9,300 Armenians were dead,[222] nearly twenty times the mortality actually estimated by the commission. A modern reader might think that these errors would be acknowledged once the true commission report was published, but that was not the way of nineteenth-century editors. No retractions appeared.[223]

THE SULTAN, IMAGE OF EVIL

As far back as the Greek rebellion of the 1820s, Americans and Europeans blamed all troubles on the Ottoman central government and its leader, the sultan. To a large extent this was a result of the failure to understand the security problems of the Ottoman Empire. If the Ottoman state had been well organized under centralized control, then indeed it would have been difficult to see how outbreaks in many provinces could have continued without central government connivance. Americans did not understand that such centralized control did not exist in the Ottoman dominions. Beset by the loss of productive regions, the need to keep large forces on its borders, European economic imperialism, and the economic ineptitude that was the condition of all developing countries, the empire simply did not have the wherewithal to exert police power effectively in all the provinces, particularly in the poor provinces of the Ottoman East. The government never had enough soldiers and gendarmes. Those who were stationed in the East were frequently not paid for months at a time. In the 1890s Sultan Abdülhamit II—no fool—knew that the Armenian Troubles could easily lead to European intervention and dismemberment of his empire, as planned by the rebels. This did not mean that he had adequate means to quash Armenian rebellion and subsequent Muslim attacks on Armenians. American newspapers, magazines, and books did not explain any of this to their readers. If the Kurds caused trouble, it was supposedly because the sultan wanted them to do so. If the empire was weak, it was because the sultan and his officials were corrupt or incompetent. If Christians were suffering, it was because the sultan had ordered it. As far as missionaries and the American press were concerned, no mitigating circumstances existed.

Completely unproven accusations that Abdülhamit ("a ferocious Mussulman barbarian, red-handed from Christian slaughter") had ordered the murders of Armenians were a staple of reports to Americans,[224] beginning with the first American Board press releases. No actual evidence of this was ever presented. Writers simply stated that the sultan had ordered massacres. The claims derived almost exclusively from letters received in America from unnamed sources. Some of the few identified sources were missionaries, some Armenians. Some of the unnamed sources are recognizable as Armenians by their use of Armenian names for cities, not the Turkish names used by press correspondents. While the authors of "reports received from the interior of Asia minor" describing forced conversions and massacres were never identified, these stories were surely sent by Armenians or missionaries.[225] Reports of the sultan's supposed extermination plans from regular news sources often used phrases such as "it is alleged" or "rumors state," which seem to have been code for Armenian assertions. A headline in the *Atlanta Constitution* stated: "Massacres Go On: No Question That the Slaughter Is by the Sultan's Order."[226] The accompanying article cited rumors in Istanbul as the source of this belief.

Although usually content to offer only assertions of government guilt, newspapers sometimes gave details and specifics (although they were often contradictory) on how the government had supposedly ordered the murders. The *Chicago Tribune* transformed the sultan's actual order to attack the rebels who had captured and killed Turkish soldiers at Zeytun into an order to kill all the Zeytun Armenians.[227] It falsely claimed that the sultan had given a formal imperial order (*ferman*) to destroy the Sasun Armenians.[228] As was so often the case, spurious quotations from Turkish officials were cited as proof. The grand vezir had supposedly declared: "To get rid of the Armenian Question is to get rid of the Armenian people," and other officials had agreed.[229] Papers alleged that the Sasun "extermination" had long been planned by the Turks, who had prepared military forces and weapons for the attack.[230] Abdülhamit supposedly would not rest until he had either converted all the Armenians into Muslims or killed them. Writings in the Christian press emphasized this, with stories of forced conversions and martyrdom for the Christian faith.[231]

Most newspapers did not bother with even spurious "facts." For example, the *New York Times* editorialized in January 1896 that the sultan wished to kill all the Armenians but that it was too daunting a task to kill them all: "To kill two millions of people in cold blood would tax even Turkish and Kurdish arms." Instead he had set upon a plan to kill the "breadwinners" and let the others starve to death.[232] By November 1896 the *Times* editor declared that the sultan was planning to kill all the Christians in the empire, not only the Armenians.[233]

The supposed evil of the sultan was presented graphically. The *New York World* printed a full-page cartoon on the front page, titled "A Standing Disgrace to the Civilized World."[234] The cartoon showed a Turkish soldier (in a costume hundreds of years out of date) dragging two screaming women before Sultan Abdülhamit II. The sultan, who is seated, is laughing. Next to him are a copy of the Quran, a sword, and a bucket with two champagne bottles. In the corner rests a pile of severed heads. The caption read: "Isn't it about time to put an end to these shocking atrocities of the barbarian sultan of Turkey?" In the absence of other material on the Ottoman Empire or its sultan, readers might think that this sort of thing was a real depiction of the sultan's pleasures. The *San Francisco Chronicle* featured a cartoon of the sultan holding a severed woman's head labeled "Armenia" in one hand, a sword in the other.[235] The *Chicago Tribune* declared that the sultan was personally responsible for massacres of Armenians, orchestrating them from the palace.[236] The article was accompanied by a cartoon showing Abdülhamit II seated on a throne topped by a skull and crossbones at a telegraph key, personally telegraphing orders for atrocities. The skull wore a fez.

The sultan's character and abilities were held to be none too good. The papers variously described him as insane, cowardly, hated by his people and his own government, and so forth. "The sultan is said to be alarmed to the verge of insanity."[237] He supposedly had been poisoned.[238] He was so afraid of his own people that he had asked the English to protect him from them.[239] A yacht was waiting near the palace to spirit the "helpless and hopeless" sultan away.[240] He was quaking in fear.[241] Abdülhamit, who was actually a very abstemious man, was accused of being an "inebriate" who was drinking heavily and a "sensualist."[242] Alternatively, the sultan was depicted as a Muslim fanatic who was completely controlled by religious leaders.[243] Newspapers constantly reported that his deposition was imminent.[244] (Abdülhamit was actually deposed, but twelve years later.) An article in the *Dallas News* alleged that the sultan had killed 150 women from his predecessor's harem by drowning them in the Bosphorus—a practice that was declared to be sanctioned by Islamic Law. He had supposedly killed "thousands of conspirators."[245] None of this actually happened, but it is doubtful that American readers would have known this.

The news about the sultan's personal life was most interesting, though ridiculous. According to the *Chicago Tribune,* Abdülhamit liked to receive visitors in his bath. When he bathed he had servants bring in his collection of stuffed birds and "impaled beetles." The sultan paid little attention to the business of state, preferring to play with his pet cockatoo. When the question of attacking Armenians came up he simply gave all authority to local commanders, not bothering with details. He loved to watch fires in the city from his palace roof. Before he ate or drank anything it was first sampled by his foster mother, who acted as his poison tester.[246] How could any reader believe such drivel? Nonetheless, an editor had thought enough of the story to print it. The reading public, schooled on generations of exotic and ridiculous tales of the "Orient," probably believed it all.

Worse than the allegations of what the sultan had done were the predictions of what he would do in the future. A cable from "an American resident in Constantinople" was sent to Boston and distributed to the press, almost surely by the American Board. The author declared that the European powers would soon dethrone the sultan, who planned "a general massacre so that he may go out in a cloud of strife and glory."[247] The *Chicago Tribune* printed a similar analysis of what Abdülhamit would do if the Europeans intervened: "The sultan vows that no Christian shall live in his empire if an English or any other fleet of warships attempts to force its way through the Dardanelles." This intelligence was based on a telegram from Berlin (author unstated) that quoted a Berlin newspaper that in turn quoted a telegram from an unknown source in Istanbul.[248]

The sultan garnered no praise for allowing missionaries and the Red Cross to minister to the Armenians. Some journals marveled at what they viewed as his inexplicable agreement to allow relief. Others stated that fear of angering America forced his hand.[249] None considered the possibility that Abdülhamit might have welcomed relief for his subjects.[250]

MISSIONARIES IN DANGER

In their books and in the reports they gave to the press, members of the missionary establishment appealed to American nationalistic feeling. In their writings, the missionaries were not only the representatives of God in the Ottoman Empire. They were the representatives of America. They were advancing American culture among the Armenians. And there was a certain amount of truth to this.

When problems arose, the missionaries appealed to American compassion not only for Armenians but for their fellow Americans in Turkey. In fact, missionaries were remarkably safe under Turkish rule. This is in many ways surprising, because missionaries were identified with the Armenians at a time when Turks and Armenians were doing battle in the 1890s, yet no missionaries were killed; all were safe or, if endangered by conflict in their regions, were protected by Ottoman soldiers. The missionary writings give no hint of this. "Peril" was the word they used most often to describe the state of the American missionaries. If they mentioned that no missionaries had been killed or even injured by Turks, this was ascribed to Turkish fear of reprisals: "Just as soon, however, as the Sultan is convinced that it would be *safe* to have them massacred under the cloak of 'a fanatical mob' that event is likely to occur."[251]

An underlying theme in American reporting was the belief that the Ottomans had designed the Armenian Troubles in order to hinder Christianization of the Ottoman Empire, "preventing the advance of Christianity."[252] The press defined this advance as the conversion of the Ottoman peoples and the spread of Christian rule, both of which were considered to be wholly desirable. Serbs, Bulgarians, Armenians, and Russians were all portrayed as doing God's work.[253] The papers did not consider the moral implications of slaughtering Muslims in the "advance of Christianity" or describe the slaughters themselves. The Turks allegedly massacred Christians as a reaction to the advance of Christianity: "The Turks were irritated by the advance of Christian civilization, and have frequently showed their hostility by the perpetration of atrocities such as barbarous people are apt to indulge in."[254]

Americans were told that a main aim of the Muslims of the East was to oust American missionaries. Writers even alleged that Armenians were being killed as a way to get rid of Americans. Newspapers asserted that Muslims threatened to murder all the Armenians unless the missionaries abandoned their posts.[255] They reported that the Ottomans had decided to expel all the American missionaries; some wrote that the order had already been given to do so.[256] Of course, this was all nonsense. The missionaries, in fact, were not as important in the scheme of things as Americans thought they were. In intercommunal warfare between Muslims and Armenians, few would have given much thought to a handful of Americans.

The position and importance of the American missionaries was built up to a fantastic extent.[257] The Associated Press, for example, stated that the Kurds were "only held in check by the missionaries." On the whole, however, the newspapers were concerned that missionaries were the planned victims of the Turks and

Kurds. The fate of American missionaries was at the forefront of American consideration of the 1890s Troubles. Newspapers and magazines painted a picture of imminent disaster for the missionaries.[258] The *Philadelphia Public Ledger* of 1895–96 contained numerous articles on the supposed dangers to missionaries. Magazines such as the pacifist journal *Advocate of Peace* portrayed the missionaries as "in great peril and fear."[259] The *New York Times* wrote in an editorial that the Ottoman government had ordered attacks on missionaries and their property in Harput (and property was indeed destroyed there).[260] Spurred by the press and the missionary establishment, the U.S. Senate passed a resolution calling for the protection of "imperiled" American missionaries.[261]

Articles often reported that missionaries were in danger because massacres of Armenians and missionaries were feared or expected: "a fanatical Muslim outbreak is imminent."[262] They did not mention how the unidentified authors knew that outbreaks would soon occur. A long article in the *New York Times* (taken from the *Independent*) listed all the American missionaries in Ottoman Asia and their stations.[263] The subheadline, "A List of the Stations and Those at Each—Some Not in Danger," could only give the impression that most were indeed in danger. The article was heavy on impending doom and expected attacks and even forced starvation.[264] The same lists were published in other newspapers. The *Philadelphia Public Ledger* had the headline "Missionaries in Peril,"[265] while the *San Francisco Chronicle* warned about "Missionaries in Danger."[266] The *Atlanta Constitution* was more dramatic: "Muslims Are Kept Busy Sharpening Their Hatchets—Missionaries Excellent Victims."[267] Careful reading of the list, however, shows that the missionaries had not actually been attacked. None had been killed or injured. Dangers to missionaries were always "imminent" or "expected" but never took place. The only report of a missionary actually suffering came from Harput: "The latest telegrams announce that they [the missionaries] are all well, and that one of their number, Mrs. Gates, is convalescing, intimating that her condition had been very serious." Although it is not mentioned in the article, she was convalescing from an operation, not from an attack by the Muslims.[268] Other articles spoke of an assault on the Reverend Dr. Thomas Christie of Tarsus, without details. It was not the missionary who really had been assaulted, however, but his "native servant," never identified, who may even have been a Muslim. The perpetrators had been arrested and sentenced.[269]

The danger was seldom real;[270] but missionaries, like the rest of the population, were indeed sometimes in danger from the general unrest. The Ottoman government took preventative measures to protect them. Fearing trouble in Bitlis, the government sent Bitlis missionaries to Van under heavy military protection.[271] The missionaries from Bitlis and the newspapers gave all the credit to the American ambassador, Alexander W. Terrell. Such action by American authorities, not the goodwill of the sultan, was always cited as the force behind the safety of missionaries. When it became evident that the missionaries would not be molested or killed, the explanation was that the sultan feared America, although what America could have done to the Ottoman Empire was never stated.[272] One paper reported that American missionaries were saved by the presence of the American warships *San Francisco* and *Marblehead,* which had been sent to the İskenderun region in answer to missionary pleas. The Turks reportedly feared United States military action and so left the missionaries alone.[273]

It should be added that not everyone believed that Ambassador Terrell had done all he could to help the missionaries. Some missionaries complained that he had not taken prompt enough action or sufficiently threatened the Turks, although it is difficult to see how he could have done more.[274] The ambassador had correctly stated that the American missionaries in Merzifon were in more danger from the Armenian revolutionaries than from the Turks and that the Ottoman government was protecting the missionaries. This was not what the missionary establishment in America wanted to hear.[275] In particular, the missionaries and their supporters complained that Terrell had (correctly) stated that demonstrations and subsequent riots in Istanbul were started by Armenian revolutionaries. The missionaries were completely wrong in denying that the revolutionaries were responsible; indeed they stated that no revolutionary organization existed in Istanbul.[276] The Reverend J. T. Johnson of Jefferson City, Missouri, preached a sermon in which he stated that Terrell should be hanged because he had become a Muslim and was aiding in the persecution of the Armenians.[277] Johnson's church sent a memorial on the subject to the State Department, but it does not seem to have taken any action. Missionaries lodged a formal complaint against Terrell, alleging, among other crimes, that he was "a man of low habits," a classic example of what would later be called a smear campaign. The State Department investigated and completely exonerated the ambassador.[278] Terrell tried to be objective in his most difficult position, calling for critics to wait for the result of the Sasun Investigation Commission to be heard before rushing to judgment. The opprobrium he received was a lesson to anyone who opposed the standard view of the Armenian Troubles. The published Sasun Commission report confirmed that he had been correct. None of the newspapers that had so criticized him mentioned this.

The papers gave the Turks no credit for their tolerance toward the missionaries. No writer wondered how the Turks, who were portrayed as evil fiends who opposed all things Christian, could allow the Christian message to be spread so freely. John Mott, the head of the Student Volunteer Movement for Foreign Missions and the World's Student Christian Federation and later world leader of the YMCA, had no hesitation in condemning the Ottomans in 1895: "There can be no real peace for the Christian people scattered throughout Asia Minor and along the beautiful Bosporus until this barbarous Ottoman Government is swept from the face of the earth."[279] In 1911 this same Reverend Mott was in attendance at the Conference of the World's Student Christian Federation, held with the approbation of the Ottoman government, in Istanbul. While there he entertained the Ottoman grand vezir for two hours at dinner with news of his Christian Federation.[280] Did he share his opinion of the Ottoman Empire with the grand vezir?

One of the most incredible facets of the missionary propaganda of the time is that even the Turks' acceptance of American relief efforts was turned against them. The situation is fairly easy to understand, at least when viewed from afar. After the troubles of 1895–96, thousands of Turks, Kurds, and Armenians in Eastern Anatolia were poorly clothed, without homes, and close to starvation, a result of the recent conflict. As even the missionaries admitted, the Ottoman government did what it could, distributing bread to Christians and Muslims alike. American and British missionary relief organizations approached the Ottoman government and said that they planned to bring relief to the Armenians only; yet the Ottomans allowed them to do so. Local Muslim officials, not to mention the Muslim hungry, must have felt bitter at seeing the food distributed only to the Christians, but the relief was allowed to go on until it was stopped not by the Ottomans but by lack of funds collected in the United States.

Instead of praise, the Turks received vilification. For example, Henry Davenport Northrop gave an account of the relief efforts of the missionary Grace Kimball, who distributed relief food in Van, in *The Mohammedan Reign of Terror in Armenia:*

> This brave woman, despite official threats and warnings, went out among the fugitives in the streets, comforted and encouraged them, gave them bread with her own hands, while they were pulling at her garments and kissing her hands and feet in gratitude. She ministered to the sick, and, cheered by her example, her missionary associates took heart of Grace and joined in the work.
>
> Again and again the Turkish Pashas and Valis [governors] insisted that the relief be stopped; the Armenians were "dogs"; "better let them die"; but the greater the opposition the higher rose the courage of the American girl.[281]

To a modern reader this stretches credulity. The government and local Turks supposedly stood in the way of one woman but could not stop her. These were the same Turks who were alleged to have ruthlessly killed Armenians and wanted all Armenians dead, yet they somehow could not stop the distribution of relief by one woman. Moreover, Kimball received funds and word of further relief to come by Ottoman government cable, forwarded and unhindered by the government that supposedly stood against her actions. This was a fine story of a noble woman (and it is true that she was dedicated and selfless), but it was nonsense. More than $1 million in relief was distributed to the Armenians of Eastern Anatolia, which could never have been done without Ottoman approval. Anyone who doubts this should consider the myriad ways in which a bureaucracy could have stopped the distribution of relief. "Sorry, the railroad track is out and the supplies cannot be sent on." "What cable of relief funds? We have received nothing." "The relief warehouse pilfered? How awful. Our authorities will look into it." Had the Turks wished to stop the relief, they could have, but they did not want to do so.

Clara Barton, the head of the American Red Cross, who herself went to investigate and oversee relief to Armenians, had nothing but praise for the aid that the Ottoman government gave to the relief effort. She cabled from Istanbul:

> Our corps of physicians and supplies left Beirut April 3 and will reach Marash the 10th. Scourge of typhoid and other diseases, from starvation and exposure, unabated. Red Cross reports just received from our expeditions, which are meeting with splendid success. No obstructions nor Turkish supervision, as has been wrongly reported. Every facility offered. Welcomed everywhere. One party working between Marash, Zeitoun, Malatya, and Harpoot. The others between Orfa, Diarbekir and Harpoot. Visiting towns and villages en route, giving assistance where most needed.[282]

Before Barton left for the Ottoman Empire the newspapers had been full of statements that the Ottoman government would not accept foreign aid for the Armenians, all of which turned out to be false.[283] Barton herself complained of the false information that circulated in the American newspapers. She marveled that the Ottomans were still willing to help her, despite the completely scurrilous reports on her mission in the American press.[284] Her statements had no effect. Even someone of her stature and respectability could not stem the flow of negative propaganda.

PUBLIC MEETINGS

In an America that had not yet seen movies or television, public meetings and oratory were established means of entertainment and education. Americans were also a churchgoing people, and sermons reached a wide audience. Meetings on the Armenian Troubles took place all across America. In large cities, meetings were held in both churches and large auditoriums. General Russell A. Alger presided over a "mass meeting" (the description used at the time) in Detroit in which he "urged that Americans should solemnly protest against the Armenian outrages, and if words were not sufficient should man their guns and go there and put a stop to it." The meeting passed a resolution reflecting his plan.[285] In Washington, D.C., Armenians addressed Presbyterian and Congregational churches with stories of "outrages."[286] "Several thousand people" met at St. Bartholomew's Episcopal Church in the Washington area to protest the "Armenian outrages."[287] Citizens of Chicago, led by the mayor, met in the Central Music Hall to condemn the Turks and call on the American government to take action.[288] The Armenian Relief Association of Philadelphia sponsored a mass meeting in which ministers, bishops, and Armenians called for the United States to take action against the Turks, declaring that this was a religious question: Islam against Christianity.[289] In New York City, both Carnegie Hall and the 1,450-seat Chickering Hall were utilized for a number of public meetings.[290] Missionaries and other ministers addressed a meeting in Faneuil Hall in Boston.[291] In Malden, Massachusetts, near Boston, a mass meeting was attended by Julia Ward Howe, William Lloyd

Garrison, the governor of Massachusetts, and a contingent of the Grand Army of the Republic.[292]

The mass meetings to advance the Armenian cause were very much the work of the missionary establishment. For example, the mass meeting of the Armenian Relief Association on April 21, 1896, had two themes: "Protect Missionaries" (listed first) and "Rescue Armenia."[293] The Episcopalian bishop of New York presided. The sponsors ("vice-presidents") were listed in the advertisement for the meeting: nineteen of the forty-two were clergymen.[294] Interestingly, the group of sponsors included editors of the *New York Times,* the *New York Post,* and the *Nation* and the managing editor of the *New York Sun,* which may reveal something of the sentiments of their newspapers. Indeed, newspapers not only reported on the mass meetings but called for them in their editorials.[295] The editors' mass meeting was one of many organized in New York by the Armenian Relief Association; the organizers and speakers were mainly clergymen or Armenians. The meetings stressed the supposed danger to missionaries.[296] These meetings were well reported in the press, taking up many columns of the news pages.

In addition to allegations of Turkish brutality, the meetings brought forth some fascinating, though false, information: "The Rev. Dr. Satterlee, rector of Calvary Church [New York], opened the meeting. He said: 'In 1840 the Mohammedans conquered Armenia, and since that time have tyrannized over the Armenians, chiefly on account of their difference in religion. The Armenian Church resembles very much the English Church, and its Patriarchs are recognized by every ruler except the Sultan of Turkey.'"[297] All this would surely have appealed to the audience, but none of it was true. Armenia had been conquered many centuries before 1840; the Ottomans recognized the patriarchs and indeed included them as community heads in the Ottoman government; the Armenians and their church were still there 800 years after the Turks began their supposed "tyranny." As for the similarities between the English and Armenian churches, anyone who attended services in both could decide.

At a public meeting held in New York on December 31, 1894, the Reverend Chauncey Depew put his feelings in words that Americans could understand: "The Turkish power is different from other powers. It is a hierarchy which endeavors to stamp out other religions than its own....Armenia is the New England of the East in thrift and industry. But to realize its jeopardy imagine our New England hemmed in by savages ready to lay it waste."[298]

Similar appeals to American sensitivities were common, although most would only have been effective for audiences with no knowledge of Armenians. Depew described the Armenians as "the Yankees of the East," whose lives and beliefs were similar to those of Americans. At yet another public meeting in New York, an Armenian pastor, the Reverend George Filian, declared: "The Armenians are as highly educated as Americans. They speak English fluently."[299] The press did not record whether the audience believed this nonsense. Filian was a popular speaker, touring America with his message and speaking in churches, at YMCAs, and in public meetings.[300]

Armenian organizations in America sponsored meetings, either alone or in conjunction with non-Armenian clergy and others. One such meeting in Chicago drew two thousand people.[301] Six hundred Armenian members and supporters of the Hunchak Party, the main organization behind the 1890s rebellions, marched through the streets of New York on July 28, 1894, adjourning to a meeting at which the Reverend Filian and others addressed them.[302] The Armenian Union and Armenian Philanthropic Society held a mass meeting in New York on November 17, 1894, at which they praised Russia, condemned England, and thanked the American press.[303]

Local Armenians as well as traveling Armenian speakers were pressed into service to give talks to local churches and mass meetings. In Chicago, Mr. N. H. Kassabian, "an agent of the Armenian Society and student at Northwestern University," drew on the audience's emotions by referring to "their daughters taken by sensual Turks to their mountain hideaways for vile and diabolic purposes."[304] In Fort Wayne, Indiana, J. R. Mooshy, an Armenian studying in Indiana to become a minister, declared that it was a Muslim's duty to kill all Christians and that the sultan, as a good Muslim, was carrying out the requirements of his faith.[305] (This completely false assertion was a staple of the attacks on the Turks.) One Mr. Chakurian addressed the Brooklyn Presbyterian Church in Oakland, California, on "the worst government in the world."[306] Rebecca Krikorian, the vice-president for Turkey of the Woman's Christian Temperance Union, came to America to solicit funds for a Home for Intemperate Women in Armenia and was asked by clergymen to describe the Armenian situation in speeches in America.[307]

Meetings in smaller cities were typically held in churches, where participants heard speakers, passed resolutions, and took up collections for Armenian relief. Thousands of these church meetings were held, sometimes addressed by local ministers, sometimes by visiting ministers, Armenians, or officials of Armenian relief organizations.[308] M. S. Gabriel (president of the Armenian Patriotic Alliance), whose incredibly prejudiced opinions are described below, toured the country, speaking in venues large and small, as did the violently anti-Turkish Reverend Frederick Greene (also described below).[309]

The headline of an article on a meeting in Syracuse more than adequately describes the tenor of the gatherings: "They Want War—Clergymen at the Mass Meeting Call for the Sword—[Rev.] Dr. Calthrop Will Enlist—Says He Will Be One of a Million Men to Teach Turkey a Lesson." (Future press reports did not indicate whether the pugnacious Reverend Calthrop had "enlisted.") Speakers at the meeting called for a united English and American army to invade and destroy the Ottoman Empire and castigated British and American politicians for not having already taken action.[310] Meetings were held in venues such as the YMCA building in Worcester, Massachusetts, where missionaries and clergymen spoke.[311] Some gatherings were only of ministers, who issued religious protests.[312] At a meeting in Paterson, New Jersey, the only speakers were clergymen;[313] this was also true of a number of other meetings.[314] One or two laymen, usually prominent politicians, spoke at many meetings.[315] At a "monster mass meeting" in Newark the clergy were joined by the governor of New Jersey.[316] The governor of Pennsylvania suggested U.S. intervention in the Ottoman Empire at an "immense mass meeting" in Lancaster.[317] Commander Frederick Booth-Tucker, head of the Salvation Army, presided at a meeting in Carnegie Hall in which clergy and missionaries spoke, read a letter from Gladstone, and expressed the hope that the "constantly accumulating horrors may yet work the downfall of that crying iniquity known as the Turkish empire."[318]

In the Churches

It is certain that the churches were avenues for attacks on the Turks. Few of the sermons given in churches have been printed, although it can be assumed that the clergy who attacked the Turks in mass meetings also did so from their pulpits. The *San Francisco Chronicle* gave nine column inches on page 1 to a sermon by a minister who confidently declared that events in Anatolia proved that the end of the world was imminent, the Ottoman Empire being the evil power represented in the Book of Revelations as having "power to torment men."[319] I have found three published sermons from the New York region. The Reverend John L. Scudder, pastor of the Congregational Tabernacle in Jersey City, New Jersey, delivered a sermon titled "Extinguish the Turk," calling for the European powers and the United States to do just that, with frequent use of terms such as "butchery," "shrieks of the dying," and "terrible evil."[320] The Reverend Dr. Charles H. Eaton, in his sermon at the Church of the Divine Paternity in New York, called for the end of all Muslim rule over Christians. He stressed the danger to missionaries, fearing that they would soon be "tortured and killed."[321] The Reverend R. L. Bachman preached a sermon in Utica, New York, in which he asked God to speed the demise of the Ottoman Empire, which he confidently expected. He ventured into demography, doubling the number of Armenians, halving the number of Muslims, and declaring that 600,000 Armenians had suffered or died in the Troubles. He described the Armenians as "bright, industrious, and moral," the Turks as "furious beasts."[322]

While few sermons on the Armenians were published *in toto,* the press reported many services and lectures in churches, typically with titles such as "Special Service in Behalf of the Armenian Sufferers."[323] For example, the Reverend Dr. Charles Parkhurst of the Madison Square Presbyterian Church suggested that England and America, as fellow Christian states, should "join hands in suppressing the Turk."[324] The Reverend Dr. T. De Witt Talmage in Washington, D.C., urged the European powers "to wipe out Turkey, that foul blot on civilization." He called upon God to lead the conquest of "the Cross over the Crescent."[325] The Reverend Z. T. Sweeney preached in Oakland, California, that the sultan was bent on either turning all Ottoman Christians into Muslims or exterminating them.[326] "Instead of the regular Sunday night devotions there were spirited addresses on the recent Armenian outrages" at the Church of the Covenant in Washington.[327] The Reverend John Peters told his flock in Brooklyn that the sultan planned to wipe out all the Christians.[328] Right Rector William White Wilson preached in St. Mark's Episcopal Church in Chicago on the subject "The Persecution of Christians in

Armenia." They were suffering for their faith, he said, just as the early Christians had suffered at the hands of the Romans.[329] The Reverend Willard Robinson, also of Chicago, was more bellicose at a meeting at the Englewood Presbyterian Church. He wanted the U.S. government to "send a fleet of gunboats up the Bosphorus."[330] Not to be outdone, Dr. Myron W. Haynes of the Englewood Baptist Church also called for gunboats and added that "with the Turk a bullet will inject the world's opinion much quicker than diplomacy."[331]

The National Societies for Christian Endeavor, a widely respected and numerous evangelical group, heard of Turkish iniquity at its national convention.[332] It sponsored a mass meeting at the Mount Vernon Methodist Church;[333] clergy, missionaries, and Armenians spoke at its large tent meeting in Washington.[334]

The annual convention of the Episcopalian Church in 1895 passed anti-Turkish resolutions and appointed a committee to examine what action was to be taken on the Armenians.[335] The New York Presbyterian Synod adopted a measure calling on President Grover Cleveland to "exercise his power to prevent the killings of Armenians in Turkey." What this meant was made plain by one speaker who demanded, to great applause, that the U.S. Navy go to Istanbul to enforce the synod's wishes.[336] The American Board, of course, held meetings and passed resolutions against the Turks.[337] The Presbyterian General Assembly, meeting in Saratoga, New York, in May 1896, considered a resolution calling for "a speedy extinction of the Islam empire." But objections were raised, saying that missionaries might suffer if the resolution passed. It was finally passed with the words "Turkish government" substituted for "Islam empire," which presumably would cause less offense.[338] The National Conference of Unitarians, meeting in Washington, D.C., passed a motion condemning the Turks and calling on England to intervene.[339] Episcopal clergymen from all over New York state gathered to condemn the Turks and to call upon the worldwide Anglican Communion to do the same.[340] An association of Baptist ministers asked the U.S. president to intervene to protect the Armenians.[341]

Frances Willard, president of the Woman's Christian Temperance Union (WCTU) and a powerful force in American religious circles, called on each Christian minister to hold a Sunday meeting once a month on the Armenian issue. She asked that resolutions be passed at each meeting and sent to the U.S. government to force it to take action.[342] The 1896 annual convention of the Woman's Christian Temperance Union featured an Armenian "mass meeting," at which the Reverend Frederick Greene, author of *Armenian Massacres or the Sword of Mohammed,* spoke.[343] The WCTU, a much more important organization in its time than might be expected, condemned the Turks for "the agony and outrage inflicted by Moslem savages upon our brother and sister Christians, whose only fault is their devotion to Christ and their loyalty to a pure home."[344]

Lest it be thought that only religious groups were affected by the Armenian drive, the Society for Ethical Culture branches in Chicago and New York also sponsored Armenian Meetings in the Chicago Grand Opera House and in Carnegie Hall. At both meetings, speaker M. H. Mangasarian attacked the Americans and Europeans for not stopping the Turks and declared, as did others, that "the Moslem believes it is a religious duty to put to death the unbeliever."[345]

THE BOOKS

Most Americans surely formed their opinions of the Turks from newspapers and the pulpit, both of which built on a long-standing prejudice. There was no lack of books on the Armenian Question, however. Bookstores and libraries contained many volumes on the issue. These presented only one side of the issue, the view of the missionary establishment, because no other view was published in America. Of all the books printed in America on the subject "Armenian" in the 1890s, 87 percent were written by the missionary establishment and 7 percent by Armenians.[346] The books presented the Armenian cause as seen by missionaries and Armenian nationalists; none included consideration of the Turkish position. (The others were from the American Red Cross and did not treat the Troubles per se.)[347]

It is not possible to describe all the books on the Armenian Troubles here. They were, in any case, similar in their main points. None admitted that Armenian rebels had started the troubles. None counted any Turkish or Kurdish dead. All dwelled on the anecdotal suffering of individuals, trusting the reader to generalize that suffering to all Armenians. All offered false statistics on the Armenian population and mortality. All stated that the Ottoman government had ordered massacres of Armenians. The books described below are representative.

The most widely known missionary establishment polemical work was the book by the Reverend Frederick Davis Greene, born in the Ottoman Empire, the son of a missionary of the American Board. The title indicated what lay within: *Armenian Massacres or the Sword of Mohammed: Containing a Complete and Thrilling Account of the Terrible Atrocities and Wholesale Murders Committed in Armenia by Mohammedan Fanatics, Including a Full Account of the Turkish People, Their History, Government, Manners, Customs and Strange Religious Beliefs, To Which Is Added "The Mohammedan Reign of Terror in Armenia," edited by Henry Davenport Northrop, D.D., the Well-Known Author.*[348] Potential readers surely knew what to expect. Despite the religious calling of the author, "thrilling accounts" might appeal to an audience that did not usually read such literature. The book was representative not only of the missionary establishment but of the feelings of the political and intellectual elite of New England, two groups that included many of the same people. Greene solicited supporters who affirmed that the material in the book was accurate, inscribing their names before the title page. They included (naturally) prominent ministers and religious officials but also a governor and an ex-governor of Massachusetts, the president of the Massachusetts School of Technology (later MIT), Julia Ward Howe (president of the Friends of Armenia), and Frances Willard, the president of the Woman's Christian Temperance Union.[349] Why these worthies were considered to have had the knowledge to judge events in the Ottoman Empire is unknown, but their support indicates that Greene and his fellows enjoyed the approbation of New England society. *The Armenian Crisis in Turkey* was sold by church groups in aid of Armenian relief.

Despite the title's promise of information on "strange religious beliefs," Greene's book covered Islam only cursorily. He stated: "The fundamental doctrines of Christianity, such as the Incarnation, the Trinity, the Atonement, and the Resurrection of Christ of Christ are specifically repudiated in the Koran. The reform of Islam as a system is, therefore, not within the range of possibility."[350] Greene wrote that Islam was guilty of evil in two ways, First, it enjoined the massacre of non-Muslims. Second, the worst elements in the characters of its adherents were brought out by Islam, "the religion of the Prophet, which, like an intoxicant, turns loose the basest passions of our nature."[351] The theological basis for these assertions was not given. Greene probably felt that it was not needed, because to him the fundamental cause of Muslim "fanaticism" and its alleged inability to reform was that Islam was not Christianity. Despite the title, the book paid almost no attention to Turkish customs, manners, history, or government. Greene's only concern was to show Turkish misrule and massacre, without any indication of environment, history, or the possibility that any Armenian might ever have committed a wrong.

Greene supplied reports of evil deeds done by the Turks without giving the names and positions of the supposed sources of the accounts. This was avowedly done to protect them, but it also made it impossible to judge them. In any case, it is obvious from the quotations that the respondents were almost never eyewitnesses. "We have word from Bitlis"; "Forty-eight villages are said to have been wholly blotted out"; and the like, including reports from Istanbul, far from the troubles.[352] Greene's depositions were like those that appeared in the press. This was to be expected, because they shared the same sources, primarily missionaries and Armenians (based on internal evidence). Deficient as these sources were, the actual quotations took up very little of a book supposedly based on primary sources: twenty-two pages of type.[353] Greene explained this as a matter of delicacy: "Enough of this Chapter of Horrors! It has been necessary to omit the most cruel details, and the stories of inhuman lust of which hundreds of pure Christian women, both matron and maid, have been the victims, shall not be allowed to soil the pages of this book, nor to defile the imagination of the reader."[354] He then proceeded to tell those cruel details, but without even paltry verification. For the next 145 pages, to the end of the book, Greene gave no sources at all, only assertions.

The method of dealing with Turks, massacres, and Christian suffering was seen often before and after Greene. When describing Ottoman history, he gave wholly invented lists of Greek, Bulgarian, and Armenian dead, with no mention that any Muslims died at the same time.[355] He presented false statistics, such as that more than half the adult male Armenians of Trabzon were killed.[356] A number of unnamed "Turkish officials" supposedly admitted that they were ordered to kill Armenians. Greene's only evidence for his assertions was in the form of letters (by unidentified authors) and the comments of missionaries and other Americans and Europeans, who rarely had seen any atrocities themselves.

Greene, or perhaps his publishers, illustrated *The Sword of Mohammed* with drawings of exotic characters. Whoever made the illustrations clearly had no knowledge of the Ottoman Empire. Turks were all dressed in the costume of bedouin Arabs. Kurds wore Indian turbans. In a drawing of the "Grotesque Dance of the Pious Dervishes," the so-called dervishes wore peaked witches' hats and had simian faces. A photograph of "Turkish Water Sellers" was obviously a studio portrait of South Arabian women. Other drawings were intended to shock or at least appeal to the emotions of the reader: small children being killed by a Turkish firing squad, Armenian women carrying away the dead bodies of their men, Armenians being slaughtered in the streets, tribesmen "receiving payments for human heads."

The long addition to Greene's volume by the Reverend Henry Davenport Northrop was even more violently anti-Turkish than the Greene portrayal. The headings of Northrop's contribution tell the story: "Barbaric Tortures," "A Tale of Horror," "Incidents of Cruelty," "No Protection to Christians," "Armenians Not the Aggressors," "Reduced to Ashes," "Systematic Extortion," "Murderers Escape," "Crimes Unpunished," "Conspirators in Crime," "A Nightmare of Horrors," "Nameless Outrages," "Prison Tortures," "Villages Raided and Destroyed," "Mutilating the Dead," "American Missionaries Attacked," and "Bloodthirsty Barbarities." His descriptions were exactly what might be expected from such titles. Northrop even stated that the Turks had systematically impoverished the Armenians,[357] when in fact all evidence from consuls and others was that the Armenians were by far the richest element in Eastern Anatolia. Any claim against the Turks was acceptable to Northrop: the Turks hated civilization; they intended "holy war" against all Christians, no Christian ever received justice in Ottoman courts. Of course, the worst claim was that the Turks were murderers who hated Armenians and meant to destroy them, based on numerous anecdotes of murderous Turks without citing any sources.

Greene's *Armenian Massacres,* which was distributed in tens of thousands of copies, was undoubtedly the most influential of the books on the Armenian Troubles,[358] but it was not the only one. The Reverend Augustus W. Williams published a book whose title, like Greene's, described its contents: *Bleeding Armenia: Its History and Horrors.* It was bound together with *Under the Curse of Islam* by the Armenian Patriotic Alliance president, Dr. M. S. Gabriel.[359] In an effort to show that the Turks had always been a blight, Williams began with a history in which mythology was presented as fact: the size of Armenian cities and the power of old Armenian kingdoms were greatly exaggerated. The Crusaders were described as holy men, solely interested in the cause of God. The Armenians had suffered because their Christian brothers had not aided them; Williams falsely claimed that an immense Byzantine army had done nothing to oppose the Seljuk Turks who attacked Armenia (that army actually tried to do so but was defeated at the Battle of Manzikert in 1071). The errors indicate that Williams knew little of Ottoman history. He declared that the janissaries took the fifth child of every Christian family when the Ottomans conquered, a many hundred–fold exaggeration,[360] and that the Crimean War was the fault of the Ottomans. Of course, according to Williams, no Muslim had ever died in Greece, in Bulgaria, or in Eastern Anatolia. For example: "The Russo-Turkish War [of 1877–78] was, from its beginning to the treaty of San Stephano, a war for religious life and freedom and singularly free from death or insult to civilian or woman, while abounding in thrilling and dramatic incident."[361] The 288,000 Turks who died and 515,000 who were exiled from Bulgaria in the war would have disagreed.

To Williams, European imperialism was the only hope, as supposedly had been proven in Greece. At Navarino, "England, France, and Russia united to crush the power of the barbarian and to set free his victims, as the wild beast would not let go his prey till it was dragged out of his teeth." But, Williams felt, the Europeans had later failed the Armenians by holding Russia back. The Europeans should unhesitatingly have aided Russian imperialism, not stood against it: "future generations will stand aghast at the hideous spectacle of three civilized nations fighting side by side with and for barbarian Moslems to crush the noble champion of their fellow Christians and fellow slaves compelled by their victories to languish beneath the yoke of these savage aliens."[362]

According to Williams, Armenians had suffered because of the fanaticism of a converted sultan. Before he ascended to the throne, Sultan Abdülhamit II supposedly "plunged into all the wickedness of the capital, and lived a life of debauchery";[363] but when he became sultan he changed into a religious fanatic who would not rest until everyone in his empire became Muslim. Abdülhamit therefore began his attacks on the Armenians.[364]

Williams described the Turks with all the usual polemic terms: "cruel severity," "barbarism," "unutterably vile," and even poetic images: "The Turk is still an aboriginal savage encamped on the ruins of a civilization which he has destroyed." He spoke of "Turks and Kurds in whose soulless bodies legions of devils seem to have taken up their abode."

> The Turk never changes. What he has always done he always will do. And as long as any Christian lands or people remain under his power and at his mercy, so long will there be discontents, disturbances, revolts and massacres. The only way to end these is to end the rule of the Turk. Reform—not to say regeneration, is an impossibility. He is an alien in race and religion. His spirit is fierce and fanatical: his rule that of the dark ages, the rule of a tyrant without conscience or remorse.[365]

The Armenians, however, were "the sole humanizing element in Anatolia," Christians who had suffered for centuries because of their faith. Williams devoted 121 pages to individual stories filled with gruesome murders and general descriptions of the Armenian Troubles of 1894–96. The stories were heart-rending, and many may have been true, although Williams offered few sources. When looked at objectively, many of his tales are hard to take seriously. For example, a married couple fled to a hillside, followed by soldiers who offered them their lives if they converted to Islam. The husband and wife refused and were killed.[366] But, since they were dead, who relayed the story: the soldiers? Interviews with Turkish soldiers and Kurdish tribesmen in which they admitted and described their deeds seem very unlikely. If the soldiers had been guilty, would they have said so to the missionaries, Armenians, or whoever reportedly collected their accounts? Williams never named the collectors of such stories, more probably their inventors, but they followed in the tradition of age-old tales of Christian martyrs, which must have lent them an air of authenticity.

The little statistical information that Williams offered does not inspire confidence in his reporting. He overstated all Armenian populations, the better to support allegations of large-scale massacre and starvation. For example, he claimed that 20,000 Armenians had fled from Eleşkirt, "near Van." That figure is many times the number of Armenians in Eleşkirt, a relatively small district that was actually 150 miles from Van by poor roads.[367] Other estimates were similarly inflated, but Williams wisely refrained from making too many personal estimates. Instead he quoted what he called "Turkish statistics" on the carnage, compiled by the government: 20,000 Armenians killed in larger towns, 60,000 killed in villages, 2,500 villages destroyed out of 3,300, 441,600 Armenians starving, a total of 521,000 Armenians either killed or starving in seven provinces, out of 716,200 total Armenians originally living in the affected area.[368] No competent observer, even the most pro-Armenian, had ever stated that three-fourths of the Armenians were dead or starving or that three-fourths of the Armenian villages were destroyed. But the real difficulty is that common sense indicates that these so-called governmental statistics were complete fabrications. Such statistics could never have been collected. And would the Turkish government have disseminated them, even if they were true? Moreover, the statistics on the Armenian population were at wide variance with actual Ottoman statistics, which were not for propaganda purposes.[369] In the entire book Williams did not cite one Muslim killed by an Armenian or make any mention of an Armenian revolt.

The accompanying section of the book by Gabriel makes Williams seem relatively tolerant. Gabriel was an out-and-out racist:

> The Turk is not a member of the best human race—the Indo-European or Arian, like the Armenians. The Turk does not belong even to the next best of races, the Semitic, like the Jews and the Arabs. He is a branch of the Mongolian race, and, as such, incapable of assimilating complex ideas and higher forms of civilization.
>
> The mental inferiority of the Turk, unfortunately matched with a religion of a very low order, has made of him what he is, worse than savages.[370]

Islam, to Gabriel, was "essentially immoral," and "the Moslem is condemned to a perpetual infancy as a moral creature."

> The Turk has no home in the European sense of the term, nor wife, nor schools, nor government. His prayers are gymnastics of lips and limbs. His

charity is a mere show—as are his prayers, and often an act of cruelty. His school is a place where the spark of Tartaric intelligence is put out under the fuel of Koranic verses. His courts are stores where justice is sold by auction. His Government is an organized brigandage and his diplomacy, falsehood and shameless hypocrisy.[371]

Gabriel's feelings are evident throughout his analysis of the Armenian Troubles. He castigated England for not doing its duty toward Ottoman Christians. Americans were all heroic. America should send battleships to force the Turks to change. I cannot comment on the factual matter in Gabriel's treatise, because it contains no factual matter, only invective.

The other Armenian authors of books printed in America painted essentially the same picture.[372] They contained incredible defamations of Islam, which they did not hesitate to call evil, and portrayed Muhammad as a rapist. Muslims, who supposedly were dying out because of their bad sexual habits, were promised a place in heaven commensurate with the number of Christians they had killed. Of course, the books included all the usual assertions that the Armenians were innocent and defenseless and that Abdülhamit II had ordered massacres, along with wholly fictitious statistics on population and mortality. Once again, no Turks or Kurds died.

Turkish Cruelties upon the Armenian Christians by the Reverend Edwin Munsell Bliss began with erroneous assertions on population and migration.[373] He claimed that half the population of Syria was Christian, Armenians were equally distributed across Anatolia, and the Muslims of Europe had left conquered territories willingly, because "they recognized that the time was at hand when the Ottoman rule in Europe must end." Bliss described contemporary Muslim belief as "predestination to evil," without any spirituality or real concept of sin. To him, the Turks were normally placid fatalists who became monsters when aroused.[374]

Bliss offered the standard missionary history of the Armenian Troubles: Kurds had robbed Sasun Armenians, who therefore could not pay their taxes. The government then ordered Kurdish tribes to attack the Armenians and sent in regular troops when the Kurds proved unable to win. They slaughtered Armenians and destroyed Armenian villages. The atrocity stories that Bliss offered were all copied from Greene's book.[375] Troubles in Istanbul were described as pure attacks on Armenians, with no mention of the killing of Turks, Armenian revolutionaries throwing bombs, or even the Ottoman Bank raid.[376] Bliss said nothing about the slaughter of soldiers and other Muslims at Zeytun and flatly denied the presence of Armenian revolutionaries in Zeytun and elsewhere. In short, his book was a summary of the missionary establishment view of events, without any reference to any other view and suppressing much evidence. Like most of the other missionary works, Bliss gave no sources or bibliography to support his assertions. It must be said, however, that he seldom engaged in the sort of invective so often seen elsewhere. Words such as "barbaric," "inhuman," and "vile" seldom appeared, except in quotations from others. Either Bliss or his publisher, however, did include a number of fanciful yet savage drawings of inhuman Turks and Kurds murdering women and children.[377]

The Story of Turkey and Armenia, edited by the Reverend James Wilson Pierce, was a collection of chapters by different authors. The first chapter, presumably by Pierce, gave a very brief history of the Turks, stressing "barbarism." It contained too many falsehoods to list them all: the sultan "needs to compel all to embrace Islam," "the Turks today are still nomadic," 2.4 million Armenians lived in the Ottoman Empire, Armenians were always "cut down" so that they did not become too powerful, and so forth.[378] The author of the following article, "The Evil of the Turk, by an Armenian," was only identified as "a recent graduate of one of the leading theological seminaries." The article began: "Why does Turkey wage perpetual war against her Christian subjects?" The answer, according to the unnamed author, was the inherent violence of the Turks. The government was corrupt and impoverished, yet the sultan supposedly was waited on by 6,000 servants. Pestilence and famine were allegedly everywhere in the empire—altogether a very displeasing picture. A later article described Sultan Abdülhamit II in terms familiar from some newspapers: "He was flung in his earliest manhood into the midst of that debauchery which makes Constantinople the cesspool of the world." But the sultan later became an ascetic and religious fanatic. Concerning the Armenians: "Probably he feels more chagrined at the incompleteness of his work than grieved because of the blood already shed."[379]

Muslims and Armenians were treated quite differently in the volume. In the Turkish home "the Turkish child is only taught the first steps toward those vicious habits of mind and body which have made his race what it is."[380] Those children allegedly grew up to be stolid and placid, until they were roused to attack Christians. On the whole, however, the author was content to offer an interesting, if overwrought, depiction of the exotic elements in Turkish life—the evil eye, marriage customs, communal baths, and other things that would appear strange to Americans. The Kurds fared even worse than the Turks at the hands of the missionary Jesse Malek Yonan, an Assyrian who did not think well of them. He described the Kurds basically as lazy robbers and murderers.[381] James L. Barton, secretary of the American Board, contributed a laudatory article describing the Armenians as "naturally religious" and "the most intelligent of all the peoples of Eastern Turkey."[382] Pierce's section on the Armenian Troubles was too similar to that of the other missionary books to warrant much comment here. He quoted clergymen and political figures at length on the evil of the Turks and pusillanimity of the Europeans, who allowed the Turks to continue to rule: "The Turk is a savage, while the statesmen are—over-civilized; he is a tyrant, while they are craven cowards."[383] "The rule of the Turk is hopelessly and remedilessly bad wherever that rule extends."[384]

The book blamed the Ottoman government for all past and present deaths of Christians, citing exaggerated numbers for deaths in the Greek rebellion and other events. It did not describe a single Armenian revolutionary or a single massacre of Turks. Individual Armenians recounted tortures, some of them highly improbable, and killings. A missionary was quoted: "The Turks have decided to dispose of it [the Armenian Question] by wiping the Armenians from the face of the earth."[385] The stories were accompanied by the usual drawings of Turks murdering Armenians.

The missionary establishment took unusual measures to bring the Armenian Troubles before the American public. Marion Harland's *Home of the Bible* was one of many works that might be called Christian travelogues, full of pictures and photographs, Bible stories, and descriptions of the strange appearance and customs of the natives of Palestine. They had a wide circulation among the religiously minded, purchased or borrowed from a library as both edifying and interesting. The publisher, the *Christian Herald,* included in the book a short section that had nothing to do with the Home of the Bible, "The Story of Martyred Armenia," by an editor of the press, George Henry Sandison.[386] Like the authors of other books by the missionary establishment, Sandison gave no definite sources for any of his assertions. He made much use of phrases such as "It is said" and "It is believed." The only named source was the missionary Cyrus Hamlin, who had not been in the Ottoman Empire for more than twenty years.[387]

Sandison repeated the scripted story seen in all such publications. The number of Armenians in the Ottoman Empire was nearly doubled, the number of Muslims similarly reduced. The Hunchaks had taken no part in the Troubles; all accusations against them were lies from the Ottoman government. Like Williams, Sandison wrote that 75 percent of all the Armenian villages in Anatolia had been destroyed by the Turks and Kurds. Abdülhamit II supposedly "had taken a vow to exterminate the Armenians."[388] Everything was allegedly done by order of the sultan, although Sandison gave no indication of how he knew that this was true. No Armenian ever did wrong in his retelling of the events at Sasun, Zeytun, and elsewhere, while all Turks and Kurds did only wrong. Once again, he gave no sources for the bloody anecdotes he recounted, including priests hacked to pieces, infants slaughtered, women burned alive, and victims disemboweled. The only good thing Sandison could say about the Turks was that they were better than the Kurds: "The Turks, although more civilized, are only one degree less cruel than the Kurds. In contrast to the Kurds and Turks alike, the Armenians were peace-loving, industrious, frugal and kindly." The Ottomans were barbarians, "unfit to be tolerated among civilized nations."[389]

Sandison's mistakes indicate that he knew virtually nothing of the history of the region or even of the Armenians. For example, he declared that the Armenian Gregorian Church was theologically and liturgically Eastern Orthodox.[390] In his version of history the Ottoman Empire and Russia had a defense treaty; Muslims had ruled all Armenia since the Crusades; "Mohammedan hordes" had taken Armenia in revenge for Armenian help to the Crusaders; the Muslims had all but suppressed the Armenian Church.[391] Most readers would not have known that so little of the work was accurate or that all of it was biased.

Robert E. Speer, the leader of the Presbyterian missions, included the Armenian Massacres in his *apologia* for missionary involvement in world affairs,[392] among what he considered to be the other great and awful events of the time, such as the Tai-Ping Rebellion and Boxer Rebellion and the Sepoy Mutiny (all, it should be noted, anti-imperialist uprisings). Providing what he considered historical background to the Armenian-Turkish strife, he began his account with the Greek rebellion against the Ottomans. Speer provided the canonical missionary establishment view of Turkish history: massacres of Greeks on Chios but no massacres of Turks in the Morea, slaughtered Bulgarians but no slaughtered Turks. Either he preferred to relate only Christian deaths or he knew no better. That style of reporting, ignoring the deaths of opponents, makes any rebellion or civil war appear to be a one-sided set of massacres.

The books on the Armenian Troubles available to Americans were not temperate. Compared to the books written by members of the missionary establishment and Armenians, newspaper articles on the Turks appear restrained. The missionaries did not hesitate to increase the numbers of dead or exaggerate the amount of destruction. The main problem with the missionary books, however, was that they never told more than one side of the story. The missionary literature depicted no guilty Christians, only guilty Muslims. None of the missionary volumes that purported to tell the recent history of the Ottoman Empire mentioned that Turks ever died at the hands of Christians. The books that related "Armenian massacres" described "past massacres of Christians" but neglected to note that Turks had been killed in those outbreaks as well. They also omitted the instances where massacres of Muslims preceded and led to massacres of Christians.

It is impossible to offer a proper evaluation of the facts in the missionary establishment's books and reports on the Armenian Troubles, because the evidence they offered was primarily anecdotal. Those assertions that can be analyzed, however, do not speak well of the missionaries' accuracy. For example, the assertion that the majority of the Armenians in the Harput region of Eastern Anatolia were forcibly converted to Islam is belied by Ottoman census statistics by religious group showing that the number of Armenian Christians did not so decline.[393] Nor, despite statements to the contrary, were missionary schools disbanded in any number. In fact, records of the American Board show that more missionary schools existed after the Armenian Troubles than before.

As for the accusations of individual murderous acts by Turks and Kurds, how can they be examined and declared true or false? They were completely taken from Armenian sources or very rarely from purported firsthand reports by unidentified missionaries. It is more than probable that many of them were true. Thousands of Armenians were killed, many more treated with great cruelty. What was missing was any balance to the story. Judged by the missionary reports, only Armenians died. Yet we know that this was not the case. Even Armenian revolutionaries (such as the leader of the Zeytun rebellion) themselves wrote of the massacres of Muslims.

THE SOLUTION

The American press suggested that the solution to all the problems of the Ottoman Empire, indeed of the entire Muslim world, was imperialism: "There is no solution to the Eastern Question until the civilized peoples rouse themselves from their cowardly sloth and put an end to the last remnant of Muslim rule."[394] Muslims, and not only Turks, were deemed incapable of ruling themselves or others. They needed the kind guiding hand of European Christians.[395] The American press painted the history of the Ottoman Empire not in black and white but in black alone. The "unspeakable Turk" had always attacked and persecuted Christians because of Islam and natural Turkish brutality. Turks had never created a proper state, a true culture, or an industry.[396] The only thing to be done about the Turks was to drive them out. The *Dallas News* wrote: "You begin to wonder, if you have any sense of international ethics at all, why this criminal state is allowed to remain among comparatively enlightened and virtuous neighbors and to continually rob and kill."[397] The *New York Times* editorialized on November 13, 1895, that the European powers should go to war with the Ottoman Empire and destroy it: this was "what the civilized world hopes for."[398] The missionary establishment organ the *Congregationalist* unhesitantly called for the destruction of the Ottoman Empire in a war in which the United States would participate.[399] *Arena* declared that all reasonable analysts agreed that not only the Ottoman Empire but all Muslim countries should be ruled by Europeans: "Missionaries, consuls, travelers of all nations unanimously declare that no Mohammedan country, under present circumstances, can be regenerated except under European superintendence." The article containing these sentiments, by Robert Stein, went on to state that all the peoples under European rule, including the Turks of Central Asia, the Egyptians, the Algerians, and the Bosnians, were happy and prosperous, with no desire for change.[400] Of course, the inhabitants of these places had revolted many times against their conquerors, but Stein mentioned no dissatisfaction. (Future revolts against this enforced benevolence also proved that his notion of the satisfaction of conquered peoples was nonsense.) *Arena* included a number of long comments by clergymen who agreed completely with Stein's assertions.

Various solutions to the problem of the Ottoman Empire were offered. Armenia should become like Bulgaria, with a European governor and its own Armenian army. It should be "protected" by Russia, with its "traditional policy of friendship toward the Armenian race and protection of Christians against Moslem outrage."[401] The *Chicago Tribune* wrote that the solution to the Armenian Troubles was twofold: Russia should take Eastern Anatolia and the Great Powers should demand that the Ottoman Empire leave Europe: "If they refused to obey the demand, then the powers should drum them out and compel them to herd with their kind in Turkestan."[402] Some, however, felt that little European action was needed. The Ottoman Empire was expected to dissolve from within at any moment, freeing the Europeans of the need to destroy it.[403] The Europeans would only need to organize the pieces of the late empire.

Britain was the focal point of both condemnation and hope in the newspapers and magazines. They lamented that the British had previously supported the Ottoman Empire against the Russians and that Great Power politics was keeping the British from cooperating with Russia in invading Anatolia.[404] Many demanded that the British see the light and cooperate with the Russians in freeing the Armenians. They praised Russia as a benefactor to the Ottoman Christians, interested only in their welfare, not Russian aggrandizement. America was not to be left out of the desired Great Power action against the Turks. The *New Orleans Daily Picayune* demanded the dispatch of "at least five or six good ships, with full crews."[405] Missionary publications were at the forefront of the demand for European and American intervention. The *Congregationalist,* for example, called for the dispatch of American ships that would contribute to the destruction of the Ottoman Empire, primarily because the end of the Ottomans would be better for missionary evangelization.[406]

Some plans to remedy the Armenians' problems extended far beyond the Ottoman Empire: "Senator Morgan of Alabama thinks it would be a good thing if the colored people in the United States were all transported to Africa and their places here filled with Armenians, who are having such a hard time in Turkey."[407]

WORLD WAR I:
THE CAPSTONE OF AMERICAN PREJUDICE

Depictions of the Turks were negative but not omnipresent in America before World War I. Outside of major American cities, years might pass without mention of the Middle East in the local newspaper. What little was known of Islam or Muslim peoples reflected a general cultural animosity toward Islam and the Turks, exacerbated by occasional periods of intense negative publicity such as the "Bulgarian Horrors" and the "Armenian Massacres" of the 1890s. Occasional mission appeals in churches demeaned the image of Muslims and other infidels. It is doubtful, however, that Islam or the Turks were much in the minds of Kansas farmers, Florida orange pickers, or workers in Chicago meat-packing plants.

All that was to change in 1915. Attacks on the Turks became staple fare in the religious, cultural, and political lives of Americans. No matter how uninterested they might be in foreign cultures or non-Christian religions, Americans could not escape constant bombardment with anti-Turkish images. They encountered them in sermons at church, in public schools and Sunday schools, and on posters in public and commercial buildings. Newspapers and magazines never let the message be forgotten.

The primary agent of this propaganda, as might be expected, was the writings and speeches of missionaries and their supporters. As it had during the Armenian Troubles of the 1890s, the missionary establishment in America took the side of the Armenians in their conflict with Turks and Kurds. Incapable of admitting that the other side might have any justification and unwilling to accept that massive numbers of Turks and other Muslims, as well as Armenians, had died, the missionaries had a vision of Armenians as solely victims and Muslims as solely villains. To aid those victims, the missionary establishment organized the most massive charitable support program ever seen in the United States. The campaign rested on the portrayal of Armenians as always-innocent sufferers and Turks as mass murderers. This message was spread across America as no campaign against one people has ever been spread before or since. The missionary establishment acted out of a charitable motive: support for starving Middle Eastern Christians. In the process it defamed the Turks, who also suffered, by ignoring their suffering and falsely laying all blame on them. Americans who saw nothing but the missionary appeals were inculcated with a strongly negative image of Turks.

The main problem with the reports of the missionary agencies was not what they said about the suffering of Armenians and Greeks. While often false or exaggerated, the reports did truthfully state that Armenians and other Christians were dying in great numbers and needed assistance. The essential call to "help the starving Armenians" was a just and needed plea. The problem was that Near East Relief never included any mention of the starving Turks. In fact, many more than half of the starving people in or from Ottoman Anatolia were Turks and Kurds, not Christians. Yet the propaganda of the missionary establishment mentioned only Christians as needing aid. Millions of Muslims were driven from their homes by Armenians, Greeks, and Russians, but the missionary establishment only reported that Armenians and Greeks had been exiled. This was an exact reflection of missionary reporting on the earlier Armenian Troubles of the 1890s, in which Muslim suffering and Armenian actions against Muslims also went unmentioned.[1]

If the impetus for the missionary establishment's campaign was charitable, the motives of the British, who were the other primary source of the anti-Turkish image, were not philanthropic. The British were at war with the Ottomans. Anything that defamed their opponents would benefit them, and they attacked their opponents with vigor and lack of respect for the truth. British government propagandists during World War I did not specifically attack Islam. Indeed they proclaimed their respect for Islam throughout the war. The reason was not altruistic; the British feared an uprising of Muslims in India and Egypt in support of the Ottomans. British attacks on Islam would have inflamed a potentially dangerous situation. The British only attacked their wartime enemies, the Turks. Missionary propaganda and British propaganda fit together well. Both were aimed at ending the rule of Turks. The British wished to defeat the Ottoman Empire in war and ultimately to seize Ottoman territory. The missionaries, themselves long supporters of British imperialism, saw in the defeat of the Turks a new opening for missionary enterprise. Each made extensive use of the other. Much of the alleged evidence quoted against the Turks by the British was taken from American missionary writings and reports. In turn, the missionaries quoted British propaganda as a support for their own assertions. Americans, who usually saw no other information on the Middle East, could not help but feel that two such sources that were in complete agreement must be correct.

The picture of wartime events in the Ottoman Empire presented by the missionaries, their supporters, and the British was entirely one-sided. A search through hundreds of books and articles published by British propagandists, church leaders, refugee aid foundations, and related organizations yields not a single example of a sympathetic portrayal of Muslim suffering. Allowing for prejudice, statements admitting Muslim suffering but blaming it on the Ottoman government might still be expected, but not even these reached the American people. Indeed, Muslim deaths were never mentioned, with one exception: the accounts of Armenians fighting in the Russian and British armies against the Turks, where they presumably killed Turkish soldiers. These Armenian fighters were praised for helping the Allied war effort. No mention was made of Muslim civilian casualties. Americans would have had no way of knowing the massive numbers of Muslim casualties.

British propaganda in America was naturally aimed primarily at Britain's main enemy: Germany. The Ottoman Turks were a secondary target. Nevertheless, it was the propaganda against the Turks that had the most lasting impact. Even during the war, some forces in America opposed the British characterizations of the Germans. German Americans naturally doubted that the land of their ancestors and relatives could be as unremittingly evil as it was portrayed. Irish Americans had no special concern for the Germans, but as a group they disliked Britain and all its works. As Americans began to rethink their involvement after World War I, people started to investigate how America had been brought into the war. Both British and American authors began to study anti-German propaganda during the war, scrutinizing wartime lies about the Germans and identifying them as such.[2] No one spoke for the Turks. No American group demanded investigation of wartime propaganda against the Turks, and academics who studied British propaganda went no further than propaganda against the Germans. Few cared about the Turks; even if they had cared, anti-Turkish and anti-Muslim prejudice was so strong that few would have listened. The "Belgian Horrors" were treated with skepticism or declared to be fakes; the "Armenian Atrocities" were accepted as completely true.

The motive for the British propaganda campaign against the Turks was first and foremost to discredit an enemy. In this it was similar to the much larger propaganda campaign against the Germans.[3] But the British had additional reasons to attack the Turks. One theme of British propaganda was always the "unfitness" of the Turks to rule in the Middle East. While British publications did not admit it at the time, British propaganda served an imperial purpose. Deprecation of Turkish administrative ability and morality led naturally to the question "Since the Turks are unfit to govern the Middle East, who is to rule in their stead?" The wartime Sykes-Picot Agreement and other compacts indicate that the Allies themselves planned to rule the Middle East. Consequently, propaganda against the Turks had a definite geopolitical objective: the appropriation of Ottoman lands. Germany was simply to be defeated; the Ottoman Empire was to be occupied.

The British also had a more immediate propaganda objective. They were anxious to manipulate American public opinion on the "Armenian Atrocities" as a counterweight to anti-Russian sentiment among Jews and other Americans. The long Russian tradition of anti-Semitism had sparked newspaper articles against the Russians all across the United States. The Russians were allies of the British, who felt that anti-Russian sentiment was damaging pro-Allied attitudes in America. The British feared that influential members of the Jewish community were in danger of coming under the German sway. To counter this, Americans, especially American Jews, had to be taught that the Ottoman Empire was as injurious to Jews and to Zionist ambitions as was Russia. The British believed that news of Armenian atrocities would drive news of Russian atrocities against Jews from the newspapers, a strategy that proved to be somewhat successful.[4] The British kept close watch on American reporting on the situation of the Jews in Russia. Their weekly press résumés always quoted articles on the subject and commented on the importance of the Armenian issue in drawing American attention away from the Jewish issue.[5]

THE WARS, 1914 TO 1923

The Ottoman Empire did not enter World War I until November 1914.[6] Largely due to fear of Russia, which was an ally of Britain and France, the Ottomans joined the Central Powers. The first battles of the war were fought in Eastern Anatolia. As Armenian revolutionaries in the Ottoman East joined the Russians against the Ottomans, Eastern Anatolia became the scene of bloody intercommunal war. In 1915 and 1916 many of the inhabitants of Eastern Anatolia were at one time or another displaced from their homes. Turks and Kurds fled Armenians and Russians; Armenians fled Turks and Kurds. Armenians revolted in Van Province and held the City of Van against Ottoman forces until they were relieved by the Russians. All across Eastern Anatolia they aided Russian invaders, attacked Muslim civilians, and disrupted Ottoman military supplies and communications. In response, fearing the effects of continuing revolt, the Ottomans ordered the relocation of much of the Armenian population of Anatolia. The Russians and Armenians also forced the exile of much of the Muslim population of Eastern Anatolia. For three years few crops were put in the ground.

World War I in the Middle East was surely one of the most deadly wars ever fought. It extended years after the armistices of 1918 that ended the war in Europe, with wars between Turks and Armenians in Eastern Anatolia until 1920 and between Turks and Greeks in Western Anatolia until 1922. Destruction of civilian property was great in both the East and the West. Farm animals were slaughtered, and years passed without crops being planted. Mass starvation followed. Cholera, typhus, and typhoid spread, resulting in high mortality. Refugees of all religious groups died in great numbers of starvation and disease.[7]

Today historians hold disparate views on the conflict between Turks and Armenians. Their perspectives divide roughly into two schools, with many variations. One holds that the Ottoman Turks, for a variety of reasons, decided on a genocide of the Armenians and effected this plan through a forced deportation. The other holds that Armenians revolted against the Ottomans in eastern, central, and southern Anatolia and that the Ottoman deportations of the Armenians were a response to wartime conditions. In the first view, Armenians died in great numbers because of Ottoman plans to murder them. In the second view, both Anatolian Muslims and Anatolian Armenians died in great numbers due to mutual murder, forced migrations of both groups, and horrible wartime conditions. The first position places blame for wartime mortality on the Turks; the second on all parties to the war, including both Armenians and Turks.

The first position was a continuation of the same one-sided accusations and tales of massacre and atrocity that had been a staple of reporting in the nineteenth century, recycled for a new generation of readers. Although the second view of history seems more accurate to me, it is not an important part of the discussion of anti-Muslim and anti-Turkish prejudice to decide who was "guilty" of the massive human losses in World War I.[8] What matters here is that Americans never learned that there were two sides to the story of World War I. In particular, Americans never saw that millions of Turks and other Muslims were killed, died of disease and starvation, or were exiled during the wars. Because of the propaganda that replaced balanced reporting in wartime America and the almost total lack of news on the "Turkish side" of the issues, most Americans formed a view of Turks that was based on prejudice, not knowledge. That view was of necessity false. The story of World War I that reached the American public was a story of suffering Christians attacked by Muslims. The other half of the story—suffering Muslims attacked by Christians—went unmentioned. The story that was told was largely the product of American missionaries and their organizations in the United States.

In fact, large numbers of Muslims died too. Six provinces of Ottoman Anatolia were delineated as "Armenia" by the Armenians and their supporters: Van, Bitlis, Erzurum, Diyarbakır, Mamuretülaziz, and Sivas. Muslim wartime suffering in these provinces was enormous. These Muslims were killed in intercommunal war by Armenians, just as Armenians were killed by Muslims, and both sides suffered greatly from disease and starvation.

Statistics on Muslim mortality are only available by province, and not every region in these provinces was in a war zone. In the zones of combat and Armenian rebellion, about 40 percent of the Muslims died (see table 8.1), as did about 40 percent of the Anatolian Armenians. Only the Armenian deaths were reported in America, cementing in the American mind the false image of Turks as genocidal monsters.

TABLE 8.1. PERCENTAGE OF MUSLIM DEAD IN THE PROVINCES OF EASTERN ANATOLIA

Province	Muslim Mortality (%)
Van	62
Bitlis	42
Erzurum	31
Diyarbakır	26
Mamuretülaziz	16
Sivas	15

Source: Justin McCarthy, *Muslims and Minorities,* p. 134. These figures are not strictly mortality but rather "population loss": the result of subtracting the population at the end of the wars from the population at the beginning of the wars. Real mortality was higher. If children born during the war years were included in the figures, the percentage dead would have been higher.

The reporting of the missionary establishment and British propaganda on the Turkish War of Independence (1919–22) similarly lacked objectivity. Defeated in World War I, the Ottoman Empire surrendered to the Allies, who attempted to force on the Turks the most onerous punishments exacted on any of the Central Powers. The Arab world was cut away from the empire, mainly to be divided between the British and French conquerors. The principles of Woodrow Wilson's "Fourteen Points," which proclaimed the self-determination of peoples, were ignored in the division of Anatolia and Eastern Thrace (the area of Europe today in modern Turkey). After much dissension and conflict, the Allies ultimately decided to grant most of Eastern Anatolia to an Armenian Republic. The French would take Cilicia, north of French-occupied Syria, and the Italians would take south-central Anatolia. Greece was allowed to take Western Anatolia and Eastern Thrace. The Turks were to be relegated to north-central Anatolia. Although Allied plans for the Ottoman capital were never finally decided, Istanbul and the straits region were occupied by the Allies, led by the British. The awards to Greece and Armenia were decided by the Allies and forced on the Ottoman government, although the prewar population of Anatolia as a whole was more than 80 percent Muslim and each province of Anatolia had a large Muslim majority.[9] None of this demographic information reached the American people. Nor did they hear the facts of the war that resulted from the Allied actions.

On May 15, 1919, Allied ships landed Greek soldiers in İzmir to begin their occupation of Western Anatolia. Massacres of Turks started on the first day of the occupation, continuing through the war that followed. The occupation and treatment of the Turks led to a Turkish national resurgence under Mustafa Kemal (later Atatürk), who organized a government at Ankara and resisted the Greek invasion. By July 1921 the Greeks had advanced almost to Ankara, where they were defeated. The next year the Turks, known as the Turkish Nationalists, drove them back in a precipitous rout.

The Allies recognized defeat. The French, defeated in Cilicia by the Turks, had already made their peace with the Turkish Nationalists. The Turks had defeated the Armenians in the East, whose homeland in Erivan had been occupied by the Bolsheviks. The British also came to terms, leaving Istanbul and the straits to the Turkish Nationalists and encouraging the Greeks to abandon Eastern Thrace. The Turkish Nationalists created a Turkish Republic, but the land they inherited was shattered by war. In both the East and the West, millions of farm animals had been killed, trees had been cut down, cities lay in ruins, and nearly one-fourth of the Muslims were dead.

As in Eastern Anatolia, where a war between the Turks and the Armenians was fought at the same time, mortality was high on both sides. When the Greeks advanced, more than 1 million Turks were forced to flee their homes as refugees. When the Greeks had been defeated and the Turks advanced, it was the Greeks' turn to flee. Like the Muslims of the occupied territories, one-fourth of the Greeks of Anatolia were dead. The missionary establishment that was the main source of information on Turkey that reached Americans reported in detail the misery and mortality of Greeks who fled their homes when the Turks defeated the Greeks. It did not report the misery and mortality of the Turkish refugees forced from their homes by the Greeks. Similar reporting described the fighting in Cilicia (parts of Adana Province and Haleb Province), where the French and Armenians fought the Turks. Americans never learned of the deaths of nearly 10 percent of Cilicia's Muslims. As with the Armenians and Greeks, most of the Muslim dead were casualties of forced migration, starvation, and disease caused by the war, as well as direct murder. Like the Christians, Muslims were raped and treated brutally by their enemies. The primary difference between the Muslims and their enemies was that Americans (and Europeans) were not told of Muslim suffering and that relief agencies very seldom came to the aid of the Muslims. They provided succor to Christians, not to all those who were in need.[10]

The result of this propaganda and one-sided reporting was more than American ignorance of Muslim suffering. It led to a firm belief that the distress of the Christians had been directly caused by the Muslims, that the Christians had been innocent victims. The picture that reached the American people was of Christian dead, never Muslim dead. Americans had no way of knowing that the agony of the war was shared by all religious groups. What was in fact a human disaster was turned into a sectarian disaster for American consumption. The portrayal was of one group of killers, the Muslims, and one group of victims, the Christians, when in fact all sides had been both killers and killed. An analogy might be the so-called Indian Wars: if, as was indeed too often the case, only the results of Indian raids on settlers' farms were reported in the newspapers, readers would have believed simply that Indians were evil people who persecuted innocent immigrants from Europe. They would have called them "uncivilized" and "savages," as, of course, they did, for both the Indians and the Turks.

9

THE AGE OF NEAR EAST RELIEF

The American Committee for Armenian and Syrian Relief (ACASR) was founded in November 1915 in response to the suffering of Christians in Eastern Anatolia. It superseded other committees such as the Committee on Armenian Atrocities,[1] which had been founded primarily by members of the Congregational and Presbyterian mission boards and other missionary organizations. The Christians to be assisted were primarily Armenians, but the ACASR was also concerned with a smaller Christian group, the Assyrians (the "Syrians" in the group's title). The Age of Near East Relief had begun.

The work of ACASR and of the Near East Relief organization that succeeded it was one of the greatest humanitarian efforts of all time. By 1930 Near East Relief and its predecessor organizations had collected $89,970,293.06 for relief efforts.[2] This was a stupendous sum, the equivalent of more than $3 billion dollars today.[3] Near East Relief also administered large sums for other organizations, including the U.S. government, totaling $116 million distributed to the needy.[4] Tens, perhaps hundreds, of thousands of Middle Eastern and Balkan Christians who might have died of starvation and disease were saved by American food and shelter.

The ACASR was led by a small group of Americans with ties to the missions in the Ottoman Empire, called together by James L. Barton, missionary leader of the American Board of Commissioners for Foreign Missions, to consider ways to help suffering Armenians. They met in New York on September 16, 1915, in the offices of Cleveland H. Dodge, a wealthy businessman and longtime supporter of missionary enterprises. While the Committee of the ACASR was avowedly nonsectarian, its guiding genius and most of its members were drawn from the missionary establishment. Its original staff came from the Laymen's Missionary Movement, whose leader, Charles Vickrey, soon took over from Dutton as executive secretary. Throughout the committee's existence its leaders and principals came primarily from the American Board of Commissioners for Foreign Missions and the Presbyterian Mission Board, and relief was distributed through the agency of those missionary groups in the Middle East and Balkans. Other religious groups such as the Laymen's Missionary Movement, the Federal Council of Churches, the YMCA/YWCA, and various additional religious organizations

TABLE 9.1. ORGANIZERS OF THE AMERICAN COMMITTEE FOR ARMENIAN AND SYRIAN RELIEF

James L. Barton	secretary of the American Board of Commissioners for Foreign Missions
Charles R. Crane	president of the Board of Trustees of the Constantinople College for Women (a missionary college)
Samuel Dutton	treasurer of the Constantinople College for Women
Cleveland Dodge	chairman of the Board of Trustees of Robert College (a missionary college in Istanbul)
D. Stuart Dodge	member of the Board of Trustees of the American University of Beirut (a missionary college)
Stanley White	secretary of the Presbyterian Board of Foreign Missions
William I. Chamberlain	secretary of the Board of Foreign Missions of the Reformed Church
Samuel Harper	beginning a mission to Russia
Frank Mason North	secretary of the Methodist Board of Missions
Thomas D. Christie	missionary in Anatolia
William I. Haven	secretary of the American Bible Society
Charles S. MacFarland	secretary of the Federal Council of [Protestant] Churches
Arthur C. James	member of the Board of Trustees of the American University of Beirut
Edward L. Smith	a secretary of ABCFM
Edwin M. Bulkley	member of the Presbyterian Board of Foreign Missions
John R. Mott	representing the YMCA (and head of a number of missionary organizations)
Rabbi Stephen Wise	chairman of the Jewish Emergency Relief Commission
George A. Plimpton	member of the Board of Trustees of the Constantinople College for Women

assisted, especially in the collection of funds, but the ACASR was in reality an agency of the Congregational and Presbyterian mission boards.

The missionary character of the organization is well demonstrated by the membership of the committee that first met on September 16, 1915, to create the organization that would become the ACASR, as shown in table 9.1.[5] All, with the obvious exception of Rabbi Stephen Wise, were members of the missionary establishment. While others were soon added to the committee, it remained a missionary organization throughout its time and through various changes in title and form.

When World War I ended, the misery of the Middle Eastern Christians continued as war was fought between the Turks and the Armenian Republic in the East and between the Turks and the Greeks in Western Anatolia. The ACASR organization expanded to meet the new situation. The American public, which during the war had devoted its energy to European as well as Middle Eastern relief, now concentrated on the Middle East. The ACASR approached Congress for its imprimatur, which came in the form of federal incorporation under the title "Near East Relief" on August 6, 1919. With the federal charter came governmental assistance, including military personnel detached to the service of Near East Relief as well as the use of ships and other equipment. Government agencies contributed large amounts of relief: flour and other foodstuffs worth 13 million in 1919 dollars. In America, government offices supported the Near East Relief appeal by displaying posters, distributing brochures, and favoring collection activities. A great benefit of the federal charter for the missionary establishment was the association of the missionary appeal with the state. Near East Relief could and did portray itself as an American not a sectarian movement. It was seen as a national movement.

By 1925 Near East Relief had records of 6,270 active committees, which contained more than 20,000 workers and volunteers. The Near East Relief executive stated that there were many more committees and workers that were not registered with the national headquarters.[6]

> Near East Relief is receiving the cooperation of practically all of the great fraternal organizations of the country, lodges, rotary clubs, Y.M.C.A., Y.W.C.A. and the Knights of Columbus; of chambers of commerce, agricultural organizations, labor organizations, and milling associations; of Government departments, State, War, and Navy; of innumerable commercial concerns, who are contributing commodities, free advertising, and other invaluable cooperation; and of newspapers and magazines, secular, religious, and fraternal.[7]

The work of Near East Relief was advanced and its message carried forth by scores of national cooperating and advisory committees, formed to spread the message throughout their organizations. They included committees for colleges; the National Parent-Teacher Association; the National Education Association; sixty-six fraternal and service organizations (such as the Elks, Masons, and Kiwanis); companies (for example, Borden, Kellogg, and Carnation); the Boy Scouts and Girl Scouts; the YMCA; women's, agricultural, and labor organizations; and others. Each of the major religious groups in America had a guiding committee for Near East Relief, including Jews, Catholics, and every main Protestant denomination from Baptists to Unitarians. In short, few aspects of American life were not enlisted in carrying the Near East Relief message. Each state had its own regional office of Near East Relief. State chairs were prominent men, mostly governors of the state.

As a direct descendant of the ACASR, Near East Relief naturally drew many of its officers and members from the parent organization. The Near East Relief Board of Trustees contained Protestant bishops, heads of Protestant colleges, the head of the Federal Council of Churches, and the missionary secretaries (heads) of both the American Board of Commissioners for Foreign Missions and the Presbyterian Foreign Mission Board. James Barton was chairman of both the ACASR and Near East Relief. Charles Vickrey was executive secretary of the ACASR and general secretary of Near East Relief. Both were clergymen and senior members of the missionary establishment.

Near East Relief was avowedly and proudly a missionary enterprise. The organization described itself as such:

> The missionary phases of Near East Relief work are not generally recognized. It is still commonly understood to be a relief organization. Its work, however, has developed a distinct missionary phase of unusual value and of a new type.
>
> Near East Relief was missionary in its origin. Missionaries revealed to the U.S. Minister in Turkey the necessity for action. He cabled the State Department, suggesting that it ask Dr. Barton, Secretary of the American Board, and others to present an appeal to the American people. From the beginning the genius and spirit of the organization have been missionary, in America it has been manned by leaders having the missionary spirit, by missionaries overseas, and the native teaching staff are nearly all graduates of the missionary colleges. Missionaries overseas and missionary secretaries in this country have exercised large influence in the committee that determines policies and administers the work. A missionary secretary has from the first been the chairman of the Board of Trustees.[8]

All the Near East Relief orphanages taught American Protestant religion and mandated Protestant worship services for the children. Near East Relief officers believed this to be one of the great benefits of the enterprise: practically, because the children so educated would become leaders in the religious and civil lives of the countries; and morally, because the children had experienced "a change from the native fatalism to the power of faith."[9]

Common Christianity was always the main call of the ACASR/Near East Relief, as illustrated by a full-page ACASR advertisement in the *New York Times*. Headed "And Jesus Said," the advertisement described the ACASR work as Christlike healing of the sick and feeding of the hungry.[10] Other ACASR advertisements also featured Bible quotations and references to the Christianity of the Armenian sufferers.[11] A Near East Relief pamphlet titled *The Cross in the East and the Church in the West* is instructive. Its cover showed a drawing of a huge cross with suffering Armenians huddled beneath it. One figure in rags raised her hands up to the cross in supplication. The pamphlet began with a quotation: "But now in Christ Jesus ye that once were far off are made nigh in the blood of Christ—Eph. 2:13." Its message was that the work of saving the Armenians should be undertaken because the Armenians were "a Christian People":

> But for the Church of Christ in America it is vastly important that the *leadership* in this great enterprise of humanity shall rest with them who are active as *Christians* in the life of the community—the pastors, the Church organizations as a whole, with all their subsidiary organizations and agencies; the local Churches, the Sunday Schools, the Missionary Societies, the Brotherhoods— all that crystallizes the Christian spirit. These are the agencies that must provide the impulse and the example, not only because this great philanthropic

work cannot be carried through without them, but for the sake of the Church of Christ itself.[12]

The message of Near East Relief was that Armenians, as well as Greeks and Nestorians, must be aided because they were Christians. The message "We Christians against the Muslims" was sometimes stated, often simply implied, but always present. It also explains why Near East Relief did not mention the need to assist Muslim orphans or starving Muslims.

One 1920 Near East Relief advertisement was headlined "Store Some of Your Money in Heaven! Don't Put It All in the Bank!":

> Two thousand years ago Jesus Christ was betrayed for thirty pieces of silver and crucified, and today, two thousand years later, Christ is still being crucified in the plains of Armenia, where the oldest Christian nation in the world, bent but unbroken under centuries of persecution, and still stubbornly refusing to renounce the Master for the heresies of Mohamet, is literally bleeding to death because no nation has yet had the moral courage to rescue her from the unspeakable horrors of Islam.[13]

The Plan of Action

The ACASR organized efficiently to bring its message to the American public. From the beginning, the relief agencies planned to carry their message throughout America through public appeals, work in schools, and especially the cooperation of churches. The central organization sent out directives on organization and work plans to local committees, stressing the need "to disseminate information continuously through the press, pulpit, and printed bulletins." The first step was to "arrange a union meeting of all the church and philanthropic organizations of the city where the situation in Western Asia can be presented." The central organization provided stereopticon slides for such meetings. After that, local committees were to "arrange for the presentation of the needs in Bible Lands before all churches, Sunday Schools, Young People's Societies. Brotherhoods, Y.M.C.A.'s, Y.W.C.A.'s, lodges, clubs, and other fraternal organizations."[14] The list was fairly complete. To a remarkable degree the instructions of the Central Committee were carried out.

In 1917 the ACASR laid out its plan for local action:

1. Prepare letters and articles based on ACASR-supplied information and place to local newspapers.
2. Publish cablegrams from the ACASR in the local press.
3. Distribute posters "in all railway stations, hotels, public bulletin boards, churches and Sunday schools throughout the community."
4. Place posters in street cars.
5. Circulate leaflets in churches and homes.

6. Make use of church programs, bulletins, and periodicals.
7. Speak with editors and make sure they are receiving ACASR literature.
8. Send communications to editors.
9. Ask businesses to devote part of their advertising space to ACASR advertising.
10. Ask local papers to set up relief funds.
11. Request that booksellers and public libraries feature books. ACASR posters would be provided for exhibits.[15]

Other methods should be used where possible: public meetings ("They will be of value chiefly as an occasion for giving publicity to the facts both from the platform and through the press"), speakers' bureaus, women's organizations, "Armenian-Syrian-Greek Parades," stereopticon slide shows in theatres and churches, house-to-house canvasses, supplements to newspapers, leaflet distribution, and Girl Collectors (using "attractive girls").

The ACASR effectively made use of pictorial propaganda. Pictures "illustrating the suffering and need in Armenia and other parts of Western Asia" were provided to schools, churches, and newspapers. They came with recommendations: to be posted on church bulletin boards, mailed to friends, used to teach children in schools, reproduced in newspapers, and so forth. As might be expected, the pictures included starving, wounded, and dead children, with captions blaming it all on Turks and Kurds.[16] Near East Relief distributed highly effective posters all across America. Seen in churches, schools, and public buildings, the posters depicted "starving Armenians."

Speakers in local churches and civic organizations were well drilled by Near East Relief. Manuals for speakers included descriptions and dubious but unrefuted statistics that could be presented to local audiences. "From a million to a million and a half people were saved from starvation in Armenia, Turkey, Greece, Syria and Palestine [by Near East Relief]."[17] In one set of talking points for speakers, Bishop James Cannon offered information on Christian orphans from Beirut passing to Near East Relief orphanages in Greece, "because the cruel, fanatical Turks would not guarantee that the lives of orphan Christian children would be safe in Turkey."[18] The bishop went on to describe the orphans' sufferings and needs. Of course, he gave no evidence that Turks persecuted orphans. It also seems odd that the orphans from Beirut were leaving a territory controlled by the French not the Turks in 1926 (six years after the last conflict between Turks and Armenians), somehow forced out by "the cruel, fanatical Turks." Readers would not have considered such fine points.

Near East Relief offered outlines of suggested speeches to local churches and other groups. The themes were those that would appeal to the American spirit, particularly the concept of national rejuvenation through learning the lessons to be taught by Americans. Speakers should apprise church members of the missionary activities of Near East Relief. They could make audiences identify with the Armenians through reminders that the Armenians had been American allies in the recent world war, which was not true (America and the Ottoman Empire had never been at war) but was undoubtedly effective.[19]

THE MESSAGE TO AMERICA

The ACASR and its successor organization, Near East Relief, were effective propagandists. Their aim was to gain funds to relieve the distress of Christians in the Ottoman Empire. In order to do so, they naturally broadcast painful and often true but one-sided stories of the Christians' suffering. Ottoman Christians were portrayed solely as innocent women and children who were starving. As in previous years, they did not mention Armenian revolt or Muslim suffering. But their publicity had another side. It was not deemed sufficient simply to support starving orphans. It was also essential to vilify the Turks. To maximize contributions, what was needed was a victim (the Ottoman Christians), a hero (the missionaries), and a villain (the Turks). Turks and Kurds were portrayed as the sole cause of the Christians' plight. From the first the committee dramatically attacked the Turks with unverified claims of atrocities. Its first circular speciously quoted Talat Paşa, the Ottoman interior minister, to the effect that he would make the Armenians "pray for massacre." Descriptions of rapes, enslavement, the murders "of nearly all able-bodied men above twelve years of age," and other atrocities were followed by an address to which funds could be sent. It is no exaggeration to say that the propaganda portrayed the Muslims as fiends who had killed the Christians or driven them to destitution purely out of hatred, without any other cause. Armenians in particular were characterized as innocent saints who had been assaulted by guilty devils. This was indisputably an effective technique. The financial success of ACASR and Near East Relief proves that. It was also effective in fixing in American minds an enduring portrait of "the Turk" as a beast.

It is impossible to be sure how much of the vilification of the Turks was only a tool of fund-raising. The image of Turks in America spread by previous work of the very missionaries who led Near East Relief was already so bad that fundraisers might have known that continued vilification was sure to be effective. But the leaders and workers of Near East Relief themselves had been the recipients of nearly a century of anti-Turkish and anti-Islamic images in books and newspapers. They had attended the seminaries in which Islam was taught as the enemy and read the books printed in the nineteenth century. They were wholeheartedly committed to the cause of Armenian nationalism. In short, they surely believed the essence of what they wrote about the Turks. They might consciously bend facts and write only what would support their cause, but unconsciously they were perhaps incapable of seeing that there was another side to the story.

The propaganda of the relief organizations fit into the pattern of wartime propaganda as practiced by the British (see chapter 10). All of the elements of psychological attack that were so prominent in British anti-German campaigns appeared in anti-Turkish campaigns. Many of the portrayals were exactly the same. Germans supposedly cut unborn babies from their mothers' wombs with bayonets; so did Turks. Germans allegedly took young girls away for horrible purposes; so did Turks. Like British propaganda, the ACASR publications quoted at length from anonymous sources ("a Lady Traveler," "a Missionary in Turkey," "a Correspondent"), who made the most damning claims of Turkish misdeeds.[20] Unsubstantiated assertions that have never appeared in identifiable sources (named sources who could be demonstrated actually to have seen the events they described) were the staple of the unidentified sources: widespread auctioning of Armenian women to the highest bidder, Armenian women being stripped naked before they were sent on deportation caravans, the rape of every woman found by the Turks, and crucifixions and other exotic tortures.[21] The ACASR was the source of much of the anti-Turkish propaganda published by the British (see chapter 10). British propagandists and the American missionary establishment exchanged "horror stories," each publishing them with minor changes.[22]

When the same stories reached America from both British and missionary sources it had the effect of making them appear all the more reliable. Just as the British propagandists and the American missionary establishment printed stories from the same sources and pretended that they corroborated each other, the missionary establishment used the U.S. State Department for false corroboration. Missionary stories were given to friendly American diplomats such as the American ambassador in Istanbul, Henry Morgenthau, who sent them on to Washington. The same stories were sent to the ACASR or the missionary boards. When cited, they appeared to corroborate each other. Occasionally this ploy was obvious. A *Dallas News* headline read: "Atrocities against Armenians Continue: Treasurer of American Relief Work Is So Advised by State Department."[23] A second assistant secretary of state had indeed sent the message to Charles R. Crane, the treasurer of the ACASR, but the message in fact had originated with Dr. William W. Peet, treasurer of the American Board, who was in Istanbul. The State Department had simply relayed Dr. Peet's message.

The ACASR suggested readings for local organizations, newspaper editors and reporters, and politicians. It most commonly mentioned its own reports and the Bryce Report on the Armenians, which had been produced by the British propaganda office. William Walker Rockwell, a professor of church history at Union Theological Seminary and director of publicity for the ACASR, prepared a long list of readings, which was published by the ACASR.[24] It included many of the negative works on Islam and the Turks by missionaries and others that are described in earlier chapters. Under the heading "Turkish Empire," the section on "History and Politics" included a number of works that depicted failings of Ottoman rule and predicted its inevitable downfall.[25] Other sections treated American missions, spoke of a "Holy War" of Islam against Christianity, and alleged Turkish intolerance. Most of the books and articles were naturally on the Armenians. The standard condemnations of Turkish rule were included, dominated by books and articles by missionaries and the propaganda works that emanated from the British Propaganda Bureau. No works that attempted any sympathy for the murders, displacement, and starvation of Turks were listed.[26]

Rockwell himself wrote stirring depictions of the Christian plight, compilations of stories without any names or places.[27] While many of the stories were undoubtedly true, it is impossible to tell which. Some of the "facts" were demonstrably wrong, such as the assertions that the Turks were deporting the Greeks and Armenians of Istanbul and that Armenian deserters from the Ottoman army were allying with the Kurds to rise up against the government (when Kurds and Armenians actually were fighting each other). Rockwell's pamphlets were typical of the ACASR literature, detailing the distress of the Christians with no reference either to the political situation or to the corresponding travails of the Turks and Kurds.

The publications of the ACASR did not stint on emotional appeals. They included descriptions of mass graves, starving children, and refugees searching through dung for undigested seeds. For example, an ACASR publication titled *Armenia: The Most Tragic Story in Human History* stated:

> There is no record in human history that, for inhuman brutality, can equal the terrible, the tragic story of Armenian persecution at the hands of the Turks. Men tortured until death relieves them, women and girls outraged and brutally killed, little children dying from hunger, from persecution and exposure; these are the facts that go to make the story.
>
> Never since the world began has there been such a reign of torture and of butchery as that to which the Ottoman hordes have subjected this helpless and unoffending nation. It is a scheme planned by high and skilled ability and carried out by low brutality.[28]

The report went on to describe "helpless people brained with clubs while little children were killed by beating their brains out against the rocks." It was a direct descendant of the missionary propaganda of the 1890s, with descriptions designed to make a powerful appeal to the public's sense of outrage. The words were well chosen for their emotive force: "inhuman brutality," "outraged women." They appealed to a desire to protect the weak but also to the long-developed racist feelings against the "Ottoman hordes." Such words had the desired effect: to increase donations to the ACASR cause. Each publication contained pleas for money to assist the suffering Christians: "Exiled from their homes, robbed of their possessions, wanderers in a desolate poverty-stricken land, their only hope for the barest necessities of life is in charity from opulent America."[29]

The ACASR printed periodic "press releases" that were part information, part pleas for funds under titles such as "Latest News concerning the Armenian and Syrian Sufferers." The releases were avowedly intended to place stories of alleged Turkish atrocities in the newspapers. The ACASR itself described its releases as "galleys released for publication in the newspapers."[30] In form, these releases were what might be called the standard pattern—reports described as coming from Americans in Ottoman Anatolia, with all names and references to place deleted: "Miss X reports on mistreatment of Armenians in Y." As such, it is hard to evaluate their veracity, but most appear to be genuine reports of events as perceived by missionary reporters. One of the ACASR sources is known through British reports: the ACASR transmitted and copied reports from the Dashnak Party in its literature.[31] The Dashnaks were the main party organizing the Armenian revolution in Eastern Anatolia and had a definite interest in painting their Turkish enemies as black as possible. The ACASR never mentioned that its sources were Armenian revolutionaries.[32] Reports alternate between descriptions of the present plight of Christian refugees and atrocity stories, including many accounts of rape and massacre. Interestingly, almost all of the reports were of atrocities committed by Kurds. They never reported on the sufferings of anyone but Christians.

As was typical in atrocity reports, the numbers of the sufferers were always inflated. Estimates of the Armenian dead and Armenian refugees routinely added up to considerably more than the prewar Armenian population.[33]

ACASR reports contained kind words for the Russians, who were praised for their assistance to the Armenians, including actions in the Van Province. Russians were portrayed as friendly, even soft and cuddly, a stark contrast to depictions of the "bloodthirsty Turk." Cossacks would "share their frugal meals" with refugees. Russian officers supposedly broke off fighting to care for Armenians. The reports told of "a Russian officer out at the front sitting crouched over a little fire that he had made out of a few sticks, and of a little girl stiff with cold and hungry, slipping into the circle of heat of the fire, and without apology snuggling up to him and going fast asleep in a moment in the kindly warmth of the fire, and of that officer sitting cramped for hours in order to let the little waif sleep in the folds of his big army coat."[34]

The ACASR publications portrayed Turks and Kurds as brutal peoples who mindlessly and without reason persecuted Armenians. They openly stated that only European pressure had kept the Turks from continually persecuting the Armenians and that the war had removed European pressure, allowing the Turks to revert to type. The pamphlets stated that the Turks themselves would ultimately pay for deporting Armenians, because "there can be little doubt that every place left vacant by an Armenian will—irrespective of the outcome of the European conflict—have to be filled by a foreigner, as the Turk has proved himself totally incapable of doing this kind of work." The professions described as being beyond Turkish capability were "doctors, dentists, tailors, carpenters...every profession or trade requiring the least skill."[35]

The very titles of ACASR publications are instructive in their emotional appeal: *The Pitiful Plight of the Assyrian Christians in Persia and Kurdistan, The Most Terrible Winter the World Has Ever Known, Armenia: The Most Tragic Story in Human History, Armenia: A Tragedy In Which the Men, Women, and Children of a Helpless Nation Are the Victims OF INHUMAN PERSECUTION AND MURDER* (capitalization in the original title).

Near East Relief falsified the Ottoman political situation: "The Turkish government recognized Mohammedanism as the national religion and the non-Moslem had no place in the political organization."[36] This was at best a half-truth. Islam was the national religion of the Ottoman Empire, just as each independent state in the Balkans and Middle East had a national religion. Christians had risen to high political place in the Ottoman Empire, however, including cabinet positions such as foreign minister; such positions were unavailable to Muslims and Jews in the Balkan states and Russia, which had sizable Muslim minorities. World War I changed this, as Christian minorities revolted against the state, but to deny that the Ottomans had a better political record on minorities than any other regional states in the matter was sheer deception.

Near East Relief painted the Armenians as a people close to saintliness. The Near East Relief organ *New Near East* in October 1921 described them as "very religious and very earnest in their devotions. Other characteristics attributed to the Armenians, by foreigners who have known them, are thrift, virility, tenacity, and indomitable perseverance . . . Another important characteristic is their love of learning, and this very often at the expense of pleasure and physical needs." "Education is a racial passion for the Armenian." Near East Relief contrasted the Armenians to the Turks, who were the enemies of education and enlightenment: "If it were true that to be a Christian in Turkey were to be a martyr, it is equally true that to be educated within the Sultan's jurisdiction is to be singled out for persecution." Armenian home life was praised as closest in the Near East to that of "the English-speaking peoples." Moreover, the Armenians were happier than the other inhabitants of the region. The Muslims had "pinched faces, pale faces, anxious faces, careworn faces, listless faces, hungry faces, sickly faces of little children, and older faces that had grown sour and sullen." The *New Near East* assured its American readers that the faces of Armenian children were neither anxious nor hungry, largely because of the efforts of American missionaries.[37]

The missionary reports that formed the bases of the ACASR press releases and publications often contained both outright falsehoods and lies of omission. As during the Armenian Troubles of the 1890s, they never admitted that Armenians had ever revolted against the Ottoman Empire or that great numbers of Muslims had died. Here is one example from an ACASR press release: "In the autumn of 1914, the Turks began to mobilize Christians as well as Moslems for the army . . . Wherever they were called, and to whatever task they were put, the Armenians did their duty, and worked for the defense of Turkey. They proved themselves brave soldiers and intelligent laborers."[38]

In fact, Armenians in Eastern Anatolia generally refused to serve. Thousands fled to Russia, where many joined the Russian forces. Others received training from the Russians and returned to the Ottoman Empire as guerrilla fighters. They were joined by young Armenians who had taken to the hills and formed armed bands, as well as by Armenian soldiers whom the Ottomans had managed to conscript. Many of these deserted to the Russians or to the Armenian bands, taking their weapons with them. Armenians indeed "proved themselves to be brave soldiers," but they fought against their own country, allied with its enemies.[39]

Another ACASR press release described the situation in Van, making no mention of an Armenian revolt there: "The Armenians [of Van] defended themselves, barricading the Armenian section of the city, in which the American Board mission premises chanced to fall, and for a month withstood the attack of the Turkish army. Beginning April 20, the siege continued until the middle of May. The Turks withdrew from Van toward Bitlis, two or three days before the Russian troops entered the city."[40] The record of the Van revolt was completely distorted. Armenian revolutionary groups met to plan their revolt one month before the war began. Rebels from Van went to Russia to consult with the Russian government then returned to organize revolt. Armenians revolted all over the Van Province then rebelled in Van City on April 20, seizing most of the city and forcing the Ottoman garrison in the Old City of Van into the citadel, where it withstood Armenian attack until forced to flee by the Russian advance. Armenians actually took and held the main Ottoman city in southeastern Anatolia and held it until the Ottomans' enemies arrived.

The ACASR report claimed that "the Armenians in the army were first brutally put to death; then followed those who had purchased exemption and nearly all able-bodied males above twelve years of age."[41] After the revolt began and they were no longer trusted, Armenians in the Ottoman army were indeed treated badly, and many died from malnourishment, disease, and murder, although "brutally put to death" is a gross overstatement. To a large extent, the same conditions held for Muslims in the army, but it is undoubtedly true that conscripted Armenians suffered a worse fate. The next statement, however, is completely false. Purchased exemptions no longer existed in the army; they had been abolished earlier at the instigation of Christian deputies in the Ottoman parliament, who felt that taking a fee from Christians in lieu of serving in the army was a sign of second-class citizenship. As for the murder of nearly all males over the age of twelve, it simply never happened. No evidence of such wholesale slaughter exists. Even if the Ottomans had wished to do such a thing, they first were fighting the Russians and the Armenian guerrillas and then were fleeing from the Russians. They would have had no time for mass murder.[42] If the mass murder had occurred, how did so many Armenians survive the war?[43]

The events of World War I in the Ottoman East are hotly debated by historians and by partisans of both the Turks and the Armenians. What is unquestionable is that the version of events propagated by the missionary establishment did not include a single Turk or Kurd massacred by Armenians. Yet in Bitlis and Van Provinces (the centers of the Armenian revolt and the murders of Muslims) the Muslim population had been killed in great numbers during and after the Russian advance, had died of disease and starvation, and had been forced to flee as refugees. At war's end 62 percent of the Muslims of Van Province and 42 percent of the Muslims of Bitlis Province were dead, yet Americans heard nothing of them.

NEWSPAPERS AND MAGAZINES

Near East Relief supporters made use of local newspapers in their campaign whenever possible, writing to the papers and inserting articles. In one pamphlet, for example, the Near East Relief organization printed brief supportive excerpts from the *Boston Transcript, Brewster [Wash.] Herald, Cleveland Plain*

Dealer, San Francisco Chronicle, New York Times, Indianapolis News, Indianapolis Star, Buffalo Express, Brooklyn Citizen, Christian Science Monitor, Leslie's Weekly, and *Newark Evening News.*[44] Media representatives were prominent on the Near East Relief Board, including John Finley of the *New York Times* and Albert Shaw of the *Review of Reviews.*[45]

No one, then or now, could properly evaluate the evidence provided in the relief organizations' press releases, which were printed verbatim or excerpted in newspapers all across America, because identification of sources was impossible. Names and places were not given. Typical of the ACASR press releases was a report that the Turks had a policy of exterminating the Armenians: "The Committee [the ACASR] says the dispatch was received through high diplomatic authority in Turkey, not American, reporting the testimony of trustworthy witnesses over wide areas."[46] Of course, this was the same accusation by unnamed sources that had been made in the 1890s.

In September 1915 the Committee on Armenian Atrocities, the direct predecessor of the ACASR, issued a statement accusing the Turks of planning extermination of all the Christians in the Ottoman Empire and providing details of supposed torture, rape, and murder, with places and names withheld.[47] The statement, continuing a form of source identification that was to become ubiquitous, was allegedly based on written affidavits from individuals whose identity was kept secret.[48] In November 1916 the ACASR produced paraphrases of documents outlining Ottoman evils, this time supposedly from Germans. Again the sources were not identified. The ACASR said the documents were available because they "had fallen into the hands of the French" and had been tested for accuracy by comparison to "reports of authoritative English observers."[49] England, of course, was at war with the Ottoman Empire; thus no English observers, authoritative or otherwise, could have made such reports. The documents, however, may indeed have come from the British: from the British Propaganda Bureau (see chapter 10).

The Committee on Armenian Atrocities sent twenty-four reports of massacres (sources unnamed) to the press and to over 120,000 churches in the United States. The newspapers printed these gruesome stories, although many were unlikely or impossible: Armenians relocated to Echmiadzin in Russian Armenia by the Turks, men lined up so that they could be killed with one bullet to save ammunition, Armenians punished by receiving 800 lashes, and so forth.[50]

The descriptions of Armenian suffering forwarded to American newspapers by the ACASR were emotional, even poetic, and must have appealed mightily to the sentiments of readers:

> There were two million Armenians when the war began. Three-quarters of a million have perished. A quarter of a million are refugees in other countries, especially in Russia. One million remain, who must be fed and clothed and put upon their feet again. And Christian America must do it. Most of the remaining Armenians are utterly destitute, emaciated, starving. Last Spring the word came

that they were living upon grass. Now the grass is gone. They feed upon carrion. The children fight upon the dung hills for fallen grains.[51]

The ACASR publicized letters from missionaries that described the most awful tortures: babies torn from their mothers then "run through by Turkish swords" or "tortured by slow fires and literally torn to pieces."[52] Turks were accused of burying babies alive in trenches dug for the purpose.[53] These became a staple of press reports.

Most of the many thousands of Armenian relief articles that appeared in America simply repeated the ACASR version of events. They had a common form: a sensational headline ("Turks Slaughter Thousands of Armenians with Axes," "Death Decreed for Armenians by the Moslems," "Armenian Women Put Up at Auction," "Turks Bury Living Babies with Corpses"), a description at varying length of atrocities and an excoriation of the Turks, wholly imaginary statistics on the number of dead and deported Armenians, and finally an appeal for funds for the ACASR or Near East Relief. Editors also used the Armenian situation for "fillers" on pages throughout newspapers. These one- or two-paragraph insertions offered "facts" without any attribution or listed source—what would be called "factoids" in some parts of today's press. They included assertions that the Turks had killed so many in one town, tortured children and raped women in another, general statements on the numbers of Armenian dead, and similar claims. Some of the short fillers were simply paragraphs taken from longer articles or press releases and used when needed to fill space.

American missionaries were frequently identified as the sources of press reports on the Armenians, although the articles seldom indicated how the missionaries had come to know what they reported and often did not even identify them by name ("a missionary in X," "the missionary Miss X").[54] One missionary reported with assurance that "the Turks and Kurds have declared a Holy War against the Armenians and vowed to exterminate them."[55] A *New York Times* article reported on news received "through missionary channels" from London that the British had plans for the Ottoman Empire that would greatly benefit Christianity. The British would drive the Turks from Istanbul and turn Hagia Sophia into a Russian Orthodox cathedral. They would give other regions of Anatolia to Christians and develop Palestine for both Christians and Jews.[56] The article did not state how news was received in London through missionary channels. Such information was often the product of cooperation between the missionaries and the British propaganda office (see chapter 10).

Today anyone who reads many of the accounts printed in American newspapers can see that they are false: impossible stories of events that could not have occurred or could not have been seen by the one making the allegation.

The ACASR sent missionary reports to newspapers, which often printed them verbatim. Newspapers also printed atrocity stories from the missionary organizations, seldom identifying the sources of the information other than to state that it had come from missionaries.[57]

Examination makes it clear that very few of the missionaries had seen what they reported and were relying on Armenian witnesses. One missionary repeated a story told by "a gentleman who had come out of Persia a few months ago" by train. This unnamed gentleman said that he had seen a column of 225,000 Armenians when the train stopped at Ani. They were suffering horribly.[58] The suffering of the Armenian refugees from Van (presumably the ones being described) was real, but the train did not stop at Ani, which was more than five miles from the rail line. Even if he meant "near Ani," this would have meant that two-thirds of the Armenian refugees in the entire Russian Empire passed by his train window while he counted the mythical 225,000, an impossible feat. But the numbers looked impressive in print.

Missionary and relief organization officer Emily C. Wheeler reported in a press release that "in the Van district alone 57,000 Armenians were killed in August [1915] alone." She did not state how she knew the number of deaths or mention that the Armenian dead were refugees, fleeing the Turks in August as the Muslims had fled the Armenians and Russians in May. Wheeler's other assertions on Turkish atrocities cast doubt on her pronouncements: "The entire district of Tiflis has been leveled [by the Turks] by fire. Women have been scorched, scalded, and burned to death." The Turks had never been near Tiflis, which was in the Russian Empire and over which the Turks had no control. Wheeler also believed that Enver Paşa had boasted that he had killed more Armenians in thirty days than Abdul Hamid had in thirty years, an unlikely boast from the Ottoman minister of war. Her source for these assertions was an Armenian missionary physician.[59]

The ACASR released a letter from "an American professor in one of the American colleges in Turkey [all missionary colleges]." The writer said that an American consul (place unnamed) was told that the Turkish government intended to exterminate the Armenians. "He further said," the professor continued, "that when the Armenians were disposed of the Greeks would be similarly treated, and after that the foreigners. A like statement was made by Enver Pasha, the Minister of War, to our ambassador, Mr. Morgenthau."[60] Although this seems an unlikely statement to make to an American consul, it might be conceivable that someone, conveniently unnamed, may have said such a thing. It is completely impossible that Enver Paşa would have said it.

The ACASR gave the press reports from Greeks and Armenians. Most of these were preposterous, although the readers of the newspapers would not know it. For example, the ACASR distributed the statement of one George Makrides of Trabzon, who alleged that the Turks had thrown 1 million Greeks into the sea, murdering them all. This event never happened, of course, and sober reflection might have shown that it was physically impossible. But readers would probably be impressed by the headline: "Million Greeks Are Massacred; Thrown into the Sea: Germans Make the Turk More Efficient in His Murders," even if they never read the article.[61]

Many of the reports ostensibly written by Christian sufferers were completely unverified, in fact (see chapter 10), with unknown sources except that they allegedly had somehow reached an American missionary or consul. Both Barton and Rock-well admitted, not publicly but in private letters, that they had no knowledge of the provenance of the stories they published.[62]

The newspapers of the time did not pay much attention to the provenance of their stories. Many news articles, especially in the smaller papers, did not give any indication of sources. Some can be identified because one paper out of many specified the source (as the ACASR, for example), while the others did not; but many sources cannot be identified.[63] Many articles were datelined New York, with no other source given, and it is hard to see how the information could have reached New York other than through the ACASR, Near East Relief, or other parts of the missionary establishment. This included stories from America. A report of Armenian women who escaped and found refuge with their relatives in Minneapolis and Milwaukee originated in New York, prominently mentioned Near East Relief, and was printed all over the country.[64]

Many reports from unnamed sources in the newspapers are obviously from missionaries: "While the source of the following information is not to be made public in fear of the serious penalties that may be inflicted upon the lives of the Honest God Fearing Americans who are seeking to spread the gospel of Christ in foreign countries, the following story of Turkish atrocities is unparalleled."[65] Some sources were identified as Americans who had lived for many years among the Armenians or used similar language, obviously referring to missionaries. These unidentified missionary reporters often gave the most incredible claims and exaggerated statistics of death and deportation. One stated that before the war began the Germans had smuggled 2,000 military officers into the Ottoman Empire disguised as "surgeons and Red Cross workers" and that the Ottoman government was planning to move to Konya, to which it had already begun to send its official records.[66] Neither ever happened. Another asserted: "Nearly 200,000 Armenian villagers between Yeni Chehir and Afion-Karahisar, in Asia Minor, have abandoned their homes and are fleeing to the mountains."[67] Readers would not have known that 200,000 was four times the number of Armenians who lived in the region.[68] Nor would they have been likely to compare this statistic to other ACASR releases stating that these same Armenians had been relocated, which, aside from the numerical exaggeration, was more accurate. The ACASR announced on November 26, 1916, that "two million destitute Armenian, Syrian, and Assyrian [*sic*] children have been aided during the past 13 months by the American Committee for Armenian and Syrian Relief."[69] Two million was more than the total population of those groups and many times the number of children.

Members of the missionary establishment themselves wrote numerous articles for American newspapers.[70] One member of the Near East Relief establishment, William T. Ellis, wrote particularly vituperative articles on the Turks.[71] In syndicated articles he presented damning and largely false caricatures of Islam. "All Moslems are united in opposition to all Christians." "Progress has been arrested [by Islam], the heritage of centuries of culture has been wasted, life has become more difficult, and the very fertility of the earth has been diminished." Ellis brought forth all the old canards of the "sensual Mohammedan," a man with "indescribable habits."[72] His articles extolled missionaries and depicted Armenian suffering without mentioning Muslim suffering.[73] He described German missionaries as spies, however.[74] Ellis even attacked the Persians, who supposedly "declared that they will not leave a single Christian alive in this part of [Western] Persia."[75] His remedy for the problems of the Near East was anything but Christian: "A reasonable number of assorted hangings [of Turks], judiciously distributed over the land, would be the quickest means of insuring peace and prosperity to Turkey."[76]

The Reverend Fred Haggard was a Baptist minister and former missionary who served as publicity secretary of the ACASR.[77] In 1917 he wrote a series of six syndicated articles that summarized ACASR propaganda: the Ottoman government's policy was extermination of Armenians. Soldiers killed Armenians with axes in order to save bullets; Armenians were crucified; Turks intended "to wipe from the earth the non-Moslem population." The Turks had been inspired to act by the Germans, while the Russians were inspired only by the purest of motives. But "the Turks have outdone their masters, the Prussians, in savage frightfulness." Haggard's quotations on the sufferings of individual Armenians all came from missionaries. He falsified the dates and facts of the Armenian relocation, alleging that it had begun "almost on the day war was declared," when in fact relocation was ordered almost seven months after the war and the Armenian rebellion (which he did not mention) began. Haggard used the entire the arsenal of ACASR press release tactics, including the ACASR headlines ("Armenia—The Word Spells Tragedy").[78]

Of course, missionaries were not responsible for all the falsehoods and half-truths ascribed to them as sources in the newspapers. Writers and editors often embellished the missionary stories, adding more damning allegations than those made by the missionaries themselves. The *Atlanta Constitution* and other newspapers ran a story headed "Untold Corpses Choke Canals and Trenches," a portrayal of the sufferings of the missionaries and Armenians who fled Van when the Russians retreated, based on the accounts of the missionary Clarence Ussher. The article writer added that "Van again is in the hands of the Russians, who are declared to have found the canals and trenches choked with untold thousands of bodies of Armenians."[79] Ussher never said that he had seen any such thing. He had fled, along with all the city's Armenians, before the Turks came. The Turks could not have killed the alleged thousands, because the Armenians had already left the city when the Turks arrived. There were no Armenian bodies in the canals and trenches.[80]

The missionaries were naturally not the only source of news on the Ottoman Empire. The British propaganda machinery was responsible for much of the information that reached America (see chapter 10). Armenian groups in America and Europe forwarded reports to the press that were often identical to those sent by the missionaries.[81] The one thing that is certain is that American newspapers and magazines, with the slightest exceptions, printed only the reports of the Ottomans' enemies. The *New York Times* was especially vociferous in its attacks on the Turks. It made little or no attempt to verify these stories: Turks had killed

100 German officers; the sultan was dying; Turks massacred the Armenians in İzmit then burned the city (it was still standing after the war); Cemal Paşa was either in Arabia organizing revolt against the Ottoman government or in Istanbul doing the same; and other fanciful tales.[82] The *Times* made its anti-Turkish and anti-German feelings obvious in what amounted to editorials but were printed as news stories. These portrayed an Ottoman Empire in which all the Muslims in the world, including the Arabs, stood against the Turks.[83] Absurdities did not bother the *Times*. It described an extremely unlikely event in Erzurum, "an extraordinary antiwar demonstration by Turkish women in Konak and Erzurum. Women threw stones and rioted for several hours, and when threatened by guards rent their garments and paraded through the streets almost in a state of nudity."[84]

Reports from Van came from an Associated Press representative who was attached to the Russian army and arrived in Van one month after the Ottoman retreat from the city. He sent completely one-sided accounts from Armenians and missionaries, recording none of the Muslim dead.[85] The AP sent similar reports concerning Erzurum after the city fell to the Russians, extolling American missionaries, Russians, and Armenians and excoriating Turks. The Erzurum reports were written in Tiflis, in the Russian Empire, far from Erzurum.[86] Reporting had the same low standards seen in the 1890s Armenian Troubles. Based on the word of one Armenian, a reporter alleged that "German and Turkish statistics which he saw in September, 1916, showed that 1,398,350 Armenians had been deported and that of that number 1,056,550 had been massacred."[87] These statistics were complete fabrications. Actual Ottoman numbers on the relocation of the Armenians were much more general, as might be expected in wartime, and gave much lower counts of both relocations and mortality.[88]

Other than a general belief in Armenian massacres, Americans, including editors, knew little about the Armenians. This sometimes resulted in laughable interpretations in the press. The *Dallas News* reported that American missionary societies all confirmed that Armenians were being massacred then proceeded to give its readers information intended to develop sympathy, calling the Armenians the "oldest Christian nation," and so forth. But the *News* got a few facts wrong. "The Armenian Church is essentially the same as the Greek Orthodox one." "The region [of the Armenians] is immediately south of the Black Sea." "The head of the Armenian Church is a Catholic."[89]

The descriptions of events in the American press were full of emotion. One story featured a box in boldfaced type: "**America Must Help Armenians**: Turkish Brutality Almost Inconceivable, Has Nearly Destroyed the Race—Infants Thrown into Fire Where Mothers Were Being Roasted Alive by the Barbarians." The article completely falsified the Turkish conquest of the city of Bitlis (which it called "Bitlic") by neglecting to mention that Armenians had rebelled and taken the city. In addition to throwing children into fires, Turks allegedly had drowned other children in lakes.[90] The Turks also supposedly were forcing the Armenians to commit unthinkable acts: "Starving Armenian Refugees deported by the Turks to Northern Arabia have actually killed and eaten their own children in some instances, Dr. James L. Barton, chairman of the American Committee for Armenian and Syrian Relief, reported today. His information came from a reliable eye witness, he said."[91]

Longer "feature" articles gave greater scope to condemnation of the Turks. For example, the *Oakland Tribune* ran an entire page, complete with drawings ("an artist's conception") of massacres, descriptions of families torn asunder, rapes, and the "Eight Commandments of the Mohammedans." The supposed "eight commandments" were quotations from the Quran in which Muhammad enjoined battle against pagans, which the *Oakland Tribune* wrongly assumed meant attacking Christians.[92] A page in the *Washington Post* blamed the Şeyhülislam, the head of the Ottoman religious establishment, for ordering the massacre of Armenians. He had supposedly dreamed of ridding Muslim lands of Christians and eventually ruling over all the world's Muslims.[93] In another full-page story, also with pictures, the *Fort Wayne Sentinel* described pillage and murder, blaming most on the Kurds, who were described as a single desert-dwelling tribe of "utter barbarity and remorseless cruelty."[94] Another full-page story featured pictures of dead and starving children, along with quotations from the British Propaganda Bureau and the Greek government and references to the Armenians' suffering Christianity and the "frenzied, fanatical intolerance" of the Muslims.[95] A full page in the *Syracuse Herald* offered the usual pictures and massacre descriptions and portrayed the Turks as ignorant brutes, who must be expected to do evil: "There is no Turkish civilization and no Turkish literature and no Turkish art."[96]

The Associated Press, which distributed press releases from missionary organizations and the ACASR/Near East Relief, also sent out press releases from Armenian organizations in America and Europe, which were printed as accurate and distributed throughout America. These stories were always from unnamed "authoritative sources" and included purported secret directives from the Ottoman government.[97] This was also true of postwar releases from the Armenian Republic.[98]

As they had in the 1890s Armenian Troubles, American newspapers printed stories taken directly from London newspapers, which were carefully controlled by the British censor (see chapter 10).[99] Newspapers also printed government reports on Armenian massacres from the Ottomans' worst enemy, Russia.[100] The *Dallas Morning News* even printed news from Armenian newspapers in the Russian Empire, although this was not done by many other papers.

ADVERTISEMENTS

The ACASR and later Near East Relief advertised in newspapers and magazines throughout the United States.[101] In addition to the ads taken out by Near East Relief, businesses took out separate ads for the organization or put pleas for Near East Relief in their own full-page advertisements.[102] Some of the advertisements were fairly innocuous, simply announcing a grave need and giving an address for donations. Some featured drawings of winsome children (presumably orphans) and did not attack the Turks much by name, although they considerably bent the facts.[103] Others, particularly the full- or half-page advertisements, were vicious. An ACASR ad headlined "Inside Facts on the Persecution of Armenia's Martyrs" appeared in newspapers all across America. It featured a long description of Armenian suffering—"thousands driven from their homes," "brutal persecution," "thousands dying from brutality"—that allegedly had come from a cable sent by Sir Gilbert Parker.[104] The ad did not mention that Parker was the head of the British propaganda effort in the United States (see chapter 10). Another ACASR ad told Americans that Armenians "fight for the clotted blood of animals" and "eat the flesh of fallen animals and men," describing Turks as murderers and rapists.[105]

As described above, the advertisements played on the religious feelings and religious prejudices of Americans: "Our God is your God, and we bare our souls for your searching eyes that you may see how we have never denied Him, nor shamed Him. When our world rocked in misery around us, in our torn and tortured bodies our hearts still cradled and sheltered the crucified Christ."[106] They stressed the emotional elements, especially the suffering and deaths of children: "their wizened little skins clinging in fear to their rattling bones, and they are crying out with gasping breath, 'I am hungry! I am hungry! I am hungry!'"[107] A Near East Relief advertisement was headlined "Poor Little Innocent Children Lie Dead in the Streets in the Far [sic] East."[108] The advertisements blamed the Turks for all.[109] An ad with a picture of a sad-looking Armenian child asked, "You Won't Let Me Starve, Will You?" It identified the girl as Shushan: "Her father was butchered. Her mother was outraged and driven naked from home; she starved to death in the desert."[110] Another ad showed a boy wrapped in what appears to be a blanket, "only one of 250,000 helpless child victims of Turkish cruelty and oppression."[111] Some advertisements told detailed stories of murder and rape by Turks.[112] Another showed a drawing of a Turk on a horse whipping Armenian refugee women—"'Let Them Die; Who Cares!' That's What the Man with the Whip Says."[113]

Many of the advertisements gave incredible figures for both the Armenian population and Armenian mortality. For example, one Near East Relief ad featured a drawing of a young emaciated boy, near starvation:

> Terror!
> Five uninterrupted years of it!
> Of brutal, beastly persecution, of cruelties innumerable and unnamable, such as only the mind of a Turk can conceive and carry out. That is the black shadow that has hung over the Armenian nation ever since the World War began.
> To tell the whole story of the sufferings of the Armenians would require as much space of this newspaper. And no newspaper would print it all.
> Of 5,000,000 Armenians, only 1,250,000 remain, and these are in the most deplorable condition. America's task—their rehabilitation—is a big one.
> America is the only nation that can help.[114]

Had the figures been true, nearly 4 million Armenians would have died. In fact, only 1.5 million Armenians lived in Ottoman Anatolia just before the war.[115] The figure of 5 million was repeated often in Near East Relief advertisements, and readers had no way to know that it was completely fictitious. Other ads also stated that nearly 4 million had been killed and some that 4 million were refugees.[116] In addition, 200,000 Greeks had supposedly died in İzmir.[117]

Some of the persecution was completely invented. ACASR and Near East Relief advertisements claimed, without giving any specifics, that "Armenians, Syrians, Greeks, Persians and Jews" had been among those persecuted by the Turks.[118] No attacks on Persians had occurred. Turkish attacks on Jews were the invention of the British Propaganda Bureau (see chapter 10), which cooperated with the missionary relief agencies.

PUBLIC MEETINGS

Public meetings were a popular form of entertainment and enlightenment in World War I America. Like their missionary establishment predecessors in the 1890s, the relief organizations made effective use of gatherings large and small to bring their message to Americans. The ACASR and Near East Relief sent speakers all over the country, usually missionaries or Armenians.[119] The meetings were held in many venues, including churches, schools, universities, civic auditoriums, and concert halls.[120] Press reports of these meetings did not usually give any numbers of those attending the meetings, except in general terms. In New York, however, James Barton (the head of the ACASR) and others addressed a mass meeting of an audience described in the *New York Times* as "thousands." The audience was told that 500,000 Armenians had been killed by the Turks and 250,000 women violated.[121] A rally for the ACASR was held at the Billy Sunday Tabernacle.[122] The *Atlanta Constitution* wrote that Clarence Ussher, whom it called "The Great Missionary" (and who was a noted publicist against the Turks), addressed "an immense audience."[123] Ussher and Barton both addressed similar meetings in various cities.

Newspaper reports indicate that the meetings were less than temperate in their consideration of the Turks. For example, Near East Relief organized a meeting of the women of Atlanta to hear speakers describe the condition of Armenian women. The speakers alleged that Muslims, "in Armenia and Assyria and everywhere where Mohammedan rule prevails, make slaves of the [Christian] women from their birth. They are sold when babies to men, who generally pay for them with Virginia leaf tobacco." This had supposedly gone on "for thirteen centuries." In recent times, the audience was told, Armenian women had been nailed to crosses and left to die or had their breasts cut off to make purses of their skin.[124] At an ACASR-sponsored meeting in Philadelphia the Reverend William F. Akerd spoke on "The Assassination of a Race." He told his audience that "800,000 skulls line the desert way from the Black Sea to the Persian Gulf and more than 2 million women and girls have been sold into slavery." The audience would not have known that this figure was nearly three times the entire prewar Armenian female population of Anatolia.[125]

A report in the *New York Times* indicates the standard of information that reached Americans:

> At the luncheon of the workers in the $30,000,000 drive of the Committee for Relief in the Near East, held in the Bankers Club yesterday, Dr. Graham Hunter, member of the Red Cross Mission to Palestine, who arrived home on Tuesday, told of conditions in the Near East and described for the first time how a community of 8,000 Armenians in a mountain village had been reduced to fifteen survivors by atrocities committed by the Turks and Kurds.
>
> Dr. Hunter said he got his story from one of the survivors, a woman school teacher, who said that not a man or a male child over seven years old was left alive. When the slaughter was over 400 women and children were all that were left. They fled into the desert where all but the fifteen died of starvation.[126]

Listeners would not have realized that a village of 8,000 in the mountains would have been an impossibility or recognized the extreme geographic improbability that the escapees would have gone from the Kurdish mountains to the desert. They might reasonably have questioned any story based on the testimony of only one woman, but such reports were standard and seem to have been universally believed.

Meetings in larger cities were often addressed by Near East Relief/ACASR speakers, local and state relief officials, and sometimes national orators designated by relief organizations.[127] The relief organizations sent Armenians across the country to speak to public meetings and in churches. In addition to stories of atrocities, the Armenians stressed the Christianity of their people and the "racial" kinship with Europeans and Americans.[128] One of the Near East Relief speakers is an example of what was heard by Americans. The Reverend Ernest C. Partridge was an ABCFM missionary who served as an agent of Near East Relief. Partridge gave lectures all across the American Middle West. In Eau Claire, Wisconsin, he spoke to the YMCA: "In 1453 the bloody hand of the Moslem was laid on Asia Minor and for 500 years has cursed Asia Minor." The Turks had never built anything and had turned their empire into "a barren blighted country."[129] Partridge told the Rotary Club of Elyria, Ohio, of Turkish misrule and castigated America "for her failure to accept her responsibility [to the Armenians]."[130] He told the Kiwanis Club of Oshkosh, Wisconsin, "of the various stages of the system of extermination of that race [Armenians] undertaken by the Turks."[131] Partridge told tales of murder and rape to the members of the First Presbyterian Church of Sandusky, Ohio, stating that the Turks intended "the complete extermination of a race of Armenian men, women, and children."[132] He gave similar lectures in churches and public meetings in many other cities.[133]

Meetings in small cities were most often held under the auspices of local clergymen, who were also usually the main speakers. Speakers in places such as Albert Lea, Minnesota, or Sandusky, Ohio, naturally had no personal knowledge of the Near East. They relied on relief organization materials. Arrangements were usually

made to collect for Armenian Relief in local churches on the Sunday following the
mass meeting.[134] The basic form of the meetings was generally the same, because
it had been set by ACASR/Near East Relief. A meeting to be held in a church
or public hall would be advertised in the local newspaper. The speaker would be
an official of ACASR/Near East Relief, who would read descriptions of Armenian suffering from missionaries and others. Speakers often made reference to the
Christianity of the Armenians and alleged that Muslims hated all Christians and
thus wanted to kill them all. A committee would be formed to oversee the collection of funds. The audience would vote on a resolution condemning the Turks and
calling on the U.S. government to do something.[135] Local newspapers took advantage of the meetings to print numerous articles on the Armenians, repeating what
was said at the convocation and quoting relief agency materials and British propaganda such as excerpts from the *Blue Book*.[136]

RELIEF DAYS

The Armenians became a national passion. Nothing since the Armenian Campaign can compare to it in scope and effect, with the possible exception of the
war bond campaign during World War II. Civic and church groups made the support of Armenian relief, and of course the damning of the Turks, a very public
matter. The Federal Council of Churches of Christ in America set aside Sunday,
May 28, 1916, as a day for the Armenian cause. The ACASR, the World's Sunday
School Association, and the International Sunday School Association also designated that day for consideration of the Armenians and collections for them.[137]
Most of the Protestant and many of the Catholic churches seem to have taken
part. President Woodrow Wilson declared October 21 and 22, 1916, as "Armenian
and Syrian Relief Days." The ACASR organized collections to be taken on Sunday, October 22, in more than fifty thousand churches. Organizers estimated that
"thousands of churches" would devote services and sermons to the Armenians.
Volunteers canvassed door to door and on city streets to collect donations.[138] The
announcement of the campaign said that 750,000 of the original 2 million Armenians had been killed or died of disease or starvation and 1 million were destitute.[139] Another presidential decree followed in 1917, designating November 10
and 11 as "Armenian and Syrian Relief Days."

All over the country the Armenian appeal touched American hearts. Collections were taken in schools, churches, businesses, and government offices. Women
donated their diamonds, which were sold for Near East Relief.[140] Others gave
automobiles, pianos, rugs, clothing, and all sorts of valuables for auction.[141] Theaters gave benefit performances for Near East Relief.[142] Merchants' and trade organization banded together to collect for Near East Relief.[143] The ACASR and Near
East Relief organized the campaign so that the image of the starving Armenians
was never far from the public mind.

"Armenian Relief Days" continued throughout the war and after. Fairs, parades,
and public gatherings featured parade floats and ACASR booths where literature
was distributed.[144] Volunteers at "tag days" accepted donations and gave donors

ACASR labels to wear.[145] Theaters gave benefit performances for the cause, sometimes presenting specifically Armenian-related plays.[146] Benefits for Armenian relief were happy public occasions, featuring vaudeville acts and bands.[147] Manhattan had 200 booths on the streets and 500 stands in department stores, hotels, and restaurants, staffed by 1,000 volunteers. The ACASR announced that 30,000 women would canvass for donations in the five boroughs of New York.[148] Near East Relief put 1,000 "solicitors" in the field to visit every house in Lowell, Massachusetts.[149]

The campaign in Atlanta in April 1919 is an example of the very public nature of the appeal. It set up forty-five booths downtown; "several hundred women" moved through offices, stores, and military camps near the city, soliciting contributions. Speakers went to every public school in the city.[150] A "great pantomimic spectacle depicting the suffering of the Armenians" was presented in the Atlanta Auditorium on April 6, 1919:

> "The Cry of Armenia" portrays the recent raid on the Armenians simply and graphically. There are three scenes: The first portraying the plot instigated by the German military representatives at the Porte for the deportation of the Armenians; the second, which is entirely in pantomime, shows how the plot was executed, with its accompanying horrors and tortures; and finally, the third scene shows the coming of Liberty, Justice and the Allies, bringing freedom to the ravished land, and how they are confronted by the refugees still in a starving condition and in immediate need of help to maintain them until they can enjoy the fruits of liberty.

The actors later went through the streets on a truck bed, presenting the spectacle to passersby. On the same day a theater presented *They Shall Not Perish,* another play on the suffering of the Armenians.[151]

In the Schools

American children were particularly targeted by the ACASR and Near East Relief. ACASR publications listed ways in which teachers should interpret materials for students and distributed pamphlets directed at students. In simple prose these told of starvation and murder. Unlike the materials for adults, material directed at children told stories of individual children with whom the American children could relate, such as "Syria of Today—My Escape: by a boy who has just reached America."[152] The portrayals were appalling, including accounts of children who watched their parents being shot.[153] Children were encouraged to create plays, dressing as Armenians and acting out their torments.

Near East Relief felt that the appeal to schoolchildren was particularly successful. "School Superintendents, versed in the history of Christian Armenia, were quick to open the doors of the schools to Armenia's pitiful story. Every school child in America came to know Armenia's worthiness and Armenia's need. They felt a brotherhood with the children of Armenia."[154] "Increasingly, principals and teachers are recognizing in the relief appeal and in the response of the children to that appeal an indispensable factor in the education and character development of children."[155] In 1920 the public schools of America gave $175,000 to Near East Relief, the equivalent of nearly $6 million today.[156]

Relief organizations made a particular appeal through Sunday schools. They gave teachers lesson plans and course materials, along with outlines of "special orders of service": worship services for children that revolved around the theme of Christian suffering and the need for relief. Pictures and reading materials for Sunday-school children were also provided.[157] The ACASR launched a major campaign for donations in the Sunday schools in October 1917 through the agency of the United Sunday Schools of America: "Suitable literature and lessons will be given the children for several weeks prior to the offering."[158]

Sunday schools of almost all major Protestant communions taught the message of Near East Relief. The organization listed twenty-five denominations as especially cooperative (see table 9.2).

TABLE 9.2. PROTESTANT SUNDAY SCHOOLS PARTICIPATING IN NEAR EAST RELIEF

Advent Christian	Free Methodist
Seventh Day Adventist	Methodist Protestant
Northern Baptist	Moravian
Southern Baptist	Presbyterian, U.S.A.
Seventh Day Baptist	Presbyterian, U.S. (South)
Church of the Brethren	United Presbyterian
Christian Church	Protestant Episcopal
Congregationalist	Reformed Church in America
Disciples of Christ	Reformed Church in the U.S.
United Evangelical	Unitarian
Evangelical Synod of N. America	United Brethren
Methodist Episcopal	Universalist
Methodist Episcopal, South	

IN THE CHURCHES

In addition to the speakers sent out by the ACASR/Near East Relief, the American Board of Commissioners for Foreign Missions and the Presbyterian Board of Foreign Missions sent speakers to churches all over the country. A few, such as Clarence Ussher, had seen some of the events in Anatolia; most had no firsthand knowledge, but all spoke with seeming authority.[159] ACASR and Near East Relief officials and designated speakers toured America, speaking at churches as well as at public meetings.[160] Churches across the country held services for the Armenians, addressed by their own ministers or by Armenian or ACASR/Near East Relief speakers. The events often included Armenian religious and secular songs.[161] Unchecked by any knowledge of the actual events, speakers were free to extemporize on the facts. Listeners were told that the Turks had killed missionaries,[162] which was not true, and even that Jesus had been in touch with the Armenians.[163]

As the missionary establishment realized, however, local pastors were their greatest potential allies. During the period of World War I Americans were a religious people, attending church regularly and assigning high status and respect to the clergy. This was naturally appreciated by the men of religion who headed the ACASR and Near East Relief, who enlisted ministers in their campaigns. The ACASR and Near East Relief held campaigns in most cities, in which pastors were asked to preach sermons on the Armenians and take up collections.[164] Ministers led local chapters of the organizations and made use of the administrative structures of their churches to spread the message. But it was the ordinary minister giving the weekly sermon who was most important to the effort.

Near East Relief and the ACASR saw the campaign to aid the Armenian and Greek as a religious cause. Not incidentally, it would most effectively appeal to the ministers, who most successfully carried the agencies' message to Americans. The agencies therefore stressed religion and religious persecution. Armenians were portrayed as "A Martyred Nation" suffering for its beliefs. Their history was depicted as a long struggle to preserve Christianity against forced conversion. The ministers did not mention that the Armenian Church had continued to exist throughout the Ottoman centuries and had official status within the Ottoman Empire.

> Armenian loyalty to Christ is the marvel of the centuries. The Armenians have been offered every inducement of favor and preferment to forsake their faith. They have been oppressed by harsh restrictions and unjust discriminations, They have been tortured and murdered—not by the hundreds, but by hundreds of thousands—in the ever recurrent orgies of religious and racial hatred. The wonder is not that a few have become Muslims but that any have remained Christian. The loyalty of the Armenians to the faith of their fathers is a modern miracle of the power of God.[165]

> Dr. James L. Barton, Secretary of the American Board of Foreign Missions says: "We are now witnessing in this twentieth century the crucifixion of the three ancient races of Christendom, all three having a large and significant part in the transmission of the word of God and of Christian tradition and the oracles of the Church down through the centuries. All three are suffering for no fault of their own, but because their lot was cast in a land where no Christian power was able to protect and because, forsooth, they would not remove the Lord Jesus Christ from their altars and put Mohammed in his place. These are the people who stretch out their hands to us for sympathy and aid."[166]

The relief organizations saw sermons as an excellent way to reach the faithful. They therefore provided ministers with complete sermons, outlines of sermons, biblical quotations, and other materials that could be easily turned into sermons on the Near East and Armenian relief. A minister might choose among short quotations in the reports from the scene, such as ACASR's "Children Starving in the

Streets" and "Suffering Children at Aleppo."[167] Near East Relief spoke of "Misery Beyond Description" and "The Land of Stalking Death."[168] Or the minister might quote from "Latest Cablegrams from Bible Lands, Suitable for Reading from Christian Pulpits."[169] ACASR publications contained short passages that might be used directly in sermons, complete with short biblical quotations that could be read and explanations of how they applied to the Near East situation. The organizations also provided complete services, which needed no alterations.[170] They instructed pastors to put up posters, send out publicity announcing their sermons, and make use of church bulletins to promote the cause.[171] Missionaries who had returned from the Ottoman Empire were sent to meetings of ministerial organizations to educate the ministers and Christian laypeople.[172]

Judging by the donations that poured out of the churches, sermons on the Near East must have been both ubiquitous and effective. All across America ministers addressed their congregations on the evils of the Turks. The booklets for pastors featured numerous condemnations of the Turks. Many of these were inaccurate or simply wrong, although neither the congregations nor the pastors would have known this. The number of deported Armenians, for example, was more than quintupled. The pastors were given excerpts from British propaganda works such as the reports by James Bryce and Martin Niepage (see chapter 10). Greeks and Jews were falsely alleged to have suffered the same deportations as the Armenians.[173] The campaign leaders placed strong emphasis on what would most cause horror among American congregations, especially the sufferings of children and rape. Of course, they made no mention of the corresponding sufferings of Muslims. It is doubtful that a single member of an American congregation ever heard of one murdered Turk or of one raped Muslim woman.

Unfortunately, few of the sermons given in churches were recorded in detail. One that was printed was the sermon of the Reverend William B. Ayers, given at the Park and Downs Congregational Church of Wollaston Park, Massachusetts, on April 8, 1917. The primary focus of his wrath was the Germans, who were accused of all the usual atrocities; but it is instructive to read why the Germans had gone wrong: because they had learned from the Turks:

> Then followed the massacre of the Armenians. Hundreds of thousands of them driven onto the desert to starve, their women and girls carted away to be ravished, ruined and devoured, by the imbecile passions of the swarthy Turk. We knew that a word from Germany would end this, and we were amazed that such a word was not forthcoming. We could not understand how Germany could allow such a thing. But now we understand fully. Germany had turned her back upon Western civilization. She had joined herself to the East as against the West, to the heathen world as against the Christian, to the Turk as against the white; her Emperor pretending to be a Mohammedan, and her statesmen becoming the champions of the faith. While destroying Belgium and making slaves of her people, while bombarding from the skies the homes of women and the cradles of children, and sinking passenger ships without warning, Germany

has been aiding Turkey with military forces while Turkey massacred a million Armenian Christians. Our Lord was constantly resorting to measures of protection for his disciples, and it would seem to be one of the duties of Christianity to protect and defend the citizens of the Kingdom.

We know now why the German mind consented to the ravishing of the Armenians. Not only had she renounced the humanitarian ideals of Western Civilization, but she had become saturated with the same consuming poison, for she did in France and Belgium what she allowed Turkey to do in Armenia. The German soldiers have sat at the feet of the Turks and learned; and well they have learned their lesson. Now the Germans are carting away the beautiful girls of France, and the fair maidens of Belgium, to what dastardly purpose we dare not think.[174]

Ayers did not stint in his racist attack on "the imbecile passions of the swarthy Turk" in the war of the Turk "against the white." The pamphlet of his complete sermon noted that it was printed by members of the church, because so many requests had come for copies. At this late date it is not necessary to comment on the minister's opinions of the Germans beyond saying that they were false. His opinions of the Turks were obviously founded on the reports of the missionaries, fortified by a liberal dose of racism and religious fanaticism. The most important point may be the effect of the sermon on the congregation, who proudly printed and distributed it. Newspaper notices of sermons in churches (short summaries of what was said) indicate that the Ayers sermon was typical. Sermon themes were the "ravishing" of Armenians, negative racial stereotypes, Islam's supposed injunction to kill Christians, and frequent comparisons of Armenians to early Christian martyrs.[175]

Near East Relief continued the traditions of the ACASR and made ministers the primary agents of its campaign and primary conduit of its message. Like the ACASR, Near East Relief provided pastors with detailed materials for sermons and suggestions for relief activities in churches, Sunday schools, and meetings of church groups. The most detailed of the Near East Relief handbooks not only presented materials for sermons but gave pastors instructions on going out into the world to address civic, commercial, educational, and other organizations.[176] They were to carry the same heartrending message evoked by the ACASR. It stressed the plight of orphans and refugees, blaming the state of both on the Turks: "They are literally being shoved off their ancestral homes into the sea—with no place to land."[177]

Ambassador Henry Morgenthau

Henry Morgenthau, one-time American ambassador to the Ottoman Empire, was an important soldier in the missionary establishment's fight against the Turks. He began serving as United States ambassador to the Ottoman Empire in November 1913 and returned to the United States in February 1916.[178] He thus appeared to have been well suited to report on the conflict between the Armenians and the Turks. This was unfortunately not the case.

The American State Department was very interested in the Ottoman Armenians. Eighty years of missionary writing on the Armenians had conditioned the Americans to think of themselves in some way as protectors of the Armenians. The Americans were also most interested in the fate of fellow Christians, for whom they had always felt great sympathy. Given that interest, it is natural to assume that the State Department expected the American ambassador in Istanbul, Henry Morgenthau, to provide detailed information on the Armenians. He seldom could give it. He collected whatever news he could find and sent it on to Washington. It was a pitifully small body of information. For example, here is Morgenthau's report on the Armenian rebellion in Van, the event that was the main cause for the relocation of the Armenians:

> [May 25, 1915] In the Eastern regions of the Empire although news is extremely scarce and unreliable, it would seem as if an Armenian insurrection to help the Russians had broken out at Van. Thus a former deputy here, one Pastermajian, who had assisted our proposed railway concessions some years ago, is now supposed to be fighting the Turks with a legion of Armenian volunteers. These insurgents are said to be in possession of a large part of Van and to be conducting a guerilla warfare in a country where regular military operations are extremely difficult. To what extent they are organized or what successes they have gained it is impossible for me to say; their numbers have been variously estimated but none places them at less than ten thousand and twenty-five thousand is probably closer to the truth.[179]

Morgenthau obviously did not have access to Turkish governmental sources of information. What he reported could have been, and probably was, extracted from the Istanbul newspapers. While it was true that insurgents had taken a large part of Van and were fighting guerrilla warfare in the countryside, Karekin Pastermajian was nowhere near Van. As to the timeliness of American diplomatic information, on the night of May 16/17 the last Ottoman troops had left Van. By May 25, when Morgenthau wrote that the insurgents "are said to be in possession of a large part of Van," they had already taken the entire city, the Russians had arrived, and the Ottoman army was in full retreat.

Except for a few sentences sent to the Americans (from Bulgaria, not from Eastern Anatolia) by the Dashnak Party (the ones who were leading the rebellion) and a few sentences from missionaries,[180] the excerpt above was all that Morgenthau knew of the Van rebellion.

The State Department might have considered Morgenthau's lack of knowledge abysmal had it not already decided without evidence that the Turks were guilty. It expected from Morgenthau reports that would justify its preconceived notions. The initial cables on the Armenians usually went from Washington to Morgenthau, not Morgenthau to Washington. These were most commonly cables from the State Department telling the ambassador that reports of "Armenian massacres" had reached Washington. Some of the Washington cables simply stated that massacres had occurred in a place, with no sources given. Other messages to Morgenthau forwarded or cited letters from the Armenian patriarch in Echmiadzin, the Dashnak Party, Aneurin Williams (MP) of the British Armenian Committee, the British and French governments, both at war with the Ottomans, and similar informants. The sources were similar in that none of them had actually seen what they described and all had political reason to defame the Ottomans. If the original sources of information were listed at all (assuming they existed), they were described as "an eyewitness," "a letter received from Constantinople," and so forth.[181] The Dashnaks also wrote directly to Morgenthau and to consuls, complaining of Turkish actions without naming sources.[182]

Morgenthau was instructed to tell the Ottoman government not to allow massacres. It is perhaps instructive that he was not actually ordered to investigate the truth of the rumors of massacres. Nor was he asked about Muslim losses. Washington assumed that the rumors were correct. In any case, Morgenthau had already told the State Department that he had no way to investigate.

A small number of consular and missionary reports on Armenian troubles, written soon after the events, did reach Morgenthau.[183] The missionary reports were transmitted to the American Board and the ACASR, which was allowed to pick from consular reports both for its own use and to forward to the British Propaganda Bureau.[184] Once again, however, the consuls had not seen the massacres that they reported as fact.[185] They did see deportations and sometimes violent incidents against individual Armenians, which they presumably reported fairly accurately, but their information on supposed massacres was drawn from Armenians and missionaries, who seldom claimed to have witnessed what they related. The missionaries and consuls usually indicated that they were simply relaying what they had been told. The Reverend J. E. Merrill, for instance, wrote of the troubles at Zeytun from Antep (85 miles away by road) and gave no indication that he had been to Zeytun.[186] Others wrote from Aleppo (165 miles from Zeytun) and even from Beirut (350 miles away).[187]

Later Morgenthau was to make a collection of missionary and some consular reports. It is important to differentiate between these and contemporaneous reports. Reports written by consular officials, not intended for use except in their government, would have value if they had witnessed what they described. Reports written after the fact or intended for political use are necessarily much less valuable. The only contemporaneous accounts that the Americans possessed were hearsay, often based on the word of a single informant. Nevertheless, Morgenthau forwarded missionary reports to the ACASR and (usually through the ACASR) to the British propaganda office.[188]

After returning to America, Morgenthau set himself up as the primary American expert on the Middle East. He entered wholeheartedly into the missionary establishment's campaign, joining the ACASR Board and touring America for the ACASR and later for Near East Relief. The contents of his speeches were much the same as those of the other ACASR speakers, although he did add touches such as accusing the Turks of "massacres in the Holy Land."[189] Some of

Morgenthau's claims stretched credulity to the breaking point. In a New York address in 1916 he contended that the Turkish government had invited him to become the minister of commerce and agriculture in the Ottoman cabinet.[190] In another 1916 speech he claimed that the Turks were willing to sell Palestine.[191] In a 1917 address Morgenthau declared that he wanted to wipe out Turkish power not only in Europe but in Asia as well, leaving the Turks nothing.[192] In 1920 he alleged at a Near East Relief meeting (on the sole strength of a letter from a friend) that the Turkish crown prince had stated publicly that the Armenians would be exterminated.[193] In 1922 Morgenthau asserted that the victorious Turks planned "to overrun Europe."[194]

Morgenthau's primary contribution to the evil image of Turks came through his book *Ambassador Morgenthau's Story*.[195] It was well written, because the actual author was Burton J. Hendrick, an accomplished journalist and author, although he was not mentioned on the title page.[196] Contributions came from Morgenthau's two Armenian assistants. Robert Lansing, the American secretary of state, read the manuscript and made suggestions for changes. The book was based on the diary Morgenthau kept and his letters while ambassador, however, with significant changes from the actual events recorded there.[197]

One the most evident marks of both missionary and British propaganda was the revelation of secret plans of the Turks and Germans that supposedly were conveyed to someone who in reality appeared to have had no way to have heard them. Thus in his British propaganda book Faʿiz El-Ghusein avowed that he had learned of the secret deliberations of the Ottoman Cabinet while he was in a Diyarbakır prison (see chapter 10), and missionaries in Eastern Anatolia stated that they knew what transpired in Ottoman cabinet meetings. In Morgenthau's case, the fabrications were reported conversations with Germans and Turks. While sitting together with Morgenthau on a bench by the Bosphorus on a pleasant day the German ambassador to the Ottoman Empire, Baron Hans Freiherr von Wangenheim, described secret German high-level meetings at which the Germans planned to start the war.[198] Wangenheim also casually mentioned to Morgenthau that the Germans were planning to steal the art treasures of Paris, that Germany planned to starve the French, that Germany was planning to unleash a Muslim Holy War against the Allies, that Germany was planning to seize a large part of the Ottoman Empire, that the Germans were forcing the Turks to treat the Christians harshly, and so forth.[199] The Austrian ambassador, however, confided to Morgenthau that Germany and Austria would probably lose the war.[200]

Although not a single American reviewer of the Morgenthau book raised the question,[201] would the German and Austrian representatives have said such things to an American ambassador? Were they such poor diplomats or, indeed, idiots?

If we believe Morgenthau, the German and Austrian representatives were positively closed-mouthed when compared to the Ottomans. The fabrications on the Ottomans in *Ambassador Morgenthau's Story* centered on the alleged decision of the Ottoman central government to order the extermination of the Armenians. Morgenthau reported that he had heard of the plan from the lips of Talat Paşa, the Ottoman interior minister: "'It is of no use for you to argue,' Talaat answered, 'we have already disposed of three quarters of the Armenians; there are none at all left in Bitlis, Van, and Erzurum. The hatred between the Turks and the Armenians is now so intense that we have got to finish them. If we don't, they will plan their revenge.'"[202] Without stating how he knew what Talat said in private conversations, Morgenthau reported: "Talaat's attitude toward the Armenians was summed up in the proud boast which he made to his friends: 'I have accomplished more toward solving the Armenian problem in three months than Abdul Hamid accomplished in thirty years!'"[203]

Even if the Ottomans had really had such a momentously evil plan, it is impossible that an Ottoman minister would casually relate it to a foreign ambassador. It is clear that Morgenthau lied about his dealings with Talat. In order to create a setting in which readers might believe that Talat would exchange confidences with him, Morgenthau wrote that he met with the minister almost daily, when in fact his own diaries show that the two only met in substantive consultation eight times in six months. In order to present Talat as an evil man, Morgenthau stated that Talat, actually a religious man, was an atheist. The diary that Morgenthau kept while ambassador was supposedly the basis of the book, but the diary mentions no Ottoman admissions of extermination plans.[204] Significantly, Morgenthau did not forward the "admissions of guilt" that Ottoman ministers supposedly made to him to the State Department at the time.

Morgenthau's motives in joining the Armenian crusade are impossible to discover. Most of what is known of his motivation has been based on his own writings, which (as noted above) cannot be trusted. One of his motives may have been a desire for public acclaim. He was the sort of person who hired a clipping agency to collect mentions of himself in newspapers across America and kept the clippings in scrapbooks.[205] More likely, Morgenthau, like other Americans, simply believed what he was told by the Armenians and missionaries. His book indicates that he discounted what Talat and Enver Paşas told him of the Armenian revolt, and the embassy records show that he neither received nor sought information on Muslim suffering. His views on "races" surely contributed to his views on the Turks; Morgenthau was a racialist who ascribed his own "eugenic" feelings to the Turks:

> In order to accomplish this great reform, it would not be necessary to murder every living Christian. The most beautiful and healthy Armenian girls could be taken, converted forcibly to Mohammedanism, and made the wives or concubines of devout followers of the Prophet. Their children would then automatically become Moslems and so strengthen the empire, as the Janissaries had strengthened it formerly. These Armenian girls represent a high type of womanhood and the Young Turks, in their crude, intuitive way, recognized that the mingling of their blood with the Turkish population would exert a eugenic influence upon the whole.[206]

Morgenthau felt that the Turks were barbaric at their core. The Turks of his day were "a remarkable development in race psychology—an almost classical instance of reversion to type," who had "reverted to the barbaric conceptions of their ancestors."[207] The Armenians presented quite a contrast: "Everywhere they are known for their industry, their intelligence, and their decent and orderly lives," "superior to the Turks intellectually and morally."[208] While such feelings might not have an approving audience today, they would have been more sympathetically received in an America that accepted "eugenic influences."

Ambassador Morgenthau's Story was tremendously effective propaganda. It had a wide circulation: by July 1919 the book had sold more than 22,000 copies. It was serialized in the popular *World's Work* magazine (circulation 120,000) and in newspapers (with a combined circulation of 2.6 million).[209] Newspapers that did not run the complete book printed extensive selections, usually choosing the falsified Talat Paşa quotations.[210] *McClure's Magazine* offered the book free with a one-year subscription.[211] Newspapers all across America ran articles on the book and laudatory reviews.[212]

Books of the Missionary Establishment

Not all missionary writings on the Turks during the war period were promulgated by the ACASR and Near East Relief. Members of the traditional mission boards, individual missionaries, and mission supporters also wrote books and articles on the Middle East. Traditional publishers of missionary materials such as the Fleming H. Revell Company and Doran brought out missionary reports and republished British propaganda. While these books were not directly produced by the relief agencies, they were recommended by relief publications.

The Tragedy of Bitlis by Grace H. Knapp was typical of the missionary volumes. The first section of the book concerned the revolution of Armenians in Van, the largest city in southeastern Anatolia, and the Ottoman siege of the rebels. In historical fact, the Armenians killed or forced to flee all the Muslims of the city then held Van until the Russian army could arrive. Upon the Armenian revolt, Kurds outside the city killed Armenians. A general bloodletting ensued. In *The Tragedy of Bitlis*, however, Americans would have read only of dead Armenians—not a single murdered Muslim appeared. In fact, the entire Armenian rebellion was not mentioned, as if the Ottomans simply had decided to put one of their own cities under siege in order to kill Armenians. The section on Van began: "The siege of Van began on the 20th of April, early in the morning."[213] Since this was purportedly a firsthand account, Knapp must have deliberately omitted the cause of the siege as well as the deaths of Muslims. The book went on to document what were undoubtedly the very real sufferings of the missionaries and Armenians, avoiding reference to the equal suffering of Muslims and any mention that the Muslims were reacting to the Armenian attacks on Muslims that began the intercommunal conflict.

Knapp collaborated with another missionary, Clarence D. Ussher, in another book on the Van uprising, *An American Physician in Turkey: A Narrative of*

Adventures in Peace and in War. The book abounded with justifications for
Armenian actions, admitting, for example, that Armenian revolutionary groups
stockpiled weapons but denying that they planned to use them. The leaders of revolutionary parties only looked for peace. They were in fact loyal to the government (why then did they become revolutionaries in the first place?). Nowhere
does the historical record support Ussher's claims; self-described revolutionaries
naturally were planning revolution.[214] Muslims, in contrast, were described as anx-
iously and always awaiting the order from the sultan to murder Armenians. In one
respect, however, Ussher did rise above the other missionary authors: he did admit
some Armenian massacre of Muslims, even if it was in only four sentences in a 339-
page book and even though he justified the massacre ("We remembered what they
had endured from the Turk all their lives").[215] Ussher had such hatred for the Turks
that even the American ambassador spoke of "his innate dislike of Turks and his
inordinate fanaticism."[216]

The War Journal of a Missionary in Persia, published by the Presbyterian
Church, told of the efforts of missionaries in a region invaded by both the Russians and the Ottomans.[217] The heroes were the missionaries and Russians. The
oppressed were the Christians. Except for mentioning that the Muslims were in
fear of the Russians, the book said nothing about Muslim losses. It also failed to
note that the Christians in question were military allies of the Russians who had
killed Muslims.

The missionary H. L. Gates (later president of Robert College, the missionary university in Istanbul) edited and published *Ravished Armenia: The Story of
Aurora Mardiganian.*[218] Perhaps realizing that the only evidence for Mardiganian's
story was her word, in his introduction Gates cited the Bryce Report and other
British propaganda (see chapter 10) as support for her tale. He also described what
he styled as the natural superiority of the Armenians over the Turks and the Armenian love of Americans. The book was made into a movie and shown in American
theaters as part of the fund-raising campaign.[219]

Robert E. Speer, the secretary of the Presbyterian Foreign Mission Board, made
his assertions in *The Gospel and the New World* on the events of the war following the standard practice of accusing without evidence or real citation. For
example: "A capable and just minded observer in Mosul reports on forced prosti-
tution of Christians, forced conversions, massacres, and even cannibalism among
the Muslims." Speer spared no emotion in his appeal: "And the horror of murder
and beastly cruelty by which the Armenians were slaughtered less mercifully than
sheep, were accompanied by every possible physical destruction, moral atrocity
and religious sacrifice."[220]

Prominent among the books recommended by ACASR was the short book
by Herbert Adams Gibbons, *The Blackest Page in Modern History.* Gibbons
stated that he had lived in the Ottoman Empire from 1908 to 1913 and thus knew
of what he spoke. He did not mention that he had been employed as a missionary
teacher in Anatolian mission schools and at Robert College in Istanbul. As a historical analysis, *The Blackest Page of Modern History* was more than deficient.

Gibbons listed nine sources for his work, all either missionary or British propaganda works. He did not quote evidence directly for any of his assertions, which is understandable, because he stated as true many things that he could not possibly have known to have happened. For example, he asserted, without identifying his sources, that he had intimate knowledge of messages that passed from the Ottoman central government to provincial leaders and back, asserting with feigned certainty what he could never have seen.[221]

The book stated demonstrably false "facts" that not even the most ardent Armenian nationalist would countenance. For example, he alleged that all "the virile masculine Armenian population still left in the cities and villages" had been killed by the Turks, as were those in the Ottoman army, leaving only women and children. Gibbons stated that Armenian revolutionaries had never been a threat to the Ottomans; indeed, they were small groups that had never had a following among any Armenian leaders or the Armenian people of the Ottoman Empire. He did not mention the Armenian rebellion in the East or even the occupation of Van by the Armenians. In fact, his only statement about Van was that Armenians were a majority in the Van Province.[222] In fact, they were less than one-third of the population.[223] Turks were described as "pitifully ignorant," with a "frenzy of blood lust." Gibbons blamed the instigation of crimes on Turkish leaders, however, because "the Turks are not, like the Arabs, a fanatical people by nature": small praise for the Turks, but none for the Arabs.[224]

Of course, very few Americans reading Gibbons's work could have known that so much of it was invention or that Turks had ever suffered at the hands of Armenians. But perhaps the title of the book should have made some expect that they were reading propaganda, not history.

Gibbons also wrote *The New Map of Europe*, which contained extensive sections on the Ottoman Empire. In addition to alleging that Turks were at fault for every problem in modern Middle Eastern and Balkan history, he described Turks as "racially" deficient and naturally dangerous, a mix of "racial and religious fanaticism."[225] His treatments of the rebellions in Macedonia in the early twentieth century and the Balkan Wars in 1912–13 were completely one-sided. Because Gibbons considered only Christians sympathetically and gave no population numbers, readers would never have known that the majority of the population in Macedonia was Muslim. Thus he portrayed the Muslims of Ottoman Europe as no more than overlords properly evicted by the populace, when in fact the Muslims were the majority of that population. His discussions of the Balkan Wars, like the other missionary publications, were silent on Muslim losses. In fact, during and immediately after the Balkan Wars, 27 percent of the Muslims of Ottoman Europe died and a further 35 percent were exiled forever from their lands.[226] Muslims suffered more than Christians did, but their losses were not mentioned. The result was propaganda, not history.

In another purported history, William H. Hall, a missionary working at the Syrian Protestant College, accused the Turks of carrying out a policy of extermination against people throughout the centuries.[227] Naturally he offered no

evidence or proof. Hall described Middle Eastern Muslims with stress on negative elements of their culture. His most damning assertions concerned Armenian
relations with Turks. In Hall's work, no Muslims were ever attacked or killed. To
make a case for the existence of an Armenia, Hall doubled the numbers of Armenians in Anatolia and quadrupled the numbers deported. The Muslim population, the majority, was not enumerated. James Barton contributed a chapter to
the volume in which he called for America to accept a mandate over the region.
He wrote that the greatest benefit of an American mandate would be increased
opportunities for missions.

Bertha S. Papazian's *The Tragedy of Armenia* was published by the Congregational Church's publishing house (the Pilgrim Press), with an introduction by
James Barton.[228] The first third of the book was an interesting though often imaginary history of the Armenians. Papazian described the early Armenians as democrats, one sect of whom were actually Protestants in the fifth century, making
them the inventors of Protestantism long before Martin Luther and John Calvin.
The Armenians were superior because they were Aryans, praised for their "racial
purity," whereas the Turks were "marauding nomads from Central Asia, possess-
ing no culture of their own, and of an inferior mentality." Papazian painted such
a bleak picture of Armenian life under Turkish rule that it seemed truly amazing that the Armenians survived 800 years of it. Her comments on the Armenian Troubles were what might be expected. Modern Armenian history was "the
untiring spirit of the Armenians again at work in the cause of human freedom,"
thwarted by the Turks.[229] Papazian had no personal knowledge of any of the events
of World War I, so her book was made up of excerpts and paraphrases from missionary and British propaganda books, with much talk of dead women and children and of Turkish love for "lust and blood." No Armenian, of course, ever did
any wrong—not only during World War I, but throughout history.[230]

In his 1916 book *Leavening the Levant*, the Reverend Joseph K. Greene, a
retired American Board missionary, blamed all the alleged evils of the Turks on
their religion: "Naturally the Turks have many good qualities. They are fond of
children, of dumb animals, of flowers. They are kind and hospitable, cleanly and
temperate. It is their religion as taught by the example of Mohammed which, on
occasion, incites them to rage and cruelty."[231] To establish that Muhammad was
the real cause of the troubles in the Middle East, Greene cited all the canards
about Muhammad's sexuality and sinfulness that had been common missionary
views for generations. His view of Turks as kindly children of nature corrupted
by their religion was contrasted with an appreciation of Middle Eastern and Balkan Christians as more capable and intelligent than the Turks, more able to live in
the modern world. Greene's reports on Armenian-Muslim conflicts were fanciful
creations that mightily magnified the numbers of Armenian sufferers and did not
mention Turkish suffering at all.

Samuel Zwemer, one of the most vituperative critics of Islam (see chapters 4 and
5), wrote no less than four books on Islam and Muslims from 1915 to 1919, including what is perhaps the single book most prejudiced against ordinary Muslims,

Childhood in the Moslem World, and *Mohammed or Christ,* a program for battling the "evil" of Islam.[232]

Samuel Graham Wilson, a minister who had studied at Princeton Seminary and been a missionary in Persia, contributed *Modern Movements among Moslems,* which followed in the long tradition of anti-Turkish works. The book was filled with the traditional false history, such as sultans' plans to kill all Ottoman Christians, and greatly exaggerated statistics on Christian mortality throughout Ottoman history. Wilson made much use of invective: "infernal brutality and devilish lust, rapine, murder, and barbarity."[233] No Muslims had ever died in the one-sided massacres he described. Wilson blamed the Ottoman government for much but felt that Islam was the base cause of the evil, which would not be cured until the Muslims converted to Christianity.

Conclusion

Near East Relief turned support for Armenians and a caricature of evil Turks into an American national myth. Supporting Americans and excoriating Turks came to be a safe cause for politicians and newspaper editors. The American people, predisposed to think ill of Turks and other Muslims by centuries of propaganda and prejudice, had heard nothing to change their minds. Playing to American prejudices to support their cause, the missionaries were almost the sole source of information on events in the war between the Armenians and the Turks. Very few Turks lived in America. Anything said against the Turks was accepted. Politicians who spoke against them were not accused of prejudice; they were praised for their compassion toward the Armenians. It makes no practical difference whether the politicians and editors or, indeed, even the missionaries themselves believed everything that they said and wrote. Correspondingly, the missionaries falsified the record by entirely ignoring the suffering of Turks.

In the period after World War I, Near East Relief was mainly occupied with refugees, including Greeks and Armenians in the East and West of Anatolia. The fund-raising organs of Near East Relief and the churches as well as the popular press described in detail the sad lives and frequent deaths of these refugees but never described the corresponding suffering of the Muslim Turkish refugees in the same places at the same time. For example, in a number of issues the *New Near East* described the poor conditions of the 10,000 Greek refugees in Istanbul, who were housed at the Selimiye Barracks while they awaited transit to Greece.[234] The reports vividly described their hunger and high mortality. They did not describe the 75,000 Turkish refugees also in Istanbul, living in conditions of equal or worse suffering, with no American relief organization to care for them.[235] The only refugees who counted were Christian refugees.

The missionaries and their supporters were indeed partisans. They served not as a neutral source of news and information but as a propaganda vehicle for one side of a war. They intended to tell the story that made their own side look best: the Russians, the British, and their local allies—the Armenians and the Greeks. Like any government propaganda bureau, the ACASR/Near East Relief never intended to tell the whole truth. It intended to tell the stories that produced the greatest indignation against the Turks and thus brought in the most money to their cause. The last thing the missionary establishment wanted was to tell the other side of the story. Just as it is impossible to imagine the British Propaganda Bureau in World War I printing accurate stories showing that Germans were not torturing babies in Belgium, the missionaries could not be trusted to tell the truth about the Middle East. Claiming that "Armenians and Muslims are engaged in a bloody civil war in which both sides have committed horrible atrocities. Send money to aid the Christians" would not have been quite so successful in attracting funds.

What is most important is that nothing was brought forth to counter the great national myth of the evil Turk. The propaganda of the ACASR and Near East Relief was to become the single greatest factor in defaming the Turks in American history.

THE CRESCENT OR THE CROSS?   *The Philadelphia Inquirer*, 1922

Newspaper cartoon: "The Crescent or the Cross?" *Philadelphia Inquirer,* 1922

NEW USE FOR OUR MINISTER TO TURKEY

Newspaper cartoon: "New Use for Our Minister to Turkey," *Library of Congress Collection,* 1885

"A STANDING DISGRACE TO THE CIVILIZED WORLD

Isn't It About Time to Put an End to These Shocking Atrocities of the Barbarian Sultan of Turkey?"

New York World, **1895**

Newspaper cartoon: "A Standing Disgrace to the Civilized World," *New York World*, 1895

"Coming Home"

"The Helping Hand"

Newspaper cartoon: "American Despair at the Turkish Victory over the Greeks," *Dallas Morning News*, 1922

Near East Relief advertisement: "They Shall Not Perish," 1918

Terror!

Five uninterrupted years of it!

Of brutal, beastly persecution. Of cruelties innumerable and unnameable, such as only the mind of a Turk can conceive and carry out. That is the black shadow which has hung over the Armenian nation ever since the World War began.

To tell the whole story of the sufferings of Armenia would require as much space as this entire newspaper. And no newspaper would print it all,

Of 5,000,000 Armenians, only 1,250,000 remain—and these are in a most deplorable condition. America's task—their rehabilitation—is a big one.

America is the only nation that can help.

It is your privelege to give—and give generously—to the Near East Relief Campaign. Mail your check today.

NEAR EAST RELIEF

1 Madison Avenue
Make checks payable to Cleveland H. Dodge, Treasurer.

Near East Relief advertisement: "Terror!" 1920

Excerpt from Near East Relief advertisement: "Let Them Die," 1919

Movie poster: Ravished Armenia, 1920

THE PROPAGANDA BUREAU:
THE BRITISH AND THE TURKS

*In a national emergency we [the British] can be as untruthful as, or more
untruthful than, anybody else. During the war we lied damnably. Let us
be clear about that.*[1]

—*Harold Nicolson*

The missionary establishment directed one of the two campaigns of vilification
against the Turks. The other campaign was directed by the propaganda arm of the
British government. Although their aims were somewhat different, the two campaigns had one common purpose: creation of anti-Turkish sentiment in America.
They cooperated with each other to achieve that end.

WELLINGTON HOUSE

From its beginning the British propaganda enterprise was secret, unknown to
the British or foreign public. The administrative system changed during the course
of the war. Through most of the war, British wartime propaganda was in the hands
of the Foreign Office. A war propaganda bureau was established by the Foreign
Office in 1914 at Wellington House. Its director was C. F. Masterman.[2] Soon after
David Lloyd George became prime minister in December 1916, he reorganized
the propaganda machinery. Propaganda efforts were placed under the Department of Information in February 1917.[3] Col. John Buchan, popular novelist and
military writer for the *London Times*, led the department, with Masterman as
deputy. In March 1918 propaganda was placed within a Ministry of Information,
headed by Lord Beaverbrook (Max Aitken). Hubert Montgomery, originally head
of the Foreign Office News Department, was originally in charge of press propaganda. As of February 1917 he became head of the Administrative Division of
the Department of Information and Buchan's deputy, in charge of "policy matters
relating to propaganda." He held the same office under Lord Beaverbrook in the
Ministry of Information. Despite changes in administration, the creation of propaganda for the United States essentially remained in the hands of the same group
of officials, primarily drawn from the Foreign Office, known collectively as "Wellington House."[4]

Wellington House drew on some of the best minds in the British government. The historian Arnold Toynbee was an advisor to Wellington House from 1914 and sat until 1917 on the committee that met daily to set its policies. He was joined on the policy committee by eminent historians Lewis Namier and J. W. Headley Morley, Oxford classicist Edwyn Bevan, and others.[5] Private and public figures and members of ostensibly nongovernmental patriotic organizations cooperated with or acted under the direction of the official propagandists.[6] British universities provided propaganda pamphlets and expertise.

By the standards of the time the British propaganda effort was a major undertaking. By 1917 Wellington House had a staff of fifty-four and could call on help from other departments and ministries. It sent an average of four hundred articles to the world's press every week.[7] The first report (June 1915) of Wellington House listed the distribution of approximately 2.5 million copies of books, pamphlets, and other written propaganda in seventeen languages. The second report (February 1916) listed 7 million copies circulated. By the end of the war, nearly three thousand different pamphlets, periodicals, and other propaganda literature had been distributed, an incredible 106 million copies in all.[8] All of the distribution was clandestine. A few official government publications were circulated by the propagandists, but all the rest were produced, subsidized, and distributed in secret. Regarding the "campaign to place the case of Britain and her Allies before neutral countries," Wellington House notified the Treasury that "such pamphlets will contain nothing to show that His Majesty's Government is in any way connected with their issue. Nor indeed will the publishing firms be brought into direct relations with a Government Department; all such arrangements are made through a well-known literary agent who has kindly placed his personal services gratuitously at Mr. Masterman's disposal."[9] Wellington House made special deals with publishers and printers, however, and even bought printing machinery for its contractors.[10]

The work of Wellington House was obviously viewed as worthwhile and successful. The Treasury, despite wartime claims on expenditures, seems to have always acquiesced to the Propaganda Bureau's requests for ever-increasing funding. The initial funding of Wellington House was £10,000, soon increased to £20,000, then £40,000, then £50,000—all in the space of a few months. Wellington House had expended £115,000 by October 1916, so £145,000 was allocated a month later.[11]

After the war the British were not proud of what they had done. The records of the Propaganda Bureau were destroyed in an effort to erase the historical record. The work was not perfectly done, however. A small amount of material was forwarded through the Foreign Office and retained in Foreign Office files.[12] For example, the Foreign Office kept copies of reports on propaganda activity sent through the British Embassy in Washington, which reveal something of the extent of the propaganda effort in America. Some "secret" publications, such as the list of sources of British accusations concerning treatment of the Armenians, were sent to Foreign Office officials and for some reason filed and never returned to Wellington House. Some of the official Wellington House reports were kept in the files of the Treasury and the Foreign Office News Department. Arnold Toynbee took away his own records of propaganda work, probably illegally, which surfaced decades later. The record of all the work of Wellington House will never be complete, but enough of the record exists to document the propaganda against the Turks.

Propaganda in America: A Secret Campaign

The British had a great advantage in propagandizing in the United States. They shared the same language, and many Americans were sympathetic to Britain.

The British felt that secrecy was essential to their propaganda operation in America. Therefore they never admitted that they were responsible for the distribution of propaganda materials. Instead materials were funneled through individuals and organizations in the United Kingdom and friends in the United States.[13] Because activities in America were recognized as being of paramount importance, Sir Gilbert Parker was put in charge of a special branch for propaganda in the United States. Parker was a Canadian who had moved to England in 1900, become a member of Parliament, and been knighted by the king. In 1915 he wrote a popular defense of Britain's positions in the war in which the Ottoman Empire was treated as a virtual colony of Germany, translating popular feelings against Turks and Muslims into anti-German sentiment (a common theme in British wartime propaganda).[14] Parker was an extremely popular novelist; each of his books sold hundreds of thousands of copies in America. Married to a wealthy American, he had entrée to many levels of American society.[15]

Parker was in charge of the campaign from 1914 to 1917.[16] He was succeeded in 1917 by Geoffrey Butler of the Foreign Office and the Department of Information.[17] Their appointments were never made public. Parker described his activities in a report to the British government: his agency was in close touch with Americans who could influence public opinion, particularly journalists, editors, and "people of eminence." These people were cultivated through personal correspondence not only by the British but by Americans, "confidential friends of the cause, of position and influence." These friends gave Parker advice and helped with distribution of materials. In addition to dispensing Wellington House materials, Parker and his confidential friends arranged for articles by friendly American journalists in London to be distributed to smaller American newspapers. It was of utmost importance to make use of Americans, knowingly or unknowingly, to distribute propaganda: "to secure voluntary offers of assistance from Americans interested in the cause of the Allies for the distribution of official, semi-official, and missionary literature."[18]

The materials that Parker distributed were always sent as if he was engaged in personal distribution of information or were distributed by intermediaries.[19] He had 170,000 addresses on his list of Americans by 1917 and supplied 555 American newspapers and 557 public libraries with Wellington House propaganda.[20] The amount of material distributed in America was massive, but the

British could count on the patriotic owners of Cunard and other steamship lines to make deliveries.[21] Woodrow Wilson's government knew of Parker's position but seems to have been pleased with it.[22] Parker himself summarized the effect of his efforts:

> In fact we have an organization extraordinarily widespread in the United States, but which does not know it is an organization. It is worked entirely by personal association and inspired by voluntary effort, which has grown more enthusiastic and pronounced with the passage of time… Finally, it should be noticed that no attack has been made upon us in any quarter of the United States, and that in the eyes of the American people the quiet and subterranean nature of our work has the appearance of a purely private patriotism and enterprise.[23]

Foreign Office letters contain lists of propaganda material sent to the United States and broadly distributed. In July 1916 the British distribution list of very important persons indicated that their propaganda reached throughout the leading members of American society (see table 10.1).[24] And this was only the list of distribution to "opinion makers." Most of those on the list received copies of all the propaganda material, and some asked for and received additional copies for distribution. While it is impossible to ascertain exactly who received the propaganda or whether all distributions were as extensive as the list for July 1916 indicates, it is obvious that the British material reached throughout the upper levels of American society.[25]

TABLE 10.1. OPINION MAKERS OF AMERICAN SOCIETY WHO RECEIVED BRITISH PROPAGANDA

Public men generally	1,847	Bishops	250
Scientific men	1,446	Historical societies	214
Lawyers, etc.	1,445	Law schools	166
YMCA officials	830	Clubs	108
Senators and representatives	680	Judges	81
Libraries	619	State superintendents of public instruction	35
Newspapers	555	Distinguished men (for distribution to others)	585
College presidents	339	Others and miscellaneous	2,212
Financiers	262		

Newspapers across America received materials from Parker. Though he avowedly wrote as a private citizen, some editors must have realized that he was not an unofficial source. As an example, Parker sent a letter to the editor of the *Indianapolis Star*:

My dear Sir,

I feel sure you will not regard this letter as an impertinence. Though unknown to you personally, you are aware that there is a considerable public in the United States which reads my books, and that my associations with the country have been intimate. I do not feel, therefore, that I am addressing you as an entire stranger; and I beg you not to think me intrusive when I venture to send you the official papers which set forth the correspondence between the English and German Governments before and at the time the war broke out; together with the speeches of the Prime Minister, of the Foreign Minister, an interview with Mr. Winston Churchill, and a pamphlet by Sir Edward Cook which condenses the official papers.[26]

The *Indianapolis Star* gave no indication that this was anything other than the action of a patriotic British subject. Like other American newspapers, the *New York Times* received the same letter. The *Times* printed it as a letter to the editor, which it obviously was not intended to be. The newspaper commented that it already had the materials Parker sent and had printed some of them.[27] Nevertheless, it praised Parker's attacks on Turks, Germans, and Austrians.[28]

Extremely few American newspapers acknowledged that Parker was anything but a civilian. The description of him in the *Syracuse Herald* was representative: "Sir Gilbert Parker, one of the world's most famous novelists and now immensely important among the British civilians who are striving to aid their nation in its great struggle with Germany, the other day acceded in my cable request for a long distance interview. The result [a page-long piece] follows."[29] The *Herald,* like the *New York Times* and other newspapers,[30] saw fit to print the Parker article as if it had been sent only to that newspaper. *The Daily Northwestern* of Oshkosh, Wisconsin, reported that the same article was a letter that Parker had written to his "American friends."[31] In reality, the British had given the article to the Associated Press for distribution in America.[32] Other articles by Parker were sent by press services or simply forwarded to local newspapers, addressed "to the editor."

Most editors either did not think it odd that a private individual would be writing to American newspapers in order to distribute British official propaganda or did not care. It must be also said that it was not uncommon, then or now, for committed believers in a cause to send materials to the press. Many editors were grateful to have received Parker's material. In editorials the *Hartford Courant* thanked Parker for the pamphlets he had sent: "and they are very welcome."[33] The *Times-Democrat* of Lima, Ohio, thanked him as well.[34] In Massachusetts the *Fitchburg Daily Sentinel* noted with pleasure that the Fitchburg Historical Society had received nearly a hundred books and pamphlets on England's part in the war, "gifts from Sir Gilbert Parker."[35] The books included works from British propagandists such as Arnold Toynbee and Lord James Bryce as well as the works of British politicians. The *Sentinel* does not seem to have wondered at Parker's interest in Fitchburg, Massachusetts. The *Decatur Review* printed a letter from Parker to president George Emory Fellows of Millikin University as if it were a personal honor for the president to have received it from "the eminent British author and statesman." Parker wrote that he had received Fellows's name from academic friends in Britain and, of course, included propaganda books and articles. Obviously, the university president and the newspaper felt that this was purely personal correspondence.[36]

Not everyone was fooled. In an editorial critical of British propaganda the *Reno Evening Gazette* wrote: "There is not a newspaper office in this country that is not in constant receipt of newspapers and pamphlets from Sir Gilbert Parker, the British press representative, as well as circular notes from him. England's efforts to influence public opinion have been strenuous and there is no indication that they have ceased."[37] Upon receipt of a packet from Parker, the *Atlanta Constitution* wrote: "A remarkable series of publications designed to arouse world sympathy is emanating from the evidently well-organized British Press Bureau under the direction of Sir Gilbert Parker."[38] Parker responded in a letter that this was untrue: "I control no press bureau. The work I do does not include the direction of a press bureau."[39] He did not include any description of the work he did. In his letter (written from London) Parker stated: "I have long been a reader of the Atlanta Constitution," which seems unlikely. That he was apprised of an offending sentence in an Atlanta, Georgia, newspaper, however, speaks of the thoroughness of his organization.[40]

Parker continued to deny his work until America joined the Allies in 1917. He told reporters in New York in January 1917: "Neither England nor France will establish any press bureau in the United States." After the United States had entered the war, however, Parker admitted publicly and proudly that "from the day the war broke out I have had American publicity in my charge." He did not state directly that he had worked for the Propaganda Bureau but did say that his work "was always approved by the British Government."[41]

Parker himself sent substantive opinion pieces under his own name on various issues of the war to American newspapers.[42] Some of these were printed as if they were unique to that newspaper with descriptions such as "Specially written by Sir Gilbert Parker,"[43] even though this was never the case. Long and short articles by Parker were forwarded from London, and he was quoted extensively by American journalists in London.[44] Because of the destruction of the archival record, it is impossible to tell if these letters were directly written by the propaganda office and given to journalists and editors or if they were solicited by press agencies, especially the Associated Press. It is likely that they were "planted" with the American reporters. In any case, they appeared in newspapers across America.[45]

British newspapers (as discussed below) were at the mercy of the official Press Bureau and thus could be trusted to carry the message of British propaganda to America. Parker arranged for newspaper exchanges that brought the British press to American towns.[46]

Wellington House was successful in turning respected American organizations into its agents.

> These agencies, now defending the interests of the Allies and doing our work for us without peril of attack, since it is done by Americans, are the direct outcome of the policy steadfastly pursued over the last nine months, of influencing those people of authority and position in the United States who would influence others. One of the most powerful agencies to assist us has been the Carnegie Endowment for International Peace, of which President Nicholas Murray Butler (of Columbia University) is the head. It has distributed our official and semi-official papers in large quantities to a selected list of people in the United States, and is distributing Lord Bryce's Report on German atrocities at the present time. Also the National Security League, brought into touch with us by one of our correspondents, is distributing Lord Bryce's Report in very large numbers and in the same way.[47]

The News from London

The most important British propaganda advantage was effective control of most war news that reached America. The British cut the telegraph cable from Germany to America early in the war, leaving the cable to Britain as the only communications channel across the Atlantic. The British government placed censorship in the hands of an official Press Bureau. The Press Bureau and sometimes other agencies controlled and carefully censored the cable, the life blood of journalism. As H. C. Peterson has written:

> This national censorship of the British was important to the United States because the news passed by this censorship was the version of the news which American newspapers printed. With the cables to Germany cut, American newspapers had to secure their war news where it was available—and that was in England. The only way in which they could get complete and dependable news was to buy the advance sheets of London newspapers. Otherwise they were limited to official communiqués from the British or French governments. News obtained from other European countries had to be filtered by the British censor also. Hence it can be seen that it was truly the British news that became the American news.[48]

If American journalists working in London wanted to see their articles sent to America for publication and wanted to continue to be employed, they must perforce send only reports that matched the British censor's ideas of what should be seen in the United States. Therefore the journalists were cooperative. In his official analysis of the British propaganda machinery, Lord Robert Cecil commented: "The friendliness which we have encountered at the hands of the American press representatives forms a fund upon which we can draw in the case of awkward or undesirable telegrams which the correspondents in London propose to send. We can almost always get such telegrams modified and not infrequently stopped altogether with their consent."[49] Cecil added: "It might astonish some outside observers if they knew how much we had succeeded in stopping [articles] that might have been disadvantageous to us in the press of the United States."[50]

Although it is impossible to know exactly how many American dispatches were rejected or altered by the censors, a representative of the Associated Press, an organization that was on the whole friendly to the Allied cause,[51] estimated in 1915 that 75 percent of the dispatches of American correspondents in Central Europe were destroyed by the British.[52] News from the Middle East must have suffered a similar fate.

The British newspapers themselves were always subject to censorship, to which journalists sometimes objected. The Press Bureau also provided news releases. These were often the sources of London newspaper articles, even though journalists also complained that the articles provided and subsequently printed were often inaccurate.[53] Active censorship was seldom necessary, however. The British press was wholeheartedly behind the war effort and seems not to have scrupled at printing even outright lies in the national interest. The "press barons" who controlled the most important newspapers were actively involved in propaganda work. At one point, the owners of the *Daily Express, Times,* and *Daily Telegraph* were actually put in charge of propaganda in neutral countries, including America.[54]

The British adopted an effective "carrot and stick" approach to the American press. British propaganda agents kept careful track of American public opinion. They read and analyzed major American newspapers daily for articles and opinions that were judged either "pro-ally" or "pro-German" and sent weekly analyses to London.[55] Newspapers that the British viewed as pro-German or even dangerously neutral, such the Hearst newspapers and the *Chicago Tribune,*[56] were denied facilities, not given interviews with political leaders and generals, and not taken on battlefield tours until they cooperated, which they ultimately did. The newspaper and press agencies that were favored, in contrast, were courted and given privileged access. They were provided with canned articles from the official Press Bureau,[57] real interviews with important Britons,[58] and faked "interviews" with British statesmen that could be quoted or paraphrased in American newspapers.[59] Journalists not only were given advanced copies of British newspaper articles but were allowed to take the information from the newspaper proofs and forward it to America, unattributed, as their own work. The job of favored journalists was easy, facilitated by the British. The job of those not favored was almost impossible.

The British made a special and very productive effort to influence the press agencies, developing lasting personal contacts with the heads of the Associated Press and United Press.[60] Editorials were especially prone to British influence. The National Editorial Services provided editorials to newspapers across the United States, which the editors printed as their own. That organization very willingly courted the British for information. The National Editorial Services approached the British Propaganda Bureau through its representative in America, Sir Gilbert Parker, asking for materials to use in editorials. The service mentioned Wellington

House in this correspondence, showing that it understood exactly what it was doing.[61]

The destruction of the archival record makes it impossible to tell which articles on the Ottoman Empire in American newspapers were written by or influenced by the British propagandists.[62] Some articles definitely appear to have been British work. For example, an article in the *New York Times* ("How Turkish Empire Should Be Made Over after the War") stated that it was "Written for the New York Times by a Student of Turkish Affairs."[63] The article touched all the points considered important by the propagandists: massacres, the Turk as "sensuous, lustful, deceitful, and incorrigible," and so forth. It was the suggestions for the restructuring of the Ottoman Empire, however, that most suggested British manufacture. The article gave a detailed description of what was to be given to Russia, England, and France, what was to be left to the Turks, and what was to be made "international": Jerusalem and its environs. The suggestions for division of the empire were remarkably similar to those that the British brought to the negotiation of the Sykes-Picot Agreement, entered into by Britain and France two months earlier.

One good indication of the hand of British propaganda was the insertion of an anti-German message into supposed news from the Ottoman Empire. Stories that depicted the Germans as murderous butchers, including allegations that they sold Armenians and Assyrians into slavery,[64] bear the mark of Allied propaganda. One article from the *London Morning Post,* reprinted in America, contended that Germans had been responsible for the great Ottoman loss to the Russians at the battle of Sarıkamış in December 1914. This was untrue: the Sarıkamış debacle was entirely the fault of Enver Paşa, the Ottoman minister of war. The article provided a supposed account from a Turkish colonel, a prisoner of war, telling of German ill-treatment and even murder of Turks, and included a highly unlikely quotation from him: "There is no true Turkey now. It is only a German province, which the Germans are carrying down with them in their own ruin. Our armies have neither clothing nor food. Germany, which before the war thrust gold galore upon us, now sits on our necks and eats our bread."[65]

Other articles taken from London newspapers contended that Germans had killed 300 Turks (their allies) at Suez and that the Turks hated the Germans and blamed them for the war.[66] In an article originating in London, the "Reuter [*sic*] correspondent with the Dardanelles fleet" quoted an Ottoman Armenian prisoner of war to the effect that the Germans caused the Turks to kill the Armenians.[67] Germans were alleged to have killed Armenians with artillery.[68]

Another indication of British influence on the American press was the large number of articles admittedly based on British governmental sources. For example, an article from London printed in many newspapers alleged that 6,000 Armenians had been killed at Van (but, as usual, included no dead Muslims). It was based on "a dispatch received in official quarters in London."[69] Such dispatches "received in official quarters in London" were the sources of a number of other articles claiming nefarious deeds by the Turks.[70] Letters (by unnamed authors) received by British politicians that damned the Turks were printed in America.[71] Speeches by British leaders forwarded by the Associated Press or other reporters were sometimes excerpted and sometimes printed verbatim in American newspapers. These obviously had propaganda purposes. A particularly egregious example of this was the parliamentary speech by Lloyd George on December 20, 1917, in which he stated that Britain had no territorial ambitions in the Middle East but only wanted to free the people "from the dominion of Turkey."[72] The *Christian Science Monitor* reported: "In a message to the American committee for Armenian relief, Mr. Balfour declares that of the 1,800,000 Armenians in the Ottoman Empire two years ago 1,200,000 have been massacred or deported."[73]

Some articles on the Turks taken from London newspapers and reprinted or summarized in the American press bore all the hallmarks of the Propaganda Bureau, as seen in known propaganda publications (described below): stories of individual suffering, statements about secret deliberations of the Ottoman government that could not have been known, sources identified only as "Miss B——" or "Mr. F——."[74] Of course, some of the articles quoting directly from London newspapers might also have originated with the propagandists. In any case, they were cleared by the British censor. None of them strayed from the government line.[75]

Anglophile newspapers in the United States obviously cooperated fully with the British. The pages of newspapers such as the *New York Times* and *Washington Post* were full of British propaganda. Newspapers took articles from London newspapers, as they had in the past, and no articles favorable to the Turks were allowed by the British press censor. These articles were presented as factual, even though common sense should have indicated that the news was suspect. Britain was at war with the Ottomans, so British newspapers had no reporters in the Ottoman Empire. Where did they get their news? An article from the *London Times* printed in American newspapers, for example, was written by a *Times* correspondent in Bulgaria, who supposedly had intimate knowledge of events in Eastern Anatolia.[76] Other British newspapers quoted in America seldom even bothered to say who had written the piece or where the reporter was stationed. One thing is certain: none of the British reporters had seen what they reported to be the truth. The British Official Press Agency was a constant source of news for the American press. For many events in the Ottoman war, it was virtually the only source. Reports on the Turkish attack on the Suez Canal came to America through it.[77] So did reports on the fighting in Iraq and Gallipoli.[78]

It was not necessary for the American press to obtain its news from London. The British propaganda organization in America provided it for them, often in ready-to-use articles. In secret messages to London, the British propagandists in America described their methods of planting stories in the American press:

1. By supplying articles and statistical paragraphs to the large newspapers who make what is termed their own "lay-outs," often incorporating photographs.

2. By supplying matrices [finished article pages or articles] to the less important newspapers which will print them.

3. By sending out special articles and fill-ups to select lists of newspapers, arranging their selection in such a manner that rival journals in any one town do not get the same article.

4. By sending out special articles to religious and other specialized periodicals.

5. By supplying material to the International News and the Western Newspaper Union, who, in their turn, send out matrices and what is termed "boiler plate" to groups of newspapers approximating in all 13,000.

6. By utilizing the services of the Associated Press, the United Press, the International News Agency and the Central News whenever the nature of the communication which we have at our disposal gives it a news value.[79]

In addition to de jure and de facto censorship, the American press had formidable difficulties in trying to get accurate news from the Middle East. With few exceptions, no American reporters were on the scene. There were usually no American reporters in the war zones in Iraq, Eastern Anatolia, or Palestine, except those few attached to the Allied armies. As had been the case in the 1890s, the few American journalists in the Ottoman Empire remained well away from the fighting, almost always in Istanbul. The writers in Istanbul had little accurate information from war zones many hundreds of miles away. If they reported the Ottoman government version of wartime events, their reports very seldom survived the difficulty of getting that news to America. Official Ottoman government reports would have been a corrective to one-sided reporting. Even if they were also propaganda, at least the propaganda of both sides would have been printed. But the Ottoman view could not get through.[80]

The primary sources for news of the Ottoman Empire that was allowed to pass through the British, as always, were missionaries and Ottoman Christians. Thus what arrived in America from the Ottoman Empire was the view of missionaries and local Christians, especially Armenians. Missionaries presented the Armenians' view to the press. The individual Americans who sent their own reports from the Ottoman Empire, almost without exception, were missionaries. The British naturally allowed missionary reports and journalists' articles based on missionary reports through their censorship, because the British and the missionaries were allies in making the Turks look as bad as possible. The majority of reports seen in America, in any case, did not originate in the Ottoman Empire. With rare exceptions, the only reports from the Ottoman theaters of war in American newspapers were unsigned articles with the dateline "London" or "[city such as Tiflis or Moscow] by way of London." Naturally, these reports were condemnations of the Ottomans. The British campaigns were always portrayed in a good light, even when they were losing, which is an indication of the accuracy of the reports. Both at Gallipoli and on the Iraq front, for example, the accounts continued to indicate that the British were winning until the final reports, which stated that they had lost.[81] The same standard of reporting was seen in articles on Ottomans and Armenians.

THE TURKS IN BRITISH PROPAGANDA

The British prime minister, David Lloyd George, personally and specifically ordered the Propaganda Bureau to deal with the Turks: "My Dear [John] Buchan, When you take in hand the question of Allied and Neutral propaganda, I am anxious you should pay attention to the futility and iniquity of the Turk."[82] Lloyd George directed that special attention be paid to what he called the Turk's "incapacity for good Government; his mis-rule, and above all, his massacres of all the industrious population." The prime minister wanted the Turks to be portrayed as "a blight on the whole territory which they have occupied" and called the Ottoman Empire "one of the worst empires that had ever lived because it has retained its unity only at the price of blotting out two or three ancient civilizations and of repressing its subject races with quite exceptional ferocity." Lloyd George wanted special attention to be focused on the Armenians.[83] He was concerned that the propaganda be surreptitious: "I need hardly point out that it is very important that all this should be done gradually and that the articles should be spread over a considerable period of time, so as not to make it too obvious what we are driving at."[84]

The Foreign Office file that contained Lloyd George's letter to Buchan was annotated with a note: "Sir Mark Sykes' article in the 'Times,' the 'Fighting Turk,' is just what we want." The article in question, one of the few whose provenance is completely recorded in the British archives, was an excellent example of the workings of British propaganda. In January 1917 the British decided to do something about one positive image of the Turks. After the Mesopotamian and Gallipoli campaigns, British soldiers reported that the Turks were "clean fighters," who fought well and treated their British captives properly. A veteran of the Gallipoli campaign had praised Turkish fighters in the British parliament. Some American newspapers had even carried articles on the "clean-handed manner" of the Turkish soldier.[85] The Foreign Office felt that this was an undesirable image for an enemy. Sir Mark Sykes, who had written books on the Middle East before the war, was solicited to write something to demonstrate that the Turks were not clean fighters.[86] (At first the request caused some confusion. Wellington House wrote to the Foreign Office asking why in the world it would want to have an article proving that the Turks were clean fighters. This misapprehension was corrected.)[87] Sykes wrote the article and submitted it to the Foreign Office for approval.

After a certain amount of editing, the Sykes article was placed in the *Times* on February 20, 1917. It was an exemplar of propaganda. "The Turk" was described as "a merciless oppressor, " "a remorseless bully," "pure barbarian[s]," "degenerate," someone who "has strewn the earth with ruins." Historical accuracy was not a particular concern. The Mongols who destroyed Iraq were falsely described as Turks to set up a historical precedent for what was alleged to be happening in the present day. Quotations from leading members of the Ottoman government were freely fabricated. The article was stylishly written.[88] Once the article had appeared in a reputable newspaper, the Foreign Office arranged for offprints to be published. Lloyd George's letter provided the impetus for widespread distribution. The *Times* patriotically gave the government a good price.[89] In the United States, 32,000 copies were distributed.[90]

John Buchan took the job of anti-Turkish propaganda firmly in hand. While the British had published and otherwise distributed much anti-Turkish propaganda before 1917, Lloyd George's direct intervention seems to have given them new purpose. Buchan directed the propaganda apparatus to give particular attention to the Turks.[91]

> <u>Mr. Montgomery</u>[92]
>
> We must organize an elaborate campaign in Britain, in Allied countries, and to a limited extent in neutral countries on the text, "The Turk must go." If Turkey in its present form disappears the German <u>drang nach osten</u> fails, and with it the major purpose with which Germany entered the war. We may have difficulty with the Allies and neutrals on some of our peace terms, but the impossible position of Turkey is a point on which we should be able to secure general unanimity. We have got to make it a platitude among Allies and neutrals.
>
> The points we must emphasize are:
>
> (a) The ancient riches and the great prosperity of Asia Minor and Mesopotamia.
> (b) The blighting influence of the Turk on the social and Commercial progress.
> (c) The incapacity of the Turk for absorbing conquered peoples or for administering equitably subject races. For this we want a historical argument and an account of the recent treatment of Jews, Armenians, Syrians and Balkan races, et cetera.
> (d) The impossibility of reforming the Turkish state. The Turk is a military power and nothing else. He has never shown any capacity for civil government.
> (e) The danger of allowing a reactionary and incompetent state to control the avenue between Europe and Asia. Such a state must always be a satellite of a reactionary military bureaucracy like Germany.
> (f) The religious element might also be pressed. Turkey at present governs a sort of museum of opposing religions, and toleration in the modern sense is alien to her theory of government.
>
> There is no necessity to present detailed themes for the future of Turkey. All we have to do is to convince people that the present situation is impossible and must be drastically dealt with.
>
> I suggest that for Britain and America we want the following:
>
> (a) Series of articles (which could be collected in pamphlets or books) dealing with the historical futility of Turkish rule.

(b) Ditto, by experts on the potentialities of Asia Minor, Mesopotamia, and Syria.

(c) Constant journalistic reminders as to recent Turkish exploits—Armenian massacres, Syrian famine, the brutalities of Enver and the Committee. The point should be made that while the Committee has made things worse, even the best elements in Turkey are incapable of setting their house in order.

The following occur to me as expert to produce material:[93]

Edwyn Bevan (Wellington House).

Sir Mark Sykes.

D. S. Hogarth.

Professor Sir William Ramsey.

Sir George Adam Smith (Aberdeen University).

Professor Browne of Cambridge (he would have to be carefully used).

Dr. John Kelman who is now in America has a good knowledge of Syria.

Blackwood has recently published two books (called, I think, "From the Gulf to Ararat" and "Through Asia Minor on Foot"). The writers struck me as good and might be used.

M. André Chévadame could help in France, but he would require to be supervised as he is Balkan-mad.

Some of the former teachers of the (American) Robert College might be got hold of. They could be approached through somebody like the President of Princeton.

Miss Gertrude Bell (now in the Intelligence Department at Basra) is a first-class authoress and might give us something.

It would be worthwhile consulting Mr. G. S. Fitzmaurice, now in the D. I. D.'s Department.

I should be very glad if you would ask Gaselee to give his attention very specially to the matter.

(Initialled) J. B. [John Buchan] 25.III.17.

Stephen Gaselee, a well-thought-of junior in the Foreign Office, did give his attention to the matter. As the resident expert, Arnold Toynbee was asked to give his suggestions for possible authors of anti-Turkish propaganda. He responded with a detailed list, including Mark Sykes, Guy Lestrange and other professors who studied the Middle East, and others. Toynbee suggested that he could find an

American to write on "the Work of American Missions in Turkey." He offered to deal with Armenia himself.[94]

Gaselee thanked Toynbee for his list and told him that Buchan would be contacting the people on the list. He added, "I send you a copy of a short memorandum drawn up by myself on the subject. It is intended for simple minds and will probably be handed to newspaper editors and others who have no particular knowledge on the subject, to serve as a guide."[95] The respect for the ever-useful editors was obviously not great. The memorandum was what might be expected. Following Buchan's outline, it stated that the Turks had single-handedly destroyed the Middle East through their rule, that the Turks were not really good or "clean" fighters, that Istanbul was too important to be left to them, and so forth, all couched in hostile language. Gaselee sent the memorandum off to editors, professors, and others, without mentioning what he thought of their simple minds.[96]

The Armenians

The primary examples of Turkish cruelty offered to the Americans were the "Armenian Atrocities." On this subject the British had an easy job, because the way had been cleared by the missionary establishment. The British propagandists and the missionaries cooperated completely in their propaganda on the "Armenian massacres." The American Board of Commissioners for Foreign Missions and individual missionaries provided the majority of the Armenian stories and documents printed and distributed by the British. The missionaries then held up the British publications as proof that what they had been contending about the Turks was true, supported by another source.

British propaganda on the Armenians and Turks began soon after the war began, long before Lloyd George's directive. From the first, the British propagandists were concerned with painting the Turks in the worst possible light. They were to be portrayed as unfit to rule an empire, incapable of setting their house in order, a blight to be eradicated. This position would not have been hard to sell in America, where more than a century of anti-Turkish polemics had said the same thing. Many of the British propaganda publications can only be called racist, stating that the Turks were ill-equipped to rule and well-equipped for massacre by nature. Others were content to provide untrue or half-true history. As in all the anti-Turkish campaigns that had gone before, the British works depended on the omission of any Turkish suffering or Turkish mortality.

Because of the destruction of the historical record it is difficult to be sure, but the plans of British propaganda seem to have changed over time. The first portrayals that came to America, at the end of 1914, were of the Armenians of Turkey flocking to the Allied cause, joining the Russians against the Ottoman government. One article claimed that Ottoman Armenians "had prepared themselves for the Russian approach by constant [military] drilling and by gathering arms secretly," Armenians had refused to accept conscription or give up their arms, 20,000 Armenian guerrillas were attacking the Ottoman forces, and the City of Van was besieged by the Armenians.[97] Ottoman Armenians had reportedly gone to Russia to fight the Turks.[98] All this was true. Articles from London and from Petrograd by way of London stated that the Muslims of the Caucasus and South Caucasus were completely loyal to the Russians: "They ask no greater boon than to be allowed to use their horses and rifles against Russia's enemies."[99] This was at best only partly true. In both types of reports, however, the hand of the British is evident: Armenians and Muslims united in their fight against the evil foe. This sort of reporting soon changed, as it became clear that a picture of completely innocent Armenians better fit the desired end of vilifying the Turks.

James, Viscount Bryce of Dechmont, was the most prominent of the British propagandists and most quoted in the American press. Bryce was a long-time foe of the Turks, friend of the Bulgarians in 1876, and founder of the Anglo-Armenian Society in 1879. He was a friend of Gladstone and the influential anti-Turkish author Edward Augustus Freeman.[100] Viscount Bryce was an inspired choice to author propaganda aimed at Americans. He had served as a popular British ambassador in Washington and had many friends in American political and religious circles. His history of the United States (*The American Commonwealth,* first published in 1888) had been well received by academics and the public. Moreover, Bryce had a reputation as an honorable man. Reviewing propaganda printed under his name, the *St. Louis Republican* had commented: "If there is a man in the entire British Empire whom the people of this nation are prepared to believe implicitly, it is James Bryce."[101] The *Washington Post* stated: "No man in Europe commands a more sympathetic audience in America than Viscount Bryce."[102]

Bryce was a believer in the Armenian cause. Seventy-six years old in 1914, he was too old to be an official member of the British Propaganda Bureau. He nevertheless worked closely with the government propagandists. Lacking the lost archival record, it is impossible to know how many of the letters and articles he sent to America were actually his own work. Judged by the deception involved in his putative authorship of the *Blue Book* (described below), it is obvious that Bryce did not scruple to send out the work of others under his own name. Whether he himself or the government propagandists were the actual source is not of primary importance; he shared a common purpose with Wellington House: to blacken the image of the Turks. Bryce advocated the common propaganda line that the Germans were at fault for the Armenians' suffering.[103] He alleged that the Germans had taken a personal hand in killing Armenians.[104] In a report sent to the American National Geographic Society and published in newspapers, Bryce called for the "neutralization" of Palestine, taking it away from the Muslims because of their "more than 14 centuries of misrule,"[105] not mentioning that this was an effective plan to ensure the security of British Egypt. Bryce told the Americans of the need for the "principality of nationality," according to which the Ottoman Empire, a multinational state, must be dissolved.[106] The hypocrisy of imperial Britain advocating such a concept seems not to have occurred to him. It would probably also not have occurred to his readers, for whom the British Empire was beyond reproach.

Information on the Armenians from Bryce was seen much more often in the American press than information from any other British source or at least any British source that was identified. He was in close contact with the American news agencies.[107] He most commonly communicated his views through long cables to editors and to press services. What he sent was often of dubious authenticity, depending on information from "an Armenian refugee worker" or "an Armenian refugee." Bryce was trusted, however, and his reports were repeated as fact in the press.[108]

Bryce's pleas in the American press were emotional, not substantive, and he was not bothered by contradicting himself. In 1915 he sent the American press a report that "virtually the whole [Armenian] nation has been wiped out,"[109] a view of Armenian mortality that he later adjusted. His submissions to the press were constant, however, in their view of the Turks and the Germans. Bryce, like the other British propagandists, blamed the Germans whenever possible, either for directing the Turks to massacre or for not stopping them.[110] Bryce said that the Turks were unfit to govern anything, that the Ottoman Empire should be destroyed, and that the Turks "should have been expelled from Europe 100 years ago."[111] Bryce's standards of evidence gathering were typical of those employed by both Wellington House and the American missionary establishment. The propagandists had the advantage of speaking to a public that had virtually no knowledge of the Ottoman Empire except what they had read in earlier attacks on the Turks. For example, Bryce offered the American press a fairly detailed (and almost totally incorrect) account of events in Van and Bitlis provinces. His telling was replete with scenes of horror: men forced to dig their own graves before they were shot, young women and children "distributed to the rabble," "women assaulted in public before the eyes of their mutilated men," and horrible tortures for all. It was true that the Armenians of Bitlis had suffered and many had died, although not with the sort of tortures alleged. Bryce, however, did not mention that Armenians were killed only after they had rebelled in Bitlis, killing and raping the Muslims of the region. Bryce's source was "an Armenian gentleman in Tiflis,"[112] far from events in Bitlis.

Bryce did not neglect the religious element in his call to oppose the Turks. A religious man himself, he undoubtedly felt this strongly. He cabled the Associated Press in America that the Turks were bent on exterminating the Armenians out of religious hatred.[113] In a signed article he compared the Armenians to the early Christian martyrs.[114] Bryce was a friend of many in the missionary establishment and often wrote to the ACASR/Near East Relief.[115] In a cable obviously intended for publication, he wrote the ACASR that the Turks intended to wipe out all Christians and Jews, leaving only Muslims in the empire. The ACASR, of course, submitted his views to the press.[116] It also forwarded to the press other cablegrams from Bryce, praising the Armenians as martyrs for their faith and condemning the Turks.[117] The messages, of course, were filled with horrific stories of Turkish wrongdoing. The ACASR stated that Lord Bryce had confirmed its own views.[118] This was natural, because most of Bryce's narratives had originated with American missionaries, as Bryce himself verified.[119] The American missionaries provided material to both Bryce and the ACASR; each then said that the evidence in the hands of the other proved it to be correct.

Many of the more ridiculous articles appearing in America seem to have been compilations of information from British and missionary sources. Some were feature articles that stressed Christian religious brotherhood with the Armenians or described a selected history of the Armenians.[120] Some were simply ridiculous, such as the supposed Turkish plan to massacre Mennonites in Syria.[121] Others (datelined London) were obviously from British sources, because American reporters would have had no way to find the information they contained. This "information" was often nonsense. For example, "British refugees" in Alexandria supposedly reported on 1917 massacres in Urfa, a city in which no British actually had been present.[122] The Turks were allegedly killing all the Armenians as they advanced in 1918, "based on statements by [unnamed] German consuls."[123] The article "Armenians Hard Hit by the Treacherous Turk" by a United Press correspondent in London (Lowell Mellett) stated: "Armenians knifed, burned, stoned, drowned and otherwise put to death by the Turks (well authenticated figures), 1,000,000."[124] Where did Mellett get his information? In the article he cited only Lord Bryce and an Armenian graduate student.

It is often difficult to believe that American editors could have accepted and printed obvious British propaganda, and not very convincing propaganda at that. For example, the Associated Press quoted a British officer in Bombay who recounted what he had heard in Iraq from a "highly educated Armenian who had escaped from the Turks." The Armenian, if he actually existed, described to the British officer scenes of cruelty and murder in many places of the Ottoman Empire. He depicted the Germans as more cruel than the Turks in persecuting the Armenians. The informant, supposedly privy to central government councils, said that he knew with certainty that the Germans were behind the troubles of the Armenians and had convinced the Ottomans to take action against them. The article did got give the name of either the British officer or the educated Armenian.[125] It stated that the information came to the Associated Press by mail, as did another article alleging that the Germans had urged the Kurds to murder Russian soldiers retreating from Anatolia after the Russian Revolution. No source was given except "by mail."[126] This sort of source was common: the *Washington Post* source on events in Van was listed only as "correspondence."[127]

Many articles in American newspapers, primarily long analyses or features, carried no identification whatever: no author, no city. It is naturally impossible to tell the origin of these, but the spirit of the British propaganda office hangs over them. For example, one long article in the *Washington Post* told how the British defeat in their first attempt to take Baghdad had been "a blessing in disguise," because it gave the British time to convince the world's Muslims what good fellows they were and that the Turks, "who are descended from the most cruel and savage foes of the prophet," were fiends.[128] It did not identify these supposed Turkish ancestors. The article compared the British to the Crusaders but said that the Muslims of Iraq welcomed British rule, which was better than the rule of the Turks, because the Arabs supposedly considered them "alien usurpers." The Iraqis were "not only contented but relieved" now that the British were there. The story bears all the marks of the British propagandists. Other unidentified articles in numerous newspapers, often complete with pictures of Jesus, carried on the same themes.[129] It is possible, of course, that such pieces were the product of humble American Anglophiles who also hated Turks and did not want to be identified, but it is unlikely. But the British propaganda had become so effective that American newspapers did print articles such as "Germany Urged Turkey to Slay the Christians" without direct British input.[130]

The basic question of where such articles could have come from, if not from British propaganda, arises. How would an enterprising if unnamed journalist in London come upon the incredible news that the Turks thought the kaiser was a Muslim, that German clergymen were converting to Islam, that Arab Christian soldiers were revolting, and other nonsense? Yet all that appeared in an article datelined only London, with no sources or verification.[131]

Many articles in American newspapers, including a number of page-long feature articles, drew completely on two sources, British newspapers and British official reports (i.e., the British propaganda machinery).[132] Indeed the British newspapers, all of which had to pass the censor, can be considered yet another set of propaganda documents. They relayed only the official line on events in the Ottoman Empire. The correspondent of the *London Times* in Dedeağaç (in Bulgaria in 1915) sent an article describing the travails of the Armenians in Eastern Anatolia, containing tales of Armenian mothers throwing their children into the Euphrates rather than see them suffer and other heart-rending stories. In America, the Associated Press distributed an article drawn from the *Times* report.[133] The article did not name sources or explain how the information reached Dedeağaç, 700 miles from the Euphrates.

In matters of propaganda against the Turks, the Associated Press was the great ally of the British. The News Department of the Foreign Office commented that it had "complete confidence" in Ben Allen, the London representative of the AP, and often asked his advice on the U.S. press.[134] As the source of many of the articles that reached newspapers in American cities, especially smaller cities, the Associated Press routinely blamed the troubles of the Armenians on the Germans, according to the British propaganda line.[135]

Associated Press reporting tended to reflect the view of the side covered by the AP reporters. Thus the reporting on the Gallipoli campaign by the correspondents lodged with the British told an ultimately false tale of impending British victory:

> Through a bold stroke the British Army has dealt the Turks a humiliating and disastrous reverse, resulting in the capture and destruction of the main lines of communication between Constantinople and the forces defending the Gallipoli Peninsula...The demoralization and the surrender of the Turkish army defending the Gallipoli Peninsula are expected in the near future. The opening

of the Dardanelles and the eventual fall of Constantinople are now said to be inevitable, and it will only be a matter of time before the Twentieth Century Crusaders will raise the standard of Christianity on the mosque of St. Sophia.[136]

No Associated Press reporters accompanied the Turks who were fighting the Armenians and the Russians in Eastern Anatolia, but the AP did place correspondents with both the British and Russian armies that were attacking the Ottomans. All of their reports were cleared through the London censor. In Eastern Anatolia the AP reporter sent back stories of Turkish massacres and Armenian and Assyrian bravery, all drawn from the testimony of individual Armenians.[137] The AP correspondent described Armenian bodies by the roads but seems not to have noticed any Kurdish or Turkish bodies.[138] His report on the Armenian rebellion at Van (drawn entirely from interviews with Armenians) completely falsified the events, attributing everything to the supposed hatred shown by the Ottoman governor.[139] An Associated Press correspondent who rode with the Russians and with the Armenian rebel leader Andranik Ozanian seems to have accepted all that he was told by the Armenians. For example, the AP reported on May 24, 1915, on the Russian occupation of Başkale, in southeastern Van Province.[140] The Armenians of Başkale were gone, so he wrote with assurance that they had been massacred by the Turks. In reality, the Russians had invaded Başkale before (in December 1914), at which time the Armenians rose up and slaughtered their Muslim neighbors. When the Russians were forced to retreat, the Armenian population, fearing reprisals, followed them. This was quite different from the reported massacres of Armenians.[141]

Almost all news from the Middle East and Balkans came through London. This included news from Eastern Anatolia, Iran, and the Russian Caucasus provinces, transmitted by the circuitous route Tiflis-Petrograd-London before they reached America.[142] The only alternative was the new wireless technology. Some reports from the Ottoman Empire managed to be sent to America by radio from Berlin, but this was an unreliable method of communication, given the state of the technology. For most journalists it was London or nothing. The *New York Times* alone printed 209 articles on Armenians datelined "London" from 1914 to 1918; only 19 articles on all topics were datelined "Constantinople." The differences were more than quantitative. Only two of the articles datelined Constantinople were on page 1, neither of them touching on troubles between Turks and Armenians. Forty-two of the articles datelined London were on page 1. The articles from London had headlines such as "Report Christians in Peril in Turkey," "Hang Christians in Street," "Whole Plain Strewn by Armenian Bodies," "Kurds Renew Massacres," and "Armenian Horrors Grow," with articles to match. The Constantinople articles mentioned Armenians only in passing and had headlines such as "Spirit of Doom Hangs over Turks" and "Pleas for Armenia by Germany Futile" or headlines on Turkish military activity in what the *Times* called Armenia.[143] It is thus likely that many of the articles datelined Constantinople actually passed through London, because they contained nothing that would offend the British censor or sometimes ("Spirit of Doom") commentary that could easily have been written by Wellington House.

The Jews

The workings of the British propaganda machinery are perhaps best seen in propaganda on the Jews of the Ottoman Empire. The choice of the Jews as a focus of propaganda would seem to be odd. The Jews whose families had lived in the Ottoman Empire for centuries, notably those whose ancestors had been expelled from Spain and Portugal, were the most loyal of Ottoman subjects. But the British felt that something had to be done about the very accurate anti-Semitic image of their allies the Russians. Press censorship easily isolated the British and French publics from knowledge of the continuing persecution of Russian Jews, including persecution of Jews in and by the Russian army. The United States was another matter. Many of the Jews in America had firsthand knowledge of Russian persecution and were unwilling to side with the Russians or to forgive those who took the Russians as their allies. The American Jewish Committee made a year-long investigation into the conditions of Jews in Russia and found damning evidence of Russian attacks on Jews and a lack of Jewish civil rights.[144] The American Jews also seem to have had excellent sources of news on Russian actions against Jews, which reached America. Even pro-Allied newspapers such as the *New York Times* felt obliged to print that news, given their readership.[145]

The British attempted three ploys to combat the American negative press on Russia and the Jews. One was diversion. Simply put, Americans were presented with the "Armenian massacres" and their supposed German sponsorship or complicity as the real massacres that should cause American concern. This was not an unworkable scheme. Then as now more sensational news drove other news from the media. American Jews and others had begun campaigns to provide aid for the Jews of Russia, and newspapers carried many articles on the campaigns. Once the campaigns for the Armenians began, however, fewer articles on the campaigns for the Russian Jews appeared. In this the missionary establishment was a great aid to the British. The missionary campaigns were at first aimed at relief for Christians. Later Jews were added to the list of sufferers, but always Middle Eastern Jews, never Russian Jews.

The second ploy was a campaign to demonstrate that the Russians were changing their ways. Articles began to appear in America (datelined only "London"), denying that the Jews of Russia were in difficulty and stressing that the middle of a war was not the time to address the problems of Russian Jews. Even Lord Lionel Walter Rothschild was quoted to that effect.[146] The Russians were reported to be treating the Jews well, beginning to end old injustices,[147] and welcoming back to their homes Jews who had fled the Russian armies as well as Jewish refugees from elsewhere.[148] While some articles continued to condemn the Russians, another campaign began to appear in the American press: the Jews of Russia could expect equal rights and an end to persecution if only the Allies won the war.[149] Articles appeared from Petrograd, London, and the United States in which Jews said that their hope was for an Allied victory, after which they were assured of reforms that would improve their status.[150] The *Jewish Chronicle* of London (discussed below) cooperated fully with the British Propaganda Bureau and shifted its initial stance on the Jews of Russia. It had at first condemned the Russians, but in articles reprinted in America it began to declare that the Russians would be instituting reforms for the Jews after the war was won.[151] The American Jewish Committee declared that equal rights for Jews in Russia were expected.[152] There was also a distinct shift in most newspaper stories from condemnation of the Russians to the treatment of Jews as victims of war, without particular blame being laid on the Russians.[153]

Like the first tactic, the third British tactic involved the Turks. One focus of this attack, the seeming support of Zionism, is too well known to need much description here. Even if the British were sincere in supporting Zionist aims in Palestine,[154] the British position, culminating in the Balfour Declaration, was indisputably an effective propaganda tool. It was not felt to be enough, however. A story of Turkish persecution of the Jews would eclipse the Russian persecutions, blacken the enemy Turks, and draw to the British camp Jews and non-Jews alike who supported the Jewish presence in Palestine.[155] For this, a wholly spurious narrative of Turkish persecution of the Jews in Palestine was invented. The centerpiece of the attack was the Ottoman relocation of the populations of Jaffa, Gaza, and other coastal cities as British forces advanced on Palestine. According to the tale, the Turks had "deported" the Jews of Gaza, Jaffa, and elsewhere in order to kill them. Some renditions extended the region of relocation to most of Palestine; some said that the Turks were planning the expulsion and death of the Jews of Jerusalem.[156] The temper of the articles that resulted can be seen in a headline from the *Washington Post:* "Unspeakable Cruelties of War Where Christ Preached Love and Kindness 2000 Years Ago." The article wrote of the Turks "visiting massacre and havoc on the people of the Holy Land."[157]

British newspapers printed stories on Palestine's Jews that were quoted in American newspapers.[158] The *Jewish Chronicle* of London began a campaign against the Turks. In articles reprinted and excerpted in America, the *Chronicle* wrote that the Turks were planning the destruction of the Jews of Palestine: "The Turkish Governor, Djemal Pasha, has proclaimed the intention of the authorities to wipe out mercilessly the Jewish population of Palestine, his public statement being that the Armenian policy of massacre is to be applied to the Jews."[159] (Cemal, of course, had made no such statement.) The *Jewish Chronicle* proclaimed that the Turks had evacuated the Jews of Gaza and Jaffa as part of their persecution.[160] The *New York Times,* among other newspapers, quoted a *London Daily News* article from Cairo stating that the Turks, "prompted by Berlin," had "undertaken the systematic destruction of the entire work of Jewish colonization."[161] A "special cable to The *New York Times*" from London stated that the Turks had robbed all the Jews who were evacuated from Jaffa, destroyed their homes, and hanged all who resisted.[162] The *Washington Post* headlined: "Turks Rob, Slay Jews: Terrible Scenes Mark Expulsion of 1,600 from Jaffa."[163] The *Christian Science Monitor* wrote:

"Information that has been gained by the *Christian Science Monitor* indicates that the Turks have commenced a series of atrocities against the Jews of Palestine similar to those perpetrated upon the Armenians and the Syrians."[164] Newspapers in smaller cities and towns copied an Associated Press article that accused Turks of "terrible torture," "mutilated bodies," and "dead in large numbers strewed the roadway."[165] A number of articles stated that only the Jews had been evacuated, with obviously evil intent, not the Muslims.[166] The reports appeared from 1915 to 1917, continuing well after the alleged events.[167]

The hand of the propagandist seems obvious in some of the articles. For example, an article with the dateline "Cairo, Egypt, Friday, July 20 (Correspondence [note: not Correspondent] of the Associated Press)" was a long statement from "an official in touch with all these sources [on Palestine]." The official wrote of the Turks' "stupendous wickedness," which was aimed at all those "not of Turkish blood." He declared: "The disaster that befell the Armenian population is now being meted out to the mixed non-Turkish population of Syria and Palestine. Families are being massacred, towns and territories evacuated, communities plundered and given over to pillage." The article stated that Jerusalem was soon to be looted and that the only hope of the people of Palestine was a speedy British victory.[168] Reports that listed no sources, such as the one that "all the leading men" of Jaffa had been "convicted by a German court-martial and hanged with many members of their families,"[169] also seem to have been the propagandists' work. The inclusion of the Germans makes this all the more likely.

None of it was true. The two sources of the reports of Turkish cruelty were the British government and the *Jewish Chronicle*. Although the information was never released to the American public, the facts were known to the U.S. Department of State. The American government had read the stories of cruelties in Palestine, including the claim that a massacre was planned for Jerusalem (a report from the *Jewish Chronicle* that was repeated in the New York newspapers). The State Department asked the American ambassador in London to ascertain the source of the stories. Questioning the British, the ambassador was told that the stories had originated with the British High Commission in Egypt, which had telegraphed them to the *Jewish Chronicle*.[170]

The U.S. government, sure that the Turks must have been guilty, asked the government of neutral Sweden (which had diplomatic representation in the Ottoman Empire) to investigate the claims against the Turks.[171] The Swedish were joined by other neutrals (Norway, Denmark, and Spain) in their investigation. Their reports stated that the allegations of cruelties to Jews in Palestine were false. The Ottomans had evacuated not only the Jews but all the inhabitants of the coastal towns, because they knew they were in danger from British and French artillery and naval bombardment (both of which then occurred). The final Swedish report stated: "Apart from the difficulties and hardships inherent in the situation, there was no rioting nor systematic ill-treatment of the Jewish population and above all there was no such thing as massacres."[172]

The Ottomans had evacuated a population in danger of death. Their proper action had been turned into a massacre by the propaganda machine.[173] Perhaps needless to say, the evidence exonerating the Ottomans did not appear in the American press. Some newspapers reported the American request that Sweden investigate the condition of the Jews in Palestine, saying that it was part of a "vigorous protest" against the Ottomans by the U.S. government.[174] None reported the results of the investigation.[175]

It was no accident that the *Jewish Chronicle,* a London publication, was prominent in the transmission of the false information on Palestine. The editor of the newspaper, L. J. Greenberg, had approached the Foreign Office to offer his services. Thomas Wodehouse Legh, Lord Newton, the assistant undersecretary for foreign affairs, spoke to Greenberg and reported: "He is ready to conform with any indication of policy which may be given to him from the Foreign Office."[176] And conform he did.

It is impossible to know how much Wellington House had to do with these stories and to what degree they originated with other British agencies. It seems to be the case that the tales originated in British-controlled Alexandria, Egypt.[177] An organized distribution system for propaganda was obviously in place, almost surely part of Parker's connections to American newspapers. How else would newspapers in small cities such as Syracuse, New York, quote articles on the Turks from the *Jewish Chronicle* in London without any mention of source other than the dateline "London"?[178] Is it likely that editors in Syracuse would ordinarily be readers of the *Jewish Chronicle?* The material must have been sent to them by the British or perhaps by American journalists in London. The publicity campaign of the missionary relief organizations joined in, disseminating stories of the Turks attacking Jews and even reporting that the Turks destroyed cities that were actually destroyed by British bombardments, "according to information received from Cairo, Egypt, by the Committee for Armenian and Syrian Relief."[179]

WELLINGTON HOUSE PUBLICATIONS

As described above, most specifics of the British publication campaign against the Turks are impossible to obtain, because the British destroyed almost all of the records of their propaganda offices immediately after the war.[180] One critical bit of evidence survived, however. An important list of the books secretly written for, subsidized by, or distributed at British government expense by the Propaganda Bureau was mistakenly retained in two places: one incomplete handwritten list sent with other volumes to the Foreign Office Library, probably because it was bound and looked like a book, and a complete printed list that found its way to the Imperial War Museum. Other documents, such as the records of stories "placed" with journalists and communications with those who cooperated with British propaganda effort, have been lost.

The registers of propaganda publications titled "Wellington House Publications" were lists of works subsidized and distributed by Wellington House.[181]

Amidst a much larger number of anti-German publications, the documents cataloged the following publications concerning the Ottoman Empire:

E. F. Benson, *Crescent and Iron Cross,* London: Hodder and Stoughton, 1918; New
York: Doran, 1918.

E. F. Benson, *Deutschland über Allah*, London and New York: Hodder and Stoughton, 1917.

British Palestine Committee, *Palestine, Reprint of article from November 24, 1917,*
London: Hayman, Christy, and Lilly, 1917; New York, Doran, 1918.

The "Clean-Fighting Turk," a Spurious Claim, reprinted from *The Times* of February 20, 1917.[182]

Israel Cohen, *The Turkish Persecution of the Jews*, London: Passmore and Sons, 1918.

The Commercial Future of Baghdad, London: Complete Press, 1917.

Edward Cook, *Britain and Turkey,* London: Macmillan, 1914.

Delegates of the Red Cross, *Turkish Prisoners in Egypt,* London: Cassell, 1917.

Leon Dominian, *The Frontiers of Language and Nationality in Europe*, New York:
Henry Holt, 1917.

Faʿiz El-Ghusein, "Bedouin Notable of Damascus [*sic*]," *Martyred Armenia*, London: C. Arthur Pearson, 1917; New York: Doran, 1918.

*General Sir Edmund Allenby's Despatch of 10th December, 1917, on the Operations
in Egypt and Palestine from 28th June, 1917, till the Capture of Jerusalem (11th
December, 1917)*, reprint from *The London Gazette* of January 22, 1918, London,
H. M. Stationery Office, 1918.

S. Georgevitch, *Serbia and Kossovo* [no information].

*Germany, Turkey, and Armenia: Selections of Documentary Evidence Relating to
Armenian Atrocities,* London: J. J. Keliher & Co., 1917.

Great Britain, Palestine, and the Jews: Jewry's Celebration of Its National Charter,
London, The Zionist Organization, 1918; New York: Doran, 1918.

Great Britain, Palestine, and the Jews: A Survey of Christian Opinion, London: The
Zionist Organization, 1918; New York: Doran, 1918.

A. P. Hacobian, *Armenia and the War,* London: Hodder and Stoughton, 1917;
New York: Doran, 1917.

E. W. G. Masterman, *The Deliverance of Jerusalem*, London: Hodder and Stoughton, 1918; New York: Doran, 1918.

Basil Mathews, *The Freedom of Jerusalem*, London and New York: Hodder and
Stoughton, 1918.

Esther Mugerditchian, *From Turkish Toils: An Armenian Family's Escape*, London:
C. Arthur Pearson, 1918; New York: Doran, 1918.

Martin Niepage, *The Horrors of Aleppo, Seen by a German Eyewitness*, London: T.
Fisher Unwin, 1917.

The Ottoman Domination, London: Fisher Unwin, 1917.

Canon Parfit, *Mesopotamia: The Key to the Future,* London: Hodder and Stoughton, 1917; New York: Doran, 1918.

Pavle Popovic, *Serbian Macedonia,* London: The Near East Limited, 1916.

Report on the Pan-Turanian Movement, Intelligence Bureau, Department of Information, London: October 1917.

R. W. Seton-Watson, *Serbia, Yesterday, Today and Tomorrow: A School Address,* London: Vacher and Sons, 1916.

George Adam Smith, *Syria and the Holy Land,* London: Hodder and Stoughton, 1918; New York: Doran, 1918.

Harry Stuermer, *Two War Years in Constantinople,* London: Hodder and Stoughton, 1917. New York: Doran, 1917.

Subject Nationalities of the German Alliance (with a Map Drawn from German Sources), London and New York: Cassell and Co., 1917.

Syria during March 1916: Her Miseries and Disasters, London: Sir Joseph Causton and Son, 1916.

S. Tolkowsky, *The Jewish Colonisation in Palestine,* London: Zionist Organization, 1918.

Arnold J. Toynbee, *Armenian Atrocities: The Murder of a Nation,* London and New York: Hodder and Stoughton, 1915.

Arnold J. Toynbee, ed., *The Treatment of Armenians in the Ottoman Empire, 1915– 1916,* London: H. M. Stationery Office, 1916.

Arnold J. Toynbee, *Turkey: A Past and a Future,* London: Hodder and Stoughton, 1917; New York: Doran, 1917.

Arnold J. Toynbee, *The Murderous Tyranny of the Turks,* London: Hodder and Stoughton, 1917; New York: Doran, 1917.

Josiah Wedgwood, M. P., *With Machine-Guns in Gallipoli,* London: Darling and Sons, 1915.

Chaim Weizmann and Richard Gottheil, *What Is Zionism?* two chapters from *Zionism and the Jewish Future,* London: The Zionist Organization, 1918.

J. S. Willmore, *The Welfare of Egypt,* London: Hodder and Stoughton, 1917.

The publications listed in the documents are only books or large pamphlets. They do not include press releases, articles, and other materials. The general themes of the propaganda are consistent from work to work:

- Turks are illegitimate rulers who have destroyed all lands in which they have ruled. European rule over the Middle East would be far preferable.
- Turks are Muslims who hate all other religions, particularly Christianity. They have always treated Christians badly.
- Turks are guilty of inhuman atrocities against Christians, including mass murder and awful sexual crimes.
- The Germans stand behind Turkish evil deeds, either because they ordered the deeds or because they had the power to stop them and refused.
- The mass of the people of the Ottoman Empire look to the British for salvation. This includes Muslims, who appreciate the good government that the British have given Muslims in Egypt and India.

Wellington House publications were most often published by Hodder and Stoughton in Britain. The American publisher was Doran, a company that was partly owned by Hodder and Stoughton, although Hodder and Stoughton also published some volumes in New York under its own imprint. According to Wellington House, George H. Doran, head of the publishing company, was "in close cooperation with Mr. Geoffrey Butler, in New York, and has been in touch with Lord Northcliffe—the head of the American Mission." "Messrs. Doran have produced and distributed a large number of books and pamphlets for Wellington House in the U.S.A., and, so far as these are concerned, Mr. Doran may be said to be the representative of Wellington House."[183] Toynbee's short books against the Turks, *The Murderous Tyranny of the Turks* and *Turkey: A Past and a Future,*[184] were both republished in America by Doran, as were anti-German books by Toynbee and others. Doran also published a number of missionary tracts directed against the Turks, including work for Near East Relief. It published other propaganda literature that was not on the Wellington House list above, including other works by the British Palestine Committee. Because of the destruction of most Wellington House records, it is impossible to tell whether these were also "sponsored" by British propaganda.

Due to the destruction of the archival record, the extent of the Wellington House involvement in the production of individual pieces of propaganda in the list above is unknown. Toynbee's works were prompted by his position with the Propaganda Bureau. Based on that and a list of the other books printed by Hodder and Stoughton it seems that most of those books were instigated by Wellington House or other governmental agencies. It cannot be an accident that Hodder and Stoughton books uniformly justified British rule in Palestine and Iraq, which it was British policy to retain after the war.[185] Nor could it have been accidental that the works of Masterman, the head of propaganda, were published by that house. Other books were most likely distributed by the British because they fit into British propaganda aims. Dominian's *The Frontiers of Language and Nationality in Europe,* written for the American Geographical Society of New York by an American Armenian, was one of these. The works from the Zionist Organization were probably produced by that organization itself, although it did cooperate with the Foreign Office. But the works by Toynbee and Masterman and those without listed authors were the product of the Propaganda Bureau, as the works of Benson probably were, which read like a catalog of British political agendas. Basil Mathews produced other propaganda, not in the Wellington House list, including *Christ and the World at War* (London: J. Clark and Company, 1917), a collection of sermons that was just what might be expected from a book with such a title. Because of the close connection of the Hodder and Stoughton and Doran publishing houses with Wellington House, it is probable that most or all of their publications on the list were instigated by the British government.

The British propagandists undoubtedly sponsored other books that were not recorded in the few sources available or distributed them surreptitiously. In addition, almost no evidence exists on the pamphlets and the newspaper and magazine articles sponsored by Wellington House and planted in the press, because the records have been destroyed. Only occasionally were such materials described in archival documents. For example, Montgomery wrote: "At our request Mr. John Masefield has written a series of articles on events at the Dardanelles. The idea is that these articles should be sold to some really influential American paper, and we have little doubt that they will have a good effect."[186] The articles were approved by the British censor and forwarded to Parker. Newspapers were not interested in the long articles, so they were published as a book. The Macmillan Company published the book in America in 1916.[187]

It is tremendously frustrating to research the propaganda machinery in the British National Archives. The small number of documents that remain refer to other documents, many of which appear to be very important but no longer exist. Little is known, for example, about an entire pro-Russian and anti-Turkish propaganda campaign concerning Muslims in the Russian Empire. Toynbee wrote a detailed description to be used in the campaign, which survived, and there were plans to use it in America and the rest of the world. Toynbee also wrote an article on the subject in the *Round Table*. Reprints were to be made, seemingly along the same system used for "The Clean-Fighting Turk." No more is known, because the documents were destroyed.[188]

THE BRYCE REPORT

The most influential of the Wellington House documents, *The Treatment of Armenians in the Ottoman Empire*, usually known simply as the *Blue Book*, was also the only one that admitted some association with the British government.[189] Although the British government did not confess that the book had been written by its propaganda arm, it did publish it under its own imprimatur, as a publication presented to Parliament. It was distributed all over the United States by Parker's organization and sold in American bookstores.

The views of Viscount Bryce, the putative author of the *Blue Book,* on the Turks were not temperate:

> Turkish government has been the very worst which has afflicted humanity during the last fifteen centuries. The Turks have always been what a distinguished European historian of the last generation called them—"nothing better than a band of robbers encamped in territories which they had conquered and devastated." They have never become civilized, they have never imbibed or tried to apply any of the principles on which civilized government must be conducted. So far from progressing with the progress of the years, they have gone from bad to worse. Savages they were when they descended into Western Asia from the plains of Turkistan, savages they were when Edmund Burke so described them one hundred and thirty years ago, and their government still retains its savage and merciless character.[190]

Viscount Bryce's affection for Armenians and dislike of Turks went back four decades. Already in his book *Transcaucasia and Ararat* (1877), he had stated that the Turkish government "deserved to die," praised the Russians for their treatment of Muslims such as the Circassians (one-third of whom had died due to the Russians), gave estimates that tripled the numbers of Armenians in Ottoman lands, and generally distorted the history of the time.[191] Given his views, it would not have been odd for Bryce to produce a volume such as *The Treatment of Armenians in the Ottoman Empire,* which was avowedly his personal work. In the introductory material of the volume, he wrote that it was a personal enterprise: "I wrote to all persons I could think of likely to possess or to be able to procure trustworthy data, begging them to favor me with such data…I had the good fortune to secure the co-operation of a young historian of high academic distinction, Mr. Arnold J. Toynbee, late fellow of Balliol College, Oxford. He undertook to examine and put together the pieces of evidence collected, arranging them in order and adding such observations, historical and geographical, as seemed needed to explain them."[192] This was pure fabrication. Toynbee, working for and assisted by the Propaganda Bureau, was the actual author and Bryce the figurehead.[193] Other than his introduction, Bryce's contribution lay in forwarding documents in his possession ("Documents have been sent to Lord Bryce by Armenian friends") to Toynbee and in reviewing what Toynbee had produced.[194] The book was in no sense a private undertaking. It was in fact a government propaganda production.

The Bryce Report on Armenian atrocities was a catalog of alleged Turkish crimes against the Armenians. It contained 150 documents detailing supposed Turkish actions against Armenians, almost all of them in connection with their deportation, along with introductory materials and a history of the Armenians. It was a companion volume to the first Bryce report on the "German atrocities in Belgium," also "edited" by Toynbee.[195] That first report has been thoroughly discredited by historians.[196] All the techniques seen in the Armenian report had been refined in the earlier report on alleged German atrocities in Belgium: anonymous reports collected from "unimpeachable sources," but no physical record of what the sources really said or wrote.[197] In both reports the few statements that were accompanied by identification or some other "proof" were much more temperate than the anonymous reports. Postwar attempts to find the sources of the Bryce Report on the Germans were unsuccessful, and a Belgian postwar investigation failed to find evidence that most of the atrocities listed by Bryce ever occurred. In particular, the more spectacular crimes that tugged at the heart and turned the stomach, such as cutting off women's breasts, bayoneting pregnant women, and murdering priests, seem to have been almost entirely fabrications or, at best, exaggerations. In his analysis of wartime propaganda, H. C. Peterson described the Bryce Report on the Germans: "His report is one of the most extreme examples of 'assassination by word.' It was in itself one of the worst atrocities of the war."[198] Interestingly, the same sorts of crimes appear with regularity in the Bryce Report on Ottoman Armenians.

The two Bryce reports, along with additional books by Toynbee and others, were part of a well-constructed British propaganda effort.[199] They were successful attempts at painting Britain's enemies black and thus affecting the outcome of the war. In the case of the Germans, they were instrumental in bringing the United States into the war against "the Hun." In the case of the Turks, they were instrumental in promoting the lasting stereotype of Turks as vicious killers. The British propaganda against the Germans has been thoroughly studied and labeled for what it was: wartime propaganda with little veracity. But the propaganda against the Turks has never been subjected to the same scrutiny and continues to form one of the bases of anti-Turkish prejudice to this day.[200]

The Bryce allegations against the Germans were based on depositions supposedly taken from Belgian refugees in the United Kingdom and British and Allied servicemen. No names were given, ostensibly to protect the families of the accusers, though why the Allied soldiers could not be identified was not explained. The Bryce Report on the Armenians followed the same basic principles. Bryce printed reports and analyses from unidentified sources supposedly within the Ottoman Empire. Like all other British propaganda publications, the work of Bryce and Toynbee never mentioned a single dead Muslim. To them, the only dead were Armenian and Assyrian Christians. Given their aims and their sources, this was not surprising.

Who were Bryce and Toynbee's sources? The names or original copies of the "sources" on German atrocities never have been discovered or published, giving some critics cause to wonder if at least some of the reports were pure fabrications. In a like manner, the report on the Armenians mainly listed its informants by coded letters and descriptions ("Mr. A," "Miss B," "A Foreign Resident," etc.). The names of the informants were omitted, ostensibly to protect them from reprisals. The British did keep records of the sources, however; these were misplaced in Foreign Office records and not destroyed with other propaganda office registers. They were discovered by chance among unrelated documents.[201]

Had the sources of the evidence been offered at the time of publication, the Bryce Report on the Armenians would have been seen as propaganda, not the evidence of neutrals. The main sources of atrocity stories were in fact American missionaries and Armenians.[202] Of the 150 accounts in Bryce's book, 59 were written by missionaries and 52 were written by individual Armenians or copied from Armenian newspapers. The majority of the documents from missionary and Armenian sources were sent by James L. Barton, head of both the American Board and the American Committee for Armenian and Syrian Relief, and by William Rockwell, the lead propagandist of the ACASR.[203] Toynbee had initiated contact with the ACASR in February 1916 and had found the ACASR leaders more than willing to cooperate.[204] Many of the stories that the ACASR provided had been used in ACASR publications. Barton, in particular, engaged in an extensive correspondence with Toynbee, furnishing documents, suggesting sources, and giving advice.[205] The other sources of documents were Boghos Nubar, leader of an

Armenian independence organization,[206] and Léopold Favre, a Swiss professor of medieval languages.[207]

Very few of the missionary authors were identified as such in the text. Most of them were identified as "foreign residents" or "foreign travelers," with no indication that they were missionaries with long ties to the Armenians.[208] Words and titles in the documents were changed so that the persons who provided information were not identified as missionaries. For example, in one document the phrase "Dr. C., coming from Constantinople, gave me the further information which he had obtained either at the American Embassy at Constantinople or in Missionary circles" was changed to "Dr. C., coming from Constantinople, gave me the further information." In the same document, "missionaries" was changed to "correspondents"; "a missionary at Mardin" became "a resident at Mardin." The author was identified only as "an Armenian formerly resident in Turkey," omitting to mention that he had not left the Istanbul region. "Dr. C." was a Canadian missionary for the ABCFM who had never actually seen what he described.[209] An American missionary or missionary's wife or sister reporting on an area away from the mission station would be called an "American traveler" even if the individual had not been an eyewitness to the events described. Readers would probably have assumed that the "traveler" was visiting from America, but this was not the case.

Toynbee and Bryce used other subterfuges as well. For example, a Greek professor at the Armenian missionary college at Mersovan (whose student body was almost entirely Armenian) who was the author of three documents was described in two of them as a "Professor at the College of X [sic]" and in the third document only as "a traveler, not of Armenian nationality."[210] Readers would naturally assume that these were two different authors, both of them neutral and one perhaps a professor in Britain or America. In fact they were all written by a Greek professor, who might very likely share the sentiments toward Turks of many other Greeks, particularly those employed by American missionaries to teach Armenians. In his introduction, Bryce stated categorically that his respondents did not know each other, a somewhat duplicitous statement when in fact his respondents were sometimes the same person. The archival record proves that Toynbee was aware that *Blue Book* sources knew each other and exchanged stories.[211] It is clear that Toynbee and Bryce deliberately lied.

Readers of the Bryce Report had no way to know how closely many of the sources were tied to the Armenian cause. The *Blue Book* described writings of the Armenian patriarch, for instance, only as the work of an "authoritative source." Most incredibly, 7 of the 150 documents were the work of the Dashnak Party. The Dashnaks had organized revolutions against the Ottoman government for decades and were the main party of revolutionaries fighting against the Ottomans in Eastern Anatolia at the time. The Dashnak source was never identified. Other documents were taken from articles in Armenian newspapers controlled by Dashnak sympathizers. A number of other documents were forwarded by Armenian political representatives, such as Boghos Nubar.[212]

The lack of authentication in the Bryce Report was outrageous. According to secret British records, most of the nonmissionary informants were known to the British only as Armenians, with no other information on their bona fides or veracity. Bryce wrote in the *Blue Book* that he knew all of the documents' authors, but fourteen (nearly ten percent) of the narratives had no known authors; the British had no idea who the authors were but included the stories anyway. In addition, American consuls and missionaries acknowledged that other reports, which they forwarded without attribution, were based on stories from unknown persons.[213] In creating the *Blue Book,* Toynbee first selected documents then made an effort to discover the names of authors. Some names were found; others were not. James Barton, who had provided more documents than anyone else, said that information on the sources of many of the reports he had sent Toynbee was "not in our possession."[214] Some of the sources that Barton could identify were not very satisfying: "a citizen of a friendly power," "an American official," "a German missionary." Barton often knew who had forwarded a document, usually a missionary or an American consul, but not who had written it.[215] At least one high British propaganda official questioned the standard of evidence of the materials sent by Barton: "I gather that Barton himself has no very clear sense of evidence, judging by his own treatment of the documents (keeping no record of names suppressed, and so on)."[216]

The Reverend William Walker Rockwell, who sent many documents to Toynbee and used some of them in his own ACASR propaganda, responded to Toynbee's request for information on sources. He identified some as coming from the Dashnaks, an American consul he could not identify, and missionaries. Even the Dashnak reports, he stated, were "not in their original form." For a number of sources, Rockwell simply wrote: "Don't know; wish very much that I did."[217]

Other providers of documents also did not know the provenance of many of them. Léopold Favre wrote of documents from "anonymous," "one who could get away [from the Turks]," "an eyewitness," and so forth.[218] Boghos Nubar stated that all he knew about one letter was that it was printed, without signature, in a Bulgarian journal. Another was written by the Armenian minister Thomas Mugerditchian, who was working in Cairo for British Intelligence.[219] Three reports had come from "journals," but Nubar did not have the issues in which they appeared. He said that another three documents had come from the Dashnak Party journal *Droschak*, which was the only provenance he knew (documents 93, 103, and 109).[220] Nubar volunteered to ask the editors and wrote to *Droschak*. The editors responded with the names of the journals in which the reports had appeared or the names of those who sent the materials; but they did not give, and perhaps did not know, the names of the authors or any other details on how the authors obtained their information.[221]

Toynbee discarded some of the unknown sources but not most of them. They were printed along with the others, identified only as "X," "Y," or "Z." Because almost all other names were hidden as well, these unknowns appeared in the Bryce Report as if their identities were known but disguised.

The *Blue Book* was a characteristic piece of British propaganda. It vilified the Turks but included the Germans whenever possible as cooperating or even leading the Turks in heinous activities. As is always the case with propaganda, the *Blue Book* only included sources from one side of the issue and was none too careful at checking those sources.

The effect of the Bryce Report was significant. Bryce, who had served as British ambassador to Washington, was a friend of Woodrow Wilson and the author of respected scholarly books.[222] He was considered an influential friend of America, and his word carried much weight. The Bryce Report on the Germans had been one of the factors convincing America to join the war. The Armenian report, which supported the missionary campaign against the Turks, had similar great effect. Missionary works on the Turks and Armenians often used phrases such as "Now our old friend Ambassador Bryce has proven our contentions."

The use of the Bryce Report in America created an interesting relationship. The report itself was largely drawn from missionary and Armenian narratives, though it usually did not identify the missionary sources as such.[223] The missionary establishment was also publishing information from Armenians and missionaries (see chapter 9). To convince American readers of the veracity of their reports, missionary organizations referred readers to the British reports. It appeared that they had found independent verification of their claims. In fact, the Bryce Report was drawn from those same missionary and Armenian reports.

In America, the Bryce Report on the Armenians was a major part of the campaign against the Turks. The British distributed parts of the Bryce Report to American newspapers in advance of publication. Gilbert Parker reported: "The New York *Times,* Philadelphia *Public Ledger,* and the Chicago *Herald*...devoted much space to the advance sheets of 'these Armenian horror stories.'"[224] Indeed they did. Before the book was published the *New York Times* had already dedicated two entire pages to it, filled with praise and complete agreement. It repeated as fact the assertions that Bryce and Toynbee had made in the page proofs sent to the *Times:* all the sources were known, none supposedly had any reason not to be completely truthful, and all evidence was considered—although nothing that advocated another position was included in the *Blue Book.*[225] Once the book was available, *Current History,* a monthly magazine feature of the *New York Times,* made the Bryce Report the centerpiece of a series on anti-Turkish articles, quoting the entire lengthy introduction of the Bryce Report and summarizing the most ghastly portions of the book.[226] The *New Republic* praised Bryce on his selection of sources and evidence, without mentioning that most of the sources were anonymous, then went on to summarize the material and condemn the Turks.[227] G. P. Putnam's Sons, publisher of the *Blue Book* in the United States, advertised the book in major and minor newspapers alike, stating that it was available in "all booksellers." It sold at least 1,000 copies in the United States. This was a small part of the total given out. In addition to the 3,000 copies that were sent to the ACASR for distribution,[228] Wellington House sent Parker 15,000 copies for dispersal to eminent Americans. Other copies were sent directly from Wellington House with a letter from Bryce.[229] It sent 200 additional copies to American newspaper editors.[230] Recognizing that they would carry more weight if forwarded by Americans, Wellington House sent these press copies (preaddressed to editors) to the ACASR, which distributed them.[231]

The ACASR was the willing assistant of the British propagandists in distributing the *Blue Book.* Before it was printed, Barton cabled Toynbee, suggesting publicity for the book in America.[232] As the book was in production, Toynbee sent page proofs to Walker and Barton for editorial comment and publicity.[233] Using the page proofs sent from London, the ACASR distributed a review of the book to the American press. Barton wrote Toynbee that the *New York Times* had been particularly helpful.[234] The British propagandists were well pleased with the ACASR publicity. Toynbee wrote: "Dear Dr. Barton, The reception of the Armenian Report in the American Press has been magnificent. I should like to thank you warmly for all you have done to make it such a success."[235] In addition to the 200 books sent to editors of the main newspapers, the ACASR sent the book to other papers. Charles Vickrey, the executive secretary of the ACASR, wrote Toynbee thanking him for a list of 280 newspapers and magazines that Toynbee had suggested for ACASR distribution of the book. Vickrey said that he was distributing the book to those and to 200 "other publications that do not chance to be on your list." He added: "I am endeavoring to see that every editor and molder of public opinion in the country has a copy."[236]

Other Wellington House Publications: A Selection

Wellington House used the Bryce Report as the basis of other propaganda publications. Under his own name Toynbee himself wrote four short books against the Turks, including *The Murderous Tyranny of the Turks* and *Turkey: A Past and a Future.* In *Armenian Atrocities,* he summarized the charges and evidence that he placed in the Bryce Report but made a great effort to blame all on the Germans, using evidence such as "cables from Cairo" and letters in New York Armenian publications to try to prove his point. In *Turkey: A Past and a Future,* Toynbee was more temperate in laying blame, accusing the Germans only of complicity, not of ordering the deaths of Armenians. He compared the Turks to the Germans, to the benefit of neither. The quality of the scholarship is indicated by the map that accompanies the book, which shows all Eastern Anatolia as "Armenian" in population, when more than three-quarters of the population of the region was in fact Muslim. Both books were printed in Britain and America through the Wellington House connection with Hodder and Stoughton/Doran.

Another Wellington House book based on the Bryce Report was *Armenia and the War* by A. P. Hacobian, which featured a preface by Bryce. Twelve percent of the book was taken up by quotations from the Bryce Report. The remainder was stated to be the product of "an Armenian gentleman belonging to a family originally from Ispahan in Persia, but now settled in England. He speaks with intimate knowledge as well as patriotic feeling."[237] Once again an anonymous informant is cited, and this time a member of an Armenian family from Isfahan in Iran (far from any Turkish-Armenian conflicts).

Armenia and the War repeated basic themes of British propaganda. Germany was largely at fault for siding with the Turks and agreeing to massacres. The Muslims of the world would welcome political rule by Britain, France, and Russia— all three of which had supposedly been a blessing to the Muslim populations they ruled. An entire chapter was devoted to a refutation of the "clean-fighting Turk," quoting Mark Sykes. The author made a plea for America to enter the war. The hand of Wellington House is obvious. Other sections of the book describe Armenians and Turks from a racialist viewpoint. The virtues of the former and vices of the latter were supposedly irredeemable features of their national characters, which nothing can change: "The Turk as a race has added yet another and vaster monument to the long series of similar monuments that fill the pages of his blood-stained history, in proof of the unchangeable brutality of his nature. You cannot reason or argue with him. Nor can you expect justice or ordinary human feelings from such a nature."[238] As proof Hacobian presented a selective and inaccurate history that included tactics such as portraying the Mongols as Turks to demonstrate the constant nature of "the Turk." This allowed him to portray the Bryce Report as yet another confirmation of basic Turkish character.

E. F. Benson's *Deutschland über Allah* offered no evidence, even spurious evidence, against the Turks. The book simply stated that the Turks were guilty of massacres of Armenians and that further actions against Greeks, Kurds, and other non-Turks were underway. Moreover, the Turks were alleged to be bad Muslims who had perverted Islam as the Germans had perverted Christianity. Benson vilified the Germans by asserting that they knew all about Turkish villainy, could have stopped it, and did nothing. If the Germans had complained, he stated, the Turks need only have reminded the Germans of what they did to the Belgians. Benson reproached the Germans for their purpose in supporting the Ottomans, which was to take over the Middle East after the war, a humorous criticism in the light of Britain's own intentions.[239]

Germany, Turkey, and Armenia is an interesting piece of propaganda because it is difficult to see how it could have been taken seriously.[240] The book was published with no author, editor, or sponsor listed. Some of the material was taken from the Bryce Report, and most of the other material was anonymous ("Fräulein O," "a German Eye-witness," "two Swiss ladies"), describing no source of the material. The majority of the reports were labeled as originating from German missionaries. Like their American colleagues, they only noticed dead Christians, never dead Muslims. The most incredible part of the book is two short "Reports by Mohammedan Officers" ("A. B." and "C. D."), which reported entirely spurious orders to kill Armenians. One of the orders was supposedly from the Şeyhülislam (the chief religious leader of the Ottoman Empire), a more than unlikely occurrence, given that he never had the power or the position to give such orders. The book of course gave no indication of how these reports reached England. Neither the language nor the form of the reports was typical of Turkish documents or even letters. For the officers to have had access to the secret documents they would have needed to have been high officials, yet they made mistakes such as saying that an officer of the Ottoman General Staff was assigned as the administrator of a small city. And if the two had been high officers, could the British and American public have believed that they were somehow secretly sending reports on the Armenians to the British? The answer is probably yes. Those who read the propaganda would have no way of checking its veracity.

As seen in the Bryce Report, the British purportedly used natives of the Middle East (if Hacobian, a resident of England whose family came from Iran, so qualified) who could be seen to be a source of authoritative evidence. The putative author of *Martyred Armenia,* Faᶜiz El-Ghusein, described himself as "a Bedouin, a son of one of the Heads of the tribe of El-Sulût, who dwell in El-Lejât, in the Haurân territory." He stated that he had studied in Istanbul then became a member of the Ottoman bureaucracy: "I was attached to the staff of the Vali [governor] of Syria (or Damascus), on which I remained for a long while. I was then Kaimakâm [district administrator] of Mamouret-el-Aziz (Kharpout), holding this post for three and a half years, after which I practiced as a lawyer in Damascus… I then became a member of the General Assembly at that place, representing Haurân, and later a member of the Committee of that Assembly." The author said that he had been accused of being a rebel, arrested, and brought to Antalya, "where persons accused of political offenses were tried." He was acquitted of the charge, but Cemal Paşa (governor of Syria) kept him imprisoned in Diyarbakır, where he was finally released. In Diyarbakır all types of officers and civilians allegedly came to him and told him of awful deeds done to Armenians. He somehow escaped to Basra and then to Bombay, resolved to tell the story of the Armenians.

The difficulties with the Ghusein story would not have been noticed by many outside the Ottoman Empire. According to official registers, no one named Faᶜiz had ever been *kaymakam* (administrator of a small district) of Harput (Kharpout). It is possible, of course, that he was *kaymakam* for such a short time that he was never entered in the published lists, although he stated that he had held the post for more than three years. The only verification of his story was his own testimony. Even according to his own account he never rose above the level of a *kaymakam,* who would never have had access to government secrets or high-level decisions. By his own admission in a later work he was indeed a rebel against the government, a member and high official of an Arab nationalist secret society.[241] At the time when he supposedly wrote *Martyred Armenia* he was most definitely a rebel against the government.

Ghusein wrote of matters he could never have known, including secret meetings of the highest government officials and secret plans in Istanbul, and on unlikely topics, such as the histories of Armenian deputies to the Ottoman parliament from the Istanbul district and Armenian revolutionary leaders whose paths never crossed his. For someone with such allegedly comprehensive knowledge he made surprising mistakes, such as placing cities in the wrong provinces. He showed an amazing if fanciful knowledge of events, at one point describing not only what goods were taken from Armenians and by whom but to whom they were delivered in Istanbul—all this reportedly learned from far away in a Diyarbakır prison. Some of his information was demonstrably false, such as the Ottoman settlement of Balkan War refugees in the Armenian city of Zeytun, which never took place. On the whole, the small book is a catalog of unproven Turkish misdeeds told in horrific vignettes, including questionable observations such as Turkish soldiers copulating with Armenian corpses.

Who actually wrote *Martyred Armenia* will probably never be known. It may have been Ghusein or it may not have been. It is instructive that the book came out of (or at least was stated to have come from) British India and then was published by the secret hand of Wellington House.[242] All that is known for sure is that the text was sent to Wellington House from War Office representatives in Cairo, not Bombay.[243] The War Office commented: "I think it ought to be rather good propaganda in America and Canada where they seem interested in the Armenians."[244]

From Turkish Toils: An Armenian Family's Escape was reportedly an extended letter from Esther Mugerditchian.[245] She was the wife of an Armenian Protestant pastor who had served in the British consular corps and, although it was not stated in the book, was serving in Army Intelligence with the British forces in Egypt.[246] The book was "translated from the Armenian," with no mention of the translator. Its foreword (again by an unknown hand) blamed the Germans for the Armenian troubles, although German misdeeds were never mentioned in the text—typical evidence of British propaganda work. The text itself was an excellent piece of propaganda, mixing believable elements (Ottoman soldiers torturing Armenians so that they would reveal arms caches) with other elements that, on analysis, seem questionable (unlikely feats of torture, speeches made to Armenians by ordinary Turkish soldiers in which they revealed high-level, long-held secret plans to exterminate Armenians to which they had somehow become privy, etc.). All of this somehow reached Esther Mugerditchian.

The Turkish Persecution of the Jews repeated all the propagandists' falsehoods about Turkish supposed actions against the Jews in Palestine, never mentioning British bombardments and Turkish assistance to the relocated Jews.[247]

The Ottoman Domination was a short anonymous work reprinted from the *Round Table* magazine. It was primarily a set of slogans: "The breaking up of Turkey is not the destruction of a living commonwealth, but a liberation of enslaved peoples from prison." "[The Turks'] hand was against every man's, and none they conquered became reconciled to their rule." "The first phase of Ottoman policy towards subject peoples was neglect, the Hamidian [rule of Abdülhamit II] was attrition; but the Young Turkish phase is extermination."[248] It claimed that the Turks first had killed 2 million Armenians (considerably more than existed in the empire) and now were beginning to exterminate the Arabs.

Syria during March 1916: Her Miseries and Disasters was a set of translations of articles first published in Cairo, which was under British control and press censorship at the time. It related the supposed terrors of life in Ottoman Syria. Directed primarily toward Arab sympathies (and thus not published in the United States), the book advanced the thesis that the British had real affection for the Arabs, while the Turks were the opposite: "The Young Turks bear deeper malice against the Arabs than against any other race in Turkey."[249] The characterizations were less than subtle attacks on the Turks, or, as they were called, "Constantinopolitan blackguards."[250]

British propaganda on the Middle East had purposes other than vilification of the Turkish enemy. It also cast the British in the best possible light. Edward Cook's *Britain and Turkey* was a justification of the British declaration of war against the Ottoman Empire. J. S. Willmore's *The Welfare of Egypt* was intended to justify British rule over Muslims. According to Wellington House, the book "shows that the Mussulman prefers to be under English rule."[251] *Turkish Prisoners in Egypt* by Delegates of the Red Cross fairly accurately portrayed British humane care for prisoners of war. Pavle Popovic's *Serbian Macedonia* and S. Georgevitch's *Serbia and Kossovo* were pamphlets supporting Serbian political positions, including the absurd assertion that the Macedonians were really Serbians. The publications on Jerusalem and those of the Zionist Organization were distributed both to elicit Jewish support, particularly in the United States, and to provide justification for British occupation of Palestine. They included testimonials by British politicians and leaders supporting Zionism and Zionist statements supporting Britain and thanking it for the Balfour Declaration, which had promised a "national home" for the Jews in Palestine. It is important to note that Britain had already committed itself diplomatically to long-term occupation in the Arab world when these publications were distributed.[252]

The Missionary Establishment and British Propaganda

The British propagandists realized that the missionary establishment was their strongest ally in the United States. They shared a common goal: the eradication of the Ottoman Empire. Arnold Toynbee wrote a memorandum on the subject of propaganda against Turkey in the United States. He set forth a plan in which the British were to make use of the American affection for the missionary enterprise by portraying the Turks as antimissionary and anti-American. Toynbee summarized the plan in a cipher telegram to Geoffrey Butler, the chief propagandist in America in 1917. Americans were to be told that the Turks had "confiscated colleges and hospitals" and otherwise acted against missionary interests. The assertions were not true, but they fit well into the claims being propagated by the missionaries. Toynbee stressed the American missionary connection with the Armenians, saying that more should be done to convince Americans that their national interests had been hurt by the Turkish government, which was "openly anti-American." He especially wanted propaganda in America that would counter the German assertion printed in some American newspapers that the British wanted to annex Ottoman territories, "which might embarrass us considerably at the peace settlement." Of course, that was exactly what the British did plan to do. Toynbee simply did not want it known. (He was also anxious that British disclaimers of territorial ambitions in the Middle East should not encourage the "extreme Zionists" who wanted a Jewish state in Palestine.) Toynbee recognized the potential usefulness of the missionary establishment in disseminating the British message. He advised Butler in America: "Machinery for propaganda already exists, for example, in American Committee for Armenian and Syrian Relief, Chairman Barton, 14 Beacon Street, Boston."[253]

As seen above, Parker made use of his connections to distribute missionary literature. The ACASR, in turn, sent British propaganda to the American press. For example, the ACASR forwarded to the American press a cable from John Masefield, "the famous English writer," stating that one-third of the Armenians had been massacred or died of starvation and disease.[254] The press release did not state how Masefield could know this, but it is easy to see the hand of the British propaganda machine. Lord Bryce received atrocity stories from the missionary establishment. He then sent those stories and others back to the ACASR, which made sure they found their way into print.[255] In his book *Armenian Atrocities,* Toynbee quoted ACASR materials and thanked the ACASR for its assistance.[256]

The previous chapter describes some of the close connections between the ACASR/Near East Relief campaign and the British propaganda efforts. The ACASR bibliographies prominently included British propaganda. The Bryce Report was sold in churches and at ACASR/Near East Relief gatherings. The ACASR sent pamphlets containing excerpts from British propaganda works to pastors across America. The missionary establishment surely provided one of the main conduits through which British propaganda reached the United States.

One of the most prominent marks of British propaganda was the effort to blame the Germans for the supposed crimes of the Turks. Thus the ACASR printed that the Turks had killed Christians on orders from the Germans, a favorite story of the British propagandists: "It was not long after the war broke out that the Turk heard his own and his master's voice, and obeyed. 'This time,' he boasted, 'I'll destroy Christianity by killing and exiling its members wherever found in my Empire. Nor will my hatred spare the Jew.' It was his master's way of terrifying the world in the hope that the world might fall at his feet and in a burst of agony cry out— '*Enough.*'"[257] James Barton and others sent accounts that blamed the Turks and Germans for colluding to destroy Armenians.[258]

Once America entered the war, Near East Relief and missionary organization press statements took advantage of the American feeling against the Germans to portray the Turks as willing agents of the Germans in attacking Christians. The American Board reported that "Germany is making every effort and with tangible results to incite the Tatars and Turks to unite in an attack on the Armenians and Georgians." The Armenians and Georgians were "in imminent peril of being massacred by the Turks and Tatars."[259] The missionaries described a German master plan to conquer the Muslim world by destroying the Christians who would have resisted the supposed evils of "the Hun." To anyone with knowledge of Germany or of the Ottomans this is a ludicrous charge, completely unsupported by anything in the historical record. The American public did not know the reality, however, and had been fed a steady diet of anti-German propaganda. Near East Relief ads described the Germans ("the Master Pirates" and "perfect sinners") as endorsing and even directing the attempted extirpation of Christians.[260]

In an incredible statement, James Barton, head of both the American Board and the ACASR, placed the blame on Germany for the "holy war, accompanied by all the horrors of Moslem fanaticism." He stated that the Germans were inciting "the Tatars in Russia to institute a massacre upon the 1,600,000 Armenians and the 1,350,000 Georgians dwelling in the Transcaucasus." But, for Barton, the German plan went further: "Had the expectations of the Kaiser and the Sultan been realized, the world would have witnessed a carnival of slaughter in India, Persia, Russia, Turkey, Egypt, all North Africa, and wherever Moslems dwell in considerable numbers, surpassing in savagery and horror anything recorded of Tamerlane or Genghis Khan."[261] In a letter to the *New York Times,* Barton reiterated his claims against the Germans: "And yet it is evident there is one revelation of the spirit of the Hun which descends to lower depths of depravity than anything previously recorded...I refer to the prolonged and concerted attempt of the German Kaiser to arouse to its utmost height of fury and fanaticism the Moslem world and to hurl it with all of its traditional cruelty against Christians and non-Moslems wherever found."[262]

When he wrote that statement in 1918, Barton had been a confidant and ally of the British propaganda machinery for years. Many of the stories in the *Blue Book* had been forwarded by Barton. Cooperation between the British and the missionary establishment was complete. The British, for example, sent advance prepublication copies of the *Blue Book* so that the ACASR could include it in bibliographies and begin publicity for it. Once the book was published, the ACASR sold the Bryce Report all over America for one dollar. The bibliographies and press releases of the ACASR included nearly all the books of Wellington House.[263]

The Effects of British Propaganda

One of the most telling facets of British propaganda against the Turks is that it has been ignored in scholarly publications on wartime propaganda. Every serious scholarly study of British propaganda during World War I rightly labels British propaganda against the Germans as a carefully constructed attack on the truth in the interests of victory. The same studies do not even consider British propaganda against the Turks, except when it also was an attack on the Germans. What British propagandists did to the Germans they also did to the Turks, yet no one has seemed to care. That is why British propaganda against the Germans has been condemned while calumnies against the Turks live on. The infamous Bryce Report against the Turks is republished and quoted as gospel while the Bryce Report against the Germans lies uncited on dusty library shelves.[264] Annotated bibliographies on World War I or on genocide as a topic prominently feature British propaganda publications, without any identification of them as what they were.[265] The common rules of historical criticism, which include verification of sources, have not been applied.

As was the case with the propaganda of the missionary establishment, the main problem with British propaganda was what it did not include: Armenian revolt and Turkish mortality. Understandably, the British propagandized only the worst about the Turks. In the interests of defaming an enemy, the propagandists omitted massacres of Turks and Kurds from the record and freely invented Turkish crimes. No Turk ever died in the books, articles, and press releases distributed by the propagandists. Armenian revolts at Van, Urfa, and elsewhere and subsequent battles between Turks and Armenians were always treated as one-sided massacres. This is completely understandable; the British were concerned with winning a war, not with telling the truth.

POLITICS AND THE MISSIONARY ESTABLISHMENT

The final attack on the image of the Turks came in the war between Greece and the Turkish Nationalists, the Turkish War of Independence. The Allies at the Paris Peace Conference had allowed the Greek army to invade the region of İzmir (also known by its classical name, Smyrna) in southwestern Anatolia. The Greeks had soon gone beyond their Allied mandate, ultimately seizing almost all of Western Anatolia. The atrocities of the Greek invasion as well as the Armenian Republic's occupation of northeastern Anatolia sparked Turkish resistance. The missionary establishment mounted a new propaganda offensive against the Turks.

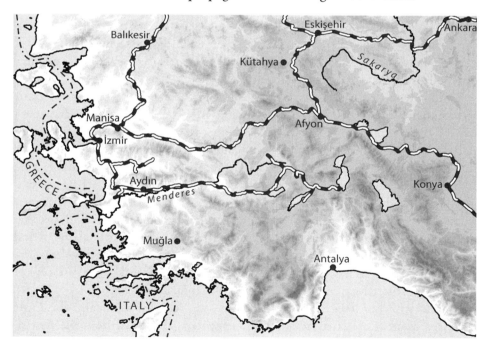

11.1 Southwestern Anatolia, 1914

Historians are fortunate to have very exact details of the Greek invasion and its effects. From the first it involved the massacre of Muslims and the disloca- tion of the Turkish population. European and American observers, including

British merchants and diplomats and American, French, and British naval offi-cers, observed the conduct of the Greek troops who landed at İzmir (Smyrna) on May 15, 1919. They recorded that the slaughter of Turks began within hours of the Greek landings and continued as the Greeks pressed inland. Ottoman officials and military leaders in İzmir were immediately killed. Turks ultimately resisted but did nothing initially. Turkish forces, for example, allowed the Allies peace-fully to occupy the forts that commanded İzmir's harbor. Turkish soldiers and gendarmes did nothing to stop the Greek landings.[1] Instead, following orders from Istanbul, they allowed themselves to be disarmed and then were often killed.

The most damning analysis of the Greek atrocities came from their allies. The leader of Ottoman Islam, the Şeyhülislam in Istanbul, lodged a complaint with the Allies over treatment of the Turks in İzmir. In an unusual action, they agreed to create a commission to investigate. The commission was headed by French, Ital-ian, British, and American members (American plenipotentiary Admiral Mark Bristol). It blamed Greek soldiers for the massacre of defenseless Turkish civilians. While not excusing Turkish attacks on Greeks, the commission placed the blame for the disaster firmly on the Greeks.[2]

The Allied commission's report stated that the pretext for the Greek invasion had been false: "The inquiry has proven that the general situation of Christians in the vilayet of Aydin [the province of which İzmir was capital] has been satis-factory since the armistice and that they [Christians] have not been in danger." It labeled the Greeks as being responsible for subsequent unrest and atrocities: "In the person of the civil Supreme Authority representing it in Smyrna, the Greek Government is responsible for the serious disturbances which bathed the country in blood while the Greek troops advanced."[3]

Unfortunately for the Turks, it was the Greek and missionary story that became known to the Americans. Ottoman documents never appeared in American news-papers. The commission report was so damning that the Allies refused to release it. A British Foreign Ministry official commented: "The Greeks come out so badly that the less we publish the better."[4] The Commission of Inquiry's findings were suppressed, so no one saw the condemnation of Greek actions. A few newspa-pers announced the existence of the commission,[5] but only one printed informa-tion on its conclusions (see below). The report on the commission's findings seen in America was an Associated Press article carried by newspapers in all major and most minor cities. The article quoted Greek prime minister Eleftherios Venizelos, stating that the commission had been unfair and that the Greeks were innocent of wrongdoing, but gave none of the commission's conclusions.[6]

The story of the Greek invasion that Americans received was a false one. Only a limited number of actual news reports appeared (almost all from the Associ-ated Press), filled with factual errors and saying nothing about the suffering of Turks. Journalists who might have wished to report accurately were hampered by being far from the battle. Most articles describing events originated in Athens or Salonica in Greece. These articles (also almost exclusively written by the Associ-ated Press) were drawn from Greek governmental sources.

Before the Greek invasion a report from the Associated Press and another news service told the American public, completely falsely, that Turks were attacking Greeks in Western Anatolia: "Information from what is considered trustworthy sources describes the condition of the Greeks in the Smyrna district as extremely critical. Bands of Turkish soldiers and civilians are overrunning the region, murdering and pillaging."[7] The article, datelined Athens and with headlines such as "Turks Decapitate Greeks" and "Turks Massacre Greeks," appeared all across the country. The *Christian Science Monitor* printed as authoritative a press release from the Greek Legation in Washington announcing that Turks were attacking Greeks in the İzmir district.[8] Other pieces declared that disaster would result and Christians would be massacred unless the Greeks were allowed to take control.[9] In a continuation of wartime assertions, the Turks were said to be planning the massacre of all the Christians.[10]

Editorials in newspapers small and large set the stage for Greek incursion by asserting that İzmir was Greek and should be united with Greece. The *Reno Evening Gazette* stated that "Smyrna is Greek and always has been. Nine-tenths of its population speaks no other language."[11] The *New York Times* editorialized: "In the Sanjak [district] of Smyrna alone there are 450,000 Greeks, more than double the number of Turks," adding: "May the new Hellenism flourish like the old!"[12] The United Press syndicate wrote: "The occupied territory [İzmir region] is populated almost wholly by Greeks."[13] For the McClure Newspapers Syndicate the widely published author Frank Simonds wrote: "Nor can he [the Turk] lay any claim to the shores of the straits and the Sea of Marmara based upon race or self determination. Outside of Constantinople the Greek is in a clear majority, within the city the Greeks are the most considerable element and the Turks only a relative small minority." Thus, Simonds asserted, the Greeks should be given all of Western Asia Minor, Thrace, and Istanbul. "This would mean the restoration of the Byzantine Empire."[14] Simonds may have had in mind the completely invented population statistics presented by Prime Minister Venizelos and quoted in American newspapers. Venizelos claimed that more Greeks than Turks lived in the areas occupied by Greece.[15]

In fact, Ottoman population registers showed that Istanbul Province was 62 percent Muslim and 23 percent Greek, Western Anatolia 79 percent Muslim and 14 percent Greek, Western Thrace 55 percent Muslim and 38 percent Greek.[16] These statistics are the most authoritative available, having been taken by the government for administrative purposes, not for propaganda, and were recognized as such at the time. The British Foreign Office, Naval Intelligence, and Army Intelligence all considered the data to be the best available,[17] although David Lloyd George preferred to quote the Greek statistics publicly for political purposes. The statistics offered by Venizelos have been conclusively proven to have been forgeries, fabricated by the Greek government for propaganda purposes.[18]

Once the invasion had begun, newspapers across America carried erroneous stories that Turks had resisted the Allied forces at the İzmir landing and that

Turkish soldiers had fought pitched battles with Greek and Allied troops in the streets of İzmir.[19] Greeks had supposedly won the (actually nonexistent) battles and were restoring order. The articles made no mention of massacres of Turks or ongoing problems. As the Greeks moved inland and began to meet actual Turkish resistance, American newspapers justified their actions as pacific and well meaning. The AP reported: "The statement is made by the Greeks that their purpose is to restore order and take a census."[20] Turkish villagers were supposedly welcoming the Greeks.[21] Turkish resistance forces were allegedly attacking both Greeks and Jews and forcibly enrolling Turks in their army, killing those who refused.[22] Some claimed that Turks were killing Greeks and mutilating their bodies.[23] The AP reported that two Turkish armies (actually nonexistent at the time) were approaching to attack the Greeks, "violating the Armistice" (when it had been the Allies and Greeks who had violated the Armistice).[24] The Greeks were nevertheless alleged to be triumphing everywhere and bringing peace.[25] The articles originated from Greece, usually from Salonica.

In fact, many of the reports on the events of the Greek invasion and occupation came from Greece. Press releases from the Greek government were printed or cited without question.[26] A story sent from Athens wrote that "fanatic Moslems, drunk with blood, beheaded the bodies of Christians and carried their bloody trophies through the streets."[27] The Greek legation at Washington contended that the Turks had killed 700,000 Greeks even before the İzmir troubles began.[28] The Associated Press reported, based on Greek allegations, that Turks were burning Greek prisoners alive.[29] A report from Athens said that Muslim villages were petitioning the Greeks "to protect them against the atrocities and outrages of Musselman bands."[30] As had been the case with stories from Armenians, statements from Greek organizations in America and Europe were printed as fact.[31] *The Christian Science Monitor* ran a long page-1 story headlined "Splendid Record of Greek Rule in Smyrna Region." Indeed, all was supposedly well in İzmir, perhaps because the story's sole source was "a prominent Greek diplomatist."[32]

The Missionary Establishment and the Greeks

Other than statements of praise and satisfaction with the Greeks,[33] the missionary establishment at first had little to say about the Greek occupation. It conducted no campaign to aid the Greeks because the Christians seemed to be winning, and no one in Near East Relief was about to organize a campaign for the more than 1 million Turkish refugees who had fled from the Greeks.[34] This changed when the Greeks lost.

As the Greek army neared the Nationalist capital at Ankara, the Turks made their stand, defeated the Greeks, then finally pursued them as they fled across Western Anatolia. The fleeing Greek army virtually disintegrated as it dashed to ports and escaped to Greece. As the Greeks fled they destroyed everything in their path. The advancing Turks saw a virtual desert. Much of Western Anatolia was in ruins: 2 million animals lost, 140,000 buildings destroyed; by war's end, 540,000 Turks had died, along with 300,000 Greeks.[35] As the Turks pursued their enemy toward İzmir, where the fleeing soldiers would be rescued by Greek and Allied boats, they saw the devastation and slaughter caused by the Greeks. The Turks unquestionably reached İzmir with vengeance in their hearts, and many took their revenge.

Whether they acted out of lack of hatred or out of a desire not to be seen as barbarians in Europe and America, Turkish Nationalist officials did all they could to restrain acts of revenge. They were largely successful with the soldiery but failed with the inhabitants of the İzmir region. Greek and Armenian civilians fought Turkish soldiers as they entered the city. Turkish mobs attacked Greeks and Armenians in the streets. Most of the Christian population of the city fled on Allied boats. Nationalist soldiers were finally able to restore order. Disaster struck, however, when the city (largely constructed of flammable wood structures) began to burn. The question of who started the blaze, which was probably actually multiple fires set separately, has never been satisfactorily resolved. Neutral observers later absolved the Turkish authorities of setting fire to the city. In any case, it was odd to think that the Turks would deliberately destroy the city they had just conquered.[36] The American press, however, blamed the Turks for the fire.

For the missionary establishment the Greek defeat was the final disaster, and the missionaries mobilized for a new campaign. The Armenians who had for so long been the focus of the missionary enterprise had been defeated in the East and were gone from Eastern Anatolia forever. Now the Greeks, the hope of all those who longed for the end of Turkish rule, had lost. The missionary establishment responded with a blast of propaganda. Near East Relief busied itself with spreading its own version of the Turkish victory. Its reports mainly described the need for relief supplies for Greek and Armenian refugees while totally ignoring corresponding needs of Turkish refugees, just as ACASR/Near East Relief had done throughout World War I. They added spurious stories of summary executions of Christians and of Turks who burned refugees then buried them in buildings, which they dynamited to destroy the evidence.[37] The Near East Relief publication *New Near East* told stories of Greeks living in fear, awaiting massacre, and called the Greek flight from İzmir "the blackest page in modern history." Its pages were filled with dire predictions of what might happen to Christians if the Turks had their way. It quoted missionaries and Near East Relief workers as knowing that the Turks planned to massacre all the remaining Christians.[38] Facts were limited, but fearful prophecy abounded.[39]

American missionaries and Near East Relief workers sent many accounts of Turkish attacks on innocent Greeks in İzmir back to America through their organizations and the American press, especially the Associated Press. They stressed that the attacks were made by Turkish soldiers: "Wherever there was a company of Turkish soldiers massacres of persons not Turks followed."[40] Most of the actual reports were of robbery, but their headlines wrote of massacre.[41] The most damning accounts came from Greece. The Greek official news agency report on İzmir printed in the American press told of horrible atrocities and alleged that Mustafa Kemal had lost control of his army.[42] The Greek metropolitan of İzmir and ten priests were reported to have been buried alive, "because they refused to embrace Islamism."[43] Near East Relief brought out the old accusations against the Turks: "Young Greek and Armenian girls are being torn from their families and disappear from sight."[44]

As always, the assertions of missionary and Near East Relief workers were printed as fact. Near East Relief officials supposedly investigated the massacre before the fire started and decided that the number had been 1,000 or 2,000. They gave no indication of how they reached that figure; but in the midst of the battles during the Turkish attack how could they have investigated at all?[45] The Greek government quoted the missionary estimate, identifying the missionary source only as an "American investigator."[46] In any case, the number was soon inflated to 2,000, the figure that the newspapers generally accepted. Some gave much higher estimates. A United Press story from "Armenian sources" wrote that 70,000 had been killed in İzmir but admitted that the estimate was unconfirmed.[47] The Associated Press quoted John Manola of Near East Relief as its authority in stating that at least 120,000 had been killed at İzmir.[48] The usual patent falsehoods and absurdities were printed, such as the alleged operation of slave markets for Christian girls in Istanbul. The article did not mention that the city was under Allied occupation and control at the time.[49] Associated Press reporters attached to the Greek army contended that it was the Turks who had burned Turkish villages, when the fires had actually been the work of the Greeks, as the diplomatic record shows.[50]

The standard charges that the Turks started the İzmir fire came from American missionaries: "Miss Mills, matron of the American [Missionary] College for Girls, declares she saw an officer of the Turkish regular army enter a house carrying several cans of petrol. Soon after he came out, the house burst into flames."[51] The officer mentioned by Mills somehow became a sergeant in the transition to other newspaper articles, and that story was repeated endlessly.[52] With few exceptions (seen below), newspapers reported that the Turks had burned İzmir to "cleanse" it of Greek associations.

Near East workers said that Turkish soldiers were "under strictest orders not to permit the escape of any of the Greek or Armenian refugees." It was difficult to reconcile this statement with the assertion by these same relief workers that 60,000 Christians had been evacuated (September 16, 1922). So one article reported that the Turkish guards "were diverted by giving them cigarettes and talking to them in their native tongue."[53] In fact, only young males considered potentially dangerous were often, but by no means always, stopped from leaving.

Mark O. Prentiss, special representative of Near East Relief in Turkey, reported that the Turks had sent "secret agents" into occupied territories who took photographs of important Greeks and compiled dossiers. According to Prentiss, the Turks had then killed 12,000 of these Greeks in İzmir and were waiting to kill 8,000 Greeks of Istanbul who were in their dossiers. The only solution, he felt, was that "three quarters of a million people must be evacuated from Istanbul."[54] In fact, of course, the killings never took place when the Turks regained Istanbul. Even including refugees, Istanbul had nowhere near 750,000 Christians.[55] The ludicrous idea that the Turks had photographed 20,000 Greeks for their imaginary dossiers was seemingly considered credible by the editors who printed Prentiss's comments. (Given the photographic technology of the time, the Turkish agents would have needed to ask Greek officials to stand still while they took their pictures.)

Once İzmir had been taken, newspapers reported on what they believed were the new Turkish plans. The Turks allegedly were allying with the Soviets, planning a worldwide Muslim uprising, or both; as one headline put it: "Shadow of Terrible Turk Hanging over Europe."[56] The *San Francisco Chronicle* headlined on page 1: "Russians Ready to Join Turkey against British: Entire Moslem World Mobilizing to Harass British Forces."[57] The *Los Angeles Times* in large type on page 1 headlined: "Leon Trotzky Will Send Armies to Aid [Turkish] Nationalist Leader."[58] The *New York Herald* wrote in a headline: "Turks May Start Holy War."[59] Newspapers carried dark predictions of a continuation of the world war if the victorious Turks were not immediately checked, this time a war in which the Turks were "the advance guards of the Mohammedan world in arms, supported and incited by Russia."[60]

Missionaries and Near East Relief speakers gave talks across the United States, spreading the missionary establishment's version of the İzmir tragedy. Mark L. Ward and Bishop James Cannon of Near East Relief were particularly active.[61] The Federal Council of Churches appealed to 150,000 churches in America in a campaign for American intervention to aid Greeks and Armenians and force an independent Armenia. Near East Relief and Armenian-American organizations joined the campaign.[62] Near East Relief and the Federal Council of Churches called joint meetings to protest the victory of the Turks. They demanded that the United States intervene, although they offered no specifics on how this might be done. One meeting in 1922, held at the Yale Club in New York, heard Bishop Cannon declare that "the object of the Kemalist advance into Europe was the extermination of Christians."[63] Mass meetings were held all over America to condemn the Turks, many under the aegis of members of the national and local committees of Near East Relief.

Perhaps the most prominent mass meeting took place in New York in 1922, at the Cathedral of St. John the Divine under the auspices of the Federal Council of Churches, with 3,000 in attendance.[64] It was "presided over by John H. Finley, editor [actually associate editor] of the New York Times."[65] James L. Barton, Robert E. Speer, and Harry Emerson Fosdick addressed the meeting.[66] Of the four organizers, only Fosdick was not a member of the central Committee of Near East Relief; he was a well-known Baptist clergyman. Barton was the Near East Relief chairman, Finley its vice-chairman. The mass meeting adopted resolutions condemning the Turks. An organizational meeting was called by the Church Relations department of Near East Relief, leaders of fifteen Protestant churches (Baptist, Methodist, Presbyterian, Lutheran, Reformed, Congregationalist, Episcopal, and others), and the Federal Council of Churches. The delegates elected Dr. Stanley White, head of the Presbyterian Board of Foreign Missions, as head of a campaign to bring the issue of an Armenian National Home once again to the forefront of American policy.[67] Smaller cities had less exalted speakers but more interesting speeches, such as the speech delivered in Kennebec, Maine: "The Bloody Turk: God Decrees His Doom? 'He Shall Come to His End and None Shall Help Him.' Daniel II 11:45." The newspaper described this as a "thrilling lecture," which it probably was.[68]

The missionary author Herbert Gibbons contributed a series of articles to the *Christian Science Monitor,* all featured on page 1.[69] Gibbons wrote overwhelming exaggerations of Christian suffering in the Greek-Turkish War, seasoned with the occasional outright lie. He claimed that the Turks were exterminating the Greek population of Anatolia and that a "secret committee" of the Nationalists was organizing massacres. According to Gibbons, the Nationalist Turks under Mustafa Kemal were the same people who had plunged Turkey into World War I, the Turks would not allow Near East Relief to aid the Greeks, and the Turks of Anatolia opposed the Nationalists. He seemed convinced that the Turks believed that "the Greek Government is the best and most helpful friend of the Turkish people."[70] The Turks, Gibbons wrote, were not joining the Nationalists, which was one of the reasons the Turks would surely be defeated by the Greeks.[71] His hopes for Greek victory colored his military judgment: "The Nationalists do not have the army they boast of, and are too weak from the military point of view to oppose the Greeks."[72] Both history and future events proved him wrong on all counts.

Most of Gibbons's assertions cannot be corroborated, because he gave no sources for them. The only sources he did offer were missionaries. They may or may not have been telling the truth on the mistreatment of Greeks, but one thing is certain—they never admitted that any Turks had suffered or died. For them, the only ones who suffered were Christians. Many of Gibbons's claims can easily be proven wrong. The Greeks were not exterminated: the Greek census of 1928 listed 850,000 Anatolian Greeks who had come to Greece, most of them in the Greek-Turkish population exchange.[73] They had not been killed. Far from being one with the government that had brought the empire to war, Mustafa Kemal, the leader of the Nationalists, was an enemy of Enver Paşa.[74] The Turks had not stopped Near East Relief aid to Greeks. James Barton, head of Near East Relief and no friend of the Turks, wrote of the agreement between the Turkish Nationalists and Near East Relief to provide exactly that aid. Barton noted that the Turks even gave stores of grain to Near East Relief.[75] As for Gibbons's belief that the Turks did not support Mustafa Kemal and were not joining his cause and that the Greeks would surely triumph, the Turkish Nationalist victory speaks for itself.

CILICIA AND THE PONTUS

In addition to İzmir, missionaries wrote or spoke on two other events—the Turkish defeat of the French in Cilicia and the relocation of Black Sea Greeks. The Turkish Nationalists feared that Greeks in the Black Sea region (the Pontus) would revolt and would open a second front against the Turks, cooperating with

Greek soldiers sent to the region by ship. They had some reason to fear: Greek guerrilla bands were operating in the region, attacking Turkish villages, and officials of the Greek Orthodox Church in Trabzon had called for a Greek Pontic Republic. The Allies at the Paris Peace Conference had given Greek warships permission to pass into the eastern Black Sea.[76] The Greek government had at least a plan to invade the Black Sea region;[77] but in hindsight it probably did not have the wherewithal to mount an offensive there. The Turks, however, expected a Greek Black Sea invasion. In response, they relocated 15,000–30,000 Greeks from what they considered danger zones. By no means were the majority of the Pontic Greeks forced out. Nevertheless, those who were relocated suffered greatly. Mortality due to disease and exposure was high.

The difficulty with the missionary reports was their exaggeration and unbelievable assertions that they knew the intentions of the Turks. The missionaries engaged in the usual numerical escalation. A Near East Relief plea declared that "there are 200,000 Christian white girls held in slavery worse than death by Turks and Kurds."[78] One missionary wrote: "Of 30,000 who left Sivas 5,000 died before reaching Harput."[79] (Ottoman population records just before the war showed 728 Greeks living in the city of Sivas.) The missionary and Near East Relief official Dr. Mark H. Ward of Harput was most often heard condemning the Turkish expulsion from the Black Sea region. Ward alleged that 30,000 had been deported from the Trabzon region and that only 8,000 had survived but gave no indication as to how he had gained that information.[80] He contended that the Turks ordered the forced migration as "a deliberate plan to exterminate the minorities." Ward stated that the Turks were sending the refugees east from Harput to Van and Bitlis. Another missionary report maintained that the refugees were being sent to Erzurum and Sarıkamış, nowhere near Van and Bitlis. Ward claimed to have heard from "a Turkish official at the head of the educational department [*sic*] that the Turks intended extermination."[81] The *New York Times* reported: "'There are 300,000 Greeks and 100,000 Armenians in Asia Minor,' said Dr. Ward. 'All are doomed unless the civilized world comes to their rescue. The Kemalist policy is that of extermination of the Christian minorities.'"[82] (Oddly enough, Ward underestimated the number of Greeks by nearly 400 percent, which shows his lack of knowledge.)

As always, some of the missionary reports were truly absurd. Dr. George E. White, a Near East Relief representative, charged that "Turkish officials decimated the Greek population along the Black Sea Coast, 250,000 men, women, and children living between Sinope and Ordou, without the shedding of blood but by 'parboiling' the victims in Turkish baths and turning them half-clad out to die of pneumonia or other ills in the snow of an Anatolian winter."[83]

Only the *Chicago Tribune* seems to have had the courage to publish the other side of the story. The Turkish governments in Ankara and Istanbul denied all, stating that both Greeks and Muslims had died from hunger and exposure in the Harput region. The Turks asked why no one had written about the massacres of Turks by Greeks. Perhaps more importantly, the *Tribune* wrote: "Florence

Billings, the Near East Relief agent at Angora, telegraphs that she has been in constant touch with Kharpout [Harput] for months and that no atrocities have been committed there."[84]

By their own admission, the missionary sources stated that the Turks allowed the missionaries to aid the Black Sea refugees. All evidence indicates that this was true, but the missionaries also had a practical reason for admitting Turkish assistance, If the Turks had not allowed the missionaries and Near East Relief to help, then why should anyone send money to the missionary and relief organizations? Indeed, if the Turks were not sympathetic, why were the relief workers needed at all? But the admission that the Turks wanted the refugees cared for undercut the descriptions of Turkish barbarities. If the Turks had wanted the Christians killed, why did they let Near East Relief feed and care for them?[85]

The missionary reports on the Black Sea relocations were exaggerations of real Christian suffering caused by Turks, for which the Turks bore responsibility. But their reports on the sufferings of Armenians in Cilicia were a case of blaming the Turks for the deaths of Christians caught up in war and completely omitting the deaths of Muslims—reporting only one side's battle mortality and calling it a massacre.

The wartime Sykes-Picot Agreement had designated Cilicia (south-central Anatolia, including Adana, Antep, Maraş, and Urfa, which extended somewhat beyond historic Cilicia) and more northern regions to France. At the end of World War I the British in Syria turned Cilicia over to the French. Because they did not have sufficient French troops to occupy the territory, they made use of Armenian volunteers, who formed the Armenian Legion. When these arrived in Cilicia, as attested in French reports, they immediately began to attack and harass Muslims. The French could do virtually nothing to respond to Muslim complaints. French general Jules C. Hamelin called these complaints "unfortunately most well-founded, against all sorts of [Armenian] excesses against the population (robbery, armed attacks, pillaging, murders)."[86] The French attempted to disband the Armenian Legion, but the legionnaires simply remained in Cilicia and continued their "excesses." Armenian refugees flooded into the area. Attacks on Muslims continued, with entire villages burned and high mortality.[87] Local Muslims responded with attacks on the Armenians, and a civil war ensued.

Although the American press described all those who resisted the French and Armenians as Turks, in reality they were Turks, Kurds, and Arabs—the Muslims of Cilicia. Before the war they had been 84 percent of the total population of the region.[88] They organized into a fighting force strong enough to attack the French and drive them out of much of the conquered land. The French ultimately gave up, signed a treaty with the Turkish Nationalists, and evacuated the region, followed by the Armenian population (December 1921).[89]

The battles in Cilicia were not at the forefront of reporting from Turkey in the European and American press until the battle of Maraş. Maraş, at the farthest distance of French occupation, was both the scene of concerted Armenian attacks on Muslims and an area in which the Nationalist forces felt they could defeat the

French. The war began with guerrilla actions and escalated into an attack on the French garrison by local Turks and Arabs and Kurdish tribes.

Armenians and Muslims were both caught in the middle of a war, although the missionaries, as always, wrote only of Armenian deaths. The missionaries could not completely disguise the nature of the situation, however. One relief worker, M. E. Dougherty, stated that the French bombarded the Muslim quarters of Maraş then set them on fire, after which the Muslims attacked the Armenian Quarter. She also mentioned in passing that Armenians from other cities had come into Maraş to obtain ammunition from the Armenian caches there. Dougherty stressed Armenian mortality but listed no Muslim deaths.[90] One Associated Press story containing selections from the journal of the Reverend C. F. H. Crathern described the hostilities: "French troops, aided by Armenians, battled with Turkish Nationalists for possession of the city, more than half of which was burned during the engagement, which brought a terrible loss of life."[91] The fighting went on for twenty-two days, but Crathern reported only the deaths of Armenians—and reported them in gripping detail. He went on to describe the incredible suffering of the refugees from Maraş. Crathern did not allege that the Turks had tried to stop the refugee columns or hamper them in any way, but he also did not mention that the Turks had agreed to the evacuation.

With the exception of descriptions of what he had not seen (stories of massacres, a reported death toll of 20,000 Armenians), what the Reverend Crathern wrote was true. The lie came in the omission of the Muslim dead and the interpretation of battles as massacres. For example, Crathern described one battle between 2,000 Armenians and the Turks in which the Turks only succeeded by burning the church from which Armenians were firing. (The *Los Angeles Times* reported the battle for the church as a Turkish massacre of Armenians with "burning oil.")[92] He said it was a massacre, but it was obviously a battle in which both sides fought and the Turks won.[93]

The Reverend Crathern's story was typical of the interviews that missionaries gave to the press. All of them told of the suffering of Armenians, never Muslims, and stressed the dangers to Americans, although all Americans escaped Maraş unharmed.[94] Near East Relief released cables from missionaries stating that the Turks were killing Armenians. One cable was supposedly from the Reverend Marion C. Wilson, "stationed at Marash." It stated that hundreds of Armenians were being massacred daily and that Maraş was cut off, with all the roads blocked, which raises the question of how Wilson was able to send his telegram.[95] Wilson, whose description of events indicated that he could not have seen the massacres he described, as usual mentioned no Muslim dead. He related a story that the French evacuated "without the knowledge of the Turks," when in reality the evacuation had been arranged with the Turkish forces. Wilson wrote that only 2,000 Armenians went with them and that 8,000 had died, leaving 10,000 behind. He stated that the Turks did not kill these Armenians, on the condition that they gave up their arms.[96] Other missionaries said that 5,000 had left with the French.[97] The missionaries and relief workers were generally confused and contradictory about events and mortality. Two missionaries reported that 5,000 Armenians had been killed.[98] Others said that 16,000 or even 20,000 had been massacred.[99] These sorts of wild and inflated guesses characterized the missionary reporting. One story alleged that 8,000 of the 10,000 Armenians in Maraş had been killed, along with 15 Turks (a remarkably small number in twenty-two days of fighting).[100]

Despite their differences in the facts of the Maraş incident, one thing was true of all the missionary accounts—they described Armenian deaths but almost no Turkish deaths. If we define "massacre" as the killing of innocents, then massacres took place on both sides. Most mortality undoubtedly came as a result of cannon fire and the burning of the city. More deaths came when the French abandoned the city. The blizzards that raged as the columns trudged away from Maraş were a disaster for the refugees. What occurred, though, was war, not massacre. The exaggerated missionary counts of mortality should have been called deaths, not massacres.

Throughout the Maraş affair the press labeled the Turkish Nationalist forces and local forces as rebels against what they considered to be justified French rule. Imperialism over Muslim peoples was always considered just. Nowhere did the press describe the overwhelmingly Muslim character of the population or consider the possibility that Muslims might be fighting for the rights of the majority.

A Small Change

For the first time, not all went against the Turks in the American press. Reports of the suffering of Greeks and Armenians filled the newspapers, but with a subtle change from previous anti-Turkish campaigns. A small minority of articles began to consider or at least mention that the Turks might not have been completely guilty.[101] Most newspaper reports of events in İzmir definitely attacked the Turks. Anyone reading only the headlines would have had no doubt as to guilt: "Turks Slay as Town Burns," "Turks Massacre 2,000 Christians," "Massacre in Smyrna." This was as it had been throughout World War I. A number of accounts, however, even reports from wire services, now included small mentions of another side to the story. For example, an Associated Press article primarily quoted "Greek official circles" who stated that the Turks had started the İzmir fire but also quoted Turkish Nationalist sources stating that the fires had been the result of gunfire between Turkish soldiers and Greeks and Armenians who fired on them from buildings. Allowing that "a number of lives have been sacrificed," the article noted that "the reports of horrible massacres appear to depend largely upon possible exaggerated statements of terrified refugees."[102] A United Press story wrote that Turks had massacred Greeks, that Americans in İzmir were in danger, that some Americans might have been killed (which was not true), and that the Turkish sergeant had probably started the fire but also included one sentence stating that Turks said Armenians had started the fire.[103] Such articles contained very little even-handed journalism, but previous reporting would not have included Turkish statements at all. It should be added that many newspapers excised the Turkish comments before they printed the stories. Most articles, of course, only blamed the Turks.[104]

The missionary story of events in Maraş was published on page 1, but occasionally the Turkish government's denial of massacres was printed somewhere in the inside pages of some newspapers, with the want ads or the cartoons.[105] One Associated Press article even printed the actual words of the Ottoman foreign minister, who stated that the fighting had begun with Armenian attacks on Muslims, including widespread massacres in the countryside, and the French arrest of Ottoman officials. Great Muslim mortality resulted from French cannon fire on Muslim districts. As evidence of the lack of Turkish intention to massacre, he offered the following: "The truth of the statement that there was no organized massacre is evident, as after the definite evacuation of Marash [by the French], calm was reestablished and the Armenians there enjoy the protection of the very persons they attacked with such hatred."[106] Although the foreign minister requested that the Allies name a commission to investigate the actual events in Maraş, a commission was never created.[107] The statements of the foreign minister are completely supported by the diplomatic record.[108]

This report is one of the few that published Ottoman assessments. The Allies in command in Istanbul, whose own diplomats and soldiers had corroborated the Turkish assertions, refused to allow the Turks to publish the documents they had amassed on the Maraş events, even in Turkish-language newspapers.[109] Nevertheless, this was a rare occasion on which the Turks were heard in America, even if very few newspapers ran the story. Only the *Chicago Tribune* gave its own accurate analysis that "the Armenians committed such atrocities against the Turks that fell into their power that they were disarmed by the French authorities" and that deaths of Armenians had been retaliation for Armenian actions against Turks.[110] The *Tribune* printed the reports of American relief workers in Haçin in Cilicia who said that the Turks had no intention of fighting the Armenians there until the Armenians took the side of the French and became enemies. The workers stated that they had tried to act as intermediaries brokering peace but that the Armenians had refused.[111] As in the case of the Greek-Turkish conflict, the *Tribune* was determined to tell both sides of the story in Cilicia.

Other articles began to appear that cast doubt on the story that the Turks had started the İzmir fire. An American naval officer stated that the fire had started in the Armenian Quarter and that the only fires started by Turks were "back fires"—smaller fires intended to stop the main conflagration by denying it fuel. (This might even explain the famous story of the Turkish sergeant starting the fire.) The author wrote of rapes and the terrors of the Greek exodus but also wrote that fighting in the city had begun when Greeks fired on Turkish soldiers and threw hand grenades.[112]

Some admitted that Turks had been killed by Greeks. A number of American newspapers printed an interview with the British scholar Marmaduke Pickthall in which he described Greek attacks on Turkish officials, soldiers, and civilians in İzmir.[113] A United Press article quoted extensively from Turkish representatives at armistice talks and stated that 1 million Turks were homeless.[114] The International News Service published part of a report by two Near East Relief members,

Annie I. Allen and Florence I. Billings, that documented Greek destruction and killings in Western Anatolia.[115] Almost all editorial writers remained resolutely anti-Turkish, but one *Indianapolis Star* editorial accurately accused the Greeks of massacres and the destruction of Turkish villages.[116]

At least two American newspapers printed the comments on Greek attacks on Turks by Viscount St. Davids (John Philipps), the British head of the Board of the Ottoman Railway. He told of systematic destruction and murder by Greek soldiers: "'The Greeks deserved all they got and more,' he said. 'King Constantine's servants are very bad fighters, but they are first class at robbery, arson, and murder.'"[117] Remarkably, one of the two newspapers that printed this story was the *New York Times.* The *Times* had been and remained firmly against the Turks. As late as August 1922, it wrote in an editorial: "The Turk remains a Central Asian nomad, skilled only in war, in diplomacy and in a low grade of agriculture. The war of Greek and Turk is a war of progress against stagnation."[118]

Mark Prentiss of Near East Relief (the man who had believed the Turks kept dossiers with photographs) did not think well of the Turks but was even-handed. He reported on the misery of the Greeks of İzmir but told the American press that the Greek army had caused starvation and suffering among the Turks. In describing the events in Smyrna, he wrote of the actions of Turkish mobs but spoke well of the regular Turkish soldiers: "I made a personal investigation and could find nothing resembling an organized massacre by the troops on the quay." He himself had been saved from a mob by Turkish soldiers.[119] The few stories such as this that acknowledged who had actually attacked the Greeks in İzmir painted a picture quite different from that of an organized attack by Turkish soldiery. One other story demonstrated that the actions against Greeks were by mobs of Turks taking their revenge for Greek actions against Turks. It stated that Turkish soldiers had been assigned to protect the Christians but could not always do so in the face of the mobs.[120]

The *Chicago Daily News* and *San Antonio Light* were able to discover the substance of the Inter-Allied Report. They properly summarized it as laying blame on the Greeks for "conducting themselves in a disgusting manner." The article, like the commission report, blamed both Greek civilians of İzmir and Greek regular soldiers for murder and pillage.[121] Some papers printed a short notice on the admission by the British undersecretary of foreign affairs that British sailors had seen Greeks committing massacres of Turks in İzmir.

Someone who read only the *New York Times* headline "Tells How Turks Robbed Orphans" would assume the worst of the Turks, but the article itself quoted from the Near East Relief worker Susan D. Orvis, who told a different story: "She said there was no doubt that the Greeks and Armenians had been guilty of cruelty in Turkish towns and villages in Asia Minor when they were in control of the country, and said that she had an orphanage filled with Turkish children in Caesarea that contained as many children as there were in the Greek and Armenian orphanages." As for the Turks who robbed orphans, she stated that one convoy was indeed robbed but that Turkish officials arrested the attackers and that "not a single child of the 600 Greeks and 2,000 Armenians [in her convoy] was lost by death or accident." In another convoy fifteen out of a thousand had died.[122] Such a story was a rarity, but a welcome one.

While public meetings against the Turks went on across the country, at least one real debate took place. The NEA Service, a Scripps-Howard agency, sent out a printed record of a debate between a New York Turkish businessman and a Greek politician that had been sponsored by the Foreign Policy Association.[123]

The *Chicago Tribune* stood out among American newspapers in its coverage of the war. The *Tribune* had a man on the ground, John Clayton, who observed and reported on actual conditions. He wrote on both Greek and Turkish refugees and said that both were starving. He reported on the Greek destruction of cities such as Uşak, Alaşehir, Manisa, and Aydın: "North and East, wherever the Greek troops pass villages and towns, they ply the torch." Unlike other reporters, he gave the stories of those who had witnessed the Greeks at work: "The shuddering tales of death and ruin and cruelty are told not by propagandists, but by Christians and Americans who witnessed various revolting deeds. An army out of hand, particularly an Oriental army, is capable of terrible things."[124] Clayton was also one of the few who reported that much of the death in İzmir was due to disease.[125]

The *Chicago Tribune* even had the courage to take on Near East Relief. Paul Williams, *Tribune* correspondent in Istanbul, wrote that Near East Relief was arranging fake telegrams from Anatolia. He contended that the telegrams were first sent from New York with the instructions "send us the following telegrams." The telegrams were then distributed to American newspapers. Williams's sources were reportedly officers in the U.S. Navy cable office, which sent and received the messages. The story cannot be substantiated beyond his assertions, but it is remarkable that the statements were printed at all.[126]

The articles that somewhat exonerated the Turks were very few and were often buried on back pages. It is instructive to consider what might have been included but was not. Two local newspapers in Pennsylvania printed a letter from Dr. James L. Park, who had been in İzmir when the Turks arrived and had toured the line of Greek retreat immediately after the Greeks had been defeated. He wrote that the Turks who entered İzmir carried out looting and killing, "but it could not be called an organized massacre." In explanation, he noted that "the Greeks had destroyed every town they could reach on their retreat from the interior, over a distance of 300 miles." Park told of evil Turkish acts in İzmir and was no friend of the Turks, whom he called savages, but he wrote that the "civilized Greeks do similar and worse things, and differing only in that they do it on a larger scale, and with more refined cruelty and with greater scientific, systematic thoroughness. I tell you, and I wish you could have it published, that what the Turks did in Smyrna is mild in comparison with what the Greeks did a few days before." Park knew the climate in America: "I know I will be asked, when I return, by missionary, Christian Endeavor and other societies to speak, but I am sure I will not be asked after about one week, for what I am going to say will not be popular."[127]

The United States Government and the Missionary Establishment

During the presidency of Woodrow Wilson, much of the United States government was at the service of the missionary establishment. The missionaries had a firm supporter in the president. Wilson himself was ideologically and religiously an ally of Europeans and Christians against non-Christians and those he viewed as lesser peoples. Himself the grandson of a missionary and son of a Presbyterian minister, Wilson was an enthusiastic supporter of the ACASR/Near East Relief and the missionary establishment.[128] He was personally close to Near East Relief officials such as Cleveland H. Dodge, the Near East Relief treasurer; James Barton, the head of both the ACASR and Near East Relief; John Mott, YMCA leader and Near East Relief board member; and Charles Crane, an ACASR official who had been vice-chairman of Wilson's election campaign. In June 1917 Wilson had stated to Rabbi Stephen Wise of Near East Relief that "when the war will be ended, there are two lands that will never go back to the Mohammedan apache. One is Christian Armenia and the other is Jewish Palestine."[129] Not surprisingly, the Near East Relief organization praised Wilson particularly for his dedication to the Armenian cause.[130]

In essence the U.S. government knew little of events in the Middle East other than what was transmitted by missionaries and local Christians. America had its diplomats in the Ottoman Empire, but they gave the government little usable information on the Middle East. The American politicians who were to participate in the peace conferences at the end of the war knew almost nothing of the region. Devoid of any real intelligence-gathering apparatus, the United States was dependent for its knowledge of the Near East on whatever "experts" could be found. True academic experts were almost nonexistent, as American universities with the rarest of exceptions simply did not teach anything on the modern Middle East. Quite naturally, the American government looked to the only source that had consistently concerned itself with the Near East: the missionary establishment. The large majority of the experts called upon to inform the government were either missionaries or people closely tied to the missionary establishment. The best example of this was the Inquiry, a detailed collection of fact and opinion that was to form the intellectual basis of American actions at the postwar peace conferences. The Inquiry collected or commissioned informative pieces on whatever areas of the world were likely to be discussed at the conferences. Its work can be regarded as the "state of the art" of American governmental understanding of the world.

Ten scholars were drafted as experts in the Western Asia (Ottoman) section of the Inquiry (see table 11.1).[131] Collectively, the members of the Inquiry section on the Near East were distinguished by their lack of any knowledge of the contemporary Near East.

Two members working in another section of the Inquiry staff, however, did have personal knowledge of the Ottoman Empire: Leon Dominian and William S. Monroe. Both served in the Balkan Europe Section of the Inquiry and

TABLE 11.1. TEN SCHOLARS WHO SERVED ON THE INQUIRY

William L. Westermann	head of the Western Asia Section: professor of ancient history at the University of Wisconsin
Dana C. Munro	professor of medieval history at Princeton
Dana G. Munro	Ph.D. in Latin American history and politics
Arthur I. Andrews	president of Tufts College; no expertise or experience in the Near East
Royal B. Dixon	anthropologist specializing in North American Indians
Ellen C. Semple	anthropologist and geographer; no expertise or experience in the Near East
F. H. Newell	mining engineer with the U.S. Geological Survey
David Magie	professor of classics at Princeton
Abraham V. W. Jackson	professor of ancient Indo-Iranian languages at Columbia
L. H. Gray	instructor in Indo-Iranian languages at Princeton, specializing in medieval and ancient literature

contributed to the Western Asia Section as well. Monroe was a professor of psychology who also wrote travelogues. He had visited the Ottoman Empire and on the basis of his limited experience alone had written a book called *Turkey and the Turks,* which illustrated more of his mentality than of the Near East.[132] Monroe's book was sometimes correct in one section, when he had read the right sources, which was then followed by a section full of laughable historical inaccuracies. He wrote much about "race types" and of the "superior intelligence" of "Aryan types." Greeks were called the most intelligent of all the "races" of the Ottoman Empire but were "untrustworthy." Armenians were portrayed as almost as intelligent as Greeks but were "cowards." Various non-Christian peoples vied for the bottom of the intellectual ladder. Monroe stated that Kurds were less intelligent than Armenians or Persians because they had mixed their "Aryan" blood "with Semitic and Mongolian races." "The Turk is distinguished neither by the ability to construct nor create, and he does not imitate well." The Jews of Turkey "represent the very lowest physical, mental, and moral types of the Hebrew race." Monroe wrote well and could be funny: "In the range of his intellectual interests and the depth of his sympathies for the refined pleasures of life—music, drama, art, and the like— the Turk is even more circumscribed than the average American business man—a mental state which suggests excessive stupidity."[133] But the prejudice lay heavy, overcoming the humor.

Leon Dominian was an Armenian who had graduated from the missionary college in Istanbul (Robert College) and then came to America. By profession a geographer who worked for the American Geographical Society, he had written a book on European ethnic geography: *The Frontiers of Language and Nationality in Europe.* The book indicated his position on the Turks: "The Turk, child of the ungrateful Asiatic steppelands, has always been the heartily despised intruder." "They knew that their nomad's tent was pitched only for a while on the continent [Europe] in which they sojourned as conquerors and as strangers." "The state they [the Turks] founded had a weak head and no heart whatever." "Turkey [in Asia] is still a vast field in which the Turk has pitched his tent and merely waits, knowing that the day is not far off when he will have to break camp and seek new pasturages for his herds and flocks."[134] At that time the Turks had been in Anatolia for almost nine hundred years, in Europe for more than five hundred years, and had long abandoned nomadic ways. Dominian described Turks as "weak," "incompetent," and "bloodthirsty murderers." As might be expected, Greeks and especially Armenians were portrayed in a considerably better light. They had art, culture, and commerce, which were not mentioned for the Turks. The dominant impression in Dominian's work was that it was fully appropriate to drive the Turks out of both Europe and Anatolia.

Dominian was assigned topics on "The Mohammedan World" and "Turkey." For the Muslim world he made the simple assertion that "social conditions in Islam have compelled European powers to control and police Mohammedan lands."[135] In his very long contribution on "Turkey," Dominian took care to divide the population by "races": "Armenoid," "Semitic," "Turkish," "Mediterranean," "Mixed Turkish & Indo-European," and others.[136] Population data were drawn from the spurious "Armenian Patriarchate Statistics" and various European estimates. Some of the population figures had been compiled forty years earlier and were wrong even then but were treated as if they were true in 1918.[137] A map of Eastern Anatolia showed the area as populated by Armenians, with scattered Turkish and Kurdish settlements.[138]

With the dubious exception of Monroe and Dominian, the Inquiry members who analyzed the Ottoman Empire were completely out of their depth. They called on those Americans that they assumed knew most about the Middle East: members of the missionary establishment.

James Barton contributed extensive analyses. The title of one of his contributions indicates the nature of his reports: "The Turkish Government—Analysis of Its Inherent Evil."[139] The report featured historical errors, such as the notion that in the Turkish concept of government all were slaves of the sultan.[140] Barton's opinion on that government was unequivocal: "There can be only one conclusion, which is that Turkey as an independent nation should be eliminated."[141] He felt that the Turks, unlike the Ottoman Christians, were inherently unfit to rule:

> The Armenians, Georgians, Greeks, Syrians and Jews are virile races with great powers of recuperation. They are industrious, have large families, are hopeful and law-abiding. They are not quarrelsome. The first four races named [i.e., not the Jews] are intellectually strong and capable of unlimited advancement in every department in the sciences, arts and professions. They would quickly respond to every opportunity for improving their present deplorable state and would, from the first, constitute a powerful force for law, order and progress.

The Turks and Kurds, Barton felt, could only provide unskilled labor.[142] For Barton, the Turks' administration of an empire for many centuries did not seem to prove that they any real skills.

Barton provided the Inquiry with statements on the Armenians from American missionaries.[143] The American Committee for Armenian and Syrian Relief provided papers from its Committee to Work on Reconstruction after the War. The committee's recommendations included a call for a foreign mandate over all Anatolia and the South Caucasus and the demand that all Turkish officials be driven from power.[144] This was called for because "the Turks are incapable of ruling themselves" and "the majority of the intelligent Turks of Konia would welcome a foreign protectorate."[145] The Inquiry studies also included works drawn up for it by other missionaries. For example, Harvey Porter of the Syrian Protestant College wrote: "The governing class have never shown ability as rulers of subject races and latterly have acknowledged this by endeavoring to exterminate them." Porter felt that all the past successes of the Ottomans had been due to the "racial qualities" of officials drawn from Christian stock; the only good rulers of Turkey had "little Turkish blood."[146]

The Inquiry consulted Armenian nationalists and even British propagandists, including documents from the Wellington House list of propaganda publications.[147] In a paper designed to advocate an American Mandate over Eastern Anatolia and the Caucasus, Boghos Nubar, Armenian national representative, provided a study of Turkish "cultural and economic inferiority"—a Turkish "insufficiency" that led to the Turk's "inability to govern himself."[148] Nubar provided completely false statistics stating that Turks were only 25 percent of the population in the Ottoman provinces that made up his Armenia, Kurds 24.5 percent, and Armenians 39 percent.[149] It should be noted that no Turks and no pro-Turkish sentiments were included in the Inquiry studies.

The members of the Inquiry Western Asia Section themselves summarized the material they collected. Dana C. Munro wrote a negative analysis of "Turkey in Asia: Social Science Data," in which he painted a grim picture. He made use of no Ottoman sources.[150] David Magie wrote: "The Turkish Government gradually decided to eliminate the troublesome [Armenian] question by eliminating the Armenians and found allies among the Kurds."[151] Without justification, Magie stated that 1890s massacres were done by order of the government.[152] The most detailed summations of the Inquiry positions were written by Ellen Churchill Semple and by the Western Asia Section director, William L. Westermann.

In "The Partition of Asiatic Turkey,"[153] Ellen Churchill Semple explained the Inquiry's suggestion that the Ottoman Empire be completely ruled by non-Turks, preferably Europeans. According to Semple, Armenians should be given a state, under foreign guidance, because of their "economic and cultural ascendancy" and because they had "a national consciousness based on a national history." It should be one of four separate states carved from Asiatic Turkey, all ruled over by a European power. To justify her claim for an Armenian state that was to stretch from the Black Sea to the Mediterranean, she provided absolutely absurd population figures, claiming, for example, that Armenians were 50–74 percent of the population in "the district immediately surrounding Lake Van." Her bibliography listed only European and Armenian sources, including works from the British propagandists.[154]

Westermann blamed the problems of the Turks partly on race, because "the Turks are not pure-blooded. They are hardly a race."[155] He laid most blame, however, on Islam. Westermann wrote of "failures" of the Turks, in which Islam was a prominent cause. Indeed his chapters were titled "Faults in" various places. The loss of the empire in the war was blamed purely on poor government, with no mention of the superior military capabilities of the empire's opponents. He described the Ottoman rule as "anarchy which prevails throughout the country side in almost all districts."[156] Westermann listed as his sources popular histories and books by Morgenthau, Edwin Pears, H. F. B. Lynch, and Zwemer—not a collection designed for an unbiased view. He did not include any Ottoman sources or any that were friendly to the Turks or even neutral.

Readers could look in vain for any sympathy for the Turks in the Inquiry—no mention of Turkish suffering or Turkish mortality. To the Inquiry researchers, the Armenians and Greeks were never guilty; the Turks were so guilty and so blighted by their religion and "race" that they were irredeemable unless Europe or America ruled over them. It is no wonder that the American government was so firmly set against the Turks, given the sources of its information and the feelings of its president. At first U.S. governmental support provided much-needed supplies and diplomatic support for the relief agencies. In the end, however, no amount of support for the missionaries could force America to rule over Turkey, the missionary establishment's final aim.

Politics

Oddly enough, the first diplomatic triumph of the missionary establishment during World War I was beneficial to the Ottoman Empire. Greatly affected by the propaganda of the missionaries and the British, public and political sentiment in 1917 was in favor of declaring war on the Ottoman Empire as well as on Germany. The missionary establishment viewed this as an impending disaster, fearing that the result would be closure of American missions. They were thus in the difficult position of advocating that America should not punish the Turkish devils, in order that God's work could continue. Congress was in the mood to declare war on the Ottomans, but the missionaries had strong friends in the Wilson administration. In particular, Cleveland H. Dodge, a major financial backer of the Presbyterian missions, had the ear of President Wilson. James Barton was also heeded.[157] Largely through their intercession, the United States never declared war on the Ottoman Empire. This was the missionaries' only beneficial act toward the Ottomans.

Throughout World War I the missionaries and their supporters were precariously balanced between the need for neutrality within the Ottoman Empire so that the mission could continue and the antipathy toward the Turks that they preached in the outside world. In their publications they praised Russian, British, and Armenian enemies of the Ottomans while they damned the Turks. Only on one occasion, however, did the missionaries actually take military action. In Urmia, Iran, $100,000 of relief money was diverted to buy arms and support a "Christian Army" to fight the Turks.[158] The missionaries mainly stayed out of Ottoman internal politics. The Ottomans responded by allowing the transfer of funds, operation of orphanages and schools, and other mission activities. After the war, though, the missionary attitude changed.

After World War I the anti-Turkish feeling that was the main tool of the relief organization was an unassailable image in America. The Suffering Armenian and the somewhat less prominent Suffering Greek had become shibboleths for politicians and newspaper editors as well as the clergy. To take anything other than a sympathetic stand toward Near East Relief or to show sympathy for the Turks would have been the path to political doom. But it is not necessary to assume that politicians, editors, and other public figures needed ulterior motives to support Near East Relief or to accept the vilification of Turks. Like the general public, they had never heard any side of the Armenian-Turkish or Turkish-Greek relations other than the one spread by the missionaries. As noted above, this sentiment led to congressional approval of the missionary project, a national charter for Near East Relief, and funding for relief efforts.

The missionary establishment mobilized to affect American policy. Abandoning their advocacy of American neutrality once the Ottoman Empire had been defeated, the missionaries tried to bring America into the war that flared in 1919 between the Turks and the Armenian Republic (formed out of what had been Russian Armenia during the Russian Revolution). After World War I the situation in the Southern Caucasus and northeastern Anatolia was fluid. Three new nations—Georgia, Armenia, and Azerbaijan—claimed some of the same territories. Armenia also claimed the land around Kars, which had been lost by the Ottoman Empire to Russia in 1878 and which the Turks wanted back. The leaders of Near East Relief did not hide their sympathies. They advocated the triumph of the Armenians in all cases, as exemplified by the writings of the missionary Ernest A. Yarrow.

Yarrow was first assistant then chief of staff of Near East Relief in the Caucasus. In January 1920 the *Journal of International Relations* printed his observations on events in the three republics of the Southern Caucasus: Georgia, Azerbaijan, and Armenia.[159] Yarrow's comments were intended to affect the political process in Britain and America. His unabashed aim was to convince the British to send an army to the Caucasus and aid the Armenian cause as Armenians and Azeri Turks fought over land. Yarrow wholeheartedly wanted to reverse the British policy of noninterference in the Caucasus.[160] He complained that the British had taken the ammunition they seized from Turks in Kars and given it to the Russian White army, instead of leaving it to the Armenians. He further denounced the British for allowing the Muslims to take Nahçivan from the Armenians:

At the time the British withdrew, the whole district of Nakhetchivan, which had been assigned to the Armenians, was being conquered by force by the Tartars [Azerbaijani Turks] and there was severe fighting going on not far from Erivan with the Armenians trying to resist this advance. I was told personally by those in charge that the British had strict orders not to send troops into Armenia, although at that time they had considerable forces in the other two republics. This was a patent pussy footing on their previously stated policy of maintaining the status quo.

Yarrow said that the British had to change their intentions and bring in an army: "There *must* be an armed force here."[161]

Yarrow's siding with the Armenians against their enemies was consistent with Near East Relief policies. His method of drawing sympathy for the Armenians was also consistent with Near East Relief practice: only the troubles of Armenians were mentioned, never those of their opponents; it was assumed that Europe and America had a duty to assist Armenia. The facts were bent more than a bit. Yarrow's declarations of British strength in the region in 1920 were erroneous. The British did not have the requisite armed forces in the area, so they could not have intervened. The British were indeed preserving the status quo, however, by not attempting to give Nahçivan to the Armenians. Nahçivan was overwhelmingly Muslim Turkish in population. The "Tartars" who "conquered by force" were in fact the residents of the region, who refused to give it to the Armenians. Not even the Allies had "assigned" the region to the Armenians at the time. Yarrow also failed to mention that the ammunition seized in Kars was taken from the Turkish inhabitants, who were a clear majority of the population, that the British had given the Kars region to the Armenian minority after they had disarmed the Turkish majority, and that the British had left much of the ammunition to the Armenians.[162]

In reality, despite Allied help in claiming the Kars region, the Armenians could not hold lands in which they were a clear minority. Yarrow wanted the British to assist them. This is a fair example of Near East Relief policy. It is also indicative of the type of reports that reached America from the South Caucasus, almost all of which originated with Yarrow and his missionary relief colleagues. Like the World War I propaganda, their reports were not temperate. Yarrow predicted that "the whole Armenian race will be exterminated" if the Turks triumphed.[163] Articles by missionaries and relief workers or quoting them constantly stressed that the Armenians were "surrounded by hostile Turks, Kurds, and Tartars, and face almost total extermination."[164] Crops had not been planted during the war, and all the peoples of Eastern Anatolia and Trans-Caucasia (Azerbaijan, Georgia, and Armenia) faced starvation. Near East Relief reports only cited Armenian hunger and alleged, without offering any evidence, that the Turks were deliberately starving the Armenians.[165] Many reports stated that the Turks of Anatolia and Azerbaijan (the "Tartars") were uniting to destroy the Armenians. Enver Paşa, the Ottoman ex-minister of war, was reported to be in the Caucasus, raising an army to attack Armenians.[166] He had supposedly gathered a force of "100,000 Turks, Kurds, Tartars, and other Mohammedans" who were planning "to swoop down and exterminate."[167] (In fact, Enver was in Europe at the time.)[168] The *Times-Picayune* of New Orleans did not feel that it was Enver who was raising the armed force; it was the Bolsheviks in league with Mustafa Kemal.[169] The *Atlanta Constitution* reported that Mustafa Kemal was operating in the Caucasus in August 1919, attacking Armenians and hindering relief supplies.[170] In reality, neither Mustafa Kemal nor any Turkish Nationalist forces were in Trans-Caucasia then.

An American Mandate

At war's end, most of the missionary establishment coalesced behind a drive to put America directly in charge of what remained of Anatolia. The missionaries pressured the U.S. government to take the region as an American "mandate," similar to the mandates that France and Britain took in the Arab world, which were in fact colonial occupation. The missionary establishment disagreed over the form of the mandate, some recommending long-term rule over all of Anatolia and the Caucasus, others a shorter rule over Armenia alone.[171] The thrust of the establishment's argument was that if America did not take the mandate ("doing its duty to the Armenians") anarchy would rule over Anatolia and Trans-Caucasia.[172] Christians would be killed, perhaps all Christians in Anatolia even "exterminated."[173]

Seventy-five bishops of American churches, primarily Methodist and Episcopalian, asked President Wilson in 1919 to accept an American mandate over Armenia.[174] The American Committee for the Independence of Armenia, which despite its name became a lobbying group for an American Mandate over Armenia, contained twelve members of the Near East Relief/ACASR Boards, including the Near East Relief chair, James Barton, and general secretary, Charles Vickrey. The committee also attracted a number of American politicians. It was led by Near East Relief board member and ambassador James W. Gerard.[175] Another major lobbying group, the Armenian-American Society, was founded by the onetime ACASR representative Walter George Smith and led by Smith and George R. Montgomery, the missionary minister who had been an authority for the Inquiry and the American committees of investigation (see below). Its board also contained many members of the Near East Relief Board.[176] Although they later were to differ on the form of the mandate, groups at first lobbied for American mandates.[177]

James Barton, leader of Near East Relief, spearheaded the campaign for an American mandate. He addressed public meetings and gave press interviews declaring that American control was the only hope for Armenians and, indeed, for all the peoples of the region: "Only under the mandate of America could Armenia expect unity, independence, and safety from annihilation."[178] Barton reported, as usual without naming sources, that the Turkish Nationalists were planning extermination of the Armenians in Cilicia and elsewhere as soon as the Allies left.[179] They would do this in alliance with the Bolsheviks, whom the Turks ("an army of murderers," "professional brigands," "malcontents of every kind") were supposedly going to allow to advance into Anatolia.[180] Peace could only come, Barton stated, if Americans took over the Ottoman Empire as well as what had been Russian Armenia, Georgia, and Azerbaijan.[181] Other members of the missionary establishment joined the call and reported to the American press that atrocities could be expected if the Americans did not fulfill their "duty to the Armenians."[182]

Ambassador Morgenthau was firmly behind the U.S. mandate scheme. His assertions echoed those of the missionaries. In numerous speeches and articles he declared that the Ottoman Empire should be dismembered, with separate mandates for Istanbul, Armenia, and the rest of Anatolia, preferably all under the United States.[183] With a certain lack of prescience Morgenthau confidently predicted that the Turks would present no problems for an occupier: "We here in the United States must realize that Turkey has at last shot her bolt. She is finished."[184]

The missionary establishment leaders and tactics that had begun the Armenian campaign took up the new cause. William Walker Rockwell, instrumental in beginning the anti-Turkish campaign of the ACASR, campaigned and wrote for the assumption of an American mandate over Armenia.[185] Rockwell assured his readers that Armenia would be Armenian because they were the largest population group there: "In 1914 the population of Turkish Armenia was estimated at 3,100,000, of which 1,403,000 were Armenians, 943,000 Turks, 482,000 Kurds, and the balance other elements." This was complete nonsense. The actual prewar population of Turks and Kurds in what was called Turkish Armenia was 3.9 million out of a total population of 5 million.[186] Rockwell added: "The Turkish Government has recently appropriated a sum equivalent to $15,000,000 with which to induce the Kurds and Tartars of Persia and Caucasus to move into Armenia, with a view of insuring a Moslem majority." No such appropriation existed, and in any case neither the Ottoman government nor the Turkish Nationalists had the money. Other writers assured the American public that all the people of Anatolia, including the Turks, wanted an American mandate.[187]

Newspapers, especially those traditionally most friendly to the missionary establishment, took up the mandate campaign. *Current Opinion* called for American intervention in Armenia, based on wholly fictitious evidence: Armenia had sizable oil and coal deposits waiting to be developed, the Armenian army was 150,000 strong and had defeated the Turks, and so forth. None of this was true; if it had been true, it would raise serious questions as to Armenia's helplessness.[188] Henry Wales of the *Chicago Tribune* news service wrote from Paris: "The United States can avert a Turkish holy war and avert the slaughter of more thousands of Armenians by declaring itself regarding the question of a mandate in Asia Minor immediately."[189] The *New York Times* and the *Christian Science Monitor* were particularly dedicated to promoting the cause. The *Monitor* ran many articles quoting missionaries and Armenian politicians, scholars, and organization heads (no Turks, of course). All called for some form of mandate and stated that massacre of Armenians would be the result if a mandate was not accepted.[190]

A long article in the *Christian Science Monitor* presented the analysis of the missionary J. Herbert Knapp of Near East Relief. He suggested that all the people of

Turkey would accept a new order in which Ottoman Europe and Istanbul were given to the Greeks, as well as separate lands being designated in Anatolia for Armenians and Kurds. Whatever territory was left for the Turks would accept all the old Capitulations and foreigners' extraterritorial rights. As he described it: "The old government is in power and Mustafa Kemal is merely a figurehead for a clique of these reactionaries." (Knapp was a fervent prohibitionist and believed that all Turkey's past ills had been due to drunkards among the ruling class.)[191] Other articles, disseminated by news services, also claimed that the Turks would welcome an American mandate.[192]

The *New York Times* ran its own missionary and Armenian articles advocating the mandate,[193] including a full page by James W. Gerard, head of the American Committee for the Independence of Armenia. Gerard asserted that America should take the mandate because the Armenians were brother Christians and that there would be war if America did not take the mandate, but perfect peace if America did so. Not taking the mandate would mean the loss "of a great opportunity for the propagation of Anglo-Saxon civilization in the Near East." America would have no military obligation ("a few thousand marines"), because the Armenians would build a large army themselves. Gerard's arguments were bolstered, of course, by absurd population statistics.[194] Others wrote confidently that an American mandate would be an easy task, requiring no more than one regiment of troops: "The Turks are thoroughly humbled and subdued and will hardly make much trouble."[195] The usual false reports of massacres and Turkish plans for them became more prominent when the mandate became an issue. Missionaries such as Ernest Yarrow reported unspecified massacres of Armenians to the American press. He wrote that Armenia would be "crucified" unless America came there "in force."[196] Near East Relief representatives alleged atrocities against Armenians all over Eastern Anatolia and the Caucasus, although the specifics of their stories almost always involved starvation among Armenian refugees, omitting, of course, any mention of starvation among Turks and Kurds.[197]

The Associated Press interviewed the prime minister of the Armenian Republic, who gave his unqualified support of an American mandate: "Whatever America decides is best for us we will follow out."[198] Prime Minister Venizelos of Greece favored an American mandate for Armenia (not the rest of Anatolia, much of which he wanted for Greece).[199] All of the Western powers at the peace conferences made clear that they wanted America to take the mandate.[200]

COMMISSIONS OF INQUIRY

Two American investigation commissions were sent out to investigate conditions in the Near East—the King-Crane Commission and the Harbord Mission. Both returned reports advocating an American mandate and were heavily influenced by the missionary establishment.

The leaders of the King-Crane Commission were Charles Richard Crane and Henry Churchill King.[201] Both went to the Middle East with considerable commitment to the Armenian cause. Crane, who had made his fortune as an industrialist in plumbing fixtures, was a trustee of Robert College and president of the board of the Constantinople Women's College, both American Protestant missionary establishments. He had served as treasurer of the ACASR and was a board member of Near East Relief. Henry King was a minister in the Congregational Church, the religious group that was the foundation of the American Board, and an official of the Federal Council of Churches. He also had ties to Near East Relief and to the missionary establishment. As president of Oberlin College he had sponsored a meeting there of the American Board of Commissioners for Foreign Missions and had himself served as a director of the ABCFM.[202] He was a particular friend of James Barton, the secretary of the American Board and head of Near East Relief.[203] Neither King nor Crane can be considered to have been neutral on Armenian or Turkish affairs.

The primary expert on Anatolia of the King-Crane Commission was the Presbyterian minister Dr. George Montgomery. In Montgomery's case, the term "expert" is misleading. He had been a Congregationalist pastor and a professor of French language and philosophy and had written books of what would today be called psychology. His academic expertise had nothing to do with the Middle East, although he had been born of missionary parents in Ottoman Anatolia (in Maraş) and had served in 1916 as a special assistant to the U.S. ambassador in Istanbul, Henry Morgenthau. Morgenthau's opinions on Turks and Armenians resonated in Montgomery.[204] Indeed, he may have been instrumental in fixing Morgenthau's anti-Turkish biases. His own writings indicate a deep prejudice against Muslims in general and Turks in particular. In the report he prepared before the commission set out, he wrote that Muslim empires "grew and prospered as long as there was loot to be divided." He stated that Islam was a completely selfish religion that could not be reformed and that Muslims could always be expected to fight against Christians and Christianity.[205]

Affected by Montgomery and others, the commission prepared itself before departure by reading the experts' recommendations as the essential works on the subject of Turks and Armenians: the reports of Near East Relief, British propaganda's *Blue Book* on the Armenians,[206] and *The Frontiers of Language and Nationality in Europe* by Leon Dominian.[207] Commission members were to make extensive use of the "position papers" prepared by the Inquiry. It would be difficult to imagine a more one-sided version of history than the one available in the recommended reading of the members of the King-Crane Commission.

Even before the commission began its investigations it was clear what the conclusions of its report on the Armenians would be. King, in Paris before leaving for the East, gave a report to President Wilson in which he outlined his feelings that an independent Armenia should be created and that Turks would continue to kill Armenians unless this occurred.[208] Montgomery advised that the commission should not go at all, because they already knew everything that was needed to come to conclusions and make recommendations.[209]

The report of the King-Crane Commission attacked the Turks, particularly the Ottoman record with Armenians. It is remarkable that the members of the commission felt themselves competent to speak on the Armenian issue at all, because they made so little effort to go to the scene of the Armenian-Turkish troubles and investigate. The commission's travels were primarily in the Arab provinces of the Ottoman Empire. Its report stated that members had discovered all they needed to know about conditions in Anatolia by studying relevant materials and holding meetings in Paris and Istanbul. Although they had briefly visited only one area of the Armenian-Turkish conflict, Cilicia (south-central Anatolia, around the city of Adana), they considered themselves knowledgeable enough to declare unequivocally that Turks had massacred Armenians throughout Anatolia. Of course, they made no mention of the Armenian massacres of Turks. King and Crane alleged that the massacres had been centrally organized by the Ottoman government: "And these massacres [of Armenians] have been due to deliberate and direct government actions, in which the Turkish people themselves have been too willing to share. They have not been crimes of the passion of the moment. And they have involved cruelties horrible beyond description."[210]

The solution to the Turkish-Armenian troubles, according to King and Crane, was a separate Armenian state, carved out of Eastern Anatolia. Using phrases such as "historical mis-government," "age-long misrule," and "this blighting influence of Turkish rule," they contended that Turks were incapable of any rule per se, even over themselves, and certainly not over Armenians or other Christians:

> The reasons for a separate Armenia, then, may be said to be: because of the demonstrated unfitness of the Turks to rule over others, or even over themselves; because of the adoption of repeated massacres as a deliberate policy of State; because of almost complete lack of penitence for the massacres, or repudiation of the crime—they rather seek to excuse them; because practically nothing has been done by the Turks in the way of repatriation of Armenians or as reparations to them—a condition not naturally suggesting a repetition of the experiment of Turkish rule; because, on the contrary, there is evidence of intense feeling still existing against the Armenians, and implicit threatening of massacre; because there has been sufficient proof that the two races cannot live peaceably and decently together so that it is better for both to have separate states... In the interest of the Armenians, of the Turks, and of the peace of the world alike, the formation of a separate Armenian State is to be urged.[211]

After numerous other statements against the Turks and in favor of the Armenians, King and Crane declared that the Armenian state they proposed could not be truly independent but should be placed under the "tutelage" of a Western state. They suggested that the United States take up a mandate for Armenia. Not coincidentally, this was the position favored by American missionaries. As justification for their opinions, King and Crane cited no fieldwork or observation of their own. They could not do so, because their commission had not visited Eastern Anatolia. Instead they offered extensive quotations from a few Western and Armenian sources. Separate mandates were to be created for Istanbul and for what remained for the Turks, but they would be unified in an unspecified way under one mandatory. King and Crane recommended that these mandates also be taken by the United States.

The King-Crane Report had an effect on the deliberations of the American government, but its effect on the American public came primarily through newspaper articles. King and Crane both told the newspapers that their commission had recommended an American mandate for at least Armenia and that all the people of the Ottoman Empire wanted America to be in charge. They put forth the standard story of Turkish-Armenian relations.[212] The King-Crane Report was not released by the U.S. government, probably because it made suggestions for independence in the Arab Middle East that were anathema for America's British and French allies. Its full impact on the public could not come until 1922, when the *New York Times* obtained a copy from former president Wilson.[213] The Harbord Mission was to have a greater impact.

The mission of the Harbord Mission (officially the American Military Mission to Armenia) differed from that of the King-Crane Commission.[214] King and Crane had been directed to prepare a general study of the Near East. General Harbord was specifically charged with studying the situation of Armenians (not, it might be noted, the people of Eastern Anatolia and the Caucasus but "Armenia").

The members of the American Military Mission to Armenia were mainly American military men.[215] They were joined by civilian technical experts in fields such as engineering. One Armenian, Lt. A. Khachadoorian, and one Turk, Professor Hussein (Pektaş), were official members.[216] Another Armenian, Major Haig Shekerjian, joined the mission in Anatolia as a de facto member. Lieutenant Khachadoorian was an important member of the mission. He was a naturalized American citizen, listed on the mission record as "born in Aintab, Armenia," who had previously worked with an American aid mission to the Armenian Republic.[217] As is evident in the archival record of the Harbord Mission, the commission greatly relied upon Khachadoorian. He drew up many of the mission reports that were the raw material of the final report, filled with negative comments on the "character" of the Turks but few data.[218] Khachadoorian also was a member, often the leader, of fact-finding missions that were sent to regions not visited by the entire mission. Hussein Bey, the sole Turk, was certainly unrepresentative of Turkish public opinion. He was anything but a Turkish Nationalist. A founding member of the "Turkish Wilsonian League," he publicly supported an American mandate for Anatolia. Nevertheless, despite his agreement with the aims of the Americans, the archival records of the commission make no mention of his role in the mission's deliberations. Other than his inclusion in lists of commission members, the only substantive mentions of him in the mission's archival papers are a record of the hotel room he occupied in Tiflis and a note that he had been lost and left behind by the commission in Aleppo (he was returned by the British).[219] The records also show that he was paid $150 for his services.[220]

Most importantly, the only interpreters to accompany the mission were Armenians—Aram Kojassar, Dikran Ohanessian, and Dikran Serijian. Only a few Turks who knew foreign languages spoke for themselves, and these were almost all in Istanbul. All of the comments of Turks who were questioned in Eastern Anatolia, the scene of the Armenian-Turkish troubles, were filtered through the Armenian translators.

Before they left for their investigations, commission members were given a list of persons to consult in Paris and on site in Istanbul, Anatolia, and Trans-Caucasia who would give "reliable information."[221] They included Boghos Nubar (head of an Armenian national delegation at the Paris Peace Conference), Avetis Aharonian (president of the Armenian Republic), Hovhannes Kachaznuni (prime minister of the Armenian Republic), Charles Crane, James Barton, Herbert Gibbons, and the Armenian patriarch and other Armenians in Istanbul.[222] The opinions that might be expressed and the advice that might be given to commission members by Armenian churchmen, generals, and politicians are obvious. All the other suggested sources of information were tied to the missionary establishment. The mission also was given a complete list of the American missionaries then in Anatolia and the Caucasus so that they could be consulted. Only one Turk, the prime minister of Azerbaijan, was mentioned as a possible source of information, but not a single Ottoman Turk or any other Muslim was included on the list of persons to be consulted.

The position papers on the Turkish-Armenian troubles that were given to the Harbord Mission were more detailed than those prepared for the King-Crane Commission, but they were similar in substance. Population statistics, all-important in studying the feasibility and morality of creating an Armenia in Anatolia, were completely drawn from Armenian sources,[223] except for one set of fabricated figures that had been commissioned by the Greek government.[224] Armenians were described as "progressive humanity," while Turks were "medieval barbarity."[225] Historical essays ignored any inhuman actions by Armenians, neglected to mention that any Turks had died at the hands of Armenians, and said nothing of Armenian rebellion against the Ottoman government. Turks, when mentioned at all, were always portrayed in the worst possible light, but little was actually said about the lives or history of Turks or other Muslims. A reader of the position papers might be led to believe that the Armenians had been the overwhelming majority in the East rather than, in reality, a distinct minority.

Most of the material was only on Armenians or by Armenians, even those few sections specifically devoted to Turks. For example, the section titled "Turks in the Caucasus" in the book-length position paper on Trans-Caucasia given to the mission members contained three typed pages of comments on the Turks (mainly on the administration of Azerbaijan), two pages of statistics from Armenian sources, then seven pages of letters, all written by the Armenian guerrilla leader Andranik![226] The lengthy section on "Armenians of the Caucasus" was written by an Armenian (without documents from Ottoman or Azerbaijani sources). Throughout the position papers, the primary input was from missionaries and Armenians. As was the case with the King-Crane Commission, the sources of information indicate the intentions of the members of the mission long before they set foot in the area.

In Anatolia and the Caucasus, the Harbord Mission met primarily with local notables, especially Christians. Their purposes and their biases would have been obvious to the few Muslim representatives they consulted, since their method of "investigation" ensured that they would only be told what they wanted to hear. As the Armenian historian Richard Hovannisian has written: "As in other places, Harbord met with local notables, whenever possible in the presence of Armenian and other Christian representatives, to solicit opinions on the political settlement, and to emphasize American interest in the well-being of Armenian survivors."[227]

The fact-finding procedure makes it easy to imagine the answers that Harbord would have received to his questions. Muslim "notables" were selected then questioned by mission members, accompanied by members of the Armenian community, with whom the Turks had been at war for five years, and by armed guards. The only way for Muslims to give testimony was through the Armenian interpreters. In addition, although the actual questions asked have not survived, comments by mission members make it clear that they were not questions intended to discover what had actually happened in the East since 1914. Instead, they were intended to find out what stood in the way of the intended creation of an Armenia in Eastern Anatolia. When mission members talked to Turks at all it was about political matters; and the Turks they spoke to were usually, but not always, enemies of the old Ottoman system who hoped to gain politically or who felt that capitulation was necessary for survival.[228] They simply did not talk to the Turks who had suffered at the hands of Armenians. How could they have done so? Imagine the responses that General Harbord—accompanied by armed men in uniform and local Armenian leaders—would have received as he spoke to "local notables" through Armenian interpreters. Even if a few had been able to explain themselves and had been interpreted properly, it is doubtful that anyone would have listened—the Americans' minds had been made up long ago.

It is difficult to imagine a less productive approach to discovering the truth. Yet the approach made sense given the intention of the mission: to investigate ways to aid in the fulfilling of the aspirations of the Armenians. Bringing back findings on the actual events of the war in Eastern Anatolia was no part of the plan of the members of the mission, who believed that they already knew the truth. In reality, the Harbord Mission was not a fact-finding commission at all.

The final report of the Harbord Mission, like that of the King-Crane Commission before it, was based on the material its members read and the mind-set they developed before the mission ever set out.[229] Much of the report dealt with matters that the mission had never really investigated. It delved extensively into history, which was told without reference to any Turkish sources. If the report mentioned Turkish wartime deaths, it was as deaths in combat. Armenian deaths, in contrast, were uniformly stated to be the result of massacre, with little or no consideration given to starvation and disease. The report cited absolutely no proof, perhaps because the commission members assumed that none was needed. The mission archival and printed materials contain no evidence that mission members ever even attempted to investigate the historical record of the Turkish-Armenian troubles, yet they felt confident in making historical assertions.

General Harbord was not above bending the truth to make his points. For example, he categorically stated the absurdity that "the purpose of the [Turkish] Nationalists" was to obtain an American mandate over the Ottoman Empire.[230] The only Turks who had spoken in favor of an American mandate over Anatolia to Harbord were a few, such as King-Crane's Hussein Bey, who seem to have been chosen precisely because they held such views (professors at the main American missionary college in the Ottoman Empire might be well disposed toward things American). The man who arguably spoke for the Turks, Mustafa Kemal, leader of the Turkish Nationalists, had taken care not to accept a U.S. mandate when he spoke with Harbord. He asked for economic aid if possible but especially for American adherence to the principles of Wilson's "14 Points."[231] Harbord also stated that "official reports of the Turkish Government say 1,100,000 Armenians have been deported." He asserted that 1,500,000 Armenians had been killed.[232] Both statements were fabrications. Not only do they contradict all other reports of the Ottoman or Turkish governments (no sources were offered by Harbord), but they are statistical nonsense.[233]

Harbord even falsified the reporting of Americans. The Harbord Mission did not go to the worst areas of wartime loss in Eastern Anatolia, and he obviously realized that this was a disadvantage to his report. His statement on the mission's travels obfuscated that fact: "All of the vilayets [provinces] of Turkish Armenia were visited except Van and Bitlis, which were inaccessible in the time available, but which have been well covered by Captain Niles, an army officer who inspected them on horseback in August, and whose report corroborates our observations in the neighboring regions."[234] His statement that they had visited all the vilayets of Turkish Armenia except Van and Bitlis was deceptive, because even many areas of northeastern Anatolia that were called "Armenia" were visited only by subgroups of the commission. The subgroups were usually led by Shekerjian or Khachadoorian (who drew up reports of the subgroups).

Harbord's statement about the investigation of Van and Bitlis, the provinces where Muslims had suffered the most at the hands of Armenians, by Captain Niles was completely false. Captain Emory Niles, along with Arthur Sutherland, had assuredly visited those provinces, but his report completely contradicted Harbord's statement. Niles and Sutherland wrote:

> At first we were most incredulous of the stories [of massacres of Muslims by Armenians] told us, but the unanimity of the testimony of all witnesses, the apparent eagerness with which they told of wrongs done them, their evident hatred of Armenians, and, strongest of all, the material evidence on the ground itself, have convinced us of the general truth of the facts, first, that Armenians massacred Musulmans on a large scale with many refinements of cruelty, and second that Armenians are responsible for most of the destruction done to towns and villages.[235]

Niles and Sutherland had laid blame on the Armenians. Their report, which gave extensive details of murder and destruction by Armenians, in no way corroborated Harbord's observations. Harbord was lying, although no one at the time was to know. The Niles and Sutherland report was suppressed and was only found by accident in the American archives decades later, among newspaper clippings, rough drafts of reports, and general detritus of the Harbord Mission.

The Harbord Report did not advocate an Armenian mandate per se. It stated that a mandate over Armenia, however defined geographically, was impractical. The region was too small, too remote, and too poor. Instead, the commission wrote, the mandate should cover all of Anatolia and Istanbul and preferably all of Trans-Caucasia (Armenia, Georgia, and Azerbaijan) as well. It did not recommend that America should take the mandate but wrote an extensive list of pros and cons on American involvement.[236] This did not stop some newspapers from stating that the Harbord Report actually supported a U.S. mandate.[237] Harbord himself seemed to be in favor of an American mandate. At least he wrote that such a mandate was needed and that all the peoples of the region wanted it.[238]

The Mandate Fails

It would appear that the reports of the King-Crane Commission and Harbord Mission would have been a telling factor in favor of an American mandate. Woodrow Wilson was convinced that an American mandate was needed and probably had been so convinced before he sent out his commissions. In May 1920 Wilson sent a special message to Congress, asking to be given authority to accept the mandate.[239] His message was an emotional plea to aid Armenians.

The American Senate was not convinced. While the American public was sympathetic to the Armenians and the powerful missionary establishment lobbied fiercely for the mandate, Americans had no desire to take on massive foreign responsibilities. American newspapers had at first spoken well of the idea of an American mandate.[240] But they soon began to have qualms over the cost and needed military commitment.[241] Isolationism and fear of entering a quagmire in the Middle East trumped sympathy for the Armenians. On May 29, 1920, the Senate rejected a mandate by a vote of fifty-two to twenty-three.[242] It also rejected a missionary initiative to make a loan to the Armenian Republic. Even Woodrow Wilson rejected the missionary establishment's exhortation to declare that the United States would regard any attack on Armenia as an attack on the United States—an impossible suggestion, given that the Armenian Republic was about to be swallowed by the Bolsheviks and was in a region where America could not possibly project its power. In 1922 Near East Relief formally asked Congress to pressure its wartime Allies to intervene in Turkey and worked for the dismissal of the American high commissioner in Istanbul, Admiral Mark Bristol, whom they viewed as unfriendly to missionaries and Armenians.[243] Both efforts failed.[244]

The American mandate was always a quixotic concept. As the Senate was voting against the mandate, Turkish Nationalist troops under Kâzim Karabekir were making their final preparations to attack the last part of Anatolia occupied by the Armenian Republic: the Kars-Ardahan region. By November 1920 it had all been taken by the Turks.[245] The Gümrü (Alexandropol) Agreement was signed by the Turkish Nationalist government and the Armenian government on December 3, 1920. The Armenians ceded all lands to the 1878 borders. Immediately afterward, the Bolsheviks took control of the Armenian Republic. The Moscow Agreement of March 16, 1921, and the Kars Treaty of October 13, 1921, confirmed the borders between Turkey and Georgia and Armenia as they remain today. On October 20 the Ankara Agreement between France and the Turkish Nationalists allowed the Turks control over Cilicia, which was completely occupied by December. All of the region that the Allies called "Turkish Armenia" was under Turkish control. By the time any American forces could have arrived there they would have been faced by a unified population that was in control of its territory and had proved that it would resist foreign conquest. No one knew in 1920 who would win the war between the Greeks and the Turks, but it was obvious that neither the Greeks nor the Turks would accept American control. If the Americans were to take up their mandate they would have to do it in war, as an invasion force.

The missionary establishment had foundered on its own naïveté. It had assumed that the support of President Wilson and the overwhelming hatred of Turks in America would ensure that the United States accepted the mandate, ignoring Wilson's declining power in Washington. Buoyed by its sense of Christian destiny, it had presumed that passing an American mandate would be a relatively easy task. The establishment had originally estimated that 10,000 American troops would be needed for a mandate. Any evidence to the contrary was ignored, even the seemingly obvious fact that the British and French, with many times that number of troops, had been unable to control Anatolia and the Caucasus.[246] Harbord had thrown cold water on the establishment's idealistic estimate with his (actually very conservative) estimate of 59,000 men and a five-year cost of $756 million. The wiser heads in the U.S. Senate probably disliked the Turks as much as the missionaries did, but they knew a bad deal when they saw one.[247]

Even after the Senate had rejected membership in the League of Nations and its mandate schemes, voices still called for American intervention.[248] Barton still called on the United States to take action in the "pacifying of Armenia" through armed intervention. "Unless we are ready to do something to help save the situation and do it soon, we must expect other reports of widespread atrocities from all over the Turkish Empire as the Turks proceed to eliminate by massacre all non-Moslem peoples from the country and leave Turkey for the Turks and the Turks alone." Not to act, said Barton, "will place this country in the position of Pontius Pilate."[249] Morgenthau predicted disaster not only in Turkey but in Eastern Europe, because America had failed to do "its duty." He declared the contagion would spread: "Millions of Jews in Russia and Poland would be murdered in the next few years, because the 'wild people' of Russia will feel that since the Turk was not punished there was nothing to prevent them from ridding themselves of those they termed aliens and foreigners."[250]

THE LAST ACT FOR THE MISSIONARY ESTABLISHMENT

The missionaries' political hopes for the Armenians were thwarted forever by the victories of the Turkish Nationalists in Anatolia and the Bolsheviks in the Caucasus. An independent Armenia was not to be. The United States was not to take up a mandate for Armenia. At first the word used was "betrayal." Missionary establishment speeches and press articles complained bitterly of the Allied *modus vivendi* with the new situation in the Near East. Then everything changed.[1]

The leaders of the missionary establishment came to the realization that they had lost. Once the Turks emerged victorious, Near East Relief and the writings and speeches of missionaries changed radically. The purpose of anti-Turkish propaganda had always been to protect the mission and to offer material aid to native Christians, and the old tactics had been directed to that end. Now, with Turks in charge of Anatolia and with the future of the mission in their hands, attacking Turks was no longer a viable tactic. In response, one-half of the traditional fundraising tactic—vilifying Turks—all but disappeared.

In the 1920s the focus of Near East Relief fund-raising changed radically. Near East Relief created the National Golden Rule Committee. Donations had dwindled, and it was impossible to contend that support for the Armenian and Greek causes would ever be politically successful. Moreover, Near East Relief was now dependent on the goodwill of the Turkish government and even the Soviet government.[2] The organization therefore transformed itself, abandoning most political propaganda and becoming more strictly charitable. It hit upon the idea of setting aside one Sunday a year (in December) as "Golden Rule Sunday," a focus for collections for Christian orphans. The National Golden Rule Committee included some of the most prominent men and organizations in America,[3] but it was led by the missionaries and missionary supporters who were in charge of Near East Relief and was endorsed by major missionary organizations. The honorary chairman was Cleveland H. Dodge, treasurer of Near East Relief and chair of the Board of Trustees of Robert College (the American missionary college in Istanbul), and James Barton chaired the Board of Trustees. John Finley, associate editor of the *New York Times* and Near East Relief Board member, chaired the Advisory

Council. Daily work was in the hands of the executive chairman, Charles Vickrey, who was also the general-secretary of Near East Relief.

Golden Rule solicitations were disseminated widely. All the publicity tools honed by Near East Relief in the past were utilized, including advertisements, press releases, prewritten editorials to be used by newspapers, posters and bill-boards, and coloring and essay contests in schools.[4] Very little of this directly vilified the Turks. Golden Rule publications still contended that the Turks were responsible for Christian suffering, but atrocity stories were missing. The emotional appeal now centered on pictures of hungry children. This surely helped cement the negative image of Turks in the minds of Americans. The propaganda, however, was not what it had been.

When campaigning for the Golden Rule, Near East Relief conveniently forgot that it had advocated American military intervention in the Near East. Instead it said that American aid would be successful in the Near East precisely because America "has gone to the Near East with a hand of ministry and not a mailed fist."[5] The rest was praise for all that America had done and descriptions of continuing need. The transformation was drastic. By 1924 the Near East Relief organ *New Near East* sometimes even grudgingly praised Turkish efforts: "Certainly there can be no apology for the past, and there are those who despair of any sincere and permanent change of heart in the Turk. Nevertheless, he seems to be making a desperate effort to deserve a place in the fellowship of nations, and thus far what has been accomplished in the way of self-government is an achievement that provokes admiration."[6]

The abrupt change in the missionaries is surprising. They accepted not only the Turks but the Soviets, recently damned as atheistic enemies of Armenian nationalism. In the case of the Soviets, the support was not even grudging. The *New Near East* declared unblushingly that "the present national leaders in Moscow have stated quite frankly and publicly that their chief aim above everything else is to ascertain and effect the will of the majority."[7] Such praise for the Soviets was repeated often by the missionary establishment.[8] Ernest Yarrow suggested that it would be "a gracious act" if Turkey gave the Kars region to the Soviets, who would in turn use it to settle Armenians.[9] Ignoring the naïveté of such a suggestion, the new position of the missionaries can be seen to illustrate what had always been the case. The missionaries were men and women who kept their primary purpose, the survival of the mission, firmly in mind. They were activists who always acted primarily to that end. Indeed, although it seems an odd thing to say about religious leaders, their actions indicate that they believed the end always justified the means.

Lausanne

The question of American acceptance of the Lausanne Treaty demonstrated the change in the missionary establishment. It also signaled the end of the power of the missionaries.

The Lausanne Treaty of July 24, 1923, recognized Turkish sovereignty approximately within the borders of today's Turkey.[10] Armenian and Greek claims to land in Turkey were abandoned by the Allies, although the Turks guaranteed religious freedom in their new borders. No mention was made of returning Armenians to Anatolia, and Greece and Turkey agreed to a population exchange.[11] All of the wartime hopes of the missionary establishment were lost. As might be expected, the missionaries, who had been impotent observers at the Lausanne Conference, at first excoriated the agreement. Then it all changed. James Barton declared that the Armenians had not received justice but stated that the new Turkey had to be accepted.[12] He went so far as "to point out errors and exaggerations which had appeared in the earlier propaganda."[13]

The reason for the about-face was, as it had always been, the continuation of the mission. At the Lausanne Conference, İsmet İnönü, the Turkish negotiator, had called in William Peet, director of the American Board of Commissioners for Foreign Missions in Turkey, and Barton to tell them that Turkey wanted the American schools and medical work to continue. Barton felt reassured.[14] The mission would no longer be proselytizing or converting, but it would continue. At the meeting of its National Council in October 1923 the ABCFM voted to continue its work in Turkey.

The question was whether the U.S. Senate, charged by the Constitution with ratifying all foreign treaties, would accept the treaty. The United States was not a party to the original Lausanne Treaty, but the substance of the treaty, in the form of an American-Turkish Treaty, was presented to the U.S. Senate on May 3, 1924.[15] If it did not accept the treaty, the Turks intimated and the missionaries feared, the mission would be evicted from Turkey. The missionary establishment mobilized to get the treaty passed.

In December 1926 the National Council of Congregational Churches and the American Board wrote to the Senate, asking it to pass the treaty.[16] The heads of the missionary institutions in Turkey voiced their support.[17] In addition, 150 prominent churchmen and churchwomen signed a petition to the U.S. Senate, asking that the treaty be accepted, "because this seems to us to be clearly in accord with our Christian teaching and the Christian spirit." They spoke highly of the new regime in Turkey. Those who signed included prominent ministers such as Henry Sloane Coffin and Reinhold Niebuhr, many serving missionaries, the leaders of the mission, the heads of the missionary colleges in Turkey, and many of the surviving members of the first ACASR board, such as James Barton, Cleveland Dodge, and Charles Crane. Many signers undoubtedly acted in the spirit of their Christian ideals. The statement also noted, however, that "without ratification it is impossible to have the fullest representation of American interests in commercial, educational, religious, and all humanitarian affairs."[18] Prominent members of the missionary establishment such as John Finley, Robert Speer, John Mott, and many others signed other ratification requests. The American Bible Society and the foreign directors of the YMCA and YWCA also signed pleas for ratification.[19] Even one of the Armenian-American organizations, the Armenia-America Society, urged

ratification, although the Committee for the Independence of Armenia strenu-
ously opposed it.[20]

Not all the one-time members of the missionary establishment agreed with the
missionaries. They were unwilling to deal with the despised Turk in order to save
a mission in which they had little part. It cannot be coincidental that the Congregationalists, who sent most missionaries to Turkey, supported ratification, but 110
bishops of the Protestant Episcopal Church, which had no missionaries or institutions in Turkey, signed a statement opposing the treaty and any recognition of
Turkey.[21] A telegram to the Senate from religious leaders who had once wholeheartedly supported Near East Relief and the anti-Turkish crusade "stated there
was determined opposition to the treaty by the Northern Baptist Church, Methodist Episcopal Church South, the Reformed Church and the bishops of the Episcopal Church." The telegram read: "It [the treaty] condones wholesale murders by
Kemalists" and "abandons untold thousands of Christian girls, now in Moslem
hands, to their fate."[22]

Meetings (many organized by American-Armenian organizations) condemned
the Lausanne Treaty. At one meeting in New York, Professor Albert Bushnell
Hart (see chapter 5) declared: "Turkey has never been a civilized power. Turkey
is not a power that can be responsible for carrying out a treaty of civilization." At
the same meeting, ambassador James Gerard of the American Committee for the
Independence of Armenia took the position that American missionary work in
Turkey actually would be damaged if the treaty was passed, because the missionaries would now be subject to Turkish laws—an interesting view, given the stand
of the missionaries themselves. He further stated that Turkey would not be safe
for Americans because a civil war was imminent.[23] (Of course, there was no civil
war.) Bishop Rennie McInnes, Anglican bishop of Jerusalem, spoke in the United
States, claiming that America had not done its duty by refusing the mandate. If the
United States had been involved, he believed, none of what he called the troubles
in Anatolia (the Turkish resurgence under Mustafa Kemal) would have occurred:
"If the United States had had five hundred men in Asia Minor the trouble would
not have happened."[24] McInnes obviously had great belief in the abilities of Americans, five hundred of whom would succeed where hundreds of thousands of others had failed.

The missionary establishment had done its work in vilifying the Turks too well.
In vain did Barton and others plead—accurately—that the Lausanne Treaty was
only beneficial to America.[25] The sort of religious appeal that had been a staple of
the relief agencies was now used against them. Opposition to the treaty centered
on what senators and the public believed to be the crimes of the Turks that had
been invented or amplified by those who now wanted Turkey to be a friend. Senator William H. King of Utah, once a prominent supporter of the relief agencies
and a continuing enemy of the Turks, led the attack on the treaty in the Senate:
"Let me remind you that under the pending treaty the Turks would be permitted
to establish, without hindrance, schools in the United States to convert Christians
or Jews to Islam."[26]

The Senate defeated the Lausanne Treaty on January 18, 1927. Fifty voted in favor, thirty-four against, six short of the needed two-thirds majority.

Rent by internal dissension, the missionary establishment had failed to secure what its leaders most wanted. Turkey did not in fact expel the missionaries or close their schools, although their numbers were diminished.[27] A remnant of the mission remains in Turkey to this day. But the ability of the missionary establishment to affect American policy in the Middle East and to influence the American image of the Turks had ended.

A Sea Change

With the campaign for the Lausanne Treaty the missionaries had turned from enemies of all things Turkish to supporters of Turkey. Had the leopard changed its spots? That is more than unlikely. Barton and his colleagues could not have felt much different about the Turks than they had a few years earlier. What had changed was the reality in which the missionaries were now forced to live. The Armenians were gone from Anatolia. The atheistic Soviet masters of new Armenia would not tolerate missionaries. The new Turkish government would only tolerate them on its own terms. They could operate schools and hospitals, facilities that were to be open to all, but they could not be involved in ethnic separatism or politics. Although the Turks never stated it, anti-Turkish propaganda obviously would mean the end of the mission. The missionaries proved to be more dedicated to the mission than to conversion or to the Armenian cause. If becoming the friends of the Turks was the price for the continuation of the mission, so be it.

The cold calculation of institutional survival, however, is not the whole story. The Congregationalists, Presbyterians, and other liberal American denominations had changed. New generations of missionaries came to Turkey infused with the ideals of the social gospel. Their purpose was to do good for humanity, not only for Christians, and they came without the intellectual baggage of their predecessors. They may have remained convinced of the superiority of Christianity, but they did not allow their beliefs to interfere with their work. The missionary teachers, book publishers, and doctors became an integral part of the advancement of the Turkish Republic. Robert College (today Boğaziçi University) became the training ground for generations of Turkish engineers, scientists, and humanities scholars. Turkish women received a fine education in the Istanbul Women's College. A number of the new missionaries studied Islam seriously and tried to bridge the gap between Islam and Christianity. Several made a great contribution to Turkish scholarship, especially through their work on dictionaries. The missionaries were fewer than in the high days of the mission, but the new missionaries made a lasting contribution to Turkey.

13

Epilogue:
The Myth of the Terrible Turk Lives On

The missionary establishment and the British propagandists created an enduring Myth of the Terrible Turk. Like other myths, whether dangerous or harmless, it became so engrained in the minds of believers that it was accepted without investigation or rational consideration.[1] For nearly two centuries Americans were exposed to the myth of the Turk as a brutal murderer. The myth built on a dislike of Muslims that had developed for nearly a millennium before Americans adopted it. It is doubtful that any people except the Jews were slandered so consistently or for such a long time as were the Turks.

American acceptance of the Myth of the Terrible Turk is understandable. No matter how naïve and illogical such prejudices may seem today, they were not at all unusual in their time. Americans accepted many such myths: the drunken (but poetic) Irishman, the lazy Mexican, the Yellow Peril, the avaricious Jew, and the panoply of prejudices that were attached to African Americans. The Myth of the Terrible Turk may have been more caustic than the others, and those who believed it more filled with loathing, but it was one myth among many. Unfamiliarity with the Turks surely fed the myth: very few Turks lived in America. The presence of Jews, Irish, Mexicans, and Chinese perhaps moderated the strength of the myths attached to those groups. Not all other Americans came into contact with them, but those who did could see their common humanity and that the myths simply did not apply to those they knew. Not so for the Turks. All people knew of them was what they read, which was none too edifying.

While it may be understandable that Americans of the nineteenth and early twentieth centuries accepted what they were told about the Turks, it is astonishing that the prejudices against the Turks live on in the twenty-first century, both in popular culture and in histories and textbooks.

The Turk in American Popular Culture

The force of the Myth of the Terrible Turk is felt in American popular culture. While the Public Broadcasting System airs programs portraying the Turks as perpetrators of genocide, it does not even consider showing any program offering a different view.[2] Newspapers review and praise books that denigrate the Turks but avoid considering books that disagree with their preconceived positions.[3] Despite great gains in cleansing film and television of overt prejudice, negative stereotypes of Turks have remained. Oliver Stone's *Midnight Express* (1978) brought the myth of the violent Turk to millions with "artistic license." *Lawrence of Arabia* (1962) skewed history to describe Turkish oppressors on the screen. The evil computer bent on the destruction of all humanity in the television show *Terminator: The Sarah Connor Chronicles* was named "Turk," as was the violent protagonist (Robert De Niro) in the movie *Righteous Kill* (2008). The series *MASH* portrayed America's Turkish allies in the Korean War as crazed soldiers. Turks have overwhelmingly resisted the calls of Al-Qaeda to oppose the West, but the popular television show *24* depicted a family of Turks as Islamic terrorists. *The West Wing* represented Turkey as an Islamic radical state. The totally evil villain in *The Usual Suspects* (1995) was a Turk. Atom Egoyan's film *Ararat* (2002) is loosely based on the book *An American Physician in Turkey* by Clarence Ussher, a missionary so blinded by his prejudice that even his English and American contemporaries spoke of "his innate dislike of Turks and his inordinate fanaticism."[4] The film depicted Turks as genocidal murderers. Even the Beatles, in *The Yellow Submarine* (1968), made the Turks into villains—monsters wearing fezzes.

In 1932 one hundred Princeton students took part in a survey of cultural stereotypes.[5] The students were asked to choose five traits from a list of eighty-four words that might describe qualities typical of certain nationalities. The ten most common results chosen for Turks were less than complimentary (see table 13.1). Other groups fared better. The first choices for Germans were "scientifically-minded" and "industrious"; for the English, "sportsmanlike" and "intelligent"; for Americans, "industrious" and "intelligent"; and so forth. Of the groups considered, the students' opinion of the Turks was by far the worst.[6] While it is doubtful that Princeton students were completely representative of the general populace, the general opinion of Turks probably was at least similar.

TABLE 13.1. DESCRIPTIONS OF TURKS IN 1932 SURVEY

Cruel	54.0%	Deceitful	14.9%
Very Religious	29.9%	Sly	13.8%
Treacherous	24.1%	Quarrelsome	13.8%
Sensual	23.0%	Revengeful	13.8%
Physically Dirty	17.2%	Superstitious	12.6%

Source: Daniel Katz and Kenneth Braly, "Racial Stereotypes of One Hundred College Students," *Journal of Abnormal and Social Psychology* 28 (1933–34): 280–90.

The study was repeated a generation later (in 1950) at Princeton, with 333 student respondents.[7] They selected the same traits for Turks: "cruel," "sensuous," "treacherous," and so forth. Once again they considered Turks the "worst" of all the ethnic groups.

In 1990 a survey was taken of 304 students at the University of Louisville, a group more representative of the American public than were their Princeton counterparts.[8] Society had progressed enough since the earlier surveys that students were unwilling to admit to prejudices, so the questions were necessarily indirect. Students responded to questions such as "Which would you most like to meet?" and "Which would you least like to meet?" from a group of nationalities (Turks, Cambodians, Colombians, English, French, Germans, Nigerians, and Russians), some of whom were chosen for their recognized negative images at the time. The Turks came in last. Only 2 out of 304 respondents would have most liked to meet a Turk, whereas 69 (23 percent) listed the Turk first among those they would least like to meet, again the worst showing. When asked to describe each group based on "what you have seen in newspapers, on television, and in the movies," 38 percent said that the image of the Turks fit the categories "not nice" or "very bad people." It is doubtful that the negative image has much diminished since 1990.

The missionaries and British propagandists did their work well. The Myth of the Terrible Turk has become part of American culture.

The Myth Taken as History

No reasonable person today repeats the nineteenth-century slanders against African Americans, Jews, or Native Americans. Historians have thoroughly examined past generations' beliefs on Manifest Destiny, slavery, imperialism, and the "racial" qualities of peoples. Their findings have found their way into the media and the textbooks, changing what were once firmly set American opinions of others. Not so in the case of the supposed crimes of the Turks. Some historians of the Middle East have begun to question and disprove the conventional view of the Turks, but their studies have not reached the schoolbooks. The slanders of 100 years ago are still quoted in today's textbooks as unquestioned truth. Standard textbooks still tell the traditional one-sided histories of the Greek, Bulgarian, and Armenian rebellions. Although the textbooks are more temperate in their language than their counterparts were long ago, they tell the same tale: Christians always innocent, Muslims always guilty.[9] As always, the textbooks make no attempt to justify their positions or cite sources. Part of the reason for this is that textbook authors have been borrowing from each other and repeating the same stories for ages.

Judged by the standards of modern historical investigation or even by common sense, it is astonishing that the books and articles that formed the Myth of the Terrible Turk would be readily accepted today. Nineteenth- and early twentieth-century Americans, including American historians, did not have access to all the facts. They did not know that the Turks were largely exonerated by independent European commissions that investigated Turkish actions in Sasun, Palestine, and İzmir. The reports were hard to find, and historians and newspaper writers had no particular desire to look. But modern writers, who should know of the commissions, must take their findings into account. The Sasun Commission, the Palestine Commission, and the Smyrna Commission all found that the Turks had been the victims of lies. Whenever the record is scrutinized, the reports of the missionaries and the press turned out to be false or, at best, greatly exaggerated: clearly the other missionary and newspaper reports should therefore have been considered questionable.

Common sense should have led to a questioning of everything written by or sponsored by the British propagandists. Of course the British propagandists lied. Lack of respect for the truth is the essence of any wartime propaganda bureau. Propagandists, even those enlisted in a good cause, are concerned with the victory of their nation, not with truth. Naïveté, affection for the British, and overall lack of knowledge may explain why Americans at the time were receptive to the propaganda but not its acceptance by later, more cynical generations who understood that governments lie. Soon after World War I scholars began to dissect the British propaganda about the Germans, finding it to be full of direct lies and half-truths. Yet no one seems to have considered that those who lied about one of their enemies, the Germans, would also have lied about their other enemy, the Ottomans. The tactics used in attacks on the Germans were also used in attacks on the Ottomans: unknown sources that not even the British could identify, outright lies on the identities of other sources, completely invented reports of secret governmental deliberations, invention of massacres, suborning of supposedly independent journalists, suppression of any news that did not fit the official view.

Common sense should also have led to questioning of the missionary establishment's accounts of the Turks. Educated in seminaries where Muslims and Islam were vilified, dedicated to the Ottoman Christians and inimical to the Ottoman Muslims, the missionaries should always have been seen as a questionable source. Books such as the Reverend Pierce's *The Story of Turkey and Armenia* should have been rejected as historical evidence because of their unnamed sources and stories like "The Evil of the Turk, by an Armenian," and their absurd assertions, such as that Turks educated their children in "evil habits of body and mind." Contemporaries might have been seduced by racism, but should today's scholars take seriously missionary authors who blamed the Turks' supposed crimes on the "mental inferiority" of the "Mongolian race"? Who can take seriously a book such as the Reverend Greene's *Armenian Massacres or the Sword of Mohammed,* with its drawings of Turks with faces like monkeys and Arabs with bags filled with the heads of dead Armenians? Surely the missionaries' repeated comparison of Ottoman Christians to early Christian martyrs or the comparison of Turks to American Indians should have made anyone question the mind-set of the writers.

Would scholars in any other field of study base their writings on so many accounts written by "an American resident at Constantinople," "a friend who has lived in Turkey," "a letter received in Boston," "reports of English observers," "a gentleman who has come out of Persia," or "a missionary," all of them unnamed? Yet these are the sources that form the bases of far too many histories today.

The work of the missionary establishment and the British propagandists has now been filtered through generations of books and media articles. Textbook writers and journalists have accepted the work of their earlier counterparts without analysis. What the earlier authors wrote of the Turks, stripped of the more racist comments, is what later students and newspaper readers have read. Authors have not felt the need to investigate the truth of assertions about the Turks, because "everyone knows about the Turks." Writers of histories specifically on the Balkans and the Middle East have repeated the slanders about the Turks because they copied earlier writers. If asked why they did it (which until very recently they never were), they could have pointed to their bookshelves and responded: "Look at these books. They all say the Turks massacred the Armenians, Greeks, Serbs, and Bulgarians. How could they all be wrong?" They were all wrong because they were all ultimately drawn from the missionaries and the propagandists. History that is wrong in the beginning does not become right because it is copied for generations; but history quoted over generations, whatever its veracity, becomes the accepted version of events, as perhaps best seen in the histories of the Bulgarian insurrection and World War I.

Contemporary newspapers that described the 1877–78 Russo-Turkish War in Bulgaria printed gory and often fanciful tales of Turkish misdeeds. They even praised the Russians for ridding Europe of "the Turk," with no mention of their methods. Yet in that war 19 percent of the Muslims, mainly Turks, died, only 2 percent of the Christians. In addition, 34 percent of the Muslims of Bulgaria only survived as refugees in the Ottoman Empire, never to return to their homes. Not included in that figure were the Turks of the Dobruja (today in northeastern Romania), where the Turkish population declined by an astounding 83 percent. More than half the Turks of Bulgaria either died or were exiled. If the press reports had been unprejudiced, this would have been a stirring account of human loss. It was a story that was never reported.

Historians who described "Bulgarian Horrors" in the textbooks of the nineteenth and early twentieth century must simply have repeated what they had learned in the press. They did not know Middle Eastern languages, so Ottoman reports were closed to them. Diplomatic reports were sealed and unavailable. But how can we explain the lack of information on Turkish suffering in the history books of our time?[10] The most accessible of the documents on Bulgaria (those in the British National Archives) contain extensive reports on the murder of the Turks of Bulgaria that have been unsealed for generations. Indeed authors of histories of the period of the Russo-Turkish War of 1877–78 have made extensive use of some of the British records. Yet they do not seem to have seen the accounts of murders and persecution of the Turks. More likely, they may have known that writing sympathetically of Turkish suffering would not be well received.

It is remarkable that present-day histories of World War I also repeat the missionary and British propaganda position without citation.[11] It can only be assumed that the authors, considering the Ottoman war to be only a sideshow, have simply repeated the traditional myths without investigation. Their books certainly give no indication that they know much of what transpired in the Middle East during the war. A student who wishes to investigate World War I in the Middle East or study the Armenian Question will find that standard bibliographies include the writings of the missionary establishment and the British propagandists without consideration of their questionable reliability.[12] The Armenian-Turkish conflict of World War I is taught to American schoolchildren as a genocide of the Armenians, with no mention of either Armenian rebellion or Turkish mortality.[13] Whenever a press article appears on Armenians, including pieces on modern politics that have nothing to do with the events of 1915, reporters dutifully include the assertion that 1.5 million Armenians (more than the entire Armenian population of Ottoman Anatolia) died in the World War I period. How many of them note that nearly 3 million Turks and Kurds died in the same period—and of the same causes? Many scholarly treatises question the missionary and propaganda works, but these sources are seldom cited in the bibliographies or in the history that is taught to students or appears in the press.

It is the same for all the wars, whether the Christians were Bulgarians, Greeks, Armenians, or Serbs: the Christians were always innocent, the Turks always guilty. Turks are portrayed only as killers, when in fact Turks and other Muslims suffered far more deaths than the others in all of the conflicts. The story of the deaths of more than 5 million Turks and other Ottoman Muslims and the exile from their homelands of 5 million more from the 1820s to the 1920s is one of the worst examples of inhumanity in history.[14] It is little known today.

The Myth Survives

At the end of World War I and the Turkish War of Independence the Turks effectively ceded world public opinion to their critics. The Turks had been left with a largely ruined country whose people had memories of relatives who had been killed, homes that had been destroyed, and entire lands such as Bulgaria, Greece, and Russian Armenia from which their people had been forcibly evicted. Many voices called for revenge. The leader of the Turks, Mustafa Kemal Atatürk, wisely and sometimes ruthlessly clamped down on all irredentism and ethnic hatred. He told the Turks to forget, or at least not to disseminate, the history of their suffering but instead to work to create a new land in what remained to them. Consequently they did not respond to attacks in America and Europe. They did nothing to oppose the false history that was almost universally believed.

What had been a wise policy in 1923 became a disaster in later years. The Turks hoped that the problem would simply disappear over time. Not until Armenian terrorist organizations began to assassinate Turkish diplomats in the 1980s did the Turks wake up and realize that their negative image had never gone away. American and European newspapers printed all the mythology of 1915 in explaining why Armenian radicals were murdering Turks. The message was that, even though taking revenge was wrong, the murderers had historic cause for their actions. Instead of eliciting sympathy for those whose diplomats were being killed, American media once again attacked the image of the Turks.[15] The Turkish side was not told. Like their ancestors, Americans read that World War I Turks had been killers, never the equally true story that Turks also had been victims. In response, Turks began to open archives and publish books on the Armenian Question, but it was very late to begin to oppose a myth of overwhelming strength that had grown for centuries.

Anyone who tries to question such a myth faces an uphill battle. The classic example is the fight against the set of myths that supported anti-Semitism. Organizations such as the Anti-Defamation League battled for generations against that myth; an incredible amount of labor produced much success. Until very recently the Turks had nothing to compare to the Anti-Defamation League. Throughout the nineteenth century Turks had little contact with America; only the occasional ambassador to Washington was there to defend his people. And he was distrusted as an official spokesman for a country that was assumed to lie about its sins. Most importantly, virtually no Turks lived in America, so Americans could not see the common humanity they shared with the Turks. There are more Turks in America today and more unbiased historians, but the Myth of the Terrible Turk has become so fixed in the American mind that it may take generations before it is finally laid to rest.

Notes

Chapter 1, The Missionaries Depart

1. *The Holy Land an Interesting Field of Missionary Enterprise: A Sermon Preached in the Old South Church, Boston, Sabbath Evening, October 31, 1819, Just before the Departure of the Palestine Mission,* pp. 26–28. In letters home, intended to gain contributions for his mission, Fisk continued to vilify the Turks after he had left for the Ottoman Empire. See "Extract of a letter from Rev. Mr. Fisk, one of the American Missionaries in Palestine, to a Gentleman in Middlebury, Vt. dated Smyrna, Sept. 16th, 1821," *Boston Recorder,* February 16, 1822, p. 27: "Think of a country, in which, in case of public disturbance, one half the community can murder whomsoever they please of the other half with impunity ... Think of a country, in which an armed man will meet a peaceable inoffensive citizen in the street of a populous city at mid-day, & shoot him dead on the spot, and then sit down quietly and smoke his pipe in sight of the corpse, while even the guards of the city are passing by."

2. Fisk, *The Holy Land,* p. 29.

3. Levi Parsons, *The Dereliction and Restoration of the Jews: A Sermon Preached in Park Street Church, Boston, Sabbath, October 31, 1819, Just before the Departure of the Palestine Mission,* p. 16.

4. Ibid., p. 12. For an account that is informative of the American mind-set on the early missionaries, see Daniel O. Morton, *Memoir of Rev. Levi Parsons.*

5. On the importance of the evangelical movement in America, see Mark A. Noll, "The American Revolution and Protestant Evangelicalism," *Journal of Interdisciplinary History* 23, no. 3 (Winter 1993): 615–38.

6. For some reason, it was erroneously believed that Pope Boniface III assumed the requisite power in 606 (Oliver Wendell Elsbree, *The Rise of the Missionary Spirit in America, 1790–1815,* p. 125), a claim that would surprise most Catholics and all historians. Pope Gregory the Great (590–604) would seem to have been a better choice for a powerful pope. Muhammad had not yet begun his prophecy in 606, and the Turks were still in Central Asia.

7. George Bush, *The Life of Mohammed: Founder of the Religion of Islam, and of the Empire of the Saracens,* p. 55. The belief that the Muslims and Roman Catholics were the agents of the Antichrist continued up to the time of the American Civil War, although it gradually became less prominent. See Lewis Cheeseman, D.D., *Ishmael and the Church* (Philadelphia: Parry and McMillan, 1856). Today Turks are

not cast as the Antichrist, but the Middle East still figures mightily in popular mil-
lenarian Christian belief, as exemplified in the writings of Tim LaHaye and Jerry B.
Jenkins, Hal Lindsey, and others.

8.   This belief is generally tied to Jonathan Edwards and Samuel Hopkins (who char-
     acterized it as "willingness to be damned for the glory of God"). See "A Dialogue
     between a Calvinist and a Semi-Calvinist," in *The Works of Samuel Hopkins, D.D.,*
     vol. 3 (Boston: Doctrinal Tract and Book Society, 1852), p. 148.

9.   Jedidiah Morse, Samuel Worcester, and Jeremiah Evarts in the *Panoplist* (Novem-
     ber 1811), quoted in Elsbree, *The Rise of the Missionary Spirit in America,* p. 128. Els-
     bree has an extensive discussion on the place of interpretations of Revelations in
     the history of the New England missions. See also Sereno Edwards Dwight, *A Ser-
     mon Delivered in the Old South Church, Boston, before the Foreign Mission Society,
     January 5, 1820* (Boston: Crocker and Brewster, 1820).

10. Of course, the expectation of the Second Coming and the place of the Middle East
     in God's plan were never forgotten. The missionaries and mainstream Protestant
     theologians simply stopped speaking of it. It has periodically reoccurred up to our
     day, and books have continued to be published on the topic throughout the nine-
     teenth and twentieth centuries and in the twenty-first century.

11. This belief is prevalent in much of the missionary literature and fits well into the
     American self-image as a chosen people and the "Novus Ordu Seclorum" (new
     order of the ages). For a summary of the belief, see Samuel W. Fisher, D.D., *God's
     Purpose in Planting the American Church: A Sermon before the American Board of
     Commissioners for Foreign Missions at the Meeting in Boston, Mass., October 2, 1860*
     (Boston: T. R. Marvin and Son, 1860). Fisher's sermon was a combination of mil-
     lennialism and racialism. For an example of the nineteenth-century literature, obvi-
     ously a fringe belief, see John Thomas, M.D., *Anatolia; or, Russia Triumphant and
     Europe Chained…* (Mott Haven, N.Y.: Published by the Author, 1854).

12. While it was surely true that Islamic Law forbade conversion from Islam and that
     the Jewish leaders firmly opposed conversion, the paucity of conversions in later
     times (when Muslims and Jews were under European colonial rule) suggests that
     the major reason was simply that Jews and Muslims had no wish to convert. For
     one of the earliest and most interesting descriptions of the missionaries' views of
     classical Christianity in the Ottoman Empire and its powers to foil conversions, see
     the descriptions in Eli Smith and H. G. O. Dwight, *Missionary Researches in Arme-
     nia,* chapter 1, p. 464. The American edition is Eli Smith, *Researches of the Rev. E.
     Smith and Rev. H. G. O. Dwight in Armenia.*

13. Smith and Dwight, *Missionary Researches in Armenia,* p. 464. See also Cyrus Ham-
     lin, "The Oriental Churches and Mohammedans," in American Board of Commis-
     sioners for Foreign Missions, *Missionary Tracts,* no. 11 (Boston: Marvin, 1853). For a
     summary of the prevalent opinion of the Eastern churches, see J. Hawes, D.D., *The
     Religion of the East* (Hartford: Belknap and Hamersley, 1845), especially pp. 111–22.

14. Smith, *Researches of the Rev. E. Smith and Rev. H. G. O. Dwight in Armenia,* p. 465.

15. Smith and Dwight, *Missionary Researches in Armenia,* p. 21.

16. Smith, *Researches of the Rev. E. Smith and Rev. H. G. O. Dwight in Armenia.* See also William Goodell, *Forty Years in the Turkish Empire; or, Memoirs of Rev. William Goodell, D.D.*

17. Smith and Dwight, *Missionary Researches in Armenia,* pp. 461–62.

18. Smith, *Researches of the Rev. E. Smith and Rev. H. G. O. Dwight in Armenia,* p. 462.

19. These statistics include wives (142 of the 535 total) and the missionaries at the American missionary colleges—Robert College, American College for Girls, and Syrian Protestant College (Harlan P. Beach and Burton St. John, *World Statistics of Christian Missions,* pp. 66–67). See also the best collection of missionary statistics: Uygur Kocabaşoğlu, *Kendi Belgeleriyle Anadolu'daki Amerika: 19 Yüzyılda Osmanlı İmparatoluğu'ndaki American Misyoner Okulları.*

20. Beach and St. John, *World Statistics of Christian Missions,* p. 81.

21. The best study of the missions in the Ottoman Empire remains Robert L. Daniel, *American Philanthropy in the Near East.* Though it considers only one period in depth, Jeremy Salt, *Imperialism, Evangelism, and the Ottoman Armenians, 1878–1896,* gives a feeling for the missionaries' orientation. A seldom-cited but valuable unpublished doctoral dissertation by Helen McCready Kearney ("American Images of the Middle East, 1824–1924: A Century of Antipathy") gives a very complete description of the views of the early missionaries (pp. 31–65). See also Kocabaşoğlu, *Kendi Belgeleriyle Anadolu'daki Amerika;* Robert L. Daniel, "American Influences in the Near East," *American Quarterly* 16, no. 1 (Spring 1964): 72–84; Salt, *Imperialism, Evangelism, and the Ottoman Armenians,* especially pp. 30–39; and Joseph L. Grabill, *Protestant Diplomacy and the Near East.* A number of the books cited in this chapter and in later chapters gave the missionary establishment's own view of the missions. See also Rufus Anderson, *History of the Missions of the American Board of Commissioners for Foreign Missions;* James S. Dennis, *Foreign Missions after a Century;* Edwin Munsell Bliss, *The Missionary Enterprise: A Concise History of Its Objects, Methods and Extension;* William Ellsworth Strong, *The Story of the American Board,* especially pp. 196–226 and 385–412; David Brewer Eddy, *What Next in Turkey: Glimpses of the American Board's Work in the Near East;* Joseph K. Greene, *Leavening the Levant;* and Florence A. Fensham, Mary I. Lyman, and Mrs. H. B. Humphrey, *A Modern Crusade in the Turkish Empire.* The American Board published an *Annual Report* (Boston, annual).

Chapter 2, Turks and Muslims in Early America

1. Given space constraints, it is not possible to consider the long history of antipathy and misunderstanding between Islam and Christianity here. The topic has been thoroughly studied elsewhere. See Clinton Bennett, *Victorian Images of Islam* (London: Grey Seal, 1992); Norman Daniel, *Islam and the West: The Making of an Image,* and *Islam, Europe and Empire;* Kenneth M. Setton, *Western Hostility to Islam and Prophecies of Turkish Doom;* R. W. Southern, *Western Views of Islam in the Middle Ages;* John Victor Tolan, ed., *Medieval Christian Perceptions of Islam* (New York: Routledge, 2000), and *Saracens: Islam in the Medieval European Imagination* (New York: Columbia University Press, 2002); and Aslı Çırakman, "From

Tyranny to Despotism: The Enlightenment's Unenlightened Image of the Turks," *International Journal of Middle Eastern Studies* 33, no. 1 (February 2001): 49–68.

2. The sermons cited here were all drawn from the Readex Early American Imprints series. This is an invaluable resource, especially because it allows computerized searches. Without it, this research would be a Herculean task, for the ministers gave extremely long sermons. I have kept citation of sermons to a minimum here. Their points were repetitious, and their titles were so long that it would take an additional volume to list them all. For a detailed and instructive view of Americans and Islam, see Fuad Shaban, *Islam and Arabs in Early American Thought: The Roots of Orientalism in America.* Shaban actually considers the subject well beyond early America.

3. Aaron Burr, *The Watchman's Answer to the Question, What of the Night...* (New York: S. Kneeland, 1757), p. 20.

4. This combined citation of those who were considered the greatest enemies of true Christianity was ubiquitous. The usage was current in England and had probably been borrowed from dissenting clergy there. For an example, see William Dyer, *Christ's Famous Titles, and A Believer's Golden Chain...* (Philadelphia: Stewart and Cochran, 1793), p. 192.

5. Charles Chauncy, *The New Creature Describ'd...* (Boston: Rogers and Edwards, 1741), p. 46.

6. Jonathan Mitchell, *A Discourse of the Glory to Which God Hath Called Believers...* (Boston: B. Green, 1721), p. 115.

7. Samuel Nowell, *Abraham in Arms...* (Boston: John Foster, 1678), p. 13.

8. Elijah Parish, *The Excellence of the Gospel...* (Newburyport, Mass.: A. March, 1798), p. 9. The blood-drinking Turks are called "Tatars."

9. Increase Mather especially stressed this point.

10. William Lynn, *The Blessings of America...* (New York: Thomas Greenleaf, 1791), p. 14.

11. Cotton Mather, *Small Offers towards the Service of the Tabernacle in the Wilderness...* (Boston: R. Pierce, 1689), p. 29.

12. Cotton Mather, *The Wonderful Works of God Commemorated...* (Boston: S. Green, 1689). Most of the ministers cited here were Calvinists, but others also used the Turks as a negative example. Perhaps the strangest comparison to the Turks came from the Reverend Jeremiah Walker, who did not approve of predestination and Calvinism. In order to show the evils of such beliefs, he spoke of the "Calvinistic Papists" and the "Calvinistic Turks," without explanation (Jeremiah Walker, *The Fourfold Foundation of Calvinism Examined and Shaken...* [Richmond, Va.: John Dixon, 1791], p. 3).

13. Samuel West, *A Sermon Preached before the Honorable Council...* (Boston, John Gill, 1776), p. 53.

14. Increase Mather, *The Duty of Parents to Pray for Their Children...* (Boston: B. Green, 1703), pp. 24–25.

15. Thomas Boston, *Human Nature in Its Fourfold State, in Several Practical Discourses* (Philadelphia: Peter Stewart, 1790), p. 357. On the association of sinning

Christians, see also Richard Mather, *A Farewel Exhortation…* (Cambridge, Mass.: Samuel Green, 1657), pp. 12, 22.

16. "'While men, like fiends, each other tear / In all the hellish rage of war.' See how *these* Christians love one another! Wherein are they preferable to Turks and Pagans? What abomination can be found among Mahometans or Heathen, which is not found among Christians also?" (John Wesley, *Sermons on Several Occasions in Four Volumes* [Philadelphia: J. Crukshank, 1794], p. 200). See also John Wesley, *The Works of the Rev. John Wesley, M.A., Late Fellow of Lincoln-College, Oxford,* vol. 1 (Philadelphia: Melchior Steiner, 1783), pp. 116–17.

17. For examples, see Cotton Mather, *Things to Be Look'd for…* (Cambridge, Mass.: Samuel Green, 1691); Increase Mather, *The Doctrine of Divine Providence Opened and Applied* (Boston: Joseph Brunning, 1684); and John Gill, *Three Sermons on the Present, and Future State of the Church…* (Salem, Mass.: E. Russell, 1777).

18. Elhanan Winchester, *The Three Woe Trumpet…* (Boston: John W. Folsom, 1794).

19. Ibid., p. 19. Winchester had a strict timetable for the Turks' destruction. He undertook great theological and historical gymnastics to fit the Turks into the plan, elevating inconsequential Turkish principalities to great kingdoms, describing minor Ottoman conquests as major, and neglecting major events in Ottoman history, but his historicity is not the question here. American and British believers would not have recognized the factual problems with his treatise.

20. Ibid., pp. 21–23.

21. Ibid., p. 24. This sentiment was found in many sermons. See, for example, Sermon VII, in "Lycurgus III," in *XIV Sermons on the Characters of Jacob's Fourteen Sons* (Philadelphia: William Spotswood, 1789), p. 21.

22. Jonathan Edwards, *The Millennium…* (Elizabethtown: Shepard Kollock, 1794), pp. 276, 296.

23. John Gill, *Three Sermons…* (4th ed., London and Boston: Green and Russell, 1756), p. 75.

24. Cotton Mather, *Unum necessarium Awakenings for the Unregenerate; or, the Nature and Necessity of Regeneration…* (Boston: Duncan Campbell, 1693), pp. 36–37. Although in later chapters I have avoided the more fanciful and apocalyptic visions of the Ottoman Empire, they were never missing in America up to World War I. See, for example, Arthur C. Daniells, *The World War: Its Relation to the Eastern Question and Armageddon* (Nashville: Southern Publishing Association, 1917). Daniells was a missionary and secretary of the World Conference of Seventh Day Adventists.

25. Some British geographies were superior to those written in America, chiefly because they were mainly concerned with facts, or what they believed to be facts, rather than dwelling on the type of moral analysis found in the books of Samuel Griswold Goodrich, Jedidiah Morse, and others. See, for example, E. Blomfield, *A General View of the World: Geographical, Historical and Philosophical* (Bungay: C. Brightley and T. Kinnersley, 1807). Some of the British volumes were published in America as well, such as John Pinkerton's *Modern Geography*. Pinkerton did not think much of the government and religions of the peoples of the Ottoman Empire: judges were all venal, the Greek Church was "in the last steps of

degradation" (p. 342), and so forth. He did identify many laudable characteristics of the various inhabitants, however. In general, he simply recorded facts on political and physical geography.

26. Harvey Newcomb, *The False Prophet; or, an Account of the Rise and Progress of the Mohammedan Religion*. Newcomb was a Congregational minister and pastor who wrote a number of uplifting books for children and a *Cyclopaedia of Missions* (New York: C. Scribner, 1854). See also the very popular fictitious tale of Aly ben-Hayton, printed first in Britain then in America: *The Conversion of a Mehometan to the Christian Religion, Described in a Letter from Gaifer, in England, to Aly ben-Hayton, His Friend in Turkey* (7th ed., New London, Conn.: T. Green, 1775).

27. *An Entertaining History of Two Pious Twin Children . . .* (New-Market, Va.: S. Henkel, 1816), "translated from the German."

28. Jedidiah Morse, *The American Universal Geography, or, a View of the Present State of All the Empires, Kingdoms, States, and Republics in the Known World, and of the United States of America in Particular*, p. 387 (first published in 1793: Jedidiah Morse, *The American Universal Geography, or a View of the Present State of All the Empires, Kingdoms, States, and Republics in the Known World, and of the United States of America in Particular* [Boston: Isaiah Thomas and Ebenezer T. Andrews, 1793]). References to *The American Universal Geography* here are to the later edition. Jedidiah Morse, *Geography Made Easy* (New Haven: Meigs, Bowen & Dana, 1784). The Library of Congress holds twenty-eight editions of Morse's geographies and histories, including only those that consider Europe, the Middle East, or the world. It should be noted that many editions are not in the Library of Congress collection.

29. Morse, *The American Universal Geography*. For further information on Morse, including a complete bibliography of his works, see Robert H. Brown, "The American Geographies of Jedidiah Morse," *Annals of the Association of American Geographers* 31, no. 3 (September 1941): 145–217. On concepts of geography in the early United States, see Geoffrey J. Martin, "The Emergence and Development of Geographic Thought in New England," *Economic Geography* 74, special issue (1998): 1–13, which contains a useful bibliography. Scholarly studies of Morse and other geographers have concentrated on their geographies of America.

30. Jedidiah Morse, *Compendious and Complete System of Modern Geography or a View of the Present State of the World*, p. 510. Other geographies of Morse's time mainly satisfied themselves with physical descriptions of the world's regions, although when they came to the Middle East they included short sections on "the Imposter" Muhammad, Islam, and the Turks. What little Middle Eastern history they contained was almost universally wrong. See, for example, Daniel Adams, *Geography; or, a Description of the World . . .* , pp. 304–13.

31. Morse, *Compendious and Complete System*, p. 600.

32. Nathaniel Dwight, *A Short But Comprehensive System of the Geography of the World . . .* , p. 93.

33. Royal Robbins, *The World Displayed in Its History and Geography . . .* (New York: Savage, 1833), pp. 316–17, 96–97.

34. Robbins and others felt no qualms about repackaging their writings under new titles. See *Outlines of Ancient and Modern History, on a New Plan* (Hartford: E. Hopkins, 1830). His books went through many editions.

35. "Turkey in Europe," in Roswell Smith, *Modern Geography, for the Use of Schools, Academies, Etc., on a New Plan*, p. 254.

36. J. A. Cummings, *An Introduction to Ancient and Modern Geography, on the Plan of Goldsmith and Guy; Comprising Rules for Projecting Maps, with an Atlas*, p. 104.

37. S. Augustus Mitchell, *Mitchell's School Geography*, pp. 273–74. The same sentiment was repeated, often in the same words, in Mitchell's other books. See *A General View of the World*, p. 512. Mitchell was primarily concerned with physical geography.

38. William C. Woodbridge, *Modern School Geography*, p. 297. The same sentiment is repeated, often in the same words, in Mitchell's other books. Interestingly, for the image of Turks and the topic of plagiarism, almost the same phrasing ("The Turks are too slothful and indolent to apply themselves to manufactures") is used in many books by other authors. See, for example, Benjamin Workman, *Elements of Geography, Designed for Young Students in That Science*, p. 136.

39. William C. Woodbridge, *A System of Universal Geography*, p. 312.

40. Robert Davidson, *Geography Epitomized*, p. 39. The couplets are supposed to rhyme; perhaps either "proceed" or "laid" was pronounced differently in early America.

41. *Historical and Descriptive Lessons, Embracing Sketches of the History, Character and Customs of All Nations: Designed as a Companion to Goodrich's, Woodbridge's, Morse's, Smiley's, and Other School Geographies*, pp. 186–88 (no author listed).

42. Woodbridge, *Modern School Geography*, p. 296.

43. *Historical and Descriptive Lessons, Embracing Sketches of the History, Character and Customs of All Nations*, p. 188.

44. George Bush, *The Life of Mohammad: Founder of the Religion of Islam, and of the Empire of the Saracens*. The book was published in numerous editions, beginning in 1830. Bush's literary output, more than twenty volumes, was mainly devoted to Christian spirituality and explications of the Old Testament. See also a book whose title speaks for itself: *The Life of Mahomet; or, the History of That Imposture Which Was Begun, Carried On, and Finally Established by Him in Arabia and Which Has Subjugated a Larger Portion of the Globe Than the Religion of Jesus Has Yet Set at Liberty*.

45. Bush, *The Life of Mohammad*, pp. 136, 159, 161. Bush was not alone in his depiction of Muhammad's sensuality, which was to remain a common theme of critics of Islam for a century. Donald Fraser wrote: "The Arabs… were libidinous beyond most of their species, and no individual among them felt that propensity stronger than their prophet" (*A Compendium of the History of All Nations*, p. 160).

46. Bush, *The Life of Mohammad*, pp. 157, 172, 181–209.

47. This can be compared to the theology of the devil, who was evil incarnate but, like all creatures, fit into the divine plan.

48. Washington Irving, *Life of Mahomet*; American edition: *Mahomet and His Successors, Irving's Works*, vol. 6 (Hudson edition).

49. Irving, *Mahomet and His Successors*, pp. 62–68, 112–30, 204, 299–300.

50.   Ibid., pp. 337–43.

51.   And this list does not include all editions.

52.   The Library of Congress holds forty-four editions of Goodrich's geographies and histories that consider Europe, the Middle East, or the world. It should be noted that many editions are not in the Library of Congress collection. Goodrich or "Peter Parley" was listed as the author of all of these, but he had extensive help from a team of writers and borrowed freely, without citation, from others.

53.   Samuel Griswold Goodrich, *Peter Parley's Universal History for Families,* pp. 355–56. This selection is repeated exactly in other Goodrich histories. Much of the historical content on the Turks and the Ottoman Empire is simply wrong. As late as 1854 Goodrich alleged, for example, that the Ottomans rose by defeating the Great Seljuk Empire and taking over its lands, when in fact two centuries separated the two empires. (See *Peter Parley's Common School History,* p. 159, which repeats similar stories in the *Universal History* and other works, and *A History of All Nations, from the Earliest Periods to the Present Time; or, Universal History: in Which the History of Every Nation, Ancient and Modern, Is Separately Given.*)

54.   Goodrich, *Peter Parley's Universal History for Families,* p. 362.

55.   Samuel Griswold Goodrich, *The World and Its Inhabitants, by the Author of Peter Parley's Tales.*

56.   Goodrich, *Peter Parley's Universal History for Families,* pp. 353–54.

57.   Ibid., pp. 354, 355.

58.   Ibid., pp. 365, 131–32, 348–50, 258–59.

Chapter 3, The Greek Rebellion

1.   *Blackwood's Magazine,* excerpted in the *Christian Register,* January 13, 1827, p. 8, also in the *Western Recorder,* January 16, 1827, p. 12. I categorize the press of this period as newspapers, because of their appearance and style of publication, but many were periodicals that appeared weekly or less often.

2.   Justin McCarthy, *Death and Exile: The Ethnic Cleansing of Ottoman Muslims,* pp. 10–13. Many of those who wrote on the Greek rebellion did not include Turkish mortality in their histories. The best of the near-contemporary authors gave some detail of the massacres: George Finlay, *History of the Greek Revolution* (London: W. Blackwood and Sons, 1861); and Thomas Gordon, *History of the Greek Revolution.* See also Alfred Lemaître, *Musulmans et Chrétiens: Notes sur la guerre de l'indépendance grecque*; and W. Alison Phillips, *The War of Greek Independence.*

3.   The news was already old when it arrived, so magazines, published less frequently, were not much different from newspapers as sources of information.

4.   There were exceptions: the *Washington Gazette* and other newspapers printed an article from France that correctly noted that those called Greeks elsewhere were in fact many different peoples who opposed each other ("Late Foreign News: From France," *Washington Gazette,* August 31, 1821, p. 2).

5.   For example, the Persians were said to be in alliance with the Russians in 1822 ("The Latest News from Europe," *Christian Watchman,* February 9, 1822, p. 35). No such alliance existed, although it was reported in many papers.

6.   "Foreign Compendium: The Greeks," *Masonic Mirror and Mechanics' Intelligencer,* January 22, 1825, p. 3.

7.   "Interesting Notes respecting Greece, from the Commercial Advertiser," *Philadelphia Recorder,* January 29, 1825, p. 334. For the record, the Ottoman family lives on today, although no longer reigning.

8.   At Corinth ("Extract of Letters from an American Gentleman, to His Friend in Boston," *Saturday Evening Post,* August 2, 1823, p. 2).

9.   "Gen. Jarvis, Capt. Miller and Dr. Howe," *Zion's Herald,* September 21, 1825. Americans who had gone to Greece to aid the Greek cause reported that 200,000 Turks had been killed, 200,000 Greeks were under arms, but help was needed from America ("The Greeks and Turks," *Zion's Herald,* September 21, 1825, p. 3).

10. For example, a "battle on the plains of Parthenia," which may never have actually have taken place and in which the Turks reportedly lost 3,000 men and the Greeks 500 (*Genius of Universal Emancipation,* November 11, 1826, p. 63).

11. "Late Foreign News," *Pittsfield [Mass.] Sun,* July 18, 1821, p. 2. The "news" also appeared in the *Charleston [S.C.] City Gazette and Daily Advertiser, Camden [S.C.] Gazette,* and other papers. See also "Constantinople," *Bennington Vermont Gazette,* July 17, 1821, p. 2. Educating children on the evils of the Turks was not neglected. See, for example, "George Maniates, the Greek Orphan Boy," *Youth's Companion,* October 24, 1828, pp. 85–86.

12. See, for example, *Niles Weekly Register,* December 8, 1827, p. 226.

13. "Extract from a Letter from Smyrna, Dated 9th May, Received by the Torpedo, at Baltimore," *Boston Daily Advertiser,* August 25, 1821, p. 2.

14. "The Greeks," *Christian Repository,* February 13, 1824, p. 388.

15. *Boston Commercial Gazette,* July 9, 1821, p. 3. This allegation of plans to kill all Ottoman Christians was printed in many newspapers and magazines.

16. Even when the Greeks had engaged in internecine war, the Americans refused to accept that it was occurring. See, for example, "The Revolution of the Greeks," *Boston Recorder,* January 10, 1824, p. 5.

17. See, for example, "Interesting from Greece," *Boston Recorder and Telegraph,* May 20, 1825, p. 83.

18. *Saturday Evening Post,* July 23, 1825, p. 3.

19. *Western Luminary,* August 10, 1825, p. 77. On İbrahim Paşa's supposed losses near Missolonghi, see the report of 400 Egyptian troops lost in the *Boston Gazette,* excerpted in *Zion's Herald,* September 21, 1825, p. 3; and the *New York Observer,* excerpted in *Zion's Herald,* November 16, 1825, p. 3. Note that *Zion's Herald* excerpted both reports. On January 4, 1826, the same paper reported the number lost to have been 1,500. For similar coverage, see *Boston Recorder and Telegraph,* August 26, 1825, p. 139; and *Christian Watchman,* September 16, 1825, p. 163.

20. *New Harmony [Ind.] Gazette,* July 5, 1826, p. 327.

21. "A Greek who recognized him, took aim at him, and gave him a wound of which he died some days later" (*Zion's Herald,* June 21, 1826, p. 3).

22. "News from Greece," *Escritoir; or, Masonic and Miscellaneous Album: Being a Periodical Journal,* October 21, 1826, p. 311.

23. "Missolonghi Fallen!" *Zion's Herald*, June 28, 1826, p. 3.

24. For example, supposed victories at Athens, in which the Greeks were driving the Turks before them ("Political: Foreign," *Western Recorder,* July 31, 1827, p. 123). Athens had actually fallen on June 5, 1827.

25. For an example of complaints on British inaction, see "From the *Connecticut Herald*, The Greeks," *Norwich [Conn.] Courier,* October 2, 1822, p. 2.

26. For an example of the call for Russian intervention, no matter what Russia's intentions, see "Russia, Turkey, and the Greek Christians," *Christian Spectator,* September 1, 1822, pp. 502–3.

27. Editorial, *Eastern Argus,* October 23, 1821, p. 2.

28. "Greece," *Literary Casket,* May 27, 1826, p. 62.

29. "Good News from Greece!" *Christian Intelligencer and Eastern Chronicle,* December 28, 1827, p. 207. See also "Destruction of the Turco-Egyptian Fleet," *Western Recorder,* December 25, 1827, p. 207; and "General Intelligence: Greece," *Christian Watchman,* February 15, 1828, p. 27.

30. "The Greeks and the Turks Relatively Considered, by an English Resident at Smyrna," *Atheneum,* May 15, 1824, p. 156.

31. At the beginning of the rebellion, before American support for the rebels coalesced, Greek massacres of Turks were at least briefly mentioned in some newspapers. The *New-York Spectator* reported: "It is also said that the Greek Islands and the Morea have revolted and massacred many of the Turks" ("Latest from England," *New-York Spectator*, June 12, 1821, p. 2). The *American Mercury* reported on February 11, 1822, that the Greeks had killed twenty thousand Turks when they took Tripolizza. The *Mercury* excused the action because seven bishops and six hundred other Greeks had been murdered ("Brussels, Dec. 13," *American Mercury,* February 11, 1822, p. 2). See also "From the Commercial Advertiser: From France," *New York Telescope,* August 4, 1827, p. 40. One article ("National Character: The Turks," *New-York Mirror*, January 3, 1824, p. 182) actually portrayed the Turkish government and system honestly—not praising it but setting it out factually. It quoted the twenty-eighth letter of Donald Campbell to his son (from *A Journey over Land to India* [Philadelphia: T. Dobson, 1797]). A newspaper in Lexington, Kentucky, admitted that the Greeks had slaughtered Turks but excused them on the grounds of the necessity of war ("From Late Foreign Journals, Received at the Office of the National Gazette, Greece," *Western Luminary,* October 13, 1824, p. 220). Another article admitted that the Turks had some good qualities: primarily they were more daring and more honest than the Greeks and had fewer "petty and contemptible vices." The Greeks should triumph, however, because they were innately much more intelligent than the Turks: "in intellectual qualities, the indispensable basis of great virtues, they [the Turks] are incomparably inferior to their former slaves" ("From the *London Weekly Review*: Present State of Greece," *Port-Folio,* November 1, 1872, p. 411).

    With these exceptions, an extensive search of hundreds of articles has revealed only very occasional mentions of massacred Turkish civilians, all of them justified as revenge or as a necessity of war. Deaths of Turkish soldiers, in contrast, were overstated and celebrated.

32. From an unnamed "American gentleman in the Mediterranean," who reported what he was told by Greek rebels. It was printed as fact in the newspapers ("The Greek War, from the *National Intelligencer,* 16th Inst.," *United States Catholic Miscellany,* September 25, 1888, p. 135).

33. "Turkish Woman," *Masonic Mirror and Mechanics' Intelligencer,* May 20, 1826, p. 164.

34. "Cruelty of the Turks," *United States Catholic Miscellany,* July 3, 1822, p. 40. This was one of the few articles available from Roman Catholic sources. It shows that Catholics, though relatively few in number, shared the feelings of the Protestants. The article, however, was excerpted from the *London Morning Chronicle.* Its unnamed author also stated that the Greeks were never intoxicated and never quarreled among themselves.

35. "Greeks and Turks," *Boston Recorder,* "from the *Mount Zion (Ga.) Missionary,*" March 18, 1822, p. 42, also copied in the *Christian Watchman,* March 16, 1822, p. 54; "Greeks and Turks, from the *Missionary,*" *Religious Intelligencer,* March 23, 1822, pp. 678–79.

36. Evi L. Psarrou, "The Chiotes Role in the Early Years of the Greek War of Independence," http://freespace.virgin.net/c.mcclernon/Chiots.pdf.

37. In 1881 the Ottoman government recorded 35,106 Greeks on Chios. Based on the evaluation of nearby Aydın Province, this was probably an undercount of 20 percent, making a Greek population of the island approximately 42,000 (Kemal H. Karpat, *Ottoman Population, 1830–1914,* p. 130; Justin McCarthy, *Muslims and Minorities,* p. 12). The population of Chios was 54,000 in 2005. The total population per square kilometer of similar islands in 1881 shows that estimates of 100,000–120,000 Greeks on Chios were absurd: Lesbos, 30/km²; Kos, 54/km²; Rhodes, 26/km²; and Chios 53/km². It should be borne in mind that the figures in the 1820s would have been considerably lower, due to population increase reflected in the 1881 numbers. Yet a Chios population of 120,000 in the 1820s would have meant 132/km²—more than twice the population density in 2005.

38. "Russia, Turkey, and the Greek Christians," *Christian Spectator,* September 1, 1822, pp. 502–3.

39. "Scio," *Missionary Herald* (May 1823): 159.

40. "Greeks and Turks," *Christian Watchman,* August 7, 1822, p. 143. The *Watchman* later moderated its view somewhat, to 25,000 men killed and 41,000 women and children taken away ("From the *Boston Daily Advertiser,* The Revolution of the Greeks," *Christian Watchman,* December 20, 1823, p. 1). The number alleged to have been taken away as slaves varied: 41,000 in the *Watchman,* 10,000 (all female) in the *Niles Weekly Register* (August 3, 1822, p. 358), 30,000 in the *Boston Recorder* ("From the *Boston Daily Advertiser,* Second Year of the Greek Revolution," December 27, 1823, p. 205; also copied, without attribution, in the *Christian Register,* January 2, 1824, p. 84), and similar estimates.

41. Charles Jelavich and Barbara Jelavich (*The Establishment of the Balkan National States* [Seattle and London: University of Washington Press, 1977], p. 44) give a figure of 3,000 killed, which seems reasonable.

42. See, for example, "From the *New Monthly Magazine,* Horrid Massacre at Scio," *Philadelphia Recorder,* June 26, 1824, p. 260; "The Greeks: The following address from the Greeks at Constantinople, to their brethren in London, cannot be read without the deepest emotion. Constantinople, May 26, 1822," *Niles Weekly Register,* August 17, 1822, p. 389.

43. "Wide spreading [*sic*] massacres at the islands of Scio, Ipsara, Candia (the ancient Crete), and Cyprus—where more than fifty thousand were put to death in cold blood" (Timothy Pickering, John Howard, D. A. White, Philip Chase, et al., "The Greeks," *Universalist Magazine,* April 26, 1828, pp. 177–78).

44. See, for example, "Greece," *Saturday Evening Post,* July 13, 1822, p. 2.

45. *Christian Watchman,* July 2, 1825, p. 120.

46. "From the Boston Gazette: Latest from Europe: Corfu, April 23," *American Mercury,* July 10, 1821, p. 2.

47. "The Greeks," *Zion's Herald,* January 1, 1824, p. 1.

48. The best description and analysis of the American response to the Greek revolt is the unpublished Ph.D. dissertation by Charles L. Booth, "Let the American Flag Wave in the Aegean: American Responds to the Greek War of Independence (1821–1824)." Booth studies the American response, not the historical events of the rebellion. See also Edward Mead Earle, "American Interest in the Greek Cause," *American Historical Review* 33, no. 1 (October 1927): 44–63; see especially Earle's intelligent analysis (pp. 61–63).

49. Daniel Webster, *Mr. Webster's Speech on the Greek Revolution.* See also "View of Public Affairs," *Christian Spectator,* January 1, 1824, p. 56; "Mr. Webster's Speech," *Christian Watchman,* January 31, 1824, p. 31; and "Greek Question," *Niles Weekly Register,* January 21, 1824, pp. 342–49. The sentiments of John Quincy Adams are in "Official Documents: Conditions and Prospects of the Greeks," *Niles Weekly Register,* January 10, 1824, p. 298.

50. Earle, "American Interest in the Greek Cause," pp. 48–49.

51. No author listed [Edward Everett], "Art. XX, The Ethics of Aristotle," *North American Review* 17, no. 41 (October 1823): 404. For good examples of this sort of appeal, see Pickering et al., "The Greeks," pp. 177–78; and William W. Miller, esq., *An Address for the Benefit of the Greeks, Delivered in Newark, New Jersey, Jan. 13, 1824* (Newark: Tuttle and Co., 1824). For examples of meetings and orations in aid of the Greeks in New York state, see the *New York Daily Advertiser,* quoted in "Grecian Emancipation," *Niles Weekly Register,* December 7, 1822, p. 215; "Cause of the Greeks," *Western Recorder,* January 6, 1824, p. 3; and "Call from the Greeks," *Religious Intelligencer,* January 20, 1827, p. 537. The 1827 meeting in New York City demanded that the U.S. Congress immediately appropriate $50,000 of public funds for the Greeks.

52. "The Greeks," *Religious Miscellany,* May 14, 1824, p. 271 ($38,000 by November 1824).

53. *Miscellaneous Cabinet,* December 27, 1823, p. 200. On the various American meet-
     ings and donations, see Earle, "American Interest in the Greek Cause," pp. 49–52,
     58–61.

54. "Succour to the Greeks," *Ariel,* June 30, 1827, p. 39; "General Intelligence: Greece,"
     Christian Watchman, February 15, 1828, p. 27.

55. "New Haven, January 3, the Greeks," *Religious Intelligencer,* January 3, 1824,
     pp. 487–89.

56. For example, "Marco Botzari, the Achilles of the Modern Greeks," *New Monthly
     Magazine and Literary Journal: American Edition* (June 1823): 441–45, also in *Ath-
     eneum,* February 1, 1824, pp. 341–45; F. G. Halleck, "Marco Bozzaris (poem)," *Phil-
     adelphia Album and Ladies' Literary Gazette,* October 15, 1828, p. 160; "Greece,"
     Christian Watchman, November 22, 1823, p. 199; "Rhigas, the Greek Patriot," *Athe-
     neum,* September 15, 1824, pp. 477–81; "Greek Sketches," *Albion,* August 5, 1826,
     p. 57; and "Theodore Colocotronu," *North American,* September 1, 1827, p. 123.

57. For example, "Romantic Adventures of Twenty-two Greek Prisoners," *Zion's Her-
     ald,* January 28, 1824, p. 3. It is not possible to give all the examples of these types of
     stories, usually each printed in a number of sources.

58. "Greece: Martyrdom of a Monk," *Christian Watchman,* April 7, 1826, p. 1.

59. "Rev. Jonas King, late a missionary in Palestine," in a letter to the ABCFM, in "the
     Suffering Greeks," *Boston Recorder,* February 9, 1827, p. 1; also in *Religious Intelli-
     gencer,* March 3, 1827, p. 631.

60. The press reported numerous stories of courageous Greek womanhood. In addition
     to those given below, see, for example, "Heroism," *Literary Casket,* September 16,
     1826; "The Greek Girl," *Philadelphia Album and Ladies' Literary Gazette,* June 25,
     1828, p. 27; and "The Euthanasia: A Story of Modern Greece," *Album, a Journal of
     News, Politics, and Literature,* November 15, 1828, pp. 180–81.

61. See, for example, "An Intrepid Greek Female," *Christian Watchman,* June 4, 1825,
     p. 104; "General Intelligence: Foreign," *Zion's Herald,* August 22, 1827, p. 135; and
     "The Greeks," *Philadelphia Album and Ladies' Literary Gazette,* April 2, 1828,
     pp. 348–49.

62. [No title], *Saturday Evening Post,* August 2, 1823, p. 2.

63. "From the *Philadelphia Mercury:* The Greek Virgin," *Philadelphia Album and
     Ladies' Literary Gazette,* December 19, 1827, pp. 225–27. For a particularly example,
     see "The Faithful Greek," *Manuscript,* February 1, 1828, pp. 161–88.

64. "Singular Vengeance," *Saturday Evening Post,* October 18, 1823, p. 1.

65. "The Turkish Insurrection," *Essex [Mass.] Patriot,* July 28, 1821, p. 2. The article also
     appeared in the *American Mercury, New Hampshire Patriot and State Gazette, Con-
     necticut Courant, New-Hampshire Gazette,* and *Farmers' Cabinet.* For examples of
     similar editorials, see "The Greeks," *Essex [Mass.] Register* (from *National Advo-
     cate*), September 5, 1821, p. 1; and *Lincoln [Nebr.] Intelligencer,* November 29, 1821.

66. As was the custom of the Balkans and Middle East from time immemorial, reb-
     els were punished by being slaves. The Turks took Greek slaves, many of them
     undoubtedly innocent. The Greeks made captured Turks slaves as well. No
     prisoner-of-war camps existed; captured soldiers on either side were ultimately

either killed or enslaved, as were a large number of civilians. One American newspaper article mentioned a Turkish slave: *New York Telescope,* November 19, 1825,
p. 100, reported that a Turkish slave on a Greek warship had set fire to the powder
magazine and blown up the ship, inspiring the local Greeks of Candia to kill 200
Turkish slaves and prisoners. This report was unusual (the only one I have found),
because stories of Greeks enslaving Turks or killing Turkish prisoners were not the
sort of news printed in American newspapers.

67.   [No author listed], "Art. XX, The Ethics of Aristotle," *North American Review* 17,
no. 41 (October 1823): 392.

68.   Ibid., p. 420.

69.   Sereno Dwight (son of the president of Yale, Timothy Dwight) was a lawyer and
minister who taught at Yale, pastor of the Park Street Church in Boston and a
respected preacher, president of Hamilton College, and chaplain to the U.S. Senate.

70.   "The Greek Revolution," *Boston Recorder,* May 8, 1824, pp. 74–75. See also *Christian Watchman,* May 8, 1824.

71.   On the expectation of missionary conversion of the Greeks, see "Religious Considerations on the Appeal from Greece," *Christian Spectator,* May, 1828, pp. 235–
39; and "Greeks and Turks, from the *Missionary,*" *Religious Intelligencer,* March 23,
1822, pp. 678–79.

72.   The fine arts are not considered here because they cannot have had much effect on
the America of the 1820s, although they did have some effect. See *The Greek Slave*
(created by Hiram Powers in 1846), an extremely realistic full-sized statue of a
naked woman in chains (Corcoran Gallery, Washington, D.C.). On the European
art about revolution, see Nina Maria Athanassoglou-Kallmyer, *French Images from
the Greek War of Independence, 1821–1830* (New Haven, Conn.: Yale University
Press, 1989).

73.   Percival [*sic*], "Liberty to Athens," *New-York Mirror,* January 29, 1825, p. 216.

Chapter 4, The Religion of The Turks

1.   Although the missionary concept of Islam permeates all anti-Muslim works, the
most detailed writing on the subject was in Samuel M. Zwemer, *Islam: A Challenge
to Faith.* See also Zwemer's short attack in Samuel M. Zwemer and Arthur Judson Brown, *The Nearer and Farther East,* pp. 1–34; and Zwemer's *The Moslem Doctrine of God.* Zwemer (1867–1952) was a missionary in Arabia and Egypt from 1891
to 1929, along with periods of instruction at American seminaries during that time.
In addition to being a most prolific author, he was an organizer of groups dedicated
to converting Muslims and in later life a professor at Princeton Theological Seminary. Although he was the most influential American opponent of Islam, Zwemer
was no dedicated student of Muslim theology. His attacks were mainly a matter of
picking and choosing quotations that supported his case, although they did not do
so very well. He first assumed that the Calvinist theology of God, as understood
by the Reformed Church, was correct then showed how the Muslim theology disagreed and thus was wrong. Arthur Judson Brown (1856–1963) was secretary of the
Presbyterian Board of Foreign Missions, head of many Presbyterian and mission

organizations and conferences, and a member of the Board of Trustees of Near East Relief (see chapter 9).

2. In evaluating the missionaries' view of Muslims it is essential to understand that they were, in their own belief, at war with Islam, fighting the so-called Mohammedan Peril in the world. Far from diminishing, Islam was growing, taking on converts among peoples whose souls were also claimed by the missionaries, particularly in Africa. Islam was rapidly expanding in sub-Saharan Africa. Despite all their claims against Islam, the missionaries could see that it was strong in the Muslim world, even if they seldom admitted it. Islam was a strong enemy. See Zwemer, *Islam: A Challenge to Faith,* pp. 233–40.

3. The percentage is based on seventy-seven of the eighty-eight books listed in the Online Computer Library Center (OCLC) Worldcat database (www.oclc.org/worldcat). OCLC lists the number of copies of each book in libraries. All books printed in the United States, written by American authors, and with more than one present-day library holding were counted. Multiple editions were only counted once. This is by no means a perfect accounting of all books that touched on Islam. It depends on catalogers' judgments on which books dealt with the subject of Islam. Some ephemeral books may not have been included. The evidence is so overwhelming, however, that small changes would have little effect on the conclusions drawn here.

4. By no means are all the books that touched on Islam and Muhammad discussed here. Many were simply too ridiculous to consider. For example, in a small book intended for a general religious audience (*The Life of Mohammad*), the Methodist clergyman, editor, and professor of systemic theology, Thomas O. Summers, was often simply wrong in his attempt to portray Turkish and Muslim history and customs. He thought the Ottomans and Seljuks were separate peoples (not the names of ruling families, as was actually the case) who somehow "blended." Tibet was a part of "Tartary." The Circassians had no religion (by 1876 they were Muslims). The "priesthood" had nothing to do with education (in fact, the Muslim men of religion, the *ulama*, controlled education and were the teachers). Summers's portrayal of Islam itself was of the same quality as his description of Muslim history. His biography gives no indication of study of Islam, travel to the Middle East, or knowledge thereof.

5. Printed in Samuel M. Zwemer, E. M. Wherry, and James L. Barton, eds., *The Mohammedan World of Today,* p. 277.

6. This analysis is drawn from Oliver Wendell Elsbree, *The Rise of the Missionary Spirit in America, 1790–1815,* which gives more detail on the development of American Calvinism and its impetus to the development of mission.

7. William Goodell, *The Old and the New; or, the Changes of Thirty Years in the East, with Some Allusions to Oriental Customs as Elucidating Scripture,* p. 23. Goodell (1792–1867) was a missionary in the Ottoman Empire for almost all his adult life, from 1823 to 1865, and established both the Beirut and Istanbul missions, yet he was capable of sentiments such as these. The missionaries seem to have been so blinded by their own assumptions and beliefs that they could not see what was

around them. Like all religions anywhere, at any time, the "oriental religions" were of course extremely concerned with morality. The morality that concerned them, however, was not the morality of Calvinist New Englanders. Goodell's opinions in reality reflected the belief that "only morality that teaches the true rules is true morality, and only I and my fellows know what those rules are": "With us there can be no religion without morality—but with them [Middle Eastern Christians], the religious has very little (or perhaps I should say nothing) to do with the moral character" (Goodell, *The Old and the New,* p. 29).

8.   Robert E. Speer, *Missionary Principles and Practice,* p. 329; and Samuel M. Zwemer, *Islam: A Challenge to Faith,* pp. 142–47.

9.   The Reverend H. H. Jessup, "Introductory Paper," in Zwemer, Wherry, and Barton, *The Mohammedan World of Today,* p. 15.

10.   W. St. Clair Tisdall, *The Religion of the Crescent: Being the James Long Lectures on Muhammadanism,* p. 72. See Zwemer, *Islam: A Challenge to Faith*, chapter 5, for a detailed analysis of what was felt to be the purely formulaic nature of Muslim prayer.

11.   By no means did the missionaries subscribe to these changes that were overtaking Christianity. The missionaries in the field disliked and obviously feared new trends in biblical criticism. The danger was that higher criticism of the Bible would give ammunition to Muslim critics of Christianity by questioning biblical inerrancy. Most missionaries in Herrick's collection of missionary opinions (George F. Herrick, *Christian and Mohammedan: A Plea for Bridging the Gap,* pp. 207–10; see note 24 below) felt that critical study of the Bible was a definite danger: "The effect is bad. They use modern methods of Biblical criticism against Christianity and Christians." "When modern Biblical scholarship takes the form of destructive criticism it confirms the Mussulman in his claim that the Christian Scriptures were corrupted." "The effect produced upon Mohammedans by modern Biblical scholarship is unfavourable, if not disastrous." Some of the missionaries surveyed, however, were forced to admit that Muslims seemed to have no knowledge of biblical criticism, and it seems doubtful that the efforts of the school of higher criticism were much known among Muslims. The real problem may have been closer to the missionaries' hearts. They had not scrupled to apply every possible tool of criticism to Islam. They did not wish to consider the same techniques applied to Christianity.

12.   Herrick, *Christian and Mohammedan,* p. 16. See also Robert E. Speer, *Missions and Modern History: A Study of the Missionary Aspects of Some Great Movements of the Nineteenth Century,* vol. 1, pp. 265–78.

13.   A few missionaries attempted to describe the beliefs of Islam as they were, without fabrications or constant commentary on the evils of Muslims and their religion. One of the best of these was one of the first, Horatio Southgate, who in 1840 described Islamic belief in detail and with few value judgments (*Narrative of a Tour through Armenia, Kurdistan, Persia, and Mesopotamia, with an Introduction and Occasional Observations upon the Condition of Mohammedanism and Christianity in Those Countries*). Another exception to the almost universally negative portrait

of Islam was *Living Religions; or, the Great Religions of the Orient from Sacred Books and Modern Customs* by the Reverend J. N. Fradenburgh, a Methodist minister. Fradenburgh, who held a Ph.D. as well as doctor of divinity degree, was a scholar who attempted to present non-Christian religions as their adherents believed them. Understandably, giving his calling, he extolled Christianity above all other religions, but his treatment of Islam was fair. The book does not appear to have been especially popular. OCLC lists 53 holdings. For comparison, Zwemer's attack on Islam, *The Moslem World,* is held by 464 libraries.

14. Tisdall, *The Religion of the Crescent,* p. 56. Tisdall, like some of the other religious commentators on Islam quoted here, was English. English writers formed most of the philosophic basis of American Protestant teachings and beliefs on Islam and were taught in the seminaries. They are both representative of and fundamental to American beliefs.

15. Ibid., p. 58. This phrase caught the missionaries' fancy and was repeated often. "The God of Christianity is a God of Love, the God of Islam is an Oriental despot" (Annie Van Sommer, ed., *Our Moslem Sisters: A Cry from Lands of Darkness Interpreted by Those Who Heard It,* p. 27). The fundamental difference in ethics led to a rejection of even the elements of Islam that might have found favor with many Christians. For example, the Muslim conception of an all-powerful God who spoke to humans through prophets should have been common ground. Much of the similarity was negated in the missionary mind, however, by the "unitarian" concept of God in Islam and the total rejection of the Trinity. This was not only a philosophical point but a practical one. The Trinitarian Congregationalists of New England were fighting an ongoing theological battle with their own Unitarians, who in the early days of the missions to the Middle East had claimed many Congregationalist churches and who rejected the entire concept of missions.

16. Indeed, Islam accepts the prophets of the Old Testament and Jesus himself as prophets of God.

17. Caesar Farah, *Islam: Beliefs and Observances,* pp. 110, 111. The quotation is from the Quran (11:52).

18. While all Christians would have found the Muslim paradise objectionable, many accepted physical pleasures of a sort, such as hymns of the Golden Fountain and the Golden Street. The Congregationalists and Presbyterians were not among this group.

19. Tisdall, *The Religion of the Crescent,* p. 63.

20. Celaleddin Rumi (Mevlana), "Gone to the Unseen" (www.mevlana.com):

> At last you have departed and gone to the Unseen.
> What marvelous route did you take from this world?
>
> Beating your wings and feathers,
> you broke free from this cage.
> Rising up to the sky
> you attained the world of the soul.

You were a prized falcon trapped by an Old Woman.
Then you heard the drummer's call
and flew beyond space and time.

As a lovesick nightingale, you flew among the owls.
Then came the scent of the rose garden
and you flew off to meet the Rose.

The wine of this fleeting world
caused your head to ache.
Finally you joined the tavern of Eternity.
Like an arrow, you sped from the bow
and went straight for the bull's eye of bliss.

This phantom world gave you false signs
But you turned from the illusion
and journeyed to the land of truth.

You are now the Sun—
what need have you for a crown?
You have vanished from this world—
what need have you to tie your robe?

I've heard that you can barely see your soul.
But why look at all?—
yours is now the Soul of Souls!

O heart, what a wonderful bird you are.
Seeking divine heights,
flapping your wings,
you smashed the pointed spears of your enemy.

The flowers flee from Autumn, but not you—
You are the fearless rose
that grows amidst the freezing wind.

Pouring down like the rain of heaven
you fell upon the rooftop of this world.
Then you ran in every direction
and escaped through the drain spout . . .

Now the words are over
and the pain they bring is gone.

Now you have gone to rest
in the arms of the Beloved.

21. George Bush, *The Life of Mohammed: Founder of the Religion of Islam, and of the Empire of the Saracens*, p. 161. This view of Muhammad was the standard for generations and was not restricted to East Coast Calvinists. For example, the first page of the introductory chapter of Summers, *The Life of Mohammad*, calls Muhammad "the greatest, most successful imposter that ever cursed the earth" and alludes to his place in the End of Days, which was described as imminent.

22. This was not universally the case. Some prominent critics still stressed Muhammad's "depravity." In his *Oriental Religions and Christianity* (New York: Charles Scribner's Sons, 1892), a series of lectures at the Union Theological Seminary, the Reverend Frank F. Ellinwood made use of all the vituperative calumnies of earlier generations. He categorically rejected any attempts to see Muhammad according to the new "science of religion." Ellinwood was the secretary (director) of the Board of Foreign Missions of the Presbyterian Church.

23. Touching on the subject of Muhammad's personal life in a leading missionary magazine, Zwemer wrote: "We must pass the matter over, simply noting that there are depths of filth in the prophet's character which may assort well enough with the depraved sensuality of the bulk of his followers" (Zwemer, *Islam: A Challenge to Faith*, p. 45).

24. Herrick, *Christian and Mohammedan*. Herrick (1834–1926) was also an instructor at the Mission Theological Seminary at Harput and president of Anatolia College at Merzifon. The list of the questions:

    1. Among Moslems of your acquaintance is there any considerable number somewhat familiar with the history of Christianity?
    2. Do such men distinguish between the history of Christianity and that of so-called Christian nations?
    3. Do they regard the Crusades as justifiable on the ground of Christian zeal, or as enterprises of wanton aggression on the part of Europe, like Napoleon's African campaign?
    4. Have you found Moslems sensitive to the moral degeneracy of Mohammed's later life?
    5. Are they appreciative of the amazing moral contrast between the life of Jesus and that of Mohammed?
    6. As to controversial methods, do you invite them or only accept them when challenged?
    7. What, in Christian attitude and conduct, have you found to repel Moslems?
    8. What have you found to win them?
    9. What effect is produced upon Moslems by Modern Biblical Scholarship, when this is known to them?
    10. Can converts from Islam be kept as leaven among their own peoples?

11. Is it harder to convert Moslems to Christianity than to convert heathen, and if so, why is it?

12. Are you more charitable to Moslems who are convinced of the truth of Christianity, but are unready to make open confession of their new faith, than you would be to men in Western lands, and if so, why?

List of Correspondents

Rev. J. R. Alexander, D.D., American United Presbyterian Mission, Pres. of College for Boys, Assiout, Egypt.

Rev. Johannes Avidaranian, Philipopolis, Dutch Orient Mission.

Rev. W. Bader, Malabar, India, Evangelical Miss. Lit. Soc., Basel.

Rev. H. N. Barnum, D.D., ABCFM, Harpoot, Turkey, since 1858; died in 1909.

Rev. Lyman Bartlett, ABCFM, Caesarea and Smyrna, 1867–1903.

Dr. Arthur K. Bennett, M. D., Ref. Church Arabian Mission, Bassorah.

Rev. T. Bomford, C. M. S. Sec'y, London. Formerly Missioner in India.

Miss C. E. Bush, ABCFM, Harpoot, 1870 until 1906.

Rev. Robert Chambers, D.D., ABCFM, Bardezag, Turkey, since 1870.

Rev. Thomas D. Christie, D.D., ABCFM, Pres. Tarsus Institute College.

Rev. James S. Dennis, D.D., Missionary of Presbyterian Church, Beirut, Syria. Author of "Missions and Social Progress," etc.

Rev. W. S. Dodd, M.D., ABCFM, Talas Hospital, Founder and Director; now in Konia.

Rev. H. O. Dwight, LL.D., ABCFM, in Turkey 1871–1901 Sec'y A. B. S., New York.

Rev. W. A. Farnsworth, D.D., ABCFM, Fifty years Missionary at Caesarea.

Rev. W. Goldsack, Australian Baptist Mission, Bengal.

Miss G. Y. Holliday, American Presbyterian Mission, Tabreez, Persia.

Dr. F. J. Harpur, C. M. S., Nile Itineracy, Egypt.

Dr. L. M. Henry, American United Presbyterian Mission, Assiout, Egypt.

Mrs. Helen M. Herrick, ABCFM, Constantinople.

Rev. J. H. House, D.D., ABCFM, Salonika.

Rev. Olaf Hoyer, Danish Church Mission, Arabia.

Rev. S. M. Jordan, American Presbyterian Mission, Teheran, Persia.

Prof. D. S. Margoliouth, Oxford, England. Author of "Life of Mohammed."

Rev. E. M. McDowell, American Presbyterian Mission, Van.

Rev. J. P. McNaughton, ABCFM, Smyrna.

Rev. H. T. Perry, ABCFM, Sivas.

Rev. H. H. Riggs, ex-Pres. Euphrates College.

Rev. H. C. Schuler, American Presbyterian Miss., Resht, Persia.

Rev. Ahmed Shah, C. M. S., Hannipur, India.

Rev. J. G. Shammas, Syrian Pastor, Oorfa; died 1909.

Miss Corinna Shattuck, ABCFM, Oorfa; died 1909.

Rev. W. A. Shedd, D.D., American Presbyterian Mission, Urumiah, Persia.

Miss M. Y. Thompson, American United Presbyterian Mission, Cairo.

Miss Elizabeth Trowbridge, ABCFM, Aintab.

Rev. S. V. R. Trowbridge, ABCFM, Aintab.

Rev. R. H. Weakley, "C. M. S. & B. & F. B. S." Alexandria, Egypt; died 1909.

Rev. H. U. Weitbrecht, D.D., Church Mission Society, Lahore, India.

Rev. E. M. Wherry, D.D., American Presbyterian Mission, Lodiana, India.

Rev. S. G. Wilson, D.D., American Presbyterian Mission, Tabreez, Persia.

Rev. G. E. White, D.D., ABCFM, Marsovan.

Dr. J. C. Young, U. F. Church of Scotland Mission, Sheikh Othman.

Rev. S. M. Zwemer, D.D., Reformed. Church Mission, Bahrein—Arabia.
Author of "Cradle of Islam," etc.

25. The Reverend W. Bader, quoted in Herrick, *Christian and Mohammedan,* p. 118. On Muhammad's supposed degeneracy, see also Robert E. Speer, *The Light of the World: A Brief Comparative Study of Christianity and Non-Christian Religions,* pp. 186–94.

26. Napier Malcolm, *Five Years in a Persian Town,* pp. 64, 65, quoted in Robert E. Speer, "The Issue between Islam and Christianity," in John R. Mott, ed., *The Moslem World of To-day [sic],* p. 345.

27. Herrick, *Christian and Mohammedan.*

28. Macdonald (1863–1943) was head of the Mohammedan Department at the Kennedy School of Missions at Hartford and also was lecturer at the University of Chicago, Wellesley College, Oberlin College, and the Berkeley Theological School at Yale. Despite a fascination with all that was "strange" (including saints and popular belief in magic) in Islam, he was a true scholar who knew his material. See also his *The Religious Attitude and Life in Islam,* particularly the preface and final chapter.

29. Duncan Black Macdonald, *Aspects of Islam,* p. 63.

30. Ibid., p. 72.

31. Tisdall, *The Religion of the Crescent,* p. 121.

32. In a speech to the Nashville Missions Convention in 1905, quoted in Zwemer, *Islam: A Challenge to Faith,* p. 118, and in Zwemer and Brown, *The Nearer and Farther East,* p. 68.

33. T. J. De Boer, quoted in Zwemer, *Childhood in the Moslem World,* p. 163.

34. "How often I have heard Arabian children dispute concerning the details of the [Islamic] ritual, as if they were professors of Moslem law and jurisprudence, meanwhile utterly ignorant of the real significance of prayer and too proud and self-righteous to have consciousness of sin or the need of a Saviour" (Zwemer, *Childhood in the Moslem World,* pp. 184–85).

35. Tisdall, *The Religion of the Crescent,* p. 88. See also Speer, "The Issue between Islam and Christianity," in Mott, *The Moslem World of To-day,* particularly pp. 348–55, for examples of missionary thinking on sin in Islam.

36. James S. Dennis, *Christian Missions and Social Progress: A Sociological Study of Foreign Missions,* vol. 1, p. 447.

37. Herrick, *Christian and Mohammedan,* p. 95.

38. See Rana Kabbani, *Europe's Myths of Orient;* and Reina Lewis, *Rethinking Orientalism: Women, Travel, and the Ottoman Harem* (New Brunswick, N.J.: Rutgers University Press, 2004). Americans did read stories on the supposedly lascivious Turks, both popular and pornographic (e.g., *The Lustful Turk*), although it is doubtful that the pornography, which was mainly British in origin, had a very great circulation in America. Titillating stories had a wider audience. There were far too many of these to cite here, and only examples are given. The *Saturday Evening Post* included in its long run a number of stories casting the Turks as villains. Readers found evil Turkish overlords and noble Christians, often a Christian man and woman whose love was thwarted by the lascivious designs of a pasha. See, for example, Burr Thornbury, "The Pacha's Plot," *Saturday Evening Post,* August 19, 1871, pp. 1–3, and in following issues; Prentiss Ingraham, "An Adventure with Turks," *Saturday Evening Post,* October 11, 1873, p. 8. See also "Some Turkish Slave Stories," *Frank Leslie's Popular Monthly* 14, no. 2 (August 1882): 138–43; "Life in a Harem," *National Police Gazette* 37, no. 164 (November 13, 1880): 11; Anthony Hope, "Phrosos," *McClure's Magazine,* serialized in vol. 7 (1896); Robert Barr, "The Pasha's Prisoner," *McClure's Magazine* 15, no. 1 (May 1900): 35–45; Eleanor Stuart, "A Life-Long Look: A Story of the Hareem," *McClure's Magazine* 37, no. 2 (June 1911): 164–78; and "Thirty Years in the Harem," *Literary World* 3, no. 5 (October 1, 1872): 70–71.

39. Dennis, *Christian Missions and Social Progress,* vol. 1, p. 91.

40. Henry Harris Jessup, *The Mohammedan Missionary Problem,* p. 49.

41. It may admittedly be difficult for today's readers, particularly those who have lived among Muslims, to believe that anyone could say such things, but they were stated and presumably believed. For example, see Tisdall, *The Religion of the Crescent,* pp. 193–98.

42. In reading literally hundreds of missionary works, I have found only one instance where an author admits "the proverbial love of the Turkish father for his children," citing the example of a father who deeply loved his daughter (Van Sommer, *Our Moslem Sisters,* pp. 194–95). For a rare alternative, nonmissionary view, see Jerome Van Crowninshield Smith, *Turkey and the Turks.* Smith was a biographer, travel writer, artist, and mayor of Boston. He did not hesitate to criticize the Turks for real and imagined transgressions and thought little of Islam, but he was willing to identify Turkish good points as well.

43. Zwemer, *Childhood in the Moslem World,* p. 37.

44. Ibid., pp. 173–74. "As our missionaries have traveled among these [Turkish] homes, how few are the faces in which happiness and confidence are to be found. Disease has stamped its heavy hand upon their features. Girlhood and childhood are shadowed by the woes of wifehood and motherhood to come. The clutch of Islam is on their hearts in this life and in the next" (David Brewer Eddy, *What Next in Turkey: Glimpses of the American Board's Work in the Near East,* p. 153).

45. Speer, *Missionary Principles and Practice,* p. 29.

46. Julius Richter, quoted in Zwemer, *Childhood in the Moslem World,* p. 52.

47. Quoted in Zwemer, *Childhood in the Moslem World,* p. 173. Zwemer declared that all Muslims around the world were immoral (Samuel M. Zwemer, *The Moslem*

Problem and Peril: Facts and Figures for the Layman, p. 13; this is a nineteen-page pamphlet "for Christian laymen"). See also A. E. Zwemer and S. M. Zwemer, *Moslem Women* (West Medford, Mass.: Central Committee on the United Study of Foreign Missions, 1926); and Henry Harris Jessup, *The Women of the Arabs, with a Chapter for Children.*

48. Mary Schauffler Labaree, *The Child in the Midst,* p. 47. This book is a catalog of "crimes against children" in all parts of the non-Christian world. All are depicted as morally evil, with variations by country.

49. Ibid., p. 4.

50. On the actual relatively low incidence of polygamy among Turks in the Ottoman Empire, see Justin McCarthy, "Age, Family, and Migration in Nineteenth-Century Black Sea Provinces of the Ottoman Empire," *International Journal of Middle Eastern Studies* 10, no. 3 (August 1979): 309–23; and Alan Duben and Cem Behar, *Istanbul Households: Marriage, Family, and Fertility, 1880–1940* (Cambridge: Cambridge University Press, 1991).

51. Zwemer, *Childhood in the Moslem World,* p. 142. See also Joseph C. Hartzell and Samuel M. Zwemer, *The Call of Moslem Children: The Story of the Neglected Children of the Mohammedan World.* For an earlier example of the religious view of all the real and imagined social evils of Asia, including the Middle East, see Ross C. Houghton, *Women of the Orient.*

52. Herrick, *Christian and Mohammedan,* p. 66. Note especially the use of the offensive world "cult." *Missionary Review of the World* (October 1898) wrote: "Their fasting is productive of two distinct evils wherever observed: it manufactures an unlimited number of hypocrites who pretend to keep the fast and do not do so, and in the second place the reaction which occurs at sunset of every night of Ramadan tends to produce reveling and dissipation of the lowest and most degrading type" (quoted in Zwemer and Brown, *The Nearer and Farther East,* pp. 34). *The Nearer and Farther East* offered a catalog of supposed Muslim evils in summary form, intended for Christian study groups ("The Social Evils of Islam," pp. 36–69). The purpose of the section is listed under "Helps for Leaders, Lesson Aim": "To show the hopeless character of Islam for the present life and to show its moral bankruptcy" (p. 65).

53. Van Sommer, *Our Moslem Sisters,* pp. 27–28. This book is a collection of articles by individual missionaries, whose names were kept secret, so it is impossible to identify who wrote what, except to say that all the writers were Christian missionaries. Most, if not all, appear to have been Americans.

54. Chapter 3, "From under the Yoke of Social Evils," in ibid.

55. Labaree, *The Child in the Midst,* pp. 47–49.

56. Jessup, *The Women of the Arabs,* pp. 8–10.

57. Jessup, *The Mohammedan Missionary Problem,* p. 49. It is not surprising that Jessup (1832–1910) saw only the worst in Muslims. He felt that the "Mohammadan" was a "man of unrestrained passion, full of falsehood and blasphemy, impure in his private character, jealous, unforgiving, and uncharitable" (H. H. Jessup, "Mohammedanism," *Missionary Herald* 56 [1860]: 85, quoted in Usama Makdisi, "Reclaiming

the Land of the Bible," *American Historical Review* 102, no. 3 [June 1997]: 691). The Makdisi article (pp. 680–713) is an excellent consideration of the missionaries and the Arabs, particularly in Syria and Lebanon.

58. J. Murray Mitchell and William Muir, *Two Old Faiths,* pp. 126–27 (the American edition of Muir's *The Rise and Decline of Islam* [London: Religious Tract Society, 1883]).

59. Mitchell and Muir, *Two Old Faiths,* p. 140. Mitchell and Muir also offered a sexual interpretation (p. 123) for the success of the Muslims: "The religion of Mohammed, on the other hand, gives direct sanction to the sexual indulgences we have been speaking of. Thus it panders to the lower instincts of humanity and makes its spread the easier." See also Eddy, *What Next in Turkey,* p. 24. The assertion that Islam forced conversion was common in American schoolbooks (see chapter 5).

60. E. M. Wherry, *Islam; or, the Religion of the Turk,* pp. 4–5.

61. Wherry (1843–1927) was also leader of missionary societies and moderator of the India Presbyterian Church.

62. Wherry, *Islam; or, the Religion of the Turk,* p. 60. Wherry's opinions bordered on the absurd, or at least would appear so to those who knew something of the religion, unlike the Americans of his time. He felt, for example, that the beliefs of Sufis (Muslim mystics) "amounted to atheism" (p. 55).

63. Thomas Laurie, *The Ely Volume; or, the Contributions of Our Foreign Missions to Science and Human Well-Being,* p. 453. According to Laurie, this was supposed to have been a common occurrence in the 1810s.

64. Frederick Davis Greene, *Armenian Massacres or the Sword of Mohammed,* pp. 458–67.

65. See the section "Racism" below and chapter 5.

66. "After twelve centuries of Islam, the Arabs are still what Mohammed found them, a nation of robbers" (John Murdoch, *The Religions of the World* [London and Madras: Christian Literature Society for India, 1902], pp. 165–66, quoted in E. M. Wherry, *Islam and Christianity in India and the Far East,* p. 119).

67. The idea of superiority of one's own people is evident in all societies, and Americans partook of it with vigor: thus "Novus Ordo Seclorum."

68. Robert E. Speer, *Christianity and the Nations,* p. 25.

69. On the contrary, missionaries stated that Japan was politically and economically doomed unless its people accepted Christianity. (See, for example, ibid., pp. 28–30.)

70. As seen in preceding and following chapters, this was a common belief held by geographers, historians, and other laypeople, not only missionaries. For an exposition of the missionary view, see Zwemer, *Islam: A Challenge to Faith,* pp. 129–31, 173–79.

71. Wherry, *Islam; or, the Religion of the Turk,* p. 61.

72. Interestingly, in earlier ages Muslims had characterized Europeans as dirty, because they did not bathe very often.

73. Zwemer, *The Moslem Problem and Peril,* pp. 12–14.

74. Van Sommer, *Our Moslem Sisters,* p. 153.

75. Speer, *Christianity and the Nations,* p. 280.

76. See also Speer's *The Light of the World,* pp. 220–37. Speer (1867–1947) was a leader of the Protestant church establishment in the United States. He served as secretary of the Presbyterian Board of Foreign Missions, moderator of the Presbyterian Church in the United States, and president of the Federal Council of Churches of Christ in America.

77. "Civilization has hid her face in every land where Islam has ruled undisturbed" (Eddy, *What Next in Turkey,* p. 30). "As concerning Mohammadenism,... where its armies have taken and conquered regions of the world which were already Christian, it has degraded their civilization" (W. Douglas Mackenzie, *Christianity and the Progress of Man: As Illustrated by Modern Missions,* p. 175). See also a British book recommended for missionaries: W. St. Clair Tisdall, *Comparative Religion,* pp. 90–101. Tisdall held that all religions other than Christianity had degraded humanity. Only Christianity had led to spiritual "progress" and eventually to social and economic progress as well.

    If the missionaries believed Islam was behind Middle Eastern backwardness, they also believed there was a remedy: American missions. The American Board published claims that its missionaries had been primarily responsible for nineteenth-century Ottoman reform in both civil liberties and politics (Laurie, *The Ely Volume,* pp. 453–58). They also maintained that American missionaries were responsible for most improvements in the Ottoman Empire, usually by stating that improvements had not been there when the missionaries arrived—and now look. For example, it was claimed that Beirut had 8,000 inhabitants and no schools (!) when the missionaries arrived and had 80,000 inhabitants in the 1880s, plus many modern buildings and other features of a modern city. This was described as "wheeling into line with the columns led by the Protestant missionaries" (Laurie, *The Ely Volume,* p. 458). No other possible causes for advancement were mentioned.

78. Tisdall, *The Religion of the Crescent,* p. 201.

79. Macdonald, *Aspects of Islam,* p. 305.

80. Ibid., p. 307.

81. Northrop, *The Mohammedan Reign of Terror in Armenia,* pp. 469–70.

82. Macdonald, *Aspects of Islam,* p. 208. See also Speer, *Missionary Principles and Practice,* p. 23.

83. E. M. Bliss, "Turkey and the Turks," in Mott, *The Moslem World of To-day,* p. 410.

84. James S. Dennis, "The Inaccessible Fields of Islam and How to Reach Them," in E. M. Wherry, ed., *Missions at Home and Abroad,* p. 231.

85. This is a common theme in many of the books and articles cited here. See, for example, Wherry, *Islam and Christianity in India and the Far East,* p. 8; Herrick, *Christian and Mohammedan,* pp. 71–73; and James S. Dennis, *Foreign Missions after a Century,* pp. 98–99. Dennis preferred the British to others as imperialists. His *Christian Missions and Social Progress* is full of encomiums to British imperialism—too many to cite here. For consideration of the negative effects of missionaries, even on the imperialists they supported, see Jeremy Salt, "Trouble Wherever

They Went: American Missionaries in Anatolia and Ottoman Syria in the Nineteenth Century," *Muslim World* 92, nos. 3 and 4 (Fall 2002): 287–313.

86. See, for example, the detailed list of benefits in Jessup, *The Mohammedan Missionary Problem*, pp. 107–30; for the belief that European colonization was God's will, facilitating the spread of missions, see Dennis, *Foreign Missions after a Century,* pp. 308–17.

87. In "The Inaccessible Fields of Islam and How to Reach Them" (p. 22), from which the Dennis epigraph quotation above was taken, one of his main complaints about Islam was "its alliance with military power."

88. Speer, *Missions and Modern History,* vol. 1, p. 73.

89. See Robert E. Speer, *The Gospel and the New World,* chapter 3 and pp. 281–83.

90. Other explanations were considered. One missionary listed the reasons why so few Muslim women convert to Christianity (Mrs. M'Clure [*sic*], "Social Hindrances," in Annie Van Sommer and Samuel M. Zwemer, eds., *Daylight in the Harem,* pp. 93–94):

   I.   Inability to discern sin, i.e., a dead conscience.
   II. The body of sin [i.e., sin is not recognized, because it is everywhere].
   III. The lack of initiative and therefore progress in (a) home; (b) education; and (c) literature [i.e., the need for Christian schools and contact with Christians].
   IV. Lack of real fellowship [i.e., "Christian fellowship"].
   V.   Superstition.

91. Among the many missionary writings that contain these sentiments, see Speer, *Christianity and the Nations,* pp. 228–30; James L. Barton, *Daybreak in Turkey,* pp. 256–57; and Zwemer and Brown, *The Nearer and Farther East,* pp. 9–10.

92. See Jessup, *The Mohammedan Missionary Problem,* p. 17.

93. Mott, *The Moslem World of To-day,* p. 364. R. Mott was general secretary of the Young Men's Christian Association (YMCA) and honorary life president of the World Association of YMCAs. He led the Student Volunteer Movement for Foreign Missions and the World's Student Christian Federation from their creation until 1920. Both organizations were responsible for publication of works against Muslims, including books by Zwemer, Dennis, and Wherry. Mott wrote seventeen books himself. He was decorated by the United States, Czechoslovakia, France, Japan, China, Sweden, and Norway. See also Zwemer and Brown, *The Nearer and Farther East,* p. 8; and Samuel M. Zwemer, *Islam and the New Era in the Near East after the War,* pp. 24–27.

94. See Anna Y. Thompson, "Reform in Egypt," in Van Sommer and Zwemer, *Daylight in the Harem,* pp. 104–60.

95. Herrick, *Christian and Mohammedan,* p. 57.

96. For example, see Speer, *Missions and Modern History,* vol. 1, chapter 2, on the God-given nature of British rule in India, and vol. 2, chapter 13, on the need for Asians to assimilate Western culture. While never disowning his earlier statements or

disavowing imperialism, Speer did see more of the evils of imperialism after World War I. He became particularly adverse to the imperial habit of treating colonized peoples as lower orders of creation, because they too were equal children of God. This, of course, was fully consistent with his evangelical beliefs, but it was a notable improvement over his previous sentiments. See Speer, *The Gospel and the New World,* chapter 3 and pp. 281–83.

97. Speer, *Missions and Modern History,* vol. 2, p. 663.

98. Herrick, *Christian and Mohammedan,* p. 72.

99. See the detailed accounts of the Russian actions and the bibliographic sources in Justin McCarthy, *Death and Exile: The Ethnic Cleansing of Ottoman Muslims.*

100. Speer, *Missions and Modern History,* vol. 2, p. 456.

101. Ibid., vol. 2, p. 626.

102. "Persian constitutional government died at its birth because the Persians themselves are unfit for self-government... The Russian occupation of the north, the British pacification of the south, and the possible control even of the neutral zone by these Powers, will usher in a new day of liberty and progress for Persia. The American missionaries welcome Russian rule in preference to Persian anarchy" (Samuel M. Zwemer, *Mohammed or Christ,* p. 212).

103. See, for example, Zwemer, *Mohammed or Christ* (chapter 4, "Islam in Russia").

104. See McCarthy, *Death and Exile,* chapters 2, 3, 4, and 6. Judging from publications, praise for Russian imperialism was common in the American church. See William Giles Dix, *The Doom of the Crescent* (Boston: Idea and Dutton, 1853), a sermon that damns the French and English for cooperating with the Turks in the Crimean War.

105. Samuel M. Zwemer, *The Disintegration of Islam,* chapter 3. See also Samuel M. Zwemer, *The Fullness of Time in the Moslem World; or, Great Britain's National Responsibility Face to Face with the Present Opportunity in the Moslem World* (London: Bible Lands Missions' Aid Society, 1910, reprinted 1915).

106. Speer, *Christianity and the Nations,* p. 191.

107. The missionaries also availed themselves of all the benefits that imperialism gave to citizens of imperial powers. In the Ottoman Empire, they jealously guarded their treaty rights to be outside of Ottoman law and taxation. Missionaries went to the point of constructing industries that competed with local enterprises but did not pay taxes because they were protected by the Capitulations (e.g., a laundry and bakery in Istanbul).

108. "Missions and Diplomacy," originally an article in the *Missionary Review of the World* (1903), in James S. Dennis, *The Modern Call of Missions,* pp. 13–40.

109. Speer, *Christianity and the Nations,* p. 193.

110. "[Critics of missionaries state:] 'The religions of other races are good enough for them.' Then they are 'good enough' for us, for the people of 'other races' are our fellow men, with the needs of our common humanity. We have not heard, however, of any critic who believes that Islam and Hinduism and Buddhism are 'good enough' for Europeans and Americans, and we have scant respect for the Phariseeism which asserts that they will suffice for Persians and East Indians and Chinese. The fact is that the best of the ethnic [i.e., non-Christian] faiths have utterly failed to produce

high character or social purity" (Arthur Judson Brown, *The Foreign Missionary: An Incarnation of a World Movement,* p. 345 [first printed in 1907]).

111. Ibid., p. 345.

112. See, for example, the analysis of the division of Islam into "Semitic" and "Aryan" "races" in Zwemer, *Islam: A Challenge to Faith,* pp. 135–36.

113. The Reverend Frederick Davis Greene, "Causes and Extent of the Recent Atrocities," in Greene, *Armenian Massacres or the Sword of Mohammed,* pp. 436–37.

114. Zwemer, *The Disintegration of Islam,* p. 37.

115. See, for example, Labaree, *The Child in the Midst,* pp. 9–11.

116. Eddy, *What Next in Turkey,* p. 46.

117. The Reverend W. K. Eddy, "Islam in Syria and Palestine," in Zwemer, Wherry, and Barton, *The Mohammedan World of Today,* p. 65.

118. Frederick Davis Greene (*The Armenian Crisis in Turkey,* p. 142), an American missionary who had served in the Ottoman Empire, quoting Isabella Bird Bishop, *Journeys in Persia and Kurdistan* (London: John Murray, 1891, vol. 2, p. 336), as representing his own views.

119. Frank G. Carpenter, "What One May See in Armenia," in Greene, *Armenian Massacres or the Sword of Mohammed,* p. 450.

120. Eddy, *What Next in Turkey,* p. 31.

121. Zwemer, *The Disintegration of Islam,* p. 118.

122. Jessup, *The Mohammedan Missionary Problem,* pp. 22, 23. It might be noted that Jessup was not strong on history. He wrote of Arab armies invading China; of pagan Turks conquering the "empire of the Arab Caliph" then converting to Islam, not, as actually happened, converting in Central Asia; and so forth.

123. Kennedy School of Missions (Hartford Seminary Foundation), *Register of Students for 1913–14, Announcement of Instructors and Courses for 1914–15* (Hartford, Conn.: Hartford Seminary Foundation, Kennedy School of Missions, 1914); Hartford School of Missions (affiliated with the Hartford Theological Seminary), *Register of Students for 1911, Announcement of Instructors and Courses for 1912–13* (Hartford, Conn.: Hartford Seminary Foundation, Kennedy School of Missions, 1912); Henry K. Rowe, *History of the Andover Theological Seminary,* pp. 128–31. For a brief history of the Hartford Seminary's Muslim program, particularly Macdonald and Mackenzie, see Alexis Rankin Popik, "Hartford Seminary's Muslim Mission," on the website of the Macdonald Center at Hartford (http://macdonald. hartsem.edu/articles_popik.htm), originally in the *Hog River Journal* 3, no. 3 (Summer 2005). Historical catalogs of the seminaries, especially Andover, are available on Google Books (www.books.google.com).

124. On Princeton Seminary, see William K. Seldon, *Princeton Theological Seminary: A Narrative History, 1812–1992;* and David B. Calhoun, *Princeton Seminary,* vol. 2.

125. A number of bibliographies on missions were published, intended as a resource for seminarians, missionaries, and the educated public. The most valuable are in Edwin Munsell Bliss, *The Encyclopedia of Missions,* vol. 1, pp. 575–661; Dennis, *Christian Missions and Social Progress,* vol. 3, pp. 557–73; Dennis, *Foreign Missions after a*

Century, pp. 347–57; and J. Lovell Murray, compiler, *A Selected Bibliography of Missionary Literature.*

126. Rowe, *History of the Andover Theological Seminary,* p. 14.

127. See William Muir, *Life of Mahomet from Original Sources, Mahomet and Islam: A Sketch of the Prophet's Life from Original Sources and a Brief Outline of His Religion, Testimony Borne by the Coran to the Jewish and Christian Scriptures,* and others. Muir (1819–1905) was a high colonial official in British India as well as a linguist with command of Arabic sources. He was active in the evangelical campaign to convert Muslims.

128. Muir, *Mahomet and Islam,* p. 166. Note that the phrase "his religion" in the subtitle of this work would be never be accepted by Muslims.

129. Ibid., p. 244.

130. Ibid., p. 246. This consideration may best be shown by the Prodigal Son parable, in which the dutiful son represented the law and the father's treatment of the prodigal as a sign of forgiving grace.

131. Ibid., p. 249.

132. Allan Menzies, D.D., *History of Religions.*

133. G. M. Grant, *The Religions of the World in Relation to Christianity,* p. 14.

134. This was a not-uncommon position: "The Koran is a reproduction of many of the facts contained in Moses and in the Evangelists, but so modified as to suit the sinister purposes of the imposter" (Lewis Cheeseman, D.D., *Ishmael and the Church* [Philadelphia: Parry and McMillan, 1856], p. 68; Cheeseman was a Presbyterian minister in Philadelphia). For a particularly radical presentation of this view, see the Reverend John C. Clyde, *Mohammedanism a Pseudo-Christianity* (Easton, Pa.: M. J. Riegel, 1888).

135. Grant, *The Religions of the World in Relation to Christianity,* p. 24.

136. For another of the better treatments, see the short discussion in G. T. Bettany, *The World's Religions,* pp. 500–584. Bettany tried harder to be objective but still stressed the traditional condemnations and "deficiencies" of Islam.

137. Frederick William Farrar, *The Witness of History to Christ* (London and New York: Macmillan, 1870), p. 114.

138. See also James S. Dennis, *The Modern Call of Missions,* chapters 11 and 12. Dennis (1842–1914) was a Presbyterian missionary in Beirut and head of the theological seminary there.

139. See the list of readings in Brown, *The Foreign Missionary.* James L. Barton, the secretary of the American Board of Commissioners for Foreign Missions, selected the book for quotation (*Human Progress through Missions,* p. 53), as did numerous other authors. It features in all the missionary bibliographies.

140. Founded in 1886, the Student Volunteer Movement for Foreign Missions intended to publicize missionary work in order to draw college students into foreign missionary work. The effects of such organizations must have been great: they were spread all over America and centered in the universities, both public and private. The Student Volunteer Movement's convention in Des Moines, Iowa, in 1920 had 7,054 delegates, representing 949 institutions. Among other speeches, they heard

ten addresses describing the necessary decline of Islam, the imminent evangelization of Arabia, and the benefits of European domination of the Near East. The delegates returned to their colleges to spread the word (Burton St. John, ed., *North
American Students and World Advance*). This book contains a number of attacks
on Islam by speakers and authors such as Samuel Zwemer and Bayard Dodge (see
chapter 9).

141. Murray, *A Selected Bibliography*, p. 2.

142. James S. Dennis, *Social Evils of the Non-Christian World*.

143. Ibid., p. 306.

144. Frederick Denison Maurice, *The Religions of the World and Their Relations to Christianity*, pp. 39, 41.

145. Ibid., pp. 108, 173.

146. S. W. Koelle, *Mohammed and Mohammedanism*, pp. 448–58. Samuel Zwemer
recommended the book for missionaries and others (S. M. Zwemer, "A Working
Library on Islam," *Moslem World* 2, no. 1 [January 1912]: 34) but stated that it was
"somewhat one-sided," a considerable understatement.

147. A few missionaries outside the leadership of the missionary establishment did not
continuously disparage the Turks, the Ottoman government, and Islam. Mary Mills
Patrick, for example, wrote an autobiography (*Under Five Sultans*) that was mainly
an even-handed description of her labors in creating and operating the Constantinople Women's College. Although obviously occupied with the education and
welfare of Christians, she spoke well of Ottoman reforms and of a number of individual Turks. The only exceptions were an obligatory mention (pp. 281–83) of the
"Armenian massacres," of which she obviously had no firsthand knowledge, and
comments on the "tyranny" of Sultan Abdülhamit II. Even she was not capable of
juxtaposing the favor that had been shown to her missionary endeavors by the sultan with the popular European view of him. One of her descriptions (pp. 251–54) is
instructive on the actual workings of the Ottoman system: the new campus of the
Constantinople Women's College was dedicated in a ceremony on April 21, 1914.
Scarcely one year after the Balkan Wars, in which thousands of Turks had been
killed by Bulgarians and Greeks, the public ceremonies included Bulgarian and
Greek (as well as Armenian) songs, dances, and national costumes, all performed
with an official Ottoman delegation in attendance. Patrick did not comment on
what this says about the Ottoman system and character but took it for granted.

148. The Presbyterian Board of Foreign Missions was the missionary organization of the
Presbyterian Church in the United States of America, the Northern Presbyterians.
There were usually two or three mission directors serving staggered terms.

149. For example, Washington Irving's *Life of Mahomet* and *Mahomet and His Successors*.

Chapter 5, Education

1. Only 5 percent had graduated from high school in 1890. By 1920 the number had
risen to nearly 20 percent (Claudia Goldin, "America's Graduation from High

School: The Evolution and Spread of Secondary Education in the United States," *Journal of Economic History* 58, no. 2 [June 1998]: 348).

2. First edition, 1828.

3. Frederick Emerson, *The First View of the World,* pp. 106–7. Emerson's *Outlines of Geography and History, Presenting a Concise View of the World* repeated the same sentiments, in the same words.

4. Roswell Smith, *A Concise and Practical System of Geography for Common Schools,* p. 53. See also another book by Smith: *Modern Geography, for the Use of Schools, Academies, Etc., on a New Plan.* Smith's various geographies began to appear in the 1830s. He wrote a number of geographies, atlases, and other school books that were printed from 1835 to 1883. See also S. Augustus Mitchell, *Mitchell's School Geography, Mitchell's Geographical Reader* (Philadelphia: Thomas, Cowperthwait and Co., 1840), and other geographies by Mitchell; William C. Woodbridge, *Modern School Geography,* and *A System of Universal Geography.*

5. Charles Carroll Morgan, *J. H. Colton's American School Geography.* Morgan was a lay official of the Congregational Church who listed himself in *Who's Who* as being a "lifelong investigator of geographical and metaphysical problems." His descriptions of the Roman Catholic and Greek Orthodox faiths (pp. 121–22) were only slightly less prejudiced than his description of Islam and the Turks (pp. 123–24, 457, 487, 500–501).

6. *The Mother's Geography: Series of Preparatory Lessons Adapted to the Capacity of Very Young Children,* p. 48.

7. The exotic was a staple of the literature of the period, not only the literature for children. See, for example, "The Ottoman Empire," *Cincinnati Mirror and Western Gazette of Literature, Science, and the Arts* 4, no. 48 (September 26, 1835): 384–85; "The Dogs of Constantinople (from *Chamber's Journal*)," *Eclectic Magazine of Foreign Literature* 38, no. 3 (July 1856): 427–29; "A Few Words about Turkey," *Juvenile Miscellany* 5, no. 3 (January/February 1834): 310–12, whose author, while stressing the exotic for children, speaks well of the Turks' personal characteristics; "Armenia and the Armenians," *Merry's Museum and Parley's Magazine* 23 (January 1, 1852): 185–88; "Armenian Women," *Saturday Evening Post,* July 22, 1865, p. 2; "A Turkish Café," *Saturday Evening Post,* August 28, 1875, p. 6; "Turkish Etiquette and Dinner Customs," *Saturday Evening Post,* October 20, 1877, p. 7; "Turkish Superstitions," *Saturday Evening Post,* April 20, 1878, p. 7. See also note 38 in chapter 4.

8. These are the separate editions cataloged in the Library of Congress. Some editions may not be in the Library of Congress catalog. Only textbooks are included in the counts, not other books such as scholarly monographs. As might be expected, a number of textbooks were unsuccessful and had only one edition. Those are not considered here.

9. Most of the authors of primary and secondary school textbooks were not such academic luminaries. Before becoming a professor at the University of Minnesota, the most successful of these, Willis Mason West, served as a school superintendent. He did not receive the high honors of many in this list, which were reserved for those who wrote learned treatises in addition to textbooks, but he must have made

a good deal of money on his secondary-school texts. Interestingly, both West and Samuel Banister Harding, a professor at Indiana University and the University of Minnesota, did their war service with the American propaganda bureau, the Committee on Public Information.

10. Ferdinand Schevill, *A History of Europe from the Reformation to the Present Day*, pp. 476–79.

11. Ibid., p. 663.

12. Ferdinand Schevill, *History of Modern Europe,* pp. 339–41, 402–4.

13. For example, William Rabenort included only this: "The Moslems and the Christians are enemies on account of their religious differences. From time to time the Moslems have massacred Armenians and other Christians" (*Rabenort's Geography: Asia-Africa-Australia,* p. 108). Although the books cited here were those used in the public education system in America, books or editions also were specifically prepared for Catholic schools. These repeated the same view (of the Turks, of Islam, of "race," etc.) as seen in the public schools. See, for example, *The Comprehensive Geography; Benziger's Elementary Geography for Catholic Schools;* and *Benziger's Advanced Geography for the Use of Catholic Schools.*

14. Daniel C. Knowlton and Samuel B. Howell, *Essentials in Modern European History,* p. 303. They devoted a few pages to the rest of Turkish history. Others gave even less attention to the Turks. For example, Nuba Mitchel Pletcher, *An Introduction to Modern History* (Saint Paul: McGill Warner Co., 1915), mentioned Turks in only two paragraphs: one on the Greek rebellion, one on the Balkan Wars. "Early histories" and medieval histories usually only included the Turks as foils in the Crusades, always with erroneous facts (see the section "Repeating the Old Errors" below).

15. James A. Bowen, *Grammar School Geography,* section 37. See also Horace S. Tarbell, *The Werner Grammar School Geography: Part I,* p. 217, which described the Turks as "lazy and ignorant."

16. J. A. Dewe, *Medieval and Modern History,* p. 26.

17. William Stearns Davis, *A History of Medieval and Modern Europe for Secondary Schools,* p. 95. Hutton Webster's high-school text *Modern European History* also made heavy use of the "decay" concept, along with "corruption" and "decadence." Webster's brief section on Ottoman government showed a lack of understanding of the basics of the Ottoman system: to him, all Muslims were "citizens of the Ottoman Empire" and the Turks were separated from the Christians by "race" (pp. 376–77). See also his *Medieval and Modern History.*

18. James Harvey Robinson and Charles A. Beard, *The Development of Modern Europe: An Introduction to the Study of Current History,* pp. 314–15.

19. Roscoe Lewis Ashley, *Modern European Civilization: A Textbook for Secondary Schools,* p. 530.

20. Carlton H. H. Hayes and Parker Thomas Moon, *Modern History,* p. 593.

21. Some of the books available included Joseph von Hammer-Purgstall's monumental *Geschichte des Osmanischen Reiches, Grossentheils aus bisher unbenützten Handschriften und Archiven durch Joseph von Hammer,* 10 vols. (Pest: C. A. Hartleben,

1827–35); Edward Shepherd Creasy, *History of the Ottoman Turks: From the Beginning of Their Empire to the Present Time* (London: R. Bentley, 1854–56); Johann Wilhelm Zinkeisen, *Geschichte des Osmanischen Reiches in Europa* (Hamburg: F. Perthes, 1840–63); Alphonse de Lamartine, *History of Turkey* (New York: D. Appleton and Co., 1855); and Stanley Lane-Poole, *Turkey* (New York: G. P. Putnam's Sons, 1888). The textbook authors might even have consulted much earlier works, which, while deficient, were much better than what the textbook writers presented: Richard Knolles, *The Generall Historie of the Turkes: From the First Beginning of That Nation to the Rising of the Othoman Familie: With All the Notable Expeditions of the Christian Princes against Them: Together with the Lives and Conquests of the Othoman Kings and Emperours unto the Yeare 1621* (London: Adam Islip, 1620–21); and Paul Rycaut, *The Present State of the Ottoman Empire* (London: John Starkey and Henry Brome, 1667).

22. http://www.m-w.com/dictionary/civilization.

23. "When the Turks came into power civilization swiftly died in the eastern Caliphate, as it has everywhere under the Turk" (George Burton Adams, *Medieval and Modern History: An Outline of Its Development,* p. 60).

24. Willis Mason West and Ruth West, *The Story of Modern Progress,* pp. 616–17. "The Turks were incapable of civilization, in the European sense, and they have always remained a hostile army encamped among subject Christian peoples, whom their rule has blighted" (Willis Mason West, *Modern History: Europe from Charlemagne to the Present Time,* p. 185). The Wests stated that one of the reasons for this was the small Turkish presence in the Balkans: "the Turks were mere invaders and scattered rulers. They were not numerous in Europe except near Constantinople" (*The Story,* p. 416). This was completely false: the Turks had a major demographic presence in the Balkans until they were expelled from 1877 to 1913. Even tourist brochures indicate the importance of Turkish culture and architecture in the Balkans.

25. Gertrude Van Duyn Southworth and John Van Duyn Southworth, *Old World History, Book Two,* pp. 37–38. This was the only mention of the Turks in the book.

26. West and West, *The Story of Modern Progress,* pp. 86–87. Willis Mason West's earlier high-school textbook contained the same sentiments: "The Turks were to play somewhat the same part in the Saracenic world that the Teutons had played in the old Roman world,—with this tremendous difference, that even to the present day they have not assimilated civilization" (*Modern History,* p. 102). He also described the Crusaders as "armed pilgrims" with only good in their hearts, neglecting to mention their atrocities (p. 104). West was a professor of history and department chairman at the University of Minnesota and an extremely influential author of textbooks on American as well as European history. All of his texts went through multiple editions.

27. Samuel Banister Harding and Alfred Bushnell Hart, *New Medieval and Modern History,* p. 136. Hart wrote elsewhere that Turkey was "a barbaric state" with "an inferior civilization" and the Turk was "at heart still a Mongol Tartar" ("A Question of Honor," in American Committee Opposed to the Lausanne Treaty, *The Lausanne Treaty, Turkey and Armenia,* pp. 62–70).

28. Charles Downer Hazen, *Modern European History,* pp. 540–41.
29. See, for example, Merrick Whitcomb, *A History of Modern Europe,* p. 258. Comparison with America's treatment of its own minorities at the time seems not to have been important to the authors.
30. Ibid., p. 258.
31. Robinson and Beard, *The Development of Modern Europe,* p. 315.
32. See, for example, Frank J. Adkins, *Historical Backgrounds of the Great War,* pp. 190–91.
33. An earlier history is very similar and contains the same prejudices: Charles Downer Hazen, *Europe since 1815* (New York: Henry Holt, 1910).
34. See Whitcomb, *A History of Modern Europe,* p. 259; Adams, *Medieval and Modern History,* p. 364.
35. Schevill, *A History of Europe from the Reformation to the Present Day,* pp. 476–79.
36. See chapter 3, note 2.
37. Henry E. Bourne, *A History of Medieval and Modern Europe,* p. 395. It should be noted that Bourne gave evidence of very little knowledge of Ottoman history, stating, for example, that the Turks had converted to Islam in the time of Osman I (p. 162), centuries too late. Charles Hazen, although his text was very pro-Greek, acknowledged "utter atrocity on both sides" (Hazen, *Modern European History,* p. 542).
38. See the descriptions at the beginning of chapter 6.
39. Hazen, *Modern European History,* p. 546.
40. Justin McCarthy, "Ottoman Bosnia, 1800 to 1878," in Mark Pinson, ed., *The Muslims of Bosnia-Herzegovina* (Cambridge, Mass.: Harvard University Press, 1994), pp. 54–83.
41. Harding and Hart, *New Medieval and Modern History,* pp. 677–80. See also Webster, *Modern European History,* pp. 385–86. Hart's feelings against the Turks are evident in a piece he wrote in 1924: "The Turks for ages have shown a magnificent capacity to merge mixed elements into a barbarous people whose government is oppression, whose tax system is plunder, and whose idea of war is torture, fire, and blood. They are a superior race only in the sense that they have conquered and partially enslaved the earlier occupants of Europe and Asia Minor. The open sore in the Near East is the Turkish power, which for the time being finds it convenient to call itself a republic" ("Making Friends with Unrighteousness," *Forum* 72, no. 6 [December 1924]: 735). The use of "mixed" elements and "race" is instructive of his mind-set.
42. See, for example, Bourne, *A History of Medieval and Modern Europe,* pp. 454–58; Hazen, *Modern European History,* pp. 546–47; Robinson and Beard, *The Development of Modern Europe,* pp. 309–11; Hayes and Moon, *Modern History,* p. 554; and Adams, *Medieval and Modern History,* p. 381.
43. West, *Modern History,* p. 599. Under different titles and revised, the West text was printed until World War II. Each edition continued the same description, sometimes paraphrased. See West and West, *The Story of Modern Progress,* p. 618.

44. Ashley, *Modern European Civilization,* p. 537.

45. See, for example, Schevill, *A History of Europe from the Reformation to the Present Day,* p. 680. Bourne (*A History of Medieval and Modern Europe,* pp. 468–69) blamed the British for the troubles, because they had not allowed Russia to conquer Eastern Anatolia in 1878.

46. See, for example, Harding and Hart, *New Medieval and Modern History,* p. 680.

47. Adams, *Medieval and Modern History,* p. 384.

48. See Justin McCarthy, "The Population of the Ottoman Balkans," in *Proceedings of the Third International Congress on the Social and Economic History of Turkey* (Istanbul/Washington, D.C.: Isis Press, 1990), pp. 275–98; Justin McCarthy, "Muslims in Ottoman Europe: Population from 1800 to 1912," special edition of *Nationalities Papers* 38, no. 1 (March 2000); Justin McCarthy, *The Ottoman Peoples and the End of Empire,* pp. 53–60; and Barbara Jelavich, *History of the Balkans,* pp. 89–95.

49. Hazen, *Modern European History,* p. 548. See also Webster, *Modern European History,* p. 388.

50. Robinson and Beard, *The Development of Modern Europe,* p. 313. Harding and Hart (*New Medieval and Modern History,* p. 714) wrote that Muslims were only one-third of the population.

51. Justin McCarthy, *Death and Exile: The Ethnic Cleansing of Ottoman Muslims,* pp. 135–77; statistical analysis on pp. 161–64.

52. This was true of all the texts read for this study, which included all the major American history textbooks and many of the minor texts. In addition to the texts cited in this section, see Ashley, *Modern European Civilization,* p. 544.

53. For coverage of the Balkan Wars, see, for example, Robinson and Beard, *The Development of Modern Europe,* pp. xxxii–xxxvi; Hayes and Moon, *Modern History,* pp. 600–601; Webster, *Modern European History,* pp. 187–89; Schevill, *A History of Europe from the Reformation to the Present Day,* pp. 705–11.

54. For example, see Harding and Hart, *New Medieval and Modern History,* pp. 682–84. Hazen (*Modern European History,* pp. 601–4) completely erroneously blamed the Turks for "massacres" in Macedonia, which supposedly caused the wars. He wrote: "The two Balkan wars cost heavily in human life and in treasure. Turkey and Bulgaria each lost over 150,000 killed and wounded, Servia over 70,000, Greece nearly as many, little Montenegro over 10,000" (p. 606). The numbers of Turkish dead were completely wrong, undoubtedly because Hazen was only counting military deaths. His main sources on this period were Herbert Adams Gibbons, *The New Map of Europe (1911–1914): The Story of the Recent European Diplomatic Crises and Wars and of Europe's Present Catastrophe;* and Edwin Pears, *Forty Years in Constantinople: The Recollections of Sir Edwin Pears, 1873–1915* (New York: D. Appleton and Co., 1916). Both were extremely suspect sources (see the section "Histories of the Middle East" below).

55. Sadly, many of today's textbook authors are not free of these same faults. See notes 9, 10, and 12 in the epilogue.

56. Adams, *Medieval and Modern History,* p. 110. See also Edward Preissig, *Notes on the History and Institutions of the Old World* (New York: G. P. Putnam's Sons, 1906), p. 423.

57. Willis Mason West, *The Modern World,* pp. 219–20. Many sections of this book were very similar to or copied directly from West's *Modern History.* His views did not change in the later volumes: "The Saracens had permitted these pilgrimages; but the Turks, when they captured Jerusalem from the Arabs, began at once to persecute all Christians there" (West and West, *The Story of Modern Progress,* p. 87).

58. Davis, *A History of Medieval and Modern Europe for Secondary Schools,* p. 94.

59. Henry William Elson and Cornelia E. MacMullan, *The Story of the Old World: A European Background to the Story of Our Country,* p. 149.

60. Turkish armies did battle Crusaders in Anatolia and elsewhere.

61. Standard histories relate the true story of the times. See, for example, the descriptions in Bernard Lewis, "Egypt and Syria," in P. M. Holt et al., *The Cambridge History of Islam* (Cambridge: Cambridge University Press, 1970), pp. 193–97; and P. M. Holt, *The Age of the Crusades* (London and New York: Longman, 1986), pp. 16–22. The Turks are still occasionally blamed in today's textbooks, presumably by those who have not read the standard histories.

62. These essentially racist views had continued through the literature of the mid-nineteenth century. See, for example, "Turkey and Its Destiny," *Debow's Review* 2, no. 3 (March 1851): 299–314. "He [the Turk] is mild and grave, but when provoked he is infuriated. He has little fanaticism, but when his religious fervor is kindled, it becomes a brutal frenzy." "He is not habitually cruel; he is sometimes generous and humane; but he is, of all men, the most remorseless in his cruelty." "The Turk is a cold-blooded animal," "naturally arrogant, sensual and implacable," "a hypocrite in all things" (pp. 311–12).

63. Louis Figuier, *The Human Race* (New York: D. Appleton and Co., 1873), p. 240. Figuier wrote quite a bit on the politics and history of the Turks. His accounts were often absurd and generally ignorant, the equal of the geographies in describing Turkish life. Many of the descriptions, while somewhat accurate for the period three hundred years earlier, were no longer so in 1873.

64. Ibid., p. 242.

65. Friedrich Ratzel, *The History of Mankind,* 3 vols., translated by E. B. Tylor (New York: Macmillan, 1896), vol. 3, p. 552. Ratzel felt that the Turks "lacked energy and astuteness" (p. 552).

66. Robert Brown, *The Races of Mankind,* vol. 4 (New York: Cassel Petter and Galpin, 1876), p. 245. Brown was an Englishman.

67. *The Standard Library of Natural History, Embracing Living Animals of the World and Living Races of Mankind* (New York: University Society, 1908), vol. 4, pp. 255–60, and vol. 5, pp. 437–39. Greeks and Armenians were unstintingly praised (vol. 4, pp. 256–64).

68. Charles Hamilton Smith, *The Natural History of the Human Species,* pp. 326–31 and plate 32. An American edition of the book was published in 1851 (Boston: Gould and Lincoln) and in subsequent editions. Smith took part in an early aesthetic

disagreement on the appearance of the Turks. He considered them to be beautiful, whereas another racialist of his time (Charles L. Brace, *The Races of the Old World: A Manual of Ethnology* [New York: Charles Scribner, 1863], p. 327) thought they were ugly. It is doubtful that either had ever seen a Turk. Brace also believed that the number of Turks was diminishing due to polygamy, fatalism, and "unnatural vices" (p. 325). See also the mixture of racism, Christian triumphalism, and praise for the Americans as the best nation "racially" in "The Meeting of the East and the West," *American Quarterly Church Review and Ecclesiastical Register* 17, no. 2 (July 1865): 274–98. The *American Quarterly Church Review and Ecclesiastical Register* was an official publication of the Episcopalian Church.

    In the middle of the nineteenth century much of the literature on race that was available in America came from England, often republished in the United States. See, for example, Robert Knox, *The Races of Men*, in which the Turks/Tatars were placed within "the dark races of men," who were supposedly marked for eventual racial extinction.

69. Charles Edward Woodruff, *Expansion of Races*, especially pp. 92, 100.
70. Clinton Stoddard Burr, *America's Race Heritage*, especially pp. 17–27.
71. Madison Grant, *The Passing of the Great Race*, p. 204.
72. J. Deniker, *The Races of Man: An Outline of Anthropology and Ethnography*, pp. 293, 377–78. Deniker also asserted, without explanation, that it was the mixing that made the Turks of the Ottoman Empire religiously "the most fanatic of all Turks" (p. 378).
73. John Clark Ridpath et al., *Ridpath's History of the World*, vol. 4, p. 311. Ridpath felt that this supposedly superior blood should have made the Turks great, if not for "the evil influence of Islam" (p. 307).
74. Arthur de Gobineau, *The Inequality of Human Races*, translated by Adrian Collins (New York: Putnam's, 1915), pp. 127–31 (originally published in 1853).
75. Lothrop Stoddard, *The New World of Islam*, pp. 14–16. See also Seth K. Humphrey, *Mankind: Racial Values and the Racial Prospect* (New York: Charles Scribner's Sons, 1917); and Alfred P. Schulz, *Race or Mongrel* (Boston: L. C. Page, 1908), especially pp. 93–96.
76. Stoddard's "brown race" included the inhabitants of Anatolia (excluding Greeks and Armenians), North Africa, Central Asia, and western and southern Asia east to Burma. See Lothrop Stoddard, *The Rising Tide of Color against White Supremacy*, and *The Revolt against Civilization*.
77. On respect for Keane in his field, see his obituary: A. C. Haddon, "Augustus Henry Keane, LL.D," *Geographical Journal* 39, no. 4 (April 1912): 406. OCLC Worldcat lists 226 American libraries that hold copies of Keane's *Man Past and Present*. It should be noted that some of the racialist books of the time merely listed the supposed races and their skull sizes, hair types, stature, and so forth, without reference to their moral and intellectual qualities.
78. Henry Morgenthau, *Ambassador Morgenthau's Story*, p. 291.

79. For examples of racism in anthropology books, see Edward B. Tylor, *Anthropology: An Introduction to the Study of Man and Civilization;* and W. E. Rotzell, *Man: An Introduction to Anthropology.*

80. Descriptive terms differed somewhat by author. These terms are from Alexis Everett Frye, *Advanced Geography,* pp. 100–104. Some authors wrote of only four races, omitting the Malayan. Instruction on the races began at an early age. See, for example, S. Augustus Mitchell, *An Easy Introduction to the Study of Geography Designed for the Instruction of Children in Schools and Families,* pp. 30–31. The book offered students drawings of each of the races—a noble Northern European Caucasian, a reasonable portrait of a Native American, somewhat sinister pictures of a Mongolian and a Malayan, and a "golliwog" caricature of an African.

81. Frye, *Advanced Geography,* p. 103.

82. Frederick Maglot, *A Manual of Geography,* p. 61. Maglot considered the Turks to be Caucasians but did not include them in his table of Caucasian peoples (p. 63), perhaps because he could not decide if they were "Hamitic," "Semitic," or "Aryan." See also Charles Redway Dryer, *Grammar School Geography,* p. 52.

83. S. C. Schmucker, *Columbia Elementary Geography,* p. 35.

84. A. von Steinwehr, *School Geography,* p. 22. Von Steinwehr felt the Caucasians were "superior to the others in intellectual qualities" (p. 22).

85. Although the selection was extremely limited, it would have been possible to recommend books that somewhat approached objectivity. The textbooks never recommended *The Real Turk* by Stanwood Cobb (Boston: Pilgrim Press, 1914), which should be cited as one of the few writings that had anything good to say about the Turks. Cobb was an interesting person. He taught for three years (1907–10) at Robert College, the missionary college in Istanbul, and his book was published by a Congregationalist press, but he was a Baha'i whose faith affected his writings on Turks, Islam, and Eastern mysticism. Cobb liked Turks, respected Islam, and spoke well of the Turks he had known. Nevertheless, he adopted the standard view of Turkish "atrocities" that, of course, he had never seen. His views can be summarized in the description of the contents of chapter 2, "The Turks a Kindly People—Yet Still Barbarous" (p. xi).

86. Some British textbooks were reprinted in America. It is impossible to know how often these were used in classes, but they are not much found in libraries. For example, Charles Stanford Terry's *A Short History of Europe, 1806–1914* (London: George Routledge and Sons; and New York: E. F. Dutton and Co., 1915) gave extensive coverage to the European diplomacy of the Eastern Question. Because of this, Terry included short sentences on the relations between Turks and Balkan Christians. He admitted that the Greeks, as well as the Turks, had committed atrocities during the Greek rebellion. After that, however, no Christian did wrong. He cited no Muslim dead in Bosnia, in Bulgaria, or during the Balkan Wars, although he magnified Christian mortality. The more than 100 pages devoted to the Eastern Question do not include any consideration of the Ottoman political situation. The British textbook by A. J. Grant (*A History of Europe: Part III, Modern Europe* [1912], revised ed. [London and New York: Longmans, Green, and Co.,

1915]) had very little to say of the Turks, who were uniformly described as violent and unstable. This led to odd analyses such as this one (speaking of the Ottoman Empire in the nineteenth century): "In Europe the Turks were a minority, who held their dominion by the power of the sword, and made no effort to conciliate or to absorb the populations they had conquered. They despised the characteristic features of European civilization and made no effort to assimilate it. Turkey was a military despotism, without industry, without science, without liberty. Generalizations in history are always dangerous; but it is safe to say that such a state can never be stable. The Ottoman Empire had never recovered from the naval defeat which she had received at the hands of the Spaniards and their allies at Lepanto in 1571" (p. 620). Somehow the allegedly unstable state managed to last more than 600 years and did not end until 350 years after Lepanto. Like Grant, other writers complained that the Turks had not absorbed conquered peoples, ignoring the inherent contradiction between this and their view of the Turks as oppressors.

Thomas Dyer's excellent political and military history (*The History of Modern Europe*) was available in 1861. It was not an especially analytical book and contained nothing on culture and little on society, but a great deal of space was devoted to the Ottomans, putting them in their rightful place in the political history of Europe. No general textbook printed in America until the middle of the twentieth century could compare. Though reprinted in England until 1901, the book was never printed in the United States and never cited by the American textbook authors.

Only one French textbook seems to have been prominently utilized by the Americans. Many of the American history textbooks included in their bibliographies and freely abstracted from the *Histoire politique de l'Europe contemporaine* by Charles Seignobos (translated into English as *A Political History of Europe since 1815* [New York: Henry Holt, 1899]). The book's coverage of the Turks was almost exclusively political, with only short sections blaming the Ottomans for the "Bulgarian Horrors" (p. 632) and the "Armenian Massacres" (pp. 651–52). Surprisingly, Seignobos described the Greek rebellion accurately, as a set of mutual massacres in which both sides took part. After that, he did not describe the expulsion and murders of the Muslim peoples or any Turkish suffering.

87. E. A. Freeman, *The Turks in Europe*. Oddly, Freeman's textbook *General Sketch of European History*, meant for British schools, gave only brief political and military mention of the Turks. Some of these were erroneous, but the accounts were not particularly prejudiced.

88. Freeman, *The Turks in Europe*, pp. 7–11. See C. J. W. Parker, "The Failure of Liberal Racialism: The Racial Ideas of E. A. Freeman," *Historical Journal* 24, no. 4 (December 1981): 825–46.

89. Freeman, *The Turks in Europe*, pp. 20, 21, 24, 30.

90. Ibid., p. 63.

91. See McCarthy, "Ottoman Bosnia, 1800 to 1878," pp. 80–82.

92. Justin McCarthy, "The Demography of the 1877–78 Russo-Turkish War," in Ömer Turan, ed., *The Ottoman-Russian War of 1877–78* (Ankara: Middle East Technical

University and Meiji University Institute of Humanities, 2007), pp. 51–78, "Muslims in Ottoman Europe: Population from 1800 to 1912," *Nationalities Papers* 28, no. 1 (2000): 29–43, and "Ottoman Bosnia." See also Alexandre Popovic, *L'Islam Balkanique: Les musulmans du sud-est européen dans la période post-ottomane* (Berlin: Osteuropa-Institut an der Freien Universität Berlin, 1986).

93. See McCarthy, *Death and Exile,* chapter 5.

94. Freeman, *The Turks in Europe,* p. 91.

95. American textbooks on the Middle East, as opposed to those that considered it only in passing, were few until the second half of the twentieth century. Two good histories of the Ottomans were available, although neither considered events past 1880. Creasy's *History of the Ottoman Turks* was first printed in two volumes in London (*History of the Ottoman Turks: From the Beginning of Their Empire to the Present Time: Chiefly Founded on Von Hammer* [London: R. Bentley, 1854–56]). The American publication was based on the revised edition (London: R. Bentley, 1877). As stated in the title of the first edition, Creasy based his work on von Hammer-Purgstall's *Geschichte des osmanischen Reiches,* the grandfather of all Ottoman histories. There were also American publications of Stanley Lane-Poole's *The Story of Turkey,* assisted by E. J. W. Gibb and Arthur Gilman (New York: G. P. Putnam's Sons, 1888), and Edson L. Clark's *Turkey* (New York: Co-operative Publication Society, 1878). Both were excellent histories, fair and balanced. Both were works for specialists, however, full of battles, diplomacy, difficult Turkish names, and dynastic maneuverings. They were surely not suitable for students or the general public, and the textbook authors gave little indication of having read either of them. *Turkey*, despite its title, was a history of the Greeks from ancient times.

96. William Stearns Davis, *A Short History of the Near East: From the Founding of Constantinople (330 A.D. to 1922).* Davis was the author of a great number of textbooks for universities and secondary schools. His books were still in print thirty years after his death in 1930. For a further view of his opinions on the Turks, see "Why the Treaty of Lausanne Should Not Be Ratified," in American Committee Opposed to the Lausanne Treaty, *The Lausanne Treaty, Turkey and Armenia,* pp. 75–103, in which Davis predicted the imminent downfall of the Turkish Republic, spoke of the Turks as a "backward race" (p. 75), and generally showed that he had no understanding of the situation.

97. OCLC Worldcat (see chapter 4, note 3) lists 785 copies in American libraries, very extensive coverage for its time.

98. Davis, *A Short History of the Near East,* p. 169.

99. Ibid., p. 212. Davis never gave his sources, so it is impossible to know the origins of his nonsense such as "refined tortures and unspeakable immoralities." "Unspeakable" is typical of this sort of assessment; it relieves the author of having to prove his assertions. His hatred of Mehmet II was an irrationality that probably arose from Mehmet's conquest of Davis's beloved Byzantine Constantinople. He considered Mehmet's complete rebuilding of Istanbul from its decayed latter Byzantine state, as well as all Ottoman architectural glory, to be borrowed and insignificant. To him, Mehmet's works "were slight enough contribution by the Ottomans to the

world of beauty from which he borrowed much and in which he destroyed much more. Little was his success in those things which pertained not to the sword" (p. 247).

100. Davis did devote one page (pp. 246–47) to "Learning and Architecture." He attributed the best Ottoman architecture to Christian elements. Ottoman poets were "not profound and their subjects were limited." In learning, "they added nothing to what the Arabs had done before them." Anyone who doubts the complete falseness of these statements need only consult standard reference works, such as the *Encyclopedia of Islam.*

101. Davis, *A Short History of the Near East,* p. 393.

102. Ibid., pp. 123–24.

103. Many of Davis's sentiments had been expressed previously in shorter form in his textbooks and at greater length in *The Roots of the War: A Non-technical History of Europe, 1870–1914, A.D.* In *The Roots of War* Davis repeated all the faults of his own and other works: no Turk had ever died in conflicts with Christians; Abdülhamit II had ordered the massacre of Armenians, who were always innocent; Ottoman reforms had never succeeded; and, indeed, the Turks had never governed well: "In a word, the Turkish Empire [in the late nineteenth century] was not merely an Oriental despotism; it was a particularly abominable and degenerate type of Oriental despotism, and it showed no signs of becoming better" (p. 64). Davis was not one to spare the invective. "The governing class labored under two handicaps, both so serious that the problem was practically hopeless. I. They were Turks; and the Turkish race, although able to produce admirable fighters and even generals, has never been able to produce civil administrators of decent ability . . . II. They were Mohammedans" (p. 62). OCLC Worldcat lists 559 copies of the book in American libraries.

104. The book was very popular, with 587 libraries holding copies according to OCLC Worldcat. See also Herbert Adams Gibbons, *The New Map of Asia (1900–1919),* which contained much less on the Turks. His most scholarly book, *The Foundation of the Ottoman Empire: A History of the Osmanlis up to the Death of Bayezid I (1300–1403)* (New York: Century Co., 1916), while often wrong, was not offensive.

105. Herbert Adams Gibbons, *Zionism and World Peace* (Paris: Friends of the Holy Land, 1919). See also Gibbons, "Palestine and the Zionists," in *The New Map of Asia,* pp. 192–208.

106. Gibbons, *The New Map of Europe,* p. 200.

107. Justin McCarthy, *Muslims and Minorities,* pp. 7–46.

108. Gibbons, *The New Map of Europe,* pp. 207–10, 167–79.

109. Mary Theodora Whitley, *Boys and Girls in Other Lands,* p. 86.

110. David Brewer Eddy, *What Next in Turkey: Glimpses of the American Board's Work in the Near East,* pp. 186–87.

111. Many books contain such descriptions, but these particular ones were taken from Elnathan Ellsworth Strong, *Mission Stories of Many Lands: A Book for Young People,* which was published by the American Board of Commissioners for Foreign Missions in 1885 expressly to be used in Sunday schools and young people's courses.

112. See, for example, Isabel M. Blake ("formerly teacher under American Board of Commissioners for Foreign Missions, Aintab, Turkey; later, Member of American Red Cross Commission to Palestine"), *Fez and Turban Tales;* Strong, *Mission Stories of Many Lands;* and others listed in these notes.

113. Although the number of Ottoman state schools was increasing, there were indeed such Quran schools, where corporal punishment (not "beatings") was not unknown. The analysis probably reflected the upper-class origins of the missionaries and the authors. They may not have been familiar with the difficult situation of many American children at the time, including schools where corporal punishment was the norm, and the great number of children who never went to school, forced to work from an early age. This is odd, however, because other men and women of religion were justifiably campaigning against child labor and other abuses in America.

114. See, for example, Mrs. Napier Malcolm, *Children of Persia,* pp. 72–74. A letter to "My Dear Boys and Girls" at the beginning of the book tells the children that "Persian children do need to be rescued from Mohammedanism."

115. See, for example, Henry Harris Jessup, *The Women of the Arabs, with a Chapter for Children,* especially pp. 8–10.

116. Malcolm, *Children of Persia,* p. 27.

117. Amy E. Zwemer, *Two Young Arabs: The Travels of Noorah and Jameel.*

118. Samuel M. Zwemer and Amy E. Zwemer, *Zigzag Journeys in the Camel Country,* pp. 102, 103. The Zwemers appropriated the title *Zigzag Journeys* from a popular series of youth books by Hezekiah Butterworth. The series titles that touched on the Turks and Islam were *Zigzag Journeys in the Orient: The Adriatic to the Baltic* (Boston: Estes and Lauriat, 1882) and *Zigzag Journeys in the Levant, with a Talmudist Storyteller* (Boston: Estes and Lauriat, 1886). While not as deeply prejudiced as *Zigzag Journeys in the Camel Country,* the books repeated many of the standard views, including the brutality of the Turks, suffering Christians, praise for the Crusaders, and the imposture of Muhammad. They were most interested, however, in the exotic and the strange.

119. Samuel M. Zwemer and Amy E. Zwemer, *Topsy-Turvy Land: Arabia Pictured for Children* (New York: Revell, 1902), p. 20.

120. See, for example, Cora Banks Pierce and Hazel Northrop, *Stories from Far Away.*

121. Ralph E. Diffendorfer, *Missionary Education in Home and School* (New York: Abingdon Press, 1917), pp. 38, 39.

122. John Lovell Murray, ed., *Missionary Programs for Schoolboys* (New York: Student Volunteer Movement, 1914).

123. See, for example, Mary Entwistle and Jeanette E. Peters, *Musa, Son of Egypt: Programs and Stories for Primary Children,* p. 15. See also Entwistle's children's book *The Story of Musa* (New York: Friendship Press, 1929), which portrayed backward Muslims and enlightened missionaries and Christians.

124. The book was also printed by the Board of Foreign Missions of the Presbyterian Church in the USA (New York, 1908) and the American Baptist Publication Society (Philadelphia, 1908), the Publication House of the Methodist Episcopal

Church, South (Nashville and Dallas, 1908), the American Advent Mission Society (Boston, 1908), and the United Society of Christian Endeavor (Boston, 1908) as well as by various commercial presses (New York: Eaton and Mains, 1908; Cleveland: J. H. Lamb, 1908; Cleveland: Jennings and Graham, 1908).

125. Labaree, *The Child in the Midst,* pp. 42, 83, 173.

Chapter 6, The Bulgarian Horrors

1. L. S. Stavrianos, *The Balkans since 1450* (New York: Rinehart, 1958), p. 379.

2. Except as otherwise indicated, the history of the effect of the Bulgarian rebellion and following events has been taken from chapter 3 of Justin McCarthy, *Death and Exile: The Ethnic Cleansing of Ottoman Muslims,* which gives detailed documentation.

3. British National Archives, FO 195-1077, Brophy to Elliot, Burgas, May 27, 1876.

4. Estimates of Bulgarian and Muslim mortality in 1876 vary and are always confused. See the sources in McCarthy, *Death and Exile,* p. 96.

5. On the Liberal attack on the Turks, see Richard Shannon, *Gladstone and the Bulgarian Agitation, 1876;* and David Harris, *Britain and the Bulgarian Horrors of 1876,* although they are not accurate on the actual events in Bulgaria. See also Keith A. P. Sandiford, "W. E. Gladstone and the Liberal-Nationalist Movement," *Albion* 13, no. 1 (Spring 1981): 27–42. The best analysis is Richard Millman, *Britain and the Eastern Question, 1875–1878.*

6. The primary Liberal newspapers were the *Daily News, Daily Telegraph,* and *Times.* It should be noted that these were the newspapers' political persuasions in 1876–78, not necessarily later. Liberal Frank Harrison Hill was editor-in-chief of the *Daily News* from 1870 to 1886. The newspaper had been founded in 1846 specifically to express Liberal political views.

7. See the affidavit from many reporters in McCarthy, *Death and Exile,* p. 67.

8. Justin McCarthy, "The Demography of the 1877–78 Russo-Turkish War," in Ömer Turan, ed., *The Ottoman-Russian War of 1877–78* (Ankara: Middle East Technical University and Meiji University Institute of Humanities, 2007), pp. 63–66. These figures differ slightly from the calculations made in McCarthy, *Death and Exile,* pp. 88–91. This is due to the inclusion of the Mankalya district (*kaza*) in the Dobruja, which went to Romania, not Bulgaria. The Muslims of the Dobruja suffered even greater loss than those in Bulgaria. The population of the Dobruja Muslims decreased by 84 percent.

9. The major newspapers did not cite the Associated Press. It is necessary to look to the newspapers of smaller cities to see the provenance of the articles. These sometimes used phrases such as "by cable from the Associated Press," identifying the same stories and sources (such as the *London Daily News*) that appeared in the press of the major cities. See note 11 below. On the British press, see "From the Eastern Question to the Death of General Gordon: Representations of the Middle East in the Victorian Periodical Press, 1876–1885," *British Journal of Middle Eastern Studies* 28, no. 1 (May 2001): 5–24; and Nazan Çiçek, "The Turkish Response to Bulgarian Horrors: A Study in English Turcophobia," *Middle Eastern Studies* 42, no. 1 (January 2006): 87–102.

10. The instances in which this article appeared are too many to list. See, for example, "The Devastation in Bulgaria," *Atlanta Constitution,* August 14, 1877, p. 4; and "The Horrors of War," *New York Times,* August 14, 1877, p. 1. The provenance of this article's information is questionable. The article seems to say that it was written by an unnamed correspondent then forwarded by an agent of the *London Times* from Syria. The unnamed correspondent based his information on letters from unnamed persons.

11. As a demonstration of this, look at the newspapers for almost any day that Bulgaria was in the news. For example, see January 22 and 23, 1878, in the *Atlanta Constitution, Oshkosh [Wisc.] Daily Northwestern, Fort Wayne [Ind.] Daily Sentinel, Davenport [Iowa] Gazette, Galveston Daily News, Helena [Mont.] Independent,* and *Titusville [Pa.] Morning Herald,* among many others. The newspapers took different sections of larger reports, but the words were exactly the same in each. The Titusville newspaper was the only one to identify the stories as originating with the Associated Press. It always did this, and its pages show that the stories run by other papers, including in the major newspapers, were from the Associated Press.

12. The majority of articles on the massacres were taken from the British press. As examples of the many articles, see "The Bulgarian Outrages," *Chicago Tribune,* October 7, 1876, p. 9; "Butchery," *Chicago Tribune,* September 20, 1876, p. 5; "The Atrocities in Bulgaria," *New York Times,* August 20, 1876, p. 5; "The Slaughter in Bulgaria," *New York Times,* August 23, 1876, p. 5; "Atrocities in the East," *New York Times,* September 3, 1876, p. 2; and "Terrible Turkish Atrocities," *New York Times,* September 3, 1876, p. 5. This chapter contains fewer citations from small city newspapers than appear in later chapters. These smaller papers seldom contained more than short, always anti-Turkish, excerpts and paraphrases of the same articles and British sources that appeared in the larger city newspapers. Only some examples are cited here.

13. Many of the articles cited here featured atrocity stories, too many to list, and it would be useless to quote from them at any length. See, for example, "A Terrible Story," *Advocate of Peace* 8, no. 5 (September/October 1877): 34; "The Turkish Terror in Bulgaria," *Friends' Intelligencer* 34, no. 38 (November 10, 1877): 604–5; and "Bulgarian Cruelties," *Albion* 54, no. 42 (October 14, 1876): 7. One interesting article in the *Janesville [Wisc.] Gazette* ("More Turkish Barbarism," August 8, 1876, p. 1) compared the Turks to inhabitants of Mississippi and their practice of lynching African Americans ("The cruelty of the Turks is proverbial").

14. "Terrible Atrocities by Bulgaria—Turkish Barbarity [*sic*]," *Boston Globe,* August 18, 1876, p. 1. The fabrications included false renderings of the reports of British consuls. See "The War in Bulgaria," *Janesville [Wisc.] Gazette,* August 24, 1876, p. 1.

15. "The Causes of the War," *Boston Globe,* April 27, 1877, p. 4.

16. "The Cause of the Russo-Turkish War," *Chicago Tribune,* May 2, 1877, p. 4. Many other editorials in various newspapers described the Turks as "aliens" that should be evicted from Europe.

17. [No title], *Chicago Tribune,* August 7, 1877, p. 4.

18. McCarthy, *Death and Exile,* pp. 89–91, 341–43, "The Demography of the 1877–78 Russo-Turkish War," pp. 51–78, and "Muslims in Ottoman Europe: Population from 1800 to 1912," *Nationalities Papers* 28, no. 1 (2000): 29–43.

19. "About the Turkish Barbarities," *Boston Globe,* September 13, 1876, p. 4. See also "Moslem Atrocities," *Iowa State Reporter,* September 20, 1876, p. 2; and "The Atrocities in Bulgaria," *Cedar Rapids [Iowa] Times,* November 23, 1876, p. 1. These articles report on the investigations of Eugene Schuyler and Walter Baring, considered in Millman, *Britain and the Eastern Question;* and especially in Richard Millman, "The Bulgarian Massacres Reconsidered," *Slavonic and East European Review* 58, no. 2 (April 1980): 218–31.

20. For a particularly egregious example, drawn from the *London Daily News,* see "Turkish Atrocities," *Port Jervis [N.Y.] Evening Gazette,* September 13, 1876, p. 2. Like all but a few of the smaller-town newspaper articles cited in this chapter, this story appeared in a number of papers.

21. See, for example, "Foreign," *Chicago Tribune,* March 20, 1877, p. 5; "The Bulgarian Atrocities," *Chicago Tribune,* August 23, 1876, p. 5; "Destruction of Property in Bulgaria Ordered by the Turks" (only 59 words long), *Boston Globe,* July 21, 1876; and "Report of the English Commissioners on Bulgarian Outrages," *Boston Globe,* September 20, 1876, p. 4. Such brief mention was quite common, often included as a sentence or two in articles on the wars. The *Galveston Daily News,* August 13, 1876, p. 1, simply wrote: "The Turks continue massacres in Bosnia."

22. This was the rule for all reports seen in the American press. See, for example, in the *New York Times:* "Bulgarians Starving to Death," September 24, 1876, p. 9; and "Turkish Ruffianism in Bulgaria," February 26, 1877, p. 5. Many articles were mixtures of observation and Bulgarian testimony. See, for example, "The Outrages of War," *New York Times,* August 27, 1877, p. 2, which contains a number of instances.

23. "Barbarous Bashi-Bazouks," *Palo Alto [Calif.] Pilot,* July 27, 1876, p. 5.

24. See, for example, "Turkish Butchers in Bulgaria: Correspondent of the London Daily News," *Atlanta Constitution,* September 11, 1877, p. 1.

25. "Mussulmen Maddened," *Atlanta Constitution,* August 24, 1876, p. 1 (from the *London Daily News*).

26. "Turkish Outrages in Bulgaria," *New York Times,* August 27, 1876, p. 9. See also "Foreign," *Chicago Tribune,* August 23, 1876, p. 5. The best analysis of the initial reporting of the numbers of Bulgarian dead is in Millman, "The Bulgarian Massacres Reconsidered."

27. "Turkish Cruelties—Slaughter of 25,000 Warmed [*sic*] Bulgarians," *Chicago Tribune,* July 23, 1876, p. 2. The same article appeared in the *New York Times* ("Turkish Cruelties," July 21, 1876, p. 3).

28. See, for example, "The Turks Badly Defeated by the Insurgents," *Boston Globe,* April 21, 1876, p. 1; "The Old World: Severe Disasters to the Turkish Armies Reported," *Boston Globe,* August 18, 1876, p. 1; "The Turks Violate the Terms of the Armistice," *Boston Globe,* September 21, 1876, p. 5; "The Disturbed Provinces," *New York Times,* April 4, 1877, p. 5; "Foreign," *Chicago Tribune,* August 2, 1876, p. 5; "Foreign," *Chicago Tribune,* August 23, 1876, p. 5; and "Blood-Sucking Turks [*sic*],"

Atlanta Constitution, July 19, 1876, p. 1. The stories could be absurd, such as the Serbian claim that Turkish soldiers carried petroleum in their backpacks solely for the purpose of burning Serbian villages ("Latest News by Cable: The Turkish Barbarities," *New York Times,* August 10, 1876, p. 5).

29. See, for example, "The War," *Chicago Tribune,* May 19, 1877, p. 5.

30. "The Fiendish Turks," *Chicago Tribune,* August 22, 1876, p. 5.

31. This was a common theme. For one example, see "The Russo-Turkish War," *Christian Union* 15, no. 22 (May 30, 1877): 491: "If it had not been for England the Ottoman throne would not now have been west of the Bosphorus. Let us hope that this Christian nation will at last become ashamed of her alliance and endeavor to restore to these Christian provinces the rights of which she has been instrumental in depriving them." See also "Turkish Rule in Europe," *New York Times,* May 15, 1877, p. 3; and Goldwin Smith, "The Eastern Crisis," *Eclectic Magazine of Foreign Literature* (from the *Fortnightly Review*) 27, no. 7 (July 1878): 18–27.

32. "The Turks in Europe," *Chicago Tribune,* April 15, 1877, p. 4.

33. "The Ottoman Blunder," *Atlanta Constitution,* May 12, 1876, p. 1.

34. One exception was an unattributed article in the *New York Times* that stated that the Turks were capable of reform (April 15, 1877, p. 5).

35. This was an almost constant sentiment, expressed in short quotations in newspapers and given in detail in magazines (see the section "Magazines" below). See, for example, "The Turks in Europe," *International Review* 4 (July 1877): 441–58.

36. See, for example, "The Atrocities in Bulgaria," *New York Times,* September 10, 1876, p. 1; "The Atrocities in Bulgaria," *New York Times,* August 13, 1877, p. 3; "Mr. Gladstone to the Bulgarians," *New York Times,* July 28, 1878, p. 8; "Gladstone's Speech," *Massachusetts Ploughman and New England Journal of Agriculture* 36, no. 18 (February 3, 1877): 2; "Montenegro, a Sketch," *Eclectic Magazine of Foreign Literature* 26, no. 1 (July 1877): 44–57; "Gladstone on the Bulgarian Outrages," *Chicago Tribune,* August 31, 1876, p. 5; and W. E. Gladstone, "The Hellenic Factor in the Eastern Problem," *Littell's Living Age* 132, no. 1701 (January 20, 1877): 131–47.

37. "Plain Talk by Mr. Gladstone," *Advocate of Peace* 7, no. 12 (December 1876): 71. Some were even more aroused than Gladstone. Lord Shaftesbury, addressing a London meeting that was reported in America, declared that "the Turks have proved themselves to be wholly unfit to have any authority over any portion of the human race" ("The Turkish Question," *New York Observer* 54, no. 33 [August 17, 1876]: 262).

38. Only a selection of magazines can be considered here: those in the American Periodical Series. As with the newspapers, there are just too many of them for complete coverage. Obviously fringe magazines have been excluded, although they contained the same sentiments as the major publications, often more violently expressed. The *Phrenological Journal and Science of Health,* for example, was distinctly anti-Turkish.

39. Edwin L. Godkin, "The Eastern Question," *North American Review* 124, no. 254 (January 1877): 106–26. Godkin was editor of the *Nation* and had been an editorial writer for the *New York Times* and correspondent for the *London Daily News.*

40. "The Herzegovinan Question," *International Review* 3 (January 1876): 3–4. The author described the Ottoman army, courts, and so forth, in equally absurd terms.

41. Daniel S. Gregory, "The Eastern Problem," *Princeton Review* (January–June 1878): 60. The numerous factual errors in magazines are not listed here, but they indicate how little the American press knew of events. The *Saturday Evening Post*, for example, wrote of the *başı bozuk*s (reservists, often only armed Turkish villagers) and the Cossacks, completely misidentifying both and stating totally erroneously that they were essentially the same type of fighters ("The Bashi-Bazouks and Cossacks," *Saturday Evening Post* 67, no. 10 [September 29, 1877]: 3). The article defined *başı bozuk* as "light headed" when it actually means "broken headed," something of a difference, but the real meaning is "civilian fighter" or "irregular."

42. "The Suicide of the Ottomans," *Appleton's Journal* 2, no. 31 (June 1877): 538. Many of the articles listed here contain these sentiments.

43. "Oppression of Christians the Cause of Turkey's Fall," *Frank Leslie's Popular Monthly* 5, no. 4 (April 1878): 490–93, gave the starkest description of this, but the picture of desolation was found in many articles.

44. See, for example, "Servia," *Littell's Living Age* (from *British Quarterly Review*) 129, no. 1663 (April 22, 1876): 195–205; and "Christian Populations in Europe," *Littell's Living Age* (from *London Quarterly Review*) 129, no. 1666 (May 13, 1876): 387–99.

45. Edward A. Freeman, "The True Eastern Question," *Littell's Living Age* (from *Fortnightly Review*) 128, no. 1648 (January 8, 1876): 67–80, also in the *Eclectic Magazine of Foreign Literature*, vol. 23, no. 2 (February 1876): 159–74; "Present Aspects of the Eastern Question," *Littell's Living Age*, vol. 131, no. 1692 (November 18, 1876): 414–23; "Montenegro," *Littell's Living Age*, vol. 128, no. 1653 (February 12, 1876): 387–98; "The Geographical Aspect of the Eastern Question," *Littell's Living Age* 132, no. 1704 (February 10, 1877): 369–78; and Edward A. Freeman, "National Morality," *Princeton Review* (July–December 1878): 641–72.

46. Freeman, "National Morality," p. 655.

47. One rare article (in *International Review* 4 [July 1877]: 459–63) made the case that, however bad the Ottomans were, they were improving and that rule by Russia would be worse.

48. "The Turkish Provinces," *National Repository* 1 (February 1877): 97–115 (quotation on 113–14).

49. Ibid., pp. 109–10.

50. Justin McCarthy, "Ottoman Bosnia, 1800 to 1878," in Mark Pinson, ed., *The Muslims of Bosnia-Herzegovina* (Cambridge, Mass.: Harvard University Press, 1993), pp. 54–83.

51. Daniel S. Gregory, "The Eastern Problem," *Princeton Review* (January–June 1878): 54–56. Daniel Seelye Gregory (1832–1915) was a Presbyterian minister (a graduate of Princeton Seminary), professor, author, and general secretary of the Bible League of America.

52. McCarthy, *Death and Exile,* chapters 1 and 2. I have found no articles on the Crimean Tatar loss and three brief mentions of the Circassian exile and mortality. The *Chicago Tribune* quoted the Istanbul paper *Levant Herald* without describing

the horrors of the Circassian migration ("The Circassian Emigration," *Chicago Tribune*, January 20, 1865, p. 3). *Dollar Monthly Magazine* ("Circassians," *Dollar Monthly Magazine* 21, no. 4 [April 1865]: 271) devoted one sentence to the migration, undercounting it by 95 percent. The *New York Times* mentioned the Circassian plight in one short paragraph in a list of all the matters being considered by the British parliament ("England: Proceedings in Parliament," *New York Times*, June 16, 1864, p. 2). The *Times* did, however, print many articles and advertisements on the beauties of Circassian women, Circassian slave markets, and the "six beautiful Circassian girls" who had been engaged by P. T. Barnum. The Circassian girls were advertised next to the Albino Boy and the Learned Seals. The only sympathetic article came from the *London Quarterly*, reprinted in *Eclectic Magazine of Foreign Literature* ("The Circassian Exodus," *Eclectic Magazine of Foreign Literature* 63, no. 4 [December 1864]: 420–29). I found no other articles on the subject.

53.   "The Latest Cable News," *Boston Globe*, July 30, 1878, p. 1. See also similar very short reports in the *Chicago Tribune* ("Foreign," April 18, 1878, p. 2; "The Atrocity Bureau," September 16, 1877, p. 1; "Pressing Forward," July 14, 1877, p. 1).

54.   "More Atrocities Reported," *Boston Globe*, September 6, 1877, p. 1.

55.   "The Horrors of War," *New York Times*, August 14, 1877, p. 1.

56.   "The Reported Russian Cruelties," *New York Times*, July 18, 1877, p. 1. Even Gladstone, referring to this statement of complete Russian innocence, did not believe that the Russians had never done anything to the Turks ("The Atrocities in Bulgaria," *New York Times*, August 13, 1877, p. 3). The *New York Times* also published excerpts from the Ottoman minister of foreign affairs on Bulgarian atrocities against Turks ("The Atrocities in Bulgaria," August 5, 1877, p. 1).

57.   Archibald Forbes, "The Russians, the Turks, and the Bulgarians," *Littell's Living Age* (from *Nineteenth Century*) 135, no. 1748 (December 15, 1877): 643–56. The same article appeared in *Potter's American Monthly* 10, no. 74 (February 1878) ("Status of the Contesting Powers in the East," pp. 81–100). *Littell's Living Age* also printed an anti-Russian article by Louis Kossuth that painted the Turks in a positive light ("Russian Aggression," from *Contemporary Review* 136, no. 1752 [January 12, 1878]: 94–108). Laurence Oliphant's "Christian Policy in Turkey" (*North American Review* 124, no. 255 [March/April 1877]: 190–213) condemned the Russians but was mainly concerned with British policy.

58.   "Our Own Correspondent," "The Eastern Conflict," *New York Times*, August 21, 1877, p. 2; "Atrocities by Both Armies," *New York Times*, September 10, 1877, p. 1; "Executions in Adrianople," *New York Times*, September 24, 1877, p. 2. Distinction must be made between "Our Own Correspondent" and "A Special Correspondent." Neither was named, but evidence indicates that the latter was actually from the *London Times*: the same stories were identified as "special correspondent" and "a correspondent of the [London] *Times*" in different articles (see, for example, "The Burned Cities of Roumelia," *New York Times*, September 22, 1877, p. 1; and "A Pitiful State of Affairs," *New York Times*, September 25, 1878, p. 1).

59.   "The Turks in the Conquered Provinces," *Chicago Tribune*, April 27, 1878, p. 4. See also "Bulgaria," "Rekindled," and "Foreign," *Chicago Tribune*, August 23, 1876, p. 5;

and "Atrocities," *Chicago Tribune,* August 1, 1877, p. 5. In general, the *Tribune* articles were less rabidly anti-Turkish than the editorials.

60. "The Bulgarian Revenge," *Chicago Tribune,* July 18, 1877, p. 4. The editor made free with words such as "barbarian hordes" and completely falsified the situation in Ottoman Bulgaria: "To all intents and purposes the Bulgarians have been the slaves of the Turks as fully as the Africans in the South were slaves before the war." See also "At It Again," *Chicago Tribune,* July 17, 1877, p. 1. The *Tribune* did print one paragraph, without comment, from the *London Telegraph* that described tortures and murders of Turks ("Outrages upon Mussulmans in Bulgaria," *Chicago Tribune,* August 21, 1879, p. 8).

61. "The Exodus of the Turk," *New York Times,* January 22, 1878, p. 4.

62. [No title], *New York Times,* January 26, 1878, p. 4.

63. "The Mobility of Asiatics," *Littell's Living Age* 136, no. 1763 (March 30, 1878): 821–23.

64. Thompson told the audience that all the religious groups hated each other and that Muslims were taught in school that they must persecute Christians. "Turkish Cruelties," *New York Observer* 55, no. 4 (January 25, 1877): 30; "American Sympathy," *New York Observer* 55, no. 6 (February 8, 1877): 42; "Sympathy with the Bulgarians," *New York Evangelist* 48, no. 6 (February 8, 1877): 4; "General Miscellany: The Bulgarian Atrocities," *New York Times,* January 31, 1877, p. 2.

65. As seen in the major newspapers and magazines cited below, the local newspapers in NewspaperARCHIVE.com, and the American Periodical Series. Only those newspapers and magazines that published in both periods were compared. It proved impossible to make an exact comparison, because all the smaller papers covered the Armenians, but many said nothing on the Bulgarians. In addition, most of the articles on Bulgaria in the main newspapers mentioned only the Russo-Turkish War, not atrocities. Ten times is a very conservative estimate. My impression is that twenty or thirty times might be accurate.

66. The Library of Congress ("Bulgaria History Uprising 1876") lists no American books on the topic in the period, although British books and pamphlets such as those by Gladstone were surely seen. One American journalist was prominent in Liberal press reporting on Bulgaria: Januarius Aloysius MacGahan, *The Turkish Atrocities in Bulgaria: Letters of the Special Commissioner of the "Daily News."* Of course, many later books of the missionary establishment (particularly those written on the Armenian Troubles) mentioned the Bulgarian Horrors, even if only in passing, as an example of Turkish evil. For an official ABCFM example, see David Brewer Eddy, *What Next in Turkey: Glimpses of the American Board's Work in the Near East,* p. 20.

67. One, from H. J. Van Lennep, is cited below in the section "The Missionaries and the Bulgarians" (see also note 87 below). For another of the few, see the article by an unnamed missionary who served in Bulgaria, "What the Missionaries Think," *New York Observer* 54, no. 52 (December 28, 1876): 415. The author believed the Turks should be evicted from Europe but gave no evidence of things he had seen himself. Perhaps he was in fact an ex-missionary in Bulgaria.

68. "Bulgaria was entered in 1857. This field has been a very difficult one and results have not been as encouraging as in the other missions of the Society" (Stephen L. Baldwin, D.D., *Foreign Missions of the Protestant Churches* [New York: Eaton and Mains, 1900], p. 178).

69. Edirne was also a station, considered part of the European Turkey Mission. Another minister, nominally attached to the station, translated the Bible into Bulgarian in Istanbul (Rufus Anderson, *History of the Missions of the American Board of Commissioners for Foreign Missions to the Oriental Churches*, 2 vols. [Boston: Congregational Publishing Society, 1872], chapter 33). These books were seen on the Project Gutenberg website (www.gutenberg.org), which gives no page numbers. Tatyana Nestorova, *American Missionaries among the Bulgarians (1858–1912)*, pp. 28–29, gives slightly different figures: four stations with seven missionaries, three of them ordained, in 1870. The slight difference changes none of the conclusions presented here. The Nestorova book is the basic text on the ABCFM in Bulgaria. The board later committed more resources to Bulgaria. See William Webster Hall, *Puritans in the Balkans: The American Board Mission in Bulgaria, 1878–1918*.

70. Edwin Munsell Bliss, *The Encyclopedia of Missions*, vol. 1, p. 76. The numbers in all categories were constantly increasing.

71. "The Principle of Liberty," *Zion's Herald* 54, no. 21 (May 24, 1877): 164.

72. "The Turks in Europe," *Christian Advocate* 51, no. 14 (April 6, 1876): 108.

73. "Editorial Notes," *New York Evangelist* 47, no. 26 (June 29, 1876): 4.

74. See, for example, George M. Towle, "The Christian Subjects of the Sultan," *Independent* 28, no. 1415 (January 13, 1876): 1–2; "The Bulgarian Massacres," *Unitarian Review and Religious Magazine* 6, no. 4 (October 1876): 440–41; "Turkish Repentance and Promises," *New York Evangelist* 47, no. 52 (December 28, 1876): 4; and the Reverend Dorus Clark, "The Fate of Turkey," *Advocate of Peace* 8, no. 3 (March 1877): 19.

75. "Results of the Struggle," *Independent* 30, no. 1522 (January 31, 1877): 16.

76. "The Atrocities in Bulgaria," *New York Evangelist* 47, no. 34 (August 24, 1876): 7. See also "The Atrocities in Bulgaria," *New York Observer* 47, no. 37 (September 14, 1876): 7; "The Turkish Atrocities," *New York Observer* 54, no. 34 (August 24, 1876): 266; and [no title], *Zion's Herald* 53, no. 34 (August 24, 1876): 268. "The Bulgarian Sufferers," *New York Observer* 54, no. 47 (November 23, 1876): 374, quoted the *Daily News* on Bulgarian suffering and included a request for funds to be sent to the American Board for relief, a foretaste of what was to come.

77. See, for example, "The Servian War," *New York Observer* 54, no. 29 (July 20, 1876): 231; "Turkish Atrocities," *New York Observer* 54, no. 33 (August 17, 1876): 258; and "Turkish Atrocities," *Independent* 28, no. 1450 (September 14, 1876): 16.

78. "Our Missionaries in Turkey," *New York Observer* 54, no. 47 (November 23, 1876): 370.

79. Such so-called statistics were featured in many articles. See, for example, "The Russo-Turkish War: How the War Began," *Christian Union* 15, no. 19 (May 9, 1877): 419–20. Based on the articles, Bulgarian villages must have been large indeed, if thousands had been killed in each. Inaccuracies went beyond

contemporary events. One 1976 article, for example, depicted the Bulgarians as religiously ruled by the Greek Orthodox Church of Istanbul, when in fact an autocephalous Bulgarian church had been allowed six years before ("The Nationalities of European Turkey," *Christian Advocate* 51, no. 29 [July 20, 1876]: 228). It also provided wholly fanciful statistics on population. See also "The Turkish Empire in the Light of Present Events," *Christian Advocate* 51, no. 32 (August 10, 1876): 252.

80. "T. L. B.," "A Missionary's View of the Eastern Question," *New York Observer* 55, no. 1 (January 4, 1877): 7. "T. L. B." was Theodore L. Byington (1831–88), a Presbyterian minister and American Board missionary in Bulgaria from 1858 to 1867 or 1868 (sources differ). He became a pastor in New Jersey but rejoined the board in 1874, serving as editor of a weekly missionary newspaper in Bulgarian until 1885. See also "The Russo-Turkish War: How the War Began," *Christian Union* 15, no. 19 (May 9, 1877): 419–20; and "Causes of the Eastern War," *Messenger* 46, no. 19 (May 9, 1877): 1.

     One article called the Russian good intentions into question, blaming them for starting the troubles by their treatment of the Circassians, who took their revenge on the Bulgarians (Cyrus Hamlin, "Crescent and Cross," *Christian Union* 14, no. 14 [October 4, 1876]: 269–70). Many articles and letters to the editor in various newspapers and magazines heatedly criticized Hamlin for this article. See, for example, "The Turk and His Friends," *Christian Advocate* 53, no. 3 (January 17, 1878): 33–34. At least one article defended his view: the Reverend R. Wheatley, "The Unspeakable Turk!" *Christian Advocate* 27, no. 49 (December 6, 1877): 769. The best source on Cyrus Hamlin is his own book *Among the Turks*.

81. H. J. Van Lennep, "Religious Toleration in Turkey," *New York Observer* 54, no. 48 (November 30, 1876): 378. See also "Christian Sufferers by Turkish Cruelty," *New York Observer* 55, no. 5 (February 1, 1877): 34; and "How Will It End?" *Independent* 29, no. 1504 (September 27, 1877): 17.

82. "Turkish Atrocities," *Independent* 28, no. 1450 (September 14, 1876): 16; "A Bad Predicament," *Zion's Herald* 53, no. 45 (November 9, 1876): 356.

83. J. F. Riggs, "The Bulgarians," *New York Evangelist* 47, no. 40 (October 5, 1876): 2. The byline "J. F. Riggs of Constantinople" is deceptive. Riggs (1852–1918) was the son of the missionary Elias Riggs but had left Istanbul in 1874 to study and become a Presbyterian pastor in New Jersey. See also "The Missionary Opportunity in Broken Turkey," *Christian Advocate* 53, no. 8 (February 21, 1878): 120A; and "Missions," *Independent* 31, no. 1570 (January 2, 1879): 10.

84. See, for example, "Islam," *Methodist Quarterly Review* 30 (January 1878): 4–26; "Religious Intelligence: The State of the Mohammedan Religion," *Independent* 30, no. 1535 (May 2, 1878): 12; and "Islam and the Ottoman Empire," *International Review* 4 (November 1877): 790–809 (no author was given, but the article was fairly obviously written by a clergyman).

85. "Horrors and Miseries of War," *New York Evangelist* 48, no. 37 (September 13, 1877): 6. See also "The War in the East," *Independent* 29, no. 1499 (August 23, 1877): 17; and "Turcomania," *Zion's Herald* 53, no. 40 (October 5, 1876): 316, which castigated those who defended the Turks.

86. "Letters from Bulgaria (Rev. E. F. Lounsbury)," *Christian Advocate* 52, no. 35 (August 30, 1877): 548.

87. H. J. Van-Lennep [*sic*], "Turkish Barbarity," *New York Evangelist* 47, no. 39 (September 28, 1876): 2. See also H. J. Van Lennep, "The Turks Once More," *New York Evangelist* 48, no. 1 (January 4, 1877): 2. Henry John Van Lennep (1815–89) was a Congregationalist minister and missionary in the Ottoman Empire from 1839 to 1869. Concerning the Bulgarian revolution, at least one missionary, while criticizing the Turks, felt that the Bulgarian revolutionaries were little better ("The Troubles in Bulgaria," *New York Observer* 47, no. 8 [February 24, 1876]: 2). The missionary was not identified, except to say that he sent his letter from Eski Zagra.

88. "The Eastern Question," *National Repository* 3 (March 1878): 265. For an excellent example of the racism of the time and the low status ascribed to the Turks by the racists, see "Notes on the Turk," *Eclectic Magazine of Foreign Literature* 25, no. 2 (February 1877): 182–92.

89. "The Cross and the Crescent," *Messenger* 45, no. 49 (December 6, 1876): 4. This publication, from New Martinsville, West Virginia, was probably not representative of general religious sentiment.

Chapter 7, Americans and Armenians

1. NewspaperARCHIVE.com returns 16,077 results for the search "Armenia or Armenians" between 1894 and 1896. Many, of course, are duplicates, especially of Associated Press articles, but the collection does not contain the majority of American newspapers.

2. The standard history of the early days of the Armenian revolutionary movements is Louise Nalbandian, *The Armenian Revolutionary Movement.* See also Hratch Dasnabedian, *History of the Armenian Revolution Federation;* Hratch Dasnabedian, "The Hnchakian Party," trans. Mariné A. Arakelians, *Armenian Review* 41, no. 4 (Winter 1988): 22; Anahide Ter Minassian, *Nationalism and Socialism in the Armenian Revolutionary Movement;* Kamuran Gürün, *The Armenian File;* Dikran Mesrob Kaligian, "The Armenian Revolutionary Federation under Ottoman Constitutional Rule, 1908–1914" (Ph.D. dissertation, Boston College, 2003); Esat Uras, *The Armenians in History and the Armenian Question;* and Hüseyin Nazım Paşa, *Ermeni Olayları Tarihi.*

3. Nalbandian, *The Armenian Revolutionary Movement,* p. 110.

4. Quoted in Dasnabedian, "The Hnchakian Party," p. 22.

5. Their *Party Manifesto* declared the Hunchaks' aim: to "eliminate the most harmful Turkish and Armenian individuals within the government, eliminate the spies, the traitors" (quoted in ibid., p. 22). One party branch was specifically charged with terrorism.

6. The organization was first called the Federation of Armenian Revolutionaries, later the Armenian Revolutionary Federation. No one is sure of the exact date of its founding. Its first party congress was held in Tiflis in 1892.

7. Hratch Dasnabedian, *History of the Armenian Revolution Federation, Dashnaktsutiun,* pp. 31–35.

8. Nalbandian, *The Armenian Revolutionary Movement,* p. 156.

9. Another party, the Armenakans, was also involved. See Justin McCarthy, Esat Arslan, Cemalettin Taşkıran, and Ömer Turan, *The Armenian Rebellion at Van,* pp. 41–42, 60.

10. Aghassi, *Zeïtoun depuis les origines jusqu'à l'insurrection de 1895,* p. 306, quoted in Gürün, *The Armenian File,* p. 153.

11. Gürün, *The Armenian File,* p. 148.

12. Ambassador Currie, quoted in Gürün, *The Armenian File,* p. 145.

13. Accounts of the Ottoman Bank seizure, like all the other events of the Armenian Troubles, have varied greatly, depending on the source. This version has been taken from British diplomatic correspondence (FO 424/188, Herbert to Salisbury, Therapia, August 27, 1896, Herbert to Salisbury, Constantinople, August 27, 1896). It must be understood that the British chargé d'affaires, Michael H. Herbert, was distinctly pro-Armenian although aghast at the bank occupation, and this colored his views.

14. Herbert stated that the Armenians were undoubtedly the original aggressors (FO 424/188, Herbert to Salisbury, Therapia, September 9, 1896). See also "Fanatics in Istanbul" (from the *London Post*), *New York Times,* October 3, 1895, p. 1.

15. FO 424/188, Herbert to Salisbury, Therapia, August 30, 1896.

16. FO 424/188, Herbert to Salisbury, Therapia, September 2, 1896.

17. McCarthy et al., *The Armenian Rebellion at Van,* pp. 60–68.

18. The Sasun and Zeytun events are described quite differently in various books. See Dasnabedian, "The Hnchakian Party," pp. 27–30; Gürün, *The Armenian File,* pp. 137–54; Richard G. Hovannisian, "The Armenian Question in the Ottoman Empire, 1876–1914," in his book *The Armenian People,* pp. 218–26; Justin McCarthy, *Death and Exile: The Ethnic Cleansing of Ottoman Muslims;* Salahi Sonyel, *The Ottoman Armenians,* pp. 117–98; Dasnabedian, "The Hnchakian Party," pp. 27–30.

19. Cyrus Hamlin was no friend of the Ottomans (as shown below), but he accurately reported the Hunchak plan as attacking Muslims in the hope of drawing reprisals that would draw in Europeans (William L. Langer, *The Diplomacy of Imperialism,* pp. 157–58). Langer cites Hamlin's original comments in the *Boston Congregationalist,* December 23, 1893.

20. See the section "The Commission of Investigation" below.

21. Quoted in Guenter Lewy, *The Armenian Massacres in Ottoman Turkey,* p. 26.

22. Gürün (*The Armenian File,* pp. 161–62) gives the figure of 20,000, based on Ottoman statistics, and also cites a number of other estimates. Salahi Sonyel (*The Ottoman Armenians,* pp. 171–72) lists many statistics, including others who estimated 20,000.

23. "Auricular confession; absolution from sin by the priest; penance; transubstantiation; baptismal regeneration; intercession of the saints and angels; worship of the material cross, of relics, and of pictures; and prayers for the dead; all belong as much to the Armenian Church as to the Roman" (H. G. O. Dwight, *Christianity in Turkey,* p. 7).

24. Ottoman statistics listed 66,000 Ottoman subject Protestants in the empire just before World War I. Most of these were Armenians. Malachia Ormanian (*The Church of Armenia* [French edition 1910], p. 209), the former Armenian patriarch of Constantinople, gave a figure of 49,900 for all Protestant Armenians in the world, but these were extremely unreliable rough estimates. Some Orthodox and even the occasional Muslim or Jew did convert to Protestantism. The numbers were so small, however, that missionary publications trumpeted each convert.

25. Instances of the earlier confidence are too numerous to cite here, but see, for example, "Encouraging Results," *Baptist Missionary Magazine* 26, no. 11 (November 1846): 337–40; "The Evangelical Armenians of Turkey, the Reformers of the East," *Christian Review* 95 (January 1859): 1–18; "A Half Century of Foreign Missions," *New Englander* 18, no. 71 (August 1860): 711–15; and "Armenia and the Armenians," *New Englander* 33, no. 126 (January 1874): 1–14. Missionary organs, of course, were most triumphant in their predictions. See "Miscellany," *Missionary Magazine* 33, no. 10 (October 1853): 430–31. "Miscellany," *Missionary Magazine* 34, no. 3 (March 1854): 93–94; "Progress of the Gospel in Turkey," *Missionary Magazine* 37, no. 4 (April 1857): 123–24; and "Mission Work in Turkey," *Missionary Magazine* 47, no. 7 (July 1867): 211–16.

26. Robert L. Daniel, *American Philanthropy in the Near East, 1820–1960*, p. 94, which offers detailed statistics on American Board missionaries and school. Uygur Kocabaşoğlu (*Kendi Belgeleriyle Anadolu'daki Amerika: 19 Yüzyılda Osmanlı İmparatoluğu'ndaki American Misyoner Okulları*, pp. 160–62) also gives detailed tables of the schools and students. Note that student numbers vary slightly in various sources. See also William Ellsworth Strong, *The Story of the American Board*, pp. 496–97.

27. Foreign Missions Conference of North America, Committee of Reference and Counsel, *World Statistics of Christian Missions*, p. 81.

28. "Stories of Wrong," *Dallas News*, December 17, 1894, p. 1; "Armenia and the Sultan," *New York Times*, December 17, 1894. The story of Armenians chasing Kurds who had taken their sheep seems to have originated from an Armenian in Bitlis, if newspaper accounts can be believed. The *New York Times* (November 17, 1894) attributed the story to that source and obviously accepted it as true without any other evidence. On American Board meetings on Armenians, see "The Debt Cancelled," *Lima [Ohio] Times-Democrat*, October 8, 1896, p. 1.

Before the beginning of the Armenian Troubles, Turks were already being accused, albeit less often, of routinely committing crimes against Christians: "Advices from Constantinople show it is of common occurrence for the Turks to kidnap Christian girls and dispose of them to the owners of harems" ("Kidnaped by Turks," *Dallas News*, February 11, 1893, p. 2). The article gave no indication of who provided the "advices."

The position of the American Board was duplicitous. A year after the board propaganda began, its president, the Reverend Dr. Richard S. Storrs, was declaring that the board had not spoken out on the issue: "Our Boston secretaries have said nothing that would give offense [to the Turks]." He said the board had remained silent because it feared its missionaries would suffer. The secretaries (mission heads) themselves might not have spoken out, but the board surely sent out press releases against the Turks ("Persecution Must Stop," *New York Times,* November 18, 1895, p. 5).

29. "The Armenian Agitation," *New York Times,* December 21, 1894, p. 5. The Evangelical Alliance passed another resolution at a meeting in September 1894 ("Evangelists against Turkey," *New York Times,* October 1, 1895, p. 1). The head of the organization, Dr. William Ellsworth Strong, stated, "The most reliable source of information regarding the Armenian outrages was through the missionaries" ("Stay the Turk's Hand," *Washington Post,* December 24, 1894, p. 6).

30. "Baptist Missionary Union," *New York Times,* May 30, 1895, p. 10.

31. These resolutions are far too numerous to list. See, for example, "Demand Intervention in Turkey," *Washington Post,* January 13, 1896, p. 4; "An Earnest Appeal for Relief: Missionary Societies Adopt Resolutions Concerning Suffering Armenians," *Washington Post,* January 18, 1896, p. 3; and "Ask the President to Intervene," *Chicago Tribune,* November 19, 1895, p. 2.

32. "Bishops Appeal to President," *Washington Post,* February 2, 1896, p. 1.

33. To give some idea of the scope, these newspapers included the *New York Times, Galveston Daily News, Lincoln [Nebr.] Evening News, Dallas Daily News, Racine [Wisc.] Daily Journal,* and *Salem [Ohio] Daily News.*

34. "Armenia and the Sultan," *New York Times,* December 17, 1894, p. 5.

35. For example, "Assistance to Armenians," *New York Times,* August 20, 1895, p. 5; "Americans Imprisoned in Turkey," *New York Times,* September 12, 1894, p. 4; "Armenians in Distress," *New York Times,* September 14, 1895, p. 5; "Aid Must Be Sent," *Jeffersonian,* December 12, 1895, p. 2; "Missionaries' Stories," *Syracuse [N.Y.] Standard,* November 26, 1895, p. 1; "Marash Riots," *Syracuse [N.Y.] Standard,* November 28, 1895, p. 1; "Foreign!" *Hornellsville [N.Y.] Weekly Tribune,* February 7, 1896, p. 1; and "Islam or Death," *Newark [N.J.] Daily Advocate,* January 14, 1896, p. 1. Most of these articles came from the American Board, forwarded by the Associated Press.

    Other religious publications featured in the news reported in the mainstream press. The *Independent,* a religious newspaper with ties to the Congregationalist Church, was quoted verbatim in newspapers. The sources, although identified only as "trustworthy," were missionary reports. They were printed as fact without any attempt to verify their allegations. See, for example, "Kurds and Christians," *New York Times,* January 16, 1895, p. 9. This article, which dealt with abuses in tax collection, naturally concerned only Armenians who suffered from taxes, even though difficulties with the tax collector were always a problem for all inhabitants, Muslim and Christian alike. The *Times* included the subheadline "Christians Were Bought and Sold" even though the article said nothing about this untrue assertion. See also "Is It Conflict or Massacre?" *New York Times,* November 27, 1895, p. 15.

36. The articles were of varying length, depending on how much of Judson's press release was quoted. For example, "Horrible Massacres at Marash," *Williamsport [Pa.] Daily Gazette and Bulletin,* November 28, 1895, p. 1; "Fooled by the Sultan," *Salem [Ohio] Daily News,* November 28, 1895, p. 1; and "Unsafe for Christians to

Appear in the Streets of Turkish Villages," *Fort Wayne [Ind.] Gazette,* November 30, 1895, p. 1.

37. "War on Christianity," *Salem [Ohio] Daily News,* December 3, 1895, p. 1 (also in the *Warren [Pa.] Evening Democrat, Fort Wayne [Ind.] Gazette,* and other papers).

38. "Stories of Wrong," *Dallas News,* December 17, 1894, p. 1; "Armenia and the Sultan," *New York Times,* December 17, 1894, p. 5. The source of the story was given as the American Board in other newspapers.

39. See, for example, "Fifteen Thousand Armenians Slain," *Chicago Tribune,* January 2, 1895, p. 7: "Boston, Mass., Jan. 1.—A letter just received in this city from a point near the seat of the recent outrages in Eastern Turkey places the number of slaughtered Armenians at fully 15,000."

40. See, for example, "Massacre of the Armenians," *New York Times,* November 27, 1894, p. 5. From the strange description of the cause of cholera (a "stench") it is obvious that the writer was not a doctor. The American Board continued to quote the figure of six thousand to ten thousand Sasun dead that appeared in the article: "Died for His Religion's Sake," *New York Times,* December 27, 1895, p. 5.

41. See, for example, "Figures for Harpoot Province," *Washington Post,* February 22, 1896, p. 2; and "Danger at Hadjin," *Philadelphia Public Ledger,* December 25, 1895, p. 1.

42. "Armenians Sad Plight," *New York Times,* November 23, 1895, p. 9.

43. *New York Times,* December 22, 1895, p. 6.

44. "A Bath of Blood," *Atlanta Constitution,* December 30, 1895, p. 1. Although the American clergy were most prominently featured, American newspapers also quoted from British clergymen and missionaries. This was especially true of articles drawn from the British press.

45. The missionary sources were often not directly identified but the stories clearly came from missionaries (and occasionally Armenians), based on the nature of the information and the regions they came from, where the only American sources were missionaries. Sometimes the articles identified the missionary sources. See, for example, "Massacres in Armenia," *Dallas News,* December 19, 1896, p. 9. The U.S. State Department, in a complete break with usual practice, made such consular reports available to newspapers if the reports castigated the Turks. This transmission of missionary reports and their release to the press occurred even more frequently during World War I, showing the position of the American government and the lack of actual observation by its own diplomatic representatives.

46. "Conditions of Armenia," *Dallas News,* February 20, 1895, p. 6.

47. All distance references are by main roads at the time.

48. "Massacres of Armenians," *New York Times,* November 17, 1894, p. 1; "Armenians Killed," *Dallas News,* September 28, 1895, p. 3. See also "Distress in Armenia," *Dallas News,* December 10, 1895, p. 3.

49. "Report 2,000 Massacred at Sassun," *Chicago Tribune,* November 19, 1894, p. 2.

50. "The Destitution at Erzuroum," *New York Times,* December 6, 1895, p. 5. The information in *London Times* and *London Daily News* articles, excerpted or copied in American newspapers, allegedly often came from Istanbul to Vienna by wire, where

it was seen by the *Times* or *Daily News* journalists. Telegrams to Vienna and to London presumably would have had to pass the same censorship, so why was the information not sent directly to London? It is more than possible that in reality the information came from Armenian groups in Istanbul and/or Vienna. See "The Crisis Is at Hand," *Oshkosh [Wisc.] Daily Northwestern,* December 12, 1895, p. 1.

51. [No title], *New York Times,* January 5, 1895, p. 5. The correspondent claimed that twenty-nine Congregational churches in Armenia had been closed. The claim was later discredited, which the *Times* briefly mentioned in an unrelated article. Even such a limited retraction was not a common occurrence ("Armenian Fugitives Killed," *New York Times,* January 8, 1895, p. 5).

52. "Cruelty of the Turks," *Washington Post,* January 2, 1895.

53. See, for example, *New York Times,* January 30, 1896, p. 5.

54. "To Kill All Christians," *Decatur [Ill.] Review,* November 10, 1895, p. 1. The article, datelined Worchester, Massachusetts, only identified the Hunchaks as "the leading Armenian revolutionists in America."

55. For example, a nearly full-page article in the *New York Times* by Herant Mesrob Kiretchjian quoted Gladstone, Canon Maccoll, and others; none of them, including Kiretchjian, had seen any of the events they described. Yet Kiretchjian was certain that the sultan had planned all the "unnameable outrages" ("The Armenian Situation," September 1, 1895, p. 20).

56. See, for example, "Ran a Turkish Gauntlet," *New York Times,* January 2, 1896, p. 5.

57. "Armenians in New York Excited," *New York Times,* November 18, 1894, p. 5.

58. See, for example, two articles in the *New York Times* on December 27, 1895: "How the Armenians Took Zeitoun" and "Hadjin, Zeitoun, Aintab." Both were on a page dedicated to Zeytun. The latter article is particularly suspect. The author of the quotations in the article, supposedly an Armenian priest, did not seem to know whether he was writing from Zeytun or Haçin. None of the articles of this type stated how the letters escaped the Ottoman military cordon around the region.

59. See, for example, "Armenians in New York Excited," *New York Times,* November 18, 1894, p. 5.

60. The general manager of the Associated Press from 1893 to 1921 was Melville E. Stone, the son of a Methodist minister.

61. "Suffering in Armenia," *New York Times,* February 4, 1896, p. 3: "The following is a translation of a letter received at Constantinople from a trustworthy source at Caesaria, and handed to the United Press correspondent at Constantinople." *Providence [R.I.] Journal,* November 11, 1895, p. 1: "The European manager of the United Press has sent from Constantinople, under date of November 18, a statement concerning the recent massacres in Armenia, presented by an Armenian Christian man, and believed to be impartial." "Turks Villainy," *Syracuse [N.Y.] Standard,* February 4, 1896, p. 1: "London, Jan. 25—(Correspondence of the United Press). The following is a translation of a letter received at Constantinople from a trustworthy source in Caesaria." The *New York Tribune* printed an article from London citing a United Press representative in Istanbul as its source ("Terror Reigns in Armenia,"

November 17, 1895, p. 1). "Over 13,000 Killed," *New York Sun,* November 28, 1895, p. 1 (a United Press article). The *Sun* printed more United Press articles than the other newspapers seen for this study.

62. I have not found Associated Press or United Press archives. The proof that the stories came from the AP was compiled by the laborious process of comparing the stories in all the main newspapers considered here and in the smaller cities' papers, as contained in NewspaperARCHIVE.com. Many of the smaller newspapers identified the AP stories. Some even proudly stated that all their national and foreign news came from the AP. For example, in large type right under its masthead on page 1 the *Davenport [Iowa] Leader* carried the line "Telegraph Reports of the Associated Press to 4 P.M." The *Oakland Tribune* was especially assiduous in identifying the Associated Press stories (virtually all the stories the paper printed on the Ottoman Empire).

Articles from the smaller cities' newspapers sometimes have been cited here, even when the same articles also appeared in the larger cities, in order to show the extent of the coverage of the stories. For most stories, however, I have cited the major newspapers. They are easier to find and use and often contained more complete Associated Press stories, which the smaller newspapers excerpted. Smaller newspapers are also cited for the more sensational stories that were not published in the main newspapers. See, for example, "Tore Down Our Flag: America's Standard Trampled on by a Turk," *Oakland Tribune,* December 3, 1896, p. 6; see also note 75 below.

63. The *San Francisco Chronicle,* for example, cited AP articles as "Special Despatches to the Chronicle."

64. For an example of the sort of unsubstantiated rumor that the AP correspondent in Istanbul sent as news, see "Turkish Persecution," *Washington Post,* February 24, 1896, p. 4. Not one of the assertions in the article is attributed to an identifiable source; it is simply a set of unsubstantiated allegations.

65. "Sultan Has No Friends," *Oshkosh [Wisc.] Daily Northwestern,* December 4, 1895, p. 1.

66. Ibid. Other newspapers printed this. One excerpted it but still kept the mistake.

67. "Relief for the Armenians," *Reno [Nev.] Weekly Gazette and Stockman,* November 28, 1895, p. 5.

68. "A Reign of Riot," *Oakland Tribune,* October 4, 1895, p. 2. Other newspapers repeated this Associated Press story and other errors, so they were not printer's mistakes.

69. "Sultan's Scheme," *Dallas News,* June 10, 1895, p. 1.

70. "Are Ready to Revolt," *Dallas News,* May 27, 1895, p. 1.

71. "Armenian Outrages," *Galveston Daily News,* February 3, 1895, p. 5. The correspondent's report allegedly came to London in a letter, leaving questions as to how it was delivered from Eastern Anatolia. He gave an inaccurate report on revolutionaries, indicating that he was still in Eastern Anatolia in July 1895 ("Armenia and Turkey," *Galveston Daily News,* July 8, 1895, p. 1). See also "Armenian Plotters Cause Suffering," *Chicago Tribune,* February 3, 1895, p. 2.

72. "Terrible Stories of Cruelty," *New York Times,* March 11, 1895, p. 5. The Associated Press "special correspondent in Armenia" seems to have spent most of his time in the Russian Empire. Some of his reports came from Julfa, on the Russian-Iranian border, even farther away from the Armenian events than Kars, where many British reports originated.

73. "A Bloody Tale Retold," *Warren [Pa.] Evening Democrat,* March 4, 1895, p. 1. See also the correspondent's story ("Armenian Outrages," *Galveston Daily News,* February 3, 1895, p. 5) in which he stated that Armenians had attacked Turks in order to gain reprisals then went on to tell the most scurrilous tales about the Turks and Kurds, such as that they raped all young Armenian women.

74. See, for example, "Word from Armenia," *Oshkosh [Wisc.] Daily Northwestern,* February 4, 1896, p. 2.

75. "Armenia Will Fight," *Fresno [Calif.] Morning Republican,* April 18, 1895, p. 4; also in the *Warren [Pa.] Evening Democrat, Titusville [Pa.] Herald, Fitchburg [Mass.] Daily Sentinel,* and many other smaller city newspapers. Of the major newspapers considered here, only the *Chicago Tribune* printed the story ("News from Abroad," April 18, 1895, p. 7).

76. "Christendom's Shame," *Cedar Rapids [Iowa] Evening Gazette,* June 3, 1896, pp. 4, 6. The subheading of the article read "Facts Are Taken from Cold-Blooded Reports and Are Unimpeachable." Some printings identified Van Meter as author; others mentioned him in the first paragraph then printed the same copy (for example, H. H. Van Meter, "Turkish Atrocities," *Newark [N.J.] Sunday Advocate,* June 7, 1896, p. 2; and H. H. Van Meter, "Turkish Atrocities," *Lima [Ohio] Times-Democrat,* June 10, 1896, p. 2). In another article, Van Meter predicted "universal war" that would soon take place because Britain and others had neglected their duties in the Ottoman Empire ("Danger of Universal War," *Cedar Rapids [Iowa] Evening Gazette,* January 6, 1896, pp. 1, 4; "Danger of a Great War," *Chicago Tribune,* January 6, 1896, p. 2). Understandably, most major newspapers avoided these articles; of the majors considered here, only the *Los Angeles Times* and the *New York Times* ran the first, the *Chicago Tribune* the second. Other somewhat less violent articles by Van Meter were printed in the *New York Times:* "United States Insulted," June 3, 1896, p. 8, and "Devils in Human Form," November 16, 1896, p. 4.

77. "For Warfare on Turkey: Uncle Sam Proposes to Bring the Sultan to Terms," *Chicago Tribune,* January 26, 1896, p. 9, repeating a long article from the *New York World.*

78. For one of the extremely rare cases in which any American newspaper quoted from a non-Liberal London newspaper, see "Fanatics in Istanbul," *New York Times,* October 3, 1895, p. 1, which quotes from the *London Post.* The article described Armenian attacks on the Ministry of Police, law courts, and other places in Istanbul. The editor was not satisfied with the honest description given and thus included a subheadline, which read "Moslems Eager to Kill Christians," although the article mentioned nothing like that.

79. See "Fresh Armenian Outrages," *Dallas News,* May 8, 1895, p. 3. For a prime example of the news from British sources, see "10,000 Lives Taken," *New York Sun,*

November 7, 1895; and "Puppets of the Sultan," *New York Sun,* November 11, 1895, p. 1 (two long articles that quoted the *London Times, Standard, Daily News,* and others). The British sources said that the sultan, fearing assassination, promised "to proclaim a constitution" (a constitution already existed), that the sultan had found a letter on his table threatening assassination if he did not abdicate, that the sultan had ordered the extermination of all Armenians, that Austria, with British consent, was going to intervene in the Ottoman Empire, and that Britain was about to join the Triple Alliance because of Ottoman actions.

80. "Sacked by Turks," *Chicago Tribune,* September 10, 1895, p. 2. Telegraph connections from Sasun to Kars were unavailable; in any case, who would have sent the telegrams through the Ottoman governmental system?

81. "Armenian Fakes Exposed," *Washington Post,* March 8, 1895, p. 4.

82. "The Armenian Troubles: An Intimation That Reports Are Made for Political Effect," *New York Times,* March 30, 1895, p. 5. As an example of probably invented news, the *London Times* (excerpted in American newspapers) quoted a wildly improbable "statement of a Kurd" who described various bloody acts. The evidence came from "a competent and trustworthy man" ("Armenian Atrocities," *Fresno [Calif.] Morning Republican,* March 29, 1895, p. 4).

83. "Turkey," *Dallas News,* December 12, 1895, p. 6. The article stated that Armenians were forming revolutionary parties in reaction to the recent violence in Anatolia, the exact opposite of the truth, for the violence had been in reaction to the actions of the preexisting revolutionaries. France, Germany, Great Britain, and other European powers operated their own post offices and mail in the Ottoman Empire. The service was curtailed in 1909 and abolished at the start of World War I.

84. Sir Ellis Ashmead Bartlett, M.P., challenged the London papers to make available the telegrams supposedly received from the scenes of massacres. He does not seem to have received an answer to his challenge ("About Armenian Atrocities," *New York Times,* March 12, 1895, p. 5; a very small notice).

85. "More Armenians Slaughtered," *Dallas News,* September 26, 1896, p. 4. Some missionary property was burned. The *Daily News* articles depended on all the unnamed sources described above. See, for examples, articles in the *San Francisco Chronicle:* "Slaughter of the Armenians," December 17, 1895, p. 3; "More of Turkey's Dilatory Tactics," November 29, 1895, p. 1; and "Preparing for More Bloodshed," November 23, 1895, p. 2.

86. On one *Daily News* article, Herbert commented that there was "not a word of truth in the story" (FO 424/188, Herbert to Salisbury, Constantinople, September 5, 1896). On false stories in the *Daily News,* see also "No Massacre at Marsovan," *Washington Post,* February 28, 1896, p. 2.

87. "Advices to London Papers," *Dallas News,* December 16, 1895, p. 7. The same quotation was printed in other papers without reference to the *Daily News.* The American newspapers abounded with questionable reports from the *Daily News.* For example, it stated that most of the Armenian priests in and around Harput (the city and fifty-three villages) had been tortured and killed because they would not accept Islam ([no title], *New York Times,* December 17, 1895, p. 5). It reported that

Armenians had been massacred in Merzifon in February 1896 ("Marsovan's Armenians Killed," *New York Times,* February 27, 1896, p. 5), but the French consul who
investigated the claims on the scene and the American ambassador reported that
no massacre had occurred ("Marsovan Had No Massacre," *New York Times,* February 28, 1896, p. 5). The *New York Times* (excerpting from the *London Daily News*)
reported that "a secret Armenian committee at Bitlis" was organizing a mass uprising of 200,000 Armenians in the spring of 1896. The contradictions between this
and their other articles seemed not to bother the *Daily News* or the *New York
Times.* A number of similar articles predicted various revolts of Armenians and
others, particularly in Syria.

88. The voluminous reports in FO 195 never mentioned such an occurrence. English
commentators gave a very different view, although they were very seldom read in
America. One exception was the writer who provided a realistic assessment of the
Armenian place in the Troubles, blaming the Armenian agitators and revolutionaries for much of what occurred: Walter B. Harris, "An Unbiased View of the Armenian Question," *Eclectic Magazine of Foreign Literature* 62, no. 5 (November 1895):
641–49 (from *Blackwood's Magazine*). Harris was a correspondent for the *Times* of
London.

89. The *New York Sun* also printed at least one short article from Istanbul telling of
Armenian attacks on Turks ("Massacre in Erzeroum," November 2, 1895, p. 1) and
a few of the Ottoman Embassy statements. Despite its title, the article said nothing about a "massacre in Erzeroum." The *New York Times* is an example of the
changes that the news underwent as the missionary campaign gathered steam.
Although the *Times* was not the national newspaper it was later to become, it
contained more foreign news than other papers in the 1890s. Its coverage of the
Armenian Troubles began with a much more evenhanded approach than was
seen elsewhere. When the 1894 Troubles started, the *Times* was properly identifying Armenian rebels as the source of the problems in Anatolia (even though it
showed great sympathy for the Armenians) and suggesting that the reported number of Armenian sufferers was greatly exaggerated. The *Times* printed some reports
from the Ottoman embassy along with reports from the missionary establishment. Then the mass meetings in churches and public halls began to arouse public
sentiment. The *Times* started to publish the same sort of unverifiable stories that
were appearing elsewhere. It still occasionally printed statements from the Ottoman Embassy, but as short (often only one paragraph) insertions at the bottom of
pages. See, for example, "Armenians Attack Gendarmes," *New York Times,* November 5, 1895, p. 5 (forty-four words); "Turkey and Armenians," *New York Times,* January 6, 1895, p. 5 (three short paragraphs); "Turks and Armenians at War," *New
York Times,* October 30, 1895, p. 5; and "Charges against Armenians," *New York
Times,* December 2, 1895, p. 2 (three short paragraphs). Massacre stories, in contrast, were given headlines and prominent placement. Each one of a number of
New York Times articles describing massacres of Armenians was as long as all the
printed press releases from the Turkish embassy together. See, for example, "Slain
by Turkish Mobs," *New York Times,* December 2, 1895, p. 1 (twenty-seven mainly

long paragraphs from the Armenian patriarch, whose only sources were unnamed Armenians of Erzincan).

90. The *Portland Oregonian* even printed a page-1 headline, "Armenians to Blame," on November 15, 1895. The headlines on the other days, however, laid all blame on the Muslims.

91. For example, in the *New York Times,* see "Turkey's Ruling Terror," November 15, 1895, p. 5; and "Massacre of Armenians," October 29, 1895, p. 5. We know that there were many more press releases than those seen in most papers, because the *Washington Post* uniquely printed many of them.

92. The *Washington Post* ran editorials calling for calm assessment of events before rushing to judgment: "As to Those Turkish Massacres," November 20, 1894, p. 4; and "The Turkish Side of the Affair," January 9, 1895, p. 4. See also "Those Persecuted Martyrs," *Washington Post,* November 24, 1896, p. 6, a decidedly anti-Armenian editorial disguised as a news story.

93. See, for example, the *Washington Post:* "Measures to Restore Order," November 17, 1895, p. 4; "The Turkish Version," December 5, 1895, p. 9; "Official Message from the Porte," January 13, 1896, p. 4; "Outrages in Armenia: Advices to the Turkish Legation," December 20, 1895, p. 11; "Turks Allege an Armenian Plot," January 26, 1895, p. 8; "Turks Worsted by Armenians," October 4, 1894, p. 1; "Ten Villages Revolted," December 6, 1894 (second part), p. 9; and "Armenians Threaten Them," August 16, 1895, p. 1.

94. "Mussulmans Convicted," *Washington Post,* October 1, 1896, p. 9.

95. See, for example, the *Washington Post:* "Armenian Outbreak in Bitlis," October 28, 1895, p. 1; "Is There a Revolt in Armenia?" October 31, 1895, p. 3; and "Armenians on the Offensive," November 5, 1895, p.1.

96. *Washington Post:* "Armenian Patriarch Shot At," April 1, 1894, p. 19; "Armenian Plot Discovered," September 18, 1896, p. 2; "Attack on a Prelate," October 27, 1896, p. 1; "Alleged Turkish Atrocities," February 28, 1895, p. 9; and "Armenians Revolt," October 3, 1895, p. 1.

97. "The Facts about Armenians," *Washington Post,* August 20, 1895, p. 4; "Facts from Armenia at Last," *Washington Post,* January 30, 1896, p. 6. The *Washington Post* offered very interesting articles by F. Hopkinson Smith that were not much seen elsewhere. Smith blamed the revolutionaries and the missionaries for the Armenian Troubles ("The Truth about Armenia," *Washington Post,* November 2, 1896, p. 6). See also the satirical comments in "Those Armenian Victims," *Washington Post,* August 29, 1896, p. 6; "The Truth about Armenia," *Washington Post,* November 22, 1895, p. 6; and "The Post and the Armenians," *Washington Post,* November 30, 1895, p. 6. The *New York Times* ("Defending the Sultan," November 9, 1896, p. 4) editorialized against Smith, stating that he had ignored the supposed fact that "the Turk is at heart a barbarian."

98. The *New York Evening Post* was one of the very few papers that pointed out that the Ottoman government had little control over the Kurdish tribes (quoted in "The Armenian Troubles," *Chautauquan* 22, no. 5 [February 1896]: 618 [no date of publication given for the *Evening Post*]). The occasional article, although highly critical

of the Turks, admitted that Armenians had attacked first, precipitating the events that followed. See, for example, Francis de Pressensé, "The Turks in Armenia," *Chautauquan* 22, no. 5 (February 1896): 591–94. Concerning the riots in Istanbul, the *Philadelphia Record* blamed the Armenian agitators: "Their vaingloriousness and thirst for notoriety are far more despicable than the Turks" (quoted in *Chautauquan* 24, no. 1 [October 1896]: 97 [no article information given]). The Turks even had at least one champion in Memphis, Tennessee (quoted in "The Situation in Turkey," *Chautauquan* 22, no. 4 [January 1896]: 486 [no article information given]):

> There seem to be two sides to the Armenian question and it is possible that the unspeakable Turk is to some extent the victim of prejudice and the false witnessing of martyrs who have not been as free from blame as they should be. The staunchest supporters of the Armenians have admitted that in some notable instances they and not the Turks have been the aggressors and that many indefensible outrages are to be laid at their door. One difficulty in the way of arriving at the true state of the case is in the fact that the Armenian has the ear of Christendom and the Turk has not. It is well to hear the words of the Turk's friends before proceeding to dismember his country and divide it up among the powers of Christendom. One of these friends is the novelist Marion Crawford. In several places in his book [*Constantinople*] he emphasizes his opinion that the Turk is in every respect a finer character than the Armenian, and there is evidence in plenty that the Turk has many robust virtues and that the Armenian, while he may be a "Christian," in the general sense, is by no means a saint.

99. "Attacked by Kurds," *Galveston Daily News,* June 8, 1896, p. 2.
100. "Is It Conflict or Massacre?" *New York Times,* November 27, 1895, p. 15.
101. "The Partition of Turkey," *New York Times,* November 17, 1895, p. 20.
102. "Heedless of Its Fate," *Washington Post,* September 14, 1896, p. 1. The author, the Associated Press correspondent, also wrote that the real number of Armenian dead was 5,000–6,000.
103. "Turkish Crimes: A Tabulated Statement by an Official of the Government," *New York Times,* February 16, 1896, p. 5.
104. The headline writers were different persons, often with different feelings and intentions, than the authors.
105. "Disorder Is Universal: Army and Navy on the Point of Rebellion," *Dallas Morning News,* November 14, 1895, p. 1; "More Bloodletting: Massacre Treads Hard upon Massacre in the Sultan's Dominion," *Dallas News,* November 21, 1895, p. 1.
106. October 5, November 5, 12, and 15, and December 15, 17, and 19, 1895.
107. "Armenian Crimes Exaggerated," *New York Times,* May 22, 1895; "Armenian Outrages: Admiral Kirkland Reports Them as Greatly Exaggerated," *Van Wert [Ohio] Times,* May 31, 1895, p. 1. Both are very short notices.
108. "The Sultan's Responsibility," *New York Times,* June 2, 1895, p. 4.

109. "Kirkland Ordered Home," *New York Times,* October 22, 1895; "Kirkland Returns," *Cedar Rapids [Iowa] Evening Gazette,* November 25, 1895, p. 1. Kirkland was relieved of his command for that and other reasons. Ostensibly the main charge against him was that he had written a letter of congratulation to president Félix Faure of France, a personal friend, on his election. This seems to have been an unlikely cause for such drastic action.

110. See, for example, "Run Riot in Bloodshed," *Chicago Tribune,* August 29, 1896, p. 4; and "Moslem Rule Doomed," *Washington Post,* August 29, 1896, p. 1, which quoted the *London Daily News* as its main source. The *New York Times* grudgingly admitted that "the rioting originated in an organized movement on the part of the Armenian Revolutionary Committee. The revolvers and knives taken from the dead or living Armenians by the police were all of the same pattern" but alleged that the Ottomans used the Armenian attacks as an excuse for massacre ("Turkey Coaxed to Kill," *New York Times,* October 20, 1895, p. 5; "Grand Vizier of Turkey," *New York Times,* October 4, 1895, p. 5 [a dispatch from the London Central News Bureau]). See also [no title], *New York Times,* October 4, 1895, p. 5, which was a report by the Istanbul correspondent of the *Berlin Tagelatt [sic: Tageblatt]* repeating information from British officials, which was given credence because it came from the British.

111. The headline about a murdered father led a story in which an Armenian feared that his family had been murdered, not evidence that this had happened ("His Father Murdered By Turks," *Washington Post,* December 29, 1895, p. 5). Examples of this sort of story are too numerous to list here. See, for example, [no title], *New York Times,* December 22, 1894, p. 5; "The Armenian Agitation," *New York Times,* December 21, 1894, p. 5; "Kurdish Deviltry," *Racine [Wisc.] Daily Journal,* March 18, 1897, p. 6; "Atrocities of the Unspeakable Turk," *Connellsville [Pa.] Courier,* June 12, 1896, p. 7; and H. H. Van Meter, "Turkish Atrocities," *Newark [N.J.] Sunday Advocate,* June 7, 1896, p. 2.

112. *Philadelphia Public Ledger,* December 18, 1895, p. 1. For examples of confused reporting, see also the *Public Ledger* articles on November 12, 20, and 26 and December 9, 1895, or the *Chicago Tribune* articles of the weeks of December 1 and 8, 1895 on the sultan and the European powers.

113. *Philadelphia Public Ledger,* November 16, 1895, p. 1.

114. "Will It Never End?" *Steubenville [Ohio] Daily Herald,* December 16, 1895, p. 2.

115. "The Partition of Turkey," *New York Times,* November 17, 1895, p. 20.

116. "Russia's Coup," *Fort Wayne [Ind.] Weekly Gazette,* January 30, 1896, p. 3. The *Chicago Tribune* vigorously proclaimed the reality of the alliance ("Turkey May Re Allied To Russia," December 30, 1895, p. 4; "Alliance of Russia and Turkey, with France Possibly Included, Would Be a Grave Blow to England and Might Cause Declaration of War," January 24, 1896, p. 1; "Russia Is with Turkey," January 26, 1896, p. 10; "No Check on Turks," February 2, 1896, p. 9). The *Washington Post* correctly printed that this was nonsense ("Russia and the Turk," January 24, 1896, p. 1).

117. "Kurds Going to Stamboul," *New York Times,* December 13, 1895, p. 5.

118. [No title], *Philadelphia Public Ledger,* November 23, 1895, p. 1.

119. For example, "Fear Another Massacre," *New York Times,* November 18, 1895, p. 5. Articles on the supposed compiling of lists of Armenians and marking Christian doors in Istanbul and İzmir in preparation for slaughter appeared in a great number of newspapers on various dates.

120. "Sultan Waiting: Question of Guardianship Not Yet Settled: The Sultan Is in a State of Terror," *Lowell [Mass.] Daily Sun,* December 9, 1895, p. 1.

121. These stories were about civilians, not soldiers, killing Armenians. The complexities of ethnic and tribal relations in the Ottoman Empire, as might be expected, were completely unknown. This led to great problems when the newspapers attempted to write on "Kurdish marauders" or Turkish "bashi bozouks."

122. "Devils in Human Form," *New York Times,* November 16, 1896, p. 5.

123. "An Armenian," *Outlook,* quoted in *Current Literature* 19, no. 2 (February 1896): 130 (no *Outlook* publication information given).

124. "Moslem Promises," *Waterloo [Iowa] Courier,* April 15, 1896, p. 1.

125. "Another Massacre Planned," *New York Times,* September 14, 1896, p. 5, quoting the British newspaper *Plymouth Mercury.* Some other papers ran abbreviated versions.

126. "Horror in Armenia," *Warren [Pa.] Evening Democrat,* March 1, 1895, p. 1.

127. "Tells of the Torture of Armenians," *Chicago Tribune,* December 14, 1894, p. 7.

128. "Universal War," *Cedar Rapids [Iowa] Evening Gazette,* January 6, 1896, p. 4. The article, which was distributed by the Associated Press, quoted H. H. Van Meter (cited above) at great length as a qualified expert. Van Meter seems to have believed that Buddhists lived in Syria, but, to give him the benefit of the doubt, this may have been poor writing. He may have meant that Buddhists would be the next to feel Muslim atrocities after they had killed off the Christians. The article also appeared in the *Salem [Ohio] Daily News, Oakland Tribune, Galveston Daily News, Fort Wayne [Ind.] News*, and other papers. Some of the other papers ran abbreviated versions.

129. "More Massacres," *Fort Wayne [Ind.] Sentinel,* November 14, 1895, p. 1.

130. "Armenian Massacres," *Reno [Nev.] Weekly Gazette and Stockman,* November 14, 1895, p. 6.

131. "Horrible!" *Fort Wayne [Ind.] Sentinel,* November 16, 1895, p. 1. The article did not state that it was from the Associated Press, but it bore the same dateline as identified Associated Press releases: "Constantinople—via Sophia, Bulgaria." No other identifiable sources shared this dateline. The *New York Times* carried a similar report, supposedly on a massacre in "the Syrian District of Gurunden." Gürün was actually nowhere near Syria. The confusion over the name may have come from the Turkish "Gürün'den" (from Gürün) and a reporter who knew no Turkish ("Killing the Armenians," *New York Times,* November 17, 1895, p. 5).

132. Elbert Francis Bacon, "The Turks and the Armenians," *Outlook,* February 8, 1896, p. 242.

133. "Woes of the Armenians," *New York Times,* January 4, 1896, p. 5.

134. The entire district of Arapkır in 1912 had only slightly more than ten thousand Armenians, and the city had only a small part of that number. Of course, the article

may have meant the entire district of Arapkır, although it seemed to be speaking only of the city's Armenians. In that case the entire district had crowded into the city, which seems unlikely.

135. "Ottoman Dynasty: Turkish Rule Has Been the Abomination of Desolation and Nothing Else: Embodiment of Wrong," *New York Commercial Advertiser,* quoted in *Dallas News,* November 25, 1895, p. 4.

136. See, for example, *Dallas News,* January 27, 1895, p. 19, excerpted from *Youth's Companion;* "The Worst Was Not Told," *New York Times,* January 14, 1895, p. 3; and *Advocate of Peace* 12 (December 1895): 281. The *Chicago Tribune* was more temperate in its estimates, contending that only 2.5 million Armenians lived in the Ottoman Empire, still many more than the actual number ("Armenia and Its People," November 21, 1894, p. 6).

137. Justin McCarthy, *Muslims and Minorities,* p. 112. Those who doubt the calculations in my book might consult the best Armenian source on the population, which shows similar population numbers: Raymond H. Kévorkian and Paul B. Paboudjian, *Les Arméniens dans l'Empire Ottoman à la veille du génocide* (Paris: Éditions d'Art et d'Histoire, 1992).

138. The question of how Kurds or Turks supposedly appeared in the area to conduct massacres when all the inhabitants were Armenians does not seem to have bothered the writers and editors.

139. "The Armenian Horrors," *Chicago Tribune,* December 19, 1895, p. 6. See also "An Armenian on Armenia," *Chicago Tribune,* September 5, 1896, p. 10, which also gives the 100,000 figure. The figures were "substantiated" by American Board "missionary circles" in Boston ("Work of Extermination," *Lowell [Mass.] Daily Sun,* December 12, 1895, p. 1).

140. See, for example, Oliver T. Morton, "James Bryce on the Armenian Question," *Dial* 22, no. 256 (February 16, 1897): 114; Carl Albert Paul Rohnbach, "A Contribution to the Armenian Question," *Forum* (January 1908): 489.

141. "The Turks in Crete and Armenia," *Chautauquan* 23, no. 6 (September 1896): 774.

142. "Frightful Atrocities of the Turks against Armenians," *Daily Kennebec [Maine] Journal,* June 8, 1896, p. 3. Van Meter also gave wholly invented "official Turkish statistics" on Armenian deaths. Like the other Van Meter stories, this one was distributed by the Associated Press.

143. "Suffering Armenia," *Oshkosh [Wisc.] Daily Northwestern,* September 16, 1895, p. 5. "Thirteenth century" is also not correct, as various Armenian kingdoms were actually conquered by different Muslim states over a period of centuries. See George A. Bournoutian, *A Concise History of the Armenian Peoples (From Ancient Times to the Present)* (Costa Mesa, Calif.: Mazda, 2002), pp. 9–114, 117–48.

144. "Ottoman Dynasty: Turkish Rule Has Been the Abomination of Desolation and Nothing Else: Embodiment of Wrong," *New York Commercial Advertiser*, quoted in *Dallas News,* November 25, 1895, p. 4.

145. "The Armenian Massacres," *New York Times,* December 16, 1894, p. 16.

146. "The Partition of Turkey," *New York Times,* November 17, 1895, p. 20. The article also stated that Muslims were "the Ottomans," showing a lack of understanding of

the entire Ottoman system. See chapter 6 on the actual events in Bulgaria and the Muslim suffering there.

147. "The Armenian Massacres," *New York Times,* December 16, 1894, p. 16. See also "Armenia and Its People," *Chicago Tribune,* November 21, 1894, p. 6.

148. "The Armenian Horrors," *Chicago Tribune,* December 19, 1895, p. 6.

149. "Howard's Story of Armenia," *Dallas News,* March 20, 1896, p. 2. William W. Howard was a relief agent of the *Christian Herald* and a reporter for the Associated Press. See his small pamphlet *Horrors of Armenia: The Story of an Eye-Witness* (New York: Armenian Relief Association, 1896).

150. "Universal War," *Cedar Rapids [Iowa] Evening Gazette,* January 6, 1896, p. 4.

151. "Persecution Must Stop," *New York Times,* November 18, 1895, p. 5.

152. See, for example, "Armenians with Us," *Dallas News,* December 29, 1895, p. 11.

153. Examples of this sort of depiction are too numerous to cite. See, for example, M. H. Gulesian, "The Armenian Refugees," *Arena* 17, no. 88 (March 1897): 652–65; Margherita Arlina Hamm, "The Armenian Tragedy," *Peterson Magazine* 6, no. 2 (February 1896): 146–55 (Hamm was a well-known journalist and apologist for imperialism). The Woman's Christian Temperance Union preferred the term "Moslem savages" (*New York Times,* January 21, 1896, p. 5).

154. James Bryce, "The Armenian Question," *Century Illustrated Magazine* 51, no. 1 (November 1895): 153; "Women of Armenia," *Dallas News,* September 2, 1895, p. 9.

155. See, for example, "Mob Law in Constantinople," *New York Times,* February 22, 1895, p. 4.

156. "The Armenian Outrages," *Chicago Tribune,* December 11, 1894, p. 6.

157. "Something about the Armenians," *Chicago Daily Tribune,* November 3, 1895, p. 35.

158. Margherita Arlina Hamm, "The Armenian Tragedy," *Peterson Magazine* 6, no. 2 (February 1896): 149–50. It is difficult to understand how anyone who had seen Turks could make such an assessment. See also "The Women of Armenia," *New York Times,* August 18, 1895, p. 21.

159. "The Armenians," *Steubenville [Ohio] Herald,* November 24, 1896, p. 5.

160. James Bryce, "The Armenian Question," *Century Illustrated* Magazine 51, no. 1 (November 1895): 151.

161. "Terrible Tortures Armenians Suffer," *New York Times,* September 16, 1895, p. 11. Strange assertions that never appeared in diplomatic reports even reached the capital. Judson Smith, the American Board secretary, quoted "a reliable letter from an American resident in Constantinople" stating that Turks "flushed with massacre and pillage" had come to Istanbul and were inciting Muslims in the bazaars against Christians ("Unsafe for Christians," *Trenton [N.J.] Evening Times,* November 30, 1895, p. 4). See also "Aid for Armenia," *Atlanta Constitution,* November 30, 1895, p. 1.

162. Examples of these atrocity allegations are too numerous to be cited here. Some examples from large city papers: "Massacre of Armenians," *New York Times,* November 17, 1894, p. 1; "Cruelties of the Kurds," *New York Times,* June 19, 1895, p. 5; "Terrible Tortures Armenians Suffer," *New York Times,* September 16, 1895, p. 11; "Fearful Tales of Armenian Torture," *Chicago Tribune,* February 21, 1895, p. 7; "Tells

of the Torture of Armenians," *Chicago Tribune,* December 14, 1894, p. 7; "Bloody Deeds of Horrible Turks," *Chicago Tribune,* November 21, 1895, p. 4; "Turkish Savagery," *Atlanta Constitution,* December 28, 1894, p. 2; "Ordered to Kill," *Boston Globe,* February 4, 1896, p. 7; "Turks Spare Not," *Boston Globe,* December 2, 1894, p. 16; "Cruelty of the Turks," *Washington Post,* January 12, 1895, p. 3.

163. E. J. Dillon, "Armenia: An Appeal," *Eclectic Magazine of Foreign Literature* 63, no. 2 (February 1896): 194, 195 (from the *Contemporary Review*). The article was summarized in newspapers.

164. "An Appeal of the Armenians," *New York Times,* December 13, 1895, p. 5.

165. "Slaughter of Armenians," *Dallas News,* January 18, 1896, p. 2. The assertion was based on a letter that the Armenian Relief Association supposedly received from Van. The consuls in Van, who surely would have noticed, mentioned nothing of the sort. On the same theme, see the story of a heroic Armenian maiden fighting the Turks (from the *London Daily News*): "She Preferred Death to Dishonor," *New York Times,* May 13, 1894, p. 17; and "Heroism Of Armenian Women: Hundreds of Them Preferred Death to Violation by the Turks," *Washington Post,* December 7, 1894, p. 1.

166. "Slaughter of Armenians," *Dallas News,* January 18, 1896, p. 2.

167. Elbert Francis Bacon, "The Turks and the Armenians," *Outlook,* February 8, 1896, p. 242.

168. "Appeals to Civilization," *New York Times,* December 31, 1895, p. 5, printed as accurate reporting. Troubles in Trabzon were explained in the *Times* by quoting a published press release from the Armenian Relief Association, printed as accurate news. Supposedly Bahri Paşa, the governor of Van, was on his way to Istanbul, bringing with him "four of the fairest maidens of Sassoun" as a present for the sultan. After Bahri reached Trabzon, local Armenian youths heard of this and shot him, wounding him. When the Armenians said they could not find the perpetrators, the Trabzon governor, on the order of the central government, ordered a massacre.

169. "Armenians to Rebel: Sultan Hamid to Be Assailed in Constantinople," *Warren [Pa.] Evening Democrat,* April 18, 1895, p. 1. The article was taken from the Associated Press. The unnamed author was unsure whether the Armenians would succeed.

170. "Hadjin, Zeitoun, Aintab," *New York Times,* December 27, 1895, p. 5. It is interesting that the priest represented the Zeytun community but was in Haçin not Zeytun.

171. "Armenians Gain a Battle," *New York Times,* November 7, 1895, p. 1. See also "Zeitoun Finely Resists," *New York Times,* December 24, 1895, p. 5. Ottoman and European records contain no mention of a battalion ever surrendering to Armenians.

172. See, for example, the Associated Press story "It Looks Like a Massacre," *Washington Post,* December 28, 1895, p. 1. The article states that the information came from "semi-official advices," whatever that might mean.

173. "Bravery of the Zeitoun Women," *Chicago Tribune* (originally in the *New York Journal*), March 24, 1896, p. 2; [no title], *Des Moines Daily Iowa Capital,* July 17, 1896, p. 7. The article was nonsense and could not have reached the *Daily News* from encircled Zeytun, but it does show the sympathy of the American newspapers and British Liberal press.

174. "Armenians Committed Murder," *New York Times,* January 17, 1896, p. 5; and November 19, 1895, p. 5. See also "Siege of Zeitoun Laid," *New York Times,* December 20, 1895, p. 5; and "A Massacre at Zeitoun," *New York Times,* December 21, 1895, p. 5 (the massacre in the headline referred to the murder of the Turkish troops).

175. "Huge Fish Story: That's about the Size of the Turkish Report Sent Out: Gross Insult to Intelligence," *Newark [N.J.] Daily Advocate,* February 25, 1896, p. 6. Other papers that published some of the report often used quotation marks: "How the 'Wicked Armenians' Oppressed 'Peaceful Turks,'" *Tyrone [Pa.] Daily Herald,* February 25, 1896, p. 1.

176. The coverage in the *New York Times* was not as ridiculous as in other newspapers. See, for example, the complete absurdity in "Five Hundred to Die: Armenians Resolve to Give Up Their Lives," *Fort Wayne [Ind.] Sentinel,* July 5, 1895, p. 1. See also "More Massacres," *Fort Wayne [Ind.] Sentinel,* November 14, 1895, p. 1.

177. *New York Times,* November 27, 1895, p. 5; "Missionaries in Armenia," *New York Times,* March 2, 1895, p. 5; "Missionaries Now in Danger," *New York Times,* March 4, 1895, p. 5.

178. "Passports to Black Sea," *New York Times,* November 22, 1895, p. 5; "Anarchy in Eastern Turkey," *New York Times,* November 12, 1895, p. 5.

179. "Turks Training Their Guns on Van," *Chicago Tribune,* November 30, 1895. The article was datelined Julfa, Persia. It claimed, among other things, that the Ottoman regular cavalry had plundered the town of Saray, which the consuls would certainly have reported but did not. The alleged events never happened.

180. "One Thousand Dead," *Dallas News,* November 29, 1895, p. 1.

181. McCarthy et al., *The Armenian Rebellion at Van,* pp. 65–66.

182. "Many Christians Killed," *New York Times,* July 26, 1896, p. 5; "Further Massacres of Armenians," *Lowell [Mass.] Sun,* July 27, 1896, p. 4.

183. See McCarthy et al., *The Armenian Rebellion at Van,* pp. 60–68.

184. "Right to Intervene," *Fitchburg [Mass.] Daily Sentinel,* January 18, 1896, p. 8; and other papers. See also "Horrors in Turkey," *Syracuse [N.Y.] Evening Herald,* March 16, 1896, p. 2. "According to reliable advices received here, 10,000 Armenians in the Province of Van have been forcibly compelled to embrace Islamism during the past two months" ([no title], *New York Times,* September 26, 1896, p. 5). The article never stated how such information could have been known.

185. "Gladstone on Armenia," *New York Times,* June 26, 1896, p. 5.

186. [No title], *New York Times,* September 26, 1896, p. 5.

187. "Armenian Horrors," *Dallas News,* October 22, 1896, p. 2. The story supposedly came from Echmiadzin, through St. Petersburg, then to Berlin and London.

188. McCarthy et al., *The Armenian Rebellion at Van,* p. 67. The Ottoman commander, Sadettin Paşa, stated that in the province as a whole 418 Muslims and

1,715 Armenians were dead, indicating the effect of Kurdish raids on Armenian villages.

189. "The Massacre at Van," *New York Times,* October 21, 1896, p. 5. The *Marshfield [Wisc.] Times,* October 3, 1896, p. 6, offers an interesting example of how this sort of "news" reached the public. Under "Foreign Affairs" it included only one sentence on Van: "The Turks leave no Armenians alive in the Van District."

190. "Slaughtering Armenians," *New York Times,* June 25, 1896, p. 5.

191. [No title], *New York Times,* August 22, 1897, p. 5 (two paragraphs, quoting the Dashnak journal *Groshat*).

192. James Bryce, "The Armenian Question," *Century Illustrated Magazine* 51, no. 1 (November 1895): 152.

193. See the section "The Missionaries and the Armenians" above and "Affairs in Turkey," *Missionary Herald* (the American Board journal) 91, no. 1 (January 1895): 11–13. See also "Massacres of Armenians," *New York Times,* November 17, 1894, p. 1; "Terrible Stories of Cruelty," *New York Times,* March 11, 1895, p. 5; "Armenians Killed," *Dallas News,* September 28, 1895, p. 3; and "Distress in Armenia," *Dallas News,* December 10, 1895, p. 3.

194. "Affairs in Turkey," *Missionary Herald* (January 1895): 11–13; See also "Armenia and the Sultan," *New York Times,* December 17, 1895, p. 5; "Tells of the Torture of Armenians," *Chicago Tribune,* December 14, 1894, p. 7; and Elbert Francis Bacon, "The Turks and the Armenians," *Outlook,* February 8, 1896, p. 242. Baldwin, an ex-staff member of the *Independent,* was the editor of *Outlook.*

195. "Killed by Cowards," *Chicago Tribune,* November 24, 1894, p. 8.

196. "Ashamed of Christendom," *New York Times,* January 6, 1896, p. 4. The *New York Times* later changed its mind and printed an article on what it called the five Armenian revolutionary societies in Constantinople. The information, even the names of the groups, was all wrong ("Sworn to Ruin the Porte: Armenian Revolutionary Societies Active in Constantinople," *New York Times,* September 24, 1896, p. 5).

197. "Why the Massacres Were Ordered," *Washington Post,* November 27, 1894, p. 1; "Massacre of the Armenians," *New York Times,* November 27, 1894, p. 5. All of the mortality figures here were printed in many newspapers and magazines, only a few of which are cited here as examples. The standard of verification of mortality statistics is indicated by a widely printed story that 6,000 had been massacred at Sasun, according to "three private letters received in Boston" ("All True," *Colorado Springs [Colo.] Weekly Gazette,* November 29, 1894, p. 8).

198. "Ten Thousand Slain," *Washington Post,* November 27, 1894, p. 1.

199. "The Turks and the Armenians," *Congregationalist,* March 21, 1895, p. 431. The *Congregationalist* did not give the details itself, except to say that 12,000 Armenians had been killed. Instead, it recommended that readers obtain Frederick Davis Greene's *The Armenian Crisis in Turkey.*

200. "Reviewing the Armenian Trouble," *Reno [Nev.] Weekly Gazette and Stockman,* February 20, 1896, p. 6; "News from Mission Lands," *Baptist Missionary Magazine* 75, no. 4 (April 1895): 116. The *Baptist Missionary Magazine* admittedly may not

have been the most informed source. It is included to show the breadth of religious sentiment.

201. "Armenian Massacres," *Dallas News,* February 22, 1896, p. 4.

202. Elbert Francis Bacon, "The Turks and the Armenians," *Outlook,* February 8, 1896, p. 242.

203. "A Monstrous Plot," *Frederick [Md.] News,* July 15, 1895, p. 1; "Mutilated Corpses," *Dallas News,* May 15, 1895, p. 2.

204. "The Armenian Massacre," *New York Observer and Chronicle,* November 22, 1894, p. 522; "Horrors of Armenia," *Middletown [N.Y.] Daily Argus,* March 18, 1895, p. 1. These Associated Press articles, and others like them, were found in many smaller city newspapers.

205. "Revolting!" *Fort Wayne [Ind.] News,* January 5, 1895, p. 1 (the testimony of one man, in a letter sent to Boston).

206. See, for example, "Cowards Run Riot," *Chicago Tribune,* December 4, 1894, p. 5; and "Horrors of Armenia," *Middletown [N.Y.] Daily Argus,* March 18, 1895, p. 1 (the statement of one boy). Before the Sasun troubles began, American missionaries had complained to the American ambassador that they had been threatened and targeted for assassination by the Armenian revolutionaries ("Armenians against Christians: Revolutionists Had Threatened Americans Long before the Sassoun Massacre," *New York Times,* August 16, 1895, p. 5). Such matters were quickly forgotten.

207. The *New York World,* copied in the *Chicago Tribune* ("It Comes from the Consul at Van," December 5, 1894, p. 7), stated that its information on Sasun came from a missionary at Van, some distance from Sasun.

208. "Massacre of the Armenians," *New York Times,* November 27, 1894, p. 5; "The Armenian Massacres," *New York Observer and Chronicle,* December 13, 1894, p. 642.

209. See, for example, "Cruelties of the Turks," *New York Times,* June 29, 1895, p. 5: "A recital of the Sasun massacre has been made by refugees. The story has been recorded in detail and forwarded for publication in the United States. It comes from Bitlis, in the mountain region of Eastern Turkey, and may be relied upon." Note that Bitlis was the point of origin. The few stories narrated have all the marks of the yellow journalism of the time: inventive tortures and dramatic speeches by victims ("Come on, my sons; I am ready to sacrifice you to the race").

210. "The Armenian Horror," *Chicago Tribune,* November 20, 1894, p. 6.

211. These consular delegates were M. Vilbert of France, H. S. Shipley of Great Britain, and M. Prjevalsky of Russia.

212. Enclosure in Currie to Salisbury, Therapia, August 15, 1895, "Report of the Consular Delegates Attached to the Commission Appointed to Inquire into Events at Sasun," in Great Britain, Foreign Office, *Turkey, No. 1 (1895, Part 1): Correspondence Relating to the Asiatic Provinces of Turkey: Part 1, Events at Sassoun, and Commission of Inquiry at Moush* (cmd. 7894) (London: HMSO, 1895), pp. 133–46 and annexes. This volume and *Turkey, No. 1 (1895, Part 2)* contain extensive interviews, commission deliberations, and statistics. Part 2 gives English translations of the

French originals of the commission's sittings. British delegate Shipley felt that the actual number of dead Armenians was 900 ("Memorandum on the Joint Report of the Consular Delegates to the Sasun Commission of July 20, 1895" by Shipley, pp. 203–8). See also FO 424/183, which contains the report, and FO 424/181 and 182.

213. "Armenia's Death List," *Dallas News,* January 29, 1896, p. 2 (an AP report that appeared in many papers). Most articles simply avoided any mention of the commission's estimates of mortality. Instead they ran missionary reports or quotations from the *London Daily News.* See, for example, "Massacres in the Sasun District," *Chicago Tribune,* October 4, 1896, p. 13.

214. "Tells of the Massacres," *Chicago Tribune,* June 29, 1896, p. 2; "Crimes of the Turks," *New Oxford [Pa.] Item,* January 31, 1896, p. 1; and many other newspapers.

215. "Massacres in the Sasoon District," *Chicago Tribune,* October 4, 1896, p. 13. The newspapers gave much play to earlier reports by consul Cecil M. Hallward, the British consul in Van. Hallward had been sent to investigate events in Sasun, although he was never able to travel to many of the affected districts because of quarantine. "My information is, therefore, necessarily of a meager character, and I have had some difficulty in collecting any definite facts" (FO 424/178, Hallward to Currie, Moush, October 9, 1894). Nevertheless, he blamed everything on the Turks and Kurds: "There was no insurrection, as was reported in Constantinople; the villagers took up arms only to defend themselves against the Kurds." Hallward stated that 8,000 or more Armenians had been massacred (FO 78/4544, Hallward to Currie, Van, November 6, 1894). He seems simply to have taken the word of Armenians for his reports, but he gave no sources for his opinion. The story he told, however, was exactly the same as the one Armenian sources in the area were telling (see FO 424/178, Hagopian, Chairman of the Armenian Patriotic Alliance, to Kimberley, London, November 15, 1894, quoting a "letter from Bitlis"). The sultan personally complained to the British ambassador that Hallward was inciting Armenian rebellion (FO 424/178, Currie to Kimberley, Constantinople, November 9, 1894). This was probably not true, but Hallward was surely not open to anything but Armenian reports. These turned out to be completely false, as the investigation commission discovered.

216. "That Butchery Tale," *Warren [Pa.] Evening Democrat,* March 11, 1895, p. 1.

217. "Kurdish Fiendish Cruelty," *New York Times,* March 19, 1895, p. 5.

218. See, for example, "The Armenian Outrages," *New York Times,* June 1, 1896, p. 9.

219. These interviews were excerpted in a rare factual article on the Armenian Troubles in the *New York Times* ("Inventions of Armenia," October 5, 1895, p. 5).

220. "The Armenian Atrocities," *New York Times,* January 12, 1895, p. 5.

221. See, for example, "Terrible Stories of Cruelty Told to the Commission of Inquiry on the Armenian Atrocities," *New York Times,* March 11, 1895, p. 5. The *Times* did print an Ottoman government list of some of houses destroyed in Muslim villages by Armenians ("Porte's View of Armenia," February 25, 1896, p. 5).

222. "Fearful Tales of Armenian Torture," *Chicago Tribune,* February 21, 1895, p. 7.

223. The *Washington Post,* which had not printed the erroneous allegations, printed an accurate assessment of the commission's report ("Facts about Sassoun," January 29,

1896, p. 1). A Turkish embassy press release also described exactly what had begun the revolt in Sasun, but only the *Washington Post* seems to have published the account ("Ten Villages Revolted," December 6, 1894 [second part], p. 9).

224. "The Rehabilitation of the Turk," *Nation* 65, no. 1686 (October 21, 1897): 314.

225. See, for example, "More Bloodletting," *Dallas News,* November 21, 1895, p. 1.

226. *Atlanta Constitution,* November 19, 1895, p. 1. See, for example, "Still Murdering," *Dallas News,* December 11, 1895, p. 2; "Battle at Zeitoun," *Dallas News,* December 24, 1895, p. 2; and "Cruelty of the Turks," *New York Times,* December 29, 1895, p. 5.

227. "The Sultan's Inhuman Edict," *Chicago Tribune,* December 23, 1895, p. 6. The *Tribune* featured a number of articles and editorials accusing the sultan of masterminding massacres. He was also supposedly planning to starve out the Nestorian Christians ("Sultan's Scheme," *Dallas News,* June 10, 1895, p. 1).

228. "The Sultan Ordered It," *Chicago Tribune,* March 31, 1895, p. 28.

229. Theodore Peterson, B.D., "Turkey and the Armenian Crisis," *Catholic World* (August 1895): 667. Peterson, as indicated by the journal name, was the rare Roman Catholic who wrote on the Armenian Troubles. This was probably primarily because of the secondary position of Catholics in the American press at the time, not to any difference between Catholic and Protestant beliefs on the Armenians.

230. "A Monstrous Plot," *Frederick [Md.] News,* July 16, 1895, p. 1; "In a Desperate Mood," *North Adams [Mass.] Daily Transcript,* July 15, 1895, p. 4; and others. This was an Associated Press article that went out all over Europe and America.

231. See two articles in the *Congregationalist* (Boston): "The Turks and the Armenians," March 21, 1895, p. 431; and "The Cry from Armenia," August 2, 1895, p. 262; Cyrus Hamlin, "The Lessons of Armenia," *Christian Observer,* November 11, 1896, p. 20. Hamlin felt that there was a good side: the persecutions would lead the Armenians to a more proper Christianity (his own).

232. "The Red Cross in Turkey," *New York Times,* January 23, 1896, p. 4.

233. "The Sultan's Plan," *New York Times,* November 2, 1896, p. 4. Newspapers from smaller cities printed the same allegation. See, for example, "Horrible!" *Fort Wayne [Ind.] Sentinel,* November 16, 1895, p. 1.

234. *New York World,* June 30, 1895, p. 1.

235. *San Francisco Chronicle,* November 26, 1895, p. 1. The same page included an article on the sermon of a minister in Kansas, just returned from the Middle East, in which the American ambassador in Istanbul was declared to be a Muslim bribed by the Ottoman government.

236. "The Cutthroat of the East," *Chicago Tribune,* December 3, 1895, p. 4. See also "Turkey Orders the Riots," *Chicago Tribune,* November 11, 1895, p. 4, which blamed the sultan's government and said he would soon be deposed. Another *Tribune* cartoon showed the sultan cowering behind a door as the spirit of Armenia (a woman in white) pointed a finger at him and European warships steamed to his punishment. A bag of skulls rested next to the sultan's door ("The Sick Man of Europe Finds Himself in a Corner at Last," *Chicago Tribune,* September 5, 1896, p. 1). Another cartoon depicted Kurds attacking old Armenian men and women

and mothers holding babies; severed heads lay in the streets. The street in the cartoon looked like someone's fanciful idea of Old Baghdad, not Sasun ("Massacre of Armenians by the Cruel Kurds," *Chicago Tribune,* December 1, 1895, p. 14). "Massacres in the Sassoon District," *Chicago Tribune,* October 4, 1896, p. 13, featured a cartoon map with wholly imaginary statistics on Armenian deaths.

237. "Terrell Watching," *Dallas News,* November 19, 1895, p. 1. See also "Trembles with Fear," *Dallas News,* November 20, 1895, p. 1; and "Abdulhamid's End Near," *Chicago Tribune,* September 14, 1896, p. 4. These and other articles on the sultan's fear and incipient insanity were sent by the Associated Press representative in Istanbul.

238. "Trembles with Fear," *Dallas News,* November 20, 1895, p. 1 (an AP article); and "The Sultan Assassinated," *Portland Oregonian,* November 20, 1895, p. 1: a headline that somewhat overstated the case.

239. "A Continuances of Outrages," *Fitchburg [Mass.] Evening Sentinel,* November 14, 1895, p. 4. The *Lowell [Mass.] Daily Sun* reported the same supposed news: "London, Nov. 3—A dispatch in the Central News from Athens says it is rumored from Smyrna and Mitylene, Asia Minor, that the Sultan of Turkey has requested the protection of the British fleet owing to the threatening conditions in Constantinople" (November 4, 1895, p. 1).

240. "Fool of a Sultan," *Chicago Tribune,* November 24, 1895, p. 13; "Turkey in Desperation," *New York Times,* November 13, 1895, p. 5.

241. "Sultan Waiting: Question of Guardianship Not Yet Settled: The Sultan Is in a State of Terror," *Lowell [Mass.] Daily Sun,* December 9, 1895, p. 1.

242. "The Inebriate Sultan," *Trenton [N.J.] Daily Times,* November 30, 1895, p. 3; "Brooklyn to Armenians," *New York Times,* February 7, 1896, p. 16. The *Chicago Tribune* did print a fairly accurate feature article on the sultan's ceremonial life, although it did not touch on his personal life ("Sultan of the Turks," December 8, 1895, p. 42).

243. "Islamism Rules the Sultan," *Atlanta Constitution,* February 2, 1896, p. 15.

244. See, for example, "Porte in Abject Fear," *Washington Post,* March 1, 1896, p. 5; "Will The Sultan Be Deposed?" *Chicago Daily Tribune,* September 13, 1896, p. 6; "Sultan to Be Deposed," *Philadelphia Public Ledger,* December 3, 1895, p. 1. Many newspapers and many articles predicted that the sultan would soon be deposed by his own people or by the powers. The *New York Tribune* reported that all the people of the empire would soon rise up against the sultan ("The Ottoman Crisis," November 18, 1895, p. 11).

245. "Ottoman Dynasty: Turkish Rule Has Been the Abomination of Desolation and Nothing Else: Embodiment of Wrong," *New York Commercial Advertiser,* quoted in *Dallas News,* November 25, 1895, p. 4.

246. "Sultan Abdul Hamid," *Chicago Tribune,* November 25, 1894, p. 46. One year later the *Tribune* printed an article stating that the sultan, far from being indolent and unattached to affairs of state, was too involved and too anxious to know everything and that this caused trouble ("Mysterious Influence at Work," *Chicago Tribune,* December 8, 1895, p. 10). See also Frank G. Carpenter, "Tales of the Sultan," *Portland Oregonian,* December 1, 1895, p. 17.

247. "Horrible," *Fort Wayne [Ind.] Weekly Gazette,* December 5, 1895, p. 2.

248. "Scenes and Incidents of the Recent Turkish Massacres," *Chicago Tribune,* September 27, 1896, p. 41. The article, replete with drawings of Turks killing Armenians with axes and an extremely improbable impaling, declared that the sultan had ordered the massacres.

249. The *New York Mail and Express, Philadelphia Evening Star, Chicago Times-Herald, Binghamton [N.Y.] Evening Herald,* and *Philadelphia Public Ledger,* quoted in *Chautauquan* 23, no. 1 (April 1896): 110. Chautauqua was a distinctly religious institution, founded by a minister and a lay official of the Methodist Church. It began life as the Chautauqua Lake Sunday School Assembly but developed into a well-known literary organization, school for ministers, and university and published its own weekly magazine, the *Chautauquan.*

250. One of the very few defenders of the sultan was General Lew Wallace, former American ambassador to the Ottoman Empire ("Wallace Defends Turkey," *Washington Post,* January 8, 1895, p. 4).

251. Frederick Davis Greene, *The Rule of the Turk: A Revised and Enlarged Edition of The Armenian Crisis,* p. xviii.

252. *Harrisburg [Pa.] Telegram* (no date or page number given), quoted in *Chautauquan* 24, no. 1 (October 1896): 97.

253. This assumption was often stated, always in the background. For an outright declaration, see *New York Times,* January 6, 1895, pp. 21–22.

254. [No title], *New York Times,* January 6, 1895, p. 22. Papers often stated the danger to missionaries and other foreigners in headlines or brief statements, without giving any evidence. For example, a headline in the *Newark [N.J.] Daily Advocate* (November 30, 1895) read: "Foreigners in Great Danger," but the article did not mention foreigners. An article in the *Washington Post* headlined "Missionaries in Great Danger" did not describe any danger (December 20, 1895, p. 11).

255. This is the substance of many articles. Two that spell it out very clearly are in the *Providence [R.I.] Journal* (November 7, 1895, p. 3) and the *Portland Oregonian* (November 1, 1895, p. 1), which alleged that the Turks hated the missionaries not only for religious reasons but because they hated Americans in general. The Reverend S. H. Devirian, an Armenian Protestant missionary, commented: "The Turks have a superstitious and deeply imbedded hatred and suspicion of Americans and things American" ("Woes of Armenians," *Chicago Tribune,* September 1, 1895, p. 26).

256. "Expel Missionaries: Action Decided upon by the Turkish Government," *Delphos [Ohio] Daily Herald,* April 8, 1896, p. 1; "Expulsion of Missionaries," *Washington Post,* May 3, 1896, p. 3. Many such articles stretched over a year-long period. The only ones that were accurate were those in which Turkish officials or the British ambassador were directly quoted as saying that nothing would happen to the missionaries or the mission.

257. For the rare, perhaps the only, detailed criticism of the missionaries and the standard view of the Armenians to appear in the American press, see the quotations from F. Hopkinson Smith in "The Truth about Armenia," *Washington Post,*

November 2, 1896, p. 6. The original article was printed in the *New York Herald*. The *New York Times* did not reprint the article but did print a rebuttal from "a gentleman who has resided many years in Istanbul," probably a missionary ("In Defense of Armenians," November 8, 1896, p. 1). The *Times* editorialized against Smith ([no title], November 17, 1896, p. 4), as did the *Chicago Tribune* ("The Amiable Turks," December 8, 1895, p. 28). Smaller city newspapers ran short articles attacking Smith but never ran his original words. Julia Ward Howe denounced him, stating that "the recent attempt of F. Hopkinson Smith to cast opprobrium upon the persecuted Armenians . . . will forever associate his name with that of the great assassin [Abdülhamit II]" ("Armenian Society Meets," *Fitchburg [Mass.] Evening Sentinel*, December 21, 1896, p. 4). Howe was addressing the United Friends of Armenia. Her attack was carried in a number of newspapers that had not printed Hopkinson Smith's original words. Most newspapers did not mention his criticisms at all.

258. "Armenians to Be Executed," *Reno [Nev.] Weekly Gazette*, November 7, 1895, p. 5. See, for example, "American Missionaries in Danger," *Dallas News*, August 16, 1895, p. 2; "Poor Old Sultan," *Dallas News*, November 14, 1895, p. 1; "Armenians and Missionaries," *New York Times*, August 13, 1895, p. 5; "Moslems and Armenians," *New York Times*, November 4, 1895, p. 5; "Missionaries again in Danger," *Washington Post*, November 23, 1895, p. 1; and "Lives of Missionaries in Peril," *Chicago Tribune*, November 1, 1895, p. 5.

259. *Advocate of Peace* 12 (December 1895): 281.

260. "The Massacre at Harput," *New York Times*, November 17, 1895, p. 4; "American Missionaries in Peril," *Chicago Daily Tribune*, December 5, 1895, p. 2. The source of the information was the missionary establishment ("Unsafe for Christians to Appear on the Streets of Turkish Villages," *Fort Wayne [Ind.] Gazette*, November 30, 1895, p. 1). A great amount of mission property was destroyed, but no missionaries were hurt. After remonstrances from the U.S. government the Ottoman government paid for the damage.

261. [No title], *New York Times*, January 5, 1895, p. 5.

262. "Armenians Are Starving," *New York Times*, December 2, 1895, p. 2; "Armenian Commission Announced," *Dallas News*, November 4, 1895, p. 1; "More Massacres," *Fort Wayne [Ind.] Sentinel*, December 14, 1895, p. 1. See also "Fears of a Massacre," *Oakland Tribune*, October 31, 1895, p. 1. The *San Francisco Chronicle* reported on November 5, 1895 ("Horrors of a Turkish Massacre," p. 2) that the missionaries were in danger; on November 15 that the missionaries were being protected by Turkish gendarmes ("No Mercy Shown by the Turks," p. 2); and on November 23 ("Planning for More Bloodshed," p. 2) that the missionaries were in danger.

263. "Missionaries in Turkey," *New York Times*, December 22, 1895, p. 16; "Americans in Turkey," *New York Times*, December 22, 1895, p. 4.

264. The Reverend Judson Smith, secretary of the American Board, predicted imminent starvation of the missionaries ("Name Day of Prayer for Turkey," *Chicago Tribune*, November 30, 1894, p. 4).

265. "Missionaries in Peril," *Philadelphia Public Ledger*, November 19, 1895, p. 1.

266. "Missionaries in Danger," *San Francisco Chronicle,* November 22, 1895, p. 2.

267. "Muslims Are Kept Busy Sharpening Their Hatchets—Missionaries Excellent Victims," *Atlantic Constitution,* December 3, 1895, p. 1.

268. Caleb Frank Gates, *Not to Me Only,* pp. 89–92, 124.

269. "Relations with Turkey," *New York Times,* December 20, 1895, p. 16; "Americans in Turkey," *New York Times,* December 20, 1895, p. 4.

270. Stories that missionaries had been mistreated at Malatya ("Terrell Watching," *Dallas News,* November 19, 1895, p. 1), for example, were untrue. It is impossible to tell how much the missionaries actually felt themselves to be in danger. They certainly wrote that they were: "We looked death in the face, and it seemed sweet to us" (the Reverend H. N. Barnum of Harput in "The Famine in Armenia," *Stevens Point [Wisc.] Journal,* March 9, 1896, p. 3).

271. The board at one point admitted that the missionaries were being protected in their homes by soldiers, thanks solely to American intervention, but stated that it feared that the missionaries would starve ("Ready for Action," *Dallas News,* November 30, 1895, p. 1). Of course, no missionaries starved. See also "American Missionaries Safe," *Steubenville [Ohio] Daily Herald,* December 16, 1895, p. 8. Starvation seems to have had a great emotional impact on Americans. It was to appear, greatly magnified, as a centerpiece of the plea for Armenians in World War I.

272. *Albany (N.Y.) Argus,* quoted in "The Armenian Troubles," *Chautauquan* 22, no. 5 (February 1896): 618 (no date of publication given for the *Argus*); *Chautauquan* 23, no. 4 (July 1896): 483.

273. "American Missionaries Protected," *Dallas News,* May 29, 1895, p. 29. The article did not consider how the two ships protected the missionaries, most of whom were far from the ships. Perhaps the newspapers and missionaries felt that the ships would bombard coastal cities if missionaries were attacked, in effect a United States declaration of war. This appears unlikely. The American naval commander (see the section "The Hazards of Dissent" above) felt that the situation was not serious.

274. "Terrell and the Missionaries," *Washington Post,* October 26, 1895, p. 1. The U.S. government defended Terrell ("Outrages in Armenia," *Washington Post,* December 20, 1895, p. 11). See the editorial against Terrell in the *New York Times* ("Minister Terrell and the Missionaries," August 5, 1896, p. 4).

275. "Armenian Revolutionists," *Washington Post,* August 16, 1895, p. 5; "Outrages by Armenians," *Cumberland [Md.] Evening Times,* November 2, 1896, p. 1.

276. Ballard Smith, "Stands by the Turk," *Chicago Tribune,* October 16, 1895, p. 9 (reprinting an article from the *New York World*). The *Tribune* itself felt that Terrell "is so utterly unfit for his post as to be a disgrace" because of his "cowardly, crawling action" ("Terrell Should Be Recalled," *Chicago Tribune,* October 7, 1895, p. 6).

277. This was a popular story, and the newspapers did not comment on its absurdity: "Terrell a Traitor," *Syracuse [N.Y.] Standard,* November 26, 1895, p. 1; "Says Terrell Ought to Be Hanged," *Reno [Nev.] Weekly Gazette and Stockman,* November 25, 1895, p. 5; "Terrell's Removal Will Be Asked For," *Williamsport [Pa.] Gazette and Bulletin,* November 25, 1895, p. 1; and others. Of the newspapers seen, only the

Washington Post (November 27, 1895, p. 6) wrote that this was nonsense, the "silliest chatter."

278. "Charges against Mr. Terrell," *Washington Post,* May 21, 1896, p. 6.

279. John R. Mott, *Addresses and Papers of John R. Mott, Volume 2; The World's Student Christian Federation,* p. 510.

280. Ibid., pp. 512–14.

281. Henry Davenport Northrop, *The Mohammedan Reign of Terror in Armenia,* p. 433. This false accusation was repeated in newspapers. See, for example, "The Famine in Armenia," *Stevens Point [Wisc.] Journal,* March 9, 1896, p. 3; "Famine in Armenia," *Galveston Daily News,* March 1, 1896, p. 12; "The Famine in Armenia," *Davenport [Iowa] Leader,* May 20, 1896, p. 3. Despite the range of dates, these are all the same article. Kimball herself gave a very strange account of her labors in Van, including her belief that a Kurdish chieftain had put a £2,000 price on her head, statement that the British consul had single-handedly kept the Kurds from massacring the Armenians in Van City (something the consul himself never reported), and similar assertions ("Where Massacre Is King," *Dallas News,* October 18, 1896, p. 10).

282. "Relief Work in Armenia," *Delphos [Ohio] Daily Herald,* April 8, 1896, p. 1. See also "Clara Barton's Armenian Work," *Washington Post,* November 23, 1896, p. 3; "Relief Work of the Red Cross," *Washington Post,* September 13, 1896, p. 13; "Clara Barton's Success," *New York Times,* August 26, 1896, p. 9. Barton's detailed report also praised the cooperation of the Ottoman government: American National Red Cross, *America's Relief Expedition to Asia Minor under the Red Cross.* See also "Clara Barton's Success," *New York Times,* August 26, 1896, p. 9, in which Barton speaks of the assistance given to her team by Turks and, in particular, the sultan.

283. See, for example, "No Help for Armenians," *Oshkosh [Wisc.] Daily Northwestern,* January 14, 1896, p. 4; "George Kennan on Armenia," *New York Times,* January 17, 1896, p. 5; "Butcheries Not at an End," *New York Times,* January 27, 1896, p. 5; "Turkey's Treatment of Armenians," *Chicago Tribune,* August 25, 1895, p. 31; and "Red Cross Shut Out," *Dallas News,* January 15, 1896, p. 4. Some later stories admitted that Barton and other Americans were allowed to distribute aid and were afforded help (for example, "Miss Barton Is Successful," *New York Times,* February 19, 1896, p. 5; and "Porte Breaks Its Promises," *New York Times,* April 17, 1896, p. 1, which actually stated that the Porte kept its promises regarding relief, despite the title).

284. American National Red Cross, *America's Relief Expedition,* pp. 11, 12. Some articles accurately reported that Barton had been greatly aided by the Ottoman government (for example, "Clara Barton's Success," *New York Times,* August 26, 1896, p. 9). Many commentators praised Barton but neglected to consider any goodwill on the part of the Turks. See "Turkey, the Bluebeard of the Orient," *Current Literature* 19, no. 2 (February 1896): 93.

285. "Gen. Alger Is Warlike," *Washington Post,* January 13, 1896, p. 4; "To Aid Stricken Armenia," *Dallas News,* January 13, 1896, p. 2.

286. "An Address on Armenia," *Washington Post,* January 19, 1895, p. 7; "History of Armenia," *Washington Post,* December 19, 1894, p. 4.

287. "More Armenian Resolutions," *Washington Post,* December 31, 1894, p. 1.

288. "Rousing Mass Meeting," *Dallas News,* January 1, 1896, p. 6.

289. "Armenian Sufferers," *Philadelphia Public Ledger,* January 23, 1896, p. 3.

290. "England's Duty to Armenia," *New York Tribune,* November 22, 1895, p. 1.

291. "Relief for the Armenians, *Reno [Nev.] Weekly Gazette and Stockman,* November 28, 1895, p. 5; "To Aid the Armenians," *New York Times,* November 10, 1896, p. 3. Other such meetings were also held later in Chickering Hall (advertisement for one meeting, *New York Times,* April 20, 1896, p. 5).

292. "Action in American Cities," *Chicago Tribune,* December 7, 1894, p. 7; "Turkish Outrages," *Fort Wayne [Ind.] Sentinel,* December 6, 1894, p. 1. Generals and clergymen denounced the Turks at the annual meeting of the Grand Army of the Republic, an organization of Civil War veterans ("Morton Invitation to Be Discussed," *New York Times,* January 30, 1896, p. 3). On Julia Ward Howe's position, see "Shall the Frontier of Christendom Be Maintained?" *Forum* 22 (November 1896): 321–26.

293. The Armenian Relief Association was an organization of Armenians in North America. Its general secretary was Herant Mesrob Kiretchjian. Among its early supporters was the Woman's Christian Temperance Union (WCTU) and other religious organizations.

294. Advertisement for the meeting, *New York Times,* April 21, 1896, p. 2. For similar mass meetings, see "About Armenian Atrocities," *New York Times,* December 12, 1894, p. 5; "A Protest to Humanity," *New York Times,* December 19, 1894, p. 5; "Welcome to Armenians," *Perry [Iowa] Daily Chief,* October 28, 1896, p. 1; "Sympathy with Armenians," *Washington Post,* November 10, 1890, p. 1; "In Behalf of Suffering Armenia," *Washington Post,* November 22, 1895; and "Persecution Must Stop," *New York Times,* November 18, 1895, p. 5. Again the meetings are too numerous to list.

295. See, for example, "The Massacre at Harpoot," *New York Times,* November 17, 1895, p. 4; "Killing the Armenians," *New York Times,* November 17, 1895, p. 5; and "Persecution Must Stop," *New York Times,* November 18, 1895, p. 5. In calling for the mass meeting in November 1895, the *New York Times* described events in the Ottoman Empire as "atrocious massacres of Armenians by Turkish soldiers." All the people the *Times* interviewed in a long article on November 18 were Protestant religious leaders. The Reverend Dr. Richard S. Storrs, pastor of the Pilgrim Congregational Church in Brooklyn and president of the American Board, spoke of "Turkish despotism" and the danger to missionaries if the sultan became displeased with them. The pastor of the First Presbyterian Church in Brooklyn announced his sympathy with any movement "to wipe him ['the tyrannous Turk'] entirely off the face of Europe" (the Armenian Troubles were occurring in Asia, not Europe). An ex-missionary compared the Turks and Kurds to "100,000 wild Indians." Another ex-missionary gave his thoughts on Islam: "The Mohammadan religion is one which few persons seem to understand in all its bearings. It regards all persons who do not come within its folds as enemies whom it is a sacred religious duty to kill" ("Persecution Must Stop," *New York Times,* November 18, 1895, p. 5).

296. See "Americans Will Protest," *New York Times,* November 21, 1895, p. 8; and "In Behalf of Armenians," *New York Times,* November 22, 1895, p. 5.

297. "Protest for Armenians," *New York Times,* December 10, 1895, p. 5. See also "Rev. Dr. Satterlee Interested," *Washington Post,* February 17, 1896, p. 9.

298. "Armenians' Many Friends," *New York Times,* December 31, 1894, p. 5.

299. "The Worst Was Not Told," *New York Times,* January 14, 1895, p. 3. Filian also wrote a book, *Armenia and Her People* (1896). It contained the same sentiments and greatly elaborated on them.

300. See "City Notes," *Trenton [N.J.] Times,* April 25, 1895, p. 5; and "Free Lecture on Armenia," *North Adams [Mass.] Transcript,* September 5, 1896.

301. "Armenians in Chicago Protest," *New York Times,* December 10, 1894, p. 5; "Deeds of the Turk," *Chicago Tribune,* December 10, 1894, p. 1. "A meeting of Armenians in Boston thanked the clergy for their support" ("Protests against the Turk," *Washington Post,* July 29, 1895, p. 7); see also "Relief Meeting Held by Armenians," *New York Times,* January 12, 1896, p. 16.

302. "Revolutionary Armenians," *New York Times,* July 28, 1894, p. 8.

303. "Armenians Ask for Protection," *New York Times,* November 18, 1894, p. 8. See also "Cabled to Queen Victoria," *New York Times,* January 15, 1896, p. 5.

304. "Armenian Atrocities," *Racine [Wisc.] Weekly Journal,* July 18, 1895, p. 2.

305. "Cry of Armenia," *Fort Wayne [Ind.] Evening Post,* February 24, 1896, p. 1.

306. "Scriptural Sayings," *Oakland Tribune,* January 8, 1896, p. 7.

307. "Pleading for Her People," *Washington Post,* January 6, 1896, p. 9. Krikorian said she was afraid that her family had been massacred but admitted she had no evidence that this was the case. Newspapers contained almost no information on Armenian lectures in schools, but they seem to have existed. See "Armenia and Its Customs," *Washington Post,* October 16, 1896, p. 7; and "Armenian Students at the Rollstone Church," *Fitchburg [Mass.] Daily Sentinel,* April 28, 1896, p. 6. When the high-school debating club in North Adams, Massachusetts, debated the proposition: "Resolved, that the United States should interfere in behalf of the Armenians," the affirmative won ("At Adams Today," *North Adams [Mass.] Daily Transcript,* February 8, 1896, p. 3).

308. These meetings are obviously too numerous to list. I have researched those included in NewspaperARCHIVE.com and selected a geographic range as examples: "Suffering Armenians," *Fitchburg [Mass.] Daily Sentinel,* April 6, 1895, p. 6, January 26, 1895, p. 2; "For Armenians: Large Meeting Held at High Street," *Lowell [Mass.] Daily Sun,* January 13, 1896, p. 1; "Meeting for Armenians," *Decatur [Ill.] Daily Republican,* March 6, 1896, p. 8; "A Public Rally to Be Held Tomorrow Night in Behalf of Armenia," *North Adams [Mass.] Transcript,* February 6, 1896, p. 1; "Armenian Mass Meeting," *Davenport [Iowa] Daily Republican,* April 19, 1896, p. 5; "The Armenians," *Steubenville [Ohio] Daily Herald,* November 24, 1896, p. 5; "An Armenian Visitor," *Frederick [Md.] Daily News,* February 29, 1896, p. 7; "Appeal to Lord Salisbury," *New York Times,* November 18, 1895, p. 5; "Armenian Relief," *Davenport [Iowa] Leader,* April 23, 1896, p. 4; "Armenian Meeting," *North Adams [Mass.] Transcript,* February 8, 1896, p. 1; "Rebuked the Turks," *Racine [Wisc.] Weekly*

Journal, July 18, 1895, p. 5; "Suffering Armenia," *Fitchburg [Mass.] Daily Sentinel,* January 25, 1895, p. 1; "Iowa, India, and Armenia," *Waterloo [Iowa] Courier,* December 21, 1896, p. 12; "By Foul Atrocity," *Lowell [Mass.] Daily Sun,* January 15, 1896, p. 1; "Sympathy and Succor," *Newport [R.I.] Daily News,* January 23, 1896, p. 1; "Able Men to Speak," *Oakland Tribune,* January 11, 1896, p. 5; "Help for Armenia," *Decatur [Ill.] Daily Republican,* March 9, 1896, p. 8; and "The Armenian Massacres," *Alton [Ill.] Evening Telegraph,* May 26, 1896, p. 3.

Donations seem to have been made primarily through the churches, which organized contributions to Armenian Relief. Lists of contributions were seldom published, so little information on this is available. Based on what is known about the contributions, however, churches and church members were the contributors. For example, the Armenia Fund of Fitchburg, Massachusetts, had received $525,630 by March 1895. Of the thirty donations, twenty-four were identified as coming from churches or church members, three from "a friend," one from the Grand Army of the Republic, one from "Mrs. E. W.," and one listed only as "cash" ("Contribution to the Armenia Fund," *Fitchburg [Mass.] Daily Sentinel,* March 2, 1896, p. 6).

Not all the gatherings on the Armenian Troubles were large-scale "mass meetings." Social gatherings of the well-to-do often featured speeches on the Armenians by clergymen and Armenians, which were listed on the society pages and announcement pages of newspapers large and small. See, for example, "Richfield Springs," *New York Times,* August 31, 1895, p. 3; and "Special Events in Summit, N.J.," *New York Times,* January 19, 1896, p. 11. It is not difficult to imagine what was said at these gatherings, although nothing was recorded.

309. For speeches by Greene, see, for example, the *New York Times:* "In Behalf of Armenia," August 29, 1896, p. 4; "Sympathy for Armenians," February 3, 1896, p. 2; and "Brooklyn to Armenians," February 7, 1896, p. 16. On Gabriel, see "Relief Meeting Held by Armenians," *New York Times,* January 12, 1896, p. 16.

310. *Syracuse [N.Y.] Standard,* February 3, 1896, p. 5. More meetings are listed in the Syracuse newspapers. Ministers canceled Sunday evening services so that church members could attend.

311. "About Armenian Atrocities," *New York Times,* December 9, 1894, p. 5; "The Worst Was Not Told," *New York Times,* January 14, 1895, p. 3.

312. "Baltimore Ministers to Protest," *New York Times,* December 10, 1894, p. 5.

313. [No title], *New York Times,* December 22, 1894, p. 5.

314. See "Armenia Has Many Friends," *New York Times,* December 31, 1894, p. 2.

315. The U.S. Congress joined the chorus of condemnation. The resolutions included "A bill for the creation of a United States commissioner to treat with a commissioner from each Christian nation of the world for the correction of the intolerable evil, so persistently and still continuing, in the shape of the Ottoman Empire and for other purposes." According to the bill, the commissioners would meet, elect a Christian to be president of "the United States of Turkey," depose the sultan, and ensure that henceforth the United States of Turkey would be a "Christian power," "never again to be ruled by Sultan, Caliph, or any other Mohammedan ruler" (54th Congress,

1st Session, S. 2788, April 9, 1896, submitted by Mr. Gallinger). The resolution that was passed called on the European powers to take action to protect the Armenians from massacres that "the American people, in common with all Christian people everywhere, have beheld with horror." The only American action demanded, however, was protection of American citizens. Secretary of state Richard Olney responded to the congressional resolution in a report condemning the Turks, but admitting: "Except where American citizens are concerned, our government is not in possession of that authentic and impartial knowledge which would enable it to make a full response to the Senate." The American losses he listed were the burning of missionary property at Harput and Maraş and the invasion of a missionary's home ("Outrages in Armenia," *Washington Post,* December 20, 1895, p. 11). See also "An Appeal to Europe Asked," *Washington Post,* February 15, 1896, p. 4; "Congress Passes the Armenian Resolutions," *Chicago Tribune,* January 29, 1896, p. 12; "A Protest to Turkey," *Washington Post,* January 28, 1896, p. 1. In the debate on the resolution in the Senate all spoke against the Turks, but Indiana senator David Turpie outdid himself: "He was in favor of giving 'the sick man of the Bosporus the coup de grace, and of ending his life and system by dissolution and destruction'" ("Vehement Speech in Senate," *New York Times,* January 29, 1896, p. 5). Elijah Morse of Massachusetts introduced a motion in the House of Representatives calling for Americans to join with Europeans, "to wipe the Turkish government off the face of the earth and ensure the freedom and independence of Armenia" ("To Annihilate the Turk," *Chicago Daily News,* January 13, 1896, p. 2).

316. "Armenian Meeting at Newark," *Middletown [N.Y.] Daily Argus,* March 6, 1896, p. 1. On meetings in larger cities, see also "Meetings for Relief of Armenians," *Washington Post,* December 7, 1896, p. 7; "Sympathy for Armenians," *Washington Post,* January 5, 1896, p. 13; "Armenian Mass-Meeting Tonight," *Chicago Daily Tribune,* December 9, 1894, p. 10; "The Armenian Mass-Meeting," *Chicago Daily Tribune,* January 5, 1896, p. 12; and "Demand Quick Action," *Chicago Tribune,* June 22, 1895, p. 5.

317. "Strong Talk about Armenia," *Washington Post,* March 9, 1896, p. 1.

318. "In Behalf of Armenians," *Washington Post,* October 27, 1896, p. 2. Frederick Booth-Tucker, an Englishman, was territorial commander of the Salvation Army in the United States from 1896 to 1904. He also presided at a mass meeting at Carnegie Hall that drew 4,000 on October 26, 1896 ("Welcome Meeting to Armenian Refugees," *Portsmouth [Ohio] Daily Times,* October 27, 1896, p. 1).

319. [No title], *San Francisco Chronicle,* November 21, 1895, p. 1.

320. "He Would Extinguish Turkey," *New York Times,* November 25, 1895, p. 3.

321. "Is Time for Interference," *New York Times,* November 25, 1895, p. 3.

322. The Reverend R. L. Bachman, D.D., *The Armenians and Their Present Persecutions: Sermon Preached in First Presbyterian Church, Utica, N.Y., January 12, 1896* ("published by request," n.p., n.d.), pp. 4–10.

323. These services and lectures are too numerous to list. For example, in addition to those given above, "Sunday Services," *Fitchburg [Mass.] Daily Sentinel,* March 7, 1896, p. 6; "Mills Meetings," *Lima [Ohio] Times-Democrat,* May 25, 1896, p. 9;

"Theological Themes," *Oakland Tribune,* January 11, 1896, p. 5; "Augusta Churches," *Kennebec [Maine] Journal,* May 23, 1896, p. 3 (the following Sunday was set aside as a day when all churches in Augusta took contributions for the Armenians: "For Armenia," *Kennebec Journal,* May 23, 1896); "Local Intelligence," *North Adams [Mass.] Daily Transcript,* February 3, 1896, p. 3; "Local Department," *Denton [Md.] Journal,* September 5, 1896, p. 3; "Gen. Greely on Armenia," *Washington Post,* March 12, 1896, p. 6; "Unitarian Services in Bank Building Hall," *Syracuse [N.Y.] Daily Standard,* December 9, 1894, p. 2; "Tomorrow's Pulpits," *Trenton [N.J.] Times,* December 15, 1894, p. 5; and "A Month's Event," *Fitchburg [Mass.] Sentinel,* October 7, 1895, p. 1.

    I have found only one sermon that defended the Turks, although for somewhat unusual reasons. The Reverend J. S. Haldeman of the First Baptist Church in New York stated: "But the Turk was there today by the will of God, in order that the land of Palestine might keep its Sabbath and the Jews still remain in exile" ("New York Clergyman Makes a Strong Defense of the Turks," *Portsmouth [Ohio] Daily Times,* November 9, 1896, p. 1).

324. "Chasm Is Breached," *Logansport [Ind.] Daily Pharos,* December 23, 1895, p. 1 (an article that appeared in many newspapers). The theme of America and Britain joining hands to oppose and crush the Turk was common in sermons. See, for example, the sermon of the Reverend G. B. Spalding in "The Sultan a Janus," *Syracuse [N.Y.] Evening Herald,* January 27, 1896, p. 7. The rumor was also heard in diplomatic circles ("Anglo-American Alliance," *Washington Post,* September 18, 1896, p. 2; "May Unite To Save Armenia," *Chicago Daily Tribune,* February 5, 1896, p. 2).

325. "Turkish Atrocities: The Ottoman Empire Should Be Wiped from the Earth," *New Philadelphia Ohio Democrat,* January 16, 1896, p. 3. Given the chance to lead the charge himself, but fearing for his safety, the Reverend Talmage refused to go to Anatolia to see the events for himself ("Talmage and the Turk," *Washington Post,* December 1, 1895, p. 11).

326. "Talked on Turkey," *Oakland Tribune,* May 16, 1896, p. 2.

327. "Stay the Turk's Hand," *Washington Post,* December 24, 1894, p. 6.

328. "Died for Their Belief," *New York Times,* January 26, 1896, p. 9.

329. "Ready to Die for Their Faith," *Chicago Tribune,* October 14, 1895, p. 3.

330. "Warships to the Turk," *Chicago Tribune,* January 20, 1896, p. 8.

331. "What Some of the Chicago Preachers Said," *Chicago Tribune,* January 27, 1896, p. 10.

332. "Churches and Church News," *Atlanta Constitution,* May 12, 1895, p. 5. The society was an evangelical group primarily directed at youth. It claimed millions of members worldwide.

333. "Endeavorers Out in Force," *Washington Post,* November 24, 1894, p. 3.

334. "Tears for the Armenians," *Washington Post,* July 14, 1896, p. 4.

335. "Episcopal Convention," *Massillon [Ohio] Independent,* October 10, 1895, p. 1; "In a Mission Session," *Chicago Daily Tribune,* October 5, 1895, p. 9. Episcopalian bishops from all across America also circulated a letter to President Grover Cleveland demanding that the United States end diplomatic relations with the

Ottoman Empire ("An Appeal from Bishops," *New York Times,* February 2, 1896, p. 9).

336. "Still for War," *Washington Post,* October 26, 1896, p. 6. The *Post* felt that this would not be wise.

337. See, for example, "In Behalf of Missionaries," *Washington Post,* October 9, 1896, p. 1.

338. "Presbyterians at Saratoga," *Atlanta Constitution,* May 31, 1896, p. 12.

339. "Unitarian Meeting Over," *New York Times,* October 25, 1895, p. 13.

340. "To Save Poor Armenians," *New York Times,* October 8, 1895, p. 13. See also "An Appeal from Bishops," *New York Times,* February 2, 1896, p. 9.

341. "Plead for the Armenians," *Washington Post,* December 11, 1894 (second part), p. 3.

342. "Churches and Church News," *Atlanta Constitution,* May 12, 1895, p. 5. Willard felt the world was not doing enough: "The Turk is barbarous, while the statesmen are overcivilized; he is a fanatic, while they are craven cowards" ("An Appeal from Miss Willard," *New York Times,* April 22, 1896, p. 8).

343. "Will Be a Great Meeting," *Newark [N.J.] Daily Advocate,* November 4, 1896, p. 3. The Armenian Question was also raised at the 1895 WCTU meeting ("Women in the Pulpits," *Washington Post,* October 21, 1895, p. 4). Many newspapers featured news of this meeting, showing the importance of the WCTU. Greene spoke at many other Armenian meetings ("Armenian Mass Meetings," *Washington Post,* January 10, 1896, p. 7; "Tears for the Armenians," *Washington Post,* July 14, 1896, p. 4; "Compares the Powers and Nero," *Chicago Tribune,* January 6, 1896, p. 2; "Sympathy for Armenians," *New York Times,* February 3, 1896, p. 2). In addition to being a missionary and an author, Greene was secretary of the National Armenian Relief Committee.

344. "Women's Appeal for Armenia," *New York Times,* January 21, 1896, p. 5. The Armenian "pure home" theme was seen often and must relate to the ideas of Muslim and Christian homes that had been spread by missionaries and other Christian writers.

345. "Under the Heel of the Turk," *Chicago Tribune,* October 14, 1895, p. 3; "Pleading for Armenians," *New York Times,* February 17, 1896, p. 9.

346. Twenty-six and two, respectively (out of thirty). The data were drawn from the OCLC database. The other two books were by Clara Barton and the American Red Cross. The Library of Congress lists twenty-one books printed between 1890 and 1900 in the United States under the subject "Armenian Question": nineteen by Protestant clergymen or Armenians, one by the editor of the *Christian Herald,* and one by a board member of the Armenian Relief Organization (essentially an organ of the missionary establishment, along with lay members, that organized mass meetings against the Turks and collected for Armenian charities). This method of finding books on the Armenian Question is somewhat imperfect, because it does not include books that for one reason or another were not properly cataloged or were never put into the catalogs at all. Some of the books cited in this chapter fall into the former category. All of them but one were missionary establishment works. The exception was a short anonymous volume: *A Few Facts about Turkey under the Reign of Abdul Hamid II by an American Observer* (New York: n.p., 1895). This may have been an attempt by the Ottoman government to tell its side of

the story. As such it was not successful: OCLC Worldcat lists only fourteen copies in American libraries.

347. Various British writers produced books on the Armenian Crisis. Judging by lack of contemporary references to them in the press and their lack of presence in American libraries, however, they do not seem to have had much effect in America. Because of this, they are not considered here. *The Sword of Islam or Suffering Armenia* by J. Castell Hopkins (Brantford and Toronto: Bradley Garretson, 1896), a well-known Canadian writer, does not seem to have made its way to the United States, as judged by library holdings (OCLC Worldcat), and thus is not considered here at length. It featured the same prejudices and misinformation as its American counterparts: "unsparing cruelty" and "barbarism" were the hallmarks of Ottoman soldiers and the Ottoman government (pp. 32–34), a largely false analysis of Islam, and in general a "history" of the Ottoman Empire that stressed the negative and was often simply wrong. Hopkins primarily related the Armenian Troubles anecdotally. He accused the Ottoman government of complicity and blamed the British and Americans for not taking action—all the usual tales. As his book was completely without sources (not even a bibliography), it is difficult to know where he obtained his information.

348. This was the third and largest of Greene's three books on the Armenian Troubles. The first was *The Armenian Crisis in Turkey.* It was so successful that the publisher followed it with a revised edition in 1896: *The Rule of the Turk: A Revised and Enlarged Edition of The Armenian Crisis.* The Library of Congress copy of *The Rule of the Turk* states that it was the "18th thousand" of that book. The three books together must have sold several times that number. Greene was greatly praised for his work. See Robert Stein, "Armenia Must Have a European Governor," *Arena* 66 (May 1895): 368–91, which also offers a good summary of the position of the missionary establishment. Greene was a Congregationalist minister for the ABCFM, serving in "Van, Armenia," from 1890 to 1894.

349. Greene, *Armenian Massacres or the Sword of Mohammed,* pp. 1–5.

350. Ibid., p. 117.

351. The Reverend Frederick Davis Greene, "Causes and Extent of the Recent Atrocities," in ibid., pp. 431–39 (quotation on p. 437).

352. Greene, *Armenian Massacres,* pp. 12, 11.

353. Excluding pictures and Greene's commentary.

354. Greene, *Armenian Massacres,* p. 37. This was an interesting sentiment from an author whose book contained drawings of murder in the streets and sacks full of severed human heads.

355. See, for example, the list in ibid., p. 96.

356. Ibid., p. 32.

357. Northrop, *The Mohammedan Reign of Terror in Armenia,* pp. 193–94. Northrop was a Presbyterian minister who wrote dozens of popular books on religion, geography, history, and what would now be called "self-help books," including many for children. He had no special contact with the Middle East.

358. See note 348 above. The Armenian Relief Association gave out copies of Greene's book ("More about Armenia," *Warren [Pa.] Evening Democrat,* November 5, 1895, p. 2).

359. Augustus W. Williams and Mgrditch Simbad Gabriel, *Bleeding Armenia: Its History and Horrors.* Williams, later the biographer of Dwight L. Moody, was a Chicago clergyman; Gabriel was a physician and author of other books on Armenians. Both were active in Armenian mass meetings (see the section "Public Meetings" above).

360. The number of janissaries at the time was 10,000 at most, so this was demographically impossible and was not at all the way the "child levy," which was much more selective, worked.

361. Williams and Gabriel, *Bleeding Armenia,* p. 195.

362. Ibid., pp. 160, 167.

363. Ibid., p. 225.

364. "The Turkish Government itself was directly and actively responsible for the outrages in Asia Minor; it not merely permitted, but actually ordered them" (ibid., p. 247).

365. Ibid., pp. 224, 306, 159.

366. Ibid., pp. 304–5, 328.

367. Ibid., p. 311. The Armenian population of the Eleşkirt Kaza was actually less than seven thousand. See also the large estimate of Armenians dead or starving in Van Province (ibid., p. 366).

368. Ibid., p. 399. It is hard to know what Williams meant by provinces, because he often misidentified them. I have assumed that he meant Van, Erzurum, Bitlis, Mamuretülaziz, Trabzon, Maraş (Haleb), and Zeytun, which would cover the areas delineated in his book. If he meant smaller areas, my analysis would be even truer.

369. Williams stated that the statistics were for seven provinces. His figures were considerably above the population numbers recorded by the Ottomans even if they included all the Armenians in those provinces, not only those in the areas affected by the Troubles, and no one has ever asserted that all Armenians were affected. See McCarthy, *Muslims and Minorities* on the population numbers.

370. Williams and Gabriel, *Bleeding Armenia,* p. 425.

371. Ibid., pp. 425–26, 427. As what today would be called a lobbyist or public relations representative for his cause, Gabriel was prominent in denying any Armenian wrong. See, for example, his letter asserting that the Istanbul demonstrations were not arranged by "Huntchagists" but were only a call for good government ("The Exasperated Armenians," *New York Times,* October 11, 1895, p. 13).

372. For example, S. S. Yenovkian, *Martyred Armenia;* and Ohan Gaidzakian, *Illustrated Armenia and the Armenians.* Of the two, *Illustrated Armenia* is by far more filled with what can only be seen as a pathological hatred. The missionary Jesse Malek Yonan published an attack on the Kurds (*Martyrdom in the Orient*), which described the Kurd as "a veritable fiend of death" (p. 6) and similar characterizations.

373. Bliss was a missionary for the American Bible Society in Turkey from 1872 to 1888. For some reason the book was also printed under a different title (*Turkey and the Armenian Atrocities*) by different publishers.

374. Edwin Munsell Bliss, *Turkish Cruelties upon the Armenian Christians,* pp. 39, 59–63.

375. Ibid., pp. 368–83. Bliss stated: "The massacres in the fall of 1894 were absolutely unprovoked" (p. 479).

376. Ibid., pp. 384–405. This was similar to the one-sided story in the press. The *Chicago Tribune,* for example, reported that "thousands were killed" in the riots but mentioned nothing of the provocation or the Muslim dead ("Run Riot in Bloodshed," *Chicago Tribune,* August 29, 1896, p. 4). See also "Moslem Rule Doomed," *Washington Post,* August 29, 1896, p. 1. The *London Daily News* was quoted as the article's main source.

377. Bliss, *Turkish Cruelties,* pp. 448–60. One drawing (ibid., p. 306) showed Kurds stamping on crosses and on the bodies of dead children, severed heads of women, and a mother holding her baby as a Kurd is about to slaughter them. The Armenians in the drawing are mainly women. The Kurds are shooting revolvers, somewhat unlikely Kurdish possessions. For the type of praise elicited by the Bliss and Greene books, see "Turkey and the Armenian Atrocities," *Chautauquan* 23, no. 6 (September 1896): 784.

378. James Wilson Pierce, *The Story of Turkey and Armenia,* pp. 1–24. This discussion assumes that articles whose authors were not listed were by Pierce.

379. Ibid., pp. 25, 39, 91. The second article cited was by W. T. Stead, not identified in the book but famous in his time. He was an Englishman, son of a Congregationalist minister, journalist, spiritualist, and reformer.

380. Ibid., p. 122. These comments are found in the chapter on home life by Pierce, pp. 105–207.

381. Ibid., pp. 304–17.

382. Ibid., pp. 223, 224. Interestingly, in view of his later activities, Barton stated that the nature of the Armenians "would make it impossible today for the Armenians to be self-governing" (p. 224).

383. Frances E. Willard, president of the WCTU (ibid., p. 356).

384. Frances E. Clark, D.D., president of the United Society of Christian Endeavor (ibid., p. 348).

385. "From a missionary to his former students" (ibid., p. 431).

386. Marion Harland and George Henry Sandison, *Home of the Bible: What I Saw and Heard in Palestine and the Story of Martyred Armenia,* pp. 415–46.

387. In a short section (one paragraph) Hamlin was quoted as saying that his sources were letters from missionaries. He had left Istanbul, which had been his only mission station, in 1873 (Cyrus Hamlin, *My Life and Times*). By the 1890s Hamlin had some odd views. He held, for example, that the Ottoman ambassador in Washington was a Russian agent and that the Russians were behind the 1890s troubles ("Must Be Free," *Oakland Tribune,* December 8, 1894, p. 5). See also Hamlin's short article four years later, in which he blamed everything on Sultan Abdülhamit II ("The Genesis and Evolution of the Turkish Massacre of Armenian Subjects," *Proceedings of the American Antiquarian Society,* new series 12 [April 1898]: 288–94).

388. Harland and Sandison, *Home of the Bible,* p. 420.

389. Ibid., pp. 417, 420.

390. Sandison's description of the Armenian Church (ibid., pp. 417–19) either was deceitful or arose from complete ignorance. Readers would have had no way to know that the church did not share their beliefs.

391. Ibid., p. 419. One interesting "fact" in the book was that the Garden of Eden had been located in what were now the Ottoman provinces of Van, Bitlis, and Erzurum (ibid., p. 446). It must have been an extremely large garden to have encompassed so much territory.

392. Robert E. Speer, *Missions and Modern History: A Study of the Missionary Aspects of Some Great Movements of the Nineteenth Century.*

393. Northrop, *The Mohammedan Reign of Terror in Armenia,* p. 261. On the population, see Kemal H. Karpat, *Ottoman Population, 1830–1914,* pp. 107–90; and the sources listed in McCarthy, *Muslims and Minorities,* pp. 235–43.

394. Thomas Davidson, "The Creed of the Sultan: Its Future," *Forum* 22 (October 1896): 162–63. *Forum* also ran articles by Armenians calling for the destruction of the Ottoman Empire.

395. See, for example, "Turkish Misrule in Armenia," *Chautauquan* 21, no. 5 (August 1895): 650.

396. See, for example, M. M. Mangasarian, "Armenia's Impending Doom: Our Duty," *Forum* (June 1896): 452. The Turks were held to have built nothing, "with the exception of a few mausoleums and mosques," and to have produced no scholars, writers, or statesmen.

397. "Who Massacred the Armenians," *Dallas News,* January 13, 1895, p. 6 (excerpted from the *San Francisco Impress*).

398. "The Turkish Crisis," *New York Times,* November 13, 1895, p. 4.

399. "The Turks and the Armenians," *Congregationalist* 80, no. 12 (March 21, 1895): 431. The *Congregationalist* also printed a number of editorials against the Turks.

400. Robert Stein, "Armenia Must Have a Christian Governor," *Arena* 66 (May 1895): 368–91. Stein's feelings were summed up in one statement: "Lord, I thank Thee that I am not like unto these Turks!" (p. 370). *Arena* was not owned by a missionary organization, although it had a wide following among the clergy, to whom it offered reduced rates. Its articles were a combination of religion and social consciousness. Many of its contributors were Protestant clergymen. It was ultimately absorbed by *Christian Work and the Evangelist. Arena* was a progressive Christian social movement as much as a magazine. Its editor, Benjamin Orange Flower, organized the Union for Practical Progress in 1892. By 1894 it had fifty clubs throughout the United States (Thomas Bender, *Knights of the Golden Rule: The Intellectual as Christian Social Reformer in the 1890s* [Lexington: University of Kentucky Press, 1975], pp. 99–103). The Union for Practical Progress distributed circulars to clergy across America calling for an independent Armenia under a Christian governor ("An Appeal for Armenia," *New York Times,* June 1, 1895, p. 4).

401. "Editorial: The Armenian Massacres," *New York Observer and Chronicle,* November 29, 1894, p. 551.

402. "The Armenian Outrages," *Chicago Tribune,* December 11, 1894, p. 6.

403. "Moslem Rule Doomed," *Washington Post,* August 29, 1896, p. 1.

404. M. H. Gulesian, "England's Hand in Turkish Massacres," *Arena* 86 (June 1897): 271–83; *Outlook* (New York), quoted in "The Situation in Turkey," *Chautauquan* 22, no. 4 (January 1896): 486–87 (no article information given). On Great Britain's actual place in the Armenian Troubles, see Robert F. Zeidner, "Britain and the Launching of the Armenian Question," *International Journal of Middle Eastern Studies* 7, no. 4 (October 1976): 465–83.

405. Quoted in "The Situation in Turkey," *Chautauquan* 22, no. 4 (January 1896): 486 (no original article information given).

406. Quoted in "Turkish Misrule in Armenia," *Chautauquan* 21, no. 5 (August 1895): 650 (no original article information given).

407. "Current Comment," *Dallas News,* February 3, 1895, p. 4 (excerpted from the *Savannah News*). The *Savannah News* thought this was a good idea but lamented that it would never happen.

Chapter 8, World War I

1. As the next two chapters show, news of the events in Eastern Anatolia began to reach America through diplomats and newspaper reporters in Istanbul and elsewhere far from the fighting. The primary source of news was American missionaries. Missionaries also wrote and cabled America, describing the sufferings of the Armenians, not the Muslims, and calling for aid. Their call struck a responsive chord in America.

2. On British propaganda efforts in World War I, see George C. Bruntz, *Allied Propaganda and the Collapse of the German Empire;* Peter Buitenhuis, *The Great War of Words;* Harold Lasswell, *Propaganda Technique in the World War;* James R. Mock and Cedric Larson, *Words That Won the War;* H. C. Peterson, *Propaganda for War: The Campaign against American Neutrality, 1914–1917;* James Morgan Read, *Atrocity Propaganda: 1914–1919;* M. L. Sanders and Philip M. Taylor, *British Propaganda during the First World War, 1914–1918;* and J. D. Squires, *British Propaganda at Home and in the United States from 1914 to 1917.* All of these books are primarily concerned with propaganda against the Germans, not the Ottomans, but they do describe the propaganda machinery that was also used against the Turks.

3. What might be called moral considerations also were involved. The British had convinced themselves that their opponents were evil, which made propaganda against them easier because it was in a "good cause." It would be a mistake to say that all this was the result of realpolitik. See Irene Cooper Willis, *England's Holy War.*

4. Sanders and Taylor, *British Propaganda,* p. 178.

5. Great Britain, Foreign Office, "American Press Résumé," weekly, marked "Confidential." These comments are based on the résumés of the fall and winter of 1915.

6. A short selection of books on the war: Edward J. Erickson, *Ordered to Die: A History of the Ottoman Army in the First World War;* Maurice Larcher, *La guerre turque dans la guerre mondiale;* Justin McCarthy, *Death and Exile: The Ethnic Cleansing of Ottoman Muslims,* and *The Ottoman Peoples and the End of Empire;* and Justin McCarthy, Esat Arslan, Cemalettin Taşkıran, and Ömer Turan, *The Armenian*

Rebellion at Van. The literature on the military history of the Ottoman Empire in World War I is far from complete, and some of the best works (such as the Turkish General Staff histories of the war) are available only in Turkish. Nevertheless, works on the subject are far too numerous to list here.

7. McCarthy, *Death and Exile,* pp. 179–322.

8. Readers should know where an author stands, so I should state that I believe labeling "the guilty" in World War I is a futile process. All parties to the war—Turks, Kurds, Greeks, Armenians, and Russia and the other Allies—were responsible for the wartime deaths. Further, I do not believe that the historical record supports any assertion that the Ottoman government ever ordered a genocide of Armenians or any other people. This is not to say that many Muslims did not kill Armenians because they were Armenians, just as many Armenians killed Muslims because they were Muslims.

9. Only two provinces were less than three-fourths Muslim, Bitlis (67 percent Muslim) and Van (61 percent Muslim). McCarthy, *Muslims and Minorities,* p. 111.

10. Some of the medical clinics established by Near East Relief in 1919 were a notable exception. Using facilities given to them by the Ottomans and Turkish nationalists, Near East Relief doctors treated Muslims as well as Christians, especially in western and central Anatolia (George L. Richards, M.D., ed., *The Medical Work of Near East Relief: A Review of Its Accomplishments in Asia Minor and the Caucasus during 1919–20*).

CHAPTER 9, THE AGE OF NEAR EAST RELIEF

1. Charles Crane (see below) was the secretary of the committee. The Committee on Armenian Atrocities actually began the anti-Turkish propaganda described below (see "Exodus of Armenians Wholesale Butchery," *New York Sun,* October 4, 1915, p. 2; and "Report of Committee on Armenian Atrocities," a pamphlet in the Library of Congress with no date or place listed). Its work was almost immediately taken over by the ACASR. Three committees joined to make up the ACASR: the Persian War Relief Committee, the Syria Palestine Relief Committee, and the Committee on Armenian Atrocities ("Committees Join to Offer Their Aid to Armenian Refugees," *Fort Wayne [Ind.] Journal-Gazette,* November 9, 1915, p. 18). Other committees that spread anti-Turkish propaganda were eventually subsumed under the ACASR banner or cooperated fully with it (see "1,000,000 Armenians Butchered or Exiled," *New York Sun,* October 3, 1915, p. 3, which was based solely on a letter from an unknown source allegedly in Istanbul).

    On the ACASR/Near East Relief, see James L. Barton, *The Story of Near East Relief;* and Robert L. Daniel, *American Philanthropy in the Near East,* chapter 7. I have not seen Fatih Gencer, *Ermeni soykırım tarihinin oluşum sürecinde Amerikan Yakın Doğu Yardım Komitesi (Amerika Şark-ı Karib Muavenet Heyeti)* (Istanbul: Alternatif Düşünce, 2006). James Reed, *The Missionary Mind and American East Asia Policy, 1911–1915,* which examines how Protestant missionaries influenced U.S. policy and business relations with China, is useful for a study of American attitudes in this period. See also Richard Weightman, "Our Missionaries and Our

Commerce," *North American Review* 182, no. 1,095 (June 1906): 86–96, for a negative view of the influence of missionaries on American policy.

2. Barton, *The Story of Near East Relief,* pp. 438–39. This sum includes $2,076,321.25 contributed to defray operating expenses but not "receipts from interest and other sources of $1,175,918.08."

3. From 1920 to 2006, using the unskilled labor wages as the deflator. Currency conversion over time is very imprecise and depends on choosing the deflator. Depending on that choice, present-day values for this conversion range from $905 million to $13 billion (www.measuringworth.com).

4. Barton, *The Story of Near East Relief,* p. xi.

5. Ibid., pp. 4–7. The descriptions in the list are as they appeared in the source, with my comments in brackets. For an example of the organization in individual areas, see "Armenian Relief Movement Here," *Fitchburg [Mass.] Daily Sentinel,* April 3, 1916, p. 11.

6. Near East Relief, *Report to Congress for 1925,* p. 7. It would be an impossible task to identify the affiliations of all the various ACASR/Near East Relief state and local committees. Of the thirty members of the committee in Hartford, Connecticut, for example, nineteen were clergymen, one a trustee of the Hartford Seminary, and one an Armenian ("Starving Armenians Plead for Succor," *Hartford Courant,* November 29, 1915, p. 10; this article called it the "American Committee for Armenian and Servian Relief").

7. U.S. Congress, Senate, *Report of the Near East Relief for the Year Ending December 31, 1922,* p. 3.

8. Clyde F. Armitage, "Near East Relief as a Missionary Enterprise," in Near East Relief, *Investments in Life: Speaker's Handbook,* pp. 25–26.

9. Ibid., pp. 25–26. On educational cooperation with native churches, see John R. Voris, "Report on Religious Education, Near East Relief" (résumé for the Federal Council of Churches Committee on Relations with the Eastern Churches, mimeographed copy in the Library of Congress).

10. *New York Times,* January 29, 1919, p. 7. The ad copy originally appeared in the *Literary Digest.*

11. See, for example, Near East Relief ads in the *New York Times,* including "Draw Out Thy Soul to the Hungry, and Satisfy the Afflicted," October 19, 1923, p. 11 (the quotation is from Isaiah 58:10); "Another Little Child Has Shriveled Up and Died," December 22, 1919, p. 13; and "They Shall Not Perish," March 1, 1919, p. 9.

12. Near East Relief, *The Cross in the East and the Church in the West,* p. 2. The same picture was used as the cover of an issue of the *New Year East* in March 1921.

13. "Store Some of Your Money in Heaven! Don't Put It All in the Bank!" (Near East Relief ad), *New York Times,* April 4, 1920, p. XX9.

14. ACASR, *Suggestions for Local Co-operating Committees.* For an example of the ACASR organization in cities, see "Take Steps for Armenian Relief," *Fitchburg [Mass.] Daily Sentinel,* July 7, 1916, p. 12.

15. ACASR, *Armenia: The Word Spells Tragedy,* pp. 37–42.

16. ACASR, *Sixteen Striking Scenes: Illustrating the Suffering and Need in Armenia and Other Parts of Western Asia.*

17. William E. Doherty (associate general secretary, Near East Relief), "New Life in the Old East," in Near East Relief, *Investments in Life,* pp. 7–8.

18. Bishop James Cannon, Jr., "The Golden Rule Working in Syra, Greece," in Near East Relief, *Investments in Life,* p. 18.

19. "Outlines of Addresses," in Near East Relief, *Investments in Life,* pp. 31–38.

20. Little information on the actual sources of the ACASR propaganda quotations is available. I have only found one list, and the identifications in it are far from satisfactory. The ACASR sent the British Propaganda Bureau one of its press releases, "Report of Committee on Armenian Atrocities (for Publication in Papers of Monday, Oct. 4, 1915)," along with a list of the sources quoted (FO 96/212/"Key to Quotations for October 4, 1915 galley"). The majority of the sources were missionaries, as might be expected. Others were never identified: "a German missionary," "Native Sources," "Armenian sources." The largest group was described only as having been forwarded by Ambassador Morgenthau, with no further identification.

21. See, for example, American Armenian Relief Fund, *The Cry of Armenia.*

22. See, for example, "Missionary Declares Germans Supervised Armenian Deportation," *Syracuse [N.Y.] Herald,* February 6, 1916, p. 4. The story, allegedly from an unnamed missionary woman who wrote from British-controlled Cairo, blames the Germans, often a mark of the British propagandists. For someone "long a missionary" the putative source was quite confused, identifying the large number of Armenians she was describing as coming from the "city of Corfu," which did not exist. The closest name I have been able to find was the small village of Korfo, which was nowhere near the events described. For another missionary assertion that the Germans were to blame, see "Atrocities of Turk Soldiers," *Ogden [Utah] Standard,* October 9, 1917, p. 3.

23. *Dallas News,* April 4, 1916, p. 1. Another missionary article told the same false story about Turkish activities in Palestine that was seen in British propaganda (see the section "The Jews" in chapter 10): "Missionaries Say Turkey Is on Verge of Anarchy," *Syracuse [N.Y.] Herald,* March 14, 1915, p. 11.

24. William Walker Rockwell, *Armenia: A List of Books and Articles, with Annotations.*

25. Books by Leon Dominian, Herbert Gibbons, and others. See the sections "Books of the Missionary Establishment" below and "The United States Government and the Missionary Establishment" in chapter 11.

26. One official fifteen-page Ottoman pamphlet on the Armenian revolutionary parties was listed.

27. William Walker Rockwell, *The Deportation of the Armenians,* and *The Pitiful Plight of the Assyrian Christians in Persia and Kurdistan* (New York: ACASR, 1916).

28. ACASR, *Armenia: The Most Tragic Story in Human History,* p. 2. Attacks on girls were a very prominent part of ACASR stories. See the many examples cited in this chapter and "Ransoms Armenian Girls," *New York Times,* February 13, 1916.

29. ACASR, *The Most Terrible Winter the World Has Ever Known.*

30. ACASR, *Latest News concerning the Armenian and Syrian Sufferers, April 5, 1916* (New York: ACASR, 1916), p. 11. A number of these "latest news" releases were issued.

31. FO 394/40/179902, "Documents relating to the treatment of Armenian and Assyrian Christians in the Ottoman Empire and N.W. Persia: Key to names of places and persons withheld from publication," September 11, 1916.

32. Newspapers occasionally printed Dashnak reports from nonmissionary sources: for example, "Massacre of 9,000 Armenians Reported," *Dallas Morning News,* July 4, 1915, p. 2.

33. The population of Ottoman Anatolia in 1912: Muslims 14,536,142; Greeks 1,254,333; Armenians 1,493,276; Syrians, Chaldeans, and Nestorians 144,499; Jews 76,498; other 31,604; total 17,536,352 (Justin McCarthy, *Muslims and Minorities,* p. 110). These figures are by religion, because the Ottomans kept their population registration statistics by religion. Protestants are included in the Armenian figure. The inflated Armenian population and mortality numbers were to remain a staple of the accusations of genocide against the Turks. This continues today.

34. ACASR, *Armenia: An Appeal to the Citizens of the United States on Behalf of the Armenian Sufferers.*

35. Ibid.

36. James L. Barton, *The Near East Relief,* p. 7.

37. "Flagging the Flour," *New Near East* 6, no. 4 (January 1921): 11–12. One Near East Relief worker felt that in at least one quality Armenians were much superior to Americans: "Armenian girls made much better wives than Americans," because they were "less spoiled" and more likely to stay home with the children ("Ex-Service Man Says Armenia Is the Place to Look for Wife," *Racine [Wisc.] Journal-News,* March 6, 1920, p. 10). Other newspapers do not seem to have printed the story.

38. ACASR, *A National Test of Brotherhood: America's Opportunity to Relieve Suffering in Armenia, Syria, Persia, and Palestine,* p. 3. See also an article reporting on Van and western Iran, based on reports from Presbyterian missionaries, that is filled with inaccuracies: "Kill 10,000 Christians," *Washington Post,* May 15, 1915, p. 15; see also "Atrocities in Persia," *Springfield [Mass.] Daily Republican,* April 20, 1915, p. 20.

39. Material in this section was taken from Justin McCarthy, Esat Arslan, Cemalettin Taşkıran, and Ömer Turan, *The Armenian Rebellion at Van,* pp. 176–257.

40. ACASR, *A National Test of Brotherhood,* p. 6.

41. Ibid., p. 5.

42. On the Armenian revolt, see ibid. For the version of the Ottoman government on the Armenian revolt, see *Verité sur le Mouvement Révolutionnaire Arménien et les mesures gouvernementales* (Constantinople: n.p., 1916). The copy used here is in the British National Archives, FO 395/40/237817.

43. I have calculated elsewhere (McCarthy, *Muslims and Minorities,* pp. 121–30) that 59 percent of the Armenians of Anatolia survived the wars. The worst Armenian mortality occurred among refugees in the Russian Southern Caucasus, where they were not under Ottoman control (McCarthy et al., *The Armenian Rebellion at Van,* pp. 273–75).

44. Near East Relief, *By an Eye Witness: What They Saw in the Near East.*

45. Finley, president of the Presbyterian/Congregationalist Knox College from 1892 to 1899 and the State University of New York from 1913 to 1921, was head of the American Red Cross in the Near East in 1918–19 (see "Dr. Finley Tells Near East Needs," *New York Times,* April 27, 1919, p. 27). He became associate editor of the *New York Times* in 1921 and was editor-in-chief in 1937–38. Finley's views were heavily colored by his religious belief (see John Finley, *A Pilgrim in Palestine;* and "Dr. Finley Flew to Near Jerusalem," *New York Times,* November 6, 1918, p. 13). He was a board member of the Federal Council of Churches from 1921 to 1925. While New York state commissioner of education (1913–21) he was noted for quashing all dissent on the war.

46. "Death Decreed for Armenians by the Moslems," *Atlanta Constitution,* August 8, 1916, p. 1.

47. The committee members included James Barton, Samuel Dutton, John Mott, Stephen Wise, Arthur James, Frank Mason North, Cleveland Dodge, and W. Stuart Dodge, all of whom were to become ACASR board members.

48. "Tales of Armenian Horrors Confirmed," *New York Times,* September 27, 1915, p. 5. "Many of which are in the possession of the committee" was the description of the interviews. These have not ever been found, but they may be the same documents sent by Barton to Toynbee (see the section "The Bryce Report" in chapter 10). Barton admitted that he did not know many of the authors. See also "Committee Confirms Armenian Massacres," *Dallas Morning News,* September 27, 1915, p. 1; "Turks' Crimes Described as 'Worst in 1,000 Years,'" *Indianapolis Star,* October 4, 1915, pp. 1, 5; and "Surpass Anything in Modern History," *Van Wert [Ohio] Daily Bulletin,* October 1, 1915, p. 1.

49. "Expose of Turkish Atrocities Come to Light in Germany," *New Castle [Pa.] News,* November 11, 1916, p. 1.

50. "Asks for $5,000,000 to Succor Armenia," *New York Times,* October 4, 1916, p. 2; "Evidence of Turkish Atrocities in Armenia," *Dallas Morning News,* October 4, 1915, p. 1; "Call for Relief of Million Armenians in Asia," *Fresno [Calif.] Morning Republican,* October 4, 1916, p. 1; "Greatest Horrors in History," *Washington Post,* October 4, 1915, p. 5. See also "Armenian Women Put Up at Auction," *New York Times,* September 29, 1915, p. 3.

51. "Ask Aid of the Nation," *New York Times,* October 21, 1916, p. 7.

52. "Armenians Tortured over Slow Fires," *Fort Wayne [Ind.] Daily News,* September 30, 1915, p. 2.

53. "Bury Children Alive," *Washington Post,* October 15, 1917 (the testimony of the missionary Henry H. Riggs). This press agency article appeared in many newspapers large and small.

54. See, for example, "American Woman Missionary Gives Vivid Picture of Armenia's Fate: Only 213 of 5,000 Exiles Survived," *Washington Post,* February 6, 1916, p. 14. Suspiciously, the woman's name was supposedly withheld so that she would not be in danger from the Turks, but she was in Cairo under British protection when the story appeared.

55. "Armenians Loot Turk Homes in Retaliation," *Dallas News,* October 6, 1915. The missionary was Ernest Yarrow (see the section "Politics" in chapter 11).

56. "A New Palestine If the Allies Win," *New York Times,* March 22, 1915, p. 3.

57. See, for example, "Crucified by Turks," *Washington Post,* April 29, 1915, p. 1; and "Turks Crucifying and Burning Alive Many Christians," *Atlanta Constitution,* April 29, 1915, p. 1 (both from the Presbyterian Board of Missions); "More Slain by Kurds," *Washington Post,* May 1, 1915, p. 11 (from the American Board); "Million Armenians the Prey of Turks," *New York Sun,* December 15, 1915, p. 2; and other examples given below.

58. "Asks Funds to Save Million Armenians," *New York Times,* February 27, 1916, p. 14; "Dr. Hill Describes Agonies of Armenians," *Dallas Morning News,* February 12, 1916, p. 4.

59. "Are Wiping Out the Armenian Race," *Dunkirk [N.Y.] Evening Observer,* October 7, 1915, p. 1; "Enver Pasha's Boast of Bloody Butchery," *Fort Wayne [Ind.] News,* October 7, 1915, p. 1. The papers printed many distorted or simply false assertions about the events in Van. See, for example, "Second Exile for Armenians," *Waterloo [Iowa] Evening Courier and Reporter,* December 28, 1916, p. 8 (the report of an ACASR official). For another missionary account from Tiflis, see "15,000 Slain by Turks," *Washington Post,* May 7, 1916, p. 14. The article quoted Richard Hill, an ACASR representative in Tiflis, alleging that the Turks had killed 15,000 Armenians in the small town of Mamahatun, many times the number of Armenians who lived there. The article was not identified as such by the *Washington Post,* but other papers that printed it described the source: "according to a statement by Richard Hill, a local representative of the American Committee for Armenian and Syrian Relief" ("Turks Slaughtered Armenians in City," *Janesville [Wisc.] Daily Gazette,* May 1, 1916, p. 1).

60. "Turkish Atrocities Reported," *Bismarck [N.Dak.] Daily Tribune,* October 15, 1915, p. 1. It is hard to believe that any Ottoman official would really make such a statement to a foreign ambassador. A far smaller number of Armenians, not Greeks, were actually killed at Trabzon. In his book, considered below, Morgenthau actually said that it was Talat who made the statement, not Enver.

61. *Chicago Tribune,* January 1, 1918, p. 5.

62. See the extensive consideration of this in the section "The Bryce Report" in chapter 10.

63. See, for example, "Greater Part of Armenians Die," *Fresno [Calif.] Morning Republican,* October 15, 1915, p. 1. The article ascribes this analysis to Ambassador Morgenthau. His reports to the State Department were not available to the press, but Morgenthau was in contact with the missionary establishment, which was probably the source of the article. The figure of half the Armenians dying was not true even in 1923, much less in 1915.

64. "Her Thumb Bears Red Tattoo Mark of Moslem Slave," *Atlanta Constitution,* January 4, 1920, p. 7B. The article did not mention anything about the slavery of the woman with the tattoo but said that she was working in a Turkish hospital. "Armenians Arrive with Tragic Stories," *Dallas Morning News,* January 4, 1920 (part 1), p. 2.

65. "Turkish Atrocities," *Janesville [Wisc.] Daily Gazette,* August 30, 1915, p. 4. The article claimed that the Turks planned to exterminate all Christians in the empire, according to the unnamed source.

66. "Turks Depopulate Towns of Armenia," *New York Times,* August 27, 1915, p. 3. This article also appeared in smaller town newspapers for a month after it was printed in the *Times,* perhaps copied from it.

67. "Slay Armenians by Hundreds," *Chicago Tribune,* September 17, 1915, p. 2.

68. And this is assuming the maximum possible area between the two cities. The "mountains" in the region would be called hills by most.

69. "Two Million Refugees Are Fed by Americans," *Nevada State Journal,* November 27, 1916, p. 3.

70. I have avoided consideration of articles and books such as the Reverend Thomas B. Gregory, "Biblical Prophecy of Armageddon Fulfilled in Battle of Nazareth," *San Antonio Light,* October 6, 1918, p. 15; and Arthur G. Daniells, *The World War: Its Relation to the Eastern Question and Armageddon* (Nashville, Tenn.: Southern Publishing Association, 1917). I have no idea how much currency was given to such apocalyptic visions.

71. Ellis was listed in Near East Relief advertisements in 1920 as a member of the "National Committee" of Near East Relief, along with William Howard Taft, Charles Evans Hughes, Henry Morgenthau, and the leading officers of Near East Relief. He was an official of various religious organizations, including the Christian Endeavor, which had been active in opposing the Turks in the 1890s. Under the name "The Religious Rambler," he wrote articles on religion for American newspapers and magazines. His misunderstanding of events can be seen in his article attesting that Enver Paşa was organizing an army in the Caucasus to defeat the Armenians ("Raises Turkish Army," *Washington Post,* August 26, 1919, p. 4).

72. "Discusses Future of Mohammedanism," *Dallas News,* February 9, 1918, p. 5. Ellis's articles, cited here from the *Dallas News* and *Atlanta Constitution*, appeared all over America, distributed by his own press service, the Ellis Service, and the *New York Herald* company.

73. "War's Desolation Is Seen in Van, Turkey," *Dallas News,* February 17, 1918, p. 2; "Missionaries Help Cause of the Allies," *Dallas News,* September 22, 1918, p. 2; "Rescue Harem Girls," *Washington Post,* October 16, 1919, p. 8.

74. "City of Urfa Scene of Black Perfidy," *Dallas News,* November 19, 1919, p. 6.

75. "Heroism and Horror Feature This Story from Western Persia," *Atlanta Constitution,* September 14, 1919, p. A10.

76. "Hangman's Noose First Instrument of Restoration of Order in Turkey," *Atlanta Constitution*, September 20, 1919, p. 8. See also "Relief Seen in Aleppo," *Washington Post,* November 30, 1919, in which Ellis also advocates hanging as the solution to problems. Readers would not have been aware that his mistakes indicated that he knew little of the topic on which he wrote. Ellis felt, for example, that Enver Paşa was leading the Turkish resistance after the war, at a time when Enver Paşa was long gone (ultimately to die in Central Asia); gave a completely confused description of the Nestorians; wrote that a "holy war" had been announced after the war, when it

had not; said that the Indian Muslims wanted to give St. Sophia to the Christians; wrote that Enver was in league with the Bolsheviks, when in fact he fought against them; and so forth ("Critical Affairs in the East as Viewed by Competent Observers," *Portsmouth [Ohio] Daily Times,* September 13, 1919, supplement, p. 1).

77. In addition to other religious posts, Haggard served as secretary of the Laymen's Missionary Movement and the American Baptist Foreign Mission Society and secretary of the YMCA in Russia. Although his articles identified him as "Secretary, American Commission for Armenian and Syrian Relief," he was in fact publicity secretary, a lesser post. Barton (*The Story of Near East Relief,* pp. 7, 429–30) did not list him on the Board of the ACASR or Near East Relief.

78. For some of the installments, see Fred Haggard, "The Atrocities in Armenia!" *Waterloo [Iowa] Times-Tribune,* December 18, 1917, p. 9; and "The Atrocities in Armenia," *Sheboygan [Wisc.] Press*, December 17 and 21, 1917, p. 2, December 22, 1917, p. 7. Although the Haggard articles appeared all across America, the *Sheboygan Press* printed stories "written especially for the *Sheboygan Press.*" Some papers announced in advance that they would be running the Haggard series. A *Waterloo Times-Tribune* (December 15, 1917, p. 1) headline called it the "First Detailed Story of Worst Crime in Human History."

79. "Untold Corpses Choke Canals and Trenches," *Atlanta Constitution,* September 19, 1915, p. 2. For another article on Van, wrong in almost every particular, see the Associated Press report "Jevded Pasha Is Blamed for Crime," *Lincoln [Nebr.] Daily Star,* October 11, 1915, p. 2. As might be imagined, the religious press heartily joined in the attack on the Turks. Quotations are not necessary, because they are exactly what would be expected, but some headlines from articles in the *Independent* tell the story: "The Greatest of Religious Massacres," "The Assassination of a Race," "The Tottering Turk," "Our Armenian Allies," and "Must Armenia Perish?"

80. McCarthy et al., *The Armenian Rebellion at Van,* pp. 241–42.

81. See, for example, "Turks Butcher Armenians and Seize Property," *Seattle [Wash.] Post-Intelligencer,* September 25, 1915. The sources were letters from unnamed "authoritative sources in Constantinople and Athens."

82. "Says Turks Are in Despair," *New York Times,* July 11, 1915, p. 5; "The Menace of Djemal Pasha," *New York Times,* September 14, 1915, p. 2; "Here and There in the War News," *New York Times,* September 5, 1915, p. XI. In later issues the *Times* and other newspapers reported that the Armenians of İzmit were alive and were being relocated by the Ottomans. The city had not been burned. *Forum* printed the opinions of Greeks and Armenians on the supposed evils of the Turks and the imminent demise of Turkish rule. According to them, Turks were shooting German officers, the Arabs were completely disaffected from the Turks, Christians were always massacred, and so forth (Philip Catzeflis, "The Partition of Islam," *Forum* 57 [January 1917]: 33–42).

83. See, for example, "German Intrigues among Arabs Vain," *New York Times,* June 26, 1916, p. 6.

84. "Turkish Women Revolt," *New York Times,* December 14, 1914, p. 2. For examples of other fanciful *Times* articles, see "Erzurum Fanatics Slay Christians,"

November 29, 1914; and "Hang Christians in Streets," December 14, 1914, p. 2
(datelined London): "a Petrograd dispatch to the Times."

85. "City of Van Free of Turks at Last," *Dallas News,* August 14, 1915, p. 15.

86. "When the Russians Took Erzerum," *Dallas News,* June 18, 1916, supplement, p. 2.
For the same type of report from Russia, see "Tales of Torture Told by Armenians,"
New York Sun, December 5, 1915, p. 2, taken from a Tiflis newspaper and based on
unnamed sources.

87. "1,056,550 Armenians Are Slain up to September, 1916," *Dallas News,* December 6,
1918, p. 1.

88. Yusuf Halaçoğlu has made an extensive study of the Ottoman records on the relocations. Records on the relocated Armenians from some provinces were very precisely
kept, whereas in others they were much less precise. The Ottomans did, however,
attempt to know exactly how many people they were moving ("Realities behind the
Relocations," in Türkkaya Ataöv, ed., *The Armenians in the Late Ottoman Period*
[Ankara: Turkish Historical Society, 2001], pp. 109–42; *Facts on the Relocation of the
Armenians (1914–1918)* [Ankara: Turkish Historical Society, 2002]).

89. "Realm of Religion," *Dallas Morning News,* October 10, 1915 (part 3), p. 3.

90. "Armenia Symbol of Suffering for Ages," *Cambridge City [Ind.] Tribune,* February 20, 1919, p. 1. The newspapers were full of sad stories of Armenian children who
had suffered and told in heart-wrenching detail of evils committed by the Turks.
See, for example, "A Wreck from a Harem," *Lincoln [Nebr.] Evening State Journal,*
December 19, 1919, p. 10.

91. "Armenians Kill and Eat Own Children," *Fort Wayne [Ind.] News,* August 8, 1916,
p. 1; "3500 Begging," *Lowell [Mass.] Sun,* August 18, 1918, p. 2; "Cannibalism with
Refugees in Arabia," *Reno [Nev.] Evening Gazette,* August 18, 1916, p. 1; "Armenians
Eat Children in Starving Extremity," *Syracuse [N.Y.] Herald,* August 8, 1916, p. 1;
"Armenians Eat Children," *Washington Post,* August 20, 1916, p. A7. Because of its
sensational nature, this was a very popular article and appeared all over America.
The various dates of publication indicate that editors used the article to "spice up"
a dull news day. For another report of cannibalism, see "Call for Relief of Million
Armenians in Asia," *Fresno [Calif.] Morning Republican,* October 4, 1916, p. 1.

92. "Worse Than War," *Oakland Tribune,* October 31, 1915, p. 3. The "Eight Commandments" were printed in what the *Tribune* called Turkish and in English. The "Turkish" was actually Arabic.

93. Howard M. Owen, "The Man Who Incited the Armenian Massacres," *Washington
Post,* January 26, 1919, p. SM2. Others blamed the Germans. See the feature article
"Germany in Turkey," *Seattle [Wash.] Post-Intelligencer,* June 8, 1915, p. 8.

94. "Barbarities in Present War Greater Than in Caesar's Time," *Fort Wayne [Ind.] Sentinel,* November 12, 1915, p. 13. The comparison with the persecution of early Christian martyrs was often seen in the press and especially in religious writings.

95. "Starving, Homeless Christians in Asia Minor," *Fort Wayne [Ind.] Sentinel,* January
19, 1919, section 4, p. 9.

96. James Morgan, "Journeys to the Fallen Nations of Europe: The Martyrdom
of Armenia," *Syracuse [N.Y.] Herald,* December 12, 1915, p. 11. See also another

full-page Morgan piece, "Battling on Old Time Fields," *Lincoln [Nebr.] Daily Star,* January 31, 1915, editorial section, p. 1.

97. See, for example, "450,000 Armenians Reported Massacred," *Dallas Morning News,* September 25, 1915, p. 3; and "Armenians Ordered to Convert to Islam," *Dallas Morning News,* January 4, 1920, p. 3. I have cited the Associated Press stories as they appeared in the *Dallas Morning News.* The AP also printed reports from its correspondent who accompanied the Russian army fighting in Van Province. He seems to have reported what he was told by local Armenians, neglecting to mention, for example, any Armenian revolt. See "Sixty Armenians Left of Hamlet of 500—All Women and Children Gone," *Daily Kennebec [Maine] Journal,* July 12, 1915, p. 2.

98. See, for example, "2,000 Armenian Civilians Said to Have Been Killed," *Dallas Morning News,* February 14, 1920, p. 13; and "Massacres of Thousands of Armenians Reported," *Dallas Morning News,* February 27, 1920, p. 2.

99. See, for example, "Claim Armenians Are Killed by Thousands (from the *London Times* and *London Chronicle*)," *Dallas Morning News,* September 26, 1915, p. 5. The *Dallas Morning News* printed more news from British and other Allied newspapers than any of the other newspapers seen for this study (again drawn from the AP).

100. See, for example, "Turks Slaughter 10,000 Christians," *Chillicothe [Mo.] Constitution,* July 23, 1915, p. 1; and "6,000 Dead in Massacre," *Fort Wayne [Ind.] Sentinel,* May 17, 1915, p. 1. The latter article was especially ridiculous, quoting as an authoritative source the Russian consul at Urmia, who contended that the Turks had killed 6,000 Armenians in Van City, that Armenians had been driven away "as slaves," and so forth.

101. Advertisements for ACASR and Near East Relief campaigns appeared in newspapers all across America. The large and full-page ads from the central headquarters were placed in major newspapers and many minor ones. It is much easier to find advertisements in the digitized files of the *New York Times* than it is to find them in other newspapers, so the *Times* is most often cited here. Sample searches for various dates indicate that the *Times* ran more of the ads but that other papers ran many of them.

102. The newspapers were full of such ads, usually with statements such as "This space donated by William R. Compton Co."

103. For example, an ad with a drawing of a pretty, dark-eyed girl in the *Galveston Daily News* ("Has This Little Girl a Home in Your Heart?—She Has No Other") and many other newspapers described "the Syrians, inhabitants of Palestine" and the "5,000,000 Greeks under Turkish domination at the beginning of the war." In reality 1.3 million Greek Orthodox lived in Ottoman Anatolia and 600,000 in Ottoman Europe (including Istanbul). The "Greeks" of the Arab provinces were Greek Orthodox, not ethnic Greeks, because the Ottomans kept census records by religion only. But even if they were added into the Greek total, 5 million would be more than double the actual number. See McCarthy, *Muslims and Minorities,* pp. 89–99.

104. See, among many others, *Fort Wayne [Ind.] Journal-Gazette,* March 12, 1916, p. 5; and the *Newark [N.J.] Daily Advocate,* March 14, 1916, p. 7.

105. *Oshkosh [Wisc.] Daily Northwestern,* November 28, 1916, p. 5.

106. "In the Name of Pity—Give!" *Lowell [Mass.] Sun,* February 21, 1919, p. 5 (an ACASR ad).

107. "Leading Americans Plead for Relief in Near East," *Atlanta Constitution,* December 21, 1919, p. 19.

108. "Poor Little Innocent Children Lie Dead in the Streets in the Far [*sic*] East," *Lima [Iowa] Daily News,* February 26, 1920, p. 5. "Far East" was presumably an error, because the ad spoke only of Armenians.

109. See, for example, "Sentenced to Die" (Near East Relief ad), *New York Times,* April 13, 1922, p. 13.

110. ACASR ad in the *New York Times,* November 3, 1917, p. 8. This ad was repeated in other issues of the *Times* and in other papers. Shushan figured in a number of other ads in many newspapers.

111. "Burlap Bag His Only Garment" (Near East Relief ad), *Humeston [Iowa] New Era,* December 17, 1919, p. 5. The picture of the boy was used in a number of other advertisements.

112. See, for example, the story of Mooshek Vorperian (ACASR ad) in the *New York Times,* November 8, 1917, p. 9.

113. ACASR ad in the *New York Times,* March 9, 1919, p. 38.

114. Near East Relief ad in the *New York Times,* March 11, 1920, p. 7.

115. McCarthy, *Muslims and Minorities,* pp. 47–88.

116. "Shall This Child Perish?" (an ACASR ad), *New York Times,* March 4, 1919, p. 14. The ad featured a drawing of a sad-eyed small girl. See also the "400,000 Hungry Mouths" ad, *New York Times,* March 16, 1919, p. 49. The 400,000 were the children in the group of 4 million. An ACASR ad in the *New York Times,* April 3, 1917, counted 2 million refugees ("Asia Minor and Syria," p. 10).

117. "Draw Out Thy Soul to the Hungry, and Satisfy the Afflicted" (Near East Relief ad), *New York Times,* October 19, 1923, p. 11. An ACASR ad in the *New York Times* (April 3, 1917, p. 10, and in the same newspaper on other days) stated that there were 2 million "survivors," indicating complete confusion over numbers.

118. See, for example, "What It's All About" (ACASR ad), *New York Times,* February 24, 1919, p. 13.

119. Near East Relief sent Armenian refugees to speak throughout the United States. "War Nurse from Armenia Asks America's Aid," *Dunkirk [N.Y.] Evening Observer,* February 7, 1920, p. 11.

120. See, for example, "Armenian Describes Turkish Atrocities," *Dallas Morning News,* February 24, 1919, p. 5; "Armenia Dependent on America for Aid," *New York Times,* August 6, 1918, p. 13; "Organizing Relief for Armenian Christians," *Colorado Springs Gazette,* April 7, 1915, p. 5; "Missionaries Meet," *Fort Wayne [Ind.] Daily News,* October 14, 1915, p. 13; "Gives Lecture on Near East," *Hartford [Conn.] Courant,* December 18, 1921, p. 6; and "To Speak Here on Persecution of Armenians,"

Dallas Morning News, October 8, 1917, p. 4. A meeting in Syracuse ejected dissenters ("Thousands Are Protesting the Turk Atrocities," *Syracuse [N.Y.] Herald,* October 21, 1915, p. 9).

121. "Thousands Protest Armenian Murders," *New York Times,* October 18, 1915, p. 3.

122. "$115,000 to Armenia at Sunday's Meeting," *New York Times,* May 29, 1917, p. 15.

123. "Thousands Hear Tale of Horror Told by Ussher," *Atlanta Constitution,* April 1, 1918, p. 1. See also "Curb Turkey, Says Colonel," *New York Times,* May 30, 1917, p. 3.

124. "Powerful Plea Made by Woman for Armenians," *Atlanta Constitution,* March 3, 1920, p. 11. Thirteen centuries before would have been approximately the year 620.

125. "Armenia's Women: Tragedy Vaster Than Belgium's," *Chicago Tribune,* May 19, 1918, p. A5. Of course, no "desert way from the Black Sea to the Persian Gulf" existed.

126. "Report on Near East Drive," *New York Times,* January 31, 1919, p. 3.

127. These meetings are far too numerous to list. See, for example, "Armenian Sufferers to Ask Aid of Reno," *Nevada State Journal,* August 12, 1917, p. 4.

128. See, for example, "Makes Appeal for Armenians," *Waterloo [Iowa] Times-Tribune,* October 31, 1919, p. 9.

129. "To Launch Drive Here Today for Rescue of 100 Armenian Children," *Eau Claire [Wisc.] Leader,* April 29, 1921, p. 5. The Turks had arrived in Asia Minor nearly four hundred years before 1453.

130. "Rotary Club to Aid Gas Probe," *Elyria [Ohio] Chronicle-Telegram,* April 21, 1920, pp. 1, 5.

131. "Armenians Are Suffering," *Oshkosh [Wisc.] Daily Northwestern,* March 8, 1921, p. 4.

132. "Massacre of Armenians by Turks Detailed by Returned Missionary before Sandusky Audience Sunday," *Sandusky [Ohio] Star-Journal,* June 18, 1917, p. 10.

133. For example, "Armenians Are Turk Victims," *Des Moines [Iowa] News,* January 9, 1919, p. 6; no title, *Cambridge City [Ind.] Tribune,* January 2, 1919, p. 1; "Man Who Knows Turk To Be Brought Here," *Racine [Wisc.] Journal-News,* January 29, 1921, p. 1; "Mayflower," *Mansfield [Ohio] News,* May 8, 1920, p. 5; "Near East Relief Speaker to Talk at Two Meetings," *La Crosse [Wisc.] Tribune and Leader-Press,* April 20, 1921, p. 6; and "LaGrange News," *Fort Wayne [Ind.] News and Sentinel,* December 20, 1920, p. 10. Partridge gave more than one talk in many cities. In Indianapolis, he said that all Armenia's problems would be solved if the United States gave Armenia a $2 million loan ("American Loan Will Aid Armenia Solve Problem," *Indianapolis Star,* January 4, 1921, p. 1). Armenia at the time had been taken over by the Bolsheviks.

134. For an example of local appeals, see "Dr. Gage Issues an Appeal for Aid for the Starving Children of the Near East," *Cedar Rapids [Iowa] Evening Gazette,* January 4, 1921, p. 1; "Armenian and Syrian Relief Mass Meeting," *Albert Lea [Minn.] Evening Tribune,* April 8, 1918, p. 5; and "Relief Campaign to Open Tonight," *Sandusky [Ohio] Standard,* August 10, 1917, p. 9. Many such meetings were announced or reviewed in local newspapers. They must have been held in most towns of any size.

135. What the government should do was seldom detailed, and it would not have been able to do much. The real purpose of the resolutions was to unite the people in support of the relief organizations. See "Sympathy for Armenia," *Lowell [Mass.] Sun,* November 19, 1915, p. 17; and "Racinites Give Aid to War's Victims," *Racine [Wisc.] Journal-News,* October 23, 1916, pp. 1, 10.

136. For Sandusky, for example, see "Horrible Cruelty toward Women and Children to Be Told at Relief Meeting Friday," *Sandusky [Ohio] Star-Journal,* August 7, 1917, p. 9; "Armenian Horrors Told in Reports Are Almost beyond Belief," *Sandusky Star-Journal,* August 8, 1917, p. 9.

137. "Much Money Needed to Save Starving People in Turkey," *Warren [Pa.] Evening Times,* May 27, 1916, p. 1; and many other newspapers.

138. In Fresno, California, for example, volunteers for the ACASR fanned out across the city selling the American flags for the relief fund and asking for donations ("Armenian Relief Campaign Starts Tomorrow," *Fresno [Calif.] Morning Republican,* October 20, 1916, p. 7). Racine, Wisconsin, held a mass meeting and volunteers solicited the entire city ("Mass Meeting to Raise Money for Syrian and Armenian War Victims," *Racine Journal-News,* October 20, 1916, p. 1).

139. "Give Millions Today to Save Armenians," *New York Times,* October 22, 1916, p. 2; "Call for Relief of Million Armenians in Asia," *Fresno [Calif.] Morning Republican,* October 4, 1916, p. 1; "Christians in Armenia-Syria Are Starving," *Clearfield [Pa.] Progress,* October 20, 1916, p. 1, and October 21, 1916, p. 4. Wilson's 1917 decree said that there were 2 million survivors, considerably more than the entire Anatolian Armenian population of approximately 1.5 million (see note 33 above) before the war ("President Appeals for Aid for 2,000,000 Destitute Armenians," *Waterloo [Iowa] Evening Courier,* October 29, 1917, p. 1).

140. "Diamonds: Near East Relief" (Near East Relief ad), *Near East Times,* March 9, 1920, p. 4.

141. "At Auction, a Thousand Articles" (ACASR ad), *Chicago Tribune,* February 16, 1919, p. A4.

142. For example, a benefit performance of "The Book of Job: The Greatest Drama of All Time," *New York Times,* November 1, 1922, p. 26; and "Hero Land," *New York Times,* December 10, 1917, p. 13.

143. "Armenian and Syrian Relief," *New York Times,* February 3, 1919, p. 4.

144. For example, Ambassador Morgenthau spoke on "Armenian and Syrian Day" at the New York Fair, saying that Germans had helped Turks to massacre Armenians ("Says Germans Aided Armenian Killings," *New York Times,* December 11, 1917, p. 13). See also "Mass Meeting in West Hartford for Near East Relief," *Hartford [Conn.] Courant,* December 18, 1919, p. 13.

145. Tag days were held all across America. For example, see "Armenian Relief 'Tag Day' Is Held," *Christian Science Monitor,* November 24, 1917, p. 9.

146. See, for example, "The Book of Job," *Hartford [Conn.] Courant,* November 3, 1922, p. 8.

147. See, for example, "Near East Relief Benefit," *New York Times,* September 18, 1922, p. 3.

148. "30,000 Women Start House to House Canvass," *New York Times,* March 2, 1919, p. 25.

149. Advertisement, *Lowell [Mass.] Sun,* February 21, 1919, p. 1.

150. "Campaign Begins to Save Starving," *Atlanta Constitution,* April 9, 1919, p. 1.

151. "Community Dramas Today Open Relief Campaign," *Atlanta Constitution,* April 6, 1919, p. A6; "Campaign Begins to Save Starving," *Atlanta Constitution,* April 9, 1919, p. 2.

152. ACASR, *A Story That Must Be Told: Armenians Are Starving.*

153. ACASR, *Stories from Real Life.*

154. "Our Junior Contributors," *New Near East* (October 1921): 1.

155. U.S. Congress, Senate, *Report of the Near East Relief for the Year Ending December 31, 1922,* p. 3.

156. See note 3 above on currency conversion.

157. ACASR, *Armenia: The Word Spells Tragedy,* pp. 31–34.

158. "To Ask Children to Aid Armenians," *Waterloo [Iowa] Evening Courier and Reporter,* October 4, 1917, p. 8. December 10, 1917, was declared "Good Samaritan Day." Sunday schools were asked to contribute what they would usually have spent on Christmas festivities to the ACASR.

159. Many of those with no firsthand knowledge had at one time been missionaries but had returned home before the events. See "Armenian Troubles Will Be Described," *Sandusky [Ohio] Register,* November 20, 1916, p. 6; "Armenian Race Has Achieved a Miracle," *Syracuse [N.Y.] Herald,* October 23, 1915, p. 2; "Plea for Armenians," *Washington Post,* July 3, 1916, p. 2.

160. See, for example, "Dr. Charles F. Aked at the Tabernacle This Evening," *Ogden [Utah] Standard,* September 22, 1917, p. 13; and "Rev. Papazian to Tell of Armenian Atrocities by Turks," *Lincoln [Nebr.] Daily Star,* September 26, 1917, p. 4. See Barton, *The Story of Near East Relief,* pp. 471–72, for a partial list of Near East Relief speakers. Many speakers identified in newspapers were not included in his list.

161. See, for example, "Service to Aid Armenians," *New York Times,* February 6, 1922, p. 7.

162. "Woman Describes Armenian Killings," *New York Times,* December 12, 1915, p. 6.

163. Dr. Andrew Brodie of Near East Relief, speaking at the Gunton Temple Memorial Church in Washington, D.C., told the congregation that this was so and that "an Armenian bishop assured me that Jesus was invited to visit Armenia" ("Need Not Belong to Church He Says," *Washington Post,* January 22, 1923, p. 7).

164. See, for example, "Sixty Enlist to Aid Armenian and Syrian Relief Campaign Here," *Indianapolis Star,* November 9, 1917, p. 9; "Armenian Relief," *Connellsville [Pa.] Daily Courier,* December 24, 1917, p. 1; and the section "Advertisements" above.

165. Near East Relief, *The Oldest Christian Nation—Shall It Perish?: Exclusive Material for Pastors,* p. 9.

166. ACASR, *The Call of the Dying and Destitute Armenians and Syrians to the Sunday Schools of America,* p. 1. Barton, who had been a missionary in Anatolia, must have known better than to make claims implying Ottoman intolerance of Christianity. He must also have known that no Muslims would ever put Muhammad on

an altar, because they consider him a man, not God. With these falsehoods Barton was obviously playing to his audience, which would be moved by reference to crucifixion.

167. ACASR, *Practicing Bible Precepts in Bible Lands: Handbook for Busy Pastors,* pp. 16–19, 23.

168. Near East Relief, *The Oldest Christian Nation—Shall It Perish?* pp. 31–32.

169. ACASR, *Photographical Reproductions of Latest Cablegrams from Bible Lands: February, A.D. 1918.*

170. For example, ACASR, *Boys and Girls of Bible Lands*; and *Near East Relief A Million Lives Saved: Handbook for Pastors.*

171. ACASR, *Armenia: The Word Spells Tragedy, p. 45.*

172. For example, in Syracuse, New York: "Tells Revolting Tale of Massacre," *Syracuse Herald,* April 10, 1916, p. 3. "Exiled Turkish Prisoner Coming," *Syracuse Herald,* March 5, 1916, p. 23.

173. Jews were never relocated. As part of the mutual forced migration of Turks and Greeks, Greeks were deported during the Independence War, well after these alleged deportations. See the section "Cilicia and the Pontus" in chapter 11.

174. *America at War* (Wollaston, Mass.: J. G. Allen, 1917), p. 7.

175. In Washington, D.C., for example, congregants in the Ingram Memorial Congregational Church were told by a missionary who had served in East Asia (not the Near East) that Islam demanded that the Muslim "rid the world of all unbelievers in his faith" ("Tells of Armenians Slain," *Washington Post,* October 11, 1915, p. 14); and the Reverend Rosslyn Bruce preached at St. John's Church on Turkish rape and murder ("Plea for Armenians," *Washington Post,* July 3, 1916, p. 2). Bishop Frederick Kinsman of Delaware, preaching at Trinity Church in New York, compared the Armenians to early Christian martyrs ("No Peace without Force, Rabbi Says," *New York Times,* December 27, 1915, p. 2).

176. See, for example, Near East Relief, *A Million Lives Saved: Handbook for Pastors.*

177. Ibid., p. 11.

178. It should be added that this was the opposite of what he wrote in *Ambassador Morgenthau's Story* (pp. 293–300).

179. U.S. National Archives, 867.4016/71, Morgenthau to Secretary of State, Constantinople, May 25, 1915. See Justin McCarthy, "Ottoman Archives and the Armenians, with Special Reference to the Armenian Rebellion at Van," in *International Turkish Archives Symposium* (Ankara: Başbakanlık Genel Müdürlüğü, 2007), pp. 2–28.

180. These reports, which never stated their sources or how the information got to Bulgaria, are ridiculous but seem to have been taken seriously by the Americans. The Sofia Dashnaks wrote that Tahsin Bey, the governor of Erzurum, had stated that the Ottomans were responsible for the troubles in Van and that the governor of Bitlis had decreed a massacre of Armenians in Muş. No one else has ever seen such a decree, and it is doubtful that Tahsin would make such an admission to the Dashnaks, even if it had been true. In some messages the Dashnaks stated that all the Armenians of Zeytun had been killed, while in others they wrote of the deportation of the Zeytun Armenians, who seem not to have been dead after all. See, for

example, U.S. National Archives, 867.4016/95, Dashnaks in Sofia to Morgenthau, June 15, 1915, enclosure in Morgenthau to Secretary of State, July 20, 1915.

181. See, for example, U.S. National Archives, 867.4016/119, Page to secretary of state, London, August 14, 1915 (forwarded to Morgenthau); 867.4016/67, 69, 70, reports from Allies; 867.4016/65, letter from Williams, May 3, 1915; 867.4016/61, telegram, secretary of state to Morgenthau, May 3, 1915; 867.4016/51, 52, 78, telegrams to secretary of state from Armenian patriarch (forwarded to Morgenthau).

182. See, for example, 867.4016/95, Morgenthau to secretary of state, Constantinople, July 20, 1915; 867.4016/122, Morgenthau to secretary of state, August 10, 1915; enclosure from Davis at Harput, June 11, 1915.

183. It is important to separate these contemporaneous accounts from those written after the events, sometimes well after, which are abundant.

184. This is obvious from the number of "American consular reports" used by the British propagandists. But we also have the testimony of James Barton, head of the American Board, the ACASR, and Near East Relief. Barton wrote to Arnold Toynbee of the British propaganda office: "I am enclosing herewith a package of new documents which I have recently secured in person from the State Department in Washington" (FO 95/205, Barton to Toynbee, Boston, March 6, 1916). See also FO 96/205, Barton to Toynbee, Boston, March 15, 1916, and FO 95/205, Enoch F. Bell (associate secretary of the ABCFM) to Toynbee, Boston, February 16, 1916.

185. They did unquestionably see the movements of the relocated Armenians, however.

186. 867.4016/80, Morgenthau to secretary of state, June 26, 1915.

187. I am not considering here the writings of Leslie A. Davis (*The Slaughterhouse Province*, edited by Susan K. Blair, [New Rochelle, N.Y.: A. D. Caratzas, 1989]), which would take more space than is available, except to note that Davis witnessed very little of what he reported about massacres, some of which undoubtedly occurred. His reports of what he actually saw seem credible. His assumption that 15,000–20,000 Armenians from Mamuretülaziz were killed seems impossible in light of the number of deportees who survived (see Halaçoğlu, "Realities behind the Relocation," in Ataöv, ed., *The Armenians in the Late Ottoman Period*, pp. 109–42; see also note 88 above). More troubling, he says nothing of the Armenian rebellion or the murders of Muslims that prompted the deportations of which he writes. To her credit, the editor does include two brief extracts from Ottoman publications on the rebellions.

188. See FO 96/212/"Key to Quotations for October 4, 1915 (galley)" for an example of Morgenthau cables to the State Department that ended up in the hands of the ACASR and, through that organization, at the British Propaganda Bureau.

189. "Turkey Is Endeavoring to Get a Whitewash," *Galveston Daily News,* December 12, 1918, p. 2. For examples of the content of Morgenthau's speeches, see "Armenian Atrocities No Myth," *Indianapolis Star,* May 28, 1916, p. 8; "Horrors Seen by Morgenthau," *Ogden [Utah] Standard,* May 22, 1916, p. 5; and "The Armenian Question Explained by Expert," *Oshkosh [Wisc.] Daily Northwestern,* June 2, 1917, p. 5. See "Not a Cure-All," *Frederick [Md.] Post,* March 4, 1920, p. 4, for a funny but disturbing use of a Morgenthau speech by an antiprohibitionist to suggest that the Turks would not have killed Armenians if they had taken the occasional drink.

190. "Asked Morgenthau in Turkish Cabinet," *New York Times,* March 3, 1916, p. 4. Morgenthau was introduced by Cleveland H. Dodge.

191. "Found Turks Eager to Sell Palestine," *New York Times,* May 22, 1916, p. 2.

192. "Turkish Atrocities," *Lowell [Mass.] Sun,* May 28, 1917, p. 6.

193. "Allies, He Says, Are Too Easy on Turkey," *New York Times,* March 5, 1920, p. 10.

194. "Allies May Block Turk's Attempt to Cross into Thrace," *New Castle [Pa.] News,* September 11, 1922, p. 12 (an International News Service article).

195. In addition to *Ambassador Morgenthau's Story,* see Henry Morgenthau (in collaboration with French Strother), *All in a Life-time,* and *The Tragedy of Armenia* (London: Spottiswoods, Ballantyne and Co., 1919).

196. Heath W. Lowry, *The Story behind Ambassador Morgenthau's Story,* pp. 29–33. Much of the discussion of Morgenthau here was drawn from this excellent book. Hendrick was mentioned in the preface: "My thanks are due to my friend, Mr. Burton J. Hendrick, for the invaluable assistance he has rendered in the presentation of the book." Hendrick called his work on the book "ghosting" (p. 31).

197. Ibid., pp. 15–29.

198. Morgenthau, *Ambassador Morgenthau's Story,* pp. 82–89. In the same pages Morgenthau also blamed losses in the American stock market on the Germans.

199. Ibid., pp. 91–93, 161, 167, 177–78, 238–41. On other Germans who reportedly spoke to Morgenthau, see ibid., p. 375.

200. Ibid., pp. 108, 189–91.

201. Indeed, the publisher's advertisements, placed in newspapers all across America, extolled "the real story told to him [Morgenthau] by the German Ambassador to Turkey." For an example, see "Germany Quits" (advertisement), *Washington Post,* November 16, 1918, p. 7.

202. Morgenthau, *Ambassador Morgenthau's Story,* pp. 333–42, (quotation on pp. 337–38).

203. Ibid., p. 342. Morgenthau reported that other Turkish officials also confided in him. One "responsible Turkish official" told him that the Turks were planning exquisite tortures for the Armenians and that they had been consulting the records of the Spanish Inquisition in order to do the job properly (p. 307).

204. See Lowry's extensive documentation of this: *The Story behind Ambassador Morgenthau's Story,* pp. 39–70.

205. The books of clippings are in the Morgenthau Papers in the Library of Congress.

206. Morgenthau also offered an alternative reason for Turkish actions: "The Armenians have been treated as perhaps no people in history have been treated because they are the spiritual brothers of western races" (Henry Morgenthau, "Morgenthau Pleads for Helping Hand in the Near East," *Olean [N.Y.] Evening Herald,* December 18, 1919, p. 11; the article appeared in a number of newspapers, often with the same headline).

207. Morgenthau, *Ambassador Morgenthau's Story,* pp. 276, 285.

208. Ibid., p. 287.

209. See, for example, "Ambassador Tells of Turkish Diplomacy," *Galveston Daily News,* December 7, 1918, p. 4 (one part of the serialization). Circulation figures from Lowry, *The Story behind Ambassador Morgenthau's Story,* pp. 8–10.

210. See, for example, "Talaat Ordered the Armenian Massacres," *Waterloo [Iowa] Evening Courier and Reporter,* December 11, 1918, p. 7; "Made in Germany," *Des Moines [Iowa] News,* July 11, 1918, p. 6.

211. *McClure's Magazine* 51, no. 2 (February 1919): 46 (advertisement); 51, no. 1 (January 1919): 4 (advertisement).

212. See, for example, "Two Notable War Books," *Literary Digest,* December 21, 1918, p. 8.

213. Grace H. Knapp, *The Tragedy of Bitlis,* p. 30.

214. See chapter 7.

215. Clarence D. Ussher, *An American Physician in Turkey: A Narrative of Adventures in Peace and in War,* p. 285.

216. Ussher was stationed in Van. The British consul there in 1905, G. E. Tyrrell, wrote: "I myself know by experience that Dr. Ussher's statements are unreliable, and I never accept any of them without careful personal enquiry." British ambassador Nicholas R. O'Conor added: "The United States Minister, whom I spoke to, informed me that he regarded Dr. Ussher as most unreliable, and given to gross exaggeration owing to his innate dislike of Turks and his inordinate fanaticism" (FO 424/208, O'Conor to Landsowne, Constantinople, May 12, 1905).

217. Mary Schauffler Platt, ed., *The War Journal of a Missionary in Persia;* originally published in Britain as Mary Edna Lewis, *The War Journal of a Missionary in Persia,* ed. Mary Schauffler Platt (London: Board of Foreign Missions of the Presbyterian Church, 1915).

218. Aurora Mardiganian, *Ravished Armenia: The Story of Aurora Mardiganian.*

219. No copy of the film, which was shown either as *Auction of Souls* or as *Ravished Armenia,* seems to have survived. For an example of its showing, see "Turk Atrocities in 'Auction of Souls' Film," *Modesto [Calif.] Evening News,* March 1, 1920, p. 5. The movie inspired newspaper and magazine articles (see, for example, Howard M. Owen, "The Man Who Incited the Armenian Massacres," *Washington Post,* January 26, 1919, p. SM2). There was also another Near East Relief movie, *Seeing Is Believing, or Uncle America Sees It Through* ("Near East's Crisis Portrayed in Film," *Christian Science Monitor,* November 25, 1922, p. 7). See Leshu Torchin, *"Ravished Armenia:* Visual Media, Humanitarian Advocacy, and the Formulation of Witnessing Publics," *American Anthropologist* 108, no. 1 (March 2006): 214–20.

220. Robert E. Speer, *The Gospel and the New World,* pp. 48–49. The source also speaks of Armenians deported from Istanbul, which did not occur.

221. The correspondence did not appear from the Ottoman archives until the 1980s and in no way supported Gibbons's assertions.

222. Herbert Adams Gibbons, *The Blackest Page in Modern History,* pp. 20, 32.

223. See McCarthy, *Muslims and Minorities,* p. 110.

224. Gibbons, *The Blackest Page in Modern History,* pp. 49, 51.

225. Herbert Adams Gibbons, *The New Map of Europe, (1911–1914): The Story of the Recent European Diplomatic Crises and Wars and of Europe's Present Catastrophe,* p. 188. Gibbons had felt in 1916 (see note 224 above) that the Turks were "not a fanatical people by nature" but seems to have changed his mind by 1918.

226. Justin McCarthy, *Death and Exile: The Ethnic Cleansing of Ottoman Muslims,* p. 164.

227. William H. Hall, *The Near East: Crossroads of the World* ("With a final chapter by James Barton"). See also "Under the Heel of the Turk," *National Geographic* (July 1918): 51–69.

228. Papazian was born Bertha Sullivan and married Garabed H. Papazian. She at one time edited the journal *Armenia.*

229. Bertha S. Papazian, *The Tragedy of Armenia,* pp. 43, 92.

230. Judging by reviews, Papazian's book was influential in America. See, for example, "The Tragedy of Armenia," *Atlanta Constitution,* March 9, 1919, p. 3; "Armenia," *Oakland Tribune,* January 10, 1919, p. 4; and "The Tragedy of Armenia," *Biblical World* 54, no. 2 (March 1920): 201–2.

231. Joseph K. Greene, *Leavening the Levant,* p. 49. The author was the father of Frederick Greene, who wrote what was probably the most inaccurate and prejudiced missionary account of Turks and Armenians: *Armenian Massacres or the Sword of Mohammed: Containing a Complete and Thrilling Account of the Terrible Atrocities and Wholesale Murders Committed in Armenia by Mohammedan Fanatics, Including a Full Account of the Turkish People, Their History, Government, Manners, Customs and Strange Religious Beliefs, to Which Is Added "The Mohammedan Reign of Terror in Armenia,"* edited by Henry Davenport Northrop, D.D., the Well-Known Author. See the section "The Books" in chapter 7.

232. See the sections "Sin" and "The Sinful Muslim" in chapter 4.

233. Samuel Graham Wilson, *Modern Movements among Moslems,* p. 82.

234. See, for example, *New Near East* (May 1923): 16 and (April 1923): 14. The Christian refugees in Istanbul were mentioned in many articles in the missionary and popular press as well.

235. McCarthy, *Death and Exile,* pp. 304, 331, 332

Chapter 10, The Propaganda Bureau

1. Speech in the House of Commons, *Hansard,* 5th series, H. C., 331 (February 16, 1938), p. 1930, quoted in James Morgan Read, *Atrocity Propaganda: 1914–1919,* p. 187.

2. FO 395/51/marked 365, Foreign Office, March 7, 1916, "Memorandum." There was some initial confusion over the chain of command. In March 1916 it was decided that the distribution of materials from Wellington House and other agencies would come under the general oversight of the Foreign Office News Department to avoid "clash and overlap." In practice, the agencies and their staffs seem to have worked well together. Toynbee, for example, did basically the same work whether for Wellington House or for other agencies.

3. "Section B (Production). This section, under Mr. Masterman, is domiciled at Wellington House, and in an adjacent building in Buckingham Gate. It deals with literature and art, and is virtually a very large publishing establishment, which issues every form of book, pamphlet, journal, and picture, and arranges for their translation into foreign languages." "Section C (Production). This section, under Mr. T. L. Gilmour, is housed in the Lord Chancellor's Court, House of Lords, and has three main branches dealing with cables and wireless, cinemas, and press articles" (CAB 21/37, December 1, 1917, John Buchan, "The Department of Information").

4. For details on the organization of British propaganda, see George C. Bruntz, *Allied Propaganda and the Collapse of the German Empire,* especially pp. 18–24; Arthur Ponsonby, *Falsehood in War-time;* Philip M. Taylor, "The Foreign Office and British Propaganda during the First World War," *Historical Journal* 23, no. 4 (December 1980): 875–98; Alice Goldfarb Marquis, "Words as Weapons: Propaganda in Britain and Germany during the First World War," *Journal of Contemporary History* 13, no. 3 (July 1978): 467–98; Harold D. Lasswell et al., *Propaganda and Promotional Activities: An Annotated Bibliography* (Chicago: University of Chicago Press, 1969); Gary S. Messinger, *British Propaganda and the State in the First World War;* M. L. Sanders, "Wellington House and British Propaganda during the First World War," *Historical Journal* 18, no. 1 (March 1975): 119–46; and M. L. Sanders and Philip M. Taylor, *British Propaganda during the First World War, 1914–18.* Sanders ("Wellington House," pp. 144–46) provides organizational tables. See also FO 395/51, London, March 7, 1916, Masterman's Memorandum, marked "confidential." In the Department of Information, Toynbee, Bevan, Napier, and others were assigned to the Intelligence Branch. In April 1918 they were transferred to the newly created Foreign Office Department of Political Intelligence, led by Sir William Tyrrell (T 1/12333/1432, Rushiust to secretary of the treasury, Office of the Under-Secretary of State, April 6, 1918).

5. Sanders and Taylor, *British Propaganda during the First World War,* pp. 40–41.

6. Best known was the Central Committee for National Patriotic Associations, formed in August 1914, whose goal was to justify British war aims. Its honorary president was prime minister Herbert Asquith; its vice-presidents, the Earl of Rosebery (Archibald Primrose) and Arthur Balfour (Bruntz, *Allied Propaganda and the Collapse of the German Empire,* p. 19; Sanders and Taylor, *British Propaganda during the First World War,* p. 42).

7. CAB 21/37, December 1, 1917, John Buchan, "The Department of Information."

8. STAT 12/22/7, Gowers to Liddington, London, December 18, 1918 (also in T 1/11992). See also Sanders and Taylor, *British Propaganda during the First World War,* p. 108.

9. T 1/11992, Schuster to His Majesty's Treasury, London, September 30, 1914. In fact, publishers soon learned who their real masters were and often engaged in direct negotiations with the government bureaus, as seen below.

10. T 1/11992, H.M. Stationery Office to The Secretary, His Majesty's Treasury, London, September 20, 1914.

11. T 1/11992, Heath to Schuster, London, August 4, 1915; Schuster to The Secretary, His Majesty's Treasury, July 6, 1915; Heath to Gowers, London, February 19, 1916; Gowers to The Secretary, His Majesty's Treasury, October 13, 1916; Heath to Gowers, November 2, 1916.

12. The Foreign Office News Department had at least theoretical control over propaganda. The majority of the archival records used here are from that department's much vetted records (FO 395).

13. See Sanders and Taylor, *British Propaganda during the First World War,* chapter 5, from which some of this material has been drawn.

14. Gilbert Parker, *The World in the Crucible.* The British government decided that propaganda should be prepared to show that Germany wanted to colonize parts of the Ottoman Empire and Persia for its own commercial and imperialist purposes. Given British war aims, this was more than somewhat hypocritical (FO 395/139/18029, "N. N." to Seton, January 16, 1917).

15. Peter Buitenhuis, *The Great War of Words,* p. 15. Advertisements for Parker's novels often appeared in the same issues of newspapers and magazines as his war propaganda.

16. The Foreign Office succinctly described Parker's job: "Sir Gilbert Parker has a special branch of work for America, which consists principally in sending out literature to and corresponding with a wide circle of influential people, and in obtaining interviews and other material for the American press correspondents in London" (FO 395/51/marked 365, Masterman memorandum, London, March 7, 1916; see also FO 115/1866, Parker to Spring-Rice, London, September 10, 1915). Parker himself was the author of a 1915 propaganda book (*The World in the Crucible,* which was a collection of historical inaccuracies and attacks against both the Germans and the Turks). He did not credit the Turks for much initiative and blamed most of their supposed actions on German instigation.

17. Butler's work in the United States did not end when America entered the war on the side of the Allies. The Foreign Office decided to keep him in his post to continue British propaganda. See the extensive documentation in FO 395/67, especially FO 395/67/195831, "Report on Conditions in the United States and Plan for an American Publicity Campaign."

18. T 1/11992/27254, "Third Report of the Work Conducted for the Government by Wellington House," October 14, 1916; Gilbert Parker, "The United States," pp. 14–15. See the names of American organizations and eminent individuals on pp. 13–16. Princeton University's president and deans are prominently mentioned in the British diplomatic accounts as being active planners in British propaganda in America. See, for example, FO 115/1961, Perry to Spring-Rice, London, January 15, 1915. The correspondence of the British Embassy in Washington contains many examples of Americans and British subjects living in America who aided the British propaganda campaign, which they undoubtedly felt was only getting out the truth. They are too numerous to cite here, but see FO 115/1961 2186. While Parker enlisted help from Americans, his desire to keep British propaganda efforts secret kept him from accepting an offer from the Allied Relief Committee to distribute

propaganda to 700,000 Americans. He believed that the British backing of the scheme would easily become public (FO 115/2028, Parker to Newton, London, July 7, 1916).

19. The campaigns are described in the secret reports of Wellington House: "Report of the Bureau Established for the Purpose of Laying before the Neutral Nations and the Dominions the Case of Great Britain and Her Allies" (T 1/11992/1762722, July 1915), "Third Report of the Work Conducted for the Government by Wellington House" (T 1/11992/27254, October 14, 1916).

20. CAB 21/37, December 1, 1917, John Buchan, "The Department of Information."

21. T 1/11992/17627, "Report of the Bureau Established for the Purpose of Laying before the Neutral Nations and the Dominions the Case of Great Britain and Her Allies," July 22, 1915; Parker, "The United States," p. 10.

22. M. L. Sanders and Philip M. Taylor, *British Propaganda during the First World War, 1914–1918,* pp. 171–72. The library count is for 1915 and probably increased later (T 1/11992/17627, "Report of the Bureau Established for the Purpose of Laying before the Neutral Nations and the Dominions the Case of Great Britain and Her Allies," July 22, 1915; Parker, "The United States," p. 10). See the extensive coverage of U.S. government efforts to cooperate on the problem of customs dues on propaganda literature sent to America, which indicates that the American government knew what was afoot (FO 395/83/154328, 169252, 229740, and 229748).

23. T 1/11992/17627, "Report of the Bureau Established for the Purpose of Laying before the Neutral Nations and the Dominions the Case of Great Britain and Her Allies," July 22 1915; Parker, "The United States," p. 10. Although largely true, Parker's claim of anonymity was not completely accurate. His reports indicate that a significant number of Americans agreed to distribute "official and semi-official" printings in the United States, and they must have known where the materials originated. "Semi-official" may be a code word for books and pamphlets that did not bear any sign of being British publications. See T 1/11992/17627, "Report of the Bureau Established for the Purpose of Laying before the Neutral Nations and the Dominions the Case of Great Britain and Her Allies," July 22, 1915; Parker, "The United States," pp. 6, 10. Parker personally communicated with members of his "organization" (see "Declares German Domination Mania Must Be Frustrated," *Atlanta Constitution,* January 23, 1916, p. 3A).

24. FO 395/3/152363, "Propaganda in the U.S.A.: Return of Despatch by Sir Gilbert Parker for the Month of July, 1916." Similar "Returns of Despatch" for different months are found in FO 395/3, 4, and 5.

25. Like the other British propaganda, the correspondence of the British with Americans who received it was destroyed, but a few examples of American letters survived. See, for example, FO 371/2833/81607, file number 13026, a letter from the astronomer David Todd of Amherst University, suggesting which articles could be put to best use in America to combat the Turks. Materials were also provided to various groups for distribution, most notably at "Allied Bazaars" in various cities (FO 395/69/1412, Parker to Wolcott, New York, December 10, 1916; FO 395/81/195706, various telegrams and letters).

26. "Explains Britain's Case with Documents," *Indianapolis Star,* October 5, 1914, p. 3.

27. "The 'White Papers,'" *New York Times,* September 29, 1914, p. 10.

28. "Sir Gilbert Parker on German Weakness," *New York Times,* June 20, 1915, p. BR1.

29. "The War to Date, from a British Standpoint," *Syracuse [N.Y.] Herald,* August 15, 1915, p. 2.

30. "Is England Apathetic? No," *New York Times,* August 15, 1915, p. SM15.

31. "How It Looks in England: By a Canadian Englishman," *Oshkosh [Wisc.] Daily Northwestern,* December 24, 1915, p. 6. The variance of publication dates of what was essentially the same article probably indicates that they were kept and used whenever space was available or when current events made them relevant.

32. See "Statement on the War," *Lowell [Mass.] Sun,* July 31, 1916, p. 3, which does identify the Associated Press origin. The *Chicago Tribune* also cited the Associated Press ("Paints Britain Winning Fruits of Preparation," July 30, 1916, p. A2), as did the *Washington Post* ("Industries of Britain Are Second Only to the Army in High Scale of Organization," July 30, 1916, p. ES5).

33. "Our Foreign Trade Blighted?" *Hartford [Conn.] Courant,* April 16, 1915, p. 11; and "A Censor Speaks," *Hartford [Conn.] Courant,* October 22, 1916, p. 8. See also "Letter from Sir Gilbert Parker," October 13, 1915, p. 6; and "From Sir Gilbert Parker," *Hartford [Conn.] Courant,* October 1, 1915, p. 8; and "English Indifference," *Oshkosh [Wisc.] Daily Northwestern,* September 8, 1915, p. 6.

34. *Lima [Ohio] Times-Democrat,* March 6, 1916, p. 4.

35. "Gifts from Sir Gilbert Parker," *Fitchburg [Mass.] Daily Sentinel,* December 26, 1916, p. 3.

36. "Gets Letter from Gilbert Parker," *Decatur [Ill.] Review,* September 25, 1914, p. 14.

37. "The Loan Won't Be Made," *Reno [Nev.] Evening Gazette,* September 16, 1915, p. 4. On May 22, 1916, the *Gazette* called Parker the "official publicity agent of the British Government" ("The Right of Search," p. 4).

38. "How England Sees It," *Atlanta Constitution,* September 12, 1915, p. 2F.

39. "Sir Gilbert Parker Discusses Meaning 'Freedom of the Seas,'" *Atlanta Constitution,* October 24, 1915, p. 2F. The *New York Times* printed Parker's letter to the *Constitution* on October 25, 1915 ("Parker Defends Blockade," p. 4) but omitted the section in which Parker denied his press bureau. The *Times* datelines the letter "Special to the *New York Times,*" which along with the date of publication indicates that it probably had been furnished separately to the *Times.* The *Constitution* did not change its opinion. On January 23, 1916, it called Parker "head of the bureau of publicity for the British government" ("Declares German Domination Mania Must Be Frustrated," p. 3A). The *Times,* which never properly identified Parker's work, did write: "The Right Honorable Sir Gilbert Parker, M. P., whose services to the British cause have been notable in the field of publicity in the United States" ("British Deeds Told by Gilbert Parker," *New York Times,* July 30, 1916, p. X2). The *Chicago Tribune* ("Paints Britain Winning Fruits of Preparation," July 30, 1916, p. A2) used the same phrase to describe Parker, as did the *Washington Post* ("Industries of Britain Are Second Only to the Army in High Scale of Organization," July 30, 1916, p. ES5) and the *Hartford [Conn.]*

Courant ("Review of Two Years of War Authorized by European Powers," July 30, 1916, p. 10).

40. See note 55 below.

41. "Forecast of Radical Changes after War Ends," *New York Times,* June 17, 1917, p. SM2. FO 395/6 and 7 contain a number of letters from influential Americans offering advice about propaganda to Parker and complimenting him on his efforts. The authors must have realized something of his position.

42. See, for example, Sir Gilbert Parker, M.P., "What American Neutrality Has Done and What Is Expected of It," *Washington Post*, September 5, 1915, p. 5; and Sir Gilbert Parker, "Bernstorff His Mark," *Washington Post,* January 3, 1915, p. 3.

43. See, for example, "England Will Continue to Fight," *Olean [N.Y.] Evening Herald,* September 19, 1914, p. 1. The article, exactly the same in all respects (even the headline), appeared in the *Dunkirk [N.Y.] Evening Observer* on the same day (p. 7) and undoubtedly in many other newspapers.

44. See, for example, "United States and Germany Discussed," *Christian Science Monitor,* October 26, 1915, p. 9. Parker's news and appeals, of course, were more concerned with the Germans than with the Turks. "New Appeal for Starving Belgians," *Bismarck [N.Dak.] Daily Tribune,* December 4, 1914, p. 1; "Sir Gilbert Parker Appeals to Cardinal Gibbons for Belgium," *Washington Post,* December 3, 1914, p. 2; and other papers. He made sure to praise Americans: "Thanks Due to U.S.," *Washington Post,* April 16, 1915, p. 3; and other papers (news service story).

45. The articles, all on the European war, were too numerous to consider in detail in a study of propaganda and the Turks. Most took the form of reports on British success or praise for America. Some were duplicitous, such as blaming the Germans for all the sufferings of the Belgians, avoiding mention of the British blockade. One was humorous, in hindsight, blaming the Germans for "atrocity-mongering." Some examples: "Sir Gilbert Parker Appeals to Cardinal Gibbons for Belgium," *Washington Post,* December 3, 1914, p. 2; "British Tribute to Our Attitude in War," *Hartford [Conn.] Courant,* April 16, 1915, p. 11; "Urges U.S. Should Avoid War," *Washington Post,* May 2, 1915, p. 13; "United States and War Theme of London Talk," *Christian Science Monitor,* May 8, 1915, p. 3; "British War Lessons," *Washington Post,* July 25, 1915, p. 13; "Briton Calls U.S. Friendship a Great Asset," *Chicago Tribune,* October 25, 1915, p. 11; "Shows 1,000,000 in British Naval Work," *Boston Globe,* February 21, 1916, p. 5; "Sir Gilbert Parker: Says Germans Will Collapse by Autumn," *Hartford [Conn.] Courant,* January 24, 1917, p. 8; "Midsummer Will See War's End, Is Belief of Sir Gilbert Parker," *Washington Post,* March 6, 1917, p. 9; "Parker Arraigns German Proposal to Conclude War," *Ogden [Utah] Examiner,* December 14, 1916, p. 1; "Parker: Sees Kaiser's Hand in Peace Talks," *Fort Wayne [Ind.] Daily News,* January 8, 1915, p. 18; "German Use of False Flags," *New York Times,* March 6, 1915, p. 2. Note: these or very similar articles appeared in many newspapers.

46. See, for example, "English Opinion is Shifting," *Ogden [Utah] Standard,* May 20, 1915, p. 4.

47. T 1/11992/17627, "Report of the Bureau Established for the Purpose of Laying before the Neutral Nations and the Dominions the Case of Great Britain and Her

Allies," July 22, 1915; Parker, "The United States," p. 6. President Butler and the Carnegie Endowment very obviously knew that they were doing the work of the British government. Butler was a force in politics as well as academics. He ran for vice-president on the Taft ticket in 1912 and received the Nobel Peace Prize in 1931.

48. H. C. Peterson, "British Influences on the American Press, 1914–17," *American Political Science Review* 31, no. 1 (February 1937): 81. All was done in secret and was sometimes done creatively. The British Censorship Department even opened letters that contained pro-German materials, took the materials out, substituted British propaganda, and sent them on (Sanders and Taylor, *British Propaganda during the First World War, 1914–1918,* p. 109). On the British press of the period, see John M. McEwan, "The National Press during the First World War: Ownership and Circulation," *Journal of Contemporary History* 17, no. 3 (July 1982): 459–86.

49. FO 395/138/8514, Lord Robert Cecil, "British Propaganda in Allied and Neutral Countries," December 29, 1917, p. 7. Cecil was parliamentary undersecretary of state for foreign affairs.

50. Ibid., p. 7.

51. See the section "The Armenians" below and the many mentions of the Associated Press in chapters 6–11.

52. Read, *Atrocity Propaganda,* pp. 187, 188.

53. Even British newspapers complained that the Press Agency censored unnecessarily and often got the facts wrong in its press releases. See "Newspapers Laugh at British Censor," *Salt Lake [Utah] Tribune,* September 6, 1914, p. 15. Articles printed in America often appeared to be written as British press releases. They contained condemnations of Britain's enemies, of course, but they also included laudatory descriptions of British leaders (in other words, praise for the writers' superiors). They seem to have been sent to America by news services and printed verbatim. On the British press during the war, see John M. McEwan, "The National Press during the First World War: Ownership and Circulation," *Journal of Contemporary History* 17, no. 3 (July 1982): 459–86. For an example of a press release, see FO 395/52, "For Monday Morning Papers Only," August 26, 1917, on the proclamation of revolt by the Sharif of Mecca.

54. Sanders, "Wellington House," p. 128.

55. See, for example, the Foreign Office "American Press Résumé" of March 24, 1916, which lists the most important newspapers in the United States, their circulation, and their attitudes toward the Allies and the Germans; and FO 395/66/46488, which covers the 300 most important "provincial newspapers" (CO 323/775/4533, Department of Information, Foreign Office, January 1918, "A Guide to the Press of the United States"; FO 395/216/8839, "A Guide to the Press of the United States: Revised Edition"; and FO 323/775/8378, February 16, 1918, "Catholic Papers in the United States: Supplement I to Guide to the Papers of the United States"). On the "friendliness" of the American media, see the above and FO 395/4/201817, "Confidential Memorandum on the Representatives of the Press of the United States of America" (no date or author). The British were vehemently against Hearst and viewed the *Chicago Tribune* as pro-German.

Hearst was so hated and feared that the British considered an attempt to cut off his supply of newsprint but found that his paper all came from United States mills, not the Canadian mills they could control (FO 395/3/166397, Montgomery to Spring-Rice, September 8, 1916). American news services were generally trusted. The representative of the Associated Press in Great Britain was Ben Allen. "He is a man in whom we have complete confidence and we have often asked his advice on matters of policy connected with the United States Press." The United Press of America was considered "extremely friendly" (FO 395/4/201817).

56. This changed when the United States entered the war, at which point both papers changed to a pro-Allied stance. In 1916 the *New York Tribune* printed what the British considered to be anti-British articles. They watched these articles closely and brought pressure to bear on the newspaper and its editor, Frank Simonds. For examples, see FO 395/6/file 27305. Simonds was wrongly identified as a Jew, with a comment that this was one reason for his position. See especially FO 395/6/95422, Gill to Cecil (no place given), May 4, 1916; and FO 395/6/27320, "A Summary of Information Obtained in the United States, Communicated to Sir Gilbert Parker by Mr. W. A. Gill, June, 1916." By 1917 the British felt that Simonds had come around (FO 395/81/212822, Butler to Buchan, New York, October 22, 1917). He was to be a staunchly anti-Turkish reporter, particularly in the years of the Turkish War of Independence (see chapter 11, note 14).

57. A search in the Newspaper Archive of American newspapers under "Official Press Bureau" for 1914–18 yielded 2,381 entries. I did not see all of these, and some may have been for non-British "official press bureaus" (although all of the hundreds I saw were British). It must be remembered that the Newspaper Archive only catalogs a relatively small percentage of American newspapers, so the numbers were actually considerably greater.

58. See T 1/11992/17627, "Report of the Bureau Established for the Purpose of Laying before the Neutral Nations and the Dominions the Case of Great Britain and Her Allies," July 22, 1915; Parker, "The United States," p. 25; and T 1/11992/27254, "Third Report of the Work Conducted for the Government by Wellington House," October 14, 1916; Parker, "The United States," p. 13 (an extensive list).

    FO 395/3 and 5 contain detailed documentation of the relations between favored American journalists and the British government. See file 13026, especially no. 147966, "Memorandum from Private Secretary to Lord Derby," which contains an analysis of the individual journalists and press services that conduct interviews in London. FO 395/4/201817 contains a similar analysis. See also the lists of journalists kept by the British in FO 395/42/94107, "London Correspondents of American Newspapers."

59. Memorandum by H. P. Hamilton of the Treasury, July 20, 1916. "Interviews" (Hamilton's quotation marks) with officials were arranged for American newspapers. These were wholly written by the British and published in America.

60. Peterson, "British Influences on the American Press," p. 82.

61. FO 395/4, National Editorial Services, Inc., to Parker, received in the News Department in London on October 13, 1916. forwarded "with the Compliments of Sir Gilbert Parker" (no date on the letter itself).

62. For example, 2,000 cartoons provided by the propagandists were distributed to and printed in American newspapers. How many of these dealt with the Turks will never be known.

63. *New York Times,* January 24, 1915, p. XXI. The article also appeared in the *Dallas Morning News,* January 15, 1915, p. 5. The *New York Times* was not mentioned as its source, and the article came out before it appeared in the *Times,* so it could not have been copied from it.

64. See, for example, "American Doctor Burned by Turks," *Atlanta Constitution,* February 20, 1916, p. A2.

65. "Russians Literally Slay Turkish Army," *Dallas News,* January 7, 1915, p. 1.

66. "300 Turks Killed by German Allies," *Dallas News,* March 8, 1915, p. 2; "'Spirit of Doom' Hangs over the Turks," *Dallas News,* May 9, 1915, p. 5.

67. "Eyewitness Describes Armenian Atrocities," *Dallas News.* October 26, 1915, p. 3. The Armenian soldier could not possibly have seen the events he described, which supposedly took place all over Anatolia.

68. "Says Germans Train Guns on Armenians," *Dallas News,* November 27, 1915, p. 1; "Armenian Women and Children Burned Alive," *Hartford [Conn.] Courant,* November 27, 1915, p. 1. The article also appeared in a number of smaller newspapers.

69. "6,000 Massacred," *Lowell [Mass.] Sun,* May 17, 1915, p. 5.

70. See, for example, "Massacred at Van," *Seattle [Wash.] Post-Intelligencer,* May 18, 1915, p. 5; "Turks Are Murdering Armenian Christians," *Atlanta Constitution,* May 18, 1915, p. 2. The same article, probably from the Associated Press, appeared in a number of newspapers with some variations, including reports from the American Board.

71. See, for example, "Armenians Sent into the Desert by Thousands," *Syracuse [N.Y.] Herald,* September 12, 1915, p. 16, which quoted "a letter written by a man in Constantinople to Aneurin Williams, a member of Parliament." Williams was active in Armenian causes, including the Lord Mayor's Committee on Armenian Refugees.

72. "Britain's War Aims Told," *New York Times,* December 21, 1917, pp. 1–2. See also "Blames Germans for Armenian Massacres," *Dallas News,* August 12, 1917, p. 7.

73. "London Hears of Massacres of Armenians," *Christian Science Monitor,* February 26, 1917, p. 1. This was a rare instance where a message to the ACASR was made public by the sender, not the committee. It can only have been released by the British.

74. See, for example, "Terrible Evidence against the Turks," *Dallas News,* January 19, 1919 (part 3), p. 4.

75. As an example of the many articles taken directly from the London press, see "Massacre of Armenians: Correspondent of London Chronicle Describes Turkish Atrocities," *Salamanca [N.Y.] Republican Press,* April 26, 1916, p. 1.

76. "Turks Destroying Armenian People," *Atlanta Constitution,* September 26, 1915, p. A10 (written before Bulgaria entered the war).

77. For example, see "Turks Retreat in Egypt," *Atlanta Constitution,* February 9, 1915, p. 2, a press agency story that was seen in many newspapers.

78. On Iraq, see, for example, "British Take Baghdad; Turks Still Retreat," *San Antonio Light,* March 12, 1917, p. 1; and similar information in many papers. On Gallipoli, see, for example, "Allies Capture Crest of Ridge," *Lincoln [Nebr.] Daily Star*, August 3, 1915, p. 4; "Gains at Dardanelles," *Washington Post,* July 3, 1915, p. 3; and similar information in many papers.

79. FO 395/290/46, Owen to Bennett (director of propaganda, Ministry of Information, New York, November 4, 1918, "Report"). Cunliffe Owen was sent to America by Lord Beaverbrook to investigate the propaganda machinery there.

80. Examples of pro-Turkish propaganda were published in Germany (see Read, *Atrocity Propaganda,* pp. 118–19). They are not considered here, because they never reached America and had no effect on American public opinion. A very few articles on the actual events of the Gallipoli campaign written by American journalists (sent to Berlin by radio) found their way to America, but I have discovered no such articles on other subjects.

81. Examples of these reports, often taken directly from British official statements or the official Press Bureau, are numerous. See, for example, "British Victory on the Tigris," *Boston Globe,* September 30, 1915; "Turks Are Driven at Dardanelles," *Atlanta Constitution,* July 15, 1915, p. 3; and "Allies Hopeful of Victory in Turk Campaign," *Seattle [Wash.] Post-Intelligencer,* August 25, 1915, p. 5.

82. FO 395/139/42320, Lloyd George to Buchan, February 24, 1917.

83. FO 395/139/63739, Kerr (writing for the prime minister) to Gasalee, 10 Downing Street, March 22, 1917.

84. FO 395/139/42320, Lloyd George to Buchan, February 24, 1917.

85. For an example, see "The Turks in Conflict," *Oelwein [Iowa] Daily Register,* July 18, 1916, p. 2.

86. FO 395/139/18029, H. W. to Seton, January 15, 1917. Sykes had provided other articles that had the stamp of the propaganda office and appeared in the American press. See, for example, "Sir Mark Sykes on Conditions in Mesopotamia," *Christian Science Monitor,* December 18, 1915, p. 9; "War Now in Its Last Phase," *Washington Post,* March 25, 1917, p. 15; and "Jerusalem Moral Center of World Predicts Briton," *Eau Claire [Wisc.] Leader,* January 24, 1918, p. 5. These articles appeared in many papers. News services distributed articles on the Ottoman war by Sykes that were sometimes identified as coming through British official sources. See "Cradle of the World Is Scene of War's Wrath," *Gettysburg [Pa.] Star and Sentinel,* December 25, 1915, p. 9. The article, which appeared in many papers, originated with the British Official Press Bureau. Sykes was interviewed for American newspapers by H. G. Wells, who also worked for the Propaganda Bureau ("Holy Land Capture Is Significant; Means Much to All Religions," *Oakland Tribune,* December 1, 1918, p. 5). The Propaganda Bureau wrote that it was distributing articles by Sykes (FO 395/81/196706, Roxburgh to Butler, London, October 18, 1917).

87. FO 395/139/25497, Gowers to Montgomery, Wellington House, January 30, 1917.

88. FO 395/139/42313 and FO 395/139/47041. Sykes was involved with other propaganda, although whether or not these were at the behest of the Propaganda Bureau cannot be known. See, for example, "Sees Great Future for Jew and Arab," *New York Times,* December 12, 1917, p. 5.

89. £40 for 100,000 copies (FO 395/139/51086).

90. FO 395/139/47048, Gowers to Sykes, March 26, 1917.

91. FO 395/139/64927, Buchan to Montgomery, March 25, 1917, "Anti-Turk Propaganda."

92. Hubert Montgomery, Buchan's deputy in charge of administration and policy.

93. Of the group, Bevan (of Wellington House) and Sykes were active propagandists. Both wrote propaganda works. Sir William Ramsay and D. G. (not D. S.) Hogarth were archaeologists. Hogarth for a time was head of the British Arab Bureau in Cairo, joined by Gertrude Bell. None of them became Wellington House propagandists. Ramsay wrote no propaganda. He only gave interviews on the war that did not smack of propaganda. Edward Granville Browne, who had great sympathy for the Turks, was a particularly bad choice. He refused to have anything to do with the war. G. H. (not G. S.) Fitzmaurice, violently anti-Turkish and anti-Semitic, was a better choice, but no evidence survives of his working with Wellington House. Nor is there evidence of G. E. Hubbard (*From the Gulf to Ararat* [Edinburgh and London: W. Blackwood and Sons, 1916]) or W. J. Childs (*Across Asia Minor on Foot* [Edinburgh and London: W. Blackwood, 1917]) doing so. It must be remembered that any record of their assistance may have been destroyed. George Adam Smith wrote propaganda books and gave lectures in America on the Allied cause ("British Educator Tells Need of Men," *New York Times,* April 3, 1918, p. 19; "Clergy Organize for Drive," *New York Times,* April 5, 1918, p. 6; "City Brevities," *New York Times,* March 14, 1918, p. 24). Dr. John Kelman, a Free Church minister, toured America in 1917, speaking for the Allied cause. Former teachers of Robert College (the missionary school in Istanbul) had already been at work on propaganda when this was written.

94. FO 395/139/69014, Toynbee to Gaselee, April 3, 1917. See also FO 395/139/64927 for the list with suggested names; and FO 395/139/64927, "A list of possible authors of propaganda publications on the Ottoman Empire." Some of the proposed contributors are discussed in note 93 above. As always, because of the destruction of documents it is not possible to know how many people on the suggested list actually worked at the behest of Wellington House. Judged by their writings and contemporary newspapers, some surely did not: Lovat Fraser, suggested as a writer on Syria and Palestine, instead became a critic of Lloyd George's handling of the war. Some surely did cooperate with the propaganda machinery, although not necessarily on the Middle Eastern issues for which they were suggested. Arnold Toynbee obviously cooperated, as Professor Seton-Watson (see below) probably did, although Wellington House may only have made use of his work. Canon J. T. Parfit wrote propaganda articles on Iraq in the *London Evening News* that were summarized in pamphlets and a small book (*Twenty Years in Baghdad and Syria* [London: Simpkin, Marshall, Hamilton, Kent, and Co., 1916], from articles that

first appeared in the *Evening News*) and published in Britain and America as a Wellington House book. G. W. Prothero wrote propaganda books. Sir Israel Zangwill had been quoted in British and American newspapers urging Jews to support the Allies and had been one of the British authors who signed a declaration of support for the war in 1914, although he was a supporter of an autonomous or independent Jewish state, not one under the British. See also "Israel Zangwill Says 'Jerusalem Is Doomed'; Awful Catastrophe Overshadows the Jews of Palestine," *Fort Wayne [Ind.] Sentinel,* February 20, 1915, p. 13.

95. FO 395/139/69014, Gaselee to Toynbee, April 6, 1917.

96. FO 395/139/79335. This folder also contains numerous examples of Gaselee's letters to editors and others.

97. This article appeared in a number of newspapers. See, for example, "Armenians Active in European War," *Fort Wayne [Ind.] Journal-Gazette,* November 13, 1914, p. 8; "Armenians Hail Troops with Joy," *Ogden [Utah] Standard,* November 12, 1914, p. 1; "Armenians Ready to Side with Russians," *Elyria [Ohio] Evening Telegram,* November 13, 1914 (page unreadable). The *Washington Post* ("Deal Blow to Turks," November 13, 1914, p. 1) and the *New York Times* ("Turkish Armenians in Armed Revolt," November 13, 1914, p. 2) paraphrased the same article, along with other news from Petrograd through London. See also "Russians Report Land Victory," *New York Times,* November 8, 1914, p. 2.

98. "Armenian Cities Taken," *New York Times,* November 6, 1914, p. 1.

99. "Eager to Fight the Turks," *New York Times,* October 31, 1914, p. 2; "Caucasus Muslims Loyal," *New York Times,* November 3, 1914; "Russian Moslems Loyal," *New York Times,* November 6, 1914.

100. See the section "Recommended Readings" in chapter 5. For an example of Bryce's early opinions on the Turks, see "The Future of Asiatic Turkey," *Littell's Living Age* 138, no. 1777 (July 6, 1878): 3–10; and "The Near East," *Eclectic Magazine of Foreign Literature* 142, no. 1 (January 1904): 37–44. These articles are filled with factual errors and venom and with the common cry that Turkish rule must be ended.

101. Quoted in H. C. Peterson, *Propaganda for War,* p. 57.

102. "Viscount Bryce's Message," *Washington Post,* January 28, 1917, p. ES4. The editorial went on: "The allied governments could not have employed a better medium than Viscount Bryce to convey to America the reason they are determined to expel the Turks from Europe."

103. "Armenian Appeal by Bryce in Full: Plea to America for Aid Made in Form of Letter to Aneurin Williams, M. P.," *New York Times,* October 10, 1915, p. 32. Of course Bryce was also very active in opposing the Germans. See the section "The Bryce Report" below; and Viscount Bryce, "Viscount Bryce Analyzes Principals of Allies," *New York Times,* February 4, 1917, p. SM3.

104. "Says Germans Train Guns on Armenians," *Dallas News,* November 27, 1915, p. 1; "Armenian Women and Children Burned Alive," *Hartford [Conn.] Courant,* November 27, 1915, p. 1. The article also appeared in a number of smaller newspapers.

105. "Neutralize the Holy Land," *Oshkosh [Wisc.] Daily Northwestern,* April 30, 1915, p. 8.

106. "Bryce Hopes Germans Will Learn by Defeat," *New York Times,* May 30, 1916, p. 2; "Palestine a Tiny Country," *Boston Globe,* May 30, 1915, p. SM16.

107. "Viscount Bryce, formerly British Ambassador to the United States, has sent to the Associated Press a plea that America try to stop the slaughter of the Armenians" ("Plea for Armenians," *Washington Post,* September 27, 1915, p. 12).

108. See, for example, the report that 1,500 Armenian fighters who had surrendered to soldiers near Sasun were murdered, based on the report of "an Armenian relief worker" in Russia, with no indication of how the information had been transmitted ("1500 Were Massacred," *Lowell [Mass.] Sun,* January 15, 1916, p. 6).

109. "Armenian Nation Is Virtually Wiped Out," *Dallas News,* October 7, 1915, p. 1. From the 1890s to the 1920s the Armenians were said again and again to have been "virtually wiped out."

110. This was a constant theme. See, for example, "Germany Able to Save Armenians, Bryce Declares," *Syracuse [N.Y.] Herald,* October 16, 1915, p. 2.

111. "Turks Unfit to Govern, Declares Lord Bryce," *Hartford [Conn.] Courant,* January 27, 1917, p. 20; "Must Oust the Turk," *Washington Post,* January 27, 1917, p. 1.

112. "Bryce Tells of Many Outrages," *Warren [Pa.] Evening Times,* November 27, 1915, p. 1. The unnamed Armenian gentleman had supposedly received his information from refugees. Bryce's allegations were quoted in many newspapers, a few of which are cited below in notes 119 and 201.

113. "Bryce Asks Us to Aid Armenia," *New York Times,* September 21, 1915, p. 3.

114. "Former British Ambassador Compares Armenians to Early Christian Martyrs," *Victoria [Tex.] Daily Advocate,* March 8, 1917, p. 2; and many other newspapers.

115. Bryce was in direct contact with James Barton. See "Armenian Relief Urged in Appeal from Lord Bryce," *Christian Science Monitor,* October 7, 1916, p. 5; and the section "The Bryce Report" below and various mentions of missionary establishment and British cooperation in chapter 9. See also FO 800/383, Barton to Bryce, Boston, September 6, 1917.

116. "Massacred for Their Faith," *Washington Post,* March 8, 1917, p. 1; and many other papers. One of these, the *Waterloo [Iowa] Times* (March 8, 1917, p. 1), incomprehensibly headed the Bryce article "Sennussi Plans the Massacres." For another Bryce cable to the ACASR, see "Bryce Asks Aid for Victims of Massacre," *Lowell [Mass.] Sun,* November 25, 1916, p. 3.

117. "Calls Armenians Martyrs," *New York Times,* February 26, 1917, p. 8. In this article, however, Bryce stated that the Turks who persecuted the Armenians were not believing Muslims but had attacked the Armenians out of political motives. See also "Lord Bryce Reports Armenian Atrocities," *Olean [N.Y.] Evening Herald,* October 19, 1916, p. 2; "Armenians Butchered for Loyalty to Christ," *Atlanta Constitution,* March 8, 1917, p. 1.

118. "Tales of Armenian Horrors Confirmed," *New York Times,* September 27, 1915, p. 5; "Million Armenians Killed or in Exile," *New York Times,* December 15, 1915, p. 3. Bryce's statements were also "confirmed" by British religious/relief circles. See "Armenians Dying in Prison Camps," *New York Times,* August 21, 1916, p. 5.

119. In November 1915 Bryce wrote that the sources of his assertions were the American committee (the ACASR) and "an Armenian gentleman of Tiflis," as indicated in note 112 above ("Bryce Tells of Many Outrages," *Warren [Pa.] Evening Times,* November 27, 1915, p. 1).

120. See, for example, "Armenia, Land of Martyrs," *Gettysburg [Pa.] Star and Sentinel,* February 15, 1916, p. 4, an article for some reason illustrated with a picture of bedouins with guns.

121. "Fear Massacre in Syria," *Iowa City Press-Citizen,* May 16, 1916, p. 2.

122. "Tell of Deaths of Armenians," *Chicago Tribune,* September 24, 1915, p. 2. Enemy aliens were not to be found in such remote places in Anatolia in 1915. The article (datelined London) stated that it had originated with the *Morning Post*'s reporter in Alexandria.

123. "Turks Are Killing Males in Armenia," *Syracuse [N.Y.] Herald,* March 17, 1918, p. 6. The article singles out supposed massacres at "Saosun on the Black Sea," which presumably means the city of Samsun, which was not claimed as "Armenia" by anyone, even Armenian nationalists.

124. *Elyria [Ohio] Evening Telegram,* May 17, 1917, p. 4. The article was reprinted in other newspapers without the author's name. Mellett was assistant European manager for the United Press, stationed in London.

125. "Armenian Says Race Is Being Massacred," *Dallas News,* August 15, 1917, p. 5; "Armenians Buried Alive by Turks," *Stevens Point [Wisc.] Daily Sentinel,* August 15, 1917, p. 4; "Germans Rival Turks in Cruelty," *Nashua [Iowa] Reporter,* September 13, 1917, p. 6; "Germans Rival Turks in Cruelty," *New Oxford [Pa.] Item,* September 20, 1917, p. 8. If the article had any real source at all, which is doubtful, it was based on rumors current in Bombay.

126. "Germans Urge Kurds to Murder Russians," *Dallas News,* March 30, 1918, p. 4. United Press articles often used "by mail," and this may have been from the UP, although it was not identified in the *Dallas News.*

127. "Throw Off Turk Yoke," *Washington Post,* August 22, 1915, p. 9.

128. "British Reap Germany's Harvest in Turkey," *Washington Post,* March 18, 1917 (second section), p. 1.

129. See, for example, "Unspeakable Cruelties of War Where Christ Preached Love and Kindness 2000 Years Ago," *Washington Post,* April 4, 1915, p. MS8.

130. *Moberly [Mo.] Democrat,* September 2, 1919, p. 4. See also "German Guilt for Armenian Blood," *Literary Digest,* October 27, 1917, pp. 29–30. Another example of an unidentified article that appears to be British propaganda: "British Relieving Suffering Armenians: Those Who Escaped Swords of the Kurds Are Being Well Cared for by the British," *Fort Wayne [Ind.] Journal-Gazette,* July 15, 1917, p. 38. This was probably a news service article.

131. "Kaiser Has Turned Mohammedan, Is Belief of the Turks," *Colorado Springs Gazette,* December 3, 1914, p. 3.

132. For example, "Turks Kill Thousands," *Washington Post,* August 6, 1915, p. 2.

133. "Slow Death Dealt by Turks," *Oakland Tribune,* September 25, 1915, p. 1. The same article appeared in many newspapers, sometimes in an abbreviated form, although

only the *Oakland Tribune* identified that it had been forwarded by the Associated Press. The *London Times* and the Associated Press were not the only ones in Dedeağaç who were omniscient. Henry Woods wrote a report from Dedeağaç describing events in Zeytun and elsewhere for the United Press ("Atrocities of Young Turks on Armenians," *Dunkirk [N.Y.] Evening Observer,* August 2, 1915, p. 1).

134. FO 395/4/201817, "Confidential Memorandum on the Representatives of the Press of the United States of America." The same source commented that the United Press was also "extremely friendly."

135. See, for example, "Doctor Is Burned to [*sic*] Stake by Turks," *Janesville [Wisc.] Daily Gazette,* February 10, 1916, p. 9; and "Fate of Armenians Veiled in Secrecy," *Oshkosh [Wisc.] Daily Northwestern,* October 9, 1915, p. 13. The United Press International was just as friendly with the British but seems to have sent fewer dispatches on the Ottoman Empire. This is difficult to know with certainty, because many articles that may have originated with the United Press carried no UP dateline in the papers. In any case, the UP seemed to be short on expertise on the Middle East. A United Press story from Washington said that "danger of massacres of Christians in Syria has been privately reported to the State Department it was learned today. The Mennonites, a large French-Catholic group, is [*sic*] reported to be in particular danger" ("Christian Massacre," *Des Moines [Iowa] News,* May 15, 1916, p. 3). This United Press article appeared verbatim in many newspapers, Mennonites included. This was not a misprint but read as it came from the UP. Maronites, not Mennonites, were assumedly the ones in danger. The fact that the UP writer and editors could confuse Maronites with an American Protestant group shows the general ignorance of the Middle East in the media and the public they served.

136. "Turks at Dardanelles Cut Off by Allies," *New York Times,* August 22, 1915, p. 3. The article, distributed by the Associated Press, originated with the correspondent of the *Chicago News,* who was stationed with the British at Mudros. Other AP articles on Gallipoli from London include "Allies Win Gallipoli Victory," *Oakland Tribune,* August 3, 1915, p. 1; and "They Won't Make Defense," *Lincoln [Nebr.] Daily News,* March 5, 1915, p. 5.

137. See, for example, "Moslems Slay Armenians by the Hundreds," *Chicago Tribune,* April 26, 1915, p. 2, for a completely fabricated story of the events in Van Province and western Iran; "With Russian Forces in Pursuit of Turks," *Daily Kennebec [Maine] Journal,* July 6, 1915, p. 12.

138. See, for example, "Brunt of Warfare in Armenia Borne by Non-Combatants," *Janesville [Wisc.] Daily Gazette,* August 10, 1915, p. 1.

139. "Jevded Pasha Is Blamed for Crime," *Lincoln [Nebr.] Daily Star,* October 11, 1915, p. 11; "Armenians Slain by Thousands at Van," *Oshkosh [Wisc.] Daily Northwestern,* October 9, 1915, p. 17; "How 600 Year Reign of Turks at Van Came to an End," *Wichita Daily Times* (Wichita Falls, Tex.), August 13, 1915, p. 2. The governor, Cevdet, had supposedly shown his antipathy by demanding that the Armenians turn in their weapons and report for conscription. The rebellion in Çatak was represented as a massacre of Armenians. The place of the American missionaries was

misrepresented, stating, for example, that they treated Turkish wounded during the rebellion.

140. "Many Bodies Found Crammed in Wells," *Dallas News,* July 13, 1915, p. 7.

141. Justin McCarthy, Esat Arslan, Cemalettin Taşkıran, and Ömer Turan, *The Armenian Rebellion at Van,* pp. 179–80, 233–36.

142 See, for example, "120,000 Armenians Destitute," *Dallas News,* March 20, 1915, p. 9; "Of 1,200,000 Armenians Only 200,000 Are Left," *Atlanta Constitution,* October 22, 1915, p. 1. That was the route by which completely erroneous news from the Armenian rebellion at Van reached the United States (for example, "Christian Massacre Renewed in Armenia," *Dallas News,* May 1, 1915, p. 1; and "Detachment of 860 Armenians Wiped Out," *Dallas News,* May 8, 1915, p. 1).

143. These figures were gathered by searching the datelines by computerized search (Armenia *or* Armenian *or* Armenians). It was not possible to compare them to the total number of articles on Armenians in the *Times,* because so many of those were on "Shipping News," "The World of Business," individual Armenians in cities, fashion, and so forth. The articles from London and Constantinople included none of this.

144. "Jews Suffer in War," *Washington Post,* February 1, 1916, p. 2. American Jews were divided in their sympathies as the war progressed, but Jewish organizations seem to have taken the British side once Palestine had been conquered. See the article by Herman Bernstein, editor of the *American Hebrew:* "The War in the Holy Land," *Sheboygan [Wisc.] Press,* December 16, 1917, p. 4, which repeats the British propaganda. The article is full of absurdities, such as German general Erich von Falkenhayn having absolute control over Cemal Paşa: "It was reported that there was a stormy scene between the German general and the Turkish officer, which resulted in the removal of Djemal from his office as military governor of Palestine." This fit well with the British plan to portray the Germans as being in control, which was completely untrue and never happened. Also, how would Bernstein have known of the contents of the meeting? The article was syndicated by the Newspaper Enterprise Association. Note the assumption that Europeans must have been in control, presumably because it was assumed they were more competent.

145. Because of the number of Jews in New York and their importance in the city's life, the *New York Times* provides the best example of articles relating to the Jews and so has been cited here on the subject, including "Jews Ordered from Kieff," May 2, 1914, p. 1; "Russian Editor's Narrow Escape," May 10, 1914, p. C10; "Closes Schools to Jews," May 10, 1914; "Making Life in Russia Intolerable for Jewish People," June 7, 1914, p. SM9; "Jews in Russia," June 10, 1914, p. 10; "Documents Which Uncover Official Crimes in Russia," June 14, 1914, pp. SM9–10; "The Exodus from Russia and Its Meaning," July 19, 1914, p. SM7; "Poles and Cossacks Massacre Jews," January 8, 1915, p. 3; "Tells of Russians' Murder of Jews," February 4, 1915, p. 3; and "The Jews in Russia," February 14, 1915, p. 4. It is possible that the German propaganda machinery had a hand in some of these transmissions. The *Times* carried many times more news on the Jews of Palestine than did newspapers from other American cities. For more normal coverage, see the small number of articles in the

Washington Post, such as "Harassing Polish Jews," March 20, 1915, p. 9; and "Przemsyl Was Looted," September 19, 1915, p. E14.

146. "Sazonoff Denies Interview on Jews," *New York Times,* January 23, 1915, p. 2.

147. See, for example, "Russia Denies That Jews Are Persecuted," *New York Times,* March 18, 1915, p. 4; "Schools for Jews Alone," *New York Times,* October 1, 1916, p. 3; and "Problems Vex Jews," *Washington Post,* January 20, 1915, p. 3. At the same time, articles on Jewish suffering began to state more often that their condition was a result of war, not mentioning Russian oppression in particular.

148. "Russians Reassure Przemsyl Refugees," *New York Times,* March 26, 1915, p. 2; "Russia Suspends Law against Jews," *New York Times,* August 22, 1915, p. 1. While the articles condemning the Russians had mainly been smuggled out of Russia, these articles often were cleared by the Russian censor and sent by normal news channels, frequently through London.

149. See, for example, "Russian Premier Denies Massacres," *New York Times,* January 24, 1915, p. 6; "Jews Still Oppressed," *New York Times,* January 1, 1917, p. 9; "Russia Mitigates the Pale," *Washington Post,* August 22, 1915, p. 7; and "Jews Gain More Rights," *Washington Post,* September 26, 1915, p. 16. For an especially damning article that is detailed and seems to be completely factual, see "How Russian Jews Suffered in War," *New York Times,* October 29, 1916, p. E3.

150. "The Program of Reforms in Russia," *New York Times,* September 10, 1915, p. 10; "Holds Out Hope to Jews," *New York Times,* October 5, 1915; "Has Hopes for Jews in Russian Victory," *New York Times,* October 17, 1916, p. 2.

151. See, for example, "For Equal Rights for Jews," *New York Times,* November 25, 1916, p. 2.

152. "Jews in Russia Hopeful," *New York Times,* January 8, 1917, p. 2.

153. See, for example, "All the Babies Starved," *New York Times,* November 20, 1916, p. 2.

154. I do not believe that they were sincere, despite the declaration of Gen. Archibald Murray, who stated: "There can be little doubt that we should revive the Jewish Palestine of old, and allow the Jews to realize their dreams of Zion in their homeland" ("Objects of Advance into Holy Land," *New York Times,* April 15, 1917, p. 14).

155. See the British Zionist publications from Wellington House listed below and, as an example of what the British promised, the article in the *Washington Post,* identified only as coming from London: "Palestine in Waste," *Washington Post,* February 7, 1915, p. 15. Despite its title, the article was on what the British would do in Palestine after the war.

156. On the expected imminent slaughter of the Jews of Jerusalem, see "Turks Cry for Blood," *Washington Post,* March 10, 1915, p. 2; and "Palestine in War Time," *Atlanta Constitution,* December 12, 1915, p. 58, an article that came complete with references and a painting of Jesus.

157. "Unspeakable Cruelties of War Where Christ Preached Love and Kindness 2000 Years Ago," *Washington Post,* April 4, 1915, p. MS8. The *New York Times* did print an article quoting German Count Johann Heinrich von Bernstorff, the Germany ambassador to the United States, to the effect that the Ottoman government was

neither anti-Jewish, which was true, nor ant-Zionist, which was not strictly true, as it feared Zionist separatism ("Bernstorff Defends Turks," *New York Times,* March 9, 1915, p. 2).

158. A number of the American newspapers seen for this study cited a "cablegram from Cairo" as the source of the information on Palestine's Jews (see, for example, "Barbarous Acts of Jaffa Turks," *Los Angeles Times,* December 23, 1914, p. 12, which stated that the information came from a "Cablegram from Cairo to Chicago Daily News"). British sources identified an Alexandria Zionist Committee as a source. Like the other articles prevalent in the American press, the reporting on Palestine almost never identified actual sources and usually came from London (for example: "information received in Zionist circles [in Copenhagen sent via London]": "Twice Avert Eviction of Jerusalem Jews," *New York Times,* May 31, 1917, p. 12). American consul Arthur Garrels in Alexandria sent a report on the Jews of Palestine that echoed all the British accusations. His report was sent to the American Jewish Relief Committee by the State Department. He gave no sources for his report ("Cruelties to Jews Deported in Jaffa," *New York Times,* June 3, 1917, p. 23).

159. "Threatens Massacre of Jews in Palestine," *New York Times,* May 4, 1917, p. 7. The *New York Sun* (December 19, 1915, section 6, p. 5) printed an article by the religious writer William T. Ellis (see the section "Newspapers and Magazines" and notes 71 and 76 in chapter 9 and chapter 11, note 166), asserting that the Turks had expelled the Christian priests from Jerusalem and closed the holy shrines.

160. "Cruel to Palestine Jews," *New York Times,* May 8, 1917, p. 4; "Cruelties to Jews Deported in Jaffa," *New York Times,* June 3, 1917, p. 23; "Barbarity of Turks Crushing Palestine," *New York Times,* August 14, 1917, p. 9. The Germans supposedly intervened before all the Jews of Jaffa could be killed ("More Turkification," *New York Times,* May 19, 1918, p. 26) and stopped the Turks from evicting all the Jews in Jerusalem ("Twice Avert Eviction of Jerusalem Jews," *New York Times,* May 31, 1917).

161. "Turks and Germans Expelling Zionists," *New York Times,* January 22, 1915, p. 3. The same source was quoted in different newspapers in similar articles: for example, "Turks Destroy Entire Work of Colonization by Jews in Palestine," *Daily Kennebec [Maine] Journal,* January 22, 1915; and "Destroy Zion Colony," *Washington Post,* January 22, 1915, p. 2. See also "Belligerents Slaying Jews," *New York Times,* February 1, 1915, p. 3.

162. "Deport Jerusalem Jews," *New York Times,* May 16, 1917, p. 3; "Plea for the Jews of Jaffa," *New York Times,* May 22, 1917, p. 11. See also (from the *Jewish Chronicle*) "Jews of Palestine Fear Wrath of Turkish Ruler," *Lima [Ohio] Sunday News,* June 8, 1917, p. 1. On May 23, 1917, the *New York Times* printed an article headlined "Admit Jaffa Horrors" (p. 5), which was "given to the *New York Times* by the [British] Foreign Office." The article, which drew upon a report by the German Relief Society for the Jews, said nothing about "horrors" but stated that "the Turkish Commander in Chief tried to render help, and placed money at the disposal of the authorities." The *Times* did print a short article (twenty lines) quoting Cemal Paşa's statement that the Turks were spending money to aid the Palestine Jews ("Says Turks Pay the

Jews," August 30, 1917, p. 2). Probably without realizing that it was giving the lie to its previous assertions, the *Times* printed a long article ("Zionism Already Begun in Palestine," June 9, 1918, p. 26) that told of the "thriving and prosperous" Jewish communities that the British found in place when they conquered Palestine.

163. *Washington Post,* December 23, 1914, p. 8.

164. "Massacre of Jews by Turks," *Christian Science Monitor,* May 22, 1917, p. 1.

165. It has obviously not been possible to see all the American newspapers that carried stories condemning the Turks for actions in Palestine; nor is it possible to cite here all that I have seen. Only some examples are given. The same Associated Press article appeared in the *Warren [Pa.] Evening Mirror* (p. 1), the *Ogden [Utah] Standard* (p. 1), and the *Decatur [Ill.] Review* (p. 11), all on May 7, 1917. The *La Crosse [Wisc.] Tribune and Leader-Press* included the article on May 8, 1917 (p. 10). The *Iowa City Press-Citizen* printed a somewhat changed version of the same piece on May 8, 1917 (p. 4), as did the *Marble Rock [Iowa] Journal* (p. 1) on May 10. The article must have appeared in many newspapers, although most did not credit the Associated Press. For another case of the same story repeated verbatim or slightly paraphrased, see "Jews Driven Out as British Come," *Sandusky [Ohio] Star-Journal,* May 8, 1917, p. 10; "Jews in Palestine Driven from Homes," *Janesville [Wisc.] Daily Gazette,* June 18, 1917, p. 1; "Another Jew Massacre Reported as Threatened," *Indianapolis Star,* May 21, 1917, p. 5; and "Palestine Jews Fear New Massacres," *Albert Lea [Minn.] Evening Tribune,* May 21, 1917, p. 1.

166. One article did admit that the Muslims had gone but said they had "also left," with no indication of the truth that the entire population had been evacuated ("Cruelties to Jews Deported in Jaffa," *New York Times,* June 3, 1917, p. 23).

167. See, for example, "Jews Expelled, Slain, Starved in Palestine," *Chicago Tribune,* May 8, 1917, p. 4; and "Palestine Jews Are Massacred," *Los Angeles Times,* May 22, 1917, p. 13.

168. "Barbarity of Turks Crushing Palestine," *New York Times,* August 14, 1917, p. 9. This article appeared verbatim in other newspapers as well, as did the other Associated Press copy (for example, *Ogden [Utah] Standard,* August 13, 1917, p. 1; *Lowell [Mass.] Sun,* August 13, 1917, p. 1; *Fort Wayne [Ind.] Sentinel,* August 13, 1917, pp. 1, 14; and *Nevada State Journal,* August 14, 1917, pp. 1, 3). Examples of other articles that appear to be from the propagandists: "Palestine Is Now a German Province in the Fullest Sense of the Word," *Newark [N.J.] Daily Advocate,* April 20, 1915, p. 10 (an AP article); and "Says Turks Desire to Destroy Zionism," *New York Times,* October 8, 1915, p. 2. The article was entirely drawn from "a letter from Alexandria to the [London] *Morning Post.*"

169. "Germans and Turks in New Atrocities," *New York Times,* November 25, 1917, p. 4. A number of reports emanating from London contained absurdities, such as that Cemal Paşa only had Germans on his staff, that he had become very rich through stealing from Jews, and that he was burning ancient Hebrew texts. Articles like "Palestine Is Now a German Province" (the same article in the *Janesville [Wisc.] Daily Gazette,* April 15, 1915, p. 1; and the *Oakland Tribune,* April 25, 1915, p. 26) seem to have been too crazy to be printed in the major newspapers.

170. U.S. National Archives, 867.4016/316, Page to Secretary of State, London, May 9, 1917; 867.4016/316, Brylawski to Phillips, Washington, May 5, 1917; 867.4016/319, Page to Secretary of State, London, May 12, 1917; 867.4016/322, Page to Secretary of State, London, May 16, 1917; 867.4016/316a.

171. The American request assumed that the Swedes would "protest earnestly" over what they found (867.4016, Lansing to Amlegation, May 14, 1917).

172. 867.4016/340, Morris to Secretary of State, Stockholm, June 18, 1917; 867.4016/349, Swedish Legation to Secretary of State, Washington, D.C., June 27, 1917; 867.4016/343, Riano [Spanish ambassador to U.S.] to Secretary of State, June 20, 1917; 867.4016/338, Bryn of Norwegian Legation to Secretary of State, Washington, June 9, 1917; 867.4016/339; Danish Legation to Secretary of State, Washington June 13, 1917; 867.4016/363, Report of Swedish Charge d'affaires in Constantinople (name undecipherable). The American press also mentioned some of the bombardments: twenty-five words in the *New York Times* ("Bombard Turks Near Gaza," April 14, 1915, p. 2), quoting the French Marine Ministry that a French battleship and French airplanes had bombarded "an important Turkish encampment in the neighborhood of Gaza." See also "Destroys Jaffa Shipyards," *New York Times,* August 15, 1915, p. 2.

173. One voice stood up against the propaganda. Abram (Abraham in the articles) Elkus, who had been United States ambassador to the Ottoman Empire, declared that the Jews in Palestine were being treated properly and were not particularly suffering. The *New York Times* printed his statements, albeit in small articles: "Elkus Reaches Paris," June 9, 1917, p. 20; "Mr. Elkus Visits London," June 9, 1917, p. 11; "Found Turks Fair to Jews," June 18, 1917, p. 11. Perhaps the *Times* printed the articles because Elkus was prominent in the New York Jewish community. Other newspapers did not see the need to publish his opinions, except for the *Washington Post,* which printed one small article at the bottom of p. 19, under some advertisements ("No Massacre at Jaffa," June 10, 1917, p. 19). American newspapers printed news of the British bombardments of coastal cities without any mention of the timely Ottoman evacuation of civilians. See, for example, "British Attack Gaza, Take 296 Prisoners," *New York Times,* November 4, 1917, p. 2.

174. "U.S. in Protest Over Massacres," *Chicago Tribune,* May 22, 1917, p. 5; "U.S. Intercedes for Jews," *Washington Post,* July 17, 1917, p. 3.

175. I have found no mention of any exoneration in the newspapers from smaller towns. The *Washington Post* ("No Massacre of Jews," July 9, 1917, p. 3), *Atlanta Constitution* ("No Massacre of Jews," July 9, 1917, p. 8), *Hartford [Conn.] Courant* ("No Massacre of Jews in Palestine," July 9, 1917, p. 2), and *Boston Globe* ("Tales of Massacres of Jews in Palestine Denied," July 9, 1917, p. 12) did all print the same one-paragraph statement by the Swedish minister in Istanbul that allegations of massacre of Jews in Palestine were untrue. The article gave no source for his opinion and did not mention the investigation or the other neutral countries involved.

176. FO 371-2835/59898, "Report of Lord Newton's Staff on a Visit by Mr. Greenberg," March 28, 1916. The material in question concerned persecutions of Jews in Poland, but Greenberg's journalistic slant obviously applies to Palestine as well. See also

FO 371/2835/31219, Letter of Mr. Greenberg to Lord Robert Cecil, London, February 14, 1916, on the effect his publications could have on the opinion of Jews in the United States in favor of Britain and against its enemies.

177. On further British propaganda on the Holy Land, see Eitan Bar-Yosef, "The Last Crusade: British Propaganda and the Palestine Campaign, 1917–18," *Journal of Contemporary History* 36, no. 1 (January 2001): 87–109. Unfortunately, the article does not consider propaganda as it reached America.

178. See "Massacres Feared: Turks Said to Threaten to Wipe Out Palestine Jews," *Syracuse [N.Y.] Herald,* May 4, 1917, p. 12.

179. "Jaffa in Ruins at Hands of Turkey," *Frederick [Md.] Post,* August 20, 1917, p. 1. Later in the war, after the Balfour Declaration, the British formally organized what was called "Jewish propaganda" as a separate Jewish Branch of the Department of Information under Albert Hyamson, who reported to Buchan. See the extensive documentation in FO 395/86/237667. Butler reported that he had particular success in planting propaganda articles in some newspapers, especially the *New York Times* and New York Jewish publications (FO 395/86/237667: Hyamson to Montgomery, London, December 19, 1917, Bayley [for Butler] telegram to Buchan, December 18, 1917, Montgomery to Hyamson, London, December 21, 1917). The Information Ministry ordered that the propaganda from Britain was to be placed without reference to the ministry, particularly to be seen as "Zionist Literature" (FO 395/86/244217, Hyamson draft of telegram from Buchan to Butler, London, December 27, 1917).

180. This is especially true of documents after 1916. For example, the existent Reports of Wellington House end in 1916, although there must have been later reports. Unfortunately, as seen in the list below, most of the Turkish materials were printed and distributed in 1917 and 1918. It is only blind luck that the publications list described below survived.

181. Located at the Foreign Office Library. The Imperial War Museum copy is titled "Schedule of Wellington House Literature." As additional proof of the accuracy of the list, the early works on it, printed before the Third Report was created, are listed in the Pamphlets and Books Distributed section of the "Third Report of the Work Conducted for the Government by Wellington House" (T 1/11992/27254, October 14, 1916). I have included the publication information for Great Britain and the United States, much of which was not on the list.

182. I have not seen the longer book, *The "Clean-Fighting Turk": Yesterday, To-day and To-morrow [sic]* (London: Spottiswoode, Ballantyne and Co., 1918). It would appear not to be the work referred to in the list.

183. INF 4/5, Letter of Commission of Investigation of Wellington House, Anthony Hope-Hawkins, chairman. Doran was definitely concerned to make a profit from its endeavors. See FO 395/68/127595, correspondence of Buchan, Masterman, and Montgomery on Doran, and FO 305/79/159718, Butler to Buchan, New York, July 27, 1917, and accompanying letters.

184. *Turkey: A Past and a Future* was printed as a book by Doran in 1917 but originated as an article in *Round Table* 27 (June 1917): 515–47.

185. As shown by the Sykes-Picot Agreement, the Constantinople Agreement, and so forth.

186. FO 395/49/162962, Montgomery to Cook, London, May 27, 1916. FO 395/49 contains copies of the various steps (censor's office, etc.) that the articles went through. Masefield was not the only poet enlisted by British Propaganda: Alfred Noyes embarked on a speaking tour in the United States. Among his other pronouncements, he declared that "The Turk must go" (FO 395/66/60200, press clippings on his speeches). He worked in close cooperation with the News Department (FO 395/138/8514, Lord Robert Cecil, "British Propaganda in Allied and Neutral Countries," December 29, 1917, p. 11).

187. John Masefield, *Gallipoli* (New York: Macmillan, 1916). A number of American newspapers reviewed it as a "best seller."

188. FO 395/139/226240, Department of Information, Intelligence Bureau, October 17, 1917, Arnold Toynbee, "Report on the Pan-Turanian Movement"; FO 395/139/235141, Ashcroft to Gaselee, Wellington House, December 10, 1917. *Round Table* articles were reprinted with secret British subventions.

189. Arnold J. Toynbee, ed., *The Treatment of Armenians in the Ottoman Empire, 1915–1916: Documents Presented to Viscount Grey of Fallodon, Secretary for Foreign Affairs, by Viscount Bryce* (hereafter cited as *Blue Book*).

190. James Viscount Bryce, *The Future of Armenia,* reprinted from *Contemporary Review* (December 1918).

191. James Viscount Bryce, *Transcaucasia and Ararat* (London: Macmillan, 1877), pp. 405–7.

192. *Blue Book,* p. xvi.

193. Parliament was also deceived as to Bryce's and Toynbee's place in the project (FO 395/40/185932, August 26, 1916, Response to Parliamentary Question).

194. FO 96/205, Toynbee to the unnamed editor of "Quelques documents sur le sort des Arméniens en 1915," London, February 1, 1916.

195. James Viscount Bryce, *Report of the Committee on Alleged German Outrages,* and *Evidence and Documents Laid before the Committee on Alleged German Outrages.* The most ubiquitous form of the Bryce Report on the Germans was newspaper serialization in both Great Britain and the United States. In addition, many American newspapers wrote long articles paraphrasing the report on the Germans (see, for example, "Report on Alleged German Outrages," *Dallas News,* May 13, 1915, p. 1). Keith G. Robbins, "Lord Bryce and the First World War," *Historical Journal* 10, no. 2 (1967): 255–78, is instructive on some of Bryce's connections and history but not on his connection with the British propaganda machinery.

196. See especially Read's *Atrocity Propaganda,* although any modern book on the subject acknowledges that the Bryce Report on the Germans was false. Buitenhuis comments: "And yet the report, as is now generally acknowledged, was largely a tissue of invention, unsubstantiated observations by unnamed witnesses, and second-hand reports, depending far more on imagination than any other factor" (*The Great War of Words,* p. 27). See also Trevor Wilson, "Lord Bryce's Investigation

into Alleged German Atrocities in Belgium, 1914–15," *Journal of Contemporary History* 14, no. 3 (July 1979): 369–83.

197. Twenty thousand copies of the first Bryce Report had already been distributed in America by October 1916 (T 1/11992/27254, "Third Report of the Work Conducted for the Government by Wellington House," October 14, 1916, p. 12).

198. Peterson, *Propaganda for War,* p. 58.

199. Toynbee wrote two short propaganda books against the Germans and two against the Turks. All four were printed in both Britain and the United States (*The German Terror in Belgium: An Historical Record; The German Terror in France; Armenian Atrocities: The Murder of a Nation;* and *The Murderous Tyranny of the Turks*). Toynbee's books were narrative retellings of the "evidence" that went into the two Bryce Reports and cite those reports. For that reason they are not analyzed separately here. An interesting complaint was lodged against *Armenian Atrocities:* the British government delegate for administration of refugees in Egypt wrote that the pamphlet had misrepresented the supposedly sad state of Armenian refugees there and stated that the refugees were actually doing quite well (FO 96/205, Hornblower to Honorary Secretary, Armenian Refugees, Lord Mayor's Fund, Alexandria, April 14, 1916).

200. See the epilogue.

201. FO 395/40/179902 and 255780, "Documents relating to the treatment of Armenian and Assyrian Christians in the Ottoman Empire and N.W. Persia: Key to names of places and persons withheld from publication," September 11, 1916 (hereafter "Key to the Blue Book"). As far as I know, the existence of this list was first mentioned at approximately the same time in "The Bryce Report: British Propaganda and the Turks," in Kemal Çiçek, ed., *The Great Ottoman Turkish Civilization* (Istanbul: Yeni Türkiye, 2000), and in Arnold Toynbee, ed., *The Treatment of Armenians in the Ottoman Empire, 1915–1916: Documents Presented to Viscount Grey of Falloden by Viscount Bryce,* ed. Ara Sarafian. The latter volume gives quite a different view of the *Blue Book* than the one presented here. The Toynbee correspondence in writing the *Blue Book* has since been made available in FO 96/205–12, which was not available when I first researched the *Blue Book.* The key was kept very secret, but six copies of the key to the names were given to the American Embassy for the embassy's use (FO 96/206 [no name in this file copy, probably Bryce], to "The Ambassador," London, December 14, 1916). Toynbee's copies of his documents have survived in FO 96, but these were copies forwarded to him, seldom originals. Bryce made use of a small number of similar documents, with even less provenance, in 1915. See "Thousands Tortured to Death," *Indianapolis Star,* November 27, 1915, p. 1.

202. Toynbee wrote, "Some of these documents have been sent to Lord Bryce by Armenian friends, some by the American Committee" (FO 96/205, Toynbee to the unnamed editor of "Quelques documents sur le sort des Arméniens en 1915," London, February 1, 1916, requesting permission to use materials from that pamphlet).

203. See, for example, FO 96/205, Rockwell to Toynbee, New York, May 21, 1916, and Toynbee to Rockwell, June 8, 1916.

204. FO 96/205, Toynbee to Barton, London, February 1, 1916. In the same letter Toynbee asked Barton's help in obtaining materials from the Dashnak journal *Gotchnag*.

205. Letters frequently passed between Barton and Toynbee, originally concerning documents for the book then concerning publicity and distribution in America. Barton's letters were sent on the stationery of both the American Board and the ACASR. As an example, documents in FO 96/205 for one brief period: Barton to Toynbee: March 6, March 15, March 27, March 29, April 1, April 17, April 25, May 1, 1916; Toynbee to Barton: March 8, March 23, April 5, April 12, April 18, 1916. FO 96/205 and 206 contain many others. Barton himself suggested ways in which the reports might be made to appear less one-sided. He told Toynbee that one of the American missionaries who sent in a report could be called a Turkish citizen, because she had married an Ottoman Armenian, or perhaps just "one who has lived in the country for years, speaks the language of the people and knows whereof she writes" (FO 96/205, Barton to Toynbee, Boston, March 15, 1916).

206. Boghos Nubar was the leader of the Armenian General Benevolent Union, founded in Cairo in 1905. Nubar was active in propaganda during the war and in the American mandate question after the war. He led one of the Armenian delegations (the Armenian National Delegation) at the postwar Peace Conferences. See chapter 11, note 222.

207. Favre also had an extensive correspondence with Toynbee, recorded in FO 96/205 and 206.

208. See the following *Blue Book* documents: 10, 13, 23, 77, 79, 85, 91, 102, 103, 104, 108, 110, 111, 112, 114, 116, 117, 120, 123, 125, 126, 127, 128, 129, and 137. Toynbee wrote that Lord Bryce had received materials from the ACASR (Toynbee, *Armenian Atrocities,* p. 119).

209. "Key to the Blue Book," pp. 2–3, *Blue Book,* document 8, p. 17. The author, H. K. Aivazian, wrote the report in a letter to Boghos Nubar. Aivazian was a merchant who had sold provisions to the Ottoman army in the Gallipoli campaign and had gone to Athens then to British-controlled Cairo. All of his information supposedly had been obtained in Istanbul (FO 96/206, Boghos Nubar to Toynbee, Paris, June 28, 1916). It was common for the missionary reports to have been written by those who were nowhere near the scenes described, even as far away as Cairo (FO 95/205, Howard Porbett, Manager of *The Times,* to Toynbee, London, March 15, 1916).

210. *Blue Book,* documents 92, 93, and 95.

211. See, for example, FO 96/205, Toynbee to Rushdoony, London, May 16, 1916, in which Toynbee acknowledges that the "similarity of passages" in documents by Rushdoony and Knapp was explained by Rushdoony being "in touch with Miss Knapp." Toynbee printed both documents. One effect of obfuscating the missionary provenance of so many documents, of course, was to hide that the authors were indeed in touch with one another.

212. Toynbee was not able to make use of the collection of documents collected by Johannes Lepsius (*La rapport secret du Dr. Johannes Lepsius* [Paris: Payot & Cie., 1918]; and *Deutschland und Armenien, 1914–1918* [Potsdam: Tempelverlag, 1919]),

because he could not obtain them in time for publication of the *Blue Book.* Lepsius had been a missionary in Anatolia in the 1890s and was president of the German Orient Mission (*Missionary Review of the World*, new series 24 [January 1911]: 66). He was an Evangelical minister, the theological brother of the American Congregationalists and Presbyterians. In 1914 he founded the German-Armenian Society. All the information he gathered consisted of what he learned in a one-month visit to Istanbul from Armenians there, including the Armenian patriarchate, and the reports that Ambassador Morgenthau showed him. Morgenthau had been granted permission from secretary of state Robert Lansing to use his discretion in showing State Department materials to Lepsius. Morgenthau's "discretion" consisted of giving Lepsius open access to his embassy's files and copies of their contents, which suggests that he may well have been stretching the intent of Lansing's instructions to their limit (Heath W. Lowry, *The Story behind Ambassador Morgenthau's Story,* pp. 82–86).

213. Many times the consuls themselves were not identified. Statements furnished by Barton often were only identified with titles, such as "a consular report to Washington" or "an American official" (FO 96/205, Barton to Toynbee, Boston, March 6, 1916).

214. FO 96/205, Barton to Toynbee, Boston, April 25, 1916. See also FO 96/205, Barton to Toynbee, April 1, 1916, Toynbee to Bell, London, March 2, 1916. Barton admitted his lack of knowledge in a number of letters (for example, FO 96/205, Barton to Toynbee, Boston, May 1, 1916):

> My dear Mr. Toynbee,
>   I very much regret that we are unable to fill in the blanks in the documents that our committee published in galley form for the press under date of October 4, 1915. Most of these documents are not here; in fact, many of them are not accessible to us. I doubt if the names of many of the places would be especially significant.
>   In Mrs. Christie's notes, the names have not been furnished to us.
>   Hastily but very faithfully yours,
>   James L. Barton

215. FO 96/205, Barton to Toynbee, Boston, March 6, 1916. See also FO 96/205, Barton to Toynbee, Boston, April 25, 1916.

216. FO 96/205, Masterman to Bryce, June 16, 1916. This letter to Bryce, which appears to be a file copy, has no name or signature. Based on internal evidence and comparison with other Masterman letters, however, the letter appears to have been from Masterman. It should be noted that not all missionaries were as deficient as Barton in recording sources. The Board of Foreign Missions of the Presbyterian Church in the USA provided few documents to Toynbee, but it knew the authors, all missionaries (FO 96/205, Scott to Toynbee, New York, May 16, 1916).

217. FO 96/206, Rockwell to Toynbee, July 8, 1916.

218. FO 96/205, Favre to Toynbee, Geneva (no date on the letter but February 1916). See also FO 96/205, Toynbee to Favre, London, March 6, 1916.

219. The Mugerditchian piece (*Blue Book,* document 134, p. 530, where his name was spelled Tovmas K. Muggerdichian, and "Key to the Blue Book," p. 25) is particularly instructive. It was drawn from an interview in Cairo with "Miss A," who saw nothing herself but "collected information from trustworthy sources." Mugerditchian wrote nothing of the Armenian revolt and subsequent battle in Urfa but stated that the Turks ordered the Armenians to be massacred. This was accomplished mainly by the Germans: "The German artillerymen destroyed the Armenian quarters, the church and everything, thus putting an end to the Armenian population at Ourfa" (p. 530). The hand of the British propagandists is obvious. On Mugerditchian, see also the section "Other Wellington House Publications: A Selection" and note 246 below.

220. FO 96/206, Boghos Nubar to Toynbee, Paris, June 28, 1916.

221. FO 96/206, "Redaction du Droschak" to Boghos Nubar, Geneva, July 31, 1916. The editor of the Armenian journal *Ararat* also did not have identification of some of the documents Toynbee took from that journal (FO 96/205, Editor of *Ararat* [signature unreadable] to Toynbee, London, February 9, 1916). The editor suggested that Toynbee make use of the "Patriarchate Statistics" by Marcel Léart, which he falsely stated had come from the patriarchate. They were actually created by Krikor Zohrab, a member of the Dashnak Party, for his book *La question arménienne à la lumière des documents* (Paris: A. Challamel, 1913), in which he used the pseudonym Marcel Léart. For an analysis of these statistics, see Justin McCarthy, *Muslims and Minorities,* pp. 53–57, 84.

222. The most well known was *The American Commonwealth* (New York: Macmillan, 1888), which went through many editions in America and was still being reprinted in 2008.

223. Bryce did acknowledge publicly that he and Toynbee had received much assistance from missionaries, although the book did not identify the great number of missionary sources: "Among the Americans to whom Lord Bryce acknowledges indebtedness in compiling the work are Dr. J. L. Barton, Chairman of the American Committee for Armenian and Syrian Relief; the Rev. G. T. Scott, Assistant Secretary of the Board of Foreign Missions of the Presbyterian Church in the United States; Dr. Herbert Adams Gibbons; Dr. William Walker Rockwell of the Union Theological Seminary, New York; the Rev. Stephen Trowbridge, Secretary of the American Red Cross Committee at Cairo; and the Rev. I. N. Camp, a missionary in the service of the American Board of Commissioners for Foreign Missions" ("Lord Bryce's Report on Armenian Atrocities: An Appalling Catalogue of Outrage and Massacre," *New York Times,* October 8, 1916, p. X2).

224. Quoted in Peterson, *Propaganda for War,* p. 243. Peterson felt that the American public was more receptive to "German horrors."

225. "Lord Bryce's Report on Armenian Atrocities: An Appalling Catalogue of Outrage and Massacre," *New York Times,* October 8, 1916, pp. X2–X3. The *Times* also published reviews and advertisements for Toynbee's other books on the war and the Armenians.

226. *Current History* 5 (November 1916): 321–34.

227. *New Republic* 9, no. 117 (January 27, 1917): 350–53.

228. Toynbee wrote to Barton, asking how many copies he wanted. Barton asked for 3,000 (FO 96/206, Toynbee to Bryce, September 22, 1916). See also FO 96/206, Toynbee to Barton, London, October 18, 1916.

229. See the samples of the letters sent to the press. These sample letters do not have a date or author. They are listed here by folio numbers: FO 96/206 #269 and #378.

230. FO 96/206, "Armenian Documents," Folios #287–88:

"Armenian Documents" [i.e., the *Blue Book*] Distribution:

1.	Official, Blue Cover in Paper	
	Foreign Office	1,500
	Stationery Office	6,000
	for Weyman's and Parliament	
2.	Official, Blue Cover in Boards	
	Sir Gilbert Parker	15,000
	American Press	200
	Wellington House—Presentation	300
	American Relief Committee	3,000
	Nubar Pasha	400
3.	American Edition—Putnam.	1,000
	Blue Cover in Boards	
4.	English Edition—(unofficial), Hodder and Stoughton, Cloth	
	For Sale	5,000
	English Press	250
	Wellington House (Steamships, etc.)	1,500
	Grand Total	34,150

An additional 500 copies were retained at Wellington House for further use. OCLC WorldCat lists 1,437 copies of the *Blue Book* in American libraries today, a very high number for a 1916 publication.

231. FO 96/206, Toynbee to Barton, London, November 4, 1916; Vickrey to Toynbee, November 20, 1916; and Barton to Toynbee, November 22, 1916.

232. FO 96/206, "Copy of cablegram from Dr. Barton, sent to Mr. Toynbee on the receipt of the proof of Lord Bryce's preface by the American Relief Committee," London, no date.

233. FO 96/205 and 206 contain many letters from Toynbee on the page proofs, which were also sent to Favre and Nubar. See, for example, FO 96/205, Toynbee to Boghos Nubar, June 20, 1916, and FO 96/205, Toynbee to Rockwell, June 20, 1916.

234. FO 96/206, Barton to Toynbee, Boston, October 9, 1916.

235. FO 96/206, Toynbee to Barton, London, November 4, 1916.

236. FO 96/207, Vickrey to Toynbee, January 6, 1917.

237. Bryce preface, in A. P. Hacobian, *Armenia and the War,* p. xiii.

238. Ibid., p. 31.

239. Benson was a well-known novelist with no expertise on the Middle East other than what he had gained as an archaeologist in Greece and Egypt in the 1890s.

240. *Germany, Turkey, and Armenia: A Selection of Documentary Evidence Relating to the Armenian Atrocities from German and Other Sources.* On German documents, see the publications of Johannes Lepsius: *Les massacres d'Arménia* (Paris: Payot & Cie., 1918) and *Deutschland und Armenien, 1914–1918* (Pottsdam: Tempelverlag, 1919).

241. On Ghusein, see Eugene Rogan, "Asiret Mektebi: Abdulhamid's School for Tribes (1892–1907)," *International Journal of Middle Eastern Studies* 28, no. 1 (February 1996): 103–4:

> Faᶜiz al-Ghusayn (1883–1968), an Aşiret Mektebi/Mülkiye graduate of 1899, was the only alumnus in Çankaya's sample to be dismissed from the civil service—by his account, for refusing to comply with a request to interfere in parliamentary elections to advance the government's candidate. Dismissed in 1912 or 1913, he nonetheless published an Ottoman-loyalist school textbook in Damascus in 1913–14—perhaps to ingratiate his way back into government service. Back in Damascus, al-Ghusayn took up a law practice and mixed with such proponents of Arabism as Shukri al-ᶜAsali and ᶜAbd al-Wahhab al-Inkhzi; thereafter he claimed to have refused subsequent invitations to return to state service. Shortly after the Ottoman entry into World War I, al-Ghusayn was approached by two members of the secret Arab nationalist society, al-Fatat. On joining al-Fatat (he quickly rose to its central committee), al-Ghusayn effectively departed from the Ottomanist camp. Although in later life al-Ghusayn attributed Arab-nationalist motives to his actions, he fits the profile of disappointed aspirants to power who, having played all of their Ottomanist cards and lost, turned to Arabism.

> In 1918 Ghusein was serving as secretary to Emir Faysal (Eliezer Tauber, *The Formation of Modern Syria and Iraq* [London: Frank Cass, 1995], p. 403).

242. "We are publishing it with Messrs. C. Arthur Pearson's imprint—and the firm are prepared to take 7,000 copies" (FO 395/137/227880, Ashcroft to Gaselee, London, November 29, 1917). Critics have noted that in a previous work I stated of Ghusein that "there was no such person." The statement was originally made in a speech then included in an article, and I misspoke. I had intended to indicate that the person described by Ghusein did not exist as described—that I believed he (or someone) had created much of his history. I should have described Ghusein as I have done here, being more specific in my language.

243. No one knew how the book had appeared in Cairo. According to the War Office, Ghusein was supposedly in Bombay; but the British admitted that they had not seen him and did not know his whereabouts (FO 395/137/227880, Gaselee to Ashcroft, December 1, 1917). FO 395/137 contains extensive documentation on the process of publishing the book. It is obvious that no one attempted to substantiate the truth of the work; nor were the British concerned about Ghusein himself. They were not even sure how to spell his name. The War Office provided other articles to the Propaganda Office. These were unsigned analyses that were forwarded by London to various countries. See, for example, FO 395/47/214716, "Turkish Nationalism."

244. FO 395/137/237621, Cooper to Gaselee, London, March 13, 1918. Bryan Cooper was a major in Army Intelligence: MI7, the section that dealt with propaganda.

245. The author's name is spelled incorrectly as Megerditchian in the book.

246. FO 141/468 contains extensive correspondence with and about Thomas K. Mugerditchian, concerning his request for a pension from the British government.

247. Israel Cohen, *The Turkish Persecution of the Jews.*

248. *The Ottoman Domination,* pp. 7, 13–14.

249. *Syria during March 1916: Her Miseries and Disasters,* p. 4.

250. Ibid. Wellington House also sponsored other publications. *The Commercial Future of Baghdad* was just what its name implied; "Serbian Macedonia" was a reprint of a relatively short letter to the editor of the *Near East* that gave the Serbian nationalist view; "With Machine-Guns in Gallipoli" was strictly a short story of actual fighting, reprinted from the *Westminster Gazette.* Martin Niepage was a teacher at the German Technical school at Aleppo (see FO 395/40/6382323 and 203755, Rumbold to Montgomery, Berne, October 2, 1916, on the usefulness of the Niepage pamphlet on Armenians as propaganda against the Germans). It should be noted that Niepage's testimony was considered suspect by at least part of the Wellington House establishment. When compiling the *Blue Book,* Arnold Toynbee refused to use the Niepage pamphlet. He wrote: "I gather that it is chiefly a collection of evidence at second-hand, Dr. Niepage having been at Beirout several months after the deportations occurred" (FO 296/206, Toynbee to Bryce, London, September 22, 1916). Harry Stuermer was representative of the *Kölnische Zeitung* in Istanbul. On Canon Parfit, see note 94 above. Israel Cohen was a prominent English Zionist and sometime secretary of the English Zionist Federation.

251. "Schedule of Wellington House Literature," p. 49.

252. For example, the Sykes-Picot Agreement. The Zionist publications are the most accurate of the lot, portraying Zionist settlement through accurate descriptions. They are not particularly good propaganda for the British and very seldom mention Great Britain at all. Richard Gottheil was in contact with the British propaganda machinery to elicit publication of Zionist materials, which declared that Zionists wished Palestine to be part of the British Empire. The Zionists and the British did not trust each other (FO 395/78/133102, Gaselee to Montgomery, July 9, 1917; see also FO 395/86/244217, Hyamson draft of telegram from Buchan to Butler, London, December 27, 1917).

253. FO 395/67/93112, Toynbee to Roxburgh, Wellington House, May 3, 1917, Montgomery to Spring Rice, cipher telegram, London, May 7, 1917. Although Toynbee had written this memorandum, it was copied under Montgomery's name, not Toynbee's, and sent to Butler in America (FO 115/2186, cipher from Montgomery, May 5, 1917).

254. "Third of Armenians Wiped Out," *Tyrone [Pa.] Daily Harold*, February 22, 1917, p. 7.

255. See notes 115–19 above.

256. Toynbee, *Armenian Atrocities*, pp. 22, 23, 68, 119.

257. "What It's All About" (ACASR ad), *New York Times*, February 24, 1919, p. 13.

258. For example, "Sees No Good in Declaration of War on Turkey," *Hartford [Conn.] Courant*, December 17, 1917, p. 20.

259. "3,000,000 in Peril of Turk Massacre," *Washington Post*, March 17, 1918, p. 20.

260. "They Shall Not Perish," *New York Times*, March 1, 1919, p. 9. Others joined in the attack. See "Says Germans Aided Armenian Killings," *New York Times*, December 11, 1917. The reputation of the Turks was so bad by the time America entered the war that association with the Turks was used against the Germans in propaganda.

261. "Germany's Aims in Asiatic Turkey," *Christian Science Monitor*, March 6, 1918, p. 1.

262. James L. Barton, "Kaiser and Sultan," *New York Times*, July 14, 1918, p. 41.

263. As seen in the previous chapter, the Rockwell bibliography on the Armenians contained the British propaganda works. Toynbee forwarded to him a set of page proofs of the Bryce Report. Rockwell must have been in close contact with him (William Walker Rockwell, *Armenia: A List of Books and Articles, with Annotations*).

264. For examples of this, see Taner Akçam, *A Shameful Act* (New York: Metropolitan Books, 2006); Richard Hovannisian, ed., *The Armenian People from Ancient to Modern Times*; Vahakn N. Dadrian, *The History of the Armenian Genocide* (Providence, R.I.: Berghahn Books, 1995).

265. The Wellington House publications are still a basic element of histories and advocacy by Armenian scholars. The following list of the Wellington House books includes those that were particularly on the Armenians. Every one of these books except one is in the standard bibliography of Armenian history published by Professor Richard Hovannisian (*The Armenian Holocaust: A Bibliography Relating to the Deportations, Massacres, and Dispersion of the Armenian People, 1915–1923* [Cambridge, Mass.: Armenian Heritage Press, 1978]). The only one that is not is *Deutschland über Allah* by Benson, perhaps because of its provocative title.

> E. F. Benson, *Crescent and Iron Cross*
> E. F. Benson, *Deutschland über Allah*
> Faʿiz El-Ghusein, "Bedouin Notable of Damascus [sic]," in *Martyred Armenia*
> *Germany, Turkey, and Armenia: A Selection of Documentary Evidence Relating to Armenian Atrocities from German and Other Sources*
> A. P. Hacobian, *Armenia and the War*
> Esther Mugerditchian, *From Turkish Toils*

Martin Niepage, *The Horrors of Aleppo*

Harry Stuermer, *Two War Years in Constantinople*

Arnold J. Toynbee, *Armenian Atrocities: The Murder of a Nation*

Arnold J. Toynbee, ed., *The Treatment of Armenians in the Ottoman Empire, 1915–1916*

Arnold J. Toynbee, *Turkey: A Past and a Future*

Arnold J. Toynbee, *The Murderous Tyranny of the Turks*

See also "The Armenian Genocide: A Bibliography," Armenian Research Center, University of Michigan Dearborn (http://www.umd.umich.edu/dept/armenian/ facts/gen_bib1.html). The bibliographies of the books in note 264 above also contain most of the Wellington House books.

Chapter 11, Politics and the Missionary Establishment

1. The sources are too extensive to list here. Most European and American primary sources are in FO 371/4218–22 and FO 371/4157, which contain British, American, and other reports. For complete documentation, see Justin McCarthy, *Death and Exile: The Ethnic Cleansing of Ottoman Muslims,* pp. 258–66, 306–12. On the Greek invasion as a whole, see Arnold J. Toynbee, *The Western Question in Greece and Turkey: A Study in the Contact of Civilisations.*

2. "Estimate of Responsibilities, Constantinople, 11 October 1919," in Çağrı Erhan, "Greek Occupation of İzmir and Adjoining Territories: Report of the Inter-Allied Commission of Inquiry (May–September 1919)," *SAM Papers* (Center of Foreign Affairs of the Republic of Turkey, Center for Strategic Research), no. 2/99, April 1999 (http://www.sam.gov.tr/sampapers.php), pp. 48–50.

3. The report of the so-called Smyrna Commission was kept secret for many years after the war. Turks obtained a copy and published it in Paris in 1920 (*Les Grecs à Smyrne—Nouveaux témoignages sur leurs atrocités: Un document official probant*). No one in the press seems to have noticed. The English version was finally published in 1947 (United States, Department of State, *Papers Relating to the Foreign Relations of the United States: The Paris Peace Conference, 1919*, vol. 12). Because the document was relatively unknown, American officials could flatly lie about it. William Westermann, chief of the Near Eastern Division of the American Peace Commission, reported on January 28, 1921, among other false statements, that the commission "could not settle the question as to who began the firing" in answer to a question as to whether the Greeks or the Turks started the massacre at İzmir (Edward Mandell House and Charles Seymour, eds., *What Really Happened at Paris* [New York: Charles Scribner's Sons, 1921], pp. 468–69). See the commentary and copy of the text in Erhan, "Greek Occupation of İzmir and Adjoining Territories."

4. FO 371/4222, no. 146629, cover sheet, p. 2.

5. "Smyrna Landing Is to Be Investigated," *Christian Science Monitor,* July 23, 1919, p. 1; "Allies Consider Smyrna Problem," *Bridgeport [Conn.] Standard-Telegram,* September 12, 1919, p. 17.

6. Some of the newspapers that carried the AP story: "Premier Venizelos Says Hearing on Smyrna Disorders Was Unfair," *San Antonio Light,* November 29, 1919, p. 16; "Report of Slaughter by Greeks Is Denied," *Indianapolis Star,* November 9, 1919 (part 2), p. 1; "Venizelos Defends Greece," *Washington Post,* November 9, 1919, p. 10; "Venizelos Wants New Smyrna Investigation," *New York Times,* November 16, 1919, p. 2.

7. "Turks Murdering Greeks in Smyrna," *Bridgeport [Conn.] Standard Telegram,* March 21, 1919, p. 12; "Turks Decapitate Greeks," *Washington Post,* March 21, 1919, p. 3; "Turks Massacre Greeks," *New York Times,* March 21, 1919, p. 3; "Greeks in Turkey Forced into Army," *Washington Post,* June 16, 1918, p. R7. With rare exceptions, all the articles from the period immediately before and immediately after the Greek invasion came from the Associated Press. As with most AP articles, they are found in very many newspapers. For reasons of space, only a few are listed here. A number of citations are often included to show that both major and minor newspapers carried the stories.

8. "Greeks in Smyrna District Attacked," *Christian Science Monitor,* Match 22, 1919, p. 1.

9. "Turks Are Responsible for the Disorders in Europe," *Fort Wayne [Ind.] Journal-Gazette,* April 18, 1919, p. 1 (note that the article was not on Europe at all). The article also appeared in "Disorder Laid to Turks," *Christian Science Monitor,* April 19, 1919, p. 2, and many other papers. It was a report of statements by Miriam Savasly, chair of the Armenian National Union.

10. "Turkey Threatens Greater Massacres If Empire's Cut Up," *Bridgeport [Conn.] Standard Telegram,* August 19, 1919, p. 10.

11. [No title], *Reno [Nev.] Evening Gazette,* March 14, 1919, p. 4.

12. "Greeks of Asia Minor," *New York Times,* January 18, 1919, p. 10. Another *New York Times* editorial admitted that the Greeks were a minority in the whole territory they wanted, which extended far beyond the district of İzmir awarded Greece by the Peace Conference. The *Times* stated that the enlarged district was two-to-one Turkish (actually more than five-to-one) but said that the Greeks should get it anyway, because they were "the principal progressive element" and "the dominant race" ("The Greeks in Smyrna," *New York Times,* November 29, 1919, p. 10).

13. "Greek Forces Land at Smyrna," *Lima [Ohio] News,* May 16, 1919, p. 1.

14. "Allies Risk New Wars in Settling the Eastern Question," *Syracuse [N.Y.] Herald,* January 12, 1919, p. 6. Simonds wrote elsewhere that at least half the population in the region claimed by Greece was "Hellenic" (Frank H. Simonds, "American Mandatory for Constantinople Mistake, Says Simonds," *Atlanta Constitution,* August 31, 1919, p. D5). See also Frank H. Simonds, "American Policy at Paris Brings Evil Compromise," *Waterloo [Iowa] Evening Courier,* August 28, 1919, p. 1. Simonds wrote from New York. On Simond's writing in World War I, see chapter 10, note 56. See also William T. Ellis, the syndicated religious writer, "Orient Turns to U.S.," *Washington Post,* August 17, 1919, p. 4; "Would Unite Greeks," *Washington Post,* March 20, 1919, p. 5; and "Will America Protect World's Weak People?" *Atlanta Constitution,* August 21, 1919, p. 5.

15. "Greece Would Add Three Million to Her Population," *New Castle [Pa.] News,* February 4, 1919, p. 2 (International Press); "Greece Demands Thrace, without Constantinople," *Waterloo [Iowa] Evening Courier and Reporter,* January 15, 1919, p. 7 (Associated Press). Editorials echoed the sentiment that Greeks should take the region because they were the largest population element. See also "Venizelos Warns of Armenia's Peril," *New York Times,* September 15, 1919, p. 15.

16. Dahiliye Nezareti, Sicil-I Nüfus İdare-yi Umumiyesi Müdüriyeti, *Memalik-i Osmaniye'nin 1330 Senesi Nüfus İstatistiği* (Istanbul, 1336 M). The provinces counted as Western Anatolia are Aydın, Hüdavendigâr, İzmit, Kale-I Sultaniye, Afyon, Karası, and Kütahya; as Western Thrace, Edirne and Çatalca. For an analysis of the Ottoman figures and corrections of the Ottoman undercount of women and children (which does not affect the percentages given here), see Justin McCarthy, *Muslims and Minorities.*

17. See FO 371–7879, E5735, Oliphant to Rumbold, London, June 10, 1923; Naval Staff, Intelligence Department, *Handbook of Asia Minor,* vol. 3, pt. 2, London, July 1919; FO 371-4221, no. 137567, Appendix 1: "Operations and Intelligence Survey, no. 2."

18. The statistics, created by Professor George Soteriadis of Athens University, were a fabrication. See Justin McCarthy, "Greek Sources on Ottoman Greek Population," *International Journal of Turkish Studies* 1, no. 2: 66–76; and Dimitri Kitsikis, *Propagande et pressions en politique internationale* (Paris: Presses Universitaires de France, 1963).

19. "Allied forces were landed at Smyrna last Thursday, meeting with considerable resistance from the Turks, but making themselves masters of the city" ("Italy Asked to Explain," *Decatur [Ill.] Review,* May 22, 1919, p. 1). This article and the ones that follow were printed in many newspapers. For example, this same story, datelined Paris, appeared in "300 Allies Fall as Turkish Fort Taken," *Nevada State Journal,* May 21, 1919, p. 3; "Allied Casualties 300 in Smyrna," *Washington Post,* May 21, 1919, p. 5l; "Asserts Hard Fight Took Place in Smyrna," *New York Times,* May 19, 1919, p. 17; and in the *Boston Globe, Los Angeles Times,* and others. The article was from the Associated Press. In a rare non-AP article, *Christian Science Monitor* wrote from London that an unidentified "representative of *The Christian Science Monitor*" had learned that "both Turkish troops and Muhammadan inhabitants" had resisted the Greek landing ("Resistance to Landing at Smyrna," *Christian Science Monitor,* May 26, 1919, p. 1). The *Christian Science Monitor* ("Features of Greek Landing at Smyrna," September 20, 1919) later offered a long and completely false description of events taken completely from "Greek military authorities." The dateline was London, with no indication of how the information had been obtained. In a break with its traditions, *New York Times* ("Slaughter in Smyrna," August 19, 1919, p. 18) published part of a letter from "an American educator stationed in Asia Minor" stating that the Greeks had massacred the Turks.

20. "Greeks Advancing from Smyrna and Turks Retiring," *Ogden [Utah] Standard,* May 29, 1919, p. 11.

21.   "Seek Greek Protection," *Washington Post,* August 10, 1919, p. RE10; "Turks Weary of War," *Washington Post,* July 20, 1919, p. 13.

22.   "Murders in Asia Minor," *New York Times,* July 8, 1919, p. 6.

23.   "Greeks Chasing Turks," *New York Times,* July 13, 1919, p. 17.

24.   "Turks Violate Armistice," *Evening State Journal and Lincoln [Nebr.] Daily News,* June 24, 1919.

25.   "Greek Army Driving Turkish Forces Backward," *Ada [Okla.] Evening News,* July 12, 1919, p. 1.

26.   Examples of article datelined Athens or Salonica (most from press agencies): Turks doing all the killing ("Turks Slay Greek Peasants," *Stevens Point [Wisc.] Daily Journal,* March 21, 1919, p. 5); Turks "committing many brutalities" ("Turkish Irregulars Cut Ears Off Greek Priest," *Syracuse [N.Y.] Herald,* September 24, 1919, p. 5); Turks mutilating women and children ("Greeks Driving Turks Out," *Decatur [Ill.] Review,* July 12, 1919, p. 1; "Turks Murdering Greeks in Smyrna," *Bridgeport [Conn.] Standard Telegram,* March 21, 1919, p. 6; "Greeks Not Yet Safe from Turkish Violence," *Fort Wayne [Ind.] Journal-Gazette,* April 29, 1919, p. 5; and "Report Turks Killed Many in Rodosto," *New York Times,* March 4, 1920, p. 3 [from the Greek Legation in Paris]).

27.   "Refugees in Athens Tell of Massacre," *Olean [N. Y.] Evening Times,* September 18, 1922, p. 1.

28.   "Turks Murder 700,000 Greeks," *Oneonta [N.Y.] Star,* August 30, 1921, p. 7, and other papers.

29.   "Greek Says Turks Burn Prisoners," *San Antonio Express,* November 8, 1922, p. 10 (AP story).

30.   "Seek Greek Protection," *Washington Post,* August 10, 1919, p. 10 (from the *London Times*).

31.   See, for example, "Claim Turks Plan Extermination of Greeks along Sea," *Wood County [Wisc.] Tribune,* August 10, 1921, p. 51; and "Turkish Treatment of Greeks Exposed," *Galveston Daily News*, August 14, 1921, p. 26 (Associated Press articles that were printed or excerpted in various papers).

32.   *Christian Science Monitor,* March 11, 1920, p. 1.

33.   See Barton's comments in "Greek Protection Ample for American Missionaries," *Kingsport [Tenn.] Times,* July 31, 1919, p. 1.

34.   McCarthy, *Death and Exile,* p. 303.

35.   Ibid., pp. 292–306.

36.   The most complete consideration of the İzmir fire is Heath W. Lowry, "Turkish History: On Whose Sources Will It Be Based? A Case Study on The Burning of İzmir," *Osmanli Arastirmaları* 9, no. 13 (1988): 1–29. G. H. Papazian, executive secretary of the Armenian National Union of America, claimed that the Turks had spread oil in the İzmir streets to aid the fire, based on a letter from an Armenian editor from the city ("Armenian Editor Tells of Smyrna," *Christian Science Monitor,* October 6, 1922, p. 5).

37.   *New Near East* (October 1922).

38.   "Killing by Turks Has Been Renewed," *New Near East* (May 6, 1922): 2.

39. For examples, see *New Near East* (January 1923) and "Fearful Massacres Unless Allies Stand," *Boston Globe,* November 7, 1922, p. 9.

40. Dr. J. E. Kirby, a Near East Relief official, in "Massacres of Armenians Continuing, Says Kirby," *Dallas News,* December 12, 1921, p. 6.

41. See, for example, "Asserts Atrocities in Smyrna Continue," *New York Times,* October 3, 1922, p. 47.

42. "Greeks Report Fiendish Slaughter," *New York Times,* September 16, 1922, p. 1.

43. "Moslems Bury Greek Christians Alive," *Madison [Wisc.] Capital Times,* November 2, 1922, p. 1. The article dateline was "Washington," from the AP.

44. "Allies Failure to Take Action Inspires Turk to New Outrages," *Christian Science Monitor,* September 22, 1922, p. 1. *McClure's Magazine* (55, no. 7 [September 1923]: 50–59) ran a long piece by a Near East Relief nurse, Agnes Evon, telling of the suffering of the Greeks and Armenians of İzmir, with no mention of Muslim suffering.

45. "Massacre 2,000 Christians," *Appleton [Wisc.] Post-Crescent,* September 15, 1922, p. 1 (an AP story). Stories on İzmir are too numerous to cite more than a few examples, in addition to the articles cited elsewhere in this chapter: "2,000 Christians at Smyrna Still Await Massacre," *Atlanta Constitution,* October 1, 1922, p. B8; "Smyrna Rescue Ship Brings Horror Tale," *Boston Globe,* October 10, 1922, p. 5; and "Turkish Atrocities in Smyrna District," *Christian Science Monitor,* September 14, 1922, p. 1.

46. "2,000 Massacred by Turks," *Lowell [Mass.] Sun,* September 15, 1922, p. 1. The Greek Legation in Washington distributed a press release claiming a more than unlikely alliance of Turkey, Germany, and Russia ("Russ and Berlin Back the Turk," *Oelwein [Iowa] Daily Register,* September 20, 1922. p. 1).

47. "Russia and Bulgaria May Join Turks," *Fayetteville [Ark.] Daily Democrat,* September 16, 1922, p. 1.

48. "Puts the Victims at 120,000," *New York Times,* September 16, 1922, p. 1. The original story was in a *London Times* dispatch from Athens. See also "Izmir in Ruins from Fire Set by Turks; Victims Are Said to Number 120,000," *New York Herald,* September 16, 1922, p. 1. The *Boston Globe* reported that the 120,000 figure came from a missionary ("Smyrna Massacre Victims 120,000 Reports American Relief Agent," September 18, 1922, p. 1). The *Dallas News* set the figure of killed at 150,000 ("Over 150,000 Persons Perish When City of Smyrna Destroyed," September 18, 1922, p. 1). The *Los Angeles Times* wrote: "More Than 100,000 Greeks and Armenians Slain in Asia Minor" (September 17, 1922, p. 2). It edified its readers with a map entitled "Where the Turks Are Running Amuck in Asia Minor." The *Los Angeles Times* page-1 banner headline on the same day read: "Hordes of Islam Determined to Defy Allies."

49. "U.S. Woman Saves 500 Greek Girls from Being Sold," *Hammond [Ind.] Times,* October 10, 1922, p. 6.

50. "Turks Have Halted Greeks' Advance," *New York Times,* July 26, 1921, p. 13. A similar allegation appeared in another AP story, "Greeks Begin the Evacuation of Smyrna," *Eau Claire [Wisc.] Leader,* September 9, 1922, p. 1. The *Chicago Tribune* gave a more honest evaluation for many of the burnings (see note 124 below). For

the history of the destruction on the Greek retreat, see McCarthy, *Death and Exile,* pp. 279–83 and 292–97, which includes extensive diplomatic records on the Greek destruction.

51. "Massacre in Smyrna" (AP story), *Fort Wayne [Ind.] New-Sentinel,* September 15, 1922, p. 1.

52. See, for example, "As Conflagration Sweeps City of Smyrna Warships Rescue Panic-Stricken Refugees," *Atlanta Constitution,* September 15, 1922, p. 1; and "14 Nationals Lost as Blaze Destroys City," *San Francisco Chronicle,* September 15, 1922, p. 1. The "14 nationals" were supposedly Americans who had been killed, but the *San Francisco Chronicle* reported two days later that all Americans were alive ("Three-Fifths of Smyrna Is Now in Ashes," September 17, 1922, p. 8).

53. "Smyrna's Ravagers Fired on Americans," *New York Times,* September 18, 1922, p. 1.

54. "Yield to Turks Now, Says Prentiss," *New York Times,* November 12, 1922, p. 1; "Turkey for Turks Given as Slogan to Relief Worker," *Atlanta Constitution,* November 12, 1922, p. 5. The *New York Herald* reported that the Turks were distributing secret massacre orders in Istanbul, disguised as information on forming neighborhood groups to fight fires ("Turks Distribute Massacre Orders," May 30, 1922, p. 1).

55. The entire urban region, including both sides of the Bosphorus and the Princes Islands, held fewer than 300,000 Christians before the war.

56. *Mansfield [Ohio] News,* September 17, 1922, p. 1.

57. *San Francisco Chronicle,* September 19, 1922, p. 1.

58. *Los Angeles Times,* September 16, 1922, p. 1. See also the United Press article "Russia and Bulgaria May Join Turks If War with Allies Develops; Constantinople Battle Is Imminent; 120,000 Christians Massacred," *Fayetteville [Ark.] Daily Democrat,* September 16, 1922. Many newspapers included statements in the articles that Russia was about to or already had sent troops to aid the Turkish Nationalists. Editorialists and cartoonists waded in. For example, the *Dallas News* on September 14, 1922, printed a large page-1 cartoon of a mounted Turk: mustachioed, wearing a fez, with a grim look in his eye, and carrying over his shoulder a scimitar dripping blood. The Turk was eyeing a city in the distance, flying from its ramparts a flag marked "Constantinople." Other cartoonists portrayed a Turk dancing with glee over the prospect of new conquests and massacres or Turks counting their victims. All the Turks looked either evil or stupid.

59. *New York Herald,* September 17, 1922, p. 5. The *Herald* ran other articles foretelling danger throughout Asia and the Balkans because of the Turkish victory.

60. One of the news service articles by Philip Gibbs: "French Intrigue and English Folly Have Brought All Europe to Brink of New War Says Gibbs," *Lincoln [Nebr.] Star,* October 1, 1922, p. 4. See also Philip Gibbs, "Gibbs Sees Danger to All Europe in Turkish Victory," *New York Herald,* September 2, 1922, p. 2.

61. See, for example, "Bishop Charges Wrong Policy Turks," *San Antonio Express,* November 8, 1922, p. 10. On Cannon's views, see "Bishop Would Use Navy Against Turks," *New York Times,* September 14, 1922, p. 3; "Work of Americans Undone by the Turk," *New York Times,* October 2, 1922, p. 3; and "Dr. Ward Will Speak at City Hall Tomorrow," *Fitchburg [Mass.] Sentinel,* September 23, 1922, p. 2.

62. "150,000 Churches to Stop Massacres," *Ironwood [Mich.] Daily Globe,* June 23, 1922, p. 7.

63. "Beg U.S. to Stop Turkish Horrors in the Near East," *Atlanta Constitution,* October 12, 1922, p. 1. Cannon, from Birmingham, Alabama, was at various times a prominent leader in the temperance movement, bishop in charge of the mission work of the Methodist Episcopal Church, member of the executive committee of the Federal Council of Churches, and chair of the Committee on Near East Relief of the Methodist Church. He was a Democrat until the party nominated a Catholic for president, when he became chair of the Southern Anti-Smith Democrats.

64. "3,000 at Cathedral Protest Atrocities," *New York Times,* September 25, 1922, p. 2; "Cathedral Meeting Asks Curb of Turk," *New York Herald,* September 25, 1922, p. 2.

65. The *New York Times* editors had been decidedly anti-Turkish throughout World War I and the Turkish Independence War. In a long commentary, Walter Littlefield, another *New York Times* editor, had labeled the Allies hypocrites for refusing to eject the Turks from Istanbul. In trying to show that the Turks should be evicted, Littlefield managed to lie about or distort the terms of the Mudros Armistice that had ended World War I, the Muslim idea of the caliphate, the population of Istanbul, Turkish affection for the city, and even the strictures of the Quran ("Repudiating the Promise to Oust the Turk from Europe," *New York Times,* March 28, 1920, p. XXXi). In another commentary he wrote that "the Greeks fought in the most righteous of causes" and called on Europe and America to intervene on their behalf. Even Littlefield seems to have realized that the Greek cause would not have been so righteous if, as was the fact, Greece had occupied lands where the large majority was Turkish. He solved this problem by declaring that none of the coastal provinces of Anatolia had a Turkish majority, a piece of nonsense that not even the other fervent advocates of the Greeks had alleged ("The Turk Bad Again," *New York Times,* May 28, 1922, p. 97).

66. "Churches Call on U.S. to Intervene at Once in Near East," *Atlanta Constitution,* September 23, 1922, p. 1:

> Suggestions regarding what course America ought to pursue will be made at a mass meeting of church leaders at the cathedral of St. John the Divine here Sunday.
>
> Signers to the petitions included officers of the federal council of Churches, foreign mission societies of the Baptist, Presbyterian, Methodist Episcopal and Reformed churches, Near East relief societies, committee on religious minorities, the church peace union, Armenian-American society, American board of commissioners for foreign missions, Armenian rights society of Pennsylvania; committee for Armenian independence, and of the Robert college of Constantinople, and the American university of Beirut.
>
> Dr. James L. Barton, chairman of the Near East relief, published a cablegram sent to President Harding by the Greek patriarch Meletios,

urging America to grant a government loan to supplement the relief work now going on in Smyrna.

For another appeal to President Harding by churchmen and Near East Relief leaders, see "Ask Harding to Act in the Near East," *New York Times,* June 12, 1923, p. 18. See also the description of the meeting in the *New Near East* (October 1922).

67. "Near East Relief Plea of Churches," *Christian Science Monitor,* May 19, 1923, p. 5.

68. *Daily Kennebec [Maine] Journal,* September 27, 1922, p. 4.

69. More than twenty of these articles appeared, too many to list. Gibbons's assertions listed below are taken from the following *Christian Science Monitor* stories: "Turkish Peasants against Policy of Kemal Pasha," May 26, 1922, p. 1; "Greek Massacres by Turks Continue," May 31, 1922, p. 1; "Kemalist Policy of Extermination Deliberate Plan," June 29, 1922, p. 1; and "Near East Relief Prevented from Helping Greeks," July 13, 1922, p. 1. The last of these articles was especially offensive to the Turks and particularly erroneous. For example, Gibbons quoted a missionary who stated that the Turks had not allowed Near East Relief to aid the Greeks in Harput, although they were allowed to aid Armenians. The Ottoman census just before the war registered no Greeks in Harput; nor do any Western sources on Ottoman population mention a Greek community there.

70. "Turkish Peasants against Policy of Kemal Pasha," *Christian Science Monitor,* May 26, 1922, p. 1.

71. "Turks Not Getting Many Recruits for Anatolian Campaign," *Christian Science Monitor,* May 23, 1922, p. 1.

72. "Turkish Feeling against Britain Growing Rapidly," *Christian Science Monitor,* June 23, 1922, p. 1. See also "Greeks Dominate Turkish Positions on Entire Front," *Christian Science Monitor,* June 13, 1922, in which Gibbons declared that the Greeks would win and would never leave Anatolia. He also asserted that the morale of the Greek Army was high, which historians know to be the opposite of the truth. A number of other Gibbons articles stated his confidence that the Greeks would triumph.

73. McCarthy, *Muslims and Minorities,* pp. 130–33. The number of those who went to Greece from Anatolia was actually approximately 850,000, because some had died before the 1928 census was taken. This number includes Greek refugees from immediately before World War I, many of whom returned to Anatolia then left again in the Independence War's population exchange.

74. But it was surely true that most lower-level members of the old Committee of Union and Progress supported the Nationalists, as did the overwhelming number of Turks.

75. James L. Barton, *The Story of Near East Relief,* pp. 148–60.

76. The Associated Press reported from Istanbul that the Allied high commissioners had authorized a Greek squadron of thirty-five war vessels to go to the Black Sea Coast ("Greeks Operating Ground Laid Out by Allies Commission," *Olean [N.Y.] Evening News,* June 15, 1921, p. 1). The Greeks were authorized to proceed as far as Batum. Some variants of this AP article said twenty-five ships, not thirty-five.

77. Venizelos supporters reported that such an invasion was planned ("Reveal Plan of Greek Seizure," *Ogden [Utah] Standard-Examiner,* January 5, 1921, p. 2 [an AP article]).

78. "Massacre of 7,000; a Plea for Relief," *Washington Post,* February 18, 1920, p. 9.

79. "Killings by Turks Have Been Renewed," *New York Times,* May 6, 1922, p. 2. See also "250,000 in Flight Seek Aid of U.S.," *Washington Post,* December 3, 1922, p. 75.

80. "Says 22,000 Greeks Died on the March," *New York Times,* June 7, 1922, p. 3. See also "150,000 Churches to Stop Massacres," *Ironwood [Mich.] Daily Globe,* June 23, 1922, p. 7; and "Declares Turks Plan Massacre," *Cleveland Plain Dealer,* June 4, 1922, p. 2B. Ward and his colleague were deported by the Nationalists. In one article, Fethi Bey, the interior minister of the Nationalist government, declared that Ward and Yowell had been deported because of intrigues against the Turkish government and asked why so little notice had been given to the well-documented Greek atrocities against Turks ("Fethi Bey Seeks Imperial Investigation into Atrocities," *Danville [Va.] Bee,* September 25, 1923, p. 11, on the want-ad page).

81. "Turkish Atrocities Stir Britain to Act," *New York Times,* May 16, 1922, p. 3. See also the Associated Press interview with Ward ("Tales of Turk Cruelty Told by Americans," *Ogden [Utah] Standard-Examiner,* May 5, 1922, p. 1), in which he stated: "The Turkish authorities frankly state their deliberate intention to let all the Greeks die."

82. "Starve Christians; Lay It to Allah," *New York Times,* June 25, 1922, p. E5. See also an article on the missionaries J. H. Knapp and B. Bannerman Murdoch ("Deportations of Armenians Are Described," *Bismarck [N.Dak.] Tribune,* August 1, 1922, p. 2). The headline writer had confused Greeks with Armenians. Ward's colleague in Harput, Forest D. Yowell, also stated that the Turks were planning to massacre all the Christians ("Killing by Turks Has Been Renewed," *New York Times,* May 6, 1922, p. 2). He gave no indication of how he had gained this information, although perhaps he also had spoken with the education department.

83. "Turkish Bath Weapon," *Wellsboro [Pa.] Gazette,* September 11, 1919, p. 8, and other papers. The story came from New York, but no news service was listed. The events supposedly took place in 1916 and 1917, long before actual relocations of Black Sea Greeks had occurred.

84. Larry Rue, "Near East Finds Kurd Atrocities a Curzon Myth," *Chicago Tribune,* May 19, 1922, p. 4B.

85. Reports of massacres by Turks at Harput were sent by F. D. Yowell and Mark L. Ward of Near East Relief, who also stated that Americans had felt "unjust and unfriendly treatment," although not physical attacks, at Harput. See the International News Service article: Harry L. Rodgers, "Investigate Atrocity Report," *New Castle [Pa.] News,* August 3, 1922, p. 1; and Larry Rue, "Americans Feel Moslem's Hate in Marash Area," *Chicago Tribune,* March 16, 1920, p. 5. The Rue article was written on February 22 but had been held up by French censors. It was based completely on missionary and Armenian sources but gave a feeling for the situation.

86. Hamelin to the High Commissioner, February 2, 1919, in Ministère de la Défense, État Major de l'Armée du Terre, Service Historique, Général (CR) du Hays, *Les armées françaises au Levant* (Vincennes: Le Service, 1978), p. 122.

87. French, American, and British sources on the Armenian attacks are cited in McCarthy, *Death and Exile,* pp. 242–45.

88. Counted here as Adana Vilâyeti and Antep, Maraş, and Urfa <u>sancaks</u>. For sources, see note 16 above and note 186 below.

89. On the Cilician Troubles, see Robert F. Zeidner, *The Tricolor over the Taurus: The Franco-Turkish War for Cilicia, Crucible of the National Liberation Movement* (New York: Peter Lang Publishing, 1996); Robert Farrer Zeidner, "The Tricolor over the Taurus: The French in Cilicia and Vicinity, 1918–1922," especially pp. 351–75 on the Maraş uprising; McCarthy, *Death and Exile,* pp. 202–8; and the sources in those works. Some Armenian groups contended that the French were secretly behind Turkish actions in Cilicia ("Charges Made by the Armenians," *Christian Science Monitor,* June 24, 1920, p. 1).

90. "Witness Tells of Massacres," *Christian Science Monitor,* April 14, 1920, p. 4.

91. "Marash's Reign of Terror Described by Boston Man," *Boston Globe,* March 6, 1920, p. 1. This AP story was repeated with more or less detail in other newspapers, such as "Eyewitness Tells How Armenians Were Massacred," *New York Times,* March 6, 1920, pp. 1–2; and "American Tells of Massacre at Marash," *Galveston Daily News,* March 6, 1920, p. 1. Crathern was a YMCA secretary and relief worker.

92. "Armenians Die in Burning Oil," *Los Angeles Times,* March 12, 1920, p. 7.

93. Another missionary, Mabel Elliott, described the same event but said 2,500 Armenians were in the church, of whom 22 survived ("Turks Wantonly Fired on American College," *Charleston [W.Va.] Daily Mail,* June 7, 1920, p. 7). Armenian churches in Maraş were not capacious cathedrals, and how 2,500 fit into one is unknown. Bishop Cannon of Near East Relief blamed the French for leaving Armenians to their "fearful fate" ("French Desertion Caused Massacre by Turks He Says," *Atlanta Constitution,* December 11, 1922, p. 5). For a one-sided account of the events in Maraş, see Stanley Elphinstone Kerr, *The Lions of Marash* (Albany: State University of New York Press, 1973).

94. See, for example, "Americans in Danger from Turks' Attacks," *Oshkosh [Wisc.] Daily Northwestern,* March 1, 1920, p. 11 (a United Press story). Headlines and stories always mentioned the danger to American missionaries and relief workers, usually the same people. Two Americans were killed in Antep ("Situation Most Desperate," *Christian Science Monitor,* February 23, 1920, p. 1).

95. "Situation Most Desperate," *Christian Science Monitor,* February 23, 1920, p. 1. See also "U.S. Relief Party Besieged by Turks," *Washington Post,* March 8, 1920, p. 1 (an AP story).

96. "Uprising in Armenia Graphically Described," *Charleston [W.Va.] Daily Mail,* June 10, 1920, p. 10.

97. "Turks Wantonly Fired on American College," *Charleston [W.Va.] Daily Mail,* June 7, 1920, p. 7, and other papers. The missionary source, Dr. Mabel Elliott, stated that 5,000 Armenians had left Maraş and less than half survived the trek.

98. "Women and Children Tortured at Marash," *Boston Globe,* March 1, 1920, p. 2. This article, probably from the Associated Press, appeared in a number of papers, often without identification of its missionary source. Dr. Robert A. Lambert of Near

East Relief reported from Aleppo that 1,000 Armenians had died on their march ("Thousand Armenians Perish in Snow," *Atlanta Constitution,* March 21, 1920, p. 8K). See "5,000 Massacre Total around Marash Latest," *Waterloo [Iowa] Evening Courier,* March 5, 1920, p. 1 (an AP story). The French gave the 5,000 number. See also "Panic among Armenians," *Dallas News,* June 12, 1921, magazine, p. 2.

99.   "16,000 Christians Massacred by Turks in Cilicia Province," *Cedar Rapids [Iowa] Evening Gazette,* March 1, 1920, p. 1. This story, which originated in London, appeared in a number of papers and was obviously a news service story, but the name of the service was not identified. The *Los Angeles Times* ("Kill Thousands of Armenians," April 16, 1920, p. 7) wrote that "19,000 to 24,000" Armenians had been massacred.

100. "8000 Armenians Killed in Maraş," *Tyrone [Pa.] Daily Herald,* March 29, 1920, p. 5. See also "Many Villages Besieged by Turks," *New York Times,* April 20, 1920, p. 3.

101. Some newspapers ran an Associated Press story from London quoting a letter received by the scholar Marmaduke Pickthall that gave an accurate retelling of the events of the İzmir invasion ("Greek Soldiers Murder Turks without Cause," *Centralia [Wash.] Daily Chronicle,* August 5, 1919, p. 5). See also Robert J. Prew, International News Service, "Frenchman Charges Greeks with Burning City," *Fort Wayne [Ind.] News and Sentinel,* July 28, 1920, p. 11.

102. "Turks Burned Smyrna to Cover Massacres, Is Charge by Greeks," *Titusville [Pa.] Herald,* September 16, 1922, p. 1. It is true that most of the atrocity stories that appeared in the American press were based on the reports of refugees. The stories came in from Athens in particular, but also from places as far away as Malta.

103. "Fear Yanks in Smyrna May Be among Victims," *Iowa City Press-Citizen,* September 15, 1922, p. 1; "As Conflagration Sweeps City of Smyrna Warships Rescue Panic-Stricken Refugees," *Atlanta Constitution,* September 15, 1922, p. 1.

104. See, for example, "Turks Burning, Slaughtering," *Moberly [Mo.] Monitor-Index,* September 15, 1922, p. 1 (an AP article).

105. "Turks Deny Rumor of New Massacres in Anatolia," *Boston Globe,* March 8, 1920, p. 6.

106. "Marash Massacre Is Denied by Turks," *Billings [Mont.] Gazette,* March 12, 1920, p. 2 (an AP story). See also "Turkey Denied New Massacres in Armenia," *Chicago Tribune,* March 8, 1920, p. 2. In one story the British undersecretary of foreign affairs admitted some Greek atrocities ("Admits Greeks Murdered Their Turkish Prisoners," *Bridgeport [Conn.] Standard Telegram,* June 27, 1919, p. 9). It was also printed under the comics.

107. This was not the only time the Turks requested Allied investigation. See "Turkey Requests United States to Probe Massacre of Christians," *Cedar Rapids [Iowa] Evening Gazette,* March 6, 1920, p. 3.

108. For example, see the reports by the American plenipotentiary Admiral Bristol in U.S. National Archives, 867.00/1137, 867.00/1128, 867.00/1185, and 867.00/1179 and the various British reports in FO 406/43 no. E1352 and FO 371/5044.

109. "Maraş Massacre Denied by Turks," *Bridgeport [Conn.] Telegram,* March 12, 1920, p. 16.

110. "Atrocities in the Near East," *Chicago Tribune,* July 4, 1921, p. 8.

111. "American Women Made Turks Obey," *New York Times,* July 9, 1920, p. 14 (from the *Chicago Tribune*). Almost uniquely, this article was found in the *New York Times,* perhaps because it portrayed American missionaries in a quite positive light. Characteristically, the *Times* gave the article a deceptive headline.

112. "Lieut. Morris, Hamilton Boy, Describes Massacre at Smyrna as 'Most Horrible,'" *Hamilton [Ohio] News,* October 14, 1922, p. 1.

113. "Turks Murdered and Pillaged by Army of Greeks," *Olean [N.Y.] Herald,* August 5, 1919, p. 4.

114. "Turkish Leaders Give Their Side," *Galveston Daily News,* October 9, 1922, p. 1.

115. Harry L. Rodgers, "Investigate Atrocity Report," *New Castle [Pa.] News,* August 3, 1922, p. 11.

116. "Greeks Suffer Serious Defeat," *Indianapolis Star,* September 6, 1922, p. 6.

117. "Says Greeks Burned and Pillaged Turkey," *New York Times,* September 27, 1922, p. 2. I have only been able to find this article in the *Times* and the *Daily Kennebec [Maine] Journal,* September 27, 1922, p. 4. The presence of the article in those two papers on the same day indicates that it must have been from an unnamed news service, but others did not print it.

118. "Making Turks," *New York Times,* August 7, 1922. The editorial title refers to the editor's contention that the Turks were deliberately sparing Christian children and sending them to Near East Relief orphanages, where they stayed until the age of twelve. They were then forcibly taken from the orphanages and converted to Islam; the boys were made into Turkish soldiers and the girls were sent to harems. Not even Near East Relief statements support such an absurd assertion. See also "A Black Friday," *New York Times,* December 3, 1922, p. 38, which referred to the day the Turks took İzmir.

119. Mark O. Prentiss, "Smyrna Now Faces Plague and Famine," *New York Times,* September 20, 1922, p. 1; "Says Turks Believe They 'Licked the World,'" *New York Times,* December 10, 1922, p. 23.

120. "The Night of Terror That Saved 500 Christian Girls" (an International Features Syndicate story), *Hamilton [Ohio] Evening Journal,* October 28, 1922, p. 20, and other papers.

121. Louis Edgar Browne, "Eye Witnesses Testify to Barbarities Committed by Greek Soldiery at Smyrna," *San Antonio Light,* October 23, 1919, p. 7.

122. *New York Times,* February 12, 1923, p. 8. Orvis also reported that she had heard a rumor that 50 percent had died, but her own observations make this seem impossible.

123. "Greeks and Turks Tell America They Both Fight for Liberty," *Danville [Va.] Register,* October 11, 1922, p. 4.

124. John Clayton, "Here Is First Full Story of Greek Debacle," *Chicago Tribune,* September 11, 1922, p. 3. See also John Clayton, "Hunger, Death Linger on Trail of Greek Flight," *Chicago Tribune,* November 30, 1922, p. A1; John Clayton, "Hell Sows Seed of Hate behind Smoky Smyrna," *Chicago Tribune,* October 4, 1922, p. 2;

"Atrocities in the Near East," *Chicago Tribune,* July 4, 1921, p. 8; and "Retreating Greeks Burn Towns," *Chicago Tribune,* September 6, 1922, p. 3.

125. John Clayton, "Plague Piles Up Deaths in Smyrna Ruins," *Chicago Tribune,* September 17, 1922, p. 1.

126. "Near East Relief Fakes Telegrams to Influence U.S.," *Chicago Tribune,* July 1, 1920, p. 12.

127. "Saw Smyrna's Great Fire," *Gettysburg [Pa.] Compiler,* November 18, 1922, p. 3.

128. It is well beyond the scope of this book to consider the religious views of Woodrow Wilson. John M. Rinehart, "The Making of a Christian Statesman: Woodrow Wilson's Religious Thought and Practice, 1856–1910" (Ph.D. dissertation, University of Illinois at Chicago, 2006), contains an extensive bibliography on the subject (pp. 261–72). The biographies and dissertations on Wilson contain very little on his attitudes toward the Middle East.

129. "Tells of Wilson's Armenian Pledge," *New York Times,* May 3, 1920, p. 17.

130. "Near East Relief Hails Wilson as Peacemaker," *Washington Post,* December 1, 1920, p. 1.

131. This list is summarized from Lawrence E. Gelfand, *The Inquiry: American Preparations for Peace, 1917–1919* (New Haven: Yale University Press, 1963), pp. 60–62. I have made much use of Gelfand's study in the following pages. On the Inquiry members at the Versailles Peace Conference and the plans for the future of the Ottoman Empire, see Jonathan Macauley Nielson, "American Historians at the Versailles Peace Conference, 1919: The Scholar as Patriot and Diplomat," pp. 470–83.

132. W. S. Monroe, *Turkey and the Turks: An Account of the Lands, the Peoples, and the Institutions of the Ottoman Empire.*

133. Ibid., pp. 64, 93, 63–64. Monroe's inaccuracies are beyond the discussion here, but readers in need of a laugh should consult his volume.

134. Leon Dominian, *The Frontiers of Language and Nationality in Europe,* chapters 11 and 12. Dominian was a thoroughgoing racialist, not a strange thing in his time. He castigated the Turks for their "racial" diversity ("The Peoples of Northern and Central Asiatic Turkey," *Bulletin of the American Geographical Society of New York* 47, no. 1 [1915]: 832–77).

135. Leon Dominian, "The Mohammedan World," U. S. National Archives, Record Group 265.2. References are to the number of the Inquiry Study. Inquiry Doc. 137, p. 2. He believed that no economic progress was possible in Muslim countries unless Europeans (or, presumably, Americans) took control (p. 1).

136. Leon Dominian, "Turkey," Inquiry Doc. 141, pp. 3–4. Dominian's bibliography on peoples and population included only European and Armenian sources.

137. Ibid., pp. 5–9, 86–95. Not all Inquiry population statistics were so deficient. David Magie stated that Ottoman statistics were "little more than rough and ready estimates" ("The Population of Asiatic Turkey at the Outbreak of the War," Inquiry Doc. 1005, p. 1) because the figures were drawn from lists of those liable for conscription. This was true in the 1830s but was completely false for later Ottoman population figures. Nevertheless, Magie used the Ottoman statistics available to

him (p. 32). He ran into trouble when he also used statistics drawn up by missionaries and provided by Barton. For the Greeks he also consulted the completely spurious "Greek Patriarchate Statistics," although he admitted that they were exaggerated, and for the Armenians, the equally spurious "Armenian Patriarchate Statistics." Both were forgeries (see note 18 above and note 221 in chapter 10). He also consulted various European estimates. Magie's statistics were as good as his sources. His figures for Western Anatolia were fairly good, because he had decent Ottoman sources. For Eastern Anatolia he put much credence in the false patriarchate statistics and missionary statistics and thus uniformly listed too many Armenians. Nevertheless, Magie made a genuine effort to find the truth, utilizing what data he had at hand.

Magie seems to have forgotten his careful statistical work when he wrote specifically about the Ottoman Christians in a separate Inquiry study ("The Christian Sects of the Ottoman Empire," Inquiry Doc. 1010). For the Armenians, for example, he simply copied the estimates of ex-patriarch Malachia Ormanian in *The Church of Armenia*, which were deficient but much better than the false patriarchate statistics. Magie did not even refer to the somewhat exaggerated estimates from his other paper. For the Greeks he used his own estimates, which were only slightly too large. Magie's two contributions read as if they were written by two persons who had not read each other's work. See also H. W. Bell, "The Proposed International State at the Straits," Inquiry Doc. 1012, which gives extensive population statistics for the area considered but does not list any sources for the estimates.

138. Dominian, "Turkey," no page number.

139. Inquiry Document No. 43.

140. James L. Barton, "The Turkish Government—Analysis of Its Inherent Evil," p. 5.

141. Ibid., p. 6.

142. James L. Barton, "Suggested Possible Form of Government for the Area Covered by the Ottoman Empire at the Outbreak of the War, Exclusive of Arabia But Inclusive of the Trans-Caucasus," Inquiry Doc. 42, p. 9. Barton's analysis was based completely on the place of government in Orthodox Islamic rules. He did not consider the possibility that the Turks might create a secular government, as they did. On Turkish government, see also the missionary William W. Peet, "The Working of the Turkish Government," Inquiry Doc. 460 (Peet signed his address as ACASR, New York) and no author listed (D. C. Munro?), "The Turkish Government," Inquiry Doc. 426 ("The central government exercises an absolute, irresponsible, and usually oppressive authority," p. 2).

143. "Letters from Missionaries regarding Their Experiences with the Atrocities of the Turks," Inquiry Docs. 482, 563, and 803–25.

144. ACASR, "Turkish Survey: Recommendations for Political Reconstruction," Inquiry Doc. 565.

145. Wilfred M. Post, M.D., "Commission on Reconstruction in the Near East: Report on the City and Vilayet of Konia," Inquiry Doc. 473. This type of report from the committee was furnished for many provinces. All stated the same ideas. In one of the reports the Reverend Henry H. Riggs described the Turks as "a childish race"

("Turkish Survey: The Kurds," edited by W. H. Hall, Inquiry Doc. 484). "Childishness," of course, was a quality often attributed to those that someone wished to control, including women.

146. "Outline of the History and Ethnology of the Turkish Empire," Inquiry Doc. 471.

147. For example: Toynbee's *Turkey: A Past and a Future* (Inquiry Doc. 561). Inquiry Document 458, "Report on the Pan-Turanian Movement," was produced by the British Propaganda Bureau (identified on the cover as Intelligence Bureau), Department of Information, October 1917 (see the section "Wellington House Publications" in chapter 10). Inquiry staff comments attached to the document show that the report, despite its poor statistics and unwarranted assumptions, was taken very seriously. See also "Weekly Reports on Turkey and Other Moslem Countries," Inquiry Doc. 783.

148. Boghos Nubar, "Memorandum," Inquiry Doc. 450, p. 2. On Nubar, see note 222 below. See also Leonard P. Fox, "International Protection of the Armenians in Asiatic Turkey," Inquiry Doc. 163.

149. Nubar, "Memorandum," p. 11.

150. Inquiry Doc. 427.

151. David Magie, "The Kurds of the Ottoman Empire," Inquiry Doc. 362, p. 64. Despite its title, Magie's piece dealt with much more than the Kurds. His sole source on the Kurds and Armenians was a 22-page article (S. Zarzecki, "La question kurdo-arménianne," *Revue de Paris* [April–May 1914]: 873–94).

152. Magie, "The Kurds of the Ottoman Empire," p. 64.

153. Ellen Churchill Semple, "The Partition of Asiatic Turkey," Inquiry Doc. 501. See also no author listed, "Proposal for Federation of Turkish Provinces," Inquiry Doc. 474.

154. Semple, "The Partition of Asiatic Turkey," pp. 11–12, 47, 3, 9, 14.

155. W. L. Westermann, "Historical Sketch of the Turkish Empire," Inquiry Doc. 601, p. 13.

156. W. L. Westermann, "The Government of Turkey," Inquiry Doc. 602, pp. 15–38, 163.

157. A few, such as Ambassador Morgenthau, wanted war with the Ottoman Empire, but the missionary establishment on the whole united behind the view that all the missionary properties would be seized if the United States declared war on the Ottoman Empire, although they advanced the somewhat odd view that it would be the Germans, not the Turks, who would take the properties ("Sees No Good in Declaration of War on Turkey," *Hartford [Conn.] Courant,* December 17, 1917, p. 20; "Divergent Views on Near East Situation," *New York Times,* June 29, 1918, p. 9; "Opposes War by U.S. on Turkey," *Washington Post,* December 17, 1917, p. 5; "Opposed to War on Turks," *Washington Post,* April 9, 1918, p. 6).

    Robert L. Daniel's "The Armenian Question and American-Turkish Relations, 1914–1927" (*Mississippi Valley Historical Review* 46, no. 2 [September 1959]: 252–75) is an excellent summary of this period in American domestic politics and foreign relations.

158. See Robert L. Daniel, *American Philanthropy in the Near East, 1820–1960,* p. 158; and Mary Lewis Shedd, *The Measure of a Man: The Life of William Ambrose Shedd,* p. 243.

159. E. A. Yarrow, "The Caucasus: The British Withdrawal and Present Conditions," *Journal of International Relations* 10 (January 1920): 251–55. Yarrow worked for

both the Red Cross and Near East Relief in the South Caucasus. In addition to damning the British, he somewhat glorified the place of the missionaries: "The Rev. Dr. Ernest Yarrow, a missionary stationed in Turkey, Armenia [*sic*], telegraphs from the Caucasus that eight Americans at Kars are protecting 40,000 orphans and the stores there." Yarrow also said the Georgian army was mobilizing to help the Armenians ("Eight Americans Protect Orphans against Turks," *Dallas News,* November 13, 1920, p. 1).

160. The British felt that the Americans should create a Caucasus mandate ("British Look to Us to Guard Armenia," *New York Times,* August 15, 1919, p. 15).

161. Yarrow, "The Caucasus," p. 253.

162. The population of the Russian Kars Province in 1897 was 50 percent Muslim, 25 percent Armenian, and 17 percent Orthodox. By 1920 many of the Orthodox had left (McCarthy, *Death and Exile,* p. 212*).*

163. "British Quit Armenia; People at Turk's Mercy," *Madison [Wisc.] Capital Times,* August 8, 1919, p. 2; "Armenian Race in Dire Peril," *Fitchburg [Mass.] Daily Sentinel,* April 1, 1918, p. 7. Yarrow's words were given to the press by the American Board, which received them via a U.S. government cable.

164. Charles Vickrey, "Threaten Millions in the Near East," *Waukesha [Wisc.] Freeman,* January 2, 1920, p. 5. On the supposed Turkish-Tartar plane, see "The Armenians in Peril," *Kansas City Times,* July 31, 1919, p. 2.

165. "Turks Starving Armenians," *Des Moines [Iowa] Capital,* April 27, 1919, p. 9A.

166. The Associated Press spread the story of Enver's Caucasian adventure: "Locate Enver Pasha in Caucasus, Where He Fled to Avoid Arrest," *Bridgeport [Conn.] Standard-Telegram,* October 18, 1919, p. 12. See "Turkey's Bad Boy, Enver, Is Found Hiding in the Caucasus," *New Castle [Pa.] News,* May 31, 1919, p. 11; and the syndicated articles by the religious writer William T. Ellis ("Enver Pasha Raising New Army to Crush Armenians," *Galveston Daily News,* August 26, 1919, p. 6; "Holy War Raised by Turkey as a Club," *Atlanta Constitution,* August 30, 1919, p. 13; and others), which were printed all across America. The *Washington Post* version ("Raises Turkish Army," August 26, 1919, p. 4) identified Ellis as "Special Correspondent of the Washington Post and New York Herald." Newspapers ran many similar articles. Enver seems to have been seen as an image of the Dangerous Turk.

Ellis's articles, which were long and numerous, went from the merely prejudiced to the idiotic. See, for example, "Russian Reds on Turkey's Border Planning Vast Asiatic Conquests," *Atlanta Constitution,* January 11, 1920, p. 4F, in which Ellis outlines Vladimir Lenin's plan for imminent conquests in Turkey, Persia, Afghanistan, India, and beyond. Ellis foresaw real trouble when the "Asiatic hordes" with their "ruthless barbarism" were joined with "bolshevism."

167. Thomas B. Preston, "Greatest Massacre World Has Ever Seen Feared When British Evacuate Armenia," *Atlanta Constitution,* September 28, 1919, p. F2.

168. Enver Paşa did visit Baku for one week at the beginning of September 1920, where he attended a meeting of the Congress of Eastern Peoples. He did not raise an army there in that one week.

169. "Bolsheviks Plot Holy War to Destroy British Empire," *New Orleans Times-Picayune,* August 15, 1920, p. 1. According to the article, the Russian Bolsheviks were sending 40,000 infantry and 2,000 cavalry to aid Mustafa Kemal.

170. "The Armenian Race Faces Annihilation," *Atlanta Constitution,* August 15, 1919, p. 6. The paper also printed a report (strangely, sent from Amsterdam, no source listed) that Turks had massacred 10,000 Armenians while evacuating Trans-Caucasia earlier ("10,000 Armenians Massacred by Turks," December 8, 1918, p. 14).

171. Oscar Strauss, one of the Near East Relief Trustees, however, was completely against any American mandate, as were many American politicians and business leaders. For the various mandate schemes suggested by the missionary establishment, see Daniel, "The Armenian Question and American-Turkish Relations, 1914–1927," pp. 259–60; and Gotthard Jäschke, "Ein Amerikanisches Mandat für die Türkei?" *Die Welt des Islams* 8, no. 4 (1963): 219–34. The one book dealing specifically with the American mandate question (James B. Gidney, *A Mandate for Armenia*) is unfortunately not very reliable in its history. The author seems to have swallowed much of the prejudice described in these pages. The book is useful, however, on the machinations of the executive branch and the Senate.

172. One relief worker, identified only as Chater, summarized feelings about Trans-Caucasia, stating that "the Armenians are the only people of the Trans-Caucasus within commensurable distance of self-governance, that the Georgians are a decadent people and that the Tartars are quite out of the race." He wrote: "The Armenians alone possess intelligence, business acumen and industry to an admirable degree. Without exception, the Armenians express their hope that their new republic may be assigned to the protection of the United States" ("Reports of Shocking Conditions in Armenia Are Verified by a Red Cross Official in Turkey," *Logansport [Ind.] Pharos-Reporter,* June 9, 1919, p. 7).

173. Dr. John W. O'Meera, a Near East Relief Worker, did not believe that foreign intervention in Anatolia was the problem, which was caused by "constant fighting between the various factions of Turks, Kurds, and Circassians." He believed that eventually Muslim religious leaders would restore order: "Kemal can't do it because he has not the support" ("Conditions Worse in Asia Minor," *Christian Science Monitor,* September 21, 1920, p. 6).

174. In 1919 eighty thousand Protestant and Catholic ministers sent a petition to President Wilson asking for the independence of Armenia (U. S. National Archives 867B.00/62: Polk to Ammission [Paris], Washington, March 16, 1919, telegram).

175. Gerard spared nothing in his campaign. He wrote that America should accept the mandate because the Armenians were Christians and Aryans and the mandate would demand only "a few thousand marines" ("Why America Should Accept Mandate for Armenia," in American Committee for the Independence of Armenia, *America as Mandatory for Armenia: Articles and Opinions by James W. Gerard, Frederic Courtland Penfield, John Sharp Williams, Etc.*). See the committee's *The Joint Mandate Scheme: A Turkish Empire under American Protection* (New York: American Committee for the Independence of Armenia, 1919). The committee was effectively led by Vahan Cardashian (Daniel, "The Armenian Question and

American-Turkish Relations," pp. 263–64). Gerard at first opposed a mandate for Armenia, demanding complete independence. The American Friends of Greece also had many members of the Near East Relief Board both on its Board of Trustees and on its National Committee (letterhead in Allen Papers, Library of Congress Manuscript Division). See also Mark Malkasian, "The Disintegration of the Armenian Cause in the United States, 1918–1927," *International Journal of Middle Eastern Studies* 16, no. 3 (August 1984): 349–65; "Joint Mandate a Turkish Scheme: Plan Would Tend to Destroy Armenian Nationality, Smother Christianity, and Consolidate Turk Rule, Says Mr. Gerard," *Christian Science Monitor,* December 9, 1919, p. 41; and "Armenians Decry Missionary Policy," *Christian Science Monitor,* August 1, 1921, p. 10, an interview with Cardashian.

176. Thomas A. Bryson, "The Armenia-America Society: A Factor in American-Turkish Relations, 1919–1924," *Records of the American Catholic Historical Society of Philadelphia* 82, no. 2 (1971): 83–105; Daniel, "The Armenian Question and American-Turkish Relations," pp. 263–64. On Smith's views, see "Turkish Designs upon Armenia," *Christian Science Monitor,* October 4, 1919, p. 7. On Montgomery's views, see George R. Montgomery, "Turkey and the Americans," *Current History* 17 (November 1922): 303–5.

177. Gerard and Cardashian felt that the schemes for a larger mandate would submerge independent Armenia.

178. "Urges American Mandate," *New York Times,* November 2, 1919, p. 5. See also "Urges Mandate over Turks," *New York Times,* December 8, 1919, p. 17; "Mandatory in Near East Advocated," *Christian Science Monitor,* December 8, 1919, p. 4; and "Armenia Harmed by Treaty Delay," *Christian Science Monitor,* October 11, 1919, p. 4.

179. "Turks Declare Plans to Slay Armenians," *New York Times,* February 15, 1920, p. 5. The article did not state who these Turks were. Other members of the missionary establishment, such as Sherwood Eddy, foreign secretary of the YMCA, also told of Mustafa Kemal's supposed plans for extermination ("A Touching Appeal," *Washington Post,* October 29, 1919, p. 6).

180. James L. Barton, "Turks Still at War; Civilization Threatened," *Decatur [Ill.] Review,* December 8, 1920, p. 8. The article originally appeared in the *Congregationalist.*

181. "Let America Rule Turkey Says Foreign Missionary," *Dallas News,* November 24, 1918, part 4, p. 8; "At Odds on Mandate," *Washington Post,* December 8, 1919, p. 3; "Favor U.S. Mandate for Most of Turkey," *Boston Globe,* August 30, 1919, p. 6. See also Charles H. Grasty, "Want One Mandate for All of Turkey," *New York Times,* November 2, 1919, p. 5.

182. "Reports Asia Minor Looking to America," *New York Times,* June 7, 1919, p. 6; "Urges American Mandate," *New York Times,* November 2, 1919, p. 5; "Urges Mandate over Turks," *New York Times,* December 8, 1919, p. 17.

183. "Cut Turkey Up, Plan of Morgenthau," *San Antonio Evening News,* December 12, 1918, p. 2; Richard V. Oulahan, "Urges 3 Mandates to Govern Turkey," *New York Times,* May 30, 1919, p. 2; "Peace and War (by the Associated Press)," *Janesville*

[Wisc.] Daily Gazette, May 23, 1919, p. 1. He repeated this plan in various speeches. See "Morgenthau for Turkish Mandate," *New York Times,* October 18, 1919, p. 1.

184. "Turkey Has Shot Her Bolt," *Independent* 96, no. 3648 (November 9, 1918): 159. See also "'Every Country Helped Turk to Live'—Henry Morgenthau," *Titusville [Pa.] Herald,* January 20, 1919, p. 1 (an AP article); and "Morgenthau Avers Conference Should Let Turk Nation Die," *Bridgeport [Conn.] Standard Telegram,* January 20, 1919, p. 1.

185. "American Mandate Alone Can Insure the Independence of Armenia," in American Committee for the Independence of Armenia, *America as Mandatory for Armenia,* p. 13.

186. The provinces of Van, Bitlis, Erzurum, Mamuretülaziz, Diyarbakır, and Sivas (McCarthy, *Muslims and Minorities,* p. 112). See also Raymond H. Kévorkian and Paul B. Paboudjian, *Les Arméniennes dans l'Empire Ottomane à la veille du génocide* (Paris: Éditions d'Art et d'Histoire, 1992). Figures in this volume differ only somewhat from those in *Muslims and Minorities.*

187. The following stories were from news services: Henry Wales, "America Waits, Armenians Die," *Los Angeles Times,* August 1, 1919, p. 14; "Armenians Want U.S. Mandatory," *Hartford [Conn.] Courant,* February 11, 1920, p. 20; "Rule of United States Wanted by Armenia," *Atlanta Constitution,* November 12, 1919, p. 8; "1,000 Armenian Refugees," *Galveston Daily News,* June 29, 1919, p. 29. Dr. Henry White, secretary of the Presbyterian Board of Foreign Missions, assured Americans that Armenians, Turks, and others would choose an American mandate if a vote was held ("Friend of Armenia Urges Ratification," *Christian Science Monitor,* October 10, 1919, p. 2). In a very strange editorial the *New York Times* ("Why Armenia Must Be Free," December 23, 1919, p. 8) urged against a mandate for all of Anatolia and Istanbul, because, the *Times* stated, the Turks wanted such a mandate. "The best argument against the unitary mandate—an argument that alone should be sufficient to bury it—is that the Turks want it."

188. Paxten Hibben, "Weighing Armenia in the Balance," *Current Opinion* 69, no. 1 (July 1920): 37–43.

189. "U.S. Mandate Is Chief Hope of Armenians," *San Antonio Evening News,* July 31, 1919, p. 2. The *Chicago Tribune* itself soon adopted a more balanced attitude toward the Turkish situation, as seen elsewhere in this chapter.

190. The *Christian Science Monitor* articles are too numerous to cite. See, for example, "Extermination, It Is Officially Said, Faces Armenians," October 1, 1919, p. 1; "Freeing Armenia from Turkish Yoke," February 20, 1920, p. 6; and "Renewed Appeal for Armenians," December 30, 1919, p. 6. The *Christian Science Monitor* had little idea of actual events in Trans-Caucasia or Eastern Anatolia. Its editor thought that Tartars and Azerbaijanis were distinct peoples ("The Armenians and the Tartars," editorial, *Christian Science Monitor,* May 14, 1920, p. 16).

191. "Recognition of United Turkey Is Urged as Solution in Orient," *Christian Science Monitor,* August 12, 1922, p. 7. See also "Demand for Armenian State under Protection of Allies," *Christian Science Monitor,* August 14, 1922, p. 2.

192. See Henry Wales, "Turks on Conquest Soon," *Kansas City Times,* July 31, 1919, p. 2: "The Turks, however, have the greatest confidence in America and would accept an American mandate of Constantinople, Anatolia, Armenia, and, in fact, all Turkey, as they know they would get a square deal from the Americans." See also "Turks Said to Favor American Mandate," *Atlanta Constitution,* August 30, 1919, p. 15.

193. Examples of *New York Times* articles: "Wants All Turkey under a Mandate," June 4, 1919, p. 23; "Wants U.S. to Ask Armenian Mandate," August 24, 1919, p. 25. The *Times* editor wanted a United States mandate only for Armenia, not for all of Anatolia and the Caucasus ("The Sword of Islam," August 31, 1919, p. 33). In this it echoed the position of the American Committee for the Independence of Armenia and of James Gerard and Vahan Cardashian. See the Cardashian letter "A Turkish Mandate," *New York Times,* June 5, 1919, p. 12.

194. James W. Gerard, "Why America Should Accept Mandate for Armenia," *New York Times,* July 6, 1919, p. 44; "Seek Recognition of Armenian Nation," *New York Times,* December 22, 1919, p. 6; "Wants U.S. to Ask Armenian Mandate," *New York Times,* September 24, 1919, p. 25; "Intervention Asked in Turkish Armenia," *Atlanta Constitution,* April 20, 1919, p. 6.

195. "America and Armenia," March 12, 1919, p. 5. The article drew on the analysis of Miran Sevasly, the chair of the Armenian National Council of America, whose views were presented in many articles. The *Sandusky [Ohio] Register* commented that the mandate "would be a mighty interesting adventure" ("America and Armenia," March 12, 1919, p. 4). See also "Armenians Desire American Control," *Boston Globe,* March 6, 1919, p. 1.

　　Press estimates of the number of American troops needed ranged from "a few" to 250,000. For example, see "U.S. Army May Be Sent into Armenia," *San Antonio Evening News,* September 27, 1919, pp. 1, 2. The *La Crosse [Wisc.] Tribune and Leader-Press* ("A Mandate for Armenia," September 18, 1919, p. 3) felt that "about all the troops that would be necessary for the United States to retain there would be a police force sufficiently strong to stand off marauding bands of Kurds and keep order in the community." See also "American Soldiers Wanted in Armenia," *Atlanta Constitution,* October 24, 1919, p. 15.

196. "Yarrow Tells of Far [*sic*] East Aid: America Only Can Save the Afflicted," *Oakland Tribune,* November 2, 1919, p. 2. See also "Fears Armenians May Perish Soon," *Atlanta Constitution,* October 2, 1919, p. 11.

197. Literally hundreds of these articles were published. Some spoke only of the starvation and the need for relief aid and donations; others specifically blamed the Turks. For example, an *Oakland Tribune* article was headlined "Turk Atrocities Are Reported" (April 22, 1920, p. 20). In it, Dr. A. W. Halsey, Caucasus commissioner of Near East Relief, called Turkish actions "unrivalled among the atrocities during the great war." His further comments, distributed by the Presbyterian Board of Foreign Missions, indicated that he was speaking of starvation, not massacres.

198. "Says Armenians Can Prosper If U.S. Takes Mandate for 20 Years," *Fitchburg [Mass.] Daily Sentinel,* November 21, 1919, p. 11; "Armenians Expect American

Control," *Atlanta Constitution,* September 9, 1919, p. 3; and many others on the Armenian desire for and expectation of an American mandate.

199. "U.S. Mandate for Armenia Favored," *Boston Globe,* September 15, 1919, p. 9.

200. See "Constantinople to United States," *Atlanta Constitution,* May 18, 1919, p. 1. For Turkish positions on the American mandate, see Jäschke, "Ein amerikanisches Mandat."

201. The standard work on the King-Crane Commission is Harry N. Howard, *The King-Crane Commission: An American Inquiry in the Middle East.* See also Harry N. Howard, "An American Experiment in Peacemaking: The King-Crane Commission," *Muslim World* 32 (April 1942): 122–46.

202. King's dedication to the missionary endeavor is documented in his biography (Donald M. Love, *Henry Churchill King of Oberlin* [New Haven, Conn.: published for Oberlin College by Yale University Press, 1956]). His feeling on non-Christian cultures is exemplified by the title of one of his articles: "Christianity the Only Hopeful Basis for Oriental Civilizations," *International Review of Missions* 2 (July 1913): 417–29.

203. Barton's long history and effect on Near Eastern affairs as a leader of the American missionary enterprise cannot be detailed here, but a quotation might help establish his viewpoint: "History has clearly demonstrated that Mohammedanism rests like a blight upon every country, race, or individual that it masters" (*The Unfinished Task of the Christian Church,* p. 50).

204. On Morgenthau, see the section "Ambassador Henry Morgenthau" in chapter 9.

205. Howard, *The King-Crane Commission,* p. 196.

206. See the section "The Bryce Report" in chapter 10.

207. See the section "The United States Government and the Missionary Establishment" above.

208. Howard, *The King-Crane Commission,* pp. 79, 80.

209. Ibid. He later became director of the Armenia-America Society, a lobbying group for the Armenian cause. In Montgomery's case, the term "expert" is misleading. He had been a professor of philosophy and had written books on what would today be called psychology. His expertise had nothing to do with the Middle East.

210. U.S. Department of State, *Papers Relating to the Foreign Relations of the United States: The Paris Peace Conference, 1919* (the King-Crane Report), vol. 12, p. 811.

211. Ibid., p. 814.

212. See, for example, "Resent U.S. Warning," *Washington Post,* August 28, 1919, p. 1; "President King Explains Issue of the Far [*sic*] East," *Elyria [Ohio] Chronicle-Telegram,* April 22, 1920, p. 1.

213. The sections dealing with Turks and Armenians: "How Two Americans Planned to Settle Near East Problem," *New York Times,* December 4, 1922, p. 12. The section on the Arab world: "Crane and King's Long-Hid Report on the Near East," *New York Times,* December 3, 1922, p. 33. King and Crane actually suggested three separate mandates, all governed by America: Istanbul, Armenia, and the remainder of Anatolia (for the Turks).

214. U.S. Congress, Senate, *Conditions in the Near East: Report of the American Military Mission to Armenia by Maj. Gen. James G. Harbord, United States Army*. See also United States National Archives 184.02102/5 for the typescript copy. Harbord described his mission in an article that illuminates his preconceptions and intentions: "Investigating Turkey and Trans-Caucasia," *World's Work* 40 (May 1920): 35–47.

215. There are numerous lists of mission members in the U.S. National Archives. See, for example, 184.021/42, 184.021/99, and 184.021/243.

216. He was named "Professor Hussein Bey" in the mission documents, although the Americans sometimes assumed Bey was a last name and listed him as "Professor Bey" or "Professor H. Bey" ("Mr. Hussein" would be a more accurate translation).

217. U.S. National Archives, 184.021/42.

218. For reports by Khachadoorian and their place in the mission's findings, see 184.021/208, 184.021/258, and 184.01602. His reports gave no indication that he had in fact spoken to the Turks he described. They are a compilation of general statements on supposed past Turkish misdeeds and on the nature of Turks, without evidence of their veracity (for example, see 184.021/324). In one of his reports Khachadoorian stated that the Turks of the Southern Caucasus were "not intelligent and very ignorant" (184.021/208, Khachadoorian, Memorandum for General Moseley, August 23, 1919).

219. U.S. National Archives, 184.021/51, 184.021/262.

220. U.S. National Archives, 184.021/335.

221. U.S. National Archives, 184.021/103, 184.021/97. Some of the descriptions of those to whom the mission was directed are telling, some unintentionally humorous. For example, Herbert Gibbons was characterized as one who "has great personal sympathy with the Armenians and is considered by them to be friendly." The mission was to consult one Dr. Robert Frew, because he was "highly recommended as a Scottish Parson with a wide and sane knowledge of the Near East and the Armenian Question" (184.021/102).

222. "The Armenian delegates who have been appointed to present the claims of their people at the Peace Conference are divided into two groups, one of which led by Nubar Pasha and Professor Hagopian represents the conservative and property owning element. It also represents the conservative and 'bourgeois' Armenians of Russia. The other party led by Mr. Aharonian represents the radical and revolutionary element" (867B.00/85, American Commission to Negotiate Peace, Paris, April 18, 1919, draft).

223. The mission specifically requested statistical materials from the Armenian Republic, although not from the Ottoman government (184.021/206).

224. U.S. National Archives, 184.021/129. On the statistics, see note 18 above. In the mission's paper on population, the accuracy of the Armenian figures was attested by "a Frenchman—Marcel Léart" (184.021/10). This would have proven nothing, of course, but Léart was in fact an Armenian (Krikor Zohrab) who wrote propaganda under a French pen name.

225. The characterizations of E. G. Bliss in his "Compilation of Information on Armenia" (184.021/103 and 112). Bliss was a member of the Bliss missionary family.

226. The report was drawn up by Wilbur E. Post, M.D. (184.021/86).

227. *The Republic of Armenia,* vol. 2 (Berkeley: University of California Press, 1982), p. 341.

228. Harbord spoke to both Mustafa Kemal and Kâzim Karabekir. Neither defended the old political system, but neither told Harbord what he wished to hear.

229. The complete report, in typescript, is in 184.02102/5. It was slightly changed and published as *Conditions in the Near East: Report of the American Military Mission to Armenia* by the U.S. Senate. The Senate had to pass two resolutions before the administration finally gave it a copy of the Harbord Report.

230. U.S. National Archives, 184.02102/1.

231. Howard, *The King-Crane Commission,* pp. 292–94; Claire Price, "Mustafa Kemal and the Americans," *Current History* 17 (October 1922): 116–25.

232. U.S. National Archives, 184.02102/5.

233. Only 1.5 million Armenians lived in all of Ottoman Anatolia at the beginning of World War I (McCarthy, *Muslims and Minorities,* pp. 110–12). Had Harbord said "migrated," thus including those who fled with the Russian armies or on their own by the end of the war as well, the estimate of 1,100,000 migrants would have been closer to the truth. The claim that as many Armenians were killed as existed would have left none at the end of the war, however, which was patently not the case. But Harbord's point was to blame the Ottoman government for deportations and deaths, not to explain them statistically. Whether he was simply relying on his sources or believed what he alleged is unknown. On the number of Armenians relocated by the Ottomans, see Yusuf Halaçoğlu, "Realities behind the Relocation," in *Armenians in the Late Ottoman Period,* ed. Türkkaya Ataöv (Ankara: Turkish Historical Society, 2001), pp. 109–42.

234. Harbord in U.S. National Archives, 184.02102/5, p. 2.

235. Justin McCarthy, "American Commissions to Anatolia and the Report of Niles and Sutherland," in *Türk Tarih Kurumu General Conference XI* (Ankara: Türk Tarih Kurumu, 1990), pp. 1809–52 (quotation on p. 1850).

236. In addition to the Harbord Report itself (cited above), see "Want One Mandate for All of Turkey," *New York Times,* November 2, 1919, p. 5 (the title was inaccurate: the Harbord Mission only wanted one mandate for Anatolia and Istanbul, not for "Turkey," the name used at the time for the Ottoman Empire); and "Harbord's Report Asks Expulsion of Turk from Europe," *New York Times,* April 4, 1920, p. 1. Before the Harbord Report was finally published, American newspapers erroneously reported that it called for an American mandate. See, for example, "U.S. Blamed for Trouble in Turkey," *Eau Claire [Wisc.] Leader,* March 12, 1920, p. 1 (an AP story).

     An Associated Press article stated that many members of the Harbord Commission were firmly against America taking a Near Eastern mandate. Their reasoning was that American interests lay more in Mexico and the Pacific than elsewhere, and it was in those regions that America should project its power ("America's Duty Closer Home, Not Armenia," *Ogden [Utah] Examiner,* October 23, 1919, p. 3; "Oppose U.S. Mandate," *Washington Post,* October 23, 1919, p. 3). The article was excerpted or printed in many other newspapers. Some commission members, however, wanted an American mandate. Colonel J. R. Jackson, who had been with the Harbord Mission, in an address to Near East Relief officials, declared that America must take the mandate to save the Armenians. "Says Armenians May All Be Annihilated," *Cedar Rapids [Iowa] Evening Gazette,* July 17, 1920, p. 5.

237. See, for example, "Armenia Mandate Urged in Report," *Atlanta Constitution,* March 12, 1920, p. 13; "Rule of United States Wanted by Armenia," *Atlanta Constitution,* November 12, 1919, p. 8; and "Harbord Report Said to Favor U.S. Mandate over Armenia," *New Orleans Times-Picayune,* March 12, 1920. It was also reported by the Associated Press, however, that a majority of the members of the commission did not support an American mandate ("Mission Opposes American Mandate," *New York Times,* October 23, 1919, p. 17).

238. J. G. Harbord, "Plain Facts about Asia Minor and the Trans-Caucasus," *New York Times,* February 22, 1920, p. XX1; "Armenia Desires U.S. as Mandatory," *Washington Post,* November 12, 1919, p. 12. The missionary establishment was deeply unhappy with the report, because it did not strongly call for an American mandate. James Barton declared that Harbord "had made little more than a surface investigation and had not realized the deeper significance of the problem" ("Urge Ratification," *Lowell [Mass.] Sun,* October 24, 1919, p. 6).

General Harbord became closely tied to Near East Relief. He was a sponsor of Near East Relief Appeals, which distributed his appeals to American newspapers. See, for example, "Major Harbord Renews Appeal for Near East," *Indianapolis Star,* January 10, 1922, p. 13.

239. The most detailed newspaper coverage of Wilson's message was in the *New York Times* ("Wilson Urges We Take Armenia Mandate," May 25, 1920, p. 1). All newspapers carried the story.

240. See, for example, "A Near Eastern Report," *New York Times,* October 24, 1919, p. 12; and Charles H. Grasty, "New Dangers Rising in Asia Minor Now," *New York Times,* December 5, 1919, p. 17.

241. Even the *New York Times,* which had supported American involvement, began to question it. The editor felt that America should have acted immediately after the war to do its duty but that now it was too late. The *Times* castigated Americans for this failure ("The Harbord Report," April 6, 1920, p. 10; "Testing Our Altruism," May 26, 1920, p. 10). The *Atlanta Constitution* complained bitterly that America had not done its duty in the Middle East, although its editorial did not mention taking a mandate. Instead America could have kept the Turks from victory by "counseling and cooperating in a peaceful way with the powers that represent Christian ideals and civilization," a somewhat naïve observation ("On the Old Roost," October 1, 1922, p. D2).

242. Americans were divided on the mandate question. Editors questioned the cost and commitment of personnel. See "What Is 'A Mandate over Armenia?'" *Des Moines*

[Iowa] News, June 11, 1920, p. 8. Some commentators also stated that America would simply be doing Britain's work if it intervened in Turkey: "But if we sent an army to Armenia we should fight the Turks not on behalf of the Armenians alone, rather primarily on behalf of the British, who desire to have the Turks abolished" (Frank H. Simonds, "Mediating for Armenia," *Atlanta Constitution,* December 6, 1920, p. 6). The *New York Times* editorialized against the mandate because it would deny Greece the chance to claim Western Anatolia for itself ("We Do Not Want Smyrna," March 13, 1919, p. 10). The *Times* editor wrote: "In any event, it is hard to believe that any responsible missionary authorities would desire to see the United States creating a Greek Alsace-Lorraine under American rule, in order to facilitate the spread of religious propaganda from the United States." That was, in fact, exactly what the missionaries wanted in supporting an American mandate. See also "Armenia Mandate Comes under Fire," *Atlanta Constitution,* May 30, 1920, p. 5C.

243. Bristol, in fact, did not like any of the Ottoman peoples and wrote disparagingly of Turks, Kurds, Armenians, and Greeks alike, stating that all had perpetrated massacres (Heath W. Lowry, "American Observers in Anatolia ca. 1920: The Bristol Papers," in *Armenians in the Ottoman Empire and Modern Turkey (1012–1926)* [Istanbul: Boğaziçi University Press, 1984], pp. 42–58). To Near East Relief, this was not a satisfactory position.

244. Daniel, *American Philanthropy,* pp. 164–66.

245. A very strange news item appeared in the press in December 1920. Woodrow Wilson had accepted the invitation of Paul Hymans, president of the Council of the League of Nations, to mediate "to end hostilities in Armenia." Wilson said he would send a representative ("President Accepts Mediatorship," *Waterloo [Iowa] Times-Tribune,* December 1, 1920, p. 1). This was odd, because hostilities had already ended in Armenia. Near East Relief praised Wilson's acceptance ("Near East Relief Hails Wilson as Peacemaker," *Washington Post,* December 1, 1920, p. 1).

246. The British had 80,000 troops in the Trans-Caucasus alone.

247. Some who had been members and supporters of the missionary establishment split with it over the mandate question. The American Committee for the Independence of Armenia wanted nothing less than complete independence, not autonomy under a mandate (see "Seek Recognition of Armenian Nation," *New York Times,* December 22, 1919, p. 6).

248. See "Two Ex-Envoys Urge Help for Armenia," *New York Times,* November 12, 1920, p. 9.

249. "Says Only America Can Save Armenia," *New York Times,* April 5, 1920, p. 4. See also "Christians Unsafe Where Turk Rules," *Christian Science Monitor,* March 1, 1920, p. 2.

250. "Allies, He Says, Are Too Easy On Turkey," *New York Times,* March 5, 1920, p. 10. Expressing the usual stereotypes, Morgenthau stated that Turkey itself would come to no good end, because "Turkey in the hands of the Kemalists is at the mercy of an unintelligent crew bent chiefly upon plunder" ("Turks Are Tyrants: Morgenthau View," *Christian Science Monitor,* August 6, 1923, p. 1). See also "Morgenthau Deplores Triumph of Turkey in Lausanne Parley," *Waterloo [Iowa] Evening Courier,*

July 27, 1923, p. 1 (an AP story). Instead of the Lausanne settlement, Morgenthau suggested that Istanbul be given to Soviet Russia. The suggestion was not popular ([no title], *Lincoln [Nebr.] State Journal,* January 1, 1923, p. 2).

CHAPTER 12, THE LAST ACT FOR THE MISSIONARY ESTABLISHMENT

1. See, for example, the editorial "The Armenia Decision" in the *Christian Science Monitor,* June 4, 1920, p. 18.

2. The Bolsheviks were much hated in America, and many newspaper articles condemned the Turks for accepting aid from them, which they had indeed done. See, for example, the Associated Press article "Supplies Smuggled Regularly to Turk Nationalist Army," *Olean [N.Y.] Evening Herald,* April 31, 1920, p. 6. After the Armenians had "made their peace" with the Soviets, Americans were told that Armenia had not really become Soviet: "There are about as many Bolshevists in Armenia as there are in Kansas" ("Armenia Practically Free of Bolshevists," *Charleston [W.Va.] Daily Mail,* July 4, 1920, p. 14). Soon, however, Near East Relief was praising the "Bolshevists."

3. The committee included heads of both the King-Crane Commission and Harbord Mission (Henry King, Charles Crane, and James Harbord); religious leaders from Cardinals William Henry O'Connell and Patrick Joseph Hayes to Rabbi Stephen Wise; politicians of all political sides, including Theodore Roosevelt, William Jennings Bryan, William Howard Taft, and Elihu Root; Charles W. Eliot of Harvard; journalists and writers, including Talcott Williams, Charles Dana Gibson, and John Finley; and a cast of governors, senators, and civic, business, and religious leaders. President Calvin Coolidge sent letters of support, which were printed in Golden Rule publications.

    The list of national organizations that supported Near East Relief's Golden Rule was impressive. In 1926 the Golden Rule listed "some of the more important organizations that have endorsed or are cooperating in International Golden Rule Sunday" (Charles Vickrey, *International Golden Rule Sunday: A Handbook,* pp. 86–87):

    1. Practically all General Assemblies, Conferences, Councils of nearly all denominations and church bodies.
    2. International Council of Religious Education and World's Sunday School Association.
    3. Leaders of the National Education Association.
    4. National Congress of Parents and Teachers.
    5. The General Federation of Women's Clubs.
    6. United Society of Christian Endeavor, Epworth Leagues, Baptist Young People's Union, and similar church Young People's Societies [5,500,000 members].
    7. International Advertising Association.
    8. The National Fraternal Congress of America [Kiwanis, Lions, Optimists, etc.].
    9. The Knights of Columbus.
    10. The Y. M. C. A.

11. The Boy Scouts of America.
12. The Railroad Brotherhoods.

4.   Ibid., p. 88.

5.   Near East Relief, *Suggestions and Meditations for Golden Rule Sunday,* p. 10.

6.   James L. Vance, "Youth an Indomitable Race," *New Near East* (November 1924): 13. For a general view of the American Board's position on the new Turkey, see ABCFM, *The Problem of Turkey as the American Board Sees It.* Even the *New York Times,* for years virtually the voice of Near East Relief, ran the testimony of İsmet [İnönü] on crimes done to the Turks in its February 1923 issue of *Current History.*

7.   Barclay Acheson, "An Emerging Russia," *New Near East* (November 1924): 5. In what would be an impossible type of admission during World War I, Charles Vickrey declared in 1920, just as the Armenian Republic was finally defeated, that "our experience during the last five years has been that the orphanages, hospitals, and other similar institutions under control of Near East Relief have been free from molestation by the Turks." That policy, he said, continued in the territory controlled by Mustafa Kemal ("Near East Workers Remain at Posts," *New York Times,* November 11, 1920, p. 14).

8.   See, for example, the article by Henry J. Allen, "New World Ideals and the Future Near East," *New Near East* (July 1923): 1–6, 9. Allen, an ex-governor of Kansas, hoped that the Soviet Russians would ultimately take Eastern Anatolia militarily. Such pro-Soviet sentiments would surely have been somewhat unusual in any other context.

9.   Ernest A. Yarrow and William S. Kennedy, "The Armenian National Problem," *New Near East* (October 1924): 7.

10. The status of Mosul Province was left for later World Court adjudication, and Hatay remained in French Syria.

11. Only the Greeks of Istanbul and Turks of Eastern Thrace were excepted.

12. "Recommends New Policy," *New York Times,* February 8, 1923, p. 2. The *New York Times* is cited here on the Lausanne Treaty debate because of its complete coverage, but the arguments are found in most newspapers. See, for example, in the *Boston Globe:* "Flay and Defend U.S.-Turk Treaty," March 16, 1924, p. 47; "Urges Ratification of Turkey's Treaty," November 26, 1923, p. 2; and "Aims to Defeat Turkish Treaty," November 25, 1923, p. 7; in the *Christian Science Monitor:* "Treaty with Turkey Asked by Churchmen," December 21, 1926, p. 3; "Lausanne Pact Adoption Asked," August 27, 1926, p. 5A; "Why the Lausanne Treaty Should Be Rejected," June 3, 1926, p. 16; "Bishop Decries Turkish Treaty," May 4, 1926, p. 6; "Dr. Barton Urges Lausanne Treaty Be Ratified," *Hartford [Conn.] Courant,* November 26, 1923, p. 5. See also General Committee of American Institutions and Associations in Favor of Ratification of the Treaty with Turkey, *Ratification of the Treaty with Turkey: Statements, Resolutions, and Reports in Favor of Ratification of the Treaty of Lausanne* (New York: General Committee, 1926); and *The Treaty with Turkey* (New York: General Committee, 1926).

13. Robert L. Daniel, "The Armenian Question and American-Turkish Relations, 1914–1927," *Mississippi Valley Historical Review* 46, no. 2 (September 1959): 269. Daniel gives sources on Barton's change of heart from the American Board Archives.

14. "Turks Want Our Schools," *New York Times,* December 8, 1922, p. 2; "Turks Reassure Dr. Barton," *New York Times,* January 21, 1923, p. 2.

15. See Daniel, "The Armenian Question and American-Turkish Relations," pp. 267–75, on the treaty in the Senate.

16. "Plead for Turkish Treaty," *New York Times,* December 21, 1926, p. 29.

17. "Assail and Defend Lausanne Treaty," *New York Times,* April 6, 1924, p. E2.

18. "Urge Ratification of Lausanne Treaty," *New York Times,* June 30, 1926, p. 16.

19. "Turk Treaty Brings Out More Appeals," *New York Times,* January 3, 1927, p. 6.

20. The committee published works against the treaty under the aegis of a separate organization, the American Committee Opposed to the Lausanne Treaty: *The Lausanne Treaty, Turkey and Armenia; Kemal's Slave Market and the Lausanne Treaty* (New York: n.p., 1926) (the old canards applied to the new Republic); *The Senate Should Reject the Turkish Treaty* (seen only in the Allen Papers, Library of Congress Manuscript Division, a copy that has no publication information); and *The Missionaries and the Lausanne Treaty* (New York: n.p., 1926), all published by the committee. I have not seen *The Missionaries and the Lausanne Treaty,* which is cited by Daniel in "The Armenian Question and American-Turkish Relations," p. 271.

21. "Plead for Turkish Treaty," *New York Times,* December 21, 1926, p. 29.

22. "King Denounces Lausanne Treaty," *New York Times,* January 14, 1927, p. 8.

23. "Score Turk Treaty as Disgrace to U.S.," *New York Times,* November 25, 1923, p. E1. Gerard frequently asserted the same sentiment: that Turkey would soon fall apart. See "Gerard Denounces Lausanne Treaty," *New York Times,* November 29, 1923, p. 15.

24. "Bishop McInnes on Turkey," *Kansas City Star,* October 17, 1922, p. 2.

25. "Urges Ratification of Lausanne Treaty," *New York Times,* November 26, 1923, p. 4. Some missionaries were not pleased with Barton's stand (see the letter of Henry Jessup in the *New York Times,* December 9, 1923, p. F8).

26. Quoted in a sarcastic editorial against opposition to the Lausanne Treaty in the *New York Times,* January 15, 1927, p. 14. See also William H. King, "The American Treaty with Turkey at Lausanne and the Kemalist Pan-Islamic Adventure," *Armenian Review* 26, no. 3 (Autumn 1973): 2–8. The article was originally written in 1926 and contained too many falsehoods to consider here, as King's description of Mustafa Kemal as a "pan-Islamist" should indicate. It is interesting that such nonsense would be considered reasonable enough to be reprinted in 1973.

27. Barton continued to praise Turkey (James L. Barton, letter to the editor, "Religion in Turkey: Facts Are Cited to Show Sincerity of Republic Breaking Away from Tradition," *New York Times,* May 6, 1928, p. 53).

Epilogue

1.   As used here the term "myth" has nothing to do with the popular meaning "false-hood" or "error." Nor does it mean gods and goddesses disporting themselves on Mount Olympus. *Merriam-Webster* gives as one definition of myth: "a popular belief or tradition that has grown up around something or someone; especially: one embodying the ideals and institutions of a society or segment of society." Those myths can be true or false, negative or positive: "Mexicans are lazy," "Germans are methodical," "Irish are drunkards," "English are cultured," "French are better lov-ers," "Asians always do better than others in school." The common thread in this type of myth is lack of rationality and lack of investigation of the myth's premises and evidence.

2.   PBS programs specifically on Armenians: *An Armenian Journey, The Armenians: A Story of Survival*, and *The Armenian Genocide*. At least two programs with high production values that took a more moderate stance, *A Myth of Terror and Arme-nian Revolt—Tragedy in the Middle East*, were refused by PBS. The PBS series on World War I, *The Great War*, is an egregious example of the effects of prejudice on public broadcasting. The director and writers consulted none of the recognized authorities on the war in the Middle East and, not surprisingly, repeated all the standard mythology on Turks and Armenians. The series was also incredibly incor-rect in its facts on other aspects of the war in the Middle East. When PBS, bow-ing to political pressure, attempted to show one short debate between those who believed in an Armenian genocide and those who did not, half the public television stations in America refused to air the program.

3.   Since 1990 the *New York Times* has printed fifteen reviews of books that considered the topic "Armenian genocide." Some were reviews of books on that subject, some only included the Armenians as part of larger studies, but all of them advanced the genocide thesis. All but one of the books were evaluated by sympathetic reviewers who never challenged the books' historical assumptions. No book that questioned the Armenian genocide thesis was ever reviewed in the *New York Times*. Many such books existed, including Erich Feigl, *A Myth of Terror* (Freilassing: Edition Zeitge-schichte, 1986); Kâmuran Gürün, *The Armenian File* (New York: St. Martin's Press, 1985); Yusuf Halaçoğlu, *Facts on the Relocation of Armenians (1914–1918)* (Ankara: Turkish Historical Society, 2002); Guenter Lewy, *The Armenian Massacres in Otto-man Turkey: A Disputed Genocide*; Justin McCarthy, *Death and Exile: The Eth-nic Cleansing of Ottoman Muslims*, and *Muslims and Minorities*; Mim Kemal Öke, *The Armenian Question, 1914–1923* (Nicosia: K. Rustem and Brother, 1988); Bilâl N. Şimşir, *The Genesis of the Armenian Question* (Ankara: Turkish Historical Soci-ety, 1983); Salahi Sonyel, *The Ottoman Armenians*; and Esat Uras, *The Armenians in History and the Armenian Question*. Not one of these was reviewed.

Other American newspapers also only printed sympathetic reviews of books that advanced the idea of an Armenian genocide, as shown by searches of the *Wash-ington Post, Boston Globe, Chicago Tribune*, and the nationwide records of smaller city newspapers in the online NewspaperARCHIVE.com. It would not be par-ticularly odd if popular American newspapers did not review academic books on

Middle Eastern history, which is usually the case. What is odd is that they reviewed only books taking one side of a historical debate.

4. British National Archives, FO 424/208, O'Conor to Landsdowne, Constantinople, May 12, 1905.

5. Daniel Katz and Kenneth Braly, "Racial Stereotypes of One Hundred College Students," *Journal of Abnormal and Social Psychology* 28 (1933–34): 280–90. The article gives only the top twelve choices for each group. Turks fared as poorly in other surveys taken at the time. See Helen McCready Kearney, "American Images of the Middle East, 1824–1924: A Century of Antipathy," pp. 7–30.

6. The study considered Germans, Italians, "Negroes," Irish, English, Jews, Americans, Chinese, Japanese, and Turks, who were identified as "races."

7. G. M. Gilbert, "Stereotype Persistence and Change among College Students," *Journal of Abnormal and Social Psychology* 46 (1951): 245–54. Far fewer students were willing to give answers in the second survey. These are the ratings of those who answered for the Turks.

8. Justin McCarthy, "The American Image of Turks," *Tarih* 2 (1992): 55–72.

9. Many textbooks accuse the Turks of crimes, even genocide, but never mention any of the crimes against the Turks. See, for example, Robert W. Strayer, *Ways of the World: A Brief Global History* (Boston and New York: Bedford/St. Martin's, 2009); John P. McKay et al., *A History of World Societies*, vol. 2 (Boston and New York, Bedford/St. Martin's, 2009); and Peter N. Stearns et al., *World Civilizations: The Global Experience*, vol. 2 (New York: Pearson/Longman, 2004).

10. A selection of books that describe Bulgarian suffering but not that of Turks: Richard J. Crampton, *Bulgaria 1878–1918: A History* (New York: Columbia University Press, 1983); Raymond Pearson, *National Minorities in Eastern Europe, 1848–1945* (London: Macmillan, 1983); Robert Lee Wolff, *The Balkans in Our Time*, revised ed. (New York: W. W. Norton and Co., 1974); Charles Jelavich and Barbara Jelavich, *The Establishment of the Balkan National States, 1804–1920* (Seattle: University of Washington Press, 1977); Barbara Jelavich, *History of the Balkans*, vol. 1 (London and New York: Cambridge University Press, 1983); R. J. Crampton, *A Concise History of Bulgaria* (Cambridge: Cambridge University Press, 1997); Mercia MacDermott, *A History of Bulgaria, 1393–1885* (New York: Praeger, 1962); René Ristelhueber, *A History of the Balkan Peoples* (New York: Twayne, 1971); Mark Mazower, *The Balkans: A Short History* (New York: Modern Library, 2000); Georges Castellan, *History of the Balkans: From Mohammed the Conqueror to Stalin* (Boulder, Colo.: East European Monographs, 1992). Ana Sitjak, *The Balkans*, vol. 1 (Chicago: Fitzroy Dearborn, 2001), simply reprints the New York Times articles from the time as if they were an accurate historical record, thus reinforcing all the prejudices with which they were originally written. L. S. Stavrianos, *The Balkans since 1450* (New York: Rinehart, 1958), does offer (on p. 379) one sentence stating that the Bulgarians killed Turks at the onset of the "Bulgarian Horrors" but includes only Bulgarian dead for the later events.

11. See, for example, John Keegan, *The First World War* (London: Hutchinson, 1998); Ian F. W. Beckett, *The Great War, 1914–1918*, 2nd ed. (London and New York:

Pearson/Longman, 2007); Martin Gilbert, *The First World War: A Complete History* (New York: Henry Holt and Co., 1994); C. R. M. F. Cruttwell, *A History of the Great War, 1914–1918* (Chicago: Academy Publications, 1934); and S. L. A. Marshall, *World War I* (Boston: Houghton Mifflin, 1964). Most histories of the war do not consider the Middle East at all or give it a few sentences or paragraphs. For examples of the use of missionary writings and especially British propaganda, see Taner Akçam, *A Shameful Act* (New York: Metropolitan Books, 2006); Richard Hovannisian, ed., *The Armenian People from Ancient to Modern Times*; and Vahakn N. Dadrian, *The History of the Armenian Genocide* (Providence, R.I.: Berghahn Books, 1995). Most prominent among the propaganda sources is the Bryce and Toynbee *Blue Book.*

12. Many modern bibliographies available to students list only modern works, which themselves draw from the missionary and British publication. Some bibliographies, however, prominently feature the missionary establishment and British propaganda works. The standard bibliography on the Armenians is Richard G. Hovannisian, *The Armenian Holocaust: A Bibliography Relating to the Deportations, Massacres, and Dispersion of the Armenian People, 1915–1923* (Cambridge, Mass.: Armenian Heritage Press/National Association for Armenian Studies and Research, 1978). The most easily accessible bibliographies are on the Internet: "The Armenian Genocide: A Bibliography," prepared by the University of Michigan–Dearborn for the U.S. Holocaust Museum (www.umd.umich.edu/dept/armenian/facts/gen_bib1.html and many other websites), lists the British propaganda books concerning the Armenians (the *Blue Book*, Toynbee's books, Ghusein, Mugerditchian, and others) as well as many of the missionary establishment works (Rockwell, Gibbons, Barton, Knapp, Ussher, ACASR and Near East Relief pamphlets, etc.). It also includes many of the 1890s missionary books. The bibliography on Armenians.com (www.armenians.com/Genocide/bibliography.html) lists virtually all of the British propaganda and missionary establishment books. The Internet Public Library, a consortium including well-known American universities and sponsored by major companies, offers a bibliography on "World War History." The only books listed on the Ottoman Empire in the war are on the topic "Armenian Massacres" (www.ipl.org/div/pf/entry/48548). In 2008 the Salt Lake City Public Library recommended books on World War I. All the books but one were on "Armenian Massacre"; the other was T. E. Lawrence's *Seven Pillars of Wisdom* (www.slco.lib.ut.us/Ww1.htm). George Shirian, "The Armenian Massacres of 1894–1897: A Bibliography," *Hye Etch* (www.hyeetch.nareg.com.au/genocide/oppress_p4.html), is very comprehensive. It contains all the worst of the 1890s volumes, including Pierce, Greene, Filian, and Bliss. For its bibliography on the Ottoman Empire in World War I, the website for the PBS documentary series *The Great War* provides a link to the site of the Armenian National Institute, which offers only the books one might expect. PBS recommends no other books on Turks in the war.

13. Like the work of the missionaries and the propagandists, the most well-known genocide studies program for schoolteachers, Facing History and Ourselves (www.facinghistory.org), has no mention of any dead Turks, only dead Armenians.

Curricula in various American states are similar. Students literally have no way to learn anything but the standard anti-Turkish version of history. They also cannot learn anything of Turkish suffering. Instead, Facing History accuses those who disagree with its positions of being agents of evil: "Deniers operate as agents of the original perpetrators"; "Denial is the final stage of genocide."

14. These are conservative figures. For the calculations of the total numbers, see McCarthy, *Death and Exile: The Ethnic Cleansing of Ottoman Muslims*, pp. 338–40.

15. Taking the New York Times as an example, see "Coast Jury Convicts Armenian in Death of a Turkish Envoy," January 5, 1984, p. A6; "Guilt by Citizenship," December 2, 1984, p. E24; "Turks' Embassy in Ottawa Seized," March 13, 1985, p. A1; "Armenian Guerilla Organization Calling Off Attacks on the Swiss," January 5, 1981, p. A10; and "Soiling the Altar of Freedom," August 9, 1983, p. A22. Many others were printed. The murders prompted articles and editorials on "Turkish guilt." See, for example, Karl E. Meyer, "Armenian Memory, Turkish Amnesia," April 23, 1983, p. 22; Florence Avakian, "The Armenian Dead," April 27, 1985, p. 23; "The Sorrows of Armenia," April 29, 1985, p. A16; Michael J. Arlen, "Armenians vs. Turks—Again," March 11, 1980, p. A19; "Turkish Amnesia," May 14, 1983, p. 22; Edward N. Costikyan and Robert H. Tembeckjian, "A Task for Armenians," July 29, 1983, p. A23; Marvine Howe, "'15 Massacre Still Stirs Armenian-Americans," April 28, 1984, p. 25; and "Inconvenience vs. Armenians," May 4, 1985, p. 26. Only Flora Lewis seems to have condemned "a tendency among some U.S. as well as French commentators to say that even though their methods are reprehensible, the Armenian terrorists do have a point" (August 5, 1983, p. A23).

BIBLIOGRAPHY

The number of books that cast light on the American image of the Turks is immense. The working bibliography for this project contains more than two thousand books and scholarly articles (not including articles from popular magazines and newspapers). Many of these sources, of course, proved to be unimportant. Far too many works were useful, however, to list them all here. A number of works cited in the notes are not included in this bibliography. Those that are listed here either are the most important or are representative of a type of source. For example, only a few of the sermons cited in the text are included here.

The names of the newspapers and magazines used in the study are listed here, but individual articles are cited exclusively in the notes. It would take many lifetimes to see all the American newspapers of the nineteenth and early twentieth centuries. Even then, many newspapers have disappeared over time. Although I consulted many articles in the Library of Congress newspaper collection, I mainly viewed the newspapers and magazines cited here in electronic versions. These include the online archives of the *Atlanta Constitution, Boston Globe, Chicago Tribune, Christian Science Monitor, Dallas News, Hartford Courant, Los Angeles Times, New York Times,* and *Washington Post.* Smaller newspapers were accessed through NewspaperARCHIVE.com and early American newspapers and magazines through the American Periodical Series and Early American Imprints. I believe that these afforded a good cross section of the American media in the Northeast, Midwest, and Far West. With the exception of Atlanta and Dallas, southern media were not as well represented.

Many of the articles came from news services, especially the Associated Press (AP), and were found in many newspapers. The endnotes usually cite only one of these newspapers, although they occasionally cite many instances in which the articles appeared in order to demonstrate the scope of the news. By no means were all the AP articles cited as such, only those that seemed important in context.

BOOKS

Abrams, Ray Hamilton. *Preachers Present Arms: A Study of the War-Time Attitudes and Activities of the Churches and the Clergy in the United States, 1914–1918.* Philadelphia: n.p., 1933.

Adams, Daniel. *Geography; or, A Description of the World, in Three Parts—Part I: Geographical Orthography, Divided and Accented; Part II: A Grammar of Geography, to*

Be Committed to Memory; Part III: A Description of the Earth, Manners and Customs of the Inhabitants, Manufactures, Commerce, Government, Natural and Artificial Curiosities, &c., to Be Read in Classes; Accompanied with an Atlas, to Which Is Added, an Easy Method of Constructing Maps, Illustrated by Plates: For the Use of Schools and Academies. Boston: West and Blake, 1814.

Adams, George Burton. *Medieval and Modern History: An Outline of Its Development.* New York: Macmillan, 1912.

Adkins, Frank J. *Historical Backgrounds of the Great War.* New York: Robert M. McBride and Co., 1918.

Aftandilian, Gregory L. *Armenia, Vision of a Republic: The Independence Lobby in America, 1918–1927.* Charlestown, Mass.: Charles River Books, 1981.

Aghassi. *Zeïtoun depuis les origines jusqu'à l'insurrection de 1895.* Paris: Édition du Mercure de France, 1897.

Allison, Robert J. *The Crescent Obscured: The United States and the Muslim World, 1776–1815.* New York: Oxford University Press, 1995.

American Armenian Relief Fund. *The Cry of Armenia.* New York: American Armenian Relief Fund, in cooperation with the American Committee for Armenian and Syrian Relief, 1916.

American Board of Commissioners for Foreign Missions. Almanac, 1915. Boston: ABCFM, 1915.

———. *Annual Report.* Boston: ABCFM, annual.

———. *A Book for Young People.* Boston: ABCFM, 1885.

———. *Condensed Sketch of the Missions of the American Board in Asiatic Turkey.* Boston: ABCFM, 1910.

———. *The Gospel in Asia Minor.* Boston: ABCFM, 1879.

———. *The Problem of Turkey as the American Board Sees It.* Boston: ABCFM, 1923.

American Committee for Armenian and Syrian Relief (ACASR). *America's Opportunity to Relieve Suffering in Armenia, Syria, Persia, and Palestine.* New York: ACASR, 1917.

———. *Armenia: An Appeal to the Citizens of the United States on Behalf of the Armenian Sufferers.* New York: ACASR, 1916.

———. *Armenia: Her Heartrending Cry.* New York: ACASR, n.d.

———. *Armenia: The Most Tragic Story in Human History.* New York: ACASR, n.d. (1916?).

———. *Armenia: A Tragedy in Which the Men, Women, and Children of a Helpless Nation Are the Victims OF INHUMAN PERSECUTION AND MURDER.* New York: ACASR, n.d.

———. *Armenia: The Word Spells Tragedy.* New York: ACASR, n.d. (1917?).

———. *Boys and Girls of Bible Lands.* New York: ACASR, 1917.

———. *The Call of the Dying and Destitute Armenians and Syrians to the Sunday Schools of America.* New York: ACASR, n.d., 1917.

———. *The Cry of Armenia.* New York: ACASR, 1916.

———. *The Cry of Millions, Exile, Destitute, Dying.* New York: ACASR, 1916.

———. *The Deportation of the Armenians.* New York: ACASR, 1916.

———. *Latest News concerning the Armenian and Syrian Sufferers, January 25, 1916.* New York: ACASR, 1916.

———. *More Material for Your Sermons on Bible Lands Today.* New York: ACASR, 1918.

———. *The Most Terrible Winter the World Has Ever Known.* New York: ACASR, 1916.

———. *A National Test of Brotherhood: America's Opportunity to Relieve Suffering in Armenia, Syria, Persia, and Palestine.* New York: ACASR, 1917.

———. *Photographical Reproductions of Latest Cablegrams from Bible Lands: February, AD 1918.* New York: ACASR, 1918.

———. *The Pitiful Plight of the Assyrian Christians in Persia and Kurdistan.* New York: ACASR, 1916.

———. *Practicing Bible Precepts in Bible Lands: Handbook for Busy Pastors.* New York: American Committee for Relief in the Near East, 1919.

———. *Sixteen Striking Scenes: Illustrating the Suffering and Need in Armenia and Other Parts of Western Asia.* New York: ACASR, n.d. (1916?).

———. *Stories from Real Life.* New York: ACASR, 1917.

———. *A Story That Must Be Told: Armenians Are Starving.* New York: ACASR, n.d. (1917?)

———. *Suggestions for Local Co-operating Committees.* New York: ACASR, 1916.

———. *Worker's Notebook on Armenia.* New York: ACASR, 1918.

American Committee for the Independence of Armenia. *America as Mandatory for Armenia: Articles and Opinions by James W. Gerard, Frederic Courtland Penfield, John Sharp Williams, Etc.* New York: American Committee for the Independence of Armenia, 1919.

American Committee Opposed to the Lausanne Treaty. *The Lausanne Treaty, Turkey and Armenia.* Ed. Vahan Cardashian. New York: American Committee Opposed to the Lausanne Treaty, 1926.

American National Red Cross. *America's Relief Expedition to Asia Minor under the Red Cross.* Washington, D.C.: Red Cross, 1896.

Anderson, Rufus. *History of the Missions of the American Board of Commissioners for Foreign Missions.* Boston: Congregational Publishing Society, 1875.

———. *Memorial Volume of the First Fifty Years of the American Board of Commissioners for Foreign Missions.* 5th ed. Boston: The Board, 1863.

Armenian National Union of America. *Armenia: The Armenian Question before the Peace Conference.* New York: Press Bureau, Armenian National Union of America, 1919.

———. *The Case of Armenia.* New York: Armenian National Union of America, 1919.

———. *Should America Accept Mandate for Armenia?* New York: Press Bureau, Armenian National Union of America, 1919.

Ashley, Roscoe Lewis. *Modern European Civilization: A Textbook for Secondary Schools.* New York: Macmillan, 1918.

Barton, James L. *Changing Turkey: Political and Religious Revolution.* Boston: ABCFM, 1926.

———. *The Christian Approach to Islam.* Boston: Pilgrim Press, 1918.

_____ . *Daybreak in Turkey*. Boston: Pilgrim Press, 1908.

_____ . *Human Progress through Missions*. New York: Revell, 1912.

_____ . *The Missionary and His Critics*. New York: Revell, 1906.

_____ . *The Near East Relief*. New York: Russell Sage Foundation, 1943.

_____ . *The Story of Near East Relief*. New York: Macmillan, 1930.

_____ . *The Unfinished Task of the Christian Church*. New York: Student Volunteer Movement for Foreign Missions, 1908.

Barton, James L., and Ara Sarafian. *Turkish Atrocities: Statements of American Missionaries on the Destruction of Christian Communities in Ottoman Turkey, 1915–1917*. Princeton, N.J., and London: Gomidas Institute, 1998.

Beach, Harlan P. *A Geography and Atlas of Protestant Missions*. 2 vols. New York: Student Volunteer Movement for Foreign Missions, 1901.

_____ . *World Statistics of Christian Missions*. New York: Committee of Reference and Counsel of the Foreign Missions Conference of North America, 1916.

Beach, Harlan P., and Burton St. John. *World Statistics of Christian Missions*. New York: Committee of Reference and Counsel of the Foreign Missions Conference of North America, 1916.

Benson, E. F. *Crescent and Iron Cross*. London: Hodder and Stoughton, 1918; New York: Doran, 1918.

_____ . *Deutschland über Allah*. London and New York: Hodder and Stoughton, 1917.

Benziger's Advanced Geography for the Use of Catholic Schools. New York: Benziger Brothers, 1921.

Benziger's Elementary Geography for Catholic Schools. New York: Benziger Brothers, 1921.

Berger, Meyer. *The Story of the New York Times, 1851–1951*. New York: Simon and Schuster, 1951.

Bettany, G. T. *The World's Religions*. New York: Christian Literature Co., 1891.

Black, John B. *Organizing the Propaganda Instrument*. The Hague: Nijhoff, 1975.

Blake, Isabel M. *Fez and Turban Tales*. New York: Interchurch Press, 1920.

Bliss, Edwin Munsell. *The Encyclopedia of Missions*. 2 vols. New York: Funk and Wagnalls, 1891.

_____ . *The Missionary Enterprise: A Concise History of Its Objects, Methods and Extension*. New York: Revell, 1908.

_____ . *Turkish Cruelties upon the Armenian Christians*. Philadelphia: Imperial Publishing Co., 1896 (also published as *Turkey and the Armenian Atrocities*. Philadelphia: Hubbard Publishing Co., 1896 [and by other publishers]).

Booth, Charles L. "Let the American Flag Wave in the Aegean: America Responds to the Greek War of Independence (1821–1824)." Ph.D. dissertation, New York University, 2005.

Bourne, Henry E. *A History of Medieval and Modern Europe*. New York: Longman, Green, 1905.

Bowen, James A. *Grammar School Geography*. New York: Rand-McNally, 1901.

Brace, Charles Loring. *Gesta Christi; or, a History of Humane Progress under Christianity*. New York: A. C. Armstrong and Sons, 1883.

Brown, Arthur Judson. *The Foreign Missionary: An Incarnation of a World Movement.* Revised ed. New York: Revell, 1932 (1st ed. 1907).

Bruntz, George C. *Allied Propaganda and the Collapse of the German Empire.* Rpt. New York: Arno Press, 1972 (1st ed. Stanford, CA: Hoover War Library, 1938).

Bryce, James Viscount. *The American Commonwealth.* London and New York: Macmillan, 1888.

———. *Evidence and Documents Laid before the Committee on Alleged German Outrages.* London and New York: Macmillan for H. M. Stationery Office, 1915.

———. *The Future of Armenia.* London: National Press Agency, 1918.

———. *Report of the Committee on Alleged German Outrages.* London: Macmillan for H. M. Stationery Office, 1915.

Bryson, Thomas A. *American Diplomatic Relations with the Middle East: A Survey.* Metuchen, N.J.: Scarecrow Press, 1977.

Buitenhuis, Peter. *The Great War of Words.* Vancouver: University of British Columbia Press, 1987.

Burr, Clinton Stoddard. *America's Race Heritage.* New York: National Historical Society, 1922.

Bush, George. *The Life of Mohammed: Founder of the Religion of Islam, and of the Empire of the Saracens.* New York: Harper and Brothers, 1837.

Butler, Frederick. *Sketches of Universal History.* Hartford: Cooke and Hale, 1818.

Çakir, Musa. *Anadolumuz Asla Hiristiyan Olmayacak; Misyonerler, memleketimize donumuz.* Istanbul: Eygi, 1966.

Calhoun, David B. *Princeton Seminary.* Vol. 2. Edinburgh and Carlisle, Pa.: Banner of Truth Trust, 1996.

Cohen, Israel. *The Turkish Persecution of the Jews.* London: Passmore and Sons, 1918.

The Commercial Future of Baghdad. London: Complete Press, 1917.

Committee on Armenian Atrocities. *Report.* New York: n.p., 1915.

The Comprehensive Geography. New York: P. O'Shea, 1876.

Cook, Edward. *Britain and Turkey.* London: Macmillan, 1914.

Cook, Ralph Elliott. "The United States and the Armenian Question, 1894–1924." Ph.D. dissertation, Tufts University, Fletcher School of Law and Diplomacy, 1957.

Cummings, J. A. *An Introduction to Ancient and Modern Geography, on the Plan of Goldsmith and Guy; Comprising Rules for Projecting Maps, with an Atlas.* Boston: Cummings and Hilliard, 1828.

Curti, Merle. *American Philanthropy Abroad: A History.* New Brunswick, N.J.: Rutgers University Press, 1963.

Daily News. *The War Correspondence of the Daily News.* London: Macmillan, 1878.

Daniel, Norman. *Islam and the West: The Making of an Image.* Edinburgh: Edinburgh University Press, 1960.

———. *Islam, Europe and Empire.* Edinburgh: Edinburgh University Press, 1966.

Daniel, Robert L. *American Philanthropy in the Near East, 1820–1960.* Athens: Ohio University Press, 1970.

Dasnabedian, Hratch. *History of the Armenian Revolution Federation, Dashnaktsutiun.* Translated by Bryan Fleming and Vaha Habeshian. Milan: GEMME Edizione, 1989.

Davidson, Robert. *Geography Epitomized*. Philadelphia: Joseph Crukshank, 1784.

Davis, William Stearns. *A History of Medieval and Modern Europe for Secondary Schools.* Boston: Houghton Mifflin, 1921.

———. *The Roots of the War: A Non-technical History of Europe, 1870–1914, AD.* New York: Century Co., 1918.

———. *A Short History of the Near East: From the Founding of Constantinople (330 AD to 1922)*. New York: Macmillan, 1923.

Delegates of the Red Cross. *Turkish Prisoners in Egypt*. London: Cassell, 1917.

Deniker, J. *The Races of Man: An Outline of Anthropology and Ethnography (1900; a translation of Les races et les peuples de la terre)*. New York: Scribner's, 1904.

Dennis, James S. *Christian Missions and Social Progress: A Sociological Study of Foreign Missions.* 3 vols. New York: Revell, 1897, 1899, 1906.

———. *Foreign Missions after a Century*. New York: Revell, 1893.

———. *The Modern Call of Missions*. New York: Revell, 1913.

———. *The New Horoscope of Missions*. New York: Revell, 1908.

———. *Social Evils of the Non-Christian World*. New York: Student Volunteer Movement for Foreign Missions, 1899.

———. *The Turkish Problem and the Status of Our Missionaries*. New York: Evangelist Press, 1896.

Dennis, James S., and Harlan Beach, eds. *The World Atlas of Christian Missions*. New York: Student Volunteer Movement for Foreign Missions, 1911.

Dewe, J. A. *Medieval and Modern History*. New York: Hinds, Noble and Eldredge, 1907.

Dominian, Leon. *The Frontiers of Language and Nationality in Europe*. New York: Henry Holt, 1917.

Dryer, Charles Redway. *Grammar School Geography*. Chicago: Rand, McNally and Co., 1903 (revision of 1894 original).

Dwight, H. G. O. *Christianity in Turkey*. London: James Nisbet and Co., 1854.

———. *Christianity Revived in the East*. New York: n.p., 1850.

Dwight, Henry Otis. *Constantinople and Its Problems*. New York: Revell, 1901.

Dwight, Nathaniel. *A Short But Comprehensive System of the Geography of the World: By Way of Question and Answer, Principally Designed for Children and Common Schools, Second Connecticut Edition*. Hartford: Hudson and Goodwin, 1795.

Dyer, Thomas. *The History of Modern Europe*. 4 vols. London: John Murray, 1861.

Eddy, David Brewer. *What Next in Turkey: Glimpses of the American Board's Work in the Near East*. Boston: ABCFM, 1913.

El-Ghusein, Faʿiz. *Martyred Armenia*. London: C. Arthur Pearson, 1917; New York: Doran, 1918.

Elsbree, Oliver Wendell. *The Rise of the Missionary Spirit in America, 1790–1815*. Williamsport, Pa.: Williamsport Printing and Binding Co., 1928.

Elson, Henry William, and Cornelia E. MacMullan. *The Story of the Old World: A European Background to the Story of Our Country*. Boston and New York: Thompson Brown, 1911.

Emerson, Frederick. *The First View of the World*. Boston: n.p., 1840.

―――― . *Outlines of Geography and History, Presenting a Concise View of the World*. Philadelphia: Hogan and Thompson, 1841.

Entwistle, Mary, and Jeanette E. Peters. *Musa, Son of Egypt: Programs and Stories for Primary Children*. New York: Friendship Press, 1926.

Erickson, Edward J. *Ordered to Die: A History of the Ottoman Army in the First World War*. Westport, Conn.: Greenwood Press, 2001.

Farah, Caesar. *Islam: Beliefs and Observances*. Woodbury, N.Y.: Barron's Educational Series, 1970.

Fensham, Florence A., Mary I. Lyman, and Mrs. H. B. Humphrey. *A Modern Crusade in the Turkish Empire*. Chicago: Women's Board of Missions of the Interior, 1908.

Field, James A. *America and the Mediterranean World*. Princeton: Princeton University Press, 1969.

Filian, George. *Armenia and Her People*. Hartford: American Publishing Company, 1896.

―――― . *History of the Greek Revolution*. London: W. Blackwood and Sons, 1861.

Finley, John. *A Pilgrim in Palestine*. New York: Charles Scribner's Sons, 1919.

Finnie, David H. *Pioneers East: The Early American Experience in the Middle East*. Cambridge, Mass.: Harvard University Press, 1967.

Fisk, Pliny. *The Holy Land an Interesting Field of Missionary Enterprise: A Sermon Preached in the Old South Church, Boston, Sabbath Evening, October 31, 1819, Just before the Departure of the Palestine Mission*. Boston: S. T. Armstrong, 1819.

―――― . *Memoir of Rev. Pliny Fisk*. Ed. Alvan Bond. Boston: Crocker and Brewster, 1828.

Foreign Missions Conference of North America, Committee of Reference and Counsel. *World Statistics of Christian Missions*. New York: Committee of Reference and Counsel of the Foreign Missions Conference of North America, 1916.

Fradenburgh, J. N. *Living Religions; or, the Great Religions of the Orient from Sacred Books and Modern Customs*. Cincinnati: Jennings and Pye, 1888; New York: Eaton and Mains, 1888.

Fraser, Donald. *A Compendium of the History of All Nations*. New York: n.p., 1807.

Freeman, E. A. *General Sketch of European History*. 5th ed. London: Macmillan, 1905 (1st ed. London: Macmillan, 1872).

―――― . *The Turks in Europe*. New York: Lovell, Adam, Wesson and Co., 1877.

Frye, Alexis Everett. *Advanced Geography*. Boston: Ginn and Co., 1899.

Gabriel, M. S. *The Armenians; or, the People of Ararat*. Philadelphia: Allen, Lane and Scott, 1892.

―――― . *Under the Curse of Islam*. Chicago: Publishers' Union, 1896.

Gaidzakian, Ohan. *Illustrated Armenia and the Armenians*. Boston: n.p., 1898.

Gates, Caleb Frank. *Not to Me Only*. Princeton: Princeton University Press, 1940.

General Sir Edmund Allenby's Despatch of 10th December, 1917, on the Operations in Egypt and Palestine from 28th June, 1917, till the Capture of Jerusalem (11th December, 1917). Reprint from the London Gazette of January 22, 1918. London: H. M. Stationery Office, 1918.

Germany, Turkey, and Armenia: A Selection of Documentary Evidence Relating to the Armenian Atrocities from German and Other Sources. London: J. J. Keliher and Co., 1917.

Gibbons, Herbert Adams. *The Blackest Page in Modern History*. New York and London: Putnam's, 1916.

_____. *The New Map of Asia (1900–1919)*. New York: Century Co., 1919.

_____. *The New Map of Europe (1911–1914): The Story of the Recent European Diplomatic Crises and Wars and of Europe's Present Catastrophe*. New York: Century Co., 1914.

Gidney, James B. *A Mandate for Armenia*. Kent, Ohio: Kent State University Press, 1967.

Goodell, William. *Forty Years in the Turkish Empire; or, Memoirs of Rev. William Goodell, D.D.* New York: R. Carter and Brothers, 1875.

_____. *The Old and the New; or, the Changes of Thirty Years in the East, with Some Allusions to Oriental Customs as Elucidating Scripture*. New York: M. W. Dodd, 1853.

Goodrich, Samuel Griswold. *A History of All Nations, from the Earliest Periods to the Present Time; or, Universal History: In Which the History of Every Nation, Ancient and Modern, Is Separately Given*. New York and Auburn: Orton and Mulligan, 1856.

_____. *Lights and Shadows of Asiatic History*. Boston: Bradbury, Soden and Co., 1844.

_____. *Peter Parley's Common School History*. Philadelphia: Butler and Co., 1845.

_____. *Peter Parley's Universal History for Families*. Boston: American Stationers, 1837.

_____. *The World and Its Inhabitants, by the Author of Peter Parley's Tales*. Boston: Bradbury, Soden and Co., 1845.

Gordon, Thomas. *History of the Greek Revolution*. Edinburgh and London: T. Cadell, 1832.

Grabill, Joseph L. *Protestant Diplomacy and the Near East*. Minneapolis: University of Minnesota Press, 1971.

Grant, G. M. *The Religions of the World in Relation to Christianity*. New York: F. H. Revell, 1895.

Grant, Madison. *The Passing of the Great Race*. New York: Scribner's, 1916.

Great Britain, Palestine, and the Jews: Jewry's Celebration of Its National Charter. London: Zionist Organization, 1918; New York: Doran, 1918.

Great Britain, Palestine, and the Jews: A Survey of Christian Opinion. London: Zionist Organization, 1918; New York: Doran, 1918.

Les Grecs à Smyrne—Nouveaux témoignages sur leurs atrocités: Un document officiel probant. Paris: Kossuth, 1920.

Greene, Frederick Davis. *The Armenian Crisis in Turkey*. New York: G. P. Putnam's Sons, 1895.

_____. *Armenian Massacres or the Sword of Mohammed: Containing a Complete and Thrilling Account of the Terrible Atrocities and Wholesale Murders Committed in Armenia by Mohammedan Fanatics, Including a Full Account of the Turkish People, Their History, Government, Manners, Customs and Strange Religious Beliefs, to Which Is Added "The Mohammedan Reign of Terror in Armenia," edited by Henry Davenport Northrop, D.D., the Well-Known Author*. Philadelphia and Chicago: National Publishing Company, 1896.

_____. *The Rule of the Turk: A Revised and Enlarged Edition of The Armenian Crisis*. New York: G. P. Putnam's Sons, 1896.

Greene, Joseph K. *Leavening the Levant*. Boston: Pilgrim Press, 1916.

Gürün, Kâmuran. *The Armenian File*. London: Rustem and Weidenfeld and Nicolson, 1985.

Hacobian, A. P. *Armenia and the War*. London: Hodder and Stoughton, 1917; New York: Doran, 1917.

Hall, Mary L. *Our World: First Lessons in Geography for Children*. Boston: Ginn and Co., 1891.

Hall, William H. *The Near East: Crossroads of the World*. New York: Interchurch Press, 1920.

Hall, William Webster. *Puritans in the Balkans: The American Board Mission in Bulgaria, 1878–1918*. Sofia: Cultura, 1938.

Hamlin, Cyrus. *Among the Turks*. New York: R. Carter and Brothers, 1878.

———. *My Life and Times*. Boston: Congregational Sunday-School and Publishing Society, 1893.

———. *The Oriental Churches and Mohammedans*. Missionary Tracts 11. Boston: American Board of Commissioners for Foreign Missions, 1858.

Harding, Samuel Banister, and Alfred Bushnell Hart. *New Medieval and Modern History*. New York: American Book Co., 1913.

Harland, Marion, and George Henry Sandison. *Home of the Bible: What I Saw and Heard in Palestine and the Story of Martyred Armenia*. New York: Christian Herald, 1896.

Harris, David. *Britain and the Bulgarian Horrors of 1876*. Chicago: University of Chicago Press, 1939.

Harris, J. Rendel and Helen B. Harris. *Letters from the Scenes of the Recent Massacres in Armenia*. New York: F. H. Revell, 1897.

Hartzell, Joseph C., and Samuel M. Zwemer. *The Call of Moslem Children: The Story of the Neglected Children of the Mohammedan World*. New York: Funk and Wagnalls, 1913.

Haste, Cate. *Keep the Home Fires Burning: Propaganda in the First World War*. London: Allen Lane, 1977.

Hatch, Harold A., and William H. Hall. *Recommendations for Political Reconstruction in the Turkish Empire*. New York: ACASR, 1918.

Hayes, Carlton H. H., and Parker Thomas Moon. *Modern History*. Revised and enlarged ed. New York: Macmillan, 1930 (1st ed. 1923).

Hazen, Charles Downer. *Fifty Years of Europe, 1870–1920*. New York: Henry Holt, 1919.

———. *Modern European History*. 3rd ed. New York: Henry Holt, 1919 (1st ed. 1917).

Herrick, George F. *Christian and Mohammedan: A Plea for Bridging the Gap*. New York: Revell, 1912.

Historical and Descriptive Lessons, Embracing Sketches of the History, Character and Customs of All Nations: Designed as a Companion to Goodrich's, Woodbridge's, Morse's, Smiley's, and Other School Geographies. Brattleboro, Vt.: Holbrook and Fessenden, 1828.

Hofstadter, Richard. *Social Darwinism in American Thought, 1860–1915*. Philadelphia: University of Pennsylvania Press, 1944.

Houghton, Ross C. *Women of the Orient.* Cincinnati: Hitchcock and Walden, 1877.

Hovannisian, Richard G., ed. *The Armenian People from Ancient to Modern Times.* 2 vols. New York: St. Martin's, 1997.

Howard, Harry N. *The King-Crane Commission: An American Inquiry in the Middle East.* Beirut: Khayats, 1963.

Huntington, Ellsworth. *Palestine and Its Transformation.* Boston and New York: Houghton Mifflin, 1911.

———. *Pulse of Asia.* Boston and New York: Houghton Mifflin, 1907.

Hurgronje, C. S. *The Holy War "Made in Germany".* New York and London: G. P. Putnam's, 1915.

Hüseyin Nazım Paşa. *Ermeni Olayları Tarihi.* 2 vols. Ankara: T. C. Başbakanlık Devlet Arşivleri Genel Müdürlüğü, Osmanlı Arşivi Daire Başkanlığı, 1994.

Ipema, Peter. "The Islam Interpretations of Duncan B. Macdonald, Samuel M. Zwemer, A. Kenneth Cragg and Wilfred C. Smith: An Interpretation." Ph.D. dissertation, Hartford Seminary, 1971.

Irving, Washington. *Life of Mahomet.* London: H. G. Bohn, 1850.

———. *Mahomet and His Successors.* Irving's Works, vol. 6. Hudson edition. New York: G. P. Putnam's Sons, 1868.

Jelavich, Barbara. *History of the Balkans.* 2 vols. Cambridge: Cambridge University Press, 1983.

Jessup, Henry Harris. *The Mohammedan Missionary Problem.* Philadelphia: n.p., 1879.

———. *The Women of the Arabs, with a Chapter for Children.* New York: Dodd and Mead, 1873.

Kabbani, Rana. *Europe's Myths of Orient.* Bloomington: Indiana University Press, 1986.

Kara Krikorian [Hohannes]. *Islam and Christianity Face to Face.* New York: American Tract Society, 1901.

Karpat, Kemal H. *Ottoman Population, 1830–1914.* Madison: University of Wisconsin Press, 1985.

Karpat, Kemal H., and A. Deniz Balgamış, eds. *Turkish Migration to the United States: From Ottoman Times to the Present.* Madison: University of Wisconsin Press, 2008.

Keane, A. H. *Ethnology.* Cambridge: Cambridge University Press, 1901.

———. *Man Past and Present.* Cambridge: Cambridge University Press, 1900.

Kearney, Helen McCready. "American Images of the Middle East, 1824–1924: A Century of Antipathy." Ph.D. dissertation, University of Rochester, 1975.

King, William Henry. *Turkish Atrocities in Asia Minor.* Washington, D.C.: GPO, 1922.

Kirakossian, Arman J., ed. *The Armenian Massacres, 1894–1896: U.S. Media Testimony.* Detroit: Wayne State University Press, 2004.

Kloian, Richard D. *The Armenian Genocide: News Accounts from the American Press.* 3rd ed. Berkeley, Calif.: Anto Printing, 1985.

Knapp, Grace H. *The Mission at Van: In Turkey in War Time.* New York: Prospect Press, 1915.

———. *The Tragedy of Bitlis.* New York: Revell, 1919.

Knowlton, Daniel C., and Samuel B. Howell. *Essentials in Modern European History.* Chicago: Longmans, Green, 1919 (1st ed. 1917).

Knox, Robert. *The Races of Men*. Philadelphia: Lea and Blanchard, 1850.

Kocabaşoğlu, Uygur. *Kendi Belgeleriyle Anadolu'daki Amerika: 19 Yüzyılda Osmanlı İmparatoluğu'ndaki American Misyoner Okulları*. Istanbul: Arba, 1989.

Koelle, S. W. *Mohammed and Mohammedanism*. London: Rivington's, 1889.

Koester, Frank. *The Lies of the Allies*. New York: Issues and Events, 1916.

Labaree, Mary Schauffler. *The Child in the Midst*. West Medford, Mass.: Central Committee on the United Study of Foreign Missions, 1914.

Lambert, Rose. *Hadjin, and the Armenian Massacres*. New York: Revell [ca. 1911].

Langer, William L. *The Diplomacy of Imperialism*. New York: Alfred A. Knopf, 1960.

Larcher, Maurice. *La guerre turque dans la guerre mondiale*. Paris: E. Chiron, 1926.

Lasswell, Harold. *Propaganda Technique in the World War*. New York: P. Smith, 1938.

Laurie, Thomas. *The Ely Volume; or, the Contributions of Our Foreign Missions to Science and Human Well-Being*. 2nd ed., revised. Boston: ABCFM, 1885.

Lemaître, Alfred. *Musulmans et Chrétiens: Notes sur la guerre de l'indépendance grecque*. Paris: G. Martin, 1895.

Lewy, Guenter. *The Armenian Massacres in Ottoman Turkey: The Disputed Genocide*. Salt Lake City: University of Utah Press, 2005.

The Life of Mahomet; or, the History of That Imposture Which Was Begun, Carried On, and Finally Established by Him in Arabia and Which Has Subjugated a Larger Portion of the Globe Than the Religion of Jesus Has Yet Set at Liberty. New York: Evert Duyckinck, 1813.

Lindsay, Anna R. *Gloria Christi*. New York: Macmillan, 1907.

Lowry, Heath W. *The Story behind Ambassador Morgenthau's Story*. Istanbul: Isis, 1990.

Macdonald, Duncan Black. *Aspects of Islam*. New York: Macmillan, 1911.

———. *The Religious Attitude and Life in Islam*. Chicago: University of Chicago Press, 1909.

MacGahan, Januarius Aloysius. *The Turkish Atrocities in Bulgaria: Letters of the Special Commissioner of the "Daily News"*. London: Bradbury, Agnew and Co., 1876.

MacKenzie, John M. *Propaganda and Empire*. Dover, N.H.: Manchester University Press, 1984.

Mackenzie, W. Douglas. *Christianity and the Progress of Man: As Illustrated by Modern Missions*. New York: Revell, 1897.

Maglot, Frederick. *A Manual of Geography*. Ada, Ohio: Agnew Welch, 1883.

Makdisi, Usama Samir. *Artillery of Heaven: American Missionaries and the Failed Conversion of the Middle East*. Ithaca, N.Y.: Cornell University Press, 2008

Malcolm, Mrs. Napier. *Children of Persia*. New York: Revell, 1911.

Malcolm, Napier. *Five Years in a Persian Town*. New York: E. P. Dutton, 1905.

Mardiganian, Aurora. *Ravished Armenia: The Story of Aurora Mardiganian*. Interpreted by H. L. Gates. New York: Kingfield Press, 1918.

Margoliouth, D. S. *Mohammed and the Rise of Islam*. New York: Putnam, 1905.

———. *Mohammedanism*. New York: Henry Holt, 1911.

Marr, Timothy Worthington. *The Cultural Roots of American Islamicism*. New York: Cambridge University Press, 2006.

_____. "Imagining Ishmael: Studies of Islamic Orientalism in America from the Puritans to Melville." Ph.D. dissertation, Yale University, 1997.

Masterman, E. W. G. *The Deliverance of Jerusalem*. London: Hodder and Stoughton, 1918; New York: Doran, 1918.

Mathews, Basil. *The Freedom of Jerusalem*. London and New York: Hodder and Stoughton, 1918.

Maurice, Frederick Denison. *The Religions of the World and Their Relations to Christianity*. Boston: Gould and Lincoln, 1854; New York: Macmillan, 1861.

McCarthy, Justin. *Death and Exile: The Ethnic Cleansing of Ottoman Muslims*. Princeton: Darwin Press, 1995.

_____. *Muslims and Minorities*. New York: New York University Press, 1983.

_____. *The Ottoman Peoples and the End of Empire*. London and New York: Arnold and Oxford University Press, 2001.

McCarthy, Justin, Esat Arslan, Cemalettin Taşkıran, and Ömer Turan. *The Armenian Rebellion at Van*. Salt Lake City: University of Utah Press, 2006.

Menzies, Allan, D.D. *History of Religions*. New York: S. Scribner's Sons, 1927.

Messinger, Gary S. *British Propaganda and the State in the First World War*. Manchester and New York: Manchester University Press, 1992.

Millman, Richard. *Britain and the Eastern Question, 1875–1878*. Oxford: Clarendon Press, 1979.

Mitchell, J. Murray, and William Muir. *Two Old Faiths*. New York: Chautauqua Press, 1891.

Mitchell, S. Augustus. *An Easy Introduction to the Study of Geography Designed for the Instruction of Children in Schools and Families*. Philadelphia: E. H. Butler and Co., 1866.

_____. *A General View of the World*. Philadelphia: Thomas, Cowperthwait and Co., 1846.

_____. *Mitchell's School Geography*. 2nd ed. Philadelphia: Thomas, Cowperthwait and Co., 1849.

Mock, James R., and Cedric Larson. *Words That Won the War*. Princeton: Princeton University Press, 1948.

Monroe, W. S. *Turkey and the Turks: An Account of the Lands, the Peoples, and the Institutions of the Ottoman Empire*. Boston: L. C. Page and Co., 1908.

Moranian, Suzanne Elizabeth. "The American Missionaries and the Armenian Question: 1915–1927." Ph.D. dissertation, University of Wisconsin, 1994.

Morgan, Charles Carroll. J. H. *Colton's American School Geography*. New York: Ivison, Phinney and Co., 1863.

Morgan, Hani. "The Portrayal of the Middle East in School Textbooks from 1860 to the Present." Ph.D. dissertation, Rutgers University, 2002.

Morgenthau, Henry (in collaboration with French Strother). *All in a Life-time*. Garden City, N.Y.: Doubleday, Page and Co., 1922.

_____. *Ambassador Morgenthau's Story*. Garden City, N.Y.: Doubleday, Page, 1918.

_____. *The Murder of a Nation*. New York: Armenian General Benevolent Union of America, 1974.

Morse, Jedidiah. *The American Universal Geography; or, a View of the Present State of All the Empires, Kingdoms, States, and Republics in the Known World, and of the United States of America in Particular.* Boston: Thomas and Andrews, 1813.

———. *Compendious and Complete System of Modern Geography or a View of the Present State of the World.* Boston: Thomas and Andrews, 1814.

Morton, Daniel O. *Memoir of Rev. Levi Parsons.* Poultney, Vt.: Smith and Shute, 1824.

The Mother's Geography: Series of Preparatory Lessons Adapted to the Capacity of Very Young Children. New York: W. A. LeBlanc, 1842.

Mott, John R. *Addresses and Papers of John R. Mott.* Vol. 2, *The World's Student Christian Federation.* New York: Association Press, 1947.

———, ed. *The Moslem World of To-day [sic].* London: Hodder and Stoughton, 1925; New York: Doran, 1925.

Mugerditchian, Esther. *From Turkish Toils: An Armenian Family's Escape.* London: C. Arthur Pearson, 1918; New York, Doran, 1918.

Muir, William. *Life of Mahomet from Original Sources.* London: Smith, Elder, 1894.

———. *Mahomet and Islam: A Sketch of the Prophet's Life from Original Sources and a Brief Outline of His Religion.* London and New York: Religious Tract Society, 1895.

———. *Testimony Borne by the Coran to the Jewish and Christian Scriptures.* Allahabad: North India Tract and Book Society, 1860.

Murray, J. Lovell, compiler. *A Selected Bibliography of Missionary Literature.* New York: Student Volunteer Movement, 1912.

Nalbandian, Louise. *The Armenian Revolutionary Movement.* Berkeley: University of California Press, 1963.

Near East Relief. *The American Committee for Relief in the Near East.* New York: Near East Relief, 1918.

———. *Annual Report, Published by National Headquarters.* New York: Near East Relief, 1925.

———. *By an Eye Witness: What They Saw in the Near East.* New York: Near East Relief, 1921.

———. *Church Cooperation in Near East Relief.* New York: Near East Relief, n.d.

———. *The Churches of America and Near East Relief.* New York: Near East Relief, 1923.

———. *The Cross in the East and the Church in the West.* New York: Near East Relief, 1921.

———. *Golden Rule Notebook.* New York: Near East Relief, 1924.

———. *Investments in Life: Speaker's Handbook.* New York: Golden Rule, 1927.

———. *A Million Lives Saved: Handbook for Pastors.* New York: Near East Relief, 1923.

———. *The Oldest Christian Nation—Shall It Perish?: Exclusive Material for Pastors.* New York: Near East Relief, 1920.

———. *Questions in Geography.* New York: Near East Relief, n.d.

———. *Report of Near East Relief to the Congress of the United States for the Year Ending December 31, 1920.* New York: Near East Relief, 1921.

———. *Report to Congress for 1925.* New York: Near East Relief, 1926.

———. *Seeing and Believing.* New York: Near East Relief, 1926.

———. *Suggestions and Meditations for Golden Rule Sunday.* New York: n.p., 1924.

Nestorova, Tatyana. *American Missionaries among the Bulgarians (1858–1912)*. New York: Columbia University Press for East European Monographs, 1987.

Newcomb, Harvey. *The False Prophet; or, an Account of the Rise and Progress of the Mohammedan Religion*. Boston: Massachusetts Sabbath School Society, 1834.

Nielson, Jonathan Macauley. "American Historians at the Versailles Peace Conference, 1919: The Scholar as Patriot and Diplomat." Ph.D. dissertation, University of California at Santa Barbara, 1986.

Niepage, Martin. *The Horrors of Aleppo, Seen by a German Eyewitness*. London: T. Fisher Unwin, 1917.

Noll, Mark A. *A History of Christianity in the United States and Canada*. Grand Rapids, Mich.: W. B. Eerdmans, 1993.

Northrop, Henry Davenport. *The Mohammedan Reign of Terror in Armenia*. Philadelphia and Chicago: National Publishing Co., 1896. (Bound together with Frederick Davis Greene's Armenian Massacres or the Sword of Mohammed.)

Obeidat, Marwan Mohammad. "The Muslim East in American Literature: The Formation of an Image." Ph.D. dissertation, Indiana University, 1985.

Olney, Jesse. *A Practical System of Modern Geography; or, a View of the Present State of the World*. New York: Pratt, Woodford and Co., 1855 (1st ed. 1828).

Ormanian, Malachia. *The Church of Armenia*. 2nd ed. Trans. G. Marcar Gregory. London: A. R. Mowbray and Co., 1955 (French edition 1910).

The Ottoman Domination. London: T. Fisher Unwin, 1917.

Pacholl, Keith Andrew. "Bearers of the Word: Religion and Print in Early America." Ph.D. dissertation, University of California at Riverside, 2002.

Papazian, Bertha S. *The Tragedy of Armenia*. Boston: Pilgrim Press, 1918.

Parfit, John Thomas. *Mesopotamia: The Key to the Future*. London: Hodder and Stoughton, 1917; New York: Doran, 1918.

Parker, Gilbert. *The World in the Crucible*. New York: Dodd, Mead and Co., 1915.

Parsons, Levi. *The Dereliction and Restoration of the Jews: A Sermon Preached in Park Street Church, Boston, Sabbath, October 31, 1819, Just before the Departure of the Palestine Mission*. Boston: S. T. Armstrong, 1819.

Patrick, Mary Mills. *Under Five Sultans*. New York: Century Co., 1929.

Payaslian, Simon. "United States Policy toward the Armenian Question and the Armenian Genocide." Ph.D. dissertation, University of California at Los Angeles, 2003.

Perkins, Bradford. *The Great Rapprochement: England and the United States, 1895–1914*. New York: Atheneum, 1968.

Peterson, H. C. *Propaganda for War: The Campaign against American Neutrality, 1914–1917*. Norman: University of Oklahoma Press, 1935.

Phillips, W. Alison. *The War of Greek Independence*. New York: Scribner's, 1897.

Pierce, Cora Banks, and Hazel Northrop. *Stories from Far Away*. New York: Revell, 1918.

Pierce, James Wilson. *The Story of Turkey and Armenia*. Baltimore: R. H. Woodward Co., 1896.

Pinkerton, John. *Modern Geography*. Philadelphia: John Conrad, 1804.

Piper, John F. *American Churches in World War I*. Athens, Ohio: Ohio University Press, 1985.

Platt, Mary Schauffler, ed. *The War Journal of a Missionary in Persia*. Philadelphia: Women's Foreign Missionary Society of the Presbyterian Church, 1916.

Ponsonby, Arthur. *Falsehood in War-time*. New York: E. P. Dutton, 1928.

Rabenort, William. *Rabenort's Geography: Asia-Africa-Australia*. New York: American Book Co., 1918.

Read, James Morgan. *Atrocity Propaganda: 1914–1919*. New Haven: Yale University Press, 1941.

Reed, James. *The Missionary Mind and American East Asia Policy, 1911–1915*. Cambridge, Mass.: Harvard University Press, 1983.

Richards, George L., M.D., ed. *The Medical Work of Near East Relief: A Review of Its Accomplishments in Asia Minor and the Caucasus during 1919–20*. New York: Near East Relief, 1923.

Richter, Julius. *A History of Protestant Missions in the Near East*. New York: Revell, 1910.

Ridpath, John Clark, et al. *Ridpath's History of the World*. 4 vols. New York: Merrill and Baker, 1894–97.

Robbins, Royal. *The World Displayed in Its History and Geography; Embracing a History of the World from the Creation to the Present Day*. New York: H. Savage, 1833.

Robinson, James Harvey, and Charles A. Beard. T*he Development of Modern Europe: An Introduction to the Study of Current History*. Vol. 2, with supplement. Boston: Ginn and Co., 1918 (1st ed. 1908).

———. *Outlines of European History: Part II, From the Seventeenth Century to the War of 1914*. Boston: Ginn and Co., 1918.

Rockwell, William Walker. *Armenia: A List of Books and Articles, with Annotations*. White Plains, N.Y.: H. W. Wilson Co., 1916; New York: ACASR, 1916.

———. *The Pitiful Plight of the Armenians*. New York: ACASR, 1916.

———, ed. *The Deportation of the Armenians*. New York: ACASR, 1916.

Rodinson, Maxime, Europe and the Mystique of Islam. Seattle: University of Washington Press, 1991.

Ross, Frank A., C. Luther Fry, and Elbridge Sibley. *The Near East and American Philanthropy: A Survey Conducted under the Guidance of the General Committee of the Near East Survey*. New York: Columbia University Press, 1929.

Rotzell, W. E. *Man: An Introduction to Anthropology*. Philadelphia: John Joseph McVey, 1905.

Rowe, Henry K. *History of the Andover Theological Seminary*. Newton, Mass.: n.p., 1933.

Salt, Jeremy. *Imperialism, Evangelism, and the Ottoman Armenians, 1878–1896*. London: Frank Cass, 1993.

Sanders, M. L., and Philip M. Taylor. *British Propaganda during the First World War, 1914–1918*. London: Macmillan, 1982.

Sarafian, Ara, ed. *United States Official Documents on the Armenian Genocide*. 3 vols. Watertown, Mass.: Armenian Review, 1993–95.

———, ed. *United States Official Documents on the Armenian Genocide: Ambassador Morgenthau's Reports*. Watertown, Mass.: Armenian Review, 2002.

———, ed. *United States Official Records on the Armenian Genocide, 1915–1917*. Princeton, N.J., and London: Gomidas Institute, 2004.

Schevill, Ferdinand. *A History of Europe from the Reformation to the Present Day*. New ed. New York: Harcourt, Brace and Co., 1930 (1st ed. 1925).

———. *History of Modern Europe*. New York: Charles Scribner's Sons, 1905.

Schmucker, S. C. *Columbia Elementary Geography*. Philadelphia: Hinds, Noble, and Eldredge, 1909.

Seldon, William K. *Princeton Theological Seminary: A Narrative History, 1812–1992*. Princeton: Princeton University Press, 1992.

Seton-Watson, R. W. *Serbia, Yesterday, Today and Tomorrow: A School Address*. London: Vacher and Sons, 1916.

Setton, Kenneth M. *Western Hostility to Islam and Prophecies of Turkish Doom*. Philadelphia: American Philosophical Society, 1992.

Shaban, Fuad. *Islam and Arabs in Early American Thought: The Roots of Orientalism in America*. Durham, N.C.: Acorn Press, 1991.

Shabaz, Yonan. *The Rage of Islam: An Account of the Massacre of Christians by the Turks in Persia*. Philadelphia: Roger Williams Press, 1918.

Shannon, Richard. *Gladstone and the Bulgarian Agitation, 1876*. 2nd ed. Hamden, Conn.: Archon Books, 1975.

Shedd, Mary Lewis. *The Measure of a Man: The Life of William Ambrose Shedd*. New York: Doran, 1922.

Shedd, William Ambrose. *Islam and the Oriental Churches, Their Historical Relations: Students' Lectures on Missions, 1902–03*. Philadelphia: Presbyterian Board of Publication and Sabbath-School Work, 1904.

Small, Mary T. Luins. "The Printed Textbook in Colonial America." Ph.D. dissertation, Boston College, 1987.

Smith, Charles Hamilton. *The Natural History of the Human Species*. London: H. Bohn, 1859 (1st ed. Edinburgh: W. H. Lizars, 1848).

Smith, Eli. *Researches of the Rev. E. Smith and Rev. H. G. O. Dwight in Armenia: Including a Journey through Asia Minor, and into Georgia and Persia, with a Visit to the Nestorian and Chaldean Christians of Oormiah and Salmas*. Boston: Crocker and Brewster, 1833; New York: J. Leavitt, 1833.

Smith, Eli, and H. G. O. Dwight. *Missionary Researches in Armenia*. London: George Wightman, 1834.

Smith, George Adam. *Syria and the Holy Land*. London: Hodder and Stoughton, 1918; New York: Doran, 1918.

Smith, Jerome Van Crowninshield. *Turkey and the Turks*. Boston: James French, 1854.

Smith, Roswell. *A Concise and Practical System of Geography for Common Schools*. New York: Cady and Burgess, 1850.

———. *Modern Geography, for the Use of Schools, Academies, Etc., on a New Plan*. Philadelphia: Grigg, Elliot and Co., 1849.

Sonyel, Salahi. *The Ottoman Armenians*. London: Rustem, 1987.

Southern, R. W. *Western Views of Islam in the Middle Ages*. Cambridge, Mass.: Harvard University Press, 1962.

Southgate, Horatio. *Narrative of a Tour through Armenia, Kurdistan, Persia, and Mesopotamia, with an Introduction and Occasional Observations upon the Condition of*

Mohammedanism and Christianity in Those Countries. New York: D. Appleton and Co., 1840.

Special Mission of the Republic of Armenia to the United States. *Republic of Armenia: A Memorandum on Recognition of the Government of the Republic of Armenia*. 66th Cong., 1st sess., Senate Doc. 151. Washington, D.C.: GPO, 1919.

Speer, Robert E. *Christianity and the Nations*. New York: Revell, 1910.

_____. *The Gospel and the New World*. New York: Revell, 1919.

_____. *The Light of the World: A Brief Comparative Study of Christianity and Non-Christian Religions*. Medford, Mass.: Central Committee on the United Study of Missions, 1911.

_____. *Missionary Principles and Practice*. New York: Revell, 1902.

_____. *Missions and Modern History: A Study of the Missionary Aspects of Some Great Movements of the Nineteenth Century*. 2 vols. New York: Revell, 1904.

_____. *The New Opportunity of the Church*. New York: Macmillan, 1919.

_____. *The Non-Christian Religions Inadequate to Meet the Needs of Men*. Philadelphia: Board of Foreign Missions of the Presbyterian Church in the USA, 1906.

_____. *Presbyterian Foreign Missions: An Account of the Foreign Missions of the Presbyterian Church in the U.S.A*. Philadelphia: Presbyterian Board of Publication and Sabbath-School Work, 1901.

_____. *The Unfinished Task of Foreign Missions*. New York: Revell, 1926.

Speiser, Ephraim Avigdor. *The United States and the Near East*. Cambridge, Mass.: Harvard University Press, 1947.

Squires, J. D. *British Propaganda at Home and in the United States from 1914 to 1917*. Cambridge, Mass.: Harvard University Press, 1935.

Steinwehr, A. von. *School Geography*. New York: American Book Co., 1877.

St. John, Burton, ed. *North American Students and World Advance*. New York: Student Volunteer Movement, 1920.

Stoddard, Lothrop. *The New World of Islam*. New York: Scribner's, 1921.

_____. *The Revolt against Civilization*. New York: Scribner's, 1922.

_____. *The Rising Tide of Color against White Supremacy*. New York: Scribner's, 1921.

Stone, Frank A. *Academies for Anatolia: A Study of the Rationale, Program, and Impact of the Educational Institutions Sponsored by the American Board in Turkey, 1830–1980*. Lanham, Md.: University Press of America, 1984.

Strong, Elnathan Ellsworth, ed. *Mission Stories of Many Lands: A Book for Young People*. Boston: ABCFM, 1885.

Strong, William Ellsworth. *The Story of the American Board*. Boston: Pilgrim Press, 1910.

Stuermer, Harry. *Two War Years in Constantinople*. London: Hodder and Stoughton, 1917; New York: Doran, 1917.

Subject Nationalities of the German Alliance (with a Map Drawn from German Sources). London and New York: Cassell and Co., 1917.

Summers, Thomas O. *The Life of Mohammad*. Nashville, Tenn.: A. H. Redford for the Methodist Episcopal Church, South, 1876.

Syria during March 1916: Her Miseries and Disasters. London: Sir Joseph Causton and Son, 1916.

Tarbell, Horace S. *The Werner Grammar School Geography: Part I.* New York: Werner School Book Co., 1896.

Ter Minassian, Anahide. *Nationalism and Socialism in the Armenian Revolutionary Movement.* Trans. A. M. Berrett. Cambridge, Mass.: Zoryan, 1984.

Tisdall, W. St. Clair. *Christianity and Other Faiths.* New York: Revell, 1912.

_____. *Comparative Religion.* London and New York: Longmans, 1909.

_____. *The Conversion of Armenia to the Christian Faith.* New York: Revell, 1897.

_____. *The Religion of the Crescent: Being the James Long Lectures on Muhammadanism.* London: Society for Promoting Christian Knowledge, 1906; New York: E. S. Gorham, 1906 (1st ed. 1895).

Tolkowsky, S. *The Jewish Colonisation in Palestine.* London: Zionist Organization, 1918.

Toynbee, Arnold J. *Armenian Atrocities: The Murder of a Nation.* London and New York: Hodder and Stoughton, 1915.

_____. *The German Terror in Belgium: An Historical Record.* London: Hodder and Stoughton, 1917; New York: Doran, 1917.

_____. *The German Terror in France.* London: Hodder and Stoughton, 1917; New York: Doran, 1917.

_____. *The Murderous Tyranny of the Turks.* London: Hodder and Stoughton, 1917; New York: Doran, 1917.

_____. *Turkey: A Past and a Future.* London: Hodder and Stoughton, 1917; New York: Doran, 1917.

_____. *The Western Question in Greece and Turkey: A Study in the Contact of Civilisations.* London: Constable and Co., 1922.

_____, ed. *The Treatment of Armenians in the Ottoman Empire, 1915–1916: Documents Presented to Viscount Grey of Fallodon, Secretary for Foreign Affairs, by Viscount Bryce.* London: H. M. Stationery Office, 1916.

_____, ed. *The Treatment of Armenians in the Ottoman Empire, 1915–1916: Documents Presented to Viscount Grey of Fallodon, Secretary for Foreign Affairs, by Viscount Bryce.* Edited and with an introduction by Ara Sarafian. Princeton, N.J.: Gomidas Institute, 2000; Reading, England: Taderon Press, 2000.

Tylor, Edward B. *Anthropology: An Introduction to the Study of Man and Civilization.* New York: D. Appleton and Co., 1906.

Ulagay, Osman, compiler. *Amerikan Basınında Türk Kurtulus Savası.* Istanbul: İsteme, 1974.

United States Congress. Senate. *Armenia and Her Claims to Freedom and National Independence.* 65th Cong., 3rd sess., Senate Doc. 316. Washington, D.C.: GPO, 1919.

_____. *Conditions in the Near East: Report of the American Military Mission to Armenia by Maj. Gen. James G. Harbord, United States Army.* 66th Cong., 2nd sess., Senate Doc. 266. Washington, D.C.: GPO, 1920.

_____. *Mandatory over Armenia: Report Made to Maj. Gen. James G. Harbord, Chief of American Military Mission, on Military Problem of Mandatory over Armenia, by Brig. Gen. George van Horn Moseley.* 66th Cong., 2nd sess., Senate Doc. 281. Washington, D.C.: GPO, 1920.

_____. *Report of the Near East Relief for the Year Ending December 31, 1922.* 67th Cong., Senate Doc. 343. Washington, D.C.: GPO, 1923.

United States Department of State. *Papers Relating to the Foreign Relations of the United States: The Lansing Papers, 1914–20.* 2 vols. Washington, D.C.: GPO, 1939–40.

_____. *Papers Relating to the Foreign Relations of the United States, 1919.* 2 vols. Washington, D.C.: GPO, 1934.

_____. *Papers Relating to the Foreign Relations of the United States, 1920.* 3 vols. Washington, D.C.: GPO, 1935–36.

_____. *Papers Relating to the Foreign Relations of the United States: The Paris Peace Conference, 1919.* 13 vols. Washington, D.C.: GPO, 1942–47.

Uras, Esat. *The Armenians in History and the Armenian Question.* Istanbul: Documentary Publications, 1988.

Ussher, Clarence D. (Grace Knapp collaborating). *An American Physician in Turkey: A Narrative of Adventures in Peace and in War.* Boston and New York: Houghton Mifflin, 1917.

Van Duyn Southworth, Gertrude, and John Van Duyn Southworth. *Old World History, Book Two.* Syracuse, N.Y.: Iroquois Publishing Co., 1929.

Van Sommer, Annie, ed. *Our Moslem Sisters: A Cry from Lands of Darkness Interpreted by Those Who Heard It.* New York: Revell, 1907.

Van Sommer, Annie, and Samuel M. Zwemer, eds. *Daylight in the Harem.* Edinburgh and London: Oliphant, Anderson and Ferrier, 1911.

Vickrey, Charles. *International Golden Rule Sunday: A Handbook.* New York: Doran, 1926.

Wade, Mary H. *Our Little Armenian Cousin.* Boston: Page, 1902.

_____. *Our Little Turkish Cousin.* Boston: Page, 1902.

Waldo, Fullerton L. *Twilight in Armenia.* New York: Near East Relief, 1920.

Webster, Daniel. *Mr. Webster's Speech on the Greek Revolution.* Washington City: John S. Meehan, 1824.

Webster, Hutton. *Medieval and Modern History.* Boston: D. C. Heath and Co., 1919.

_____. *Modern European History.* Boston: D. C. Heath and Co., 1920.

Wedgwood, Josiah. *With Machine-Guns in Gallipoli.* London: Darling and Sons, 1915.

West, Willis Mason. *Modern History: Europe from Charlemagne to the Present Time.* Boston and Chicago: Allyn and Bacon, 1907 (1st ed. 1903).

_____. *The Modern World.* Boston: Allyn and Bacon, 1915.

West, Willis Mason, and Ruth West. *The Story of Modern Progress.* Boston: Allyn and Bacon, 1938 (1st ed. 1931).

Wheeler, Everett P. *The Duty of the United States to American Citizens in Turkey.* New York: Revell, 1896.

Wherry, E. M. *Islam and Christianity in India and the Far East: The Student Lectures on Missions at Princeton Theological Seminary for 1906–07.* New York: Revell, 1907.

_____. *Islam; or, the Religion of the Turk.* New York: American Tract Society, 1896.

_____, ed. *Missions at Home and Abroad.* New York: American Tract Society, 1895.

Wherry, E. M., S. M. Zwemer, and C. G. Mylrea, eds. *Islam and Missions.* New York: Revell, 1911.

Whitcomb, Merrick. *A History of Modern Europe*. New York: D. Appleton and Co., 1903.

Whitley, Mary Theodora. *Boys and Girls in Other Lands*. New York: Abingdon, 1924.

Williams, Augustus W., and Mgrditch Simbad Gabriel. *Bleeding Armenia: Its History and Horrors*. Chicago: Publishers' Union, 1896.

Williams, Talcott. *Turkey: A World Problem*. Garden City, N.Y.: Doubleday, 1921.

Williams, W. L. *Armenia, Past and Present*. London: P. S. King and Son, 1916.

———. *Armenia's Tragic Story*. London: P. S. King and Son, 1916.

Willis, Irene Cooper. *England's Holy War*. New York: Knopf, 1928.

Willmore, J. S. *The Welfare of Egypt*. London: Hodder and Stoughton, 1917.

Wilson, J. Christy. *Apostle to Islam: A Biography of Samuel M. Zwemer*. Grand Rapids, Mich.: Baker Book House, 1952.

Wilson, Samuel Graham. *Modern Movements among Moslems*. New York: Revell, 1916.

Winter, Jay. *America and the Armenian Genocide of 1915*. New York: Cambridge University Press, 2003.

Wollaston, Arthur N. *The Religion of the Koran*. London: Orient Press, 1904.

———. *The Sword of Islam*. London: John Murray, 1905.

Woodbridge, William C. *Modern School Geography*. Hartford: Belknap and Hammersley, 1844.

———. *A System of Universal Geography*. Hartford: Belknap and Hammersley, 1842.

Woodruff, Charles Edward. *Expansion of Races*. New York: Rebman Co., 1909.

Workman, Benjamin. *Elements of Geography, Designed for Young Students in That Science*. Philadelphia: John M'Culloch, 1790.

Yenovkian, S. S. *Martyred Armenia*. Cleveland: Britton Printing Co., 1896.

Yilmaz, Şuhnaz. "From Strangers to Allies: Turkish-American Relations (1800–1952)." Ph.D. dissertation, Princeton University, 2000.

Yonan, Jesse Malek. *Martyrdom in the Orient*. Chicago: n.p., 1895.

Zacher, Dale E. "Editorial Policy of the Scripps Newspapers during World War I." Ph.D. dissertation, Ohio University, 1999.

Zeidner, Robert Farrer. "The Tricolor over the Taurus: The French in Cilicia and Vicinity, 1918–1922." Ph.D. dissertation, University of Utah, 1991.

Zwemer, Amy E. *Two Young Arabs: The Travels of Noorah and Jameel*. West Bedford, Mass.: Central Committee on the United Study of Foreign Missions, 1926.

Zwemer, Samuel M. *Arabia, the Cradle of Islam*. New York: Revell, 1900.

———. *Childhood in the Moslem World*. New York: Revell, 1915.

———. *The Disintegration of Islam*. New York: Revell, 1916.

———. *Islam: A Challenge to Faith*. New York: Student Volunteer Movement for Foreign Missions, 1907.

———. *Islam and the New Era in the Near East after the War*. New York: Laymen's Missionary Movement, 1918.

———. *The Law of Apostasy in Islam: Answering the Question Why There Are So Few Moslem Converts, and Giving Examples of Their Moral Courage and Martyrdom*. London and New York: Marshall Brothers, 1924.

———. *Mohammed or Christ*. New York: Revell, 1916.

_____ . *The Moslem Doctrine of God*. Boston: American Tract Society, 1905.

_____ . *The Moslem Problem and Peril: Facts and Figures for the Layman*. New York: Laymen's Missionary Movement, n.d. (probably 1905).

_____ . *The Moslem World*. Boston: American Board of Commissioners for Foreign Missions, 1908; New York: Young People's Missionary Movement of the United States and Canada, 1908.

Zwemer, Samuel M., and Arthur Judson Brown. *The Nearer and Farther East*. New York: Macmillan, 1908.

Zwemer, Samuel M., E. M. Wherry, and James L. Barton, eds. *The Mohammedan World of Today*. Rpt. Allahabad: Chugh Publications, 1976 (1st ed. New York: Revell, 1906).

Zwemer, Samuel M., and Amy E. Zwemer. *Zigzag Journeys in the Camel Country*. New York: Revell, 1911.

Archival Sources

Great Britain National Archives. Foreign Office (FO), Cabinet (CAB), Treasury (T), Stationery Office (STAT), Colonial Office (CO), Department of Information (INF).

United States National Archives. Record Group 59, Department of State; Record Group 256.2, Records of the Inquiry.

Newspapers and Magazines

Newspapers and magazines cited more than a few times in the text are listed here, along with their place of publication. The same newspaper often slightly varied its title. At different times, for example, the *Atlanta Constitution* was also called the *Constitution* and the *Daily Constitution*. *The Lincoln Star* was sometimes also called the *Lincoln Daily Star* and the *Lincoln Sunday Star*. The most common or well-known variants are listed here.

Ada Evening News (Ada, Oklahoma)

Advocate of Peace (Boston, Massachusetts)

Albion (New York, New York)

Alton Evening Telegraph (Alton, Illinois)

American Hebrew (New York, New York)

American Mercury (Hartford, Connecticut)

Appleton Post-Crescent (Appleton, Wisconsin)

Appleton's Journal (New York, New York)

Arena (Boston, Massachusetts)

Argus (Albany, New York)

Ariel (Philadelphia, Pennsylvania)

Atheneum (Boston, Massachusetts)

Atlanta Constitution (Atlanta, Georgia)

Baptist Missionary Magazine (Boston, Massachusetts)

Bee (Danville, Virginia)

Billings Gazette (Billings, Montana)
Bismarck Tribune (Bismarck, North Dakota)
Blackwood's Magazine (Edinburgh, UK)
Boston Daily Advertiser (Boston, Massachusetts)
Boston Gazette (Boston, Massachusetts)
Boston Globe (Boston, Massachusetts)
Boston Recorder (Boston, Massachusetts)
Bridgeport Standard Telegram (Bridgeport, Connecticut)
Bridgeport Telegram (Bridgeport, Connecticut)
Bulletin of the American Geographic Society (New York, New York)
Cambridge City Tribune (Cambridge City, Indiana)
Camden Gazette (Camden, South Carolina)
Capital Times (Madison, Wisconsin)
Cedar Rapids Evening Gazette (Cedar Rapids, Iowa)
Cedar Rapids Republican (Cedar Rapids, Iowa)
Cedar Rapids Times (Cedar Rapids, Iowa)
Centralia Daily Chronicle (Centralia, Washington)
Century Illustrated (New York, New York)
Charleston Daily Mail (Charleston, West Virginia)
Chautauquan (Jamestown, New York)
Chicago Daily News (Chicago, Illinois)
Chicago Tribune (Chicago, Illinois)
Chillicothe Constitution (Chillicothe, Missouri)
Christian Advocate (New York, New York)
Christian Herald (New York, New York)
Christian Intelligencer and Eastern Chronicle (Portland, Maine)
Christian Observer (Boston, Massachusetts)
Christian Register (New York, New York)
Christian Repository (Woodstock, Vermont)
Christian Science Monitor (Boston, Massachusetts)
Christian Spectator (New Haven, Connecticut)
Christian Union (New York, New York)
Christian Watchman (Boston, Massachusetts)
Chronicle-Telegram (Elyria, Ohio)
City Gazette and Daily Advertiser (Charleston, South Carolina)
Clearfield Progress (Clearfield, Pennsylvania)
Colorado Springs Gazette (Colorado Springs, Colorado)
Congregationalist (Boston, Massachusetts)
Connecticut Courant (Hartford, Connecticut)
Connecticut Herald (New Haven, Connecticut)
Contemporary Review (New York, New York)
Current History (New York, New York)
Current Literature (New York, New York)
Current Opinion (New York, New York)

Daily Courier (Connellsville, Pennsylvania)

Daily Gazette (Williamsport, Pennsylvania)

Daily Gazette and Bulletin (Williamsport, Pennsylvania)

Daily Herald (Steubenville, Ohio)

Daily Herald (Tyrone, Pennsylvania)

Daily Iowa Capital (Des Moines, Iowa)

Daily Kennebec Journal (Augusta, Maine)

Daily News (Frederick, Maryland)

Daily News (London, UK)

Daily Northwestern (Oshkosh, Wisconsin)

Daily Republican (Decatur, Illinois)

Daily Times (Portsmouth, Ohio)

Dallas News (Dallas, Texas)

Davenport Daily Republican (Davenport, Iowa)

Davenport Gazette (Davenport, Iowa)

Davenport Leader (Davenport, Iowa)

Decatur Review (Decatur, Illinois)

Denton Journal (Denton, Maryland)

Des Moines Capital (Des Moines, Iowa)

Des Moines News (Des Moines, Iowa)

Dial (Boston, Massachusetts)

Dunkirk Evening Observer (Dunkirk, New York)

Eastern Argus (Portland, Maine)

Eau Claire Leader (Eau Claire, Wisconsin)

Eclectic Magazine of Foreign Literature (Boston, Massachusetts)

Elyria Evening Telegram (Elyria, Ohio)

Escritoir; or, Masonic and Miscellaneous Album (Albany, New York)

Essex Patriot (Haverhill, Massachusetts)

Essex Register (Salem, Massachusetts)

Evening Courier and Reporter (Waterloo, Iowa)

Evening Democrat (Warren, Pennsylvania)

Evening Gazette (Cedar Rapids, Iowa)

Evening Gazette (Port Jervis, New York)

Evening Herald (Syracuse, New York)

Evening News (Lincoln, Nebraska)

Evening News (London, UK)

Evening Post (Frederick, Maryland)

Evening State Journal and Lincoln Daily News (Lincoln, Nebraska)

Evening Times (Cumberland, Maryland)

Evening Times (Trenton, New Jersey)

Evening Tribune (Albert Lea, Minnesota)

Farmers' Cabinet (Amherst, New Hampshire)

Fayetteville Daily Democrat (Fayetteville, Arkansas)

Fitchburg Daily Sentinel (Fitchburg, Massachusetts)

Fitchburg Evening Sentinel (Fitchburg, Massachusetts)
Fortnightly Review (New York, New York)
Fort Wayne Evening Post (Fort Wayne, Indiana)
Fort Wayne Gazette (Fort Wayne, Indiana)
Fort Wayne Journal-Gazette (Fort Wayne, Indiana)
Fort Wayne News (Fort Wayne, Indiana)
Fort Wayne News and Sentinel (Fort Wayne, Indiana)
Fort Wayne Sentinel (Fort Wayne, Indiana)
Fort Wayne Weekly Gazette (Fort Wayne, Indiana)
Forum (New York, New York)
Frank Leslie's Popular Monthly (New York, New York)
Frederick Post (Frederick, Maryland)
Fresno Morning Republican (Fresno, California)
Friends' Intelligencer (Philadelphia, Pennsylvania)
Galveston Daily News (Galveston, Texas)
Gazette and Bulletin (Williamsport, Pennsylvania)
Genius of Universal Emancipation (Baltimore, Maryland)
Gettysburg Compiler (Gettysburg, Pennsylvania)
Hamilton Evening Journal (Hamilton, Ohio)
Hamilton News (Hamilton, Ohio)
Hammond Times (Hammond, Indiana)
Harrisburg Telegram (Harrisburg, Pennsylvania)
Hartford Courant (Hartford, Connecticut)
Helena Independent (Helena, Montana)
Hornellsville Weekly Tribune (Hornellsville, New York)
Humeston New Era (Humeston, Iowa)
Independent (New York, New York)
Indianapolis Star (Indianapolis, Indiana)
International Review (New York, New York)
International Review of Missions (Edinburgh, UK)
Iowa City Press-Citizen (Iowa City, Iowa)
Iowa State Reporter (Waterloo, Iowa)
Ironwood Daily Globe (Ironwood, Michigan)
Janesville Gazette (Janesville, Wisconsin)
Jeffersonian (Albany, New York)
Jewish Chronicle (London, UK)
Kansas City Star (Kansas City, Missouri)
Kansas City Times (Kansas City, Missouri)
Kennebec Journal (Augusta, Maine)
Kingsport Times (Kingsport, Tennessee)
La Crosse Tribune and Leader-Press (La Crosse, Wisconsin)
Leslie's Illustrated Weekly Newspaper (New York, New York)
Lima News (Lima, Ohio)

Lincoln Evening News (Lincoln, Nebraska)

Lincoln Intelligencer (Lincoln, Nebraska)

Lincoln Star (Lincoln, Nebraska)

Literary Casket (West Chester, Pennsylvania)

Literary Digest (New York, New York)

Littell's Living Age (Boston, Massachusetts)

Logansport Pharos-Reporter (Logansport, Indiana)

London Chronicle (London, UK)

London Quarterly Review (London, UK)

London Weekly Review (London, UK)

Los Angeles Times (Los Angeles, California)

Lowell Sun (Lowell, Massachusetts)

Mail and Express (New York, New York)

Mansfield News (Mansfield, Ohio)

Manuscript (New York, New York)

Marble Rock Journal (Marble Rock, Iowa)

Marshfield Times (Marshfield, Wisconsin)

Masonic Mirror and Mechanics' Intelligencer (Boston, Massachusetts)

Massachusetts Ploughman and New England Journal of Agriculture (Boston, Massachusetts)

Massillon Independent (Masillon, Ohio)

McClure's Magazine (New York, New York)

Messenger (Philadelphia, Pennsylvania)

Methodist Quarterly Review (New York, New York)

Middletown Daily Argus (Middletown, New York)

Miscellaneous Cabinet (Schenectady, New York)

Missionary Herald (Boston, Massachusetts)

Moberly Democrat (Moberly, Missouri)

Moberly Monitor-Index (Moberly, Missouri)

Modesto Evening News (Modesto, California)

Morning Post (London, UK)

Mount Zion Missionary (Mount Zion, Georgia)

Nashua Reporter (Nashua, Iowa)

National Advocate (New York, New York)

National Intelligencer (Washington, D.C.)

National Police Gazette (New York, New York)

National Repository (Cincinnati, Ohio)

Nevada State Journal (Reno, Nevada)

Newark Advocate (Newark, New Jersey)

New Castle News (New Castle, Pennsylvania)

New-Hampshire Gazette (Portsmouth, New Hampshire)

New Hampshire Patriot and State Gazette (Concord, New Hampshire)

New Harmony Gazette (New Harmony, Indiana)

New Monthly Magazine (London, UK)

New Monthly Magazine and Literary Journal, American Edition (London, UK, and Philadelphia, Pennsylvania)

New Near East (New York, New York)

New Oxford Item (New Oxford, Pennsylvania)

New Republic (New York, New York)

Newport Daily News (Newport, Rhode Island)

News (Frederick, Maryland)

New-Sentinel (Fort Wayne Indiana)

New York Commercial Advertiser (New York, New York)

New York Daily Advertiser (New York, New York)

New York Evangelist (New York, New York)

New York Herald (New York, New York)

New York Journal (New York, New York)

New-York Mirror (New York, New York)

New York Observer (New York, New York)

New York Observer and Chronicle (New York, New York)

New-York Spectator (New York, New York)

New York Telescope (New York, New York)

New York Times (New York, New York)

New York Tribune (New York, New York)

New York World (New York, New York)

Niles Weekly Register (Baltimore, Maryland)

Nineteenth Century (New York, New York)

North Adams Transcript (North Adams, Massachusetts)

North American (Philadelphia, Pennsylvania)

North American Review (Boston, Massachusetts)

Norwich Courier (Norwich, Connecticut)

Oakland Tribune (Oakland, California)

Oelwein Daily Register (Oelwein, Iowa)

Ogden Examiner (Ogden, Utah)

Ogden Standard (Ogden, Utah)

Ogden Standard-Examiner (Ogden, Utah)

Ohio Democrat (New Philadelphia, Ohio)

Olean Evening News (Olean, New York)

Olean Evening Times (Olean, New York)

Olean Herald (Olean, New York)

Outlook (New York, New York)

Pall Mall Gazette (London, UK)

Palo Alto Pilot (Palo Alto, California)

Perry Daily Chief (Perry, Iowa)

Peterson Magazine (Philadelphia, Pennsylvania)

Philadelphia Album and Ladies' Literary Gazette (Philadelphia, Pennsylvania)

Philadelphia Mercury (Philadelphia, Pennsylvania)

Philadelphia Record (Philadelphia, Pennsylvania)
Philadelphia Recorder (Philadelphia, Pennsylvania)
Phrenological Journal and Science of Health (New York, New York)
Pittsfield Sun (Pittsfield, Massachusetts)
Plymouth Mercury (Plymouth, UK)
Port-Folio (Philadelphia, Pennsylvania)
Portland Oregonian (Portland, Oregon)
Portsmouth Daily Times (Portsmouth, Ohio)
Post-Intelligencer (Seattle, Washington)
Potter's American Monthly (Philadelphia, Pennsylvania)
Princeton Review (New York, New York)
Providence Journal (Providence, Rhode Island)
Public Ledger (Philadelphia, Pennsylvania)
Racine Journal (Racine, Wisconsin)
Racine Journal-News (Racine, Wisconsin)
Recorder and Telegraph (Boston, Massachusetts)
Register (Danville, Virginia)
Religious Intelligencer (New Haven, Connecticut)
Religious Miscellany (Carlisle, Pennsylvania)
Reno Gazette (Reno, Nevada)
Reno Weekly Gazette and Stockman (Reno, Nevada)
Republican Press (Salamanca, New York)
Round Table (London, UK)
Salem Daily News (Salem, Ohio)
Salt Lake Tribune (Salt Lake City, Utah)
San Antonio Evening News (San Antonio, Texas)
San Antonio Express (San Antonio, Texas)
San Antonio Light (San Antonio, Texas)
Sandusky Register (Sandusky, Ohio)
Sandusky Standard (Sandusky, Ohio)
Sandusky Star-Journal (Sandusky, Ohio)
San Francisco Chronicle (San Francisco, California)
San Francisco Impress (San Francisco, California)
Saturday Evening Post (Philadelphia, Pennsylvania)
Savannah News (Savannah, Georgia)
Sheboygan Press (Sheboygan, Wisconsin)
Springfield Daily Republican (Springfield, Massachusetts)
Star (Oneonta, New York)
Star and Sentinel (Gettysburg, Pennsylvania)
Steubenville Herald (Steubenville, Ohio)
Stevens Point Daily Sentinel (Stevens Point, Wisconsin)
Stevens Point Journal (Stevens Point, Wisconsin)
Sun (New York, New York)
Syracuse Herald (Syracuse, New York)

Syracuse Standard (Syracuse, New York)

Telegraph (London, UK)

Times (London, UK)

Times-Democrat (Lima, Ohio)

Times-Herald (Chicago, Illinois)

Titusville Herald (Titusville, Pennsylvania)

Trenton Times (Trenton, New Jersey)

Tyrone Daily Herald (Tyrone, Pennsylvania)

Unitarian Review and Religious Magazine (Boston, Massachusetts)

United States Catholic Miscellany (Charleston, South Carolina)

Universalist Magazine (Boston, Massachusetts)

Van Wert Daily Bulletin (Van Wert, Ohio)

Van Wert Times (Van Wert, Ohio)

Vermont Gazette (Bennington, Vermont)

Victoria Daily Advocate (Victoria, Texas)

Warren Evening Times (Warren, Pennsylvania)

Washington Gazette (Washington, D.C.)

Washington Post (Washington, D.C.)

Waterloo Courier (Waterloo, Iowa)

Waterloo Evening Courier and Reporter (Waterloo, Iowa)

Waterloo Times (Waterloo, Iowa)

Waterloo Times-Tribune (Waterloo, Iowa)

Waukesha Freeman (Waukesha, Wisconsin)

Weekly Gazette (Colorado Springs, Colorado)

Wellsboro Gazette (Wellsboro, Pennsylvania)

Western Luminary (Lexington, Kentucky)

Western Recorder (Utica, New York)

Westminister Gazette (London, UK)

Wichita Daily Times (Wichita Falls, Texas)

Wood County Tribune (Grand Rapids, Wisconsin)

World's Work (London, UK)

Youth's Companion (Boston, Massachusetts)

Zion's Herald (Boston, Massachusetts)

INDEX